Other Auerbach Publications

Local Area Network

HANDBOOK

6TH EDITION

John P. Slone
EDITOR

CRC Press
Taylor & Francis Group
Boca Raton London New York

CRC Press is an imprint of the
Taylor & Francis Group, an **informa** business

CRC Press
Taylor & Francis Group
6000 Broken Sound Parkway NW, Suite 300
Boca Raton, FL 33487-2742

First issued in paperback 2019

© 2000 by Taylor & Francis Group, LLC
CRC Press is an imprint of Taylor & Francis Group, an Informa business

No claim to original U.S. Government works

ISBN-13: 978-0-8493-9838-4 (hbk)
ISBN-13: 978-0-367-39942-9 (pbk)
Library of Congress Card Number 98-35521

Library of Congress Cataloging-in-Publication Data

Local area network handbook / John P. Slone, editor. --1999
   ed.
         p.   cm.
      Includes bibliographical references and index.

      1. Application software--Development--Handbooks, manuals, etc.
   I. Slone, John P.
   QA76.76.D47H34   1999
   005.1–dc21   98-35521
                                                                 CIP

Visit the Taylor & Francis Web site at
http://www.taylorandfrancis.com

and the CRC Press Web site at
http://www.crcpress.com

Contributors List

THOMAS ATKINS, *Regional Systems Engineer, Extreme Networks, Cupertino, CA*
AL BERG, *Director, Strategic Technologies, NETLAN Inc., New York, NY*
ALEX BIDWELL, *President, CyberQuest Inc., Dallas, TX*
ELLEN BONSALL, *Marketing Director, U.S. Operations, ActivCard Inc., San Francisco, CA*
SMOOT CARL-MITCHELL, *Managing Partner, Texas Internet Consulting, West Austin, TX*
MARION CERUTI, *Scientist, Advanced C41 Systems, Engineering and Integration Group, Command and Intelligence Systems Division, Naval Command, Control, and Ocean Surveillance Center, RDT&E Division, San Diego, CA*
RUSSELL CHUNG, *Senior Consultant, American Eagle Group, Sunland, CA*
TIM CLARK, VICE PRESIDENT OF SALES, TAVVE SOFTWARE COMPANY, DURHAM, NC
DOUGLAS G. CONORICH, *Internet Security Analyst, Internet Emergency Response Service, IBM Corporation, Clearfield, UT*
PAUL CULLEN, *IS Technical Consultant, Norwest Audit Services, Inc., Minneapolis, MN*
JOHN FISKE, *Independent Writer, Prides Crossing, PA*
MARK N. FOLICK, *Associate Professor, MIS, University of Tennessee, Memphis, TN*
KAREN C. FOX, *Assistant Director, Computing and Telecommunications, University of Tennessee, Memphis, TN*
FREDERICK GALLEGOS, *IS Audit Graduate Advisor and Faculty Member, Computer Information Systems, College of Business Administration, California State Polytechnic University, Pomona, CA*
MICHEL GILBERT, *Senior Member, Technical Staff, Hill Associates Inc., Colchester, VT*
FRANK M. GROOM, *Professor, Center for Information and Communication Sciences, Ball State University, Muncie, IN*
KEVIN M. GROOM, *Senior Technical Associate, AT&T, Cincinnati, OH*
TOM HADLEY, *Networking Consultant, IBM Corporation, Raleigh, NC*
GILBERT HELD, *Director, 4-Degree Consulting, Macon, GA*
GARY C. KESSLER, *Director, Information Technology, Hill Associates Inc., Colchester, VT*
LAURA KNAPP, *IBM Corporation, Raleigh, NC*

WILLIAM R. KOSS, *Director of Sales, Sonoma Systems, Marlborough, MA*

JEFFREY J. LOWDER, *Network Security Element Chief, United States Air Force Academy, Colorado Springs, CO*

PHILLIP Q. MAIER, *Program Manager, Secure Network Initiative, Lockheed Martin Corp., Sunnyvale, CA*

MICHAEL J. MASTERSON, *Doctoral Student, Management Information Systems, Auburn University, Auburn, AL*

CRAIG R. MCGUFFIN, *President, C.R. McGuffin Services, Toronto, Ontario, Canada*

COLIN MICK, *Consultant, Palo Alto, CA*

J. P. MORGENTHAL, *Java Computing Analyst, nc.focus, New York, NY*

JIM MORIN, *Director, Corporate Planning and Market Development, Computer Network Technology Corporation, Minneapolis, MN*

NATHAN J. MULLER, *Consultant, The Oxford Group, Huntsville, AL*

LUC. T. NGUYEN, *Area Consulting Manager, Bay Networks, Atlanta, GA*

A. PADGETT PETERSON, *Senior Staff, Corporate Information Security Engineering, Lockheed Martin Corp., Orlando, FL*

STEVEN POWELL, *Professor, Computer Information Systems, College of Business Administration, California State Polytechnic University, Pomona, CA*

RAJ RAJAGOPAL, *Principal Scientist, MITRE Corp., McLean, VA*

RICHARD RAUSCHER, *Senior Systems/Network Analyst, H. Lee Moffitt Cancer Center and Research Institute, University of South Florida, Tampa, FL*

LAWRENCE D. ROGERS, *Vice President and General Manager, Software Systems Division, Emerald Systems Corp., San Diego, CA*

LARRY SCHESSEL, *Cisco Systems, Research Triangle Park, NC*

MARTIN SCHLEIFF, *Technical Lead, Boeing Corp., Seattle, WA*

E. EUGENE SCHULTZ, *Program Manager, SRI Consultants, Menlo Park, CA*

JOHN P. SLONE, *Chief Designer, Directory Services, Lockheed Martin Corp., Orlando, FL*

PETER SOUTHWICK, *SMTS, Hill Associates Inc., Colchester, VT*

WILLIAM STALLINGS, *President, Comp-Comm Consulting, Brewster, MA*

STEPHEN TANNER, *President, Argus Consulting, Arcadia, CA*

Contents

INTRODUCTION xi

SECTION 1   LAN BASICS: BUILDING BLOCKS OF THE
              ENTERPRISE NETWORK 1

1   Building Highly Reliable Computer Networks 3
      Richard Rauscher
2   Gigabit Ethernet 19
      Colin Mick
3   Processor Types 31
      A. Padgett Peterson
4   Server Data Bus Structures 41
      A. Padgett Peterson
5   Dynamic IP Addressing with DHCP 49
      Tom Hadley and Laura Knapp
6   LAN Connectivity Options for the Small Business 55
      Nathan J. Muller
7   LAN Printing Techniques 65
      Gilbert Held
8   An Overview of Cryptographic Methods 73
      Gary C. Kessler
9   Assessing and Combating The Sniffer Threat 85
      E. Eugene Schultz

SECTION 2   INTERCONNECTIVITY BASICS:
              PUTTING THE PIECES TOGETHER 99

10   TCP/IP Essentials 103
      Smoot Carl-Mitchell
11   Configuring TCP/IP on a Windows NT Computer 113
      Gilbert Held
12   Routing and Routing Protocols 123
      Michel Gilbert
13   Evolution to Layer 2 and 3 Switching 139
      Michel Gilbert

14 Implementing Routing, Switching, and VLANs in
Modern Corporate Networks 153
Thomas Atkins

15 Remote Access Concepts and Techniques 171
Peter Southwick

16 Remote Access Authentication 185
Ellen Bonsall

17 Working With Cisco Access Lists 199
Gilbert Held

18 Securing Your Router 209
Gilbert Held

SECTION 3   ADVANCED LAN & INTERCONNECTIVITY:
BUILDING ENTERPRISE NETWORKS FOR
THE NEW MILLENNIUM 217

19 Advances in NIC Technology 221
Gilbert Held

20 Emerging High-Bandwidth Networks 227
Kevin M. Groom and Frank M. Groom

21 ATM Access: The Genesis of a New Network 245
William R. Koss

22 Voice and Data Network Integration 259
Larry Schessel

23 RSVP: Building Blocks of the Next-Generation Internet 269
William Stallings

24 IPv6: The Next-Generation Internet Protocol 277
Gary C. Kessler

25 Internet-Based Virtual Private Networks 293
Nathan J. Muller

26 Implementing and Supporting Extranets 305
Phillip Q. Maier

27 Virtual Corporations: A Need for Integrated Control
and Perpetual Risk Assessment 317
Steven Powell and Frederick Gallegos

SECTION 4   BUILDING ENTERPRISE INFRASTRUCTURES
WITH LAN-BASED TECHNOLOGY 325

28 Windows NT Architecture 327
Gilbert Held

29 A Quick Overview of Linux 335
Raj Rajagopal

30 The Emergence of the Directory-Enabled Operating
System 343
John P. Slone

31 Enterprise Directory Services 357
   Martin Schleiff
32 Storage Area Networks 371
   Jim Morin
33 Push Technology: Impact and Issues 383
   Frederick Gallegos
34 Enterprise Deployment: Building an IP PBX
   Telephony Network 393
   John Fiske
35 Internet Security: Securing the Perimeter 401
   Douglas G. Conorich
36 Private Keys, Trusted Third Parties, and Kerberos 415
   Alex Bidwell

**SECTION 5   BUILDING ENTERPRISE SOLUTIONS WITH
             LAN-BASED TECHNOLOGY** 431

37 Web-to-Information-Base Access Solutions 433
   Marion Ceruti
38 Local Area Network Messaging 447
   Russell Chung
39 Choosing and Equipping an Internet Server 461
   Nathan J. Muller
40 Networking Features of the Java Programming
   Language 477
   John P. Slone
41 Java's Role in Distributed Computing 489
   J. P. Morgenthal
42 The Pitfalls of Client/Server Development Projects 497
   Paul Cullen
43 Creating a Paperless Workflow: A Case Study 507
   Karen C. Fox and Mark N. Folick
44 Security and Control of Electronic Mail 515
   Craig R. McGuffin
45 Applets and Network Security:
   A Management Overview 535
   Al Berg

**SECTION 6   MANAGEMENT OF LAN-BASED ENTERPRISE
             NETWORKS** 543

46 Managing Enterprise Systems Without a Strategy:
   A Case Study 545
   Michael J. Masterson
47 Proactive Performance Management 553
   Tim Clark

48   Issues in Managing Multimedia Networks 563
        Luc. T. Nguyen
49   Network Data and Storage Management Techniques 571
        Lawrence D. Rogers
50   License Tracking and Metering Software................................587
        Nathan J. Muller
51   Working with NT's Performance Monitor 599
        Gilbert Held
52   Evaluating the Performance of NT-Based Systems................609
        Gilbert Held
53   Developing a Network Security Plan 619
        Frederick Gallegos and Stephen Tanner
54   Firewall Management and Internet Attacks 629
        Jeffrey J. Lowder

ABOUT THE EDITOR..645

INDEX 647

Introduction

At the dawn of the new millennium, we find a networking landscape vastly different from that of just a few years ago. Little more than a decade ago, the term "local area network" conjured up images of computer laboratories filled with minicomputers strung together with fat yellow cables. In contrast, the term "enterprise network," if the term had been coined back then, would undoubtedly have been associated with a mainframe-centric network composed of front-end processors, remote concentrators, cluster controllers, and terminals, connected to one another through a combination of leased phone lines and point-to-point coaxial cable. The two concepts could not have been further apart.

By contrast, today's enterprise cannot effectively function without a network, and today's enterprise network is almost always based on LAN technology. In a few short years, LANs have become an essential element of today's business environment. This time in the spotlight, while well deserved, has not come without a price. Businesses now insist that LANs deliver vast, and ever-increasing quantities of business-critical information, and that they do it efficiently, flawlessly, without fail, and most of all securely. Today's network managers must consistently deliver this level of performance, and must do so while keeping up with ever-changing, ever-increasing demands without missing a beat. At the same time, today's IT managers must deliver business-critical information systems in an environment that has undergone radical paradigm shifts in such widely varied fields as computer architecture, operating systems, application development, and security.

This collective environment, in which networking and information technology work together to create LAN-based enterprise networks, is the focus of this *Local Area Network Handbook, 6th Edition*. The focus of this edition is on the enterprise aspect of LANs. Topics have been selected and organized with this in mind, providing both depth and breadth of coverage. It is intended that readers of this book not only gain an understanding of how LANs work and how to go about selecting and implementing LAN products, but also how to leverage LAN capabilities for the benefit of their respective enterprises. As with the prior editions, readers of this edition of the *Handbook* are squarely positioned at the forefront of technology.

Readers of the previous edition of this *Handbook* will find many similarities in this edition, but will find some key differences. To begin, nearly 50% of the material in this edition is new since the last edition. In addition, a new section entitled "Building Enterprise Infrastructures with LAN-Based Technology" has been added, incorporating some of the material previously contained in the "Enterprise Solutions" section, and presenting a number of new topics. Finally, perhaps the most important change in this edition is the elimination of "Security" as a separate section. Instead, security-focused chapters have been placed within each section according to the specific security topic at hand.

While the elimination of the Security section may seem counter-intuitive at first, it actually serves several purposes. First and foremost, it emphasizes the point that security topics should no longer be considered "side issues" but should be an integral component of every enterprise solution. Second, it makes it easier for the reader to find the security topics associated with a particular concept. Finally, this arrangement actually allows the inclusion of more security-related chapters than if they had all been placed within a single section.

HOW TO USE THIS BOOK

The reader's objective will determine how to get the most out of this handbook. For the reader in search of an educational manual or textbook, the organization is such that if the chapters are read sequentially, cover to cover, the topics will unfold in a logical, orderly progression. For the reader with a general grasp of most of the subject matter, but who needs more focused information, each section is organized to provide complete coverage of a topical area, with a minimum of dependence on other sections. Finally, for the reader with very specific needs, each chapter can be read independently without any loss of meaning.

Such specific needs may take several forms, and accordingly the handbook contains several types of chapters. The first such type presents basic, fundamental concepts, or information about stable technologies. Other chapters deal with more dynamic, time-sensitive subjects. These have been included to the greatest extent possible in a publication of this form, but with a strict guideline: only information indicative of a significant trend is included, and time-sensitive details are identified for the reader. A number of chapters also present case studies, describing what other people have done in certain situations with the technology available to them.

For any reader, it is suggested that the section introductions be read first. The overall organization of the book will then be clearer and the reader will be given a summary of the information presented in each chapter. Briefly, the first section of the book takes a look at what could be considered "core" technologies, such as hardware and truly local transmission technologies. Section 2 takes a look at the technologies of LAN interconnectivity. Section 3 explores some of the more challenging and advanced issues in these two areas. Following these three sections, the focus shifts to the application of LAN technology to build enterprise infrastructures in Section 4 and to build enterprise solutions in Section 5. Rounding out the book, Section 6 deals with managing LAN-based enterprise networks. As mentioned above, each section contains focused material on security issues pertinent to the theme of the section.

For all readers, this handbook is not meant to be simply read once and shelved. Every effort has been made to include only chapters that will contribute to the book's usefulness on a continuing basis, and the intent is for the book to be kept handy and referred to many times. Most of the chapters are richly illustrated, and many include such useful features as checklists and list of suggestions. An index facilitates the location of specific items of interest.

ACKNOWLEDGMENTS

As with each previous edition, I would like to express my most sincere appreciation and gratitude for all the men and women who have contributed to this book, including the authors of individual chapters and the countless others who have made indirect contributions in the form of suggestions for revisions and improvements or author referrals. Without their many hours of planning, preparation, and execution, and more importantly, without their willingness to share their ideas and experiences with others in our industry, this book would never have been possible.

In addition, I would like to extend a special note of gratitude to the readers of this and previous editions of the *Handbook*. Without the continued support of *Handbook* readers, this edition would not have become a reality. To ensure that future editions continue to meet the needs of the readers, I would welcome any feedback, whether it is a compliment or suggestions for change. You may reach me for such purposes by electronic mail at jpslone@gate.net. To the extent my schedule allows, I will acknowledge each note.

I would also like to thank the staff at Auerbach Publications, most notably Theron Shreve, for his assistance in bringing this publication together, and for his patience with me in getting through some especially difficult transition issues.

Finally, I wish to express a special word of thanks to my wife Nan, who has patiently waited more times than I can remember for me to emerge from my office after yet another session at my computer working on this book, and to my daughter Melissa, who, although in college, is too young to remember me not working on one edition or another of the *Handbook*.

John P. Slone
Orlando, Florida
May 1999

Section 1
LAN Basics: Building Blocks of the Enterprise Network

Enterprise networks, no matter how large or small, must begin with the basics. To help the LAN or IT manager who needs to make sense of the sometimes bewildering array of ever-changing technology, this section of the *Handbook* provides an overview of a number of basic LAN technologies and standards, with an emphasis on building solid, reliable LANs, from which solid, reliable, high-performance enterprise networks can be built.

Having emerged from the laboratory little more than a decade ago, LANs have now taken center stage in most enterprise networks. As such, reliability is of paramount importance for today's LAN managers. Chapter 1, "Building Highly Reliable Computer Networks," investigates several factors to consider in the fault tolerance equation. In this chapter, aspects of network infrastructure component reliability are considered from the perspective of attaining fault tolerance at each of the first three layers of the OSI model.

In addition to reliability, a key design criterion in today's LANs is performance. Although most LANs currently support transmission speeds of 10 to 100 megabits per second, today's network designer must consider the needs of the next few years. Accordingly, Chapter 2, "Gigabit Ethernet," discusses the application trends leading to the requirement for gigabit transmission capacity, describes in significant detail how the technology works, and assesses the technology's status with respect to the IEEE standardization process and industry support.

While an understanding of transmission technology is essential for today's LAN manager, it is equally important to keep in mind that the ultimate purpose of a LAN is to actually move data, most often back and forth between user workstations and servers. In building a LAN-based enterprise network, it is not sufficient to limit one's thinking to the delivery of data to or from the server's network interface card. Rather, it is important to also consider movement of the data inside the server. Chapters 3 and 4 provide insight into two important aspects of server architecture, each of which can play a significant role in overall LAN performance. Chapter 3, "Processor Types," focuses on CPU architecture, illustrating why it is essential to

1

consider more than just the CPU's model number and clock rate when designing server systems. Chapter 4, "Server Data Bus Structures," discusses the architecture of the data bus, providing insight into the complex relationship between CPU speed, network interface cards, and disk I/O. Together these chapters provide the LAN and IT managers with information needed to ensure that the server's performance is optimized.

Not all LAN-related considerations have to do with reliability or speed. As such, Chapter 5, "Dynamic IP Addressing with DHCP," addresses a topic that solves problems related to the explosion of devices connected to the global Internet coupled with the proliferation of affordable laptop computers and the resulting increase in the need to provide connectivity for mobile users. The chapter looks at the evolution of dynamic IP addressing and discusses specifics of how DHCP works in today's networks.

Until recently, the networking market was effectively closed to small businesses. LANs and enterprise networks were the exclusive domain of larger businesses that could afford to keep seasoned networking professional on their payrolls. Due in large part to the success of the IEEE 802.3 family of standards, reliable, interoperable LAN components have become both affordable and readily available, opening this market to companies of any size. Chapter 6, "LAN Connectivity Options for the Small Business," discusses options available for companies in the 2 to 100 user range. Many of these options are equally applicable to the home office, for telecommuters, or for small field offices needing to participate in the larger corporate network.

Since the earliest days of LANs, the ability to share printers has been both a popular and important application of LAN technology. Chapter 7 explains "LAN Printing Techniques," including several methods of printer attachment currently available, and discusses the factors that should be considered in evaluating the basic options.

Fundamental to any enterprise network is the need to protect the information traversing it. One of the most basic means of protecting that information is through the use of encryption. Encryption, or more accurately, the science of cryptography, while not sufficient to secure a network, is certainly essential. Chapter 8, "An Overview of Cryptographic Methods," provides a good survey of the field, providing the reader with the background necessary to understand the choices available and how to select the appropriate cryptographic mechanisms for his or her network environment.

Rounding out the section on LAN Basics is a chapter that takes a look at a serious security threat rooted in fundamental LAN management. Long regarded by LAN managers as an essential tool in the diagnostic toolbox, the sniffer has also emerged as one of the most serious threats. Chapter 9, "Assessing and Combating the Sniffer Threat," examines the nature of this threat and proposes several steps that can be taken in response.

Chapter 1
Building Highly Reliable Computer Networks

Richard Rauscher

Highly reliable computer networks are becoming increasingly essential in industries in which real-time transactions occur. The health care industry depends on information systems not only for business operations but also for critical care: Patient monitoring systems now rely on computer networks for communications. What would happen if the nurses' station didn't get a message indicating that a patient was in cardiac arrest? Law enforcement and emergency services are using information systems for every part of their function: A working computer at the dispatchers' office can be the difference between a police officer knowing if the car he just pulled over was simply committing a speeding violation or contains a wanted murderer. In these and many other instances, the computer network can be the difference between life and death.

Vendors sell products based on performance. Engineers often buy products based on performance. With the speed of common local area networks (LAN) increasing tenfold every few years, "more power" should be the slogan for the network architect of the 1990s. Does all this increased bandwidth *really* translate to any tangible benefit? That depends on network utilization and applications. Maintaining good utilization statistics helps the network engineer make this decision. These statistics may also indicate that there is no current requirement for more bandwidth. Budget money would be better spent elsewhere. It may be time to concentrate on making the computer network more reliable rather than faster.

If the network architect is building a network on which others' lives will depend, she must ask herself if she would let her life depend on this network. If the answer is "no," she needs to make immediate changes: either to the network infrastructure or to her choice of careers.

The reader may already be an expert in finding network *performance* bottlenecks. This chapter helps the reader to identify *reliability* bottlenecks. The chapter focuses strictly on network infrastructure components and only briefly mentions server and client issues. It discusses the following issues: device reliability, environmental issues, physical layer issues, link layer issues, network layer issues, and network management. The reader should have a good understanding of the functions of the Open Systems Interconnection (OSI) stack before perusing this chapter. Purchasing reliable equipment and installing redundant equipment will help the network architect build a highly reliable network.

DEVICE RELIABILITY METRICS AND RATINGS

A computer network is simply a collection of cables and electronic devices connected in a particular way to facilitate communications between two or more computers. Examining each of the components in a computer network helps readers analyze the risk (probability) of network failure.

An important but often overlooked and understudied device specification, the *mean time between failures (MTBF)*, can be used by network planners to maximize the reliability of their design. The MTBF is the only metric supplied by the manufacturer that can be used to evaluate the expected reliability of a product. In most cases, the vendor is self-reporting this information. But even assuming that the vendor is honestly disclosing its MTBF numbers, what does this number mean? Let us first examine the ways in which vendors compute their MTBF number and then use these numbers to calculate our own MTBF odds based on the network model below.

1. To get a product to market quickly (which is necessary in the competitive marketplace), the vendor is likely to take a large number of devices and run them continuously for some predetermined period. The MTBF is calculated by taking the total, cumulative running time of each device and dividing it by the number of failures. For example, if a vendor ran 10 devices for 1,000 hours each and 2 failed during that time, the total number of hours is 10,000/2 = 5,000 MTBF.
2. Vendors often do not consider an initial "burn-in" period (the initial period that a device is powered and running).
3. Vendors may or may not consider real-world effects, such as applying and removing power on a regular basis, handling during shipping, handling during installation, and so on.
4. Vendors may or may not be computing the MTBF as a function of the combined MTBF of all the devices' components, plus some operational probability of failure.
5. Vendors expect the unit to degrade below the stated MTBF after the period stated as its usable life has elapsed.

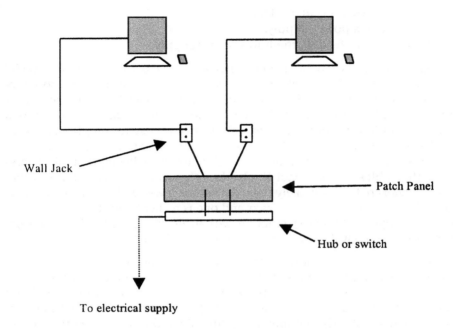

Wall Jack

Patch Panel

Hub or switch

To electrical supply

Exhibit 1.1.   A simple network diagram

The responsible network engineer will ask vendors how they compute their MTBF ratings. The engineer should not be surprised if the salesperson needs to call headquarters to obtain this information. A few rules of thumb should apply:

1. Do not trust the vendor's self-reported MTBF exclusively; read trade magazine articles about that vendor.
2. Allow a burn-in period for every device placed on the network; to effectively "burn-in" a new device, no activity is required—the device just needs to be turned on.

Analysis of a Simple Network

It would be helpful to examine the simple network model in Exhibit 1.1.

Exhibit 1.1 represents a simplified LAN model in which two computers are communicating via a hub. For simplicity, assume that this network is based on Ethernet. What can go wrong with this network? Ignoring the computers, the component parts of this network are the following:

1. Both cables from computer to wall.
2. Both cables from wall, through wall, to back of patch panel.
3. Both cables from patch panel to hub.

5

4. The hub's internal electronics.
5. The hub's power supply.
6. The power feeding the hub's power supply.

Six of the nine components of this network are cables. Without any MTBF data on the rate of failing cables, common sense is necessary. Three assumptions are necessary: (1) cables that move are more likely to break than cables that do not; (2) cables that do not move and will not break; and (3) before a cable is put into production, it is tested. Given these assumptions, cables that are subject to human interaction are more likely to move; therefore, cables that are subject to human interaction are more likely to break. Therefore, the cables that connect the back-of-the-wall jack to the back-of-the-patch panel are the least likely points of failure. If we can further assume that one of these computers is a server and one is a client and that the server is seldom subject to human interaction, we can also deduce that the cable from the server to the wall jack carries a reduced probability of failure.

Given the lack of supporting data, assume that the hub has a significantly higher probability for failure than any cable in the network. This may be because the hub is an active, electromechanical device. The hub is considered mechanical because it contains (usually) an electrical fan. That fan may have been constantly accumulating dust since the day it was turned on. That dust will clog the low-power motor. Over time, that motor may slow down or shut down completely. When the fan stops, the unit operates outside its design specifications and it probably stops running. In real networks, there may be tens or hundreds of interdependent network devices at various levels of the OSI stack.

REDUNDANCY

Often the outage of a single component, device, or link in the network can cause a larger outage. Therefore, it is useful to have a second item in place to provide service in the event that the primary item fails. This use of more than one item to perform the same task is called redundancy. Although it is true that a network functions without redundancy, a redundant network, which decreases the probability of failure, is more reliable. If redundancy is properly implemented, it can protect the network from debilitating device or link failures. The following sections of this chapter discuss how to have redundancy at a variety of levels. These levels loosely correspond to the three lower layers of the OSI stack. The lower three layers are physical, link, and network.

PHYSICAL LAYER ISSUES (OSI LAYER ONE)

Environment

Network architects occasionally have the ability to plan the construction of a new building. This can be very satisfying if done correctly. However, more often than not the network architect must construct a network in a pre-existing structure. Most of these structures, particularly older buildings, did not consider data communications during the design. Thus, communications closets may be in electrical closets, broom closets, or even ceilings and floors. The network architect must consider the total environment when analyzing the space in which the computer equipment will live. Are there any water pipes? The risks associated with water pipes are somewhat obvious. If one of them springs a leak, the organization does not want the network to go down the drain. Also, although less obvious, plumbers may occasionally need to access these pipes. In general, it is a good idea to stay away from areas in which other building infrastructure is concentrated, for it is in these areas that the most work will be done.

(As an aside, network architects should consider all building infrastructure maintenance people armed and dangerous. During the days of thick coaxial cable, this author had several run-ins with the heating and air-conditioning duct workers. At a thin coaxial cable installation, a team of painters seemed to thrive on unplugging Ethernet loopback connectors. Whether it is envy or a malicious plot to ruin the architect's good name, these people are out to destroy the network. Architects be warned.)

Power

In general, the network architect should have some basic understanding of how the power systems in the facility work. The equipment for which he is responsible must be powered. This section explores some of the power issues:

1. Is there an uninterruptible power supply (UPS)? A UPS is a mechanism that typically sits between the network devices and the facility's power supply (wall current). The UPS passes power through special circuitry that detects failures in the electrical supply and switches (within 1/60 of second) to its on-board battery. Unless the power systems have centralized redundancy, a UPS is a must. It not only keeps the network devices functioning in the event of an outage, but it can also condition the electrical current going into the network devices so to not cause unnecessary wear and tear on the device's power supply.
2. How many power supplies does the network devices have? Most modern network devices have an optional redundant power supply. If the facility has opted for the redundant power supply, the network architect should be sure that the power that feeds it is not the same power that supplies the other power supply. For example, if a communications closet has several devices, each with a redundant power supply, a reasonable UPS scheme would be to plug the primary

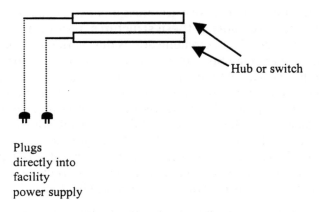

Plugs
directly into
facility
power supply

Exhibit 1.2.   No Redundant Power

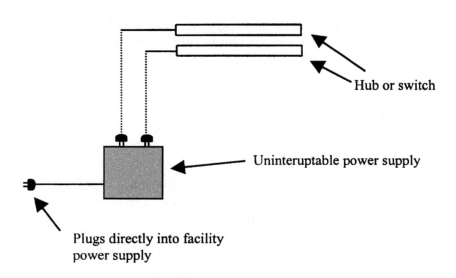

Plugs directly into facility
power supply

Exhibit 1.3.   UPS for Temporary Redundancy for Main Power Supply

power supply of each device in to one UPS and the second power
supplies of the other devices in to another UPS.
3. Do multiple, independent power systems feed the communications
   closet (e.g., power systems that come off of multiple circuit break-
   ers)? If so, network architects should take advantage of this by partitioning the power strategy across the two separate supplies.

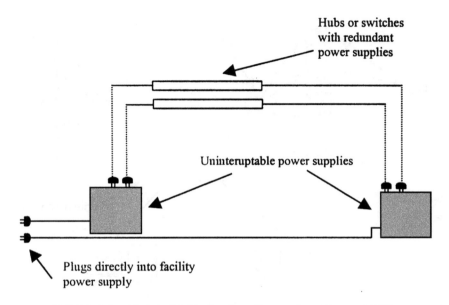

Exhibit 1.4.   Hubs with Redundant Power Supplies and UPSs

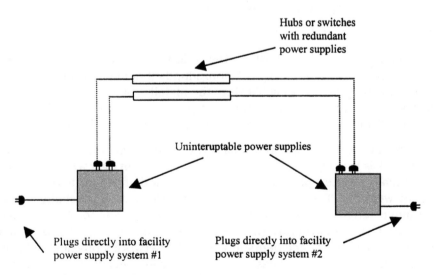

Exhibit 1.5.   Hubs with Redundant Power Supplies, UPSs, and Power Feeder Systems

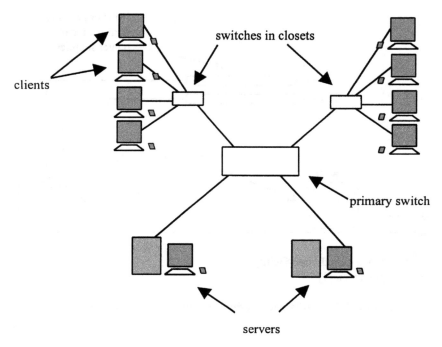

Exhibit 1.6. Typical Collapsed Star Topology

Exhibits 1.2 through 1.5 illustrate the various tiers of power supply redundancy. Exhibit 1.2 shows a typical, nonredundant configuration. Exhibit 1.3 shows the next most expensive step, the installation of a UPS. Exhibit 1.4 shows the installation of redundant power supplies into the hubs. Exhibit 1.5 shows the addition of a redundant power conduit system.

After addressing power redundancy, the next logical layer in the network stack is the physical layer. The physical medium over which bits travel (typically twisted pair or multi- or single-mode fiber optics) does not usually wear out. The breaking of a physical connection is usually caused by human activity. Construction or changes being made to other parts of the building's infrastructure (i.e., heating/air conditioning, plumbing, and electricity) can cause accidents in which the network's physical links are cut. In extreme circumstances, interference from electrical and magnetic sources can interfere with copper-based transmission media. Severe moisture can adversely affect some types of fiber-optic media.

Like power systems, various levels of redundancy can be achieved to avoid problems with physical lines being cut. Exhibit 1.6 illustrates a simple star network.

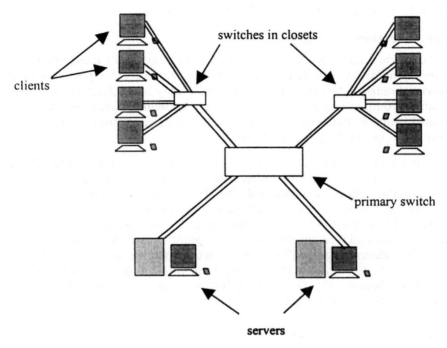

switches in closets

clients

primary switch

servers

Exhibit 1.7. Addition of Redundant Physical Connections

Each physical connection (represented by a line) is a possible point of failure for one or more clients. In this picture, there are two servers, one central switch and two closets from which clients are connected. The physical connections that can affect users here are the connections from server to switch, the connections from the primary switch to the closet switch, and the connections from the closet switches to the clients. Adding additional cables from the servers to the primary switch and from the primary switch to the closet switches reduces the probability of a failure that would affect more than one network node. It should be noted that these additional, redundant connections should follow a different physical route through the building from point A to point B. This is called route redundancy. Because cables usually fail as a result of some sort of local physical interference, there is a significant chance that the same interference would affect the redundant cable if it were to follow the identical route. The network can be made further redundant by adding additional links from the computers to the closet switches (see Exhibit 1.7).

These redundant physical paths must have software support. That support is discussed in the section on Layer 2 and 3, which follows.

11

LINK LAYER ISSUES (OSI LAYER TWO)

The Wide Area Networks

For wide area networks (WAN), the network engineer must usually secure connectivity from point A to point B via some service provider. In the world of deregulation, this service provider may be a telephone company, a power company, a cable company, or anyone willing to sell networking infrastructure. Because this is usually the telephone company, telephone company terminology is used here.

It is important for network architects to have some understanding of how their equipment is interacting with that of the local telephone company. Telephone companies coordinate all of their local connectivity for a geographical area from a central office (CO). Network architects must understand how their telephone company's COs are organized. The better they understand how the telephone company's network is configured, the more intelligently they will be able to request route redundancy through their network. Request that redundant WAN connections be routed through different COs. The section on Layer 3 provides more information about the use of redundant leased-lines

The Local Area Networks

Layer 2 (the link layer) is defined primarily by LAN definitions. These are standardized by the IEEE committee 802 and by ANSI. The IEEE 802.3 subcommittee has defined a set of standards known commercially as Ethernet. Because Ethernet is the most prevalent LAN topology type, it is used here as the primary example.

Shared Ethernet. Several vendors offer facilities for redundancy in shared Ethernet environments. These facilities vary among vendors and are not typically interoperable. Because all shared Ethernet redundancy solutions are vendor-dependent, they will not be discussed here.

Switched Ethernet. One of the more influential developments in LAN technology has been the overwhelming shift from shared media technologies to switched media technologies. An Ethernet switch is nothing more than a bridge with many ports. These ports may connect to other switches or hubs or directly to end devices. For the purposes of this chapter, the widespread use of switches has introduced a powerful tool for redundancy: the Spanning Tree Protocol.

Spanning Tree Protocol. The Spanning Tree Protocol (STP) was originally developed by IEEE subcommittee 802.1d to overcome the inability to have redundant bridges. Because Ethernet switches are simply multiport bridges, the STP can be used to facilitate the construction of highly link-redundant networks. To construct a redundant network that uses STP as a "safety net," it may be useful for readers to understand how the STP works.

Exhibit 1.8 provides a network diagram. It is a simple example in which three switches are connected via a link to one another. There is a cycle in this network. The cycle must be eliminated for the Ethernet network to function correctly. The STP algorithm works as follows:

1. Through the use of Ethernet multicast packets (called bridge protocol data unit, or BPDU), a "root" switch node is elected; this election is based on the switch with the lowest "bridge ID." The bridge ID is usually based on the media access control address of the switch.
2. For each segment that is common to more than one switch, a decision is made about which switch will forward packets to the root node. This decision is based on the switch that is closest (based on the number of hops) to the root node. The redundant links are put in "standby" mode.
3. Switches exchange BPDU packets that contain data indicating the number of hops to the root node.
4. As each switch receives BPDU packets, it evaluates the packet and compares the information to its stored perception of the network. If the new information leads to a shorter path to the root node, a new root port is identified and the old one will be shut down.
5. If a switch detects a change in the configuration of the network, a new root node may be elected (if necessary) and the calculation starts again.

Assume that the primary switch is elected to be the root node. The link that interconnects to the two closet switches would be furthest from the root node and therefore be turned off on both switches.

Recovery times when using the STP vary depending on the number of nodes in the tree, the speed of connectivity to those nodes, and various tunable parameters associated with the STP. A typical network takes more than 30 seconds to recover from a root-port outage. Many users perceive this 30-sec. delay as unacceptably long. To increase the attractiveness of Ethernet, various vendors have implemented proprietary methods to obtain a much smaller convergence time. Some vendors have claimed to reduce convergence times for large networks to less than 5 seconds.

STP is no longer limited only to Ethernet switches. Vendors have begun making network interface cards (NIC) that also recognize redundant connections. Using this technology, we can extend the use of redundancy to the leaf nodes of the network as in Exhibit 1.7. The obvious problem with Exhibit 1.7 is that the failure of any one switch would affect many computers. Exhibit 1.9 adds the redundant link between the closet switches and an additional primary switch. The failure of the primary

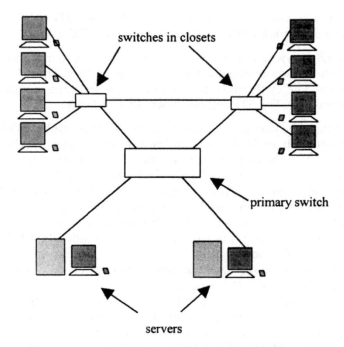

switches in closets

primary switch

servers

Exhibit 1.8.   The Switched Network with a Redundant Link

switch, a single-server-to-switch link, or any one switch-to-switch link, does not result in downtime.

LAYER THREE: THE NETWORK LAYER

In this section, readers examine Layer 3 methods for redundancy to build highly reliable networks. The Internet Protocol (IP) is the subject examined. Although only IP examples are cited, many of the same or identical concepts can be seen in Internet Packet Exchange (IPX) and Xerox Network Services (XNS) networks.

The basis of achieving IP redundancy is in learning new routes to old destinations. Exhibit 1.10 shows a corporate WAN with three sites. Site A is the primary facility and sites B and C are secondary facilities. All three sites are connected via T1 lines. For redundancy, add a third link connecting facilities B and C. Now the failure of any one link will not result in the isolation of any node. But how does IP handle this? The answer depends on the routing protocol. The simplest way to configure routing is to statically identify routes. There is one pro and several cons to static routes. The pro is that it is extremely simple and difficult to make a mistake. The con is that it is impossible to learn new routes when the primary route fails.

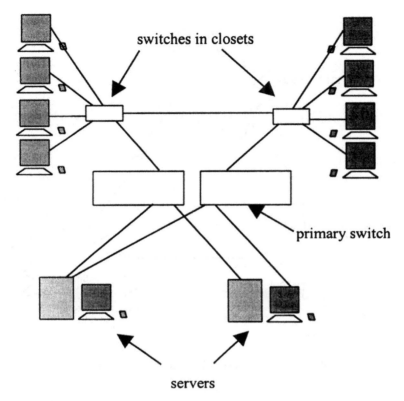

switches in closets

primary switch

servers

Exhibit 1.9. Redundant Primary Switches and Server Connections

There are three popular routing algorithms for small to medium-size networks (<500 subnets): RIP (routing information protocol), RIP2 (an improved version of RIP), and OSPF (open shortest path first). RIP sends periodic updates; OSPF updates its neighbors when something changes. Thus, if a node or link becomes inactive, OSPF will propagate that fact more quickly. For this and other reasons, OSPF will converge to a complete layer three network much faster than RIP.

NETWORK MANAGEMENT AND TESTING

The wonderful thing about automated, redundant fault-tolerant systems is that entire devices and power supplies, for example, can fail and no one will notice. Of course, at least one person needs to notice: the network manager. To build a completely fault-tolerant system would be a fool's errand if there were no network management system to inform someone that a fault had occurred. Once a fault occurs, the system is on its backup systems and just one fault away from being nonfunctional.

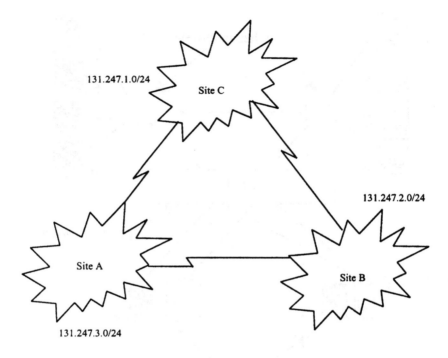

131.247.1.0/24
Site C

131.247.2.0/24

Site A

Site B

131.247.3.0/24

Exhibit 1.10.   IP Networks with a Redundant Path

After a supposedly reliable network has been configured and installed, one should always test the points of failure for which one planned redundancy. This test can be as simple as disconnecting a plug. If all goes well, the redundant systems should engage and the network management system will be notified.

BUSINESS JUSTIFICATION

Network redundancy is not inexpensive. The need for redundancy must be weighed against the cost of downtime to the organization. Redundancy can, in extreme cases, double the cost of networking. When calculating the cost of downtime, take into account not just the lost salaries of idle employees but also the indirect costs such as the public relations expenses of not being able to service customers.

THE ULTIMATELY RELIABLE NETWORK

The ideal is a LAN that will not go down under any noncataclysmic conditions (see Exhibit 1.11). To keep the complexity of the drawing minimal, the exhibit describes only a single client. There are two servers. Also as-

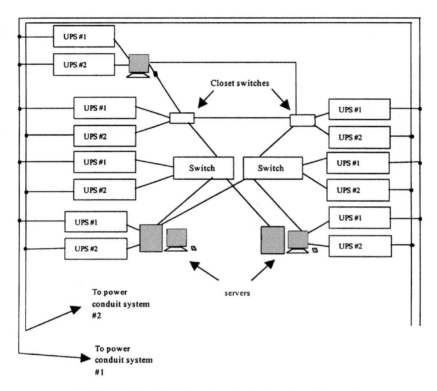

Exhibit 1.11.   The Completely Redundant Network

---

sume that those servers are OS-level redundant for each other. In other words, one server can be down and some software mechanism will cause the client to look to the other server for resources. Every device on the network has two UPSs that connect to it. Every device has a redundant power supply, and two UPSs and is powered from two independent power systems. The client computer is the only single point of failure. Assuming that is a spare client computer, and that any user could do the job equally well from the second computer, there should be no significant work loss in the event that the client computer failed.

Chapter 2
Gigabit Ethernet
Colin Mick

Although most organizations are just beginning to adopt Fast Ethernet, a newer, faster Ethernet technology is already entering the marketplace and some users are already preparing to use it. Gigabit Ethernet may seem overkill to those who are still running with shared or switched 10M-bps networks, but more than 100 network component and systems vendors are betting that there is already a market for an Ethernet technology that offers a full two orders of magnitude improvement in data rate.

The initial market for Gigabit Ethernet will be primarily to upgrade network infrastructures by providing high bandwidth links for backbones and server connections. A second market consists of vertical markets with specialized applications that require high bandwidth to the end user station.

Gigabit Ethernet is a logical backbone technology to connect existing networks built with both Fast Ethernet and 10Base-T. Modern network design practices, with their need for anywhere-to-anywhere connectivity, require high-bandwidth backbone support to ensure that users can reach servers anywhere in the organization. Today most networks use 100M-bps backbones based on asynchronous transfer mode (ATM), Fast Ethernet, or fiber distributed data interface (FDDI) technology. As requirements for bandwidth to end users increase, backbone capacity must be scaled up. Compared with other options, Gigabit Ethernet offers the simplest backbone upgrade for Ethernet-based networks; there is no translation, no fragmentation, and no frame encapsulation. New standards under development will augment Gigabit Ethernet backbones with Class of Service (COS) support.

Centralization of servers into server farms and the provision of anywhere-to-anywhere service both increase the demands on server performance. Gigabit Ethernet offers a simple upgrade to improve server performance. New Peripheral Component Interconnect (PCI) bus servers are capable of delivering data bursts at more that 1G bps and continuous data well in excess of 100M bps. Today, most servers and server farms are connected to the network via Fast Ethernet links. Gigabit Ethernet offers a low-cost upgrade that can potentially double the throughput of each server; all this takes at the server end is installation of a Gigabit Ethernet network interface card (NIC) and driver. (You also will have to add a Gigabit Ethernet repeater or switch to connect your servers to your existing network.)

0-8493-9838-X/00/$0.00+$.50
© 2000 by CRC Press LLC

Object	Bandwidth/Size	Compression ratio	Required Bandwidth
ISOCHRONOUS STREAM			
Full Motion Video (HDTV)	150M bps	50:1 (MPEG)	3M bps
Full Motion Video (NTSC)	45M bps	50:1 (MPEG)	1M bps
Voice	64K bps	8:1 (voice)	8K bps
DATA			
X-ray image	120M bits	2:1	60M bits
24-bit computer image	800M bits	100:1 (JPEG)	8M bits
20-page document with graphics	40M bits	4:1	10M bits
1 page letter	5K bits	4:1	1.3K bits
1 page scanned FAX image	1M bits	14:1	75K bits

Exhibit 2.1. Application Bandwidth Table

Graphics, image, multimedia, and video-based applications offer a ready market for Gigabit Ethernet now. Exhibit 2.1 shows the bandwidth requirements of a variety of applications.

TECHNICAL OVERVIEW

Gigabit Ethernet extends the ISO/IEC 8802-3 Ethernet family of networking technologies beyond 100M bps to 1000M bps. The bit rate is faster and bit times are proportionately shorter, reflecting the 10☐ bit rate increase. In full-duplex operation, packet transmission time has been decreased by a factor of 10; in half-duplex operation the improvement is smaller because of changes made to ensure operation over a reasonable collision domain diameter. Cable delay budgets are similar to those seen in 100Base-T,Base and the achievable topologies for half-duplex operation are similar to those available for half-duplex 100Base-T.

HOW IT WORKS

Gigabit Ethernet combines the tested and true Ethernet Media Access Control (MAC) and two different physical layer signaling technologies: 1000Base-X and 1000Base-T (see Exhibit 2.2). It also takes advantages of full-duplex operation and flow control, new capabilities added to the Ethernet MAC by the recently completed 802.3x Media Access Control sublayer, partitioning, and relationship to the ISO Open Systems Interconnection (OSI) reference model.

1000Base-X Signaling Systems

The 1000Base-X family couples the Ethernet MAC with hardware originally developed for Fibre Channel (ANSI X3.230). This approach follows the

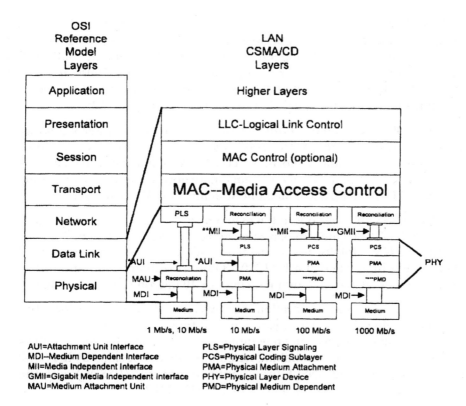

OSI Reference Model Layers

LAN CSMA/CD Layers

Exhibit 2.2. Media Access Control Sublayer Partitioning and Relationship to the ISO Open Systems Interconnection (OSI) Reference Model

one used for developing 100Base-X, where the Ethernet MAC was coupled with ANSI X3T12, encoding physical medium dependent specifications designed to carry FDDI over copper and fiber links.

Adoption of the Fibre Channel

The physical layer required modification of the interface to the Ethernet MAC, the use of 8B10B coding, and a 17% increase (from 1.0625M baud to 1.25M baud) in the speed of PHY operation to accommodate the 1000M bps data rate.

The MAC interface change was accomplished by adding a Gigabit Media Independent Interface (GMII) between the MAC and PHY layers. Similar in operation to the Media Independent Interface (MII) found in 100Base-T, the GMII is capable of supporting operation at 10M bps, 100M bps, and 1000M bps through transmit and receive paths up to 8 bits wide. A reconciliation sublayer maps signals between the MAC and the GMII.

The 1000Base-X family consists of three physical layer signaling systems: short wavelength (1000Base-SX) fiber, long wavelength (1000Base-LX) fiber, and a short-haul copper system using twinaxial cable (1000Base-CX). The signaling systems incorporate the Physical Coding Sublayer (PCS) and Physical Medium Attachment (PMA) sublayer.

1000Base-SX specifies operation over a pair of optical fibers using short-wavelength (770-860 nm) transmission and either 62.5 micron or 50 micron multimode fiber. 1000Base-LX specifies operation over a pair of optical fibers using long-wavelength (1270-1355 nm) transmission and either 62.5 micron or 50 micron multimode fiber or 10 micron single-mode fiber.

1000Base-CX specifies operation over two pairs of 150-ohm shielded, balanced tw-style cabling. This system would typically be used for jumper cables to connect devices in an equipment rack or machine room. Cables use either shielded DB-9 subminiature connectors as specified by IEC 807-3 or the 8-pin shielded ANSI Fibre Channel connector (HSSDC) with the mechanical mating interface defined by IEC 61076-103.

1000Base-T will use a DSP-based signaling system that supports operation over 100 m of 4-pair Category 5 UTP cabling as specified in EIA/TIA 568-A and ISO/IEC 11801—the same Category 5 links used for 100Base-TX operation. This portion of the standard is being developed by a separate Task Force (802.3ab) and was planned for completion at the end of 1998—some time after the completion of 802.3z.

Auto-Negotiation

All Gigabit Ethernet signaling systems use some form of Auto-Negotiation to configure both ends of the link for proper operation at start-up. 1000Base-T uses the same Auto-Negotiation technology pioneered by Fast Ethernet. This technology, described in clause 28 of IEEE802.3u, supports operation over copper links with RJ45 connectors. It ensures that stations at both ends of the link are compatible and, if so, configures them for optimal operation.

In addition to ensuring proper connection and operation and startup, 1000Base-T Auto-Negotiation can support multi-speed (100/1000M bps) capable devices, much like the 10/100 devices available for Fast-Ethernet.

1000Base-X uses a different form of Auto-Negotiation, developed by the 802.3z task force, to support full-duplex continuous signaling using 8B10B coding over 1.25-GHz links. As with the copper link version of Auto-Negotiation, it provides a means for stations at two ends of a link to exchange information describing their abilities and to then use this information to configure themselves so they can operate with one another in an optimal configuration. The auto-negotiation information is exchanged via special frames as part of the start-up process.

Once Auto-Negotiation is complete, the link is opened for communication. The basic information exchanged as part of the 1000Base-X Auto-Negotiation process is contained in a "base page" and includes support of full-duplex operation, support of half-duplex information, support of asymmetric and/or symmetric PAUSE control (needed for flow control), provision of remote fault codes to report Auto-Negotiation problems, acknowledgment that the base page has been received, and notification of additional or next pages to be sent.

The Next pages are used to exchange optional or vendor-specific information as part of the Auto-Negotiation process.

Half-Duplex/Full-Duplex

Gigabit Ethernet supports two modes of operation: the traditional half-duplex mode which uses carrier sense multiple access with collision detect (CSMA/CD), and a full-duplex mode similar to that provided by Fast Ethernet. The two modes operate and behave quite differently.

Half-duplex operation requires modifications to the MAC layer which change the treatment of small packets and can limit performance. At operating speeds above 100M bps, the MAC appends a sequence of carrier extension bits to short frames to ensure that the length of each frame event equals or exceeds the slot time. This means that the minimum frame size for half-duplex operation at 1000M bps is 4096 bit times or 512 bytes. A minimum frame size of 512 bytes ensures half-duplex operation with a collision domain of 200—the same as that provided by 100Base-T. (Failure to extend the frames would limit the collision domain to approximately 20 meters.) Extension bits are not data and are automatically stripped from frames at receipt.

A second change to the MAC enables sending burst of frames. When operating in half-duplex mode at speeds greater than 100M bps, the CSMA/CD MAC may optionally transmit additional frames (up to a total of 65,536 bits) without relinquishing control of the transmission medium. This improves the throughput during half-duplex operation—assuming there are multiple packets in a queue waiting to be sent and that upper layer protocols permit packet bursting.

PHY	IEC 807-3 TW-style copper cable	EIA/TIA-568-A Category 5 copper cabling	62.5 micron multi-mode fiber	50 micron multi-mode fiber	10 micron single mode fiber
1000Base-SX	na	na	260 meters	500 meters	na
1000Base-LX	na	na	440 meters	500 meters	3,000 meters
1000Base-CX	25 meters	na	na	na	na
1000Base-T	na	100 meters	na	na	na

Exhibit 2.3. Gigabit Ethernet Link Distances

Full-duplex operation provides for simultaneous data flow in both directions by turning off CSMA/CD as per Clause 31 of IEEE802.3. Turning off CSMA/CD allows the links to operate at full bandwidth, maximizing performance. In 10Base-T and 100Base-T, full-duplex operation is possible only on dedicated or switched links, but 1000Base-T also supports shared media full-duplex operation via Full Duplex repeaters, which are described later in this chapter.

CABLING AND TOPOLOGY RULES

Gigabit Ethernet signaling systems are designed to work with a variety of fiber and copper links.

Fiber links are dependent on the interaction between the optics and the fiber; the distances shown in Exhibit 2.3 are minimum distances. The TW-style copper users should be aware that the electrical requirements for 1000Base-CX support are more stringent than the IEC-807-3 specifications.

Gigabit Ethernet link distances assume ISO/IEC 11801 compliant fiber. Distances will vary depending on the modal bandwidth of the installed fiber. Additional details on the impact of modal bandwidth on fiber link distances are provided in Clause 38 of the standard.

Supporting 1000M-bps operation over Category 5 links raises concerns about both return loss and crosstalk, performance areas that have previously been unspecified in the US EIA/TIA-568-A cabling standard. A new addendum to that standard specifies how to measure return loss and crosstalk for both component and field testing. By the time 1000Base-T products reach the market, commercial cable testing devices should be

Model	TW-style cable	EIA/TIA-568-A Category 5 copper	Fiber	TW-style and fiber (CX & SX/LX)	Cat 5 fiber (T & SX/LX)
DTE-DTE	25	100	320	na	na
One repeater	50	200	220	210[b]	220[c]

Notes
[a]In meters, no margin
[b]Assume 25 meters of TW-style cable and one fiber link of 195 meters.
[c]Assumes 100 meters of CAT-5 and one fiber link of 110 meters.

Exhibit 2.4. Maximum Collision Domain Diameters for Half-Duplex Operation[a]

capable of evaluating these cable characteristics. Cabling experts have indicated that cabling plants that are compliant with the current version of EIA/TIA-568-A should have no problem meeting appropriate return loss and crosstalk performance levels.

Exhibit 2.4 provides collision domain diameter information for 1000M-bps half-duplex operation. Maximum collision domain diameters for half-duplex operation assume 25 m of TW-style cable and one fiber link of 195 m.

BUILDING NETWORKS WITH GIGABIT ETHERNET

Gigabit DTEs can be connected via a direct link, via CSMA/CD repeaters for shared media solutions, via full-duplex repeaters for shared media solutions, and with switches for dedicated bandwidth solutions.

Half-duplex repeaters are the traditional means for providing shared bandwidth to Ethernet users. The standard defines operation of a half-duplex CSMA/CD repeater, which supports collision domains of up to 200 m in diameter. Only one repeater can be contained within a single collision domain. Half-duplex repeaters offer an extremely low-cost method for sharing access to 1000M bps service, but they also offer reduced performance, compared with full-duplex repeaters (FDR) and switches.

FDRs, also called buffered distributors, offer the traditional low-cost shared media operation of repeaters, but with support for full duplex operation. They utilize the full-duplex flow control mechanism to arbitrate access instead of Ethernet's traditional CSMA/CD. On-board buffers store incoming packets until they can be repeated to other ports. Asymmetric flow control is used to temporarily halt the flow of incoming packets when the input buffers fill. When the buffers empty, the halted transmitting units are allowed to resume transmission. The combination of full-duplex operation, input buffers, and flow control means that FDRs can support effected shared media operation at close to 1000M bps, providing much higher throughput than traditional half-duplex repeaters.

25

Switches provide dedicated bandwidth connections and a means for connecting networks with different bandwidths. Each link in a collision domain represents a separate collision domain, and since there are no collisions, links can operate at either half-duplex or full duplex.

Gigabit Ethernet switches fall into two categories: aggregating and backbone. Aggregating switches are used to connect one or two gigabit links to a number of 100M-bps ports. Flow control is used to keep the gigabit links from overwhelming the switch buffers when a gigabit flow is directed to one or two 100M-bps ports. Backbone switches provide multiple gigabit ports and have multi-gigabit backplanes to provide wire-speed connectivity between ports. They typically have larger buffers than aggregating switches and may offer advanced features such as Layer 3 switching and virtual LANs.

MANAGEMENT OF GIGABIT ETHERNET

As with 100Base-T, Gigabit Ethernet makes use of the current 802.3 Ethernet management suite as defined in Clause 30 of 802.3u. The basic Ethernet frame format, CSMA/CD operation, and both the RMON and Simple Network Management Protocol MIBs remain virtually unchanged (although some minor changes were made.) This means most management tools should continue to work seamlessly with Gigabit Ethernet products.

SUPPORTING ORGANIZATIONS

Two multicompany organizations are significant contributors to Gigabit Ethernet technology: the Gigabit Ethernet Alliance and the Gigabit Ethernet Consortium. The Gigabit Ethernet Alliance is an organization composed of more than 120 companies to facilitate the development of the standard and provide technology marketing support. Headquartered in Silicon Valley, the GEA has supported technology development by providing mechanisms to facilitate progress on the standard between formal IEEE-sponsored meetings and to develop test suites to ensure product conformance and interoperability. The technology marketing arm of the GEA has focused on promoting Gigabit Ethernet technology through press releases, a World Wide Web site, technology demonstrations, and seminars. Since the major goal of the GEA is to support the development of the Gigabit Ethernet standard, it has a limited lifespan and may disband.

Until it disbands, the GEA will maintain a Web site (*www.gigabit-ethernet.org*), which provides information about the technology, standards status reports, and links to GEA member company sites.

In the summer of 1997, a GEA team working with staff members of the University of New Hampshire Interoperability Laboratory established the Gigabit Ethernet Consortium. Founded July 7, 1997 with 15 member companies, the GEC provides an independent forum for testing Gigabit Ethernet products for conformance and interoperability. This program will provide vendors with critical development information and provide users with the confidence that first-generation products will have a high degree of interoperability. Unlike the GEA, the Gigabit Ethernet Consortium is intended for long-term operation.

ENABLING TECHNOLOGIES

The diffusion of Gigabit Ethernet into the marketplace will be done in parallel with several enabling/facilitating technologies, much as Fast Ethernet diffused in parallel with switching. Some of these enabling technologies—full-duplex operation, flow control, and full duplex repeaters—have already been discussed, as they operate via Ethernet standards. Other enabling technologies emerging from other standards groups include Layer 3 switching, classes of service, support for time-sensitive applications, and virtual LANs.

Layer 3 switching extends the speed and power of switching technology to Layer 3 routing and is a natural outgrowth of the switching technology that appeared in the early 1990s. Until recently, most switches have operated at ISO Layer 2—making decisions based on MAC addresses. Layer 3 switches extend the speed of switching technology to Layer 3 addresses (usually based on Internet Protocol (IP)), allowing better network management and segregation of network traffic while eliminating the bottleneck of long router processing latency.

Class of service technology provides the ability to assign priorities to messages to assure the delivery of time-sensitive information. Although priorities and time-sensitive delivery have been available with other networking solutions, such as Token Ring, FDDI, and ATM, Ethernet has traditionally remained a single priority system. Work currently under way in the IEEE 802.1 High Layer Working Group (project 802.1p) and in 802.3 (proposed project 802.3ac) will soon provide a standards-based approach to attach priorities to Ethernet frames.

Transmission of voice, video, and multimedia content over networks brings its own set of problems. Solutions to these problems are coming from the Internet Engineering Task Force (IETF) via technologies such as IP Multicasting, RSVP, and RTSP. IP Multicasting is an extension to the standard IP network level protocol (RFC 1112) to facilitate the one-to-many delivery of time-sensitive information to a group of users by broadcasting datagrams to a host group identified by a single IP destination address. RSVP, the Reservation Protocol, provides a way of creating multi-hop connections across routers with a specified quality of service level to support specific data streams or traffic flows. RTSP, the Real Time Streaming Protocol, is an application-layer protocol for controlling the on-demand delivery of time-sensitive data such as audio and video. These protocols require intermediate device (router, switch) support.

VLANs are a management tool for organizing users into logical groups rather than physical ones. Since the organization is logical, individual users can be swiftly transferred from one VLAN to another via management tools. Many manufacturers already offer proprietary VLAN implementations for switches. The standard for VLAN operation, IEEE 802.1Q, is currently in development.

SUMMARY

Gigabit Ethernet is an extension of the IEEE802.3 Ethernet family of local area networking technologies. It was designed to integrate smoothly with legacy Ethernet systems, just like 100Base-T. Gigabit Ethernet offers an easy-to-use, scalable technology to expand and update legacy Ethernet Networks. Gigabit Ethernet uses the traditional Ethernet format and size and supports half-duplex (CSMA/CD) and full-duplex operation.

Gigabit Ethernet management uses the same management definition and MIBs, which means that most management tools should be able to work with Gigabit Ethernet products. Gigabit Ethernet supports operation over most LAN links including 50 and 62.5 micron multimode fiber, 10 micron, single-mode fiber, short runs of and standard EIA/TIA-568-A Category 5 copper links. This means it will work with most existing fiber and copper installations.

Gigabit Ethernet is supported by a large number of vendors. Conformance and interoperability test mechanisms for Gigabit Ethernet are already in place and tests are being developed in parallel with the standards process.

The Ethernet family of local area networking standards is developed under the IEEE 802.3 working group. The standard consists of a base volume and supplements. Fast Ethernet is currently described in a 1995 supplement containing Clauses 21-30. An additional supplement was published in late 1997 containing Clause 31 (Full Duplex and Flow Control and Clause 32—1000Base-T2) and a supplement covering Gigabit Ethernet (with the exception of 1000Base-T) was expected to be published in late 1998 (see Exhibit 2.5).

Clause	Publication	Covers	Contents
1	ISO/IEC 8802-3 (1996)	General	Introduction
2	ISO/IEC 8802-3 (1996)	General	Media Access Control (MAC) service specification
3	ISO/IEC 8802-3 (1996)	General	MAC frame structure
4	ISO/IEC 8802-3 (1996)	General	Media Access Control
5	ISO/IEC 8802-3 (1996)	General	Layer Management
6	ISO/IEC 8802-3 (1996)	General	Physical Signaling (PLS) service specification
7	ISO/IEC 8802-3 (1996)	1/10M bps	Physical Signaling (PLS) and Attachment Unit Interface (AUI) specifications
8	ISO/IEC 8802-3 (1996)	10M bps coax	Medium Attachment Unit and baseband medium specifications, Type 10BASE5
9	ISO/IEC 8802-3 (1996)	10M bps	Repeater unit for 10M bps baseband networks
10	ISO/IEC 8802-3 (1996)	10M bps coax	Medium attachment unit and baseband medium specifications, Type 10BASE2
11	ISO/IEC 8802-3 (1996)	10M bps broadband	Broadband medium attachment unit and broadband medium specifications, Type 10BROAD36
12	ISO/IEC 8802-3 (1996)	1M bps coax	Physical signaling, medium attachment, and baseband medium specifications, Type 1BASE5
13	ISO/IEC 8802-3 (1996)	10M bps topology	System considerations for multi-segment 10M bps baseband networks
14	ISO/IEC 8802-3 (1996)	10M bps CAT 3, 4, 5	Twisted-pair medium attachment unit (MAU) and baseband medium, Type 10BASE-T
15	ISO/IEC 8802-3 (1996)	10M bps fiber	Fiber optic medium and common elements of medium attachment units and star, Type 10BASE-F
16	ISO/IEC 8802-3 (1996)	10M bps fiber	Fiber optic passive star and medium attachment unit, Type 10BASE-FP
17	ISO/IEC 8802-3 (1996)	10M bps fiber	Fiber optic medium attachment unit, Type 10BASE-FB
18	ISO/IEC 8802-3 (1996)	10M bps fiber	Fiber optic medium attachment unit, Type 10BASE-FL
19	ISO/IEC 8802-3 (1996)	Management	Layer Management for 10M bps baseband repeaters
20	ISO/IEC 8802-3 (1996)	Management	Layer Management for 10M bps baseband medium attachment units
21	IEEE 802.3u (1996)	100M bps	Introduction to 100M bps baseband networks, Type 100BASE-T
22	IEEE 802.3u (1996)	100M bps	Reconciliation Sublayer (RS) and Media Independent Interface (MII)
23	IEEE 802.3u (1996)	100M bps CAT 3, 4, 5	Physical Coding Sublayer (PCS), Physical Medium Attachment (PMA) sublayer and baseband medium, Type 100BASE-T4
24	IEEE 802.3u (1996)	100M bps Cat 5, fiber	Physical Coding Sublayer (PCS), Physical Medium Attachment (PMA) sublayer, Type 100BASE-X
25	IEEE 802.3u (1996)	100M bps CAT 5	Physical Medium Dependent (PMD) sublayer and baseband medium, Type 100BASE-TX
26	IEEE 802.3u (1996)	100M bps fiber	Physical Medium Dependent (PMD) sublayer and baseband medium, Type 100BASE-FX
27	IEEE 802.3u (1996)	100M bps	Repeater for 100M bps baseband networks

Exhibit 2.5.   Ethernet Standards Status and Coverage as of Summer 1997

28	IEEE 802.3u (1996)	10M bps & 100M bps Cat 3, 4, 5	Physical Layer link signaling for 10M bps and 100M bps Auto-Negotiation on twisted pair
29	IEEE 802.3u (1996)	100M bps topology	Systems considerations for multi-segment 100BASE-T networks
30	IEEE 802.3u (1996)	Management (all of Ethernet)	Layer Management for 10M bps and 100M bps
31	IEEE 802.3x (in prep)	10/100/1000M bps	Full Duplex and Flow Control
32	IEEE 802.3y (in prep)	100M bps CAT 3, 4, 5	100BASE-T2
33	IEEE 802.3ac (in dev.)	VLAN tagging	New clause to be added to support VLAN tagging
34	IEEE 802.3z (in dev.)	1000M bps	Introduction to 1000M bps baseband networks
35	IEEE 802.3z (in dev.)	1000M bps	Reconciliation Sublayer (RS) and Gigabit Media Independent Interface (GMII)
36	IEEE 802.3z (in dev.)	1000M bps fiber & short-haul copper	Physical Coding Sublayer (PCS) and Physical Medium Attachment (PMA) sublayer, type 1000BASE-X
37	IEEE 802.3z (in dev.)	1000M bps	Auto-Negotiation for 1000BASE-X
38	IEEE 802.3z (in dev.)	1000M bps fiber	Physical Medium Dependent (PMD) sublayer and baseband medium, type 1000BASE-LX (Long Wavelength Laser) and type 1000BASE-SX (Short Wavelength Laser)
39	IEEE 802.3z (in dev.)	1000M bps short-haul copper	Physical Medium Dependent (PMD) sublayer and baseband medium, type 1000BASE-CX
40	IEEE 802.3z (in dev.)	1000M bps CAT 5	1000BASE-T
41	IEEE 802.3z (in dev.)	1000M bps	Repeater for 100M bps baseband networks
42	IEEE 802.3z (in dev.)	1000M bps topology	System considerations for multi-segment 1000M bps baseband networks

Exhibit 2.5. *(Continued)*

Chapter 3
Processor Types
A. Padgett Peterson

The two basic divisions between processors today are CISC and RISC. CISC (or Complex Instruction Set Computers) is the traditional form in which the manufacturer decides the use of the processor, designs the microcode for all of the instructions the processor will use, and implements that microcode on the chip itself, optimizing the data paths for speed. The most common CPUs today, the Intel Corp. 80x86 and Motorola Inc. 680x0 series, are examples of CISC processors.

With a CISC processor, compilers and assemblers produce code that runs for the most part directly on the processor. In turn, the CISC processor offers a rich instruction set with provision for such things as floating point arithmetic, character and string manipulations, and an array of I/O manipulations.

Beginning in the late 1970s with bit slice processors such as the AMD 2901, the RISC (or Reduced Instruction Set Computer) formed a different path. In this case the on-board microcode is limited to a very small set of instructions, typically involving only simple register and memory operations. The advantage of RISC is a small microcode store and short data paths, which give the RISC processors a decided speed advantage over their CISC relations.

For example, RISC processors are now (1998) capable of clock speeds in the 300 to 900 MHz range while their CISC relations are running at 100 to 400 MHz.

As usual, vaporware is rampant as marketeers promise 500-MHz Intel chips and 1,000-MHz Alphas. Although tomorrow may well bring such marvels, the current foundry capability (the companies that make the wafer dies from which chips are constructed) will probably make speeds not much faster than today's processors.

Although such numbers look impressive and are often used to promote models, it is important to remember that true machine throughput depends on a balance of all the components. In an application-sensitive firewall or a graphical design application, a high-speed CPU may be important, whereas for most file server applications, the load is not very heavy.

0-8493-9838-X/00/$0.00+$.50
© 2000 by CRC Press LLC

For this reason, although a well-designed server may use multiple CPUs, the purpose is more reliability in the same way redundant arrays of inexpensive drives (RAID) are used rather than pure throughput.

However, this is not without cost when real work must be done, as a RISC processor typically needs many more instructions to perform the same task that a CISC can perform with only one. An old joke in the computer industry is that the ultimate RISC does nothing at all but does it very fast.

In terms of a typical programming mix of human-computer activities, the RISC unit will be somewhat slower than the equivalent CISC. The reason is that although a full-featured operating system can be layered directly on the CISC, often the RISC instruction set must be augmented through a layer of software called an emulator.

This is best shown by the original "Power PC," which was able to emulate the Macintosh/680x0 instruction set very well but was noticeably slower when called upon for Windows/Intel duties.

However, the real power of the RISC can be found when the full set of instructions is not generally needed, as for server operations provided the software is written directly for the RISC set without requiring an intermediate emulation layer. In this case, the speed advantage, particularly for logical operations, can make up for the fact that more instructions must be executed to accomplish the same task.

For this reason, the later Intel processors, beginning with the 486 series, retain the full CISC instruction set; however, the most commonly used instructions such as Metal Oxide Varistor were optimized to be executable in a single clock cycle. This characteristic was carried forward in the Pentium and Pentium Pro series, which used even greater optimization for an overall reduction in clock cycles per instruction. For this reason, the Pentium 90 and the 486DX5-133 are approximately equal in practical speed.

MEMORY SPEED

Any discussion of CPU speed must be related to the speed at which the memory can deliver instructions to the processor. Optimally, the processor would request a memory location and on the same cycle it would be able to access that information. In practice, it does not work that way for a number of reasons.

First, a digital designer must consider that although the memory address may not be available until near the end of the requesting clock cycle, the data must be stable at the beginning of the cycle at which it is expected. Second, gate delays in the associated circuitry take time to translate the address request from the processor to the memory device assigned that location. Third, a designer must consider the reaction time of the memory device itself.

For the first PCs of 1981, with a 4.77-MHz clock cycle, 200 ns memory was adequate for a three-cycle operation. On the first clock, the address was provided to the memory circuitry, the second was allowed to provide stable information on the data bus, and on the third clock the data would be read in.

This three-clock cycle was the basis for all PC-type computers that came later. When computers are set up today, they use the same baseline, so if the user selects one wait state for memory, this means that four cycles are used instead of three.

As processor speeds went up, memory access times had to decrease because a 33-MHz bus clock provided only 30 ns per clock or 90 ns total for no-wait-state operation. Given a 20 to 30 ns gate delay, 80 ns memory often required an additional wait state to operate. The fact that the 40 ns cycle allowed by a 25-MHz clock provided the same 120 ns with three clocks that a 33-MHz unit needed four to achieve meant that for 80 ns memory, there was little real performance difference between a 25-MHz and a 33-MHz computer.

MEMORY BUSES

Another contributing factor is the bus width or the amount of data that can be transferred at one time. The Motorola 680x0 series of processors have always had a 32-bit bus width, allowing 4 bytes of data to be received in parallel, but the Intel-based processors have gone through a series of stages to get there.

Beginning with an 8-bit data bus width for the 8088 to make it compatible with 8080 and Z-80 machines, the IBM PCs and their first clones were handily outperformed by machines from those companies that designed their systems around the companion 8086 processor. The only difference was a 16-bit data bus width.

With the PC-AT and its 80286 processor, the standard bus width became 16 bits and accounted for most of the performance increase, since clock speed was increased only slightly to 6 MHz.

The introduction of the 386 made Windows possible by curing a problem in the 286—the inability to switch from virtual to real mode without rebooting. It also increased the bus width to 32 bits, achieving for the first-time parity with the 680x0 used in the Macintosh. In an attempt to use up stocks of 16-bit bus motherboards originally intended for Advanced Technology (AT) class machines, Intel also produced the 386SX, a 16-bit version and hence considerably slower than the DX.

With the introduction of the 486, things became even more confusing. Both the SX and DX versions were 32-bit but were soon joined by the 486SLC from other vendors that had a 16-bit data bus. Fortunately, few were sold.

The final entries (so far) are the Pentium and Pentium Pro processors. Superscalar architecture using submicron design rules, these super microprocessors use a 64-bit data path enabling access of 8 bytes at a time. To fully utilize this architecture, memory chip carriers have transformed from 30 pin SIMMs to 72 pin units in the last few years.

RISC units have always enjoyed an advantage in this area: The first units had a 32-bit bus width and the latest Alpha chips access a 256-bit-wide memory bus. Combined with 500 to 600 MHz clock speeds, the latest RISC stations enjoy a clear performance advantage.

CACHE

Cache memory, in an attempt to increase the processing speed of a computer by reducing the need for access to slow main memory, adds a relatively small amount of fast memory in a separate area. Whenever memory is accessed, it is also written to this store. On the next access, if it is still in the cache area, it is retrieved from there with no wait states involved. That cache memory typically has a 15 to 20 ns access time whereas main memory typically consists of 60 to 80 ns access time is indicative of the speed required for next-cycle access at a 33-MHz bus speed.

Introduced on some 386 class machines (e.g., those from Zenith Data Systems), the first caches were fully populated at 64K of RAM and materially increased effective performance the same way that disk caches in memory had done some years earlier.

Experiments showed that performance increased dramatically at first as more RAM was added, then more slowly after 128K, with a maximum "bang for the buck" at about 256K. Further increases, while assisting in some operations, were hampered by the increased activity necessary to determine whether the just-requested segment was already in cache.

The second cache was introduced with the introduction of the 486 class processor, which had 8K of on-board RAM. Located on the CPU itself, the amount was limited, but it was as fast as the processor.

As now there were two types of cache available, designations were needed: on-board cache was referred to as level 1 or simple "L1" cache; separate RAM cache on the motherboard became known as level 2 or "L2."

Unfortunately, although companies such as Texas Instruments experimented with increased L1 cache, up to 16K, others marketed products with as little as 1K, which had minimal performance effect. When combined with a "486" designated device, which was really a 386 architecture with a few added instructions, this led to 486 machines that were slower than the equivalent 386. This was further confused by a series of "486SLC" devices designed for a 16-bit data path to take advantage of leftover 386SX motherboards. Combined with a ROM change, these systems reported themselves to be 486 boards—just very slow ones.

By contrast, several vendors packaged TI 486 chips onto special substrates, allowing them to be used on true 386DX motherboards. Coupled with a driver program to enable the L1 cache, when used on a motherboard already equipped with L2 cache, speeds very close to true 486 boards can be obtained.

At the present, few chip sets permit "586" chips to be used on older 486 motherboards with a concurrent performance improvement. Unfortunately, such hybrids typically use an Industry Standard Architecture or VESA peripheral bus instead of the high-speed Peripheral Component Interconnect (PCI) bus, limiting the effective throughput.

One major reason for this limitation is that the true Pentium uses a 64-bit direct access to L2 cache, doubling the effective cache throughput and incidentally larger effective cache sizes (512 Kb is effective), though the speed improvement with a larger cache is not linear—going from 256K bps to 512K bps provides a typical speed increase of only 2 to 3%. The 486 chips and motherboards do not support this, though some "dual use" boards have been built.

If cache is an advantage to CISC-based systems, it can be of even greater assistance to RISC systems because they typically require more instructions to perform the same operation. In this case, if the entire program to be executed can be loaded in cache, then the only need for main memory is to load the program initially and retain data. In this case, the complete operation can be from cache while main memory takes the place of disk storage. For this reason and due to the drastic drop in memory prices in 1996, large cache systems are becoming popular—with cache approaching early disk drive capacity becoming common.

Again for RISC processors, the rules are different. Where Intel-based motherboards are often limited to 1 Mb of cache ("superservers" may provide more), the cache for a RISC machine is typically extended to three levels. The current Digital Equipment Corp. Alpha Station 500s have 8 Mb of L3 cache as standard and most are shipping with 256 Mb of memory.

SPEED DOUBLERS AND TRIPLERS

Given sufficient cache for most operations, it is possible for the processor to operate independently of the system within which it is operating. At the same time, ever decreasing prices for peripherals are driven by the stable bus speeds. In this case, the basic clock speed for the PC has been hardware limited to about 33 MHz.

To achieve increased internal speeds, processors now have internal clock circuits that are synchronized to the external hardware clocks but operate at two or three times the hardware clock rates. The first of these raised 25-MHz clocks to 50 MHz and 33-MHz clocks to 66 MHz.

The numbering system used by "doublers" bears some examination as it is not outwardly clear why a 486DX4-100 has a bus speed of 33 MHz rather than 25 MHz. Actually, when doublers were first introduced, it was not clear yet what the designs would allow. Accordingly, speed points were set a 2x, 2.5x, 3x, and 4x clock and numbered 2, 3, 4, and 5. Hence, a 486DX3-80 would use a 33-MHz system clock whereas a 486DX2-80 would require a 40-MHz clock. As a frame of reference, given a 33-MHz system clock, the advertised speeds would be as follows: 2, 66 MHz, 3, 80 MHz, 4, 100 MHz, and 5, 133 MHz.

The Pentium processors, advertised solely on their internal speed, made all this obsolete. Here, once again, the early practice of overdriving a chip is being used with the DS2-50 chip often found in 33-(66) MHz machines. Overdriving is popular, as often the elaborate cooling towers/fans used to cool the latest high-speed chips obscure the manufacturers' markings.

Note that overdriving was primarily a way to allow the millions of existing motherboards to receive an apparent speed improvement with little cost to the consumer. As long as processors are able to operate out of L1 and L2 cache, performance will improve, but when required to access main memory or I/O, the limit is that of the original design and the processor spends much of its time waiting for the rest of the machine to catch up.

In general, RISC machines do not use doublers, preferring to require an upgrade of all of the supporting systems when a processor speed advance is made. Because consumer price pressure does not exist for most RISCs, which are "high-end" items, this is possible today.

HEAT

Dense chips, such as those in CPUs, always run hot—often near the 85□C (185□F) limit of most plastic cases. With the introduction of the large 486 series, this became a real problem—the first 25-MHz chips were marginal. Once the 33-MHz threshold was reached, it became critical. To combat this elaborate convection, cooling towers and fans were attached.

Unfortunately, the plastic cases are not good heat conductors, and it was critical that thermally conductive grease be applied between the tower and the CPU or else the CPU often heated up even faster.

Once the 3.3v CPUs replaced the earlier 5v units, much of the problem evaporated because the 3.3v CPUs dissipate much less heat than the earlier designs. When replacing a CPU, it is essential to know the voltage the board is designed for (some accommodate both), as use of a 3.3v chip in a 5v socket is a quick way to achieve maximum smoke.

BIOS

The final element that affects processing speed is the Basic Input Output System (BIOS). Essentially an operating system on a chip, the BIOS makes an Intel box "100% compatible" (with the original IBM specification).

The problem is not the memory structure of the BIOS; it uses read-only memory (ROM) which can be faster than the common dynamic random access memory (DRAM) used for the main memory (RAM), or even the faster static RAM (SRAM). Instead, the bottleneck is usually the 8-bit data bus used to connect the CPU to the BIOS ROM.

One typical mechanism to correct this bottleneck is to copy the ROM into RAM on the 32-bit data bus, which has much faster access time. This is called shadow RAM.

However, copying is unnecessary when a true 32-bit operating system is used because all I/O is through RAM anyway and the BIOS is mapped out. When a server operating system such as UNIX or Novell Inc. NetWare is used, a small RAM savings (64K) can be achieved by turning off all ROM shadowing.

This mechanism is a legacy from the first 8088-based Intel machines that is also maintained in the interest of minimum price and compatibility with REAL mode, another 8088 requirement. RISC machines have no such limitations.

PIPELINING

The final element that must be considered relating to processor speed is the pipeline depth. The 680x0 series CPUs have always been pipelined, though the current Pentium CPUs have a similar depth. RISC processors rely heavily on pipelining for burst speed.

Essentially a "L0" cache, the pipeline works best with interleaved memory. This is a technique whereby more than one memory location is accessed on a single clock. With interleaving, when memory is accessed, the surrounding memory locations are also activated and read into the pipeline. Thus, when one instruction completes, the next has already been loaded so that no memory wait cycle is required.

Early CPUs had short pipes, but the current Pentium series chips often incorporate dual pipes of 50 instructions.

The problem is that pipes work best with in-line code. Every time a branch or jump is taken, the pipeline must be flushed and refilled. Programs with many JMPs or CALLs must often flush and refill. Taken to the extreme, the pipelined system can be slower than a system with none at all; hence, it is important to use a compiler optimized for the processor.

A poor compiler can lengthen runtimes by 20 to 30% over a well-optimized system, particularly if a very large pipe is involved.

For RISC machines, pipelining is a critical element and care is usually taken to avoid branching that would flush the pipe. Part of the speed improvements found on most RISC platforms are a result of compilers that optimize for speed rather than size. In turn, cache size becomes even more critical. Many RISC machines are designed today to operate programs entirely out of cache if possible.

BALANCE

As discussed previously, it is essential that the system be properly balanced for each of its components. Memory must be properly matched to bus speed (as shown earlier, with slow memory, slowing the clock to reduce total wait states can improve throughput). Of course, it is better to use fast memory in the first place.

A 33-MHz memory bus system can run with 80 ns RAM, but extra wait states are required. Increasing the memory speed to 60 or 70 ns can allow a reliable return to "zero wait state" operation (as demonstrated, zero really means three).

The next consideration is cache. More is generally better, though the performance increase approaches zero once the actual program length is reached. For CISC processors, 256K is a good place to start, whereas a RISC machine may benefit from a megabyte or more.

L1 cache is another case of "if enough is good, more is better." Generally, 8K is a minimum and 16K is better. Below 8K, performance drops off quickly so that a 1K L1 cache is almost useless.

Again, the problem is that too much can hurt—if the cache is large, the system may spend longer deciding whether a particular range is in cache than it would to retrieve it in the first place. Although improvement varies with instruction mix, the numbers given here have proven to be good for today's systems.

For the RISC machines "the rules are different," with large caches (4 to 8 M bytes) common. Large caches can be done effectively because the design is optimized for maximum use rather than cost sensitivity, and if the entire program can be encapsulated inside the cache, there is no need for disk access once loaded.

Thus, it is essential to properly balance the components in a system and then tune to the application mix. If one area cannot meet the system throughput design requirements, the system will be slow. Devices with too high performance will not affect throughput; however, they generally affect cost. Balance is vital.

Chapter 4
Server Data Bus Structures

A. Padgett Peterson

One of the determining features of any processor is the bus speed because any operation is limited by the slowest portion. The previous chapter discussed the relative operations of various processors and their memory subsections. This chapter discusses the relationship between the processor speeds and the bus speeds. Toward the end of the section, nonstandard structures such as the crowbars used in parallel processing operations are described.

DATA BUSES

In modern systems, memory buses are tightly incorporated into the system design and are related to the processor in use, whereas data buses used for peripherals are much more flexible. In fact, the current Peripheral Component Interconnect (PCI) bus is defined as processor-independent.

The importance of the bus speeds is paramount in a well-designed system because all I/O is via the system bus, which is shared around the peripherals: keyboard, display, disk drives, and network. Because buses are typically parallel operations similar to memory buses, two elements must be considered: bus (clock) speed and bus width. In both cases, more is better. For example, an 8-bit-wide (1-byte) bus running at 10 Mhz shows a theoretical maximum data rate of 10M byte/sec. (8 bits × 10,000,000 / 8 bits per byte). However, this assumes that the bus is simply a pipe with as much data as it can process on one end and unlimited capability to process on the other. This theoretical maximum is also sometimes known as burst or streaming mode.

In practice, real-world throughputs are somewhat less, about two thirds maximum for well-organized and balanced systems, one half or less for poorly assembled systems such as a Pentium platform with a 16-bit Industry Standard Architecture (ISA) video card and complex graphical displays. It must be remembered that any system is limited to the speed of the slowest component.

Thus, when a 32-bit PCI bus is said to have a 133M byte/sec. throughput, that is a theoretical maximum and indicates a 33-MHz clock speed (133×8/32) with no wait states. As soon as real-world factors such as the commands necessary to initiate the transfer or to acknowledge receipt or for error correction are taken into account, throughput decreases significantly, since all these factors consume cycles. If the processor itself with inherent wait states must be involved (as opposed to Direct Memory Access transfers), the effective throughput is even less.

Mainframes typically have 64- or 128-bit bus widths, whereas the systems typically used for microcomputer-based servers are smaller. Further, although some common computer bus structures such as VME or Q-Bus are both wide and fast, they are rarely used for servers. Today, the standards are VESA Local Bus (VLB) for 486-class machines and PCI for Intel Corp. Pentiums and follow on processors, Power PC, and Digital Equipment Corp. Alpha systems.

EVOLUTION OF DATA BUSES

The buses used by the IBM PC are an excellent starting point for understanding the evolution of bus structures. The first was the 8-bit PC-Bus introduced with the IBM PC, which runs at the same 4.77 MHz as the 8088-based PC. This gives a maximum theoretical throughput of about 5M byte/sec. The continuing popularity of the 3Com Corp. 3C503 Ethernet card for low-performance applications shows that this was and often still is adequate for low-performance applications and can typically provide effective net speeds around 70K byte/sec. transfer rates. In this case, the address bus had a width of 20 bits and a granularity of 1 byte, limiting access to 1M byte. Since the 8088 only had 16-bit registers, a system of 64K "segments" had to be used. On the other hand, the memory bus was only 8 bits wide so data had to be accessed one byte at a time.

The next change came in 1985 with the introduction of the PC-AT (Advanced Technology) and the 16-bit ISA architecture, doubling the memory bus width to 16 bits and increasing the bus speed (originally to 6 MHz but quickly expanded to 8 MHz and often stretched to 10 MHz). Effectively quadrupling the theoretical bandwidth, two additional cards/vendors—the WD (Western Digital) 8003 / SMC (Standard Microsystems Corp.) Elite and the NE (Novell Ethernet) 2000—became leaders. Transfer rates in the 160–280K byte/sec. over networks became common.

For marketing reasons, the ISA bus had to maintain commonality with the earlier 8-bit bus so a dual connection was used—for 8-bit boards, the original connector was maintained with a 4.77-MHz bus speed and 8-bit-wide connection. For the new 16-bit boards, a second connector was placed in line, allowing 1- bit width and 8 MHz (often pushed to 10 MHz) data rate. The design limit for the ISA bus was 8.77M byte/sec. throughput.

IBM attempted to improve again with the 1987 MCA (MicroChannel Architecture) bus: 32-bit and 10 MHz. IBM made OS/2 a common choice for servers for many years even though the proprietary nature of the bus led to high card prices, which in turn kept the PS/2 from becoming any more than a market niche. MCA did away with the familiar dual-edge connector sockets of the AT, replacing them with finer (.050 in. wide rather than .100 in.) contacts.

Few vendors took part because the market was small and MCA used an early (and user-hostile) version of what we know now as Plug-n-Play, requiring a special setup disk for each machine and each card. Some vendors responded with dual-use cards—ISA connection on one side and MCA on the other—and others built adapter cards, but none was very successful.

One element introduced with the PS/2 was widely accepted—the VGA graphics structure. However, the VGA graphics structure and the miniature keyboard/mouse connectors are about the only elements that remain today.

To counter the MCA bus, a group of vendors led by Compaq Computer Corp. supported the Extended ISA (EISA) bus—an extension of the ISA bus which promised 33M byte/sec. transfer rates and compatibility with older 286 machines—though the 33-MHz rate required burst capability. Squabbles among the vendors and lack of general acceptance by the marketplace kept EISA out of all but niche markets. One problem was that although ISA cards could be used in EISA slots, the EISA standard changed the pin assignments so that even though the sockets looked the same to the user, they were actually different and incompatible.

The final solution, which eliminated the PS/2 from serious consideration in the marketplace (though the flat memory model of OS/2 maintained its use as a server), was the VESA VL bus, which allowed a 32-bit width and even higher speed (160M byte/sec. transfer rate in Version 2) than the MCA bus. Such cards were designed to be able to be placed in a standard 16-bit ISA bus slot as well, although the speed then dropped to that of a normal ISA card.

The VESA portion required yet another connector, to be placed behind the original PC bus connector and the AT bus connector for a total of three connectors in line. In an age of ever-reducing motherboard size, this made for a very long footprint. Thus, most motherboards had only three VESA sockets, as users believed that video, disk, and network cards were the only components to require such speed.

It was also often known as Local-Bus, VESA Local Bus, or VLB, and in the beginning there were two competing standards.

Attempts have been made to extend the life of the VLB bus structure by expansion to a theoretical 160M byte/sec. data rate through the use of a

40-MHz clock. But other than the AMD 486DX-40, TI 486DX2-80, and AMD 486DX4-133, no processors are available for this use —which also requires high-speed memory to avoid the inevitable wait states.

Next to appear was the PCMCIA (PC Card) standard for notebook devices. Though rarely seen on desktop machines, the PCMCIA bus promised 33-MHz clock speeds. The early implementations ran somewhat slower. In the future, PCMCIA-capable slots may appear on the desktop to foster the use of smart cards for online electronic commerce expected to explode in 1999. The PCMCIA bus is really a parallel development and is unlikely to impact servers.

The final link is the PCI bus introduced with the Pentium processors. This utilizes a fine contact specialized connector much like the MCA but provides both 32- and 64-bit access sections and peak transfer rates of 133M byte/sec. (32 bit) or 266M byte/sec. (64 bit). The current Digital Alpha RISC processors use the PCI bus structure with some enhancements. At present, only 64-bit peripheral cards are available for disk access (SCSI-2). (Note: the access speeds such as 133M byte/sec. are the maximum theoretical throughput and are presented for establishing relationships between bus structures. Actual throughput in terms of real-world performance is often about half the theoretical capability.)

BUS LOADS

As mentioned earlier, the network card is not the only device that requires access. Although the display and keyboard require some service, these are demand devices and once operational, on a server their loads are minimal. Of course, if the server is also used as a graphical work station, this will change drastically, which is why a server should always be dedicated to that task unless the network loads are very light.

The other device that requires service is the disk storage subsystem, which also passes data. In fact, the I/O requirements are almost exactly the same as that of the network, as most data passes between these two devices with the processor acting as an intermediary.

Better disk subsystems have large caches to minimize processor loads. However, data passing from the network to the disk, or the disk to the network, must proceed via the processor along the bus. Thus, each byte must take at least two clocks to get from the input device to the processor, then another two clocks to get from the processor to the output device. Often this latency determines actual throughput.

Finally, just because the bus can support a high data rate does not mean that the system will operate at that speed; many factors determine operation speed. For instance if an ISA card such as the SMC Ultra is placed on a PCI bus machine, the speed will be that of the lowest component, in this case the

16-bit, 8-MHz PC-AT bus and not the 33-MHz, 32-bit PCI bus. Although a lower-rated device often works on a higher-rated system, typically the speed suffers over an integrated device. For today, a Pentium-based system with 32-bit PCI bus structure is adequate for low- to medium-loaded networks; for heavy loads, a RISC-based system such as the Digital Alpha with a 64-bit PCI bus would be preferred.

PERIPHERALS

Once the basic architecture has been determined, the peripherals must be considered. Oddly enough, what is visible is not that important, particularly in a server environment. For example, consider a 6x CD-ROM with a theoretical capability of 900 (6x150) K bps. Many people are dissatisfied with such devices when the real culprit is an 8-bit controller card that limits the effective throughput to approximately 400K bps.

The opposite is true of the human interface elements (keyboard, pointing device), printers, and even modems because these devices are incapable of and do not need high-speed access. For these devices, the original 8-bit PC bus is sufficient.

Really high-speed operations must, by their nature, be contained within the computer itself. The shorter the distance information must travel the better, because for nano-second response times, lead latencies (6.67 ns/ft of lead length is a good rule of thumb) become significant. Accordingly, the most critical elements must be chosen to apply a balanced load on the system when operating at its design point. For a server, these elements are CPU and memory (covered earlier), disk drive subsystem, network interface, and display controller.

DISK DRIVES

The disk drive structure needs to have the highest performance capability in a server. Until recently, there was little difference in disks because the limiting function was typically the bus and processor speed. Since 1990, the pressure has been on the disk drives with caching controllers. Extended IDE and SCSI-2 specifications and higher rotational speeds by drives all increase performance capability.

The basic limitation of any drive is the physical—the rotation speed of the spindle, the numbers of bytes per sector, and real sectors per track, and the positioning rate of the heads. Note the caveat "real" with respect to sectors per track is made because often a logical translation is made to comply with older BIOS limitations—hence the number entered into a CMOS table may bear little relation to the actual physical layout.

HISTORICAL ORIGINS

The first PC drives used the ST-506 (Seagate Technology Inc.) standard for drive manufacture. This required a separate drive and controller. The long lead lengths slowed effective throughput, and such devices were limited to effective transfer rates of about 300K byte/sec.—about the same as a 2x CD-ROM today. The theoretical transfer rate for a Modified Frequency Modulation drive with 17 512-byte sectors per track rotating at 3,600 rpm was about 510K byte/sec. but was approachable only with an interleave of 1:1. Any deviation slowed the rate down. The 3:1 interleave optimally used on an XT class machine (many use 6:1) was induced by the electronics/data bus; users have successfully run an original full-height 10-Mb drive [type 1] at 1:1 with a 386 and a good controller with a throughput of over 300K byte/sec.). Although adequate for personal computers, this was not sufficient for any except the most basic servers.

The next adoption was Enhanced Small Device Interface (ESDI), which introduced the concept of "on-disk" controllers. This allowed a theoretical transfer rate increase to 3M byte/sec., which was never approached in practice but looked good in advertising.

In the late 1980s, SCSI devices also became popular—surprisingly, as the cost was generally higher than for a similar ST-506 device and the 8-bit data bus inherent in the initial standard limited the initial devices to a peak of 4M byte/sec.

Still, this was not bad for the time and had a definite advantage in the PC environment. Whereas the standard Intel-based PC could support only two disks, the SCSI bus could support up to eight devices of any kind—disk, CD-ROM, etc. When coupled with FAST-SCSI adapters having theoretical data rates of 10M byte/sec. (real world, about 5M byte/sec.), performance was more than adequate. This has now been incorporated into SCSI-II.

In addition, because controllers had their own BIOSs to manage the disks, the Type function—which limited available disk sizes in many PCs—did not apply. For this reason, the first very large disks were primarily SCSI.

Today, SCSI-II and III standards have extended the capabilities to 16- and 32-bit bus widths for even greater theoretical capability. Currently, SCSI is the drive mechanism of choice in high-performance RISC workstations, with 64-bit data widths and extended PCI bus structures allowing RAID-configured systems to exceed 120M byte/sec. real transfer rates. Theoretical maximum is over 260M byte/sec., so some improvements are still possible without major change. This is not to be found in CISC-based workstations as yet, and the question remains whether such a workstation would be able to handle such a large throughput.

IDE

For smaller systems and lower performance servers, though the gap is narrowing, Intelligent Drive Electronics (IDE), or ATA or AT Attachment extended the ESDI promise by moving all electronics onto the drive and using the controller car merely to establish port addresses and connect the drive to the system bus.

The promise of the IDE standard was in its 16-bit data width and the speeds inherent in having the drive electronics as close as possible to the heads. A large number of sectors per track (often between 50 and 80) increases disk speeds. Rotational speeds of up to 7,200 rpm (most currently run at 4,800 rpm) coupled with 1:1 interleaving allow high throughput, usually limited by the bus structure to effectively 1M byte/sec. Later local bus controllers utilizing the Extended IDE (EIDE) standard raised this to about 3M byte/sec.—good enough for workstations and low-end servers but not for true high-performance systems.

The latest update to the EIDE specification, known as Ultra DMA or UDMA, boosts performance to match midrange SCSI drives with a burst transfer rate of 33M byte/sec. Even so, the extensions allow low drive prices, currently around $50 per gigabyte, and as such are very attractive to the consumer market because a good SCSI system also requires a high-performance controller that often costs more than the drive it supports. EIDE has no such limitation, and with BIOSs supporting large disks and Large Block Access (essentially a streaming mode) to those upgrading to such a system, the throughput seems good.

The bottom line is that for a fast RISC-based server in a high-load condition, there is no substitute for Fast Wide (64-bit) SCSI drives. For lesser applications, particularly with an Intel base, EIDE drives perform satisfactorily at a slightly lower cost.

RAID

The final note on drives involves both speed and error correction. Redundant Arrays of Inexpensive Drives (RAID) offer one solution that can enhance reliability, improve throughput, and allow hot-swapping of defective drives without having to bring the system down. For standard server operation, Level 5 or Level 6 is generally the best choice if RAID is desired.

NETWORK CARDS

Until recently, the standard was Ethernet using thick coax (aui adapter required), thin coax (RG-58 cable with BNC connections), or hub-based twisted pair using 6 pin RJ-45 connectors (4 pin RJ-11 connectors, a.k.a. telephone jacks have also been used, but they are nonstandard) at 10M bps rate or under 2M byte/sec. This level of performance can be handled by a standard ISA bus structure. In fact, it was common to connect a high-performance server to multiple networks simultaneously because the CPU and the disk structure were only lightly loaded.

Today, Fast-Ethernet, fiber distributed data interface (FDDI), and asynchronous transfer mode (ATM) are pushing network speed past 100M bps or 12M byte/sec. To support these speeds, the current servers are being stressed to keep up—particularly under heavy loads.

Ethernet is a serial network. Only one packet can be received at a time, so each must be handled in turn. For these systems, multiple CPUs and arrays of RAIDs are becoming common both for fault tolerance and for improved throughput. The bottom line is that new and emerging network systems will be able to fully oust the throughput capability of a powerful server and are no longer the bottleneck they once were.

DISPLAYS

Unless the server is to be used as a workstation, there is little need to invest heavily in display technology. Although 4 Mb of display memory coupled with high-performance graphics processors can provide impressive displays in 64 million colors, there is no need for this in a server display. A common VGA video card with 1 Mb of memory is generally sufficient even if complex graphics are utilized to support load displays.

CD-ROMS

The addition of one or more CD-ROM devices does not place a significant load on the system even in 10x (1.5M byte/sec.) systems because such high throughputs are rarely sustainable by the hardware. Like a floppy disk, CD-ROM usage differs depending on the installation, but the hardware performance level is not yet sufficient to be a strain on any modern server.

KEYBOARD AND POINTING DEVICE (MOUSE)

Because these operate at human speed, virtually any device will do, as speed/throughput is not an issue.

CONCLUSION

The main I/O will always be the bottleneck of any server installation. The main factors are disk access times and throughput and network capability. Although important, CPU speed is generally not the limiting factor. In a server environment, the first task is the design of the disk farm—with throughput a major factor. Overall system speed and network load capability, as well as necessary bus widths and speed, fall out from the design. Servers, by nature serial devices, are limited by the least capable device.

Chapter 5
Dynamic IP Addressing with DHCP

Tom M. Hadley and Laura J. Knapp

Only a few years ago most knowledge about Internet Protocol (IP) was in university computer science departments. Today most of us are altering our business plans to move our computer systems to the protocol of the Internet — Transmission Control Protocol/Internet Protocol (TCP/IP). While the movement to a single protocol reduces complexity in many areas, it also introduces a new series of challenges. In moving to IP one of the most significant changes for users of Systems Network Architecture (SNA), internetwork packet exchange, and NetBIOS is the need for each device to have a unique IP address. Initially it may appear that this would be a major stumbling block to the rollout of IP. Requiring a technician to visit each and every desktop, server, and network device to configure an IP address is a real challenge to the movement to IP. In addition, since the IP address contains the network number, any future movement of a device may require a change to the IP address. True to the heritage of TCP/IP, recognizing challenges and inventing solutions to them, IP now has a mechanism that allows the distribution of IP addresses to devices at startup. This technology is Dynamic Host Configuration Protocol (DHCP).

REVERSE ARP

As local area networks (LAN) were deployed in the mid 1980s, some early IP implementations broadcast traffic to all stations. Each device would receive the information packet (datagram) and decide if the address is the IP address of that device. This is wasteful of both network and PC resources, so the Address Resolution Protocol (ARP) was invented. A table was built in an ARP server containing IP addresses and corresponding LAN device addresses. To initiate a data transfer, the sending station could inquire for the LAN address using the IP address and direct traffic to only that specific LAN address. The first solution to IP address distribution reversed this process using the same ARP server: The station sent its own LAN adapter address, and the server returned the corresponding IP address. Hence the name Reverse ARP (RARP).

0-8493-9838-X/00/$0.00+$.50

When a LAN device starts up, it requests an IP address from the RARP server. The server looks in its table for the specified LAN address, finds its corresponding IP address, and returns it to the device. The device can now complete the start-up of the IP protocol stack with its unique IP address. Since the ARP and RARP server requests are broadcast on the LAN segment, a server is required for each LAN segment. RARP worked fine for a small group of devices, but it ran into many problems as networks grew. ARP servers contain only address pairs, so they are of no use to distribute other information.

The Internet Engineering Task Force (IETF) continued to work on a more complete solution for distributing IP addresses. This time the driving force was from network hardware manufacturers, whose devices in the 1990s began using the IP Simple Network Management Protocol (SNMP). Each managed hub, bridge, router, and gateway requires an IP address. A way was needed to distribute these addresses throughout a business and at the same time, allow additional information to be passed along with the IP address. This resulted in the BOOT Protocol (BOOTP). A BOOTP server contains configuration information. In this case, it not only contains the IP address but can also include other IP configuration information (subnet masks, gateway address, Domain Name Server [DNS] addresses), and files to execute. One of the advantages of BOOTP is that it allows many different attributes to be used to identify the device requesting an IP address, including LAN address, IP host name, or type of physical connection. Another addition allows the routers in a network to forward the BOOTP request. The use of BOOTP allowed a single server to handle the needs of an entire organization for local and remote site configuration.

Although BOOTP solved many of the distribution issues, several still remained. First, the IP addresses assigned by BOOTP have a permanent or static association with a given IP device. This is not always the optimum method of distribution, and in large organizations it can cause administrative nightmares when considering the large number of devices. This also led to inefficient use of IP address space. We have all heard the stories about running out of IP addresses, so address conservation is key to the growth of IP. A static IP address is one that is always given to the same device each time the device requests an address. If that device is taken out of service for a day, week, month, or year, no other device can use its address. Although unused, it is also unavailable to any other device. On the other hand, dynamic addresses change every time a device asks for an address. The second issue with BOOTP involves mobile users who access the network from different points. With the widespread use of subnetting within the IP network of a business, static address assignments cannot be used for mobile users. In a nutshell, BOOTP does nothing to enhance dynamic network topology, which is one of the benefits derived from an IP network.

DYNAMIC HOST CONFIGURATION PROTOCOL

As mentioned above, one of the hallmarks of TCP/IP development is to build on what went before. Because the IETF knew that BOOTP provided a large portion of what was needed to distribute dynamic IP addresses, BOOTP is at the core of DHCP. DHCP is yet another client/server environment. A server runs special code to allow it to store IP addresses, identifiers, subnet masks, gateway addresses, and other information for distribution. Most installed servers are either UNIX- or Windows NT-based, although mainframes and the AS/400 have support as a DHCP server. Administration varies by vendor, but most use a graphical interface.

A DHCP client requests an address from the server, which provides the address and other information. Microsoft Corp's Windows 95 brought DHCP to the forefront as the first mass-marketed operating system with an IP stack containing a DHCP client. In fact, Windows 95 defaults to using a DHCP server for the IP address and must be overridden to allow an address to be specified. Since 1996, most IP protocol stacks support a DHCP client. Any DHCP server can support any DHCP client regardless of type of device, operating system, or manufacturer. Also, the DHCP protocol flows through routers, so DHCP servers can be centralized for easier administration.

When a DHCP server is set up, IP addresses can be assigned in one of three different ways. Each has a role to play in your network. First, IP addresses can be placed in a manual queue. This is the original BOOTP operational mode where the IP address is static and destined for a given IP host. Every time the IP host asks for an address, it is given the same address along with other information associated with that address. This is the optimum mechanism for any device that always needs the same address such as servers, hardware devices, midrange systems, etc. The systems are accessed by IP applications that have a hard-coded IP address or have the IP address associated with a predefined domain name (DNS).

The second way to assign addresses is via an automatic mechanism. Assume that over the next six months your business is rolling out eight NT servers. A series of eight IP addresses can be set up in the automatic queue and an identifier is associated with each IP address. Over the coming months, as you bring the NT servers online, the start-up process provides the identifier to the DHCP server and asks the server for the next available address. It will be assigned and from then on every time that NT server asks for an address, it will be given the same address. The initial IP address is dynamic, but from then on the address is statically assigned. This small change from the manual process has assisted in making IP rollouts much easier. Based on your IP addressing plan, this can be a very powerful tool and can help reduce IP address management.

The third and final way to assign addresses is dynamic. This is the mechanism that will be used for most end-user systems. End users do not need the same IP address each time they log in, since they are working as a client, getting information, applications, and functionality from other servers on the network. For the end user, it eliminates the need to configure an address into the IP protocol stack on the desktop. For the administrator it eliminates administration problems moving between IP subnets, reduces trouble calls due to incorrect configuration at the user station, and allows changes in network topology without having to go to each end user and reconfigure their IP protocol. Dynamic IP addresses have also allowed Internet-service providers (ISP) to provide browser access to the public Internet without having to "code in" an IP address for each user. The address comes from the pool at dial in and is returned when the user disconnects. In addition, the user can dial in to any location and be assured a working address regardless of the subnet structure of the ISP. If you consider the number of employees that are out of the office on a daily basis due to trips, vacation, meetings, and illness, your business can use fewer addresses using DHCP and help conserve IP addresses.

HOW DOES DHCP WORK?

The process follows a second rule of the IP protocol—keep it simple. When a device is started and the IP protocol is being initialized, a DHCP Request IP Address discover message is broadcast over the network. If this request meets a router, the router forwards it on all ports in an attempt to find a DHCP server. Since servers can fail and devices cannot enter the network without an IP address, the administrator can set up multiple servers. Thus, the request may reach several DHCP servers that can respond with an address. All servers that receive the request will review it and if they can satisfy the request, will respond with an IP address. The responses will flow back through the network, and the requesting device will determine which IP address to use, usually the first received. When the workstation decides which address to use, it responds to the issuing DHCP server. That server commits the address and removes it from the available pool. Other servers that responded with an IP address that was not used will, after an acceptance timer expires, return the unused address to their available pools.

When the server distributed the IP address, other necessary addresses and information can also be sent. DNS server addresses, default router addresses, and programs to load are all representative of information that can be passed via the DHCP process. As you look at the DHCP environment, it takes away one of the major problems with a massive rollout of IP—configuration at the desktop—and automates the entire process. Another aspect of note is that when an address is delivered, it comes with a "lease" agreement. This means that the user can use the address for a specified amount of time. Halfway through the lease period, the device can request a new lease. The administrator sets the lease time and other parameters.

In an effort to improve security, the DHCP server can be set to answer address requests and set the lease period only during certain times of the day. The administrator can set certain devices to only have IP access from 7 a.m. to 7 p.m. Should one of these devices attempt to load IP and gain access to any IP application outside these times, no address would be supplied and access would be prohibited. Other features of this nature exist in the DHCP servers available today.

Another major advantage of DHCP is that it can identify the IP subnet a request comes from and ensure that an appropriate IP address is distributed. This uses the basic BOOTP relay function that includes the subnet information within the header of the DHCP IP Address Request.

MORE TO COME!

Although DHCP has allowed the tremendous growth of the Internet and the IP protocol to progress, additional function is still required. We mentioned above that the DHCP IP Address Request message could be answered by more than one DHCP server in the network. This provides a level of backup, but not true redundancy. That is, each server requires a set of addresses in each subnet range for which they can answer. If a DHCP server is down, its addresses are unavailable for any other server to use. Although backup DHCP servers are possible today, they have redundant addresses and cannot provide "hot backup" for a downed server.

New additions to the DHCP protocol are being worked on to allow DHCP server-server communications, which will again ease the job of the IP administrator. Security is still a major work item. Where DHCP is installed anyone (even a visitor with a notebook computer) can connect to your network, request an IP address, and potentially gain access to business-sensitive data. Just think about what now exists on intranet Web servers with no access controls! Finally, and perhaps the most important next move, is the ability for dynamic IP addresses assigned by DHCP to be correlated with dynamic DNS. Today the few implementations that allow DHCP and DNS correlation require that both be from the same vendor. For IP to continue its growth, DHCP and DNS must be synchronized and must support multiple vendor implementations.

WHAT SHOULD YOU DO NOW?

As you implement your IP network, be sure to plan for DHCP. Servers are available for a wide range of operating system platforms, and almost all TCP/IP implementations now support DHCP clients to dynamically obtain address setup information. The ease of administration and the elimination of end user configuration headaches are well worth the investment!

Chapter 6
LAN Connectivity Options for the Small Business

Nathan J. Muller

Small businesses of 2 to 100 users are part of the fastest-growing segments of the networking market. According to various industry estimates, there were about 1 million networked companies with 100 or fewer employees in 1996 and 300,000 more in 1997. The number of such companies is expected to grow to more than 2 million by the year 2000. The major networking vendors and many second-tier vendors are targeting this market with product lines that feature entry-level hubs, switches, printer servers, integrated services digital network (ISDN) routers, and other networking products that offer ease of use, clearly written and illustrated documentation, and technical support specifically aimed at novices.

The most popular network topology among small businesses is Ethernet because it is relatively inexpensive, easy to set up and use, and very fast. There are currently three categories of Ethernet. Standard Ethernet operates at 10M bps, which is quick enough for most networking tasks. Fast Ethernet moves data 10 times faster at 100M bps, making it ideal for desktop video, multimedia, and other bandwidth-hungry applications. The latest category of Ethernet is Gigabit Ethernet, which moves data 100 times faster than standard Ethernet, making it suited for uplinks among high-capacity hubs or switches as well as links among high-capacity servers.

Although there are other types of LANs available, (e.g., Token Ring, fiber distributed data interface, and asynchronous transfer mode, this chapter focuses on Ethernet because it is the network of choice among small businesses and will continue to be well into the future. As in any type of network, several elements merit consideration when building an Ethernet network, including cabling, media converters, network adapters, hubs, network operating systems, and routers for LAN-to-LAN communication over the wide area network (WAN).

0-8493-9838-X/00/$0.00+$.50
© 2000 by CRC Press LLC

CABLING

For standard 10Base-T Ethernet, the most popular type of network cabling is Category 5 unshielded twisted-pair (UTP) cable. This type of cable looks like the coaxial cabling that is often used to connect a VCR to a TV set and usually has 8 wires. It can be used at a maximum distance of 328 feet. A modular plug at each end (RJ45) of the cable makes interconnecting the various network devices as simple as plugging them in. Fiber-optic cabling (also known as 10Base-FL) can be used as well at a maximum distance of about 607 feet.

Fast Ethernet, or 100Base-T, is the standard that is most compatible with 10Base-T. It uses the same contention-based media access control method—carrier sense multiple access with collision detection (CSMA/CD)—that is at the heart of 10Base-T Ethernet. This level of compatibility means that no protocol conversions need to be done to move data between the two types of networks.

There are several media standards for implementing 100Base-T. They can be summarized as follows:

- 100Base-TX: a two-pair system for data grade (Category 5) UTP and STP (shielded twisted-pair) cabling.
- 100Base-T4: a four-pair system for both voice and data grade (Category 3, 4, or 5) UTP cabling.
- 100Base-FX: a two-strand multimode fiber system.

All these cabling systems can be interconnected through a hub, which helps organizations retain their existing cabling infrastructure while migrating to Fast Ethernet.

Companies with small networks usually standardize on Category 5 cabling because it is inexpensive, flexible, and adequate for short distances. It also allows companies to easily migrate to higher-speed networks without having to rewire the building. For networks that span multiple offices or floors—or must traverse noisy environments such as manufacturing facilities—fiber-optic cabling is the best choice because it offers immunity to electromagnetic interference, provides virtually error-free transmission, and is more secure than copper-based media. The maximum length for a 100Base-FX segment is about 1,300 feet.

Gigabit Ethernet, also called 1000Base-T, is limited to 328 feet per segment using Category 5 cabling. Media extensions to the Gigabit Ethernet standard use multimode fiber at up to 1,500 feet (1000Base-SX) and single-mode fiber at distances up to 9,000 feet (1000Base-LX). Optical fiber is mostly used as an uplink between stackable Ethernet hubs, but it can also be used for interconnecting servers. Gigabit Ethernet will not see widespread use among most small businesses unless they are engaged in specialized work such as

Computer-Aided Design/Computer-Aided Manufacturing or three-dimensional modeling.

MEDIA CONVERTERS

All three types of media—twisted pair, thin coax, and optical fiber—can be used exclusively or together, depending on the type of network. There are even media converters available that allow segments using different media to be linked together. For example, some media converters link 10Base-T to 10Base-2 and 10Base-T to 10Base-FL (single or multimode). There are also media converters that link 100Base-T to 100Base-FX (single or multimode). Because media conversion is a physical layer process, it does not introduce significant delays on the network.

NETWORK ADAPTERS

A computer—whether configured as a client or server—is connected to the network with an adapter called a network interface card (NIC), which comes in internal and external versions. Typically, the NIC is installed inside the computer: It plugs directly into one of the computer's internal expansion slots. Most older computers have 16-bit Industry Standard Architecture slots, so a 16-bit NIC is needed. Faster computers, such as Pentium-based machines, come standardly equipped with several 32-bit PCI slots. These PCs require 32-bit NICs to achieve the fastest networking speeds.

If a computer is going to be used with a Fast Ethernet network, it needs a network adapter that specifically supports 100M bps as well. Some NICs offer an "autosensing" capability, enabling them to determine the speed of the network and whether to run at 10M or 100M bps in half-duplex or full-duplex mode. In half-duplex mode, the computer can alternately send and receive. In full-duplex mode, the computer can send and receive at the same time, effectively doubling its throughput on a dedicated segment.

Some NICs support multiple types of media connectors. In addition to RJ45, they might also include a connector for the older British Naval Connector (BNC) interface. If a PC lacks vacant expansion slots, an external network adapter may be used, which plugs in to the computer's printer port. The adapter usually has LED indicators for such things as polarity, signal quality, link integrity, and power.

Portable computers can connect to the office LAN via a PC Card network adapter. This credit-card-size adapter communicates with the portable computer using special software drivers called socket and card services. Another set of drivers, called network drivers, enable the PC Card to communicate with the network at large. Some client operating systems, such as Microsoft Corp.'s Windows 95, provide these sets of drivers, which enables

Plug-n-Play operation; otherwise they must be installed by the user from the vendor's installation disk. Some PC Card adapters include an integral 56K bps modem that can be used for remote dial-up connection to the office LAN.

HUBS

Although it is possible to network PCs together in serial fashion using NICs with BNC T-connectors and terminators, most Ethernet networks installed today use a hub, which centralizes the cable connections from computers and other networked devices.

A hub is basically a box with a row of jacks into which the cables from the NIC-equipped computers are plugged. Most small office hubs have 4 to 16 jacks, but some may have more. Most hubs also have a dedicated uplink port, which allows the hub to be connected to other hubs as a means of accommodating growth.

Like network adapter cards, hubs are available in both standard Ethernet and Fast Ethernet versions. However, more than two hubs cannot be linked together without using some kind of switch or repeater to boost the interim signal. If three, four, or more standard hubs are uplinked together without regard for signal strength, data becomes corrupted and applications fail.

But this situation applies only to standard hubs joined together through RJ45 ports, where each hub is seen by the network as a separate entity. Stackable hubs, on the other hand, are designed to appear as a single hub to the network—regardless of how many are connected together. The linkages are implemented with one or more stacking cables that actually join the backplanes of each hub through a dedicated high-speed port. Because information does not pass through the hub's regular RJ45 ports, it is not slowed down by error correction and filtering. The result is a minimal slowdown when data moves from one hub to another.

Some switching hubs allow both 10M and 100M bps networking hardware to be used on the same network. An autosensing feature associated with each port determines the speed of the NIC at the other end of the cable and transparently bridges the two speeds together.

A small business that wants to network only a few computers together will be able to get by with a hub, some network adapters, and 10Base-T cables. If the organization anticipates significant growth in the future, a stackable 10/100 Ethernet hub is the better choice. It provides tighter integration and maximum throughput and the means to scale up to a few hundred nodes if necessary without the need for external repeaters or switches.

Hubs also come in managed and unmanaged versions. Hubs that are not manageable are easy to set up and maintain. They offer LED indicators that show the presence of send-and-receive traffic on each port, collisions, and hub utilization and power status. However, unmanaged hubs do not offer the configuration options and administrative features of managed hubs.

A management system offers ways to configure individual ports. For example, address filtering can be applied to ports to limit access to certain network resources. A management system can also provide performance information about each port to aid troubleshooting and fault isolation. Most hubs of this type support the Simple Network Management Protocol (SNMP) and the associated Remote Monitoring (RMON) standard, which makes possible more advanced network monitoring and analysis. In supporting SNMP, the hub can also be controlled and managed through a major management platform such as IBM's NetView, Hewlett-Packard Co.'s OpenView, and Sun Microsystems Inc.'s Solstice SunNet Manager.

A small business with less than 25 PCs can get by without a managed network for a limited time. But when the number of PCs increases, it becomes more economical over the long term to have a management system in place that can facilitate daily administration and provide information for troubleshooting purposes. Although this might require a dedicated administrator with technical expertise, the expense of this additional employee is more than offset by improvements in productivity made possible by high-network availability and reliability. An alternative would be to subscribe to the remote monitoring services of a vendor or carrier, in which case an SNMP-based hub management system would still be required.

NETWORK OPERATING SYSTEM

Every computer that is attached to a network must be equipped with a network operating system (NOS) to monitor and control the flow of information between users. NOSs are of two types: peer-to-peer or client/server. Examples of peer-to-peer NOSs that are commonly used by small businesses are Windows 95, Artisoft LANtastic, and Novell Inc.'s NetWare Lite. These NOSs are useful for sharing applications, data, printers, and other resources across PCs that are interconnected by a hub. Examples of client server NOSs are Windows NT and NetWare, which are used by large organizations whose users require fast network access to a variety of business applications.

PEER-TO-PEER

A simple peer-to-peer network can be built inexpensively with thin coax cabling and a 10/100 Ethernet switching hub. After the networking hardware has been installed, a peer-to-peer network software package must be installed in all the PCs. If the PCs come with Windows 95, the basic proto-cols for peer-to-peer networking are probably already installed in each sys-tem and it is a matter of configuring them through the operating system's control panel. If a different NOS is preferred, a separate package such as Artisoft LANtastic or NetWare Lite can be installed separately.

Most NOSs allow each peer-to-peer user to determine which resources will be available to other users. Specific hard and floppy disk drives, direc-tories or files, printers, and other resources can be attached or detached from the network via software. Access to each resource can be controlled in a variety of ways. For example, when configuring Windows 95 for peer-to-peer networking, a password can be applied to each shared resource. Alternatively, specific users and groups can be granted access to each shared resource.

When one user's disk has been configured so that it is "sharable," it appears as a new drive to the other users. Because drives can be easily shared between peer-to-peer PCs, applications need to be installed only on one computer instead of all computers. If the company relies on a spread-sheet application, for example, it can be installed on one user's computer and be accessible to other computers whenever it is not in use. If the spreadsheet program is not used continuously by all potential users, it makes more sense to share one copy rather than buy one for each machine. Of course, sharing applications over a peer-to-peer (or cli-ent/server) network might require a network license from the vendor, or the company risks a penalty for copyright infringement.

Peer-to-peer networks have several advantages over client/server. They are easy and inexpensive to set up and maintain, and there is no require-ment for a dedicated network administrator. Many vendors offer documen-tation that is geared for the novice, and they offer telephone support when the occasional problem is encountered.

CLIENT/SERVER

In a client/server environment such as Windows NT or NetWare, files are stored on a centralized, high-speed file server PC that is made available to client PCs. Network access speeds are usually faster than those found on peer-to-peer networks. Virtually all network services such as printing and electronic mail are routed through the file server, which allows networking tasks to be tracked. Inefficient network segments can be reworked to make them faster, and users' activities can be closely monitored. Public data and applications are stored on the file server, where they are run from client PCs' locations, which makes upgrading software a simple task—network administrators can simply upgrade the applications stored on the file server rather than having to physically upgrade each client PC.

In the client/server network, the client PCs are subordinate to the file server. The clients' primary applications and files are stored in a common location. File servers are often set up so that each user on the network has access to his "own" directory, along with a range of "public" directories where applications are stored. If two clients want to communicate with each other, they must go through the file server to do it. A message from one client to another is first sent to the file server, where it is then routed to its destination. A small business with 100 or more client PCs might find that a server-centric network is the best way to meet the needs of all users.

Take a simple task such as printing, for example. Instead of equipping each desktop or workgroup with its own printer, it would be more economical for many users to share a few high-speed printers. In client/server networks, network printing is usually handled by a print server, a small box with at least two connectors: one for a printer and another that attaches directly to the network cabling. Some print servers have more than two ports—they may, for example, support two, three, or four printers simultaneously. When a user sends a print job, it travels over the network cabling to the file server where it is stored. When the print server senses that the job is waiting, it moves it from the file server to its attached printer. When the job is finished, the print server returns a result message to the file server, indicating that the process is complete.

Another simple task that can be more economically handled by a server-centric network is the provision of gateway access to the outside world. This involves a remote-node server, which provides remote access and modem sharing. Most remote-node servers attach directly to the network cabling. They provide a bridge between the network, a modem, and an ordinary telephone line.

Remote access allows users to dial in to their home networks from anywhere in the world. Once a connection has been established over ordinary phone lines by modem, users can access any programs or data on the network as if they were locally attached to the LAN. Some remote access servers provide only access to a file server's disk drives. Others can provide access to both the file server and direct access to any PC's hard disk on the network, which saves time because it allows a remote user to communicate directly with any network user without having to go through the file server.

To prevent unauthorized access to the corporate network, the remote access server can be configured to implement appropriate security features. Password protection is the most common security feature, but hackers using automated tools can easily discover passwords. The remote access server's modems might be able to offer better protection by supporting a dial-back capability. Incoming calls are prompted for a password, and the modem calls back the originating modem using the associated number stored in its security table.

More advanced security systems are available, such as the Remote Authentication Dial-In User Service (RADIUS), which is considered one of the most effective security protocols for dial-in access. RADIUS provides a client/server architecture that supplies authentication, authorization, and session accounting for users of remote access networks, including the Internet and corporate intranets. The remote access server acts like a client to the RADIUS server.

An administrator creates user profiles, which are stored at the RADIUS server. These profiles determine the authorizations that are given to remote dial-up users. A challenge/response protocol is used during user log-on to avoid sending passwords in plain text over the communication line. When a user dials in to the network, the RADIUS server responds with a challenge. The remote client uses the challenge to perform a cryptographic operation, the result of which is sent back to the RADIUS server. At the server, a similar operation is performed, and if the result matches the client's result, the user's identity is verified. If not, access is denied.

Developed by Livingston Enterprises, RADIUS has achieved status as the worldwide de facto standard and is the Internet Engineering Task Force's proposed standard for dial-in access security (RFC 2138).

Modem sharing lets local network users dial out from their individual network computers to access the Internet, bulletin boards, and other services. After launching their favorite communications software, local users establish a link with the remote-node server over the network, which opens up an outgoing telephone line. Users' individual PCs do not need modems. Because only a few modems and phone lines are required to support a small company, this method of remote access can provide significant cost savings on equipment and lines. In the case of peer-to-peer networks, by contrast, every PC requires its own modem for access to the outside world.

ROUTERS

For LAN-to-LAN communication between remote sites, a router is needed. A router can be a stand-alone device or it can come in the form of a module that plugs in to a managed hub. Routers operate at layer 3 of the OSI reference model (the network layer). Basically, they convert LAN protocols into wide-area packet network protocols such as Transmission Control Protocol/Internet Protocol (TCP/IP), and perform the process in reverse at the remote location.

ISDN-based routers provide high-quality dial-up connections to a local Internet service provider (ISP) so that LAN traffic can be carried economically between far-flung locations over the public TCP/IP-based Internet. Some products come with scripts that detect the specific type of ISDN connection the company has before setting up the TCP/IP information on the network (70 types of ISDN circuit configurations are available, each with its own order code). Some routers even offer firewall software to protect the corporate network from intruders who might attempt to enter through the Internet.

A stand-alone ISDN access router comes with an Ethernet port for connection to the hub. It also has an ISDN port for connection to the company's network termination point at which the carrier has connected a digital line for ISDN service. Some ISDN routers also have "plain old telephone service" ports, which also allow the unit to be used for faxing. In some cases, two phone lines capable of supporting 56K bps modems can be aggregated to achieve bandwidths close to ISDN's 128.8K bps. This type of router typically costs around $500.

Some stand-alone routers offer a high degree of configuration flexibility. Depending on the software package ordered with the unit, the device's WAN port can be configured for use over leased lines, ISDN, frame relay, switched 56K service, switched multimegabit data services and X.25. This type of router typically costs around $1,000.

GETTING STARTED

One of the easiest ways for a small business to set up a LAN is to buy a starter kit. Some vendors offer starter kits for both 10Base-T and 100Base-T networks. This is a convenient, affordable solution that comes complete with the necessary hardware and cabling needed to create a two-node network.

The typical kit includes a four- or five-port stackable hub, two autosensing Ethernet 10/100 NICs, and two thin coax cables. A 10Base-T starter kit typically sells for less than $100, whereas a 100Base-T starter kit costs less than $200. Additional NICs can cost between $25 and $60. An autosensing 10/100 PC Card for portable computers costs less than $100. Starter kits for switched Ethernet are also available for under $250. A two-port switch offers two autosensing 10/100Base-T ports, two NICs and cables. The starter kits are ready to run with all major network operating systems.

To make LAN-to-LAN communication easier for small businesses, some vendors have bundled equipment together into a basic network package for secure Internet access. A package from Cisco Systems Inc., for example, consists of a firewall, a hub, and a router for approximately $2,000. A similarly provisioned package from 3Com Corp., specifically designed for nontechnical users, features a World Wide Web browser interface that can step the user through all configuration and addressing tasks.

Another way for a small business to get started with a LAN is to buy products from a local value-added reseller (VAR), which will install and configure the network to meet specific business needs. Usually, the VAR specializes in providing products from a single vendor and its authorized partners, so the offerings are tightly integrated and have a record of proven performance. A key advantage to dealing with VARs is that they also offer technical support. And if a company cannot afford the upfront cost of installing a LAN, the VAR can usually arrange an equipment lease.

CONCLUSION

Just a few years ago, building a corporate network was a daunting task undertaken only by seasoned professionals. Small businesses that could not afford to spend lavishly on technical assistance either had to struggle along without a network or try to put the pieces together themselves, often on a trial-and-error basis, until they got it right. Recognizing the growing importance of this market, many interconnect vendors have started to design products that are easy for ordinary people to install and use. In some cases, the equipment is ready to use out of the box or is self-configuring after installation. In the few instances in which manual procedures are still necessary to get the equipment configured properly, a graphical interface steps the user through the process.

Although this chapter has focused on the LAN connectivity options for small businesses, the same connectivity options are available for the home, where it is increasingly common for several desktop computers to reside. In addition to computers for one or more students, there might be one for a telecommuter, along with a docking station for a mobile professional's laptop computer. All these computers can be networked together to save money on printers and other resources, as well as the cost of Internet access.

Chapter 7
LAN Printing Techniques
Gilbert Held

PROBLEMS ADDRESSED

During the early development stage of local area networking technology, the sharing of expensive laser printers was one of the primary reasons cited for using that relatively new technology. Although the price of laser printers has significantly declined over the past decade, network printing remains an important application supported by LANs. Thus, it is important to understand the different options available for installing network printers as well as the advantages and disadvantages associated with each option. Doing so will provide data center managers with information necessary to satisfy organizational network printing requirements in a cost-efficient manner, while considering such key issues as the effect of printing on other network operations, as well as network security.

CONNECTION METHOD

There are four basic methods that can be used to connect a printer to a local area network. Those methods are:

- File server connection
- Print server connection
- Remote printer via PC connection
- Direct connection

They are presented in the order that network printing technology developed and do not represent an order of preference. The remainder of this article examines each connection method in detail to understand the advantages and disadvantages associated with each method.

File Server Connection

The first series of network operating systems that were developed provided support for network printing via the attachment of printers to the serial or parallel ports of file servers. Although this option limits the number of network printers that can be used prior to purchasing a license to operate another file server, it minimizes network traffic, which can be an important consideration when a network has a high level of activity. To understand why a file server connection minimizes network print traffic in

0-8493-9838-X/00/$0.00+$.50
© 2000 by CRC Press LLC

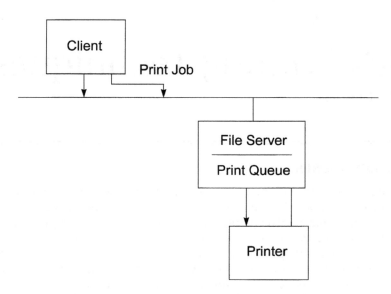

Exhibit 7.1. File Server Print Connection Data Flow

comparison to other network printing options requires a review of the flow of print job traffic.

PRINT JOB TRAFFIC

In a client/server environment, all network traffic originated by client workstations first flows to a server to include print jobs. When a print job flows to a file server, it is first placed into a print queue from which it will be serviced. Thus, the attachment of a printer directly to a file server results in a print job flowing from the client to the file server, as illustrated in Exhibit 7.1. Note that every byte in the print job only flows once on the network. As will be noted later in this article, each of the other network printing options results in every byte in a print job flowing twice on the network, in effect doubling the print job workload in terms of its impact on network traffic.

FILE SERVER ATTACHMENT PROBLEMS

Although the direct attachment of network printers to a file server minimizes the effect of print job traffic on a network, its use in this manner has a number of disadvantages. Those disadvantages include potential file server performance problems and printer access constraints.

When a file server supports directly connected printers, data leaves the server's print queues at the serial or parallel port interface speed, which is typically a fraction of the network operating rate. Because the file server must use interrupts to service print jobs exiting its print queues, the server will perform a periodic series of interrupt servicing operations for a longer period of time than if the print job was directed onto the network. This in turn adversely affects the ability of the server to perform other network-related functions. Based on a series of performance measurements conducted by the author of this article, a NetWare 3.1X or 4.X server operating on an Intel 486 50-MHz or lower performance processor will be adversely affected by at least 10% through the use of two or more directly connected printers when 20 or more pages of network printing occur per hour. Although such printing will adversely affect the performance of a file server operating on an Intel Pentium processor, the actual decrease in the level of performance was found to be so slight that it was difficult to measure, varying between 1% and 2%. Thus, if a 75-MHz or higher Pentium processor is used as the platform for an organization's file server, the file server's level of performance when printers are directly connected should be considered to be equivalent to other network printing methods that relocate network printers to other areas on the network.

A second, and for many users a more serious, problem associated with the direct attachment of printers to a file server is printer access. Most organizations consider their file servers to represent repositories of important data they wish to secure. Thus, it is quite natural for file servers to be located in access-controlled areas within a building, such as the corporate data center, a technical control center, or a similarly controlled access location. Because one of the goals of network printing is to provide convenient access to shared printers, many organizations prefer to maintain security for their file servers and eliminate this printing option from consideration. Other organizations, such as small departments where access for all employees is already controlled, may install a server in an empty office. For such organizations, the direct connection of printers to a departmental file server may represent a viable network option, especially if they are using NetWare on an Intel Pentium processor-based computer.

PRINT SERVER CONNECTION

A printer server is a computer that runs network software developed to extract print jobs from print queues residing on a file server. Through the use of a print server, network printers can be located at any location where the print server can be connected to a network. Thus, the use of a print server removes the controlled access problem associated with the direct connection of printers to a file server.

Exhibit 7.2 illustrates the data flow for a print job when printers are connected to a print server. In a client/server environment, the print job first

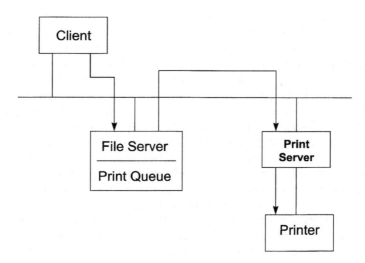

Exhibit 7.2.   Print Job Data Flow when a Printer Server is Used

flows to the file server, where it is placed into a print queue. The print server operates software that communicates with the file server, and the two servers negotiate the transmission of the print job from the print queue in the file server to the print server, where it is directed to an attached printer. Thus, the print job must flow twice on the network, first from the client workstation to the file server, and then from the file server to the print server.

If the network has a high level of utilization, a significant amount of printing can result in a degradation of network performance, especially when using graphics embedded in documents directed to the network printer. Thus, for many network managers and administrators, the choice between connecting network printers to a file server or to a print server represents one of printing convenience and security versus a degradation of network performance.

REMOTE PRINTING ON A PC

Remote printing represents a network printing technique that turns a workstation into a limited-function print server. The major differences between remote printing and a print server concern the ability of each device to perform other operations and the number of printers that can be supported. A remote printer capability is established by loading a terminate and stay resident (TSR) program on a PC connected to a network. The TSR program works in a manner similar to print server software, establishing communications with a file server and extracting jobs from print queues associated with the remote printer. The TSR program works in the background on the host PC, enabling foreground operations to continue. This enables a PC user to use his or her computer for both local and network-related operations, while network printing is performed on a printer connected to the computer. In comparison, a print server is dedicated to servicing attached printers and cannot be used for other operations.

A second difference between a remote printing TSR program operating on a PC and a dedicated print server concerns the number of printers that can be supported by each computer. Remote printing on a PC is normally limited to one per computer. In comparison, a print server is only limited by the number of serial and parallel ports that can be installed in the server.

One of the key advantages associated with the use of remote printing is its simplicity, because the installation of the TSR program can be performed in under a minute. Another advantage associated with this network printing method is the fact that many organizations have large quantities of obsolete Intel 286-, 386-, and 486-based computers. Because the remote printing processes are not processor intensive, just about any computer platform can be used to obtain a remote printing capability. This means remote printing PCs can be located within several areas of an organization to better distribute print jobs to areas where users work. In comparison, a print server that is normally used to support multiple printers does not provide the level of location flexibility typically associated with the use of remote printing PCs.

Disadvantages associated with the use of remote printing include the doubling of print job traffic and the possibility that the PC user whose computer is operating the TSR program may automatically power down his or her workstation at the end of the day, precluding the ability of other network users to use one or more printers attached to that computer. Concerning the latter, for this reason most organizations now set up a remote printer capability on unattended workstations that are left on continuously. This alleviates the problems associated with the tendency of computer users to power off their computers when they leave the office. In addition, if the organization has an inventory of older Intel 286-, 386-, or 486-based computers, those computers can be used as remote printer workstation platforms to distribute a network printing capability throughout the organization.

Exhibit 7.3 illustrates an example of the use of print server and remote printer-printer connections. In this example, it was assumed that engineering department employees were grouped in a small area and those employees had a sufficient amount of network printing to justify the use of three network printers. Thus, rather than install three separate remote printer-based computers, one computer was installed operating print server

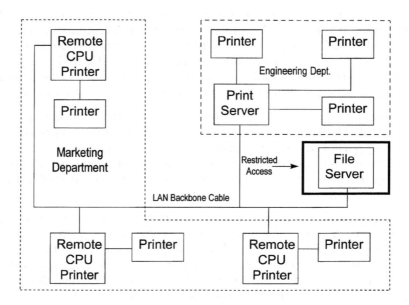

Exhibit 7.3.   Using Print Server and Remote Printer-Printer Connections

software, which enabled that computer to support the attachment of three network printers. The marketing department, which occupies the remainder of the floor shown in Exhibit 7.3, has employees spread out over an extended area of floor space. Based on an assumption that there are three convenient areas where network printing jobs could be delivered for pickup by marketing personnel, three remote printing computers were installed to service the requirements of that department. Thus, mixing the use of print servers and remote printer-based computers, allows for a degree of flexibility in satisfying the network printing requirements of organizational employees. In addition, note that access is restricted to the file server shown in Exhibit 7.3, precluding its use for convenient pickup of network printing jobs. Thus, no printers are shown as being attached to the file server. If access to the file server was not restricted, an alternative approach that could be considered would be the use of the file server for network printing to support the engineering department. However, if the file server is not located within a 15-foot radius of the location where the engineering department wants to locate network printers, the file server would have to be relocated, which may not be an easy task. The 15-foot radius limitation is based on the common use of 15-foot parallel printer cable. If serial printers are used, the radius of support can be extended to approximately 50 feet, which represents the maximum standardized drive distance for serial connections when an RS-232 interface is used.

Exhibit 7.4. Comparing LAN Printer Connection Methods

Effect on Network and End-User Operations	LAN Printer Connection Method			
	File Server Connection	Print Server Connection	Remote Printer	Direct Connection
Minimize network traffic	Yes	No	No	No
Typical printer support	Up to 4	Up to 4	1 or 2	1
Effect on file server performance	10% when non-Pentium system is used	None	None	None
Printer access	Usually restricted	More flexible	Very flexible	Extremely flexible
Requires dedicated computer	Yes	Yes	No	N/A

DIRECT CONNECTION

The fourth method for supporting network printing is via the direct connection of a printer to the network. To do so, the printer must have a network adapter and ROM code that convert the printer into a mini remote printer. This method of connection is a relatively recent development that was introduced by Hewlett-Packard in 1995, and provides users with a great deal of flexibility in supporting user network printing requirements because the necessity for having a separate printer is eliminated. Thus, this network printing method minimizes the amount of desk space required to support network printing. The disadvantages of this network printing method concern its printer support and network traffic. Because the LAN adapter and ROM code are physically inserted into a printer, support is limited to one printer. Concerning network traffic, print jobs first flow to the file server, and then from the file server to the card in the printer, doubling network traffic. Exhibit 7.4 compares the four LAN printer connection methods with respect to their effect on network and end-user operations.

RECOMMENDED COURSE OF ACTION

As indicated in this article, there are significant differences associated with the use of different methods for supporting network printing. Some network printing methods provide more flexibility in locating printers than other methods, while the use of a file server minimizes the effect of print jobs on network traffic. In developing a network printing solution to satisfy organizational requirements, it is important to understand the advantages and disadvantages associated with each method, as well as the volume of print traffic and desired printer locations. In many situations, a mixture of network printing methods may be more suitable for satisfying user requirements than the use of a single method. Thus, in attempting to match the characteristics of different network printing methods against organizational requirements, the data center operations manager should consider implementing several methods rather than a single method.

Chapter 8
An Overview of Cryptographic Methods

Gary C. Kessler

Does increased security provide comfort to paranoid people? Or does security provide some very basic protections that we are naive to believe that we do not need? During this time when the Internet provides essential communication between tens of millions of people and is being increasingly used as a tool for commerce, security becomes a tremendously important issue with which to deal.

There are many aspects to security and many applications, ranging from secure commerce and payments to private communications and protecting passwords. One essential aspect for secure communications is that of cryptography, which is the focus of this chapter. But it is important to note that although cryptography is *necessary* for secure communications, it is not by itself *sufficient*. The reader is advised, then, that the topics covered in this chapter describe only the first of many steps necessary for better security in any number of situations.

This chapter has two major purposes. The first is to define some of the terms and concepts behind basic cryptographic methods, and to offer a way to compare the myriad cryptographic schemes in use today. The second is to provide some real examples of cryptography in use today.

THE PURPOSE OF CRYPTOGRAPHY

Cryptography is the science of writing in secret code, and it is an ancient art; the first documented use of cryptography in writing dates back to Egypt, circa 1900 B.C. In data and telecommunications, cryptography is necessary when communicating over any untrusted medium, which includes just about *any* network, particularly the Internet.

Within the context of any application-to-application communication, there are some specific security requirements, including

- *Authentication*: The process of proving one's identity. (The primary forms of host-to-host authentication on the Internet today are name-based or address-based, both of which are notoriously weak.)

```
key                                key
plaintext ----------------> ciphertext ----------------> plaintext
```

Exhibit 8.1.   Secret Key (Symmetric) Cryptography

- *Privacy/confidentiality:* Ensuring that no one can read the message except the intended receiver.
- *Integrity:* Assuring the receiver that the received message has not been altered in any way from the original.
- *Non-repudiation:* A mechanism to prove that the sender really sent this message.

Cryptography, then, not only protects data from theft or alteration, but it can also be used for user authentication. There are, in general, three types of cryptographic schemes typically used to accomplish these goals: secret key (or symmetric) cryptography, public-key (or asymmetric) cryptography, and hash functions, each of which is described below. In all cases, the initial unencrypted data is referred to as *plaintext*. It is encrypted into *ciphertext*, which will in turn (usually) be decrypted into usable plaintext.

Secret Key Cryptography

In secret key cryptography, a single key is used for both encryption and decryption. As shown in Exhibit 8.1, the sender uses the key (or some set of rules) to encrypt the plaintext and sends the ciphertext the receiver. The receiver applies the same key (or ruleset) to decode the message and recover the plaintext. Because a single key is used for both functions, secret key cryptography is also called *symmetric encryption*.

With this form of cryptography, it is obvious that the key must be known to both the sender and the receiver; that, in fact, is the secret. The biggest difficulty with this approach, of course, is the distribution of the key.

There are several widely used secret key cryptography schemes, and they are generally categorized as being either *block ciphers* or *stream ciphers*. A block cipher is so called because it encrypts blocks of data at a time; the same plaintext block will always be encrypted into the same ciphertext (when using the same key). Stream ciphers operate on a single bit, byte, or word at a time, and implement a feedback mechanism so that the same plaintext will yield different ciphertext every time it is encrypted.

The most commonly used secret-key encryption scheme used today is the Data Encryption Standard (DES), designed by IBM in the 1970s and adopted by the National Bureau of Standards in 1977 for commercial and unclassified government applications. DES is a block-cipher employing a 56-bit key that operates on 64-bit blocks. DES has a complex set of rules

```
                one key                     other key
plaintext ----------------> ciphertext ----------------> plaintext
```

Exhibit 8.2.   **Public-key (Asymmetric) Cryptography Using Two Keys
                    (One For Encryption and the Other For Decryption)**

---

and transformations that were designed specifically to yield fast hardware implementations and slow software implementations, although this latter point is becoming less significant today because the speed of computer processors (and, therefore, programs) is several orders of magnitude faster today than 20 years ago. IBM also proposed a 128-bit key for DES, which was rejected at the time by the government; the use of 128-bit keys is under consideration at this time, however, although the cost of conversion will be one of the major stumbling blocks.

There are a number of other secret-key cryptography algorithms that are also in use today. Triple-DES, for example, is a variant of DES that uses either two or three different keys, coupled with three encryption steps. CAST-128 (described in Request for Comments, or RFC, 2144; CAST is not an acronym, but its name is derived from the initials of its inventors, Carlisle Adams and Stafford Tavares of Nortel) and the International Data Encryption Algorithm (IDEA) are conceptually similar to DES; both are 64-bit block ciphers using 128-bit keys. CAST and IDEA are also internationally available and, therefore, unencumbered for use by members of the Internet community. Rivest Cipher 4 (RC4), named for its inventor Ron Rivest, is a stream cipher using variable-sized keys; it is widely used in commercial cryptography products, although it can be exported using only keys that are 40 bits or less in length. RC5 is a block cipher that supports a variety of block sizes, key sizes, and number of encryption passes over the data.

Public-Key Cryptography

Public-key cryptography (PKC) was invented in 1976 by Martin Hellman and Whitfield Diffie of Stanford University to solve the key exchange problem with secret-key cryptography. Their scheme requires two keys, where one key is used to encrypt the plaintext and the other key is used to decrypt the ciphertext. The important point here is that it does not matter which key is applied first, but both keys are required for the process to work (Exhibit 8.2). Because a pair of keys is required, this approach is also called asymmetric cryptography.

In PKC, one of the keys is designated the public key and may be advertised as widely as the owner wants. The other key is designated the private key and is never revealed to another party. It is straightforward to send messages under this scheme. The sender, for example, encrypts some information using the intended receiver's public key; the receiver decrypts the ciphertext using his own private key. This method could also be used in both directions at the same time. For example, the sender could encrypt the plaintext first with his own private key and then encrypt again with the receiver's public key; this latter scheme might be used where it is important that the sender cannot deny sending the message (nonrepudiation).

The most common PKC scheme used today is RSA, named for its inventors Ronald Rivest, Adi Shamir, and Leonard Adleman, and used in hundreds of software products. The RSA scheme can be used for key exchange or encryption. RSA uses a variable size encryption block and a variable size key. The key pair is derived from a very large number, n, that is the product of two prime numbers chosen according to special rules; these primes may be 100 or more digits in length each, yielding an n with roughly twice as many digits as the prime factors. The public key information includes n and a derivative of one of the factors of n; an attacker cannot determine the prime factors of n (and, therefore, the private key) from this information alone and that is what makes the RSA algorithm so secure. (Some descriptions of PKC erroneously state that the safety of RSA is due to the difficulty in factoring large prime numbers. In fact, large prime numbers, like small prime numbers, have only two factors!) The ability for computers to factor large numbers, and therefore attack schemes such as RSA, is rapidly improving and systems today can find the prime factors of numbers with more than 140 digits. The presumed protection of RSA, however, is that users can easily increase the key size to always stay ahead of the computer processing curve.

An alternative to RSA was published by the National Institute for Standards and Technology (NIST) in 1991. The Digital Signature Algorithm is part of the NIST's proposed Digital Signature Standard (DSS), both part of the desire of the U.S. government to define a next-generation cryptography system.

Hash Functions

Hash functions, also called message digests and one-way encryption, are algorithms that, in some sense, use no key (Exhibit 8.3). Instead, they transform the plaintext mathematically so that the contents and length of the plaintext are not recoverable from the ciphertext. Furthermore, there is a very low probability that two different plaintext messages will yield the same hash value.

```
                        hash function
           plaintext ----------------> ciphertext
```

Exhibit 8.3.　**Hash Functions Using No Key (Plaintext is not Recoverable From the Ciphertext)**

Hash algorithms are typically used to provide a digital fingerprint of the contents of a file, often used to ensure that the file has not been altered by an intruder or virus. Hash functions are also commonly employed by many operating systems to encrypt passwords.

Among the most common hash functions in use today in commercial cryptographic applications are a family of Message Digest (MD) algorithms, all of which are byte-oriented schemes that produce a 128-bit hash value from an arbitrary-length message. MD2 (RFC 1319) is well-suited for systems with limited memory, such as smart cards. MD4 (RFC 1320), developed by Rivest, is similar to MD2 but designed specifically for fast processing in software. MD5 (RFC 1321), also developed by Rivest, came about after potential weaknesses were reported in MD4; this scheme is similar to MD4 but is slower because more manipulation is made to the original data. MD5 has been implemented in a large number of products, although several weaknesses in the algorithm were demonstrated by German cryptographer Hans Dobbertin in 1996.

The Secure Hash Algorithm (SHA), proposed by NIST for its Secure Hash Standard (SHS), is seeing increased use in commercial products today. SHA produces a 160-bit hash value.

Why Three Encryption Techniques?

So, why are there so many different types of cryptographic schemes? Why are we unable to do everything we need with just one?

The answer is that each scheme is optimized for some specific application(s). Hash functions, for example, are well-suited for ensuring data integrity because any change made to the contents of a message will result in the receiver calculating a different hash value than the one placed in the transmission by the sender. Since it is highly unlikely that two different messages will yield the same hash value, data integrity is ensured to a high degree of confidence.

Secret-key encryption, on the other hand, is ideally suited to encrypting messages. The sender can generate a session key on a per-message basis to encrypt the message; the receiver, of course, needs the same session key to decrypt the message.

Key exchange, of course, is a key application of public-key cryptography. Asymmetric schemes can also be used for nonrepudiation; if the receiver can obtain the session key encrypted with the sender's private key, then only this sender could have sent the message. Public-key cryptography could, theoretically, also be used to encrypt messages, although this is rarely done because secret-key encryption operates at 100 to 1,000 times faster than public-key encryption.

Public Key Certificates

As PKC becomes more commonplace, particularly for electronic commerce applications, it is important to discuss the tangential issue of repositories for public keys. Without such repositories, a sender has no way to find a receiver's public key and, therefore, cannot send encrypted messages.

Many, perhaps most, public-key systems rely on repositories of public keys called certification authorities (CA). When a sender needs an intended receiver's public key, the sender must get that key from the receiver's CA. That works OK if the sender and receiver have the same CA, but how does the sender know to trust the foreign CA? One industry wag has noted, about trust: "You are either born with it or have it granted upon you." Thus, some CA will be trusted because they are known to be reputable, such as the CA operated by BBN, CommerceNet, GTE Cybertrust Solutions Inc., the U.S. Postal Service, and VeriSign. CAs, in turn, form trust relationships with other CAs. Thus, if a user queries a foreign CA for information, the user may ask to see a list of CAs that establish a "chain of trust" back to the user.

As complicated as this may sound, it really is not in concept. Consider driver licenses. I have one issued by the state of Vermont. The license establishes my identity, indicates the type of vehicles I can operate and the fact that I must wear corrective lenses while doing so, identifies the issuing authority, and notes that I am an organ donor. When I drive outside of Vermont, the other jurisdictions throughout the U.S., Canada, and many other countries recognize the authority of Vermont to issue this "certificate" and they trust the information it contains. Some other countries may not recognize the Vermont driver license as sufficient bona fides that I can drive.

Certificates for PKC systems are defined in International Telecommunication Union Telecommunication Standardization Sector (ITU-TSS) Recommendation X.509. X.509 certificates identify the holder, the holder's rights and privileges, the issuing authority, an expiration date, the public-key data, and other information.

CRYPTOGRAPHIC ALGORITHMS IN ACTION

The paragraphs above have provided an overview of the different types of cryptographic algorithms, as well as some examples of some available protocols and schemes. Exhibit 8.4 provides an even longer list of some of the schemes employed today for a variety of functions, most notably electronic commerce. The paragraphs below will show several real cryptographic applications that many of us employ (knowingly or not) everyday for password protection and private communication.

Capstone	U.S. National Institute of Standards and Technology (NIST) project for publicly available cryptography standards that can be implemented in one or more tamper-proof computer chips (e.g., Clipper); comprises a bulk encryption algorithm (Skipjack), digital signature algorithm (DSA), and hash algorithm (SHA)
Clipper	The computer chip that will implement the Skipjack encryption scheme
CAST-128	A DES-like secret key cryptosystem using 128-bit keys
DES (Data Encryption Standard)	Secret-key cryptosystem; provides message encryption for privacy; a variant, called Triple-DES, uses multiple keys and multiple encryption/decryption passes over the message
Diffie–Hellman	First public-key cryptosystem, used for key exchange for secret-key (symmetric) cryptosystems
DSA (Digital Signature Algorithm)	Algorithm specified in the digital signature standard (DSS) proposed for Capstone; provides digital signature for the authentication of messages
IDEA (International Data Encryption algorithm)	Secret-key cryptosystem; provides message encryption for privacy
Kerberos	A secret-key encryption and authentication system, designed to authenticate requests for network resources within a user domain rather than to authenticate messages
MD2, MD4, MD5	Message Digest algorithms used for digital signature applications for message integrity
MOSS (MIME object security standard)	Designed as a successor to PEM to provide PEM-based security services to MIME messages
PCT (Private Communication Technology)	Developed by Microsoft and Visa for secure communication on the Internet; similar to SSL, PCT supports Diffie–Hellman, Fortezza, and RSA for key establishment; DES, RC2, RC4, and triple-DES for encryption; and DSA and RSA message signatures; a companion to SET.
PEM (Privacy Enhanced Mail)	Provides secure e-mail over the Internet and includes provisions for encryption (DES), authentication, and key management (DES, RSA); may be superseded by S/MIME and PEM-MIME
PEM-MIME	(See MOSS)
PGP (pretty good privacy)	Provides cryptographic routines for e-mail and file storage applications; uses Diffie–Hellman/DSS for key management and digital signatures (older versions use RSA); IDEA, CAST, or Triple-DES for message encryption; and MD5 or SHA for computing the hash value of the message
PKCS (public-key cryptography standards)	A set of guidelines for coding various security-relayed messages, designed by RSA Data Security
RC2, RC4, RC5	Secret-key cryptosystem; provides message encryption for privacy
RSA (Rivest, Shamir, Adleman)	Widely used public-key cryptosystem for encryption, authentication, and key exchange (for secret-key systems)
Secure IP (IPsec)	Comprises two mechanisms: the IP authentication header provides integrity and authentication for IP packets using MD5; while the IP encapsulating security payload provides integrity and confidentiality using DES-CBC

Exhibit 8.4.   Some Secure Communications Protocols, Cryptography Systems, and Their Primary Applications

SET (secure electronic transactions)	A merging of two protocols: SEPP (secure electronic payment protocol), an open specification for secure bank card transactions over the Internet, developed by CyberCash, GTE, IBM, MasterCard, and Netscape; and STT (Secure Transaction Technology), a secure payment protocol developed by Microsoft and Visa; supports DES and RC4 for encryption, and RSA for signatures, key exchange, and public-key encryption of bank card numbers; SET is a companion to PCT
S-HTTP (secure hypertext transfer protocol)	An extension to HTTP to provide secure exchange of documents over the Web; supported algorithms include RSA and Kerberos for key exchange, DES, IDEA, RC2, and Triple-DES for encryption
SHA (Secure Hash Algorithm)	The Message Digest (hash) algorithm in the Secure Hash Standard (SHS) proposed for Capstone
Skipjack	Secret-key (symmetric) encryption scheme proposed for Capstone
S/MIME (Secure Multipurpose Internet Mail Extension)	Adds digital signature and encryption capability to Internet MIME messages
SSL (secure sockets layer)	Developed by Netscape Communications to provide application-independent security and privacy over the Internet, allowing protocols such as HTTP, FTP (file transfer protocol), and Telnet to be layered on top of it transparently; RSA is used during negotiation to exchange keys and identify the actual cryptographic algorithm (DES, IDEA, RC2, RC4, or RSA) to use for the session; employs MD5 for message digests
TLS (transport layer security)	IETF specification intended to replace SSL; employs Triple-DES (secret key cryptography), SHA (hash), Diffie–Hellman (key exchange), and DSS (digital signatures)
ITU-T Recommendation X.509	Specification for format of certificates for public key cryptography systems; certificates map (bind) a user identity with a public key

Exhibit 8.4. *(Continued)*

Password Protection

Nearly all modern multiuser computer and network operating systems employ passwords at the very least to protect and authenticate users accessing computer and/or network resources. Passwords are not typically kept on a host or server in plaintext but are generally encoded using some sort of hash scheme. UNIX, for example, uses a well-known scheme via its crypt() function. Passwords are kept in the etc/passwd file (Exhibit 8.5); each record in the file contains the username, hashed password, user's individual and group numbers, user's name, home directory, and shell program. Note that each password results in a 13-byte hash.

Windows NT uses a similar scheme to store passwords in the Security Access Manager file. In the NT case, all passwords are hashed using the MD4 algorithm, resulting in a 128-bit (16-byte) hash value (they are then obscured using an undocumented mathematical transformation that was a

```
carol:FM5ikbQt1K052:502:100:Carol Monaghan:/home/carol:/bin/bash
alex:LqAi7Mdyg/HcQ:503:100:Alex Insley:/home/alex:/bin/bash
gary:FkJXupRyFqY4s:501:100:Gary Kessler:/home/gary:/bin/bash
todd:edGqQUAaGv7g6:506:101:Todd Pritsky:/home/todd:/bin/bash
sarah:Jbw6BwE4XoUHo:504:101:Sarah Antone:/home/schedule:/bin/bash
josh:FiH0ONcjPut1g:505:101:Joshua Kessler:/home/webroot:/bin/bash
```

Exhibit 8.5.   Sample Entries in a Unix Password File

---

secret until distributed on the Internet). Thus, the password might be stored as the hash value (in hexadecimal) 60771b22d73c34bd4a290a 79c8b09f18.

Passwords are not saved in plaintext on computer systems precisely so they cannot be easily compromised. For similar reasons, we do not want passwords sent in plaintext across a network. But for remote log-on applications, how does a client system identify itself or a user to the server? One mechanism is to send the password as a hash value. A weakness of that approach, however, is that an intruder can grab the password off of the network and use an off-line attack (such as a dictionary attack in which an attacker takes every known word and encrypts it with the encryption algorithm of the network, hoping eventually to find a match with a purloined password hash). In some situations, an attacker only has to copy the hashed password value and use it later on to gain unauthorized entry without ever learning the actual password.

An even stronger authentication method uses the password to modify a shared secret between the client and server, but never allows the password in any form to go across the network. This is the basis for the Challenge Handshake Authentication Protocol (CHAP), the remote log-on process supported by Windows NT.

As suggested above, Windows NT passwords are stored in a security file on a server as a 16-byte hash value. When a user logs on to a server from a remote workstation, the user is identified by the username sent across the network in plaintext (no worries here; it is not a secret anyway!). The server then generates a 64-bit random number and sends it to the client (also in plaintext). This number is the challenge.

The client system then encrypts the challenge using DES. Recall that DES employs a 56-bit key, acts on a 64-bit block of data, and produces a 64-bit output. In this case, the 64-bit data block is the random number. The client actually uses three different DES keys to encrypt the random number, producing three different 64-bit outputs. The first key is the first seven bytes (56 bits) of the hash value of the password, the second key is the next seven bytes in the password hash, and the third key is the remaining two bytes of the password hash concatenated with five zero-filled bytes.

(So, for the example above, the three DES keys would be 60771b22d73c34, bd4a290a79c8b0, and 9f180000000000.) Each key is applied to the random number resulting in three 64-bit outputs, which comprise the response. Thus, the 8-byte challenge from the server yields a 24-byte response from the client and this is all that would be seen on the network. The server, for its part, does the same calculation to ensure that the values match.

Pretty Good Privacy (PGP)

PGP is one of the most widely used public-key cryptography programs in use today. Developed by Philip Zimmermann and long the subject of controversy, PGP is commercially (http://www.pgp.com, San Mateo, CA) available today and is also available as a plug-in for many e-mail clients, such as Microsoft Corp.'s Exchange and Outlook, and Qualcomm's Eudora.

PGP can be used to sign or encrypt e-mail messages with the mere click of the mouse. Depending upon the version of PGP, the software uses SHA or MD5 for calculating the message hash; CAST, Triple-DES, or IDEA for encryption; and RSA or DSS/Diffie–Hellman for key exchange and digital signatures.

PGP uses a different trust model than that described above with CA and X.509 certificates. In particular, PGP relies on a local keyring and a "web of trust." PGP users maintain their own list of known and trusted public keys. If I need a user's public key, I can ask him for it or, in many cases, download the public key from an advertised server. If you hold the public key of a user, I might get the key from you. How do I know that it is valid? Well, if I trust you and you think the key you gave me is valid, then I will trust that a key you give me is OK. But trust is not necessarily transitive, so I may not trust a third party merely because you do. In any case, encryption and signatures based on public keys can be used only when the appropriate public key is on the user's keyring.

When PGP is first installed, the user has to create a key pair. One key, the public key, can be advertised and widely circulated. The private key is protected by use of a passphrase. The passphrase has to be entered every time the user accesses his private key.

Exhibit 8.6 shows a PGP-signed message. This message will not be kept secret from an eavesdropper, but a recipient can be assured that the message has not been altered from what the sender transmitted. In this instance, the sender signs the message using his own private key. The receiver uses the sender's public key to verify the signature; the public key is taken from the receiver's keyring based on the sender's e-mail address. Note that the signature process does not work unless the sender's public key is on the receiver's keyring.

```
-----BEGIN PGP SIGNED MESSAGE-----
Hash: SHA1

Hi Carol.

What was that pithy Groucho Marx quote?

/kess

-----BEGIN PGP SIGNATURE-----
Version: PGP for Personal Privacy 5.0
Charset: noconv

iQA/AwUBNFUdO5WOcz5SFtuEEQJx/ACaAgR97+vvDU6XWELV/GANjAAgBtUAnjG3
Sdfw2JgmZIOLNjFe7jP0Y8/M
=jUAU
-----END PGP SIGNATURE-----
```

Exhibit 8.6. A PGP-signed Message

Exhibit 8.7 shows a PGP-encrypted message (PGP compresses the file, where practical, prior to encryption because encrypted files cannot be compressed). In this case, public key methods are used to exchange the session key for the actual message encryption using secret-key cryptography. In this case, the receiver's e-mail address is the pointer to the public key in the sender's keyring; in fact, the same message can be sent to multiple recipients. When the destination side receives the message, the recipient must use their private key to successfully decrypt the message (Exhibit 8.8).

```
-----BEGIN PGP MESSAGE-----
Version: PGP for Personal Privacy 5.0
MessageID: DAdVB3wzpBr3YRunZwYvhK5gBKBXOb/m

qANQR1DBwU4D/TlT68XXuiUQCADfj2o4b4aFYBcWumA7hR1Wvz9rbv2BR6WbEUsy
ZBIEFtjyqCd96qF38sp9IQiJIKlNaZfx2GLRWikPZwchUXxB+AA5+1qsG/ELBvRa
c9XefaYpbbAZ6z6LkOQ+eE0XASe7aEEPfdxvZZT37dVyiyxuBBRYNLN8Bphdr2zv
z/9Ak4/OLnLiJRk05/2UNE5Z0a+3lcvITMmfGajvRhkXqocavPOKiin3hv7+Vx88
uLLem2/fQHZhGcQvkqZVqXx8SmNw5gzuvwjV1WHj9muDGBY0MkjiZIRI7azWnoU9
3KCnmpR60VO4rDRAS5uG19fioSvze+q8XqxubaNsgdKkoD+tB/4u4c4tznLfw1L2
YBS+dzFDw5desMFSo7JkecAS4NB9jAu9K+f7PTAsesCBNETDd49BTOFFTWWavAfE
gLYcPrcn4s3EriUgvL3OzPR4P1chNu6sa3ZJkTBbriDoA3VpnqG3hxqfNyOlqAka
mJJuQ53Ob9ThaFH8YcE/VqUFdw+bQtrAJ6NpjIxi/x0FfOInhC/bBw7pDLXBFNaX
HdlLQRPQdrmnWskKznOSarxq4GjpRTQo4hpCRJJ5aU7tZO9HPTZXFG6iRIT0wa47
AR5nvkEKoIAjW5HaDKiJriuWLdtN4OXecWvxFsjR32ebz76U8aLpAK87GZEyTzBx
dV+1H0hwyT/y1cZQ/E5USePP4oKWF4uqquPee1OPeFMBo4CvuGyhZXD/18Ft/53Y
WIebvdiCqsOoabK3jEfdGExce63zDI0=
=MpRf
-----END PGP MESSAGE-----
```

Exhibit 8.7.   A PGP-Encrypted Message: The Receiver's E-Mail Address is the Pointer to the Public Key in the Sender's Keyring. At the Destination Side, the Receiver Uses His Own Private Key

```
Hi Gary,

"Outside of a dog, a book is man's best friend. Inside of a dog, it's
too dark to read."

Carol
```

Exhibit 8.8.   The Decrypted Message from Exhibit 8.7

CONCLUSION ... OF SORTS

This chapter has briefly described how cryptography works. The reader must beware, however, that there are a number of ways to attack every one of these systems; cryptanalysis and attacks on cryptosystems, however, are well beyond the scope of this chapter. In the words of Sherlock Holmes (OK, Arthur Conan Doyle, really), "What one man can invent, another can discover" ("The Adventure of the Dancing Men").

Cryptography is a particularly interesting field because of the amount of work that is, by necessity, done in secret. The irony is that today, secrecy is not the key to the goodness of a cryptographic algorithm. Regardless of the mathematical theory behind an algorithm, the best algorithms are those that are well-known and well-documented because they are also well tested and well-studied! In fact, time is the only true test of good cryptography; any cryptographic scheme that stays in use year after year is most likely a good one. The strength of cryptography is the choice of the keys; longer keys will resist attack better than shorter keys. A corollary to this is that consumers should be very wary of products that use a proprietary cryptography scheme, ostensibly because the secrecy of the algorithm is an advantage; this security through obscurity posture is doomed to fail.

REFERENCES AND FURTHER READING

Kahn, D., *The Codebreakers: the Story of Secret Writing*, revised ed., Scribner, New York, 1996.
Kaufman, C., Perlman, R. and Speciner, M., Network Security: Private Communication in a Public World, Prentice-Hall, Englewood Cliffs, NJ, 1995.
Schneier, B., *Applied Cryptography*, 2nd ed., John Wiley & Sons, New York, 1996.
Counterpane (Bruce Schneier). URL: http://www.counterpane.com.
Cypherpunks Web Page. URL: ftp://ftp.csua.berkeley.edu/pub/cypherpunks/Home.html.
International Computer Security Association Web Site. URL: http://www.icsa.com.
Pretty Good Privacy Web Site. URL: http://www.pgp.com.
RSA's Cryptography FAQ. URL: http://www.rsa.com/rsalabs/newfaq/home.html.
Yahoo! crypto pages. URL: http://www.yahoo.com/Computers_and_Internet/Security_and_Encryption/.

Chapter 9
Assessing and Combating the Sniffer Threat

E. Eugene Schultz

To say that determining the real origins and magnitudes of threat is one of the most challenging problems facing information security (InfoSec) professionals is a gross understatement. The media, net news, and a myriad of other sources constantly remind us just how diverse the range of potential threats is. Internet security, intranet and extranet security, operating system-based security, information warfare, personnel security, and other important topics have all at one time or another received a disproportionate amount of attention in the 1990s, forcing InfoSec professionals to deal with these issues more than with many other competing issues. Addressing these issues is a sound strategy, but the proverbial winds of hype continually shift. All things considered, deciding what the real, relevant sources of InfoSec threat are, then assessing the resulting risk, and, finally, planning how to effectively control that risk have become more difficult than ever.

The inevitable result of all this justified attention on these diverse, sometimes sensational sources of InfoSec-related threat has been diminished attention to less dramatic, more seemingly routine sources of threat. One such source, the focus of this article, is network snooping or sniffing in which network traffic is captured without authorization. Although most InfoSec professionals understand that such a threat exists, it is easy to fall into the trap of thinking that somehow the magnitude of this threat pales compared to the other, more exciting sources of threat. An organization is likely to have provisions in an InfoSec policy that prohibit the use of sniffers without proper authorization and that may even require periodic inspections to determine whether unauthorized sniffers exist. Furthermore, unless one works in a unit whose responsibilities include networking, one is not likely to be aware of the extent to which sniffers are deployed and exactly who has access to the data that sniffers capture. Of all the sources of potential loss due to unauthorized access to systems, illegal data transfers, etc., however, none is greater in most operational environments than the deployment of unauthorized sniffers. This article explores the nature of the sniffer threat, presents solutions for combating the risk, and suggests strategies for dealing with sniffer-related incidents should they occur.

THE NATURE OF THE THREAT

How Sniffers Work

To understand the threat that sniffers present first requires understanding how sniffers work. The manner in which sniffers operate depends on the type of network. In a shared media network such as a standard Ethernet, packets sent along a network segment travel everywhere along the wire. Any host connected to a segment is capable of capturing all sessions within that segment. For example, Exhibit 9.1 depicts a sniffer-capable host. It is able to capture any traffic that goes through the network segment, regardless of the particular neighboring host or other remote host to which that traffic is destined. In other types of networks (e.g., token-ring networks), sniffers are capable only of capturing sessions sent to or through a specific device or host, that is, either the physical sniffer itself or the host that houses a logical sniffer. Exhibit 9.2 depicts this scenario in a token-ring environment. Note that only the traffic traversing the side on which the sniffer is located can be captured by the sniffer.

Types of Sniffers

The two types of sniffers are physical sniffers and logical sniffers. Physical sniffers are devices with built-in network interface hardware such that when they are installed on a network, they record all traffic. Logical sniffers are programs that run on host machines that also capture data traversing a network. In order for logical sniffers to function, the host machines that house them must have a network interface card that not only provides a physical interface to the network, but also provides packet capture functionality. This type of interface card, commonly known as a promiscuous network interface card, is built into some off-the-shelf systems, but must be installed in others.

Two types of promiscuous network interface cards exist. One can monitor all traffic going across a network segment. The other is capable only of capturing the traffic bound for or going through the host on which it is installed.

The Concern

Why do unauthorized sniffers pose such a high degree of threat? When in the hands of legitimate network administrators and other technical personnel, sniffers are an immensely valuable tool; sniffers help substantially in diagnosing and fixing networking problems (such as broadcast floods and locating points in a network in which traffic flow is disrupted). When

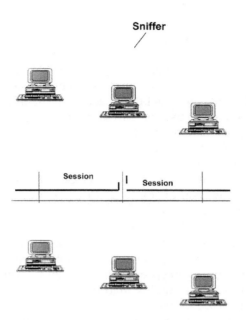

Exhibit 9.1.   A Sniffer in a Shared Media Network

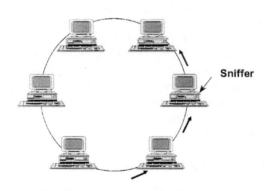

Exhibit 9.2.   A Sniffer in a Token-Ring Network

in the hands of unauthorized persons, however, sniffers are a potential security-related catastrophe waiting to happen because:

1. Many logins across networks in typical operational environments involve transmission of cleartext passwords. An intruder with access to a sniffer can quickly learn the login names, passwords, and IP addresses of host machines on which login accounts exist by examining the first portion (the "header") of each log-in packet. The

87

intruder can then establish a telnet or a similar connection to that host and attempt to log in. Unless captured passwords are obsolete (because, for example, the user whose password has been captured recently changed the password), the probability of the intruder's success in breaking into legitimate user's accounts is very high. Once the intruder breaks into an account, the intruder will have the access rights of the user whose account is now compromised, leading to the possibility of reading and copying files to which the user has access. Worse yet, the intruder now has a foothold (namely, user-level access) within a system and can attempt to use cracking tools and other methods that provide superuser access on this system. With superuser access, the attacker is able to read and copy any file stored on that system, and is in addition very likely to find attacking other machines with the network considerably easier.[1]

2. Data (including text within e-mail messages) is constantly sent from host to host within a typical network; sniffers can capture this data. If the data is not encrypted, unauthorized persons can read and copy the data. A reasonably high proportion of transmitted data in typical corporate network environments is business critical. The compromise of data such as information about pending patents, original engineering data, marketing and lease bid data, and other information can result in immeasurable loss if in the hands of a competitor or other potentially hostile party. Consider also that this type of data compromise may not directly result in direct financial loss — a competitor may obtain critical information but not use it. The media may, however, learn of the incident involving data compromise or some other negative outcome, and then release stories that can damage an organization's image. The result may be substantial indirect loss through outcomes such as lowering customer confidence in products and services offered by that organization, stockholder lawsuits, etc.

EXTENT OF THE PROBLEM

The full extent of unauthorized deployment of sniffers is (like so many other types of InfoSec-related problems) unlikely to be known or even reasonably estimated. The meaning of "unauthorized deployment" is in fact ambiguous at best; an intruder can, for example, gain access to a legitimately installed sniffer. Whereas the installer and others may have legitimate access, someone else's access to that sniffer may be unauthorized. In addition, sniffers for the most part are by nature clandestine — discovering them requires additional analysis and work that many organizations neglect. Despite complications such as these, data about deployment of unauthorized sniffers is available. The following two case studies exemplify the range of incidents that can occur as a result of unauthorized sniffers.

Case Study 1: Outbreak of Sniffer Attacks on the Internet

A widespread series of sniffer-based attacks on the Internet occurred between 1993 and 1995.[2] Attackers initially broke into host machines using automated attack scripts widely available over the Net, then exploited other vulnerabilities to gain superuser access using additional scripts. Superuser access allowed them to put unauthorized network sniffers in place. The intruders then connected to the hosts on which the logical sniffers were installed to gather log-in names and passwords, enabling them to break into additional hosts throughout the Internet. What was most noteworthy, however, was the fact that the intruders compromised hosts used by Internet service providers. These hosts were within subnets to which hub routers used in routing large volumes of Internet traffic were placed. In addition, these subnets had numerous leased line and dial-up connections. By placing sniffers on a host within the same network segment to which hub routers were connected, the attackers were able to capture all traffic that went in and out of the routers. Sniffers were often embedded in hacking toolkits that also removed indications of the intruders' activities from system logs.[3]

These attacks were devastating in that an organization could have a relatively secure, sniffer-free network that nevertheless could be compromised because of sniffers outside the network. A single user simply had to log in remotely to a machine within the network from a machine outside the network. When the traffic passed through a compromised Internet service provider's network, one or more sniffers captured passwords and other critical information. The practical significance is that sniffers within an organization's networks are only part of the total sniffer threat; sniffers *outside* an organization's network(s) can pose a significant security threat to that organization's security.

Case Study 2: An Unauthorized Gateway-Based Sniffer in a Large Corporation

Several years ago, a technical staff member for a U.S.-based Fortune 100 company discovered an unauthorized physical sniffer. Unauthorized sniffers almost always spell trouble, but the location of this particular sniffer posed an especially high risk — -it was attached to a high throughput link to the Internet immediately before (i.e., outside of) a firewall that screened incoming traffic. Whoever had planted this sniffer had the ability to capture all traffic coming into and out of this business-critical network. Soon after the sniffer was discovered and removed, an investigation ensued. Investigators determined that it had been installed by an employee who was working in collusion with another outside person in a scheme to sell corporate information. The sniffer had been in place for approximately three months before it was discovered.

The moral of this story is that physical sniffers placed anywhere can cause catastrophic results. Sniffers placed at gateways to critical networks, however, can potentially cause the greatest loss because they can capture all traffic (inbound and outbound) through the gateways. Sniffers attached to a network's backbone also entail significantly elevated risk because so much traffic traverses through the backbone.

Which pose a greater overall threat — physical or logical sniffers? Although physical sniffers pose a serious threat, they are separate, identifiable hardware devices that can be seen by someone who is physically present. Additionally, someone who is physically present at a location where network cabling (to which a physical sniffer must be attached) is accessible must install them. Someone who installs an unauthorized sniffer might be observed and subsequently reported. Furthermore, physical sniffers tend to be somewhat (but not prohibitively) expensive, making their purchase by the typical user somewhat unlikely. A more likely scenario, therefore, is unauthorized access to a physical sniffer purchased and installed legitimately by an organization, rather than the purchase and installation of such a device by a dishonest employee or contractor (although the latter possibility is nevertheless real and potentially catastrophic).

Logical sniffers in many respects comprise a more serious threat than physical sniffers. Many systems have built-in promiscuous interfaces; more commercial system administration tools than one might expect have built-in network traffic capture capabilities. Someone with access (authorized or unauthorized) to these tools could read or copy captured network traffic. Access to such tools is, however, not necessary; a perpetrator can simply gain remote access (in most cases, superuser access) to a target host, install a sniffing program, then wait until a sufficient amount of passwords or data is captured, and finally harvest the captured data. In many incidents, intruders have gone even further; they have replaced the entire kernel of a compromised system with a new, promiscuous kernel, thereby making discovery of the fact that the compromised system is now in promiscuous mode very difficult.[2]

For all practical purposes, however, the greatest threat associated with the use of logical sniffers is an everyday desktop user buying a promiscuous interface card and a sniffer program at a local computer store, then installing both on a desktop machine that connects to a corporate or other network. Commercial sniffer programs that run in environments such as DOS and Windows 95 now often cost less than $20. Sniffing in Macintosh environments is even easier; a sniffer program, Traffic Peek, is built into every Macintosh host. Windows NT 4.0 Server also offers a built-in logical sniffer, the Network Monitor (NM). Fortunately, access to this program is limited by default to administrators and also requires entry of a password.

In summary, the sniffer threat is indeed more serious than might superficially be apparent. Sniffers can be installed virtually anywhere network wires go.[4] Not only are there physical sniffers, but there are also logical sniffers, many of which can be installed by an average user without elevated privileges. In so many corporate, government, and academic environments around the world, passwords and data traverse networks in cleartext, making them perfect targets for sniffer attacks. Worse yet, only one sniffer installed in the proper location can capture a voluminous amount of data.

SOLUTIONS

The sniffer threat is insidious. It should come as no surprise, therefore, that choosing suitable control measures is by no means easy or straightforward. The following solutions are the best currently known solutions.

Policy. Policy is the basis for all effective InfoSec measures. The first and most essential step, therefore, in dealing with the sniffer threat is to ensure that one's InfoSec policy contains provisions that prohibit the installation or use of sniffers (physical or logical) on any system or network without the written approval of cognizant management. Cognizant management may possibly include line management, business unit managers, InfoSec management, or some other management function. This policy should also specify who (employees only, employees and contractors, etc.) is allowed to install sniffers and read sniffer data; include provisions for protecting sniffer data from unauthorized disclosure; and specify consequences in case someone does not adhere to it.

Encryption. The most powerful, single technical solution to the sniffer threat is the widespread deployment of network encryption. Encryption forces those who deploy sniffers without authorization to be capable of breaking the encryption to read the contents of captured packets. Tragically, the major question with respect to deployment of encryption too often centers on the strength of encryption (e.g., 40-bit versus 128-bit encryption). The result is that encryption solutions are postponed, leaving systems and data at risk. Some encryption (no matter how weak) is better than none. Relaxation of United States encryption export policies makes implementing some kind of network encryption feasible in nearly every country.[5]

Implementing virtual private networks (VPNs) is an increasingly popular method of achieving encrypted network traffic flow. Sessions between hosts can be encrypted using either private or public key encryption, thereby establishing a secure "tunnel" between them. VPNs between firewalls or routers are now used routinely in corporate intranets and in other critical network deployments. Although VPNs are generally effective in

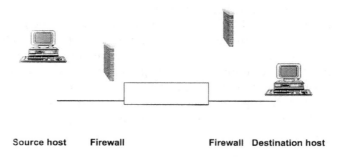

Source host   Firewall   Firewall Destination host

Exhibit 9.3.   A VPN with Link Encryption Between Firewalls

controlling the sniffer threat, the type of VPN deployed makes a significant difference in the overall effectiveness. VPNs that provide link encryption (as from one firewall to another) are not so effective in that transmissions are sent in cleartext everywhere but between the hosts that provide the link encryption (see Exhibit 9.3).

In contrast, VPNs that provide point-to-point (also known as end-to-end) encryption are more effective in that network transmissions are encrypted over every part of the route they traverse (see Exhibit 9.4).

Additionally, a problem common to both types of VPNs is that some vendors have deviated from the mainstream by developing their own, proprietary Point-to-Point Tunneling Protocols (PPTP — the protocol that provides the encrypted sessions). Consequently, two hosts that support different implementations of PPTP cannot establish a secure tunnel.

Employ One-Time Password Authentication. In one-time password schemes, a password for a user is sent across the network once, and then changed the next time a password for that user is transmitted. Several different one-time password programs exist, but one of the most effective versions is

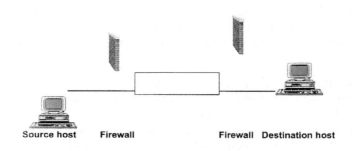

Source host   Firewall   Firewall Destination host

Exhibit 9.4.   A VPN with End-to-End Encryption

Bellcore's commercial S/KEY tool. S/KEY allows the user to choose a particular password for a given number of log-ins, but never allows a cleartext password to be sent over the network. Instead, it encrypts every password transmission. Better yet, it encrypts each password differently[6] during each log-in attempt. Even if a sniffer captures passwords, the passwords will be encrypted. The encrypted versions will be very difficult to crack because no two cyphertext passwords sent over the network will be identical.

Use Secure Ethernet Technology. As mentioned previously, standard Ethernets are shared media networks. As such, they are ideal for perpetrators of sniffer attacks. Fortunately, a relatively new development — the secure Ethernet — limits the distribution of data sent over a network. Secure Ethernets send data only to the host that each packet header indicates is the destination host. In a secure Ethernet, an attacker would have to plant a sniffer on every host within a network segment to capture all sessions. The major limitation of secure Ethernet technology is that it works only locally; once network transmissions are sent outside of the local network in which this technology is implemented, the traffic may be subject to sniffer attacks if the destination networks have not implemented secure Ethernets. Still, secure Ethernet technology offers substantial improvement in ability to defend against the sniffer threat.

Have System Administrators Regularly Inspect Hosts for Unauthorized Logical Sniffers. In particular, have them look within gateways — routers are often the hosts on which logical (as well as physical) sniffers are installed without authorization because such a large volume of traffic generally goes through routers. Logical sniffers are often installed in public directories (including temporary directories) where anyone can add files and where the sheer number of files can make finding the executable and data files for the sniffer unlikely. Using integrity checking tools such as Tripwire (for UNIX hosts) can be helpful in identifying changes to existing files if someone replaces a legitimate file with a sniffer executable. Other clues that unauthorized logical sniffers may be in place are the presence of hidden files (such as . files in UNIX hosts and $ files in Windows NT hosts), often with unfamiliar names such as ., .., .X, or others. A well-known logical sniffer program in the UNIX arena is named "rootkt," although an attacker is likely to change this name to some name that is not so easily recognized. Entries in audit logs may show that a sniffer has been installed; similarly, checking for current processes that are running on each system may reveal the presence of unknown processes that capture network or host sessions. Scanning programs such as CPM (Check for Network Interfaces in Promiscuous Mode[7]) are useful in that they can be run on Sun Microsystems hosts to determine whether they are in packet-capturing mode. Remember, however, that measures such as these help only with respect to the sniffer threat in local networks.

Frequently Inspect for Unauthorized Physical Sniffers. These sniffers can sometimes be very easy to detect. The fact that a desktop computer bearing a well-known sniffer manufacturer's name, such as Network General, is attached to the network is, for example, a dead giveaway that the computer is a sniffer. The presence of a hardware device that connects to a network cable via a vampire clamp — a type of interface that penetrates the cable's insulation where the clamp is attached — is a high probability indicator of the presence of an unauthorized physical sniffer. The most significant problems in discovering unauthorized physical sniffers are that home-made sniffer devices may not be so easily recognizable and also that sniffers can be hidden in difficult-to-access locations such as wiring closets and subflooring.

Implement Secure E-mail. Secure e-mail programs can protect the privacy of e-mail messages by encrypting the contents. Both commercial and freeware programs of this nature are widely available. As mentioned previously, United States encryption export restrictions have recently been relaxed sufficiently to allow sufficiently strong encryption throughout the world.

Prepare for and Plan to Use the IPv6 Protocol. This emerging protocol consists of an authenticating header (AH) and encrypted session payload (ESP). The ESP portion keeps cleartext data from being transmitted over networks, making data safe from sniffers. IPv6 is currently an emerging technology; however, to use this technology requires that network applications be programmed to utilize it. As a real solution to the sniffer threat, therefore, this technology is still several years away. Nevertheless, initiating efforts to investigate and utilize IPv6 as soon as possible is an excellent strategy for dealing not only with the sniffer threat, but also a wide range of other threats.

Employ Third-Party Authentication. This type of authentication requires users to authenticate to an authentication server (usually through presenting some kind of token such as a smart card), then to authenticate using the normal system authentication procedures (namely by entering a log-in name and password). With third-party authentication, even if a perpetrator captures a user's cleartext password and attempts to log in using it, the log-in attempt will fail because the perpetrator will not possess the necessary token. As strong as this measure is, unfortunately, it provides only a partial solution to the sniffer threat in that it protects against password sniffing, but does not protect data transmitted over the network.

Educate Users. Educates users about the sniffer threat and help them understand the policy the organization has in place concerning sniffers. The education and awareness effort should enable them to recognize and report illegal sniffers through proper channels. This effort can go a long way in the battle to combat unauthorized sniffers. The time and resources spent in training system and network administrators usually also have great benefits; the "gung-ho" administrator who installs sniffers with good intention but without proper authorization is in many respects the greatest source of danger.

RESPONDING TO SNIFFER-RELATED INCIDENTS

Schultz and Wack[8] maintain that responding to incidents requires six distinct phases of activity, including:

- preparation
- detection
- containment
- eradication
- recovery
- follow-up

Of these stages, detection and containment are usually the most critical in a sniffer-related incident. Detection is critical because, as mentioned earlier, any system within a network can be capturing packets without anyone's knowledge other than the person who installed it. Additionally, sniffer incidents are often extremely difficult to contain. As in Case Study 2 above, a sniffer may be running for months before it is finally detected. By the time the sniffer is found, it may have captured tens of thousands or more cleartext passwords to systems that are now subject to immediate, unauthorized access.

If an unauthorized sniffer is discovered, the first thing one should do, if at all possible, is to perform a full backup of the system on which the sniffer runs. The backup will serve as evidence in case the organization initiates prosecution of the perpetrator(s). Additionally, by including all the sniffer's executables and data files, the backup may be useful in determining how the sniffer works, what data the sniffer has captured already, and (if one is lucky) clues concerning the identity of the person(s) who have written and installed the sniffer.[9] If the sniffer is a logical sniffer, one may be able to inspect the code to determine the file(s) to which the sniffer is writing data. Inspecting log-in IDs and passwords in such files will allow one to know which accounts in which systems are most likely to have been compromised. Have the system administrators of these systems inspect logs, log-in messages, etc. to determine whether these systems have been accessed without authorization; then take any necessary evasive measures (including, if circumstances warrant, initiating system shutdown procedures) to protect these systems and the data they store. Be sure at this point to also delete any sniffer-related files within any compromised system to prevent them from being accessed and used by others.

If an unauthorized physical sniffer is discovered, handle this device as you would any other piece of physical evidence.[10] Fingerprints on the sniffer device may enable law enforcement personnel to identify the perpetrator; be sure, therefore, to have someone who is an expert in computer forensics or law enforcement be in charge of evidence handling. As in the case of logical sniffers, inspecting the output of a physical sniffer may also enable one to determine the accounts and systems that are currently most at risk.

The next step is also an extremely important one. One should now initiate an effort to change all passwords on all hosts within any network on which a sniffer has been found or through which remote log-in traffic has passed. Although the user community is likely to be less than enthusiastic about this measure, it is the only logical course of action. One sniffer may have captured passwords for any other host in the entire network, allowing the perpetrator(s) easy and immediate access. Changing all passwords is the only way to be sure that any passwords that any perpetrators have "stockpiled" are now invalid and useless.

Performing incident response procedures correctly for sniffer-related incidents may not be as easy as it seems. Consider the following case study.

Case Study 3: A Lesson Learned in Responding to a Sniffer Incident

During the massive outbreak of Internet sniffers from 1993 to 1995, a member of a national emergency response team traveled to a site in which several unauthorized logical sniffers were found. After analyzing the problem, this investigator deleted the sniffer programs, then logged in remotely as root (superuser) to a system at the site from which this team operated. Shortly afterward, this system — in addition to scores of others at the response team's site — was compromised. The investigator did not realize that additional, as yet undiscovered sniffers had been installed at the site at which the investigation was being performed. The root password to the investigator's system was transmitted in cleartext across a network segment in which an undiscovered sniffer had been installed. A perpetrator harvested this password, broke into the investigator's system as root, and planted still another sniffer on this system. This enabled the perpetrator to gather many passwords for machines at the investigator's site (in addition to a number of additional sites). The lesson learned from this series of unfortunate events is that sniffer attacks are not as easy to handle as one might suspect. One mistake, such as the one discussed in this case study, can proliferate these incidents out of control. Although the speed of response is critical, it is most important to carefully think through every step and action to avoid making the situation worse. This "lesson learned" is particularly applicable to organizations with many intranet and extranet connections.[11]

Finally, one should engage in a follow-up process to determine how the sniffer-related incident occurred and what measures (e.g., scanning hosts more frequently to see if they are in promiscuous mode) might have made the occurrence of such an incident less likely. One should also evaluate the response to the sniffer incident, identifying steps that could have been performed more efficiently and additional resources that would have been useful. One should revise incident handling procedures accordingly and, finally, write a report on the incident for future reference.

CONCLUSION

The threat of unauthorized sniffers has long been recognized in the InfoSec community. Amid all the confusion generated by the news of new, more sensational threats, it is easy to overlook the sniffer threat. Overlooking the sniffer threat is a major mistake; in many respects, a well-placed, unauthorized sniffer could easily result in more loss and disruption to an organization than any other type of incident. The proliferation of logical sniffers on many platforms represents a serious escalation in the sniffer threat. Network attackers cannot only install sniffers on remote hosts, but even the most casual, inexperienced user can now buy an inexpensive logical sniffer and install it on a desktop machine to capture critical data and passwords transmitted across network segments.

Many potential control measures for unauthorized sniffers exist. These include getting the appropriate policy provisions in place, encrypting network transmissions, using one-time passwords, implementing secure Ethernet technology, regularly inspecting for both logical and physical sniffers, installing secure e-mail, implementing network applications that utilize the IPv6 protocol, using third-party authentication, and establishing an effective user education and awareness program that helps both users and system administrators understand and combat the sniffer threat. The appropriate subset of these measures depends on the particular business and other needs of the organization. However, ensuring that an appropriate policy exists is imperative, no matter what other measures are appropriate. Encryption is the best (although not necessarily the most feasible) technical solution. Additionally, the potential for a widespread outbreak of sniffer attacks dictates that an effective incident response program that includes the appropriate procedures for combating sniffer attacks be put in place.

Notes

1. Many system administrators set up trusted access mechanisms that allow them to easily move from one machine to the other in a network without having to authenticate themselves to each machine. These mechanisms often require that those who use them have

superuser privileges on the machine from which trusted access is initiated. Although advantageous from the perspective of convenient access for system administrators, a perpetrator who gains superuser status in a single machine may also be able to exploit these mechanisms to gain unauthorized access to many other systems within the same network.

2. Schultz, E.E. and Longstaff, T.A. (1998). Internet Sniffer Attacks. In D.E. Denning and P.J. Denning (Eds.), *Internet Besieged.* Reading, MA: Addison-Wesley, p. 137–146.
3. Van Wyk, K.R. (1994). Threats to DoD Computer Systems. Paper presented at *23rd International Information Integrity Institute Forum* (cited with author's permission).
4. Sniffers could also, in fact, be used to attack wireless networks if they are planted in any host connected to such networks.
5. Laws within countries such as France and Russia restrict the use of encryption within these countries.
6. The change in encryption is the same for both the sending and receiving host, so authentication is not disrupted.
7. Available from ftp.cert.org and other ftp and Web sites.
8. Schultz, E.E. and Wack, J. (1996). Responding to Information Security Incidents. In M. Krause & H.F. Tipton (Eds.), *Handbook of Information Security Management: 1996–97 Yearbook.* Boston: Auerbach, p. S-53–S-68.
9. Authors of a sniffer tool will, for instance, write the sniffer code in a manner that manifests a particular style of programming. Software forensics experts may accordingly be able to identify the authors. In addition, the code may contain Internet addresses and other information that may enable investigators to determine the identity of any perpetrator(s).
10. Bernstein, T., Bhimini, A., Schultz, E.E., and Siegel, C. (1996). *Internet Security for Business.* New York: John Wiley & Sons.
11. An intranet is, for the purposes of this article, considered a group of internal networks that connect with each other. An extranet is a group of external networks that are linked together.

Section 2
Interconnectivity Basics: Putting the Pieces Together

Enterprise networks consist of more than just standalone LANs. Rather, they are constructed from a close alliance of traditional LAN technologies and LAN interconnection technologies. A mastery of both is essential for the network designer tasked with providing high-performance LANs in support of value-added business solutions.

Throughout the 1980s and well into the 1990s, considerable attention was given to the "Holy Grail" of interconnectivity known as the OSI reference model. It was believed by many that when OSI arrived, diverse, but OSI-compliant systems would simply "plug and play," resulting in universal connectivity. More recently, it appears that OSI has either simply disappeared or has been replaced by TCP/IP. While OSI still provides an excellent framework for understanding and discussing networks, no network or IS manager should be without at least a basic knowledge of TCP/IP. Chapter 10, "TCP/IP Essentials," provides a good primer for those not well versed in this critical technology, and can serve as a good refresher for those with some TCP/IP experience.

Although it is important to understand TCP/IP at a conceptual level in order to fully exploit its capabilities, it is equally important to be able to translate that conceptual basis into a practical implementation. Chapter 11, "Configuring TCP/IP on a Windows NT Computer," focuses on doing just that in the Windows NT environment, including discussion of both traditional static IP addressing and the newer dynamic addressing with DHCP.

Since the earliest days of internetworked LANs, the routing function has been a critical component, yet it remains one of the least understood. To provide the LAN or IT manager with the background information needed to make informed decisions about routing, Chapter 12, "Routing and Routing Protocols," provides a consistent language for discussing internetworking, describes the general model most often implemented for routing, and surveys the major network layer routing protocols in use today. The chapter concludes by describing the major types of routing platforms and the contexts in which they are used.

One of the strongest interconnectivity trends in the market today is beginning to challenge some traditional assumptions about the role of routers in enterprise networks. In particular, while LAN switches, providing switching services at the physical layer, have matured considerably in the past few years, the broader concept of LAN switching continues to evolve at a fairly rapid rate and is moving up the OSI reference model into the layers previously filled exclusively by bridges and routers. The most significant areas of development are in layer 3 switching and in the implementation of switching that takes place in a coordinated fashion between layer 2 and layer 3 switching components. Chapter 13, "Evolution to Layer 2 and 3 Switching," describes the current state of the practice in this area.

Chapter 14, "Implementing Routing, Switching, and VLANs in Modern Corporate Networks," continues our discussion of switching technologies. This chapter considers three focal points for network design—performance, management, and redundancy—and provides a comparative assessment of routing, switching, and VLANs as alternative network designs. The chapter concludes with the observation that despite (or perhaps because of) its unprecedented complexity, network design technology at the dawn of the millennium offers choices that allow designers to build networks around real-life functional requirements, rather than technology-bound constraints.

Chapter 15, "Remote Access Concepts and Techniques," wraps up our discussion of interconnectivity technologies by taking a look at access technologies available for providing interconnectivity for the small office / home office (SOHO) environment. The chapter explores typical scenarios for remote access, followed by a discussion of the hardware, software, and protocols required to support users in this environment.

The remainder of the section focuses on security issues that must be addressed when designing and implementing interconnectivity solutions. We begin our look at interconnectivity security issues with Chapter 16, "Remote Access Authentication," which considers the technologies discussed in the previous chapter from a security perspective, paying particular attention to solutions available for ensuring that the identity of the remote user is properly authenticated.

While much of this section has focused on emerging trends and alternatives to traditional LAN interconnectivity, the fact remains that most enterprise networks deployed today continue to rely extensively on the solid, proven technology of routers. As such, router security is an essential element of any network protection plan. Chapter 17, "Working with Cisco Access Lists," explores the use of access lists as a security tool. While the chapter focuses on a specific product line, the concepts discussed are generally applicable. Chapter 18, "Securing Your Router," concludes the section with a discussion of the fundamental steps needed to ensure the security and integrity of the router itself.

Chapter 10
TCP/IP Essentials
Smoot Carl-Mitchell

The Transmission Control Protocol/Internet Protocol (TCP/IP) suite of networking protocols is currently the most widely used set of protocols for internetwork communication. The name TCP/IP is derived from the most widely used protocols in the suite: TCP is a byte stream protocol that provides reliable end-to-end communication between two processes running on the same or different host systems; IP is a simple best-effort packet switching protocol that allows many different interconnected networks to share the same virtual address space and form a single internetwork. From the host's point of view, IP makes the underlying internet appear as a single virtual network.

The world's largest computer network, the Internet, uses TCP/IP as its dominant protocol suite. The Internet today is a worldwide internet. TCP/IP is also used on many corporate networks and is particularly popular with UNIX workstations. However, TCP/IP implementations can be found for almost any class of machine from PCs to supercomputers.

PROTOCOL MODELS

Like any modern communications protocol, TCP/IP is a layered protocol and follows its own layering model: the Internet model. This model resembles, but is not the same as, the more familiar Open System Interconnection (OSI) seven-layer model. Exhibit 10.1 compares the two layering models.

Working down from the top, the Internet model has a process/application layer. The OSI model has an application layer and a presentation layer where data is transformed and presented in a uniform way to an application. OSI also has a session layer where application sessions are controlled. The Internet model generally incorporates aspects of the OSI presentation and session layers into its process/application layer. The various application protocols are found at this layer. TCP/IP has defined process/application protocols for the following services, among many others:

- Telnet, for remote log in.
- File transfer protocol (FTP), for remote file transfer.
- Simple mail transfer protocol (SMTP), for e-mail transport.
- Hyptertext transfer protocol (HTTP) for World Wide Web access.

0-8493-9838-X/00/$0.00+$.50
© 2000 by CRC Press LLC

Internet Model	OSI Model
Process/Application	Application
	Presentation
	Session
Transport	Transport
Internet	Network
Network	
Link	Data Link
Physical	Physical

Exhibit 10.1.   The OSI and Internet Protocol Stacks

Below the process/application layer is the transport layer. TCP/IP's transport layer is equivalent to OSI's transport layer. This is where end-to-end protocols, which move data from one process to another process, are defined. This refers to processes, not hosts, although processes usually reside on different machines.

An end-to-end protocol may or may not be designed with features to improve data communications reliability. It may be packet-oriented or byte-stream oriented. A transport layer protocol may incorporate features for end-to-end flow control and multiplexing. The two major TCP/IP transport protocols are TCP and the User Datagram Protocol (UDP). UDP is a datagram or packet oriented protocol that adds little reliability and does not guarantee delivery.

Below the transport layer is the internet layer. This generally corresponds to the top half of OSI's network layer. This is where internetwork addressing and routing issues are handled. In the Internet model a single protocol, IP, is defined at this layer.

Below the internet layer is the network layer, corresponding to the bottom half of OSI's network layer. The network layer deals with the interface to various data link layer protocols (e.g., Ethernet and Token Ring). Essentially, this layer defines how bits are sent from one network interface to another over the same physical medium.

Below TCP/IP's network layer is the link layer. This deals with the lower-level specifications of the various network protocols (e.g., Ethernet and Token Ring), and is equivalent to OSI's data link layer.

The lowest layer in both models is the physical layer, which deals with the physical and electrical (or optical for fiber) specifications of the various network technologies.

The Internet model places an emphasis on internetworking software and not hardware. The various specifications of its network, link, and physical layers are generally borrowed from other standards; for example, the Ethernet specification occupies the physical, link, and network layers of the Internet model. The Internet model simply uses the standard Ethernet specifications and builds an interface specification on top of them for the encapsulation of IP packets over an Ethernet. It does the same for fiber distributed data interface (FDDI) and Token Ring technologies. These interfaces are specified as a part of the Internet model's network layer.

Protocol layering is not an exact science. There is nothing inherently correct in OSI's seven-layer division or the Internet model's six layers. The general idea is to rationalize a complex communications system and present it in a way that simplifies understanding. An actual implementation may or may not follow the layering model exactly.

HISTORY

No discussion of TCP/IP can be complete without a brief discussion of its history, because how the protocol suite was developed had a lot to do with its later success and widespread use.

TCP/IP evolved from work done in the network research community, in particular the late 1960s and early 1970s work on packet switching that led to the development of the ARPANET. The ARPANET (named after the Advanced Research Projects Agency of the U.S. Department of Defense) was a project designed to demonstrate the feasibility of packet switching technology to build reliable data communications systems. The system the Defense Department was interested in had to survive a nuclear attack from (presumably) the Soviet Union. Ironically, there are sites within the former Soviet Union that use TCP/IP today.

Before the ARPANET, data communications systems were built around circuit switching. To send a message from host A to host B, a path (or circuit) between A and B had to be established and all information sent along that path until the circuit was disconnected. This is the way the telephone system was designed. From a reliability standpoint this means that all intermediate nodes along that path have to be in service. If one node fails (say from a nuclear attack), then the circuit is broken and communications cannot continue until an alternate circuit is reestablished.

In packet switching, the data sent from A to B is divided into discrete chunks, called datagrams or packets. Each datagram is self-contained, that is, it contains all the addressing information it needs to get to its destination. In a packet switched network, each node forwards the datagram to the next node that is closer to the final destination. Because the addressing information of the destination is contained in the datagram itself, an intermediate switching node can examine the address to determine the next hop the datagram must take on its way to its final destination. With this method a packet can be rerouted around a failed switching node.

The ARPANET was a packet switched network, but it was a single network and it used protocols not intended for internetworking. In the mid-1970s, network researchers realized that various high-speed LAN technologies (e.g., Ethernet) were nearing widespread deployment. With LANs entering the equation, a true internet of interconnected networks became more and more feasible. TCP/IP, a true internetworking protocol suite, is the product of these changes in the networking environment.

Widespread deployment of TCP/IP occurred within the ARPANET community in the early 1980s. By 1983 the name Internet came into use as the official name of the community of interconnected networks using TCP/IP. The ARPANET was a core network in the early Internet, but it was by no means synonymous with the Internet. The ARPANET, due to its slow link speeds (56K bps), was retired in 1990. The Internet started to grow at a very rapid rate (the number of hosts and users more than doubling every year) starting in the mid 1980s and that pace of growth continues today.

THE INTERNET PROTOCOL

The Internet Protocol (IP) is the heart of the TCP/IP suite. IP provides the essential services that any internetworking protocol must provide, and all the protocols above and below it depend on its services.

IP Addressing

IP defines a virtual address space. An IP address is a 32-bit (4 byte) unsigned integer number. The convention for writing one of these addresses is to use dotted-decimal notation, that is, each byte of the address is written as a decimal number (separated by periods), for example, 192.135.128.129.

Each network interface is assigned a unique IP address. For engineering reasons and to simplify routing, an IP address is divided into two parts: network number and host number. The division between network number and host number is not fixed but is bit-encoded into the address. The IP address space is divided into five classes, A through E. Each class is encoded by using a specific bit pattern in the high-order bits of the first byte of the address.

A class A address uses the single-order byte as the network number, a class B address uses 2 bytes, and a class C address uses 3 bytes. Class D is used for multicast addresses, and class E is reserved as of this writing. Classes D and E use all 4 bytes as a network address. In general, classes A thorough C are the most widely used classes.

Regardless of the class, every host interface on the same network must have the same network number and a unique host number. Usually the address assignments are handled as system configuration parameters. The reason for this restriction is it simplifies routing. With all hosts on the same network guaranteed to have the same network number, routing can be handled by examining only the network number. Only when a packet is sent to its final destination does the host number come into play.

An extension of the original IP address format allows a further partitioning of the host number into a subnet number and a host number. Any IP network can be subnetted. Subnetting allows a single IP network number to be used on several underlying, but fully connected networks. A subnet mask is used to cover the network and subnet number. The subnet mask is locally defined, that is, a subnet can cover any of the bits of the original host number provided both the subnet number and the new host number fields are at least 2 bits wide. Where a subnet mask is defined, the routing algorithm treats the network number and the subnet number as the network number used for routing purposes.

IP Packet Format

IP also defines a specific packet format. An IP packet consists of a header followed by arbitrary data, as illustrated in Exhibit 10.2.

Only the most important fields are explained here. The HLEN field is a 4-bit field that indicates the header length in 4-byte words. An IP header is always a multiple of 4 bytes and is padded if necessary. The length field contains the total length in bytes of the entire IP packet, including the header. This is a 16-bit unsigned integer, so an IP packet can be at most 65,536 bytes long.

The TTL field contains an integer number that is decremented each time the packet passes through a routing node. This prevents a packet from looping around an internet forever. The source and destination fields

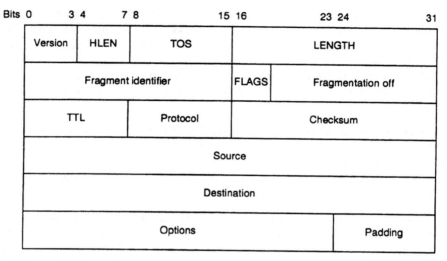

Notes:
HLEN Header length
TOS Type of service
TTL Time to live

Exhibit 10.2. The IP Packet Format

contain the source and destination addresses for the packet. The protocol field indicates the higher level protocol whose data is encapsulated within this packet. The source field indicates where the packet originated and destination field indicates the packet's final destination. The data field contains any arbitrary data and is normally provided by one of the transport layer protocols.

An IP packet is entirely self-contained. It can be routed on an internet without reference to any other packet. This has some implications for the transport layer protocols. In particular, IP does not guarantee delivery or the order of delivery. It is up to a transport layer protocol to perform these tasks.

Fragmentation and Reassembly

An IP packet can be larger than a frame of most network layer protocols. An Ethernet frame's maximum size (excluding the header) is 1,500 bytes, so an IP packet larger than 1,500 bytes will not fit into a single Ethernet frame. An IP packet can be split into smaller pieces, called fragments, which can be reassembled at the final destination. Several fields in the IP header control the fragmentation and reassembly algorithm. Fragmentation can be expensive, so most IP implementations try to avoid it. However, fragmentation allows a great deal of independence from the underlying network layer protocol's limitations.

Routing

The IP routing algorithm is extremely simple, and routing is usually performed by specialized routing nodes that do nothing else. Most IP implementations do support routing, so all that is required is to have a host node with more than a single network interface. When a node receives an IP packet, it examines the destination IP address in the IP packet header. If the address is one of the node's own interface addresses, the node processes the packet locally.

If the network or subnet number is the network number of one of the node's own interfaces, the node knows the destination is one of the locally attached networks. In this case, the node forwards the packet to the host on the local network. For a LAN, this usually means mapping the destination IP address to a data link address and framing the IP packet in a data link frame. This is done by the address resolution protocol (ARP). ARP essentially discovers the data link address of an IP configured interface by broadcasting a request for the data link address. A cache of replies is kept to eliminate ARP requests for the same address.

If the destination network number is not a locally attached network, then the routing node consults a routing table to determine where to send the packet. A routing table maps an IP network number to the IP address of the next router on the path to the final destination. The next router must be on a locally attached network. The packet is forwarded to that router, which in turn repeats the algorithm and sends the packet to its next hop.

The simple routing algorithm requires that consistent routing tables be maintained on all routing nodes in the internet. This can be done statically or dynamically. Static routes are manually created routing table entries. For an internetwork with a simple tree-like topology where a single path exists from any one node to another, static routing tables can be quite sufficient.

Dynamic routing uses a routing update protocol to keep all routers aware of the routing topology. This is particularly important in an internetwork that periodically changes its topology, or in which more than a single path exists between nodes. Use of a dynamic protocol allows the network to respond rapidly to topological changes or routing node failures.

Routing is still more art than science, in particular in a large internetwork like the Internet. Within the Internet, routing issues are very complex and the routing authority itself is distributed across the entire Internet. But for a site with a single LAN that is connected to the rest of the Internet through a single router, a simple default routing scheme will work. A default route is a route of last resort. If the destination network is not found in the routing table, the router pointed to by a default route is used instead.

Transport Protocols

TCP/IP has two principal transport layer protocols: TCP and UDP. TCP is a reliable two-way byte stream protocol and is used where total reliability is required. TCP is a very complex protocol and the details of its implementation are beyond the scope of this chapter. TCP guarantees that all bytes are received in order, doing this by building sequenced, check-summed messages that are then encapsulated within an IP packet. In essence, TCP builds a virtual circuit on top of the unreliable packet-oriented service of IP. TCP also incorporates a flow control algorithm that makes efficient use of available network band-width. This allows several TCP messages to be in flight before an acknowledgement is received for the first message. To do all this, TCP must maintain a considerable amount of state information. This state information is maintained and updated in both the TCP header as well as at each end of the connection.

UDP, unlike TCP, is an unreliable packet-oriented protocol. UDP provides a process interface to the packet delivery services of IP. The only type of reliability checking UDP does is a simple check sum of each message. Also unlike TCP, UDP has no notion of a connection. This allows a UDP message to be broadcast to all hosts on a single entry network by using the IP broadcast address. This broadcast support makes UDP very useful in applications that require a single message to be sent to multiple hosts where an acknowledgment is not required. Routing update protocols often use UDP to transmit routing updates.

Both TCP and UDP support multiplexing, that is, messages can be directed to different processes on the same host. This is supported by the port abstraction. A port is simply an integer that is associated with a process on a machine. Every TCP and UDP message header contains a source and destination port.

In the case of UDP, when a message is received the process data contained in the message is sent to the process waiting for data on the destination port. Therefore, more than one process can be sent data using UDP. All that is required is that each process wait on a different port number.

TCP elaborates on the port abstraction and allows multiple connections to the same destination port. Services such as Telnet use this facility to let multiple clients connect to the same service. For example, a Telnet server always uses a port number of 23. All Telnet clients use this well-known port as a destination field to connect to a Telnet server. The destination port in the TCP message header is concatenated with the source port and the source and destination IP addresses and protocol number (found in the IP header) to form a unique 5-tuple. This 5-tuple forms a unique connection address. When a TCP message is received, this connection address is evaluated and the data is sent to the correct process.

PROCESS AND APPLICATION PROTOCOLS

The TCP/IP protocol suite has a number of process and application layer protocols. All of these are built on top of either TCP or UDP transport. This chapter briefly describes some of the more common applications.

Telnet

Telnet is the remote terminal service of TCP/IP, allowing a user on one host to log in to another host. Telnet defines a network virtual terminal (NVT) that maps the differences between various local terminal protocols to a common canonical convention. Telnet is one of the oldest of the TCP/IP protocols and was adapted from a protocol that had the same name and that was used on the original ARPANET.

FTP

File transfer protocol (FTP) lets a user access a remote host and transfer files to and from that host. FTP also supports what is called anonymous TFP, which allows any remote user to access a carefully restricted subnet of files on a remote host. Anonymous FTP is the mechanism used by Internet archive sites to allow remote access to publicly available software.

SMTP

Simple mail transfer protocol (SMTP) permits e-mail messages to be sent from one host to another in a standard way. SMTP is not usually an end-user protocol, but is embedded in a mail transfer agent (MTA) that places received mail in a user's mailbox where it is read by a mail user agent (UA).

DNS

Domain name system (DNS) is a distributed naming service for the Internet community. DNS is primarily used to map host names to their corresponding IP interface address. DNS defines a hierarchical name space that allows distribution of naming authority. A name such as akasha.tic.com is an example of a DNS name.

Remote File Sharing

Several file-sharing systems have been built using TCP/IP. These systems are generically called transparent file access (TFA). The most popular

111

of these systems is Sun Microsystems Inc.'s (Mountain View, CA) Network File System (NFS). NFS allows sharing of remote file systems as if they were local. Another TFA system is the Andrew File System (AFS).

HTTP

Hypertext transfer protocol (HTTP) permits a user with a World Wide Web browser to access Web servers for the purpose of retrieving text, graphic images, and other objects. HTTP emerged in the mid-1990s and quickly became the most popular protocol on the Internet.

SUMMARY

The TCP/IP suite, although it is more than 15 years old, continues to grow and develop. The protocol suite was originally a research experiment and at one time it was in use only in computer laboratories and on research networks. Its use today goes far beyond just being a research tool; so much so, in fact, that now it is the engine that drives the world's largest network of networks, the Internet.

Chapter 11
Configuring TCP/IP on a Windows NT Computer

Gilbert Held

Due to the migration of many corporate networks to the TCP/IP protocol suite, it is important to understand how to appropriately configure workstations and servers to support this suite. In addition, due to the rapid growth in the use of Windows NT, which now accounts for over 60 percent of the corporate networking server market, it is also important to understand how to configure the TCP/IP protocol suite for operation on Microsoft's NT platforms. Thus, the focus of this article covers the key address that must be used to configure TCP/IP on any operating system while using the Windows NT platform to specifically illustrate how to configure this protocol suite on this popular operating system.

OVERVIEW

There are two basic methods to consider when configuring the TCP/IP protocol suite. The first method involves installing a Dynamic Host Configuration Protocol (DHCP) server that dynamically issues Internet Protocol (IP) addresses to clients that can be both workstations and servers. Most organizations that use a DHCP server do so because they may have hundreds or thousands of workstations and issuing, configuring, and maintaining IP addresses could become an administrative burden. If an organization decides to use DHCP, each workstation and server that receives an IP address from the DHCP server will still require a small degree of customization. Specifically, users or a LAN administrator will still have to manually configure each workstation to use DHCP as well as to specify the host name and domain name (which is noted later in this article).

The second method associated with configuring the TCP/IP protocol is to assign IP addresses and several additional pieces of information to each station on the network. This article primarily focuses on this latter method, illustrating the addresses and data that must be supplied to configure the TCP/IP protocol suite on a Windows NT platform. Because both Windows NT Workstation and Windows NT Server use the same method to configure the TCP/IP protocol suite, the example here is limited to configuring TCP/IP on a Windows NT server.

0-8493-9838-X/00/$0.00+$.50
© 2000 by CRC Press LLC

WINDOWS NT CONFIGURATION

From the Start menu, select Settings>Control Panel. Once the Control panel is displayed, double-click on the Network icon to display the Network dialog box. If the TCP/IP is not installed, one can do so by selecting the Protocols tab in the Network dialog box and then selecting the Add button. Once the TCP/IP protocol suite is added to the computer, the Network dialog box appears similar to the one shown in Exhibit 11.1.

The computer system used by this author was configured to support four protocols to include TCP/IP. To configure TCP/IP, first click on the network protocol entry of TCP/IP Protocol. Then click on the button labeled Properties, which the arrow cursor is located on in Exhibit 11.1.

IP ADDRESS REQUIREMENTS

Selecting the button labeled Properties shown in Exhibit 11.1 results in the display of a new dialog box labeled Microsoft TCP/IP Properties. Exhibit 11.2 shows the dialog box that has its IP Address tab illustrated. By initially focusing attention on the selectable items on the IP Address tab, note the difference between using DHCP to provide IP addresses and manually configuring workstations to support a specific IP address.

Under TCP/IP, each interface must have a unique IP address. Because a network adapter provides the interface to a network for workstations and servers, the IP Address tab shown in Exhibit 11.2 provides Windows NT users with the ability to configure an IP address for each adapter installed in a computer. If only one adapter is installed in the computer, one only has to configure an IP address or select the DHCP option discussed next. Otherwise, configure an IP address or select the use of DHCP for each adapter installed in the computer that one wants to support the TCP/IP protocol suite. Although one could theoretically configure one adapter card to obtain an IP address from a DHCP server and another adapter to be configured manually with a static IP address, this is not normally done. This is because that action would defeat the purpose of using a DHCP server because its use is designed to reduce the administrative burden associated with having to individually configure a large number of computers.

The area under the rectangular box labeled Adapter in Exhibit 11.2 provides the ability to either specify the use of a DHCP server for IP address assignments, or manually specify an IP address and other addressing information required to correctly configure the computer. By selecting the first button labeled "Obtain an IP address from a DHCP server," in effect configures the computer to obtain a dynamic IP address issued by a DHCP server. Doing so simplifies IP address management as one would not have to complete the IP addressing information required if the IP address had been manually specified. Thus, one of the key reasons for the use of a DHCP server is

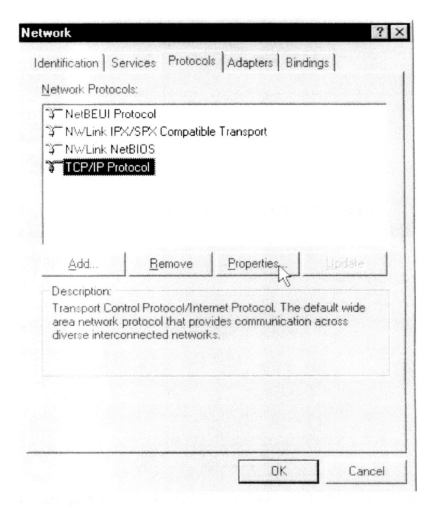

Exhibit 11.1. **Configure TCP/IP on a Windows NT workstation or server by first selecting the Protocols tab from the Network dialog box. Then select the Properties button.**

IP address administration. A second reason behind the use of a DHCP server concerns the movement of workstations and servers. For a large network with many subnets and periodical movement of workstations and servers from one segment to another, one would have to reconfigure each computer's IP address when it is moved. Because network operations can be adversely affected by duplicate IP addresses, the network manager or LAN administrator must carefully document all network changes, which creates an administrative burden that can also be alleviated by the use of a

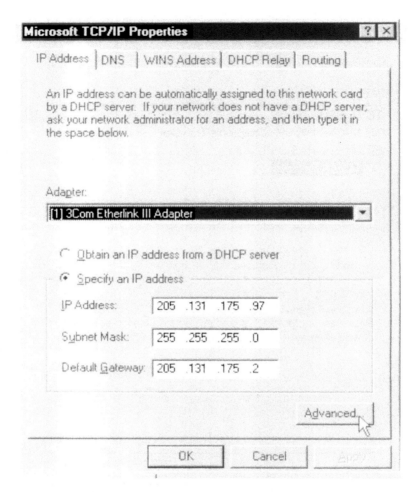

Exhibit 11.2. **The IP Address tab in the Microsoft TCP/IP Properties dialog box provides the ability to select an IP address from a DHCP server or manually specifying an IP address.**

DHCP server. However, the preceding benefits are not without cost. The use of a DHCP server requires a network manager or LAN administrator to set up a DHCP server to lease addresses for predefined periods of time. This results in the DHCP server periodically querying network devices after each device has leased an IP address for a specific period of time. As the life of the lease approaches termination, the server will communicate with the network device to extend the lease, resulting in additional network traffic. Due to the preceding, most organizations with a few hundred or less devices typically elect to use a manual IP address configuration method that results in the assignment of a static IP address for each device. The remainder of this article focuses this method of IP address assignment by examining the data elements that must be specified when one selects the Specify an IP address button as shown in Exhibit 11.2.

In examining the lower portion of Exhibit 11.2, note that three addresses must be entered in the IP Address tab when the Specify an IP address button is selected. Those addresses are the specific IP address assigned to the selected adapter card, a subnet mask, and the address of the default gateway. Each is discussed below.

IP Address

The IP address represents a unique 32-bit address assigned to the interface connected to a network. As previously discussed, because the adapter card provides the interface to the network, one can view the IP address as being assigned to the adapter card. The 32-bit IP address represents four 8-bit bytes. Because each 8-bit byte can vary in value from decimal 0 to decimal 255, an alternate method used to represent the binary value of a 32-bit IP address is through the use of four decimal digits, commonly referred to as dotted decimal notation because a decimal point is used to separate the decimal value of one 8-bit byte from another. Thus, the IP address shown in Exhibit 11.2 that has the value 205.131.175.97 actually represents a 32-bit binary number. However, because it is rather awkward to work with 32-bit binary numbers, the Internet Assigned Numbers Authority (IANA) assigns IP address space using dotted decimal numbers, which are also used by hardware and software developers to configure equipment.

Under IP Version 4 — the current version of the Internet Protocol — there are three types of IP addresses that are assigned to organizations. Those addresses are referred to as Class A, Class B, and Class C addresses. Each type of address consists of a network portion and a host portion. The network portion of the address indicates a specific network, while the host portion of the address indicates a specific host on the network. Exhibit 11.3 provides a summary of the number of bytes used to denote the network and host identifiers for Class A, B, and C addresses.

In examining the entries in Exhibit 11.3, one unanswered question concerns how one address class is differentiated from another. The answer to this question is the composition of the first byte of each address. A Class

Exhibit 11.3. Network/Host Assignments

Address Class	Network Portion (Bytes)	Host Portion (Bytes)
A	1	3
B	2	2
C	3	1

A address begins with a value of binary 0 in bit 8 of the first byte. In comparison, a Class B address begins with a value of binary 10 in bit positions 8 and 7 in the first byte, while a Class C address begins with a value of binary 11 in bit positions 8 and 7 in the first byte. This results in a Class A address ranging from 0 to 127, while a Class B address ranges from 128 to 191. A Class C address then falls in the range 192 through 255. Thus, the IP address shown entered in Exhibit 11.2 represents a Class C address.

From Exhibit 11.3, a Class C address consists of a 3-byte network portion and a 1-byte host portion. Thus, the IP address shown in Exhibit 11.2 represents host 97 on the network 205.131.175.0.

As a further review of IP addresses, it should be noted that there are two host addresses one cannot use for each address class. Those addresses are 0, which represents "this network," and a value of 255 for each host byte, which represents a broadcast address. Thus, for a Class C address, the permitted host values would range from 1 to 254, resulting in a maximum of 254 distinct interfaces being capable of being supported on a Class C network.

Subnet Mask

If one subdivides a network into two or more segments but retains one IP address for both segments, then one would use an appropriate value in the subnet mask to enable the device being configured to recognize data transmitted to the device. When one subdivides an IP network, two or more subnets are created. When this occurs, the network portion of the IP address is extended internally to the network while simultaneously reducing the host portion of the address. The extended network address represents the subnet that is used to identify a specific subnet on which a host resides.

The subnet mask represents a sequence of set bits that is logically ANDed with the IP address to determine the extended network address. Because the first or first two bit positions of an IP address indicates the type of address, it also indicates the length of the network portion of the address prior to subnetting. By subtracting the length of the IP address from the ANDed length, the device can determine the length of the subnet portion of the address and the value in the subnet portion. For example, the subnet mask of 255.255.255.0 shown in Exhibit 11.2 when ANDed with the IP address of 205.131.175.97 results in a 24-bit address. However, because the network address of 205.131.175.0 represents a Class C address that consists of a 3-byte network address and 1-byte host address, this indicates that no subnetting occurred. Thus, a subnet mask of 255.255.255.0 represents a nonsubnetted Class C address. Similarly, a subnet mask of 255.255.0.0 would indicate a nonsubnetted Class B address, while a subnet mask of 255.0.0.0 would represent a nonsubnetted Class A network address.

Default Gateway

The third IP address one must enter in the IP Address tab shown in Exhibit 11.2 is the address of the default gateway. In actuality, this address represents the address of a router. However, when TCP/IP was originally developed, the term "gateway" was used to reference a device that routed information between networks. Thus, the term "gateway" represents antiquated terminology that most hardware and software vendors elect to continue to use although the term "router" would be more accurate as the new millennium approaches.

Although one can correctly configure a network device to use the TCP/IP protocol suite by entering an IP address, subnet mask, and default gateway address, it may be desirable to enter some additional addresses. Those addresses are entered by clicking on the button labeled Advanced and selecting the tab labeled DNS. Thus, in concluding this examination of configuring TCP/IP to operate on a Windows NT-based computer platform, one can now focus attention on each additional configuration area.

ADVANCED IP ADDRESSING

By clicking on the button labeled Advanced previously shown in Exhibit 11.2, one obtains the ability to modify or remove a previous gateway address assignment or to enter additional gateway addresses. Microsoft's implementation of the TCP/IP protocol suite enables users to specify up to three gateway addresses. Exhibit 11.4 illustrates the Advanced IP Addressing dialog box, indicating the result from clicking on an Add box that is obscured by a pop-up dialog box labeled TCP/IP Gateway Address. By clicking on the Add button, one can add up to three gateway addresses that will be tried in the order they are entered.

THE DNS TAB

The second optional series of IP addressing entries is reflected by the use of the DNS tab shown in Exhibit 11.5. DNS, a mnemonic for Domain Name System, represents the translation service between near English host and domain names and IP addresses. When users surf the World Wide Web, access an FTP server, or perform another TCP/IP application that requires a destination address, they typically specify a near-English mnemonic and represent the destination and not an IP address. This is because it is much easier to remember addresses in terms of near-English mnemonics. This also means that a translation process is required to convert those near-English mnemonics to IP addresses because routing and address recognition are based on IP addresses.

If one wants employees on a private TCP/IP network or persons on the Internet to be able to access a computer through the use of a near-English mnemonic, one would use the DNS tab shown in Exhibit 11.4, to specify a

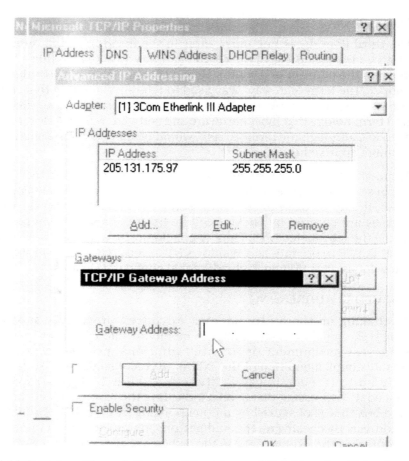

Exhibit 11.4. **Through the use of the Advanced IP Addressing dialog box, one can enter up to three gateway addresses that will be tried in the order they are entered.**

host name and domain name. In the example shown at the top of Exhibit 11.4 the host name WWW3 and domain xxx.com is shown entered. Thus, other persons can refer to the computer being configured as www.xxx.com instead of its IP address of 205.131.175.97.

If one intends to use a computer to access other computers and to only specify IP addresses, one does not have to specify any additional information. However, if one wants to use that computer to access other computers by specifying their near-English mnemonic address, then one must specify one or more DNS service addresses. Those addresses can represent the address of DNS servers operated by one's organization or a DNS server operated by the Internet Service Provider. Similar to permitting multiple

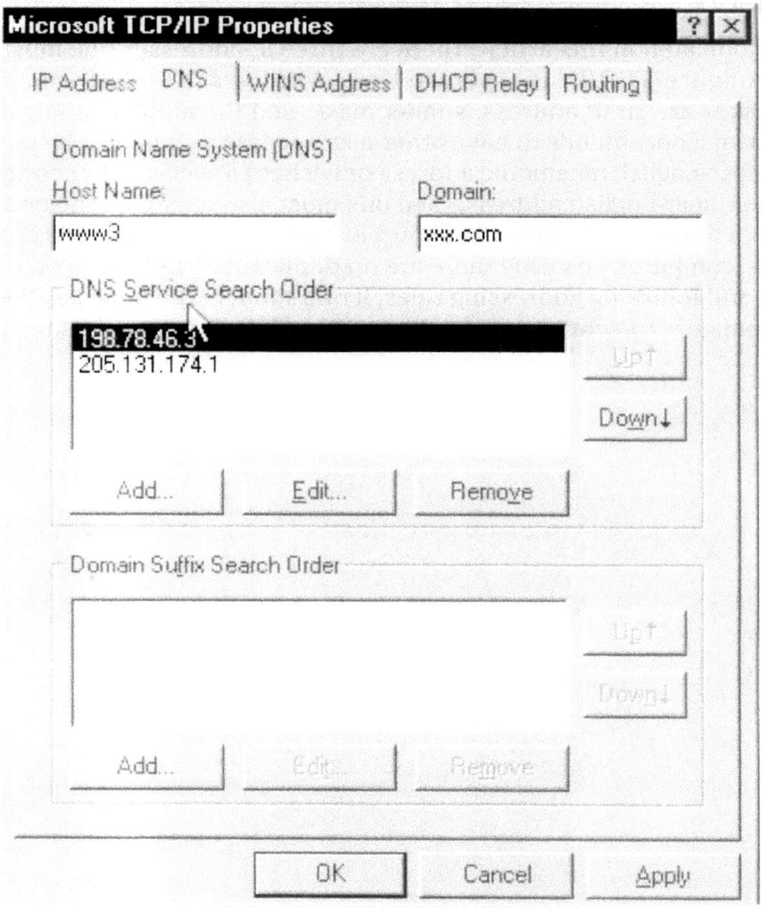

Exhibit 11.5. The DNS tab provides the opportunity to specify a near-English mnemonic to reference a computer as well as one or more addresses of DNS servers to resolve near-English mnemonic addresses entered to access other computers.

gateway addresses, Windows NT also supports the entry of multiple DNS servers. In Exhibit 11.4, two IP addresses were entered, which represents the addresses of two DNS servers. If an address resolution is required to convert a near-English mnemonic address entered to access a Web site or another TCP/IP application, the first DNS IP address will be used in an attempt to resolve the near English address to an IP address. If, after a predefined period of time, the specified address does not resolve the near-English address, the next IP address will be used in a second attempt to resolve the address.

SUMMARY

As indicated in this article, there are three IP addresses one must enter to configure TCP/IP to operate on a Windows NT platform. Those addresses are an IP address, subnet mask, and the address of a gateway. However, if one intends to have other users access a computer by referencing a near-English mnemonic address or wishes to access other computers via their near-English address, then one must also configure the computer through the use of the DNS tab shown in Exhibit 11.4. By carefully configuring the computer, ensuring there are no duplicate IP addresses on the network, and following addressing rules, if one subnets the network, then one can configure the computers to support the TCP/IP protocol suite.

Chapter 12
Routing and Routing Protocols
Michel Gilbert

In the language of the Open System Interconnection (OSI) Reference Model, a router is a Network Layer device responsible for routing traffic between subnetworks that make up a data internetwork. At its heart, a router is essentially a packet switch.

This definition relies upon a number of terms that merit exploration. The term "packet" refers to the transmission unit (known as a Protocol Data Unit) that moves from the Network Layer software in one system, across a network, to the Network Layer software in another system. A packet contains, among other things, the address of the source end station and the address of the destination end station. It is on this destination address that the router bases its decisions. End stations are the devices that generate or receive the vast majority of the packets moving through the network. They are, in essence, the reason why the network exists in the first place!

The terms subnetwork and internetwork are also not all that precisely used in the industry. For the purposes of this discussion, a subnetwork is defined as a collection of network resources that can be reached without needing to go through a router. If a message has to pass through a router to go from one end station to another, those two end stations are on differing subnetworks. And an internetwork is defined as a collection of two or more subnetworks connected using routers. This relationship is depicted in Exhibit 12.1.

In this context, the role of the router is straightforward: it receives packets transmitted by end stations (and possibly other routers) and routes them through the internetwork to the appropriate subnetwork. Once the packet has reached a router attached to the destination subnetwork, this router delivers it to the intended end station. Routers can also perform more advanced functions if the Network Layer protocol supports those functions. Some of these include the ability to fragment packets if necessary, or to notify transmitting end stations when packets are being discarded. Routers also provide some congestion control capabilities,

0-8493-9838-X/00/$0.00+$.50
© 2000 by CRC Press LLC

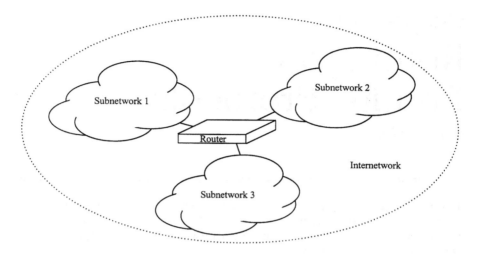

Exhibit 12.1.   Routers, Subnetworks, and Internetworks

---

although the vast majority of routers handle congestion by the simple expedient of dropping packets. Routers can also be fairly sophisticated packet filters, providing the network with a certain level of security.

Routing is sometimes confused with bridging. The distinction between the two lies in the Layer at which they operate. Routing is a Network Layer function. Routers operate on packets and make routing decisions based on the Network Layer address. Bridging is a Data Link Layer function. Bridges operate on frames and make filtering and forwarding decisions based (directly or indirectly) on the media access control address.

It is important to note that the frame is the mechanism used to get a transmission from one end station to another within the same subnetwork. Packets ride within frames and are the transmission unit used to get a message from one end station to another anywhere in the internetwork. If the two end stations are in the same subnetwork, the packet will be placed in a frame by the transmitter and sent across the subnetwork to the intended recipient, possibly crossing one or more bridges. If the end stations are not in the same subnetwork, the packet will ride in one frame from the transmitter to a router, which will make a routing decision and forward the packet across the next subnetwork in a new frame.

Within a subnetwork, bridging software has to build tables and keep track of potentially all of the devices within the subnetwork. And those tables do not usually contain entries for any end station in a different subnetwork. Routers, on the other hand, build tables that list all of the subnetworks and how to reach them.

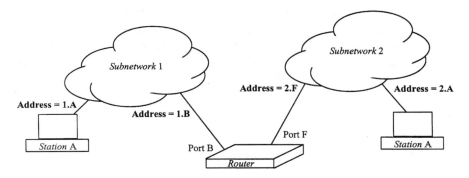

Exhibit 12.2.   Touters, Subnetworks, and Addressing

ROUTING IN THE NETWORK LAYER

The Network Layer protocol in an internetwork is responsible for end-to-end routing of packets. There are many Network Layer protocols in the industry, but they all share some common characteristics. All of them define a packet structure and an address format. All of them specify the types of service the network can provide, which may include such things as packet fragmentation, connectionless or connection-oriented service, and packet prioritization.

Key to the operation of the Network Layer protocol is the Network Layer address. The Network Layer address is hierarchically structured, with at least two basic segments defined. The first of these identifies a subnetwork, and the other identifies a particular end station within that subnetwork. Some Network Layer protocols define additional address fields, but these two fields are always present.

Each router or end station interface is assigned a Network Layer address that must be unique throughout the internetwork, much like each phone in the world must have a globally unique number so the telephone network can route the call. All of the devices that connect to the same subnetwork must agree on what the local subnetwork number is, as depicted in Exhibit 12.2. This global numbering strategy is the cement that binds the internetwork together, and makes it possible for routers to route packets.

A hierarchical address structure is only one of the things most modern Network Layer protocols have in common. The vast majority of these protocols also provide only a connectionless service and implement datagram-based networks. A connectionless service is one in which the upper layer protocol or application has no way to request an end-to-end relationship or "connection" with another end station. All it can do is provide the data to be sent and the address to which it is to be delivered. If there is any

Exhibit 12.3.   Common Network Layer Protocols

Network layer protocol	Address length	Address fields	Additional capabilities	Used in
Internet Protocol (IP)	4 octets (32 bits)	NETID (var.), Hostid (var.)	Fragmentation, nondelivery notification, subnetting	Internet, most network environments
Internetwork packet exchange (IPX) protocol	12 octets (96 bits)	Network (4), node (6), socket (2)	Automatic client addressing	NetWare
Datagram delivery protocol (DDP)	4 octets (32 bits)	Network (2), node (1), socket (1)	Automatic client addressing	AppleTalk
VINES internet protocol (VIP)	6 octets (48 bits)	Network (4), subnetwork (2)	Fragmentation, nondelivery notification, automatic addressing	VINES

acknowledgment, flow control, or sequencing of messages to be done, the upper layer protocol or application will have to do it.

A datagram-based network is one in which the routers are unable to establish end-to-end circuits on which to carry traffic. Every packet received by a router is routed independently of the ones that precede and follow it. That makes it difficult to provide any guaranteed quality of service or capacity because the routers cannot predict where the next packet will come from, when it will arrive, and where it will be destined. If a network supports end-to-end circuits, the routers would at least know that packets will arrive on an established circuit, and expected loads could be defined at the time the circuit is established.

Exhibit 12.3 summarizes four of the major Network Layer protocols in use today, and their primary characteristics. All four of these define connectionless services and implement datagram-based internetworks.

IP has one of the most complex addressing structures, largely due to its role in the Internet. The boundary between the IP subnetwork number (called the NETID) and the end station number (called the HOSTID) is not fixed. It varies depending on the class of the address and the value of the subnet mask being used. IP defines five address classes, three of which are for deploying subnetworks. These are summarized in Exhibit 12.4.

One of the more difficult concepts in IP networks is the subnet mask. Logically, the purpose of the subnet mask is to take a particular NETID and divide it into smaller subnetworks connected by routers. For example the Class B address 128.13.0.0 could be divided into 256 smaller networks designated as 128.13.1.0, 128.12.2.0, 128.13.3.0 (and so forth) using the 255.255.255.0 mask.

Exhibit 12.4.   IP Address Classes

Address class	Value of first octet	Length of NETID/use	Number of NETID	Number of HOSTID
Class A	1–126	1 octect	126	16,777,214
Class B	128–191	2 octets	16,382	65,534
Class C	192–223	3 octets	12,097,150	254
Class D	224–239	Multicast	N/A	N/A
Class E	240–255	Reserved	N/A	N/A

This is known as subnetting. Conversely, the mask can be used by routers to summarize routes. For example, all of the Class C networks from 199.12.0.0 to 199.12.255.0 could be advertised as 199.12.0.0 using the 255.255.0.0 mask. This is called supernetting, or Classless Interdomain Routing (CIDR).

IP addresses are typically manually assigned to all devices. There are exceptions, however. Most notably, the Dynamic Host Configuration Protocol (DHCP) permits a DHCP server to dynamically "lease" addresses to end stations as they come online. IP can perform packet fragmentation if necessary. A fragmented packet stays fragmented until it reaches the destination end station, where it is reassembled.

The Internetwork Packet Exchange (IPX) address has three portions. The first two portions identify the subnetwork (called the network) and end station (called the node). The third portion is called the socket and identifies a particular protocol, application, or upper layer process in the end station. IPX has a unique approach to address assignment. The local subnetwork identifier (called a network number) is assigned at the local routers. IPX clients learn this number by querying the routers, and then adopt their own media access control address as their end station identifier (called a node number). This means IPX client addressing is automatic; only servers and routers need to be programmed.

Like IPX, Datagram Delivery Protocol (DDP) has a three-part address, the subnetwork portion (called the network number) is assigned to local routers, and the end-station portion (called the node number) is dynamically assigned. What differs is the assignment mechanism. A DDP end station searches for an end station number that is not in use by any other local end station and adopts it.

VINES Internet Protocol (VIP) is more like IP, with a simple two-part address. However, VIP does not support the concept of subnet masking. And VIP addressing is 100% automated. The local subnetwork number is provided by the Virtual Networking System (VINES) server, which has the address encoded on a hardware key required to enable the server software. The VINES client requests an end station number from the local server, which provides a function similar to that of DHCP in an IP internetwork.

Like IP, VIP packets can also be fragmented if necessary. However, VIP depends on an associated protocol called the Fragmentation Protocol to do the deed. Fragmented packets are reassembled by the next router in the path before being routed onwards.

It is important to note that routing, as a Network Layer function, is performed by any device that implements a Network Layer. This includes both end stations and routers. While it may seem odd to think of an end station performing a routing function, the routing process actually begins with the device that generates the packet. This device must determine if the destination end station lies within the local subnetwork or on a different subnetwork. Destinations that lie within the local subnetwork can be reached directly via the underlying network technology. This is known as direct routing or delivery. To reach destinations that lie on a different subnetwork requires the services of a router. The end station must be able to identify a local router that can provide the service and forward the packet to that device, a process known as indirect routing.

Routers also perform direct and indirect routing, but typically this action is performed on packets generated by end stations. The router examines the destination address within a packet it has received and performs direct routing if the destination is on a local subnetwork. If the destination is not on a local subnetwork, the router performs an indirect routing operation and passes the packet on to another router.

For either a router or end station to perform direct routing, it must have a mechanism for mapping the Network Layer address of the destination end station to the corresponding address in the underlying network (e.g., the Ethernet address or the Frame Relay DLCI). IP, DDP, and VIP depend on associated protocols to build and maintain local tables that provide this mapping. Because IPX uses the value of the media access control address as part of the Network Layer address, it has no need for such a table. Once this mapping has been accomplished, the Network Layer packet is encapsulated in a frame that includes the mapped destination address and transmitted to the destination device.

To perform indirect routing, a device must have a mechanism for mapping the destination subnetwork to the Network Layer address of a local router that can forward the packet to that subnetwork. This mapping is typically achieved in one of three ways. First, the device can send a request to the local routers asking them to identify themselves if they are capable of routing a packet to the destination subnetwork. Second, a device can be programmed with a "default router" to which it will forward packets it does not otherwise know how to route. Third, the device can have a mechanism for building a table that contains the required mappings. End stations typically employ some form of the first two strategies.

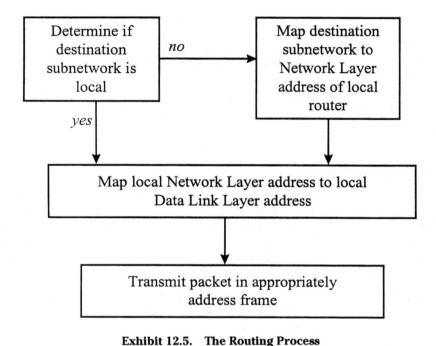

Exhibit 12.5. The Routing Process

For example, IP end stations are commonly configured to know a default router (called a default gateway in the IP community). Routers typically employ the second and/or third approach. Of course, once the Network Layer address of a local router is known, the packet can be directly routed to it by mapping that address to the corresponding local network address. This entire process is represented graphically in Exhibit 12.5.

The routing table is the key to the routing process, especially in routers. It contains the mappings that associate destination subnetworks with the address of a local router that can forward packets to, or toward, that network. The routing table lists the next hop only and typically indicates a total cost to reach that subnetwork. Cost is a reflection of the quality of the route. In general, a smaller cost means a better route. The specific meaning of the number differs from environment to environment.

The routing table contains various types of entries, which can be classified in two ways: how the entry was placed in the table, and the scope of the routing information. Entries in a routing table can be made statically or dynamically. Static routes are manually configured, and dynamic routes are automatically entered by some process in the router or end station. Static routes cannot be overwritten by a dynamically learned route.

Routing table entries can also differ in their precision. Host-specific routes are routes to a specific end station and are fairly rare. Subnet-specific routes are routes to a specific subnetwork and are the most common. Route summaries aggregate a set of subnetworks into a single entry. The default route is an "all others go here" route. In general, a router will select the "best" or "most specific" route it finds in its routing table. If there is a host-specific route for a particular end station, that is the best match. If the best match is the default route, this is the one that will be used. If there is no match at all, the router declares a routing error and discards the packet.

ROUTING PROTOCOLS

Routing protocols are responsible for providing the dynamic entries in a routing table. It is the routing protocol that monitors the network and alters the routing table when network changes occur. There are many routing protocols in the industry, and most Network Layer protocols have at least two associated routing protocols that can be used to build its routing tables. These protocols can be assessed in multiple ways.

The first assessment point is bandwidth. To build meaningful routing tables, the routers must exchange information. This act consumes bandwidth that would otherwise be used by end stations. The more bandwidth consumed by the routing protocol, the less is available to the end stations to do work.

The second assessment point is the metric the router optimizes to select routes. To select between several possible routes, a router needs a way to compare their quality. Some routers use simple hop count (i.e., the number of links or routers along the path to the destination). Others use metrics such as delay, bandwidth, or packet loss. Some protocols can even use a combination of several metrics. Delay is commonly accepted as one of the better metrics a router can use.

A third assessment point is the time the routing tables take to converge. There is always a finite period of time between the moment a network changes and the moment when the routing protocol has correctly altered the routing tables. This is a critical issue. From the moment the internetwork changes until the moment all of the routing tables are correct, packets may be misrouted along old and possibly invalid routes.

Finally, routing protocols require memory space and processing power within the router. Although today's low-cost memory and high-powered processors have made this a less critical issue, there are still some environments in which these requirements should be considered, including server-based and low-end routers.

The vast majority of modern routing protocols are classified as "distributed," meaning that the process of calculating routing tables is performed

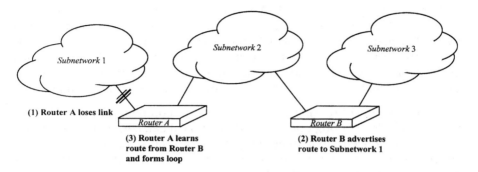

Exhibit 12.6. The Counting to Infinity Loop

by all of the routers in the internetwork. Centralized routing protocols, in which a single system makes all of the routing decisions and downloads routing tables to the routers, have only recently begun to appear in parts of the Internet and in some asynchronous transfer mode (ATM) environments. Distributed routing protocols fall into two broad classes: distance vector (DV) and link state (LS).

DV routing protocols, also called vector distance protocols or Bellman–Ford protocols, have three important characteristics. First, the routing updates they produce contain a list of destination/costs pairs. Second, those routing updates are sent neighboring devices (i.e., devices with which they share a common subnetwork). Finally, route calculation is itself distributed, with each system performing part of the calculation. In effect, these protocols extract a list of the destinations they have learned and the cost to reach them from the local routing tables and pass that information to their neighbors. The neighbors accept this calculated cost information as correct, add to the reported costs the cost of the link between themselves and the neighbor, and compare those values to the ones already in the routing table. If any of the information is better than what currently occupies the routing table, the routing table is updated.

In early implementations, DV protocols were shown to have a propensity for forging routing loops. The "counting to infinity" problem is one such loop that neighboring systems were prone to forming under specific conditions, as depicted in Exhibit 12.6. In this diagram, Router A has a route to Subnetwork 1 and Router B uses Router A to reach this subnetwork. If Router A loses the route and Router B advertises that fact before Router A can advertise the loss, Router A will accept Router B as a new route to Subnetwork 1, forming a loop. Any packet destined for Subnetwork 1 and arriving at one of these routers will Ping-Pong between them until the loop resolves.

131

To avoid this problem, most DV routing protocols implement "split horizons." Split horizons is a rule that prevents a router from advertising routes in the direction from which they were learned (i.e., downstream). It is essentially a "don't preach to the choir" philosophy. A split horizon with poisoned reverse is a version that permits advertisement of these routes, but sets the cost to "infinity" to prevent other routers from learning.

Most existing DV routing protocols transmit complete updates at regular intervals. Restricting updates to this interval can seriously impact network convergence time if something changes or fails. To improve convergence, routers are required to send updates immediately if they change any part of their routing table. This is called a "triggered" or "event-driven" update. Unfortunately, if the table update was the result of a network problem that caused a particular route to fail or become less optimal, it is possible for a router that has not yet received information about the change to reintroduce the old route into the network. To prevent this from occurring, routers are typically required to place any route that has failed into a "hold down" state. During the hold-down interval, typically three times the normal update interval, the router will refuse to accept any further updates on that route. The result is that first news (good or bad) about changes in a route travels quickly. If the news is bad news, however, the subsequent good news (i.e., a new route) is learned much more slowly.

DV routing protocols tend to be fairly simple to implement and design for, and they demand very little in terms of memory and processing power. Unfortunately, most of them are also prone to long convergence intervals and can consume significant amounts of bandwidth as the network grows large.

LS routing protocols also have three distinct characteristics. First, the routing updates contain link characteristic and status information. Second, routing updates sent by one router can potentially be seen by all routers in the internetwork, through a process similar to flooding. Finally, complete route calculation is performed by each router running the protocol.

At the heart of the LS routing protocol is the LS database. The routing updates generated and flooded by each router are stored by all routers in a local database. This database contains sufficient information to graph the network, calculate the shortest paths, and build a routing table based on those calculations. The role of the database is critical. A significant portion of any LS protocol is devoted to ensuring that the databases at all routers are synchronized. New routers entering the network have mechanisms for requesting a copy of the database from a local router, and existing routers have mechanisms for periodically verifying their database against that of another local router. Database synchronization is performed between neighboring routers that have formed a logical relationship called an adjacency.

Clearly, the size and complexity of the network can significantly impact the size of the database and the complexity of the route calculation. And even though LS updates are relatively small and only sent when changes occur, flooding can still be demanding in terms of network bandwidth. To deal with these scalability issues, LS protocols adopt mechanisms for limiting the flood of information.

First, only select routers are permitted to pass a flooded update into the network, and these routers are required to check the update against their local database before flooding, to avoid resending updates that have already been seen. Finally, networks running a LS routing protocol can be organized into areas, and many LS updates are only flooded within their assigned area. To provide routing information across area boundaries, specific routers are designated to summarize intra-area routes to other connected areas.

LS routing protocols tend to converge fairly quickly. If correctly configured, they tend to be more bandwidth-friendly than DV routing protocols and are significantly less prone to creating routing loops than DV routing protocols. However, LS routing protocols are also significantly more complex to design for and configure than DV routing protocols, and they can consume significantly more processing power and memory.

All of the classifications and characteristics of routing protocols discussed thus far apply to pretty much any routing protocol. However, there is another way of classifying routing protocols that is specific to the Internet. The Internet is essentially an internetwork of internetworks. Each internetwork is locally administered and is generally referred to as an Autonomous System (AS). On the Internet, a routing protocol that operates completely within an AS is called an Interior Gateway Protocol (IGP). However, the Internet also needs to pass routing information between these AS to bind them into a whole. Routing protocols operating between AS are called Exterior Gateway Protocols (EGP).

SURVEY OF MAJOR ROUTING PROTOCOLS

Exhibit 12.7 summarizes the key attributes of the major DV routing protocols used in the industry today. As Exhibit 12.7 indicates, the IP version of the Routing Information Protocol (RIP) optimizes hop count and generates updates every 30 seconds. Because of the problems that surface as RIP scales, this routing protocol limits the maximum length of a learned route to 15 hops. In RIP-speak, 16 means "you can't get there from here." RIP is considered an IGP and is typically used within small AS. Because RIP does not include subnet mask information in the routing updates, it can be used only in networks that either are not subnetted or have been subnetted using the same mask for all subnets. RIP cannot be used to support Variable Length Subnet Masking (VLSM) or CIDR.

Exhibit 12.7.   Summary of DV Routing Protocols

Routing protocol	Used to route	Metric(s)	Update interval	Documented by:
Routing Information Protocol (RIP)	Internet Protocol (IP)	Hop count	30 s	RFC 1058
RIP Version 2 (RIP-II)	IP	Hop count	30 s	RFC 1388
Routing Information Protocol	Internetwork Packet Exchange (IPX) protocol	Delay, hop count	60 s	Novell/Xerox
Interior Gateway Routing Protocol (IGRP)	IP	Delay, bandwidth (reliability, load)	90 s	Cisco
Enhanced IGRP (EIGRP)	IP, IPX, DDP	Delay, bandwidth (reliability, load)	Event driven	Cisco
Routing Table Maintenance Protocol (RTMP)	Datagram delivery protocol (DDP)	Hop count	10 s	Apple Computer
Routing Table Protocol (RTP)	VINES Internet Protocol (VIP)	VINES Internet Protocol (VIP)	90 s	Banyan
Border Gateway Protocol Version 4 (BGP4)	IP	IP	Event driven	RFC 1771 (and others

RIP Version II (RIP-II) was introduced in 1993 and has garnered little support in the industry. The major enhancements it brings to RIP are the inclusion of the subnet mask in the routing update, an authentication mechanism for routing updates, and information to support integration with EGP. Like its predecessor, RIP-II is considered an IGP.

The Novell Inc. NetWare (or IPX) version of RIP is much like the IP version. The three notable exceptions are the update interval, the inclusion of delay as a metric, and the fact that it builds routing tables for IPX instead of IP.

Cisco Systems Inc. has two routing protocols of its own. The Interior Gateway Routing Protocol (IGRP) builds IP routing tables, has an update interval of 90 seconds, and can learn multiple lowest-cost routes to a particular destination and balance the load across them. More significantly, IGRP optimizes a composite metric that defaults to include the total path delay weighted by the bandwidth of the narrowest link along the route. Link delay and bandwidth are statically configured at each interface on each router. The composite metric can also factor in load and reliability, but these metrics are not typically included. Like RIP, IGRP is considered an IGP and does not include the subnet mask in its updates.

Cisco's Enhanced IGRP (EIGRP) adds four new features to IGRP. First, it can build routing tables for the DDP and IPX, as well as IP. Second, it uses only event-driven updates, eliminating all periodic updates. Third, IP updates include the subnet mask, which makes EIGRP suitable for VLSM and CIDR environments. Finally, EIGRP implements the Diffused Update Algorithm, a simple, but elegant strategy for virtually eliminating the formation of routing loops in the internetwork.

The Routing Table Maintenance Protocol (RTMP) in Apple Computer Inc.'s AppleTalk has a reputation for being one of the chattiest routing protocols in the industry, with routing updates generated every 10 seconds. It can be used only to build DDP routing tables for an AppleTalk internetwork. In most other respects, it is very similar to the IP version of RIP.

Banyan Systems Inc.'s VINES implements a proprietary protocol suite that uses the VIP at the Network Layer. The Routing Table Protocol (RTP) is the most commonly encountered routing protocol in these networks. RTP optimizes delay and generates updates every 90 seconds. In recent years, Banyan has introduced Sequenced RTP, a version of RTP that eliminates periodic updates, thereby reducing bandwidth consumption.

The only EGP reviewed in this survey is the Border Gateway Protocol Version 4 (BGP4). This IP routing protocol is essentially the glue that binds the Internet backbone together. Although essentially a DV routing protocol, BGP4 adds a few new twists. First, to BGP4, a neighbor is any other BGP4 system that it can directly reach in another AS, or any other BGP4 router it is programmed to recognize in the local AS. BGP4 routers do not have to share a subnetwork to be considered neighbors. The BGP4 metric is actually a collection of attributes that describe the characteristics of a route. Also, BGP4 supports policy-based routing. That is to say, BGP4 routers can be programmed to accept or reject routes and to transmit or not transmit routing information, based on defined policies.

Exhibit 12.8 summarizes the key attributes of the major LS routing protocols in use today. LS routing protocols originated in the Advanced Research Projects Agency Network (ARPANET), and it is no surprise that the most commonly cited and used LS routing protocol appears in the context of TCP/IP. Open Shortest Path First (OSPF) is considered an IGP and is used in larger AS to build routing tables for IP routers. OSPF features strong

Exhibit 12.8.   Summary of LS Routing Protocols

Routing protocol	Used to route	Metric(s)	Documented by:
Open Shortest Path First (OSPF)	IP	Dimensionless	RFC 2178
Intermediate System to Intermediate System	IP, CLNS	Dimensionless	ISO DP 10589 and RFC 1142
NetWare Link Services Protocol (NLSP)	IPX	Dimensionless	Novell

support for building routing areas within an AS, and strong support for integration with other routing protocols as well as IP multicast. OSPF optimizes a metric that is described as "dimensionless." Each OSPF interface is assigned a cost, the meaning of which is at the discretion of the network administrator. If every interface is assigned a cost of one (1), OSPF will essentially optimize hop count. If each interface is assigned a cost proportionate to the delay experienced on that interface, then OSPF optimizes delay. OSPF Version 2, the current version of the standard, was updated in RFC 2178 in July 1997.

Intermediate System to Intermediate System (IS-IS) originated as an ISO protocol for the Connectionless Network Service (CLNS). It has been adopted by the Internet community and is used by some Internet service providers within their backbone network. It is relatively uncommon to find IS-IS in a corporate network. Like OSPF, the IS-IS metric is dimensionless and the protocol provides strong support for area-based routing.

The performance problems historically experienced over wide area network links in NetWare internetworks was one of the primary motivating factors for Novell's development of the NetWare Link Services Protocol (NLSP), which is largely based on IS-IS. In addition to building IPX routing tables, NLSP also builds NetWare's service tables, a function normally performed by the Service Advertising Protocol (SAP). Although IPX routers running NLSP retain the ability to respond to directed RIP and SAP queries, they no longer produce the bandwidth-intensive periodic updates. Recently, Novell has backed off of its emphasis on NLSP and has started to encourage the migration of NetWare environments towards the use of IP in place of IPX.

CONVENTIONAL ROUTER IMPLEMENTATIONS

A router is essentially a computer system equipped with multiple interfaces and software to perform the routing function. Within this definition, there are several platforms that can be classified as routers. The term "software router" typically refers to the use of a generic computer to provide routing. This most often occurs within the context of a server. In fact, the Windows NT Server, NetWare, and VINES servers all have an integrated routing capability, making it possible to build internetworks without the need to purchase additional routing equipment. Using those platforms to route traffic should be done with care, however. Every CPU cycle and kilobyte of memory consumed by the routing process is not available for servicing users. Software routers are typically best used in small internetworks, in branch office environments, or on the periphery of a larger internetwork.

Dedicated routers are those that come with a fixed number and type of ports. Those systems tend to have a relatively low port density, and are primarily used in smaller networks. They are also common in branch office or departmental contexts.

Modular routers implement their ports as I/O cards that can be selected to match the needs of the environment. These systems usually have a higher base sticker price than dedicated routers and tend to have higher port densities and support higher port speeds. They are commonly used in internetwork backbones.

Many modular hubs now have routing capabilities. Initially, this required the purchase of a specialized routing card that had to be inserted in the hub. Many modern hubs, however, have migrated this function to the backplane of the hub or integrated it into multiport modules.

Finally, the industry is seeing the rapid emergence of Layer 3 switches, which are essentially high-speed routers. These come in two flavors. A wire-speed router implements an internal switching fabric. Most of these systems have application-specific integrated circuits (ASIC) on each interface and distribute the routing process to these ASICs. The CPU in these systems is typically responsible for calculating routing tables and distributing them to the ASICs. They are called wire-speed routers because the latencies through the router are extremely small. Some of these platforms can route millions of packets per second.

Hybrid Layer 3/Layer 2 switches combine a Layer 2 switch with a Layer 3 router. Routing decisions are made by the Layer 3 function, as would be expected. But if a long-term flow of packets is detected, or if the end stations have the ability to request it, the router can establish a Data Link Layer connection for that flow of traffic and bypass the packet-by-packet routing decision. These systems are most commonly associated with ATM networks.

CONCLUSION

The purpose of this chapter has been to provide IT personnel with the background information they need to make informed decisions about routing options. To that end, this chapter has provided a consistent language for discussing internetworking, described the general model for routing implemented in modern networks, surveyed the major Network Layer protocols and routing protocols, and described the major types of routing platforms and the contexts in which they are most commonly used.

Chapter 13
Evolution to Layer 2 and 3 Switching
Michel Gilbert

Robert Metcalfe and D. L. Boggs did their early work on Ethernet at Xerox Corp.'s PARC Place in 1972. This local area network (LAN), destined to become the preeminent LAN technology in the world, was initially designed around a shared-medium, shared-bandwidth model. Although the idea of building LANs on a broadcast model may appear shortsighted today, it made perfect sense in the context of the time. The computers being networked were mainframes and minicomputers, and companies had a handful at most. The traffic being sent across these early networks was largely ASCII character-based data. Switches were slow and expensive. The microcomputer was still essentially a hobby toy, and the Internet was still in diapers. In this context, shared-medium and shared-bandwidth LANs made sense. Metcalfe's simple and elegant Ethernet was low-cost, low-delay, and high-speed.

Parkinson's Law, however, was destined to prove true. The emergence of the IBM PC in 1981 introduced a flood of a new system to be networked. Furthermore, the slow but steady migration from text to graphics began to ramp up load. Under these pressures, the second generation of LANs was born: dedicated media, shared bandwidth. Borrowing from the Token Ring experience, the Institute of Electrical and Electronic Engineers produced a standard for hub-based twisted pair Ethernet in 1990. This environment proved less expensive to deploy and less expensive to maintain and scale.

The third generation of LANs is the dedicated-medium, dedicated-bandwidth environment. This is the province of the LAN switch. The LAN switch takes the hub-based LAN one step further: It makes each port on the hub a distinct LAN. The three generations of LANs are depicted in Exhibit 13.1.

As we shall see, Layer 2 and Layer 3 switches are essentially bridges and routers, respectively. So reviewing the essentials of bridging and routing is in order.

Bridges operate at the Data Link Layer; they can be incorporated into a network with no changes to the operation of end stations. Bridges isolate

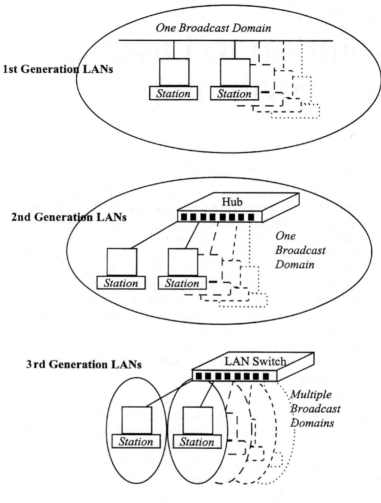

Exhibit 13.1. Three Generations of LANs

the broadcast domains, forwarding only the frames that need to cross from one LAN into another. Bridges operate on the media access control (MAC) address (directly or indirectly). The bridging software must be able to keep track of potentially every end station in the bridged network.

Routers operate at the Network Layer, routing packets from one end station to another across an internetwork. Routers interconnect subnetworks. Subnetworks can be a LAN, a collection of bridged LANs, or even a wide area network (WAN). Regardless of what it is, each subnetwork is uniquely identified by a subnetwork number. Each device has a Network

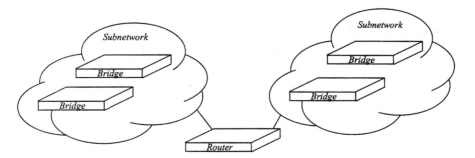

Exhibit 13.2. The Relative Scope of Bridging and Routing

Layer address that identifies the subnetwork to which it is connected, and uniquely identifies it within that subnetwork.

To place the two strategies in perspective, a bridge has intra-subnetwork scope while a router is an inter-subnetwork device, as depicted in Exhibit 13.2.

LAYER 2 SWITCHING

The birth of LAN switching occurred in 1994 when a small startup company called Kalpana introduced the EtherSwitch, a 15-port Ethernet hub with a remarkable capability. This hub could read and learn the MAC addresses of the device connected at each port. When frames were received on any port, the destination MAC address in the frame would be read and the frame would be switched to the specific port where the destination system was attached. Only frames explicitly sent to the MAC broadcast address would be forwarded on all ports. Furthermore, if the destination port was busy, the EtherSwitch would buffer the frame until the port was available.

One of the primary benefits to this approach was the freedom it gave companies to leverage their infrastructure. Significant throughput enhancements could be achieved simply by changing out the hub. In effect, each attached system was given a private Ethernet. This was the first LAN switch. What Kalpana (which has since been bought by Cisco Systems Inc.) did was to merge two concepts together: bridges and hubs. A LAN switch differs from a conventional bridge in two regards: it has the physical appearance and configuration of a hub, and it implements a switching fabric internally. This switching fabric is most often a shared memory or crosspoint switch, although other technologies are possible. It is also common for each of the interfaces on the bridge to implement an application-specific integrated circuit (ASIC) designed to make the filter forward decisions and

141

Conventional Bridge

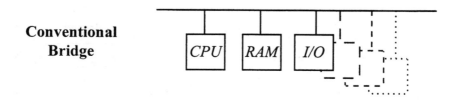

LAN Switch

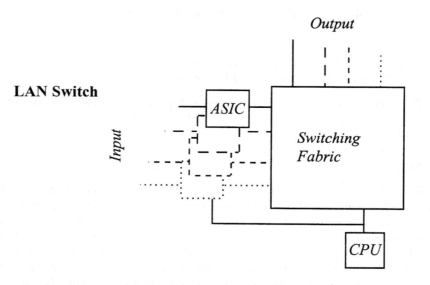

Exhibit 13.3.   LAN Switches vs. Conventional Bridges

---

feed the frames into the switch fabric. A conventional bridge, by way of comparison, is essentially a von Neumann computer optimized for bridging (Exhibit 13.3).

The introduction of the LAN switch opened the door to another development: the full-duplex LAN. Conventional LANs are effectively half duplex because of their multi-access nature. But LAN switches create private LANs with only two attached devices. This opens the door to full duplex operation, which doubles the throughput on the link. This is commonly used for server, router, and switch-to-switch links and requires specialized full-duplex adapters at each end of the link.

Another feature of the LAN switch is its low latency. Because of their architecture, conventional bridges perform store-and-forward bridging. A frame must be completely received and processed before it can be forwarded. One advantage of this approach is that any frames that are detected to be in error can be discarded before they are forwarded, reducing wasted bandwidth. Unfortunately, the disadvantage is increased latency. At 10M bps, a 1500 octet frame experiences at least 1.2 ms of delay passing through a store-and-forward bridge. A bit could travel over 350 km in that time!

LAN switches can begin to forward a frame before it is completely received. The advantage of this cut-through feature is reduced latency. The frame is delayed only long enough to read the destination address, which is at or near the front of the frame. At 10M bps, a frame is delayed a mere 0.0048 ms. A bit can travel only approximately 1.5 km in that time, a significant reduction. Unfortunately, errored frames can be detected only when the frame is completely received, so this approach will forward errored frames on into the network, which wastes bandwidth. Normally, this is not a significant problem. However, if an adapter or cable segment is faulty and produces an inordinate number of errored frames, it can seriously impact network performance.

Modern switches combine both features. They will cut through frames until errors exceed a specified level, then they will switch to a store-and-forward mode until the error level returns to a defined "normal." It is important to note that any LAN switch defaults to store-and-forward if the destination port is busy.

Another distinguishing factor between LAN switches is their ability to learn MAC addresses. If the LAN switch can learn a single address per port, the attached device can be a single end station or router. If the LAN switch can learn multiple addresses per port, the attached device can be another LAN switch, a conventional hub, or a conventional bridge. Switches typically advertise a per-port address capability and an overall address capability. Beyond several hundred addresses per port and several thousand per LAN switch, address density becomes pure specmanship. As we shall see, LAN switches have scalability problems.

It is also common for LAN switches to implement different data rates on some ports. The bandwidth required by a server, router, or uplink to another LAN switch is typically greater than that required by a conventional end station. A LAN switch makes it possible to combine ports with different data rates to give these devices more throughput, as depicted in Exhibit 13.4. When the frame format used by each LAN is the same, the switch simply uses buffers to deal with the transmission rate mismatch. For example, an Ethernet switch may implement several 10Base-T ports and one or two 100Base-T (i.e., Fast Ethernet) ports.

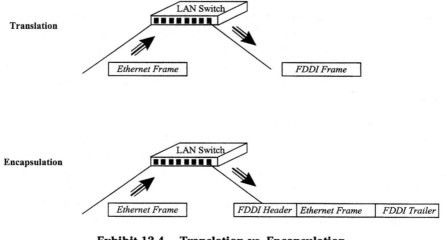

Exhibit 13.4.   Translation vs. Encapsulation

As with all interconnection devices, LAN switches have to deal with congestion issues. This is especially true on links to servers, routers, and other LAN switches, where traffic tends to concentrate. There are multiple approaches to alleviating this type of congestion. First, it is possible to increase the throughput of these links with high-speed or full-duplex connections. Most of these switches also provide for increased buffer capacity to deal with speed mismatches between interfaces. Some Ethernet switches are also able to explicitly exert congestion control using a technique known as backpressure.

When some Ethernet switches begin receiving a frame destined for a congested port, they are able to generate a jamming signal on the receiving port that forces a collision and causes the transmitter to stop, back off, and try again. This is known as backpressure. Although it can be an effective technique, it has some unfortunate side effects. Backpressure causes the transmitter to stop all transmissions until the frame at the front of the transmission queue of that device is successfully transmitted. On a link to a server or router, this stops all traffic from that device. On a link to a conventional hub, it can stop all transmissions in that hub until the congestion resolves.

It is important to note that congestion is also handled by upper layer protocols, which can exert flow control, slowing or arresting transmissions when congestion causes frame discards to occur.

LAN switches, as has been noted, are essentially high-speed bridges. Like conventional bridges, they have scalability problems associated with their bondage to the MAC address. First, as a subnetwork scales to include thousands of systems, the LAN switches must be able to handle a high number of addresses. Second, these devices all periodically generate MAC Layer broadcast frames. These frames are traditionally flooded through a bridged internetwork, which can result in a very high load in large subnetworks.

Many modern LAN switches have enhanced capabilities for directing broadcast traffic. These devices are intelligent enough to peer into the frame to determine the purpose of the broadcast and direct the transmission with a high degree of intelligence. For example, they can learn the IP address of attached stations and forward Address Resolution Protocol broadcasts only to the specified station. Or they can learn the location of Novell Inc. NetWare servers and routers and forward Service Advertising Protocol and Routing Information Protocol (RIP) broadcasts to only those systems. These advanced capabilities come at a cost, both in dollars and in performance. The LAN switch must do more processing on these broadcast transmissions, which can increase latency and reduce the throughput of the LAN switch.

A quick scan of the market is enough to show that there are many LAN switches that implement different MAC schemes. The simplest of these support MACs that implement the same frame type. This includes switches that combine the various flavors of Ethernet, or switches that combine 100VG-AnyLAN with either Token Ring or Ethernet ports. The LAN switch has no additional work to do. It can forward the same frame unchanged onto another interface.

When the MAC schemes implement different schemes, things become more difficult. There are two basic approaches: translation and encapsulation (Exhibit 13.4). In the translation approach, the LAN switch converts the frame from one format to another. Although this is possible and there are products that do it, it has consequences for performance and interoperability. To translate the frame, the LAN switch has to receive more of it before the translation can begin, which increases latency. There are also many instances when frame translation causes problems with Upper Layer interoperability, especially when Token Ring frames are translated to Ethernet or fiber distributed data interface.

In the encapsulation model, one frame type is placed within another. For example, some products on the market encapsulate Token Ring frames into Ethernet for transmission across a switched backbone. This can enable integration of Fast Ethernet or Gigabit Ethernet backbones with token ring LANs. However, the solution is proprietary and typically requires equipment from the same vendor at each end of the link.

One common way of classifying LAN switches is by the context of their intended use. To this end, they are classified as desktop, workgroup, or enterprise switches.

Desktop switches are very small, supporting as few as two ports and seldom supporting more than six. They typically implement the conventional LAN rates (e.g., 10M bps Ethernet or 16M bps Token Ring). They are stand-alone devices that implement a single MAC scheme. They are intended to provide connection of several devices on a desktop or in a small office to a workgroup or enterprise backbone.

Workgroup switches are the medium-scale devices intended to support a department or part of a department. They typically support a few dozen ports, come in a stand-alone or stackable configuration, and often provide a combination of conventional and high-speed ports. The high-speed interfaces are often used to support a local server or to provide connection to a higher-speed enterprise backbone. These devices are fully manageable, and most can be accessed in-band via a Telnet connection or a World Wide Web browser.

Enterprise (or backbone) switches are the workhorses of the corporate data network. They are typically modular platforms, although there are also stackable products. They have all of the features of a workgroup switch, but they support a significantly higher port density. Virtually all of them have asynchronous transfer mode (ATM) capability, integrated router capability, and support WAN connections. Support for virtual LANs is also common.

In selecting an appropriate LAN switch for a given environment, several factors should be considered. First, the scope of the application should dictate whether a desktop, workgroup, or enterprise switch is appropriate. Growth issues will also influence the choice between a stand-alone, stackable, or modular platform. Naturally, the switch must implement the appropriate MAC types with the appropriate media and the appropriate data rates. The size of the subnetwork should dictate the number of MAC addresses the device must be able to handle, and this condition should apply to all switches, even those at the periphery of the switched subnetwork. Port density and cost are also critical issues. Finally, low latency switches should be a priority for network environments with time-sensitive traffic or extremely high loads. Vendors provide specifications for their products, and product benchmarks can often be obtained from the Tolly Group at *www.tolly.com*.

LAYER 3 SWITCHING

Since the advent of LAN switches, the great debate has raged. Manufacturers of conventional routers claim that LAN switches lack the sophistication to build large corporate networks. The manufacturers of LAN switches claim that their products have a lower price per port, higher speeds, and the lower latencies needed to implement modern backbones. Throughout the debate, most would have to acknowledge the essential truths claimed

146

by the opposing camp. Layer 2 switching is essentially a bridging solution, with all of the implied scalability problems. Conventional routers also have comparatively high latencies because all of the packet processing is done by one or more central processing unit (CPU) that essentially form a bottleneck to traffic.

Today, the evolution to Layer 3 switching is occurring in two sectors of the market. Manufacturers of LAN switches are integrating Internet Protocol (IP) and Internetwork Packet Exchange (IPX) routing in their products. At the same time, the manufacturers of conventional routers are integrating switching technology into these platforms.

One of the key issues driving the need for higher forwarding rates and lower latencies in routers is the explosion in network data rates. ATM is capable of extremely high data rates, which only recently have been matched by Gigabit Ethernet technologies. At these high data rates, store-and-forward conventional routers would require an extremely large buffer capacity to allow the processor(s) time to process frames before forwarding. A single Gigabit Ethernet adapter could barrage a router interface with over 200,000 packets/sec. It would not take too many of these ports to overwhelm even the fastest CPU today.

The industry's answer to this problem is the wire-speed router, one of two types of Layer 3 switches. These platforms combine the latency of the LAN switch with the sophistication of the router. Wire-speed routers are simply routers that have a specialized architecture that permits them to handle packets at an incredibly high speed. Some routers achieve this using a routing cache. When the CPU processes a packet and determines a mapping between the destination address and the port on which the packet is to be forwarded, the mapping is stored in a high-speed cache. These caches are typically implemented using content-addressable memory.

Although this strategy can enhance performance, the performance enhancement is in direct proportion to the arrival pattern of destination addresses. If packets arrive with a high degree of repeatability (i.e., destined for the same subnetwork or end station), cache hits are frequent and router throughput is increased. If packets arrive randomly with little repeatability, cache hits are less common and throughput is degraded back to near conventional router levels. One example of a device that implements this approach is Cisco's 7513.

A more common approach to designing wire-speed routers is to distribute the routing function internally. These platforms borrow liberally from the LAN switching world in their architecture, implementing an internal switching fabric (typically shared memory or crosspoint) and ASIC on each port. The CPU is responsible for calculating routing tables and downloading them to the ASIC. Routing becomes a function that is local to each port.

One of the advantages to this approach is that adding modules increases the forwarding capacity of the router. These platforms claim forwarding rates as high as 100 million packet/sec. Examples of this type of architecture include Ascend Communication Inc.'s GRF 1600, which claims a maximum forwarding rate of 10 million packet/sec; 3Com Corp.'s CoreBuilder 2500 and 6000, which claim forwarding rates of up to 1.1M bps; 3Com's CoreBuilder 3500 and 9000, which claim forwarding rates of up to 64 million packet/sec; and Foundry Network's BigIron 4000 and 8000, which claim forwarding rates of 100 million packet/sec.

A second type of Layer 3 switch is the hybrid Layer 2/Layer 3 switch, sometimes called a multilayer router. These platforms initially began to appear in response to the ATM factor. ATM is a completely different technology than any of our existing LAN schemes. Where LANs are essentially connectionless, ATM is connection-oriented. While LANs operate on the datagram model, ATM requires established circuits before traffic can traverse the network. These are features common to WAN technologies, and they complicate ATM integration into the corporate backbone. To address these issues, two basic approaches have emerged. LAN Emulation (LANE) defines a mechanism for implementing a virtual LAN on an ATM backbone. Classical IP (CIP) defines a mechanism for defining a single Logical IP subnetwork over ATM.

Both of these strategies create single subnetworks; the former can be multiprotocol while the latter is limited to IP only. Although it is technically possible to build internetworks that comprise a single huge subnetwork, such bridged environments have been shown to scale poorly. Subnetworks are typically kept relatively small (i.e., a few systems to several hundred systems). As a result, both the LANE and CIP strategies need routers to interconnect these subnetworks. When multiple subnetworks reside in the same ATM fabric, end-to-end traffic can end up crisscrossing the ATM fabric multiple times before arriving at the intended destination. A similar problem has developed over conventional LANs when the LAN switches support a virtual LAN capability that makes it possible for multiple LANs to coexist in the same network fabric.

The general approach to this problem is to define a way for the end stations and routers to interact to locate and use a "shortcut" route across the underlying network. Accomplishing this requires protocols that can detect when packets are crisscrossing needlessly, identify and establish a loop-free shortcut, and direct the end stations and/or routers to use the shortcut. This is sometimes called the "route once, switch after" model. The Layer 3 devices cooperate to route the first packet and discover the shortcut; the shortcut is then assigned a "tag" or "label" that is used by the Layer 2 switching function to speed subsequent packets on their way with no further involvement by the routing function.

It is important to note that this involves a fundamental change to the general routing model. In conventional networks, an end station or router can never send a packet directly to a system that lies on a different subnetwork. It must use the services of a router. In this model, the end station begins in that mode but eventually learns a Layer 2 address (or tag) that can be used for direct communication.

As a general rule, there are two strategies for triggering the discovery of a shortcut: flow-based and topology-based triggering. In the flow-based model, the need for a shortcut is triggered when the routers detect a potentially long-term flow of traffic between two end systems. Long-term flows would include such things as Transmission Control Protocol (TCP) connections for Telnet or File Transfer Protocol, and NetWare server connections. Short-term flows would include such things as Domain Name System name queries or Simple Network Management Protocol management exchanges. Flow-based triggers have a relatively major Achilles heel: Because they are based on end station to end station flows, they can trigger a proliferation of shortcuts between the same two subnetworks in a larger internetwork.

The alternative strategy, topology-based triggering, focuses on the general structure of the internetwork itself. As traffic begins to flow between two particular subnetworks, these protocols explore the path between the two subnetworks to determine if a shortcut is warranted. If it is, and it is established, it can be used by multiple systems simultaneously. This can significantly reduce the number of shortcuts required to move traffic between the two subnetworks.

Perhaps the biggest problem with multilayer routing is the proliferation of strategies in the industry. Every vendor has its own idea for how this should be done, and there are even two standards activities underway. Exhibit 13.5 summarizes the major approaches that have emerged.

Multilayer routing really began when Ipsilon (since acquired by Nokia) introduced its IP Flows concept. Ipsilon was specifically targeting the problem of IP/ATM integration. Its solution was to integrate an ATM switch into an IP router. To the network, the IP router appeared to be at the periphery of the ATM cloud. ATM connections could be terminated at the router. End stations communicating across multiple IP subnetworks would route their packets to the router in the usual way. In addition to routing packets, the router would examine the IP addresses and TCP port information to detect long-term flows from one subnetwork to another in the ATM fabric. When these were detected, the IP router could instruct the ATM switch to establish a new circuit from source to destination that bypassed the local router. To perform this task, Ipsilon defined a protocol called the Ipsilon Flow Management Protocol. Once established, the IP router could notify the end stations to use the new circuit for the duration of the flow. Subsequent packets

149

Exhibit 13.5. Major Multilayer Routing Approaches

Protocol name	Promoted by	Layer 3 protocols	Layer 2 protocols	Label tag distribution by:
IP switching	Ipsilon (Nokia)	IP only	ATM only	Ipsilon Flow Management Protocol (IFMP)
Tag switching	Cisco	All protocols in the Cisco IOS	ATM, frame relay, LAN	Tag Distribution Protocol (TDP)
Mulitprotocol Over ATM (MPOA)	ATM Forum	Any	ATM	Next Hop Resolution Protocol (NHRP), Q.2931 signaling
Aggregate Route-based IP switch (ARIS)	IBM	IP	ATM, frame relay	ARIS protocol
Switching IP Through ATM (SITA)	Telecom Finland	IP	ATM	None
Cell Switch Router (CRS)	Toshiba	IP	ATM, frame relay	Flow Attribute Notification Protocol (FANP)
IP Switching over Fast ATM Cell Transport (IPSOFACTO)	NEC	IP	ATM	None
Multiprotocol Label Switching (MPLS)	IETF	Any (initially IP and IPX)	Any	Draft documents only

would cut through the IP/ATM hybrid, handled completely by the ATM switch with no further intervention from the router. A description of the IP Flows approach can be found in a series of Internet informational RFCs, specifically RFC 1953, 1987, and 2297. Information is also available at *www.ipsilon.com.*

It was not long before Cisco entered the fray with its own solution, which it calls Tag Switching. Unlike IP Flows, Cisco's approach is multiprotocol, supporting all of the Layer 3 protocols handled by Cisco's Internetworking Operating System. Tag Switching is also not limited to the ATM world. It can be used over frame-relay and virtual LAN environments as well. Another point of differentiation between IP Flows and Tag Switching is its triggering mechanism; Tag Switching uses topology-based triggers.

The Cisco approach differentiates between tag-edge switches, which lie at the periphery of the tag-switched environment, and tag-core switches, which lie at its heart. The Layer 3 function in these switches runs standard routing protocols (e.g., OSPF, RIP, IGRP, EIGRP, BGP4, etc.) to build local routing tables. Cisco created the Tag Distribution Protocol (TDP) to discover shortcuts and define and distribute route tags to the Layer 2 switching functions. These tags and their associated destination prefixes (i.e., subnetwork prefixes) are stored in a local Tag Information Base that is then used by the Layer 2 switching function to forward traffic. The TDP protocol requires TCP connections between the tag switches, both core and edge.

One of the strengths of the Cisco approach is the range of granularity with which tags can be defined. For example, a tag could be assigned to guide all traffic flowing from one set of subnetworks to another (extremely coarse granularity), or it could guide the traffic between two specific end station applications. This is similar to the flow-based model implemented by Ipsilon. Further information about the Tag Switching architecture can be found in Internet RFC 2105 or at *www.cisco.com.*

Multiprotocol over ATM (MPOA) is a standards-based approach to multilayer routing that originates from the ATM Forum. Like Tag Switching, MPOA supports multiple Layer 3 protocols and uses a combination of topology and flow-based triggers. Like IP Flows, it was defined specifically for ATM networks. MPOA also uses standards-based techniques for identifying and tagging shortcuts. It uses the Next Hop Resolution Protocol (NHRP) to locate the shortcuts, and Q.2931 signaling (part of the ATM UNI specification) to establish the end-to-end circuits.

One of the key features of MPOA is its close dependence on LANE. In essence, MPOA binds LANE-based subnetworks into a larger internetwork. MPOA distinguishes between MPOA clients (MPC), which use shortcuts when they can, and MPOA servers (MPS), which are routers that assist in finding shortcuts and can route traffic that does not require shortcuts. In MPOA, it is the MPC that is responsible for detecting flows. A flow is defined as a number of packets in a specified period of time that are traveling to the same subnetwork via the same local router. The MPC is the device that issues a next hop resolution request to the local MPS, where the NHRP service is usually resident. The job of NHRP is a relatively simple one conceptually: It has to locate the ATM Network Service Access Point Address (NSAPA) of the destination so that a direct ATM circuit can be established to that router, avoiding the crisscrossing syndrome. These NSAPA/subnet mappings are locally cached so they can be used for other requests.

There are numerous other strategies that have been proposed. IBM has the Aggregate Route-Based IP Switch (ARIS). This strategy was designed for IP traffic over connection-oriented Layer 2 infrastructures (e.g., ATM and Frame Relay). Telecom Finland has proposed Switching IP Through ATM (SITA) which, as the name implies, is restricted to IP over ATM environments. Toshiba enters the fray with its Cell Switch Router (CRS) strategy, which is similar to ARIS in its use of connection-oriented Layer 2 strategies and defines its own label distribution protocol called the Flow Attribute Notification Protocol (FANP). Finally, NEC, after initially embracing Ipsilon's IP Flows strategy, has now proposed the IP Flows Over Fast ATM Cell Transport (IPSOFACTO), which addresses IP flows over ATM networks. Information about these varying strategies and links to the various approaches can be found at *infonet.aist-nara.ac.jp/member/nori-d/mlr/*.

The other standards-based activity is Multiprotocol Label Switching (MPLS) sponsored by the Internet Engineering Task Force (IETF). MPLS is an attempt by the community at large to create a unifying standard. The work is in its early stages, so there is little that can be said about the final outcome of the activity. However, it is enlightening to note the scope of the activity. The workgroup is targeting three basic areas of standardization: the semantics of the labels themselves, the forwarding methods to be used by the Layer 3 and Layer 2 functions, and the strategies for distributing the labels throughout the internetwork.

The state of the union in the area of multilayer routing is largely confused. The broad array of competing approaches has resulted in little interoperability between strategies, and mixed support for the various strategies. ARIS, CRS, SITA, and IPSOFACTO have garnered little industry support at this point. IP Flows, after an energetic start, is coming under fire for some of its scalability problems and because of its limitation to ATM and IP environments. The three approaches that either have significant support or seem to have the potential to gain it are Tag Switching, MPOA, and MPLS.

As a Cisco strategic direction, Tag Switching has tremendous potential. Cisco has such a broad market presence that it has the leverage to push strongly for its solution. However, Cisco (together with IBM) is a key player in the MPLS activity, so the potential exists for these two concepts to merge in the future. MPOA is now seeing deployment and support by many vendors, but its limitation to ATM environments and its complexity (i.e., it involves three major technologies, including LANE, NHRP, and Q.2931) have brought it under fire of late.

CONCLUSION

Layer 2 switches are increasingly mature and highly interoperable. This chapter has provided an overview of the available technologies, and suggestions for features information technology personnel should examine when exploring the market for these products. Layer 3 switching is less mature. The most highly interoperable platforms are the wire-speed routers, where enhanced speed is being achieved through internal architectural changes. This chapter also summarized the various approaches to multilayer routing and underscored the strategies that seem to be taking hold in the industry.

Chapter 14

Implementing Routing, Switching, and VLANs in Modern Corporate Networks

Thomas Atkins

Corporate networks have undergone dramatic evolutionary changes over the past several years. New computing paradigms, more powerful desktop and server platforms, and the ever increasing capabilities of network equipment have altered the way network managers architect networks.

The first corporate networks consisted of large (Ethernet or Token Ring) segments connected with repeaters. The only way to extend the size of the network was to add repeaters. These simple devices regenerated local area network (LAN) signaling—allowing more users to share a network that could span a larger geographical area. Repeaters were simple devices that propagated packets (both good and error types) across the segment.

Repeater environments gave way to bridged networks. Bridges allowed network managers to divide repeated environments into two or more segments. Network users on both sides of the bridge could transparently share data, but error frames were isolated to the segment on which they originated. Bridges increased network performance by allowing the creation of multiple segments, but scalability issues plagued large networks. Installations with many bridges were difficult to troubleshoot, and broadcast storms in one location could affect users throughout the enterprise.

Eventually, routers were introduced to corporate networks. These devices solved many of the problems inherent to bridged networks. Routers control broadcasts, particularly across low bandwidth wide area network (WAN) connections, and are deployed widely in most corporate networks. However, while providing much needed scalability characteristics, routers imposed a performance penalty for processing each packet. This performance hit (typically about 20 ms) was not initially noticed on large networks (due to the other benefits provided by routers) increased traffic loads and the adoption of intranet computing eventually highlighted router performance limitations.

Switches arrived in corporate networks in the early 1990s and quickly earned a reputation as an excellent performance enhancement to router networks. Switches performed the same functions as bridges, but they were designed to forward traffic at much higher rates. Switches increased performance within the local area network (LAN) environment but rarely provided the WAN and broadcast control abilities of traditional routers. Many modern networks now contain both routers and switches—each performing separate functions to provide a combination of performance and management functions.

The latest type of device to be introduced to corporate networks are switches that can also perform router functions. This new generation of equipment (Layer 3 switch) is capable of forwarding traffic either as a switch or a router without imposing the performance penalty typically associated with routing. Layer 3 switches promise to change the way modern networks are designed for the remainder of the decade.

NETWORK DESIGN EVOLUTION

As network devices have evolved, network designs have changed to make the best use of the new capabilities afforded by the latest equipment. But even though several new types of devices have been introduced over the years, network designs have focused on three key points: performance, management, and redundancy. New devices have addressed one or more of these points, allowing network designers to further enhance portions of their networks with each new piece of equipment.

Focus on Performance

Improving performance was the first enhancement network managers could make to their developing networks years ago. Repeated environments became slower as more users were added to the same shared media. Increased traffic and contention made it more difficult for each user to access the network. When bridges arrived, performance could easily be improved. Each two-port bridge effectively doubled network bandwidth by segmenting a single repeated segment into two collision domains. Performance was increased because available network bandwidth was shared among fewer users. Broadcast traffic, however, could still propagate across the bridged domain.

As with bridges, switches allowed network managers to make further improvements in network performance. Switches were deployed in much the same way as bridges, but they were introduced long after router technology had matured.

As mentioned earlier, bridges and switches allow network managers to increase performance by segmenting collision domains into smaller segments containing fewer users. Unfortunately, these devices also propagate broadcasts, which can create problems when large numbers of bridges and/or switches are deployed in a single broadcast domain. This scalability issue, inherent to bridged/switched network designs is typically addressed by the focus on management.

Focus on Management

Two side effects of bridge/switch deployment are broadcast traffic propagation and more difficult troubleshooting. Bridges and switches are programmed to forward any broadcast packet out all ports, effectively multiplying broadcasts on the network. Each end station (e.g., PCs, servers, printers) must process every broadcast packet to see if it is the designated recipient. Excessive broadcasts (a by-product of large broadcast domains) can slow down attached devices and consume bandwidth.

Furthermore, many types of erroneous broadcast packets are also forwarded in bridged/switched environments. Because error packets can appear simultaneously on many segments, identifying and isolating error conditions can be difficult on large switched networks.

Routers (and later, VLANs) were initially used to address the scalability issues with bridges/switches. Because routers (and VLANs) are used to control the size of a broadcast domain, the extent to which broadcasts are propagated can be limited. The need to manage networks more effectively drove the implementation of router ports in most large networks.

Virtual LANs (VLANs — discussed in greater detail in the following section) are also used to control the size of broadcast domains, particularly in switched environments. VLANs can be used to limit the number of end stations in a broadcast domains, but VLANs are administrative entities — hence the "Virtual" nomenclature. Routers are still required to forward traffic between VLANs. In the third section, we will discuss when VLANs should be implemented.

Although considered necessary by most network architects, the continued deployment of routers began to slow in the latter half of the 1990s. High performance routers are expensive — often costing $120,000 and more. Also, the advanced functions performed by routers imposed a penalty of several milliseconds for every packet forwarded. Balancing the ratio of router and switch ports became something of a black science.

Focus on Redundancy

As networks proliferated in the late 1980s and early 1990s and more devices were being attached to corporate networks, the need for redundancy increased. Critical information resources were attached to networks so that extended outages could dramatically affect corporate operations. Protocols allowing redundant topologies were implemented, providing more robust network designs among routed and switched environments.

Spanning Tree Protocol (STP) was devised to allow bridges and switches to be connected in redundant topologies so that the failure of a single link or bridge/switch would not disable the entire network.

Several protocols for routers were also developed for the same purpose. Routing Information Protocol (RIP) and Open Shortest Path First (OSPF) allow routers to be connected in redundant topologies so that the failure of a single link or router would not disable the entire network.

These standard protocols allowed network managers to design much larger networks which would be more resilient to outages. Of course these new protocols also have drawbacks. Both of them require additional CPU capacity to process topology packets and to calculate routing table updates. In large networks, topology changes may take several minutes to fully propagate across all devices.

Network Device Evolution

As network designs and paradigms have evolved, the devices used to connect segments and networks have together also evolved. Briefly:

- Repeaters initially ran near wire speed for their particular medium, and the first generation of bridges were relatively slow. Bridges imposed a performance penalty.
- Bridges later became faster, and traversing router ports became network speed bumps.
- Switches appeared, operating at wire speed for several ports simultaneously and routers also became faster. However, routers remained significantly slower than switches.
- Recently, a new generation of switches has appeared that can perform both routing, and switching functions at wire speed. These new devices threaten to change once again the way networks are designed.

Given the breadth of choices available to network managers these days, how should modern networks be designed to provide the highest levels of performance, redundancy and manageability? The remaining sections will address this question.

TECHNOLOGY OVERVIEW

Broadcast Domain

A broadcast domain consists of the set of network components that will propagate broadcasts. Because broadcasts can occur at both Layer 2 (Data

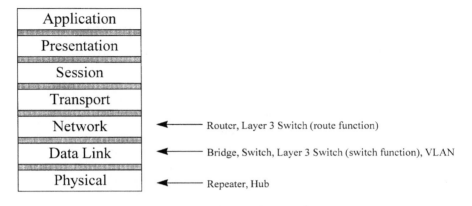

Exhibit 14.1. OSI Reference Model

Link) and Layer 3 (Network) of the Open Systems Interconnection (OSI) Reference Model, broadcast domains are defined less by protocol than by physical network topology. Specifically, any combination of segments, repeaters, bridges and switches comprise a broadcast domain. Typically routers act as boundary devices for broadcast domains (see Exhibit 14.1).

Collision Domain

A collision domain is the part of the network that will propagate a collision event. While collisions are particular to Ethernet environments, the analogous entity in a Token Ring network is a single ring. Effectively, the collision domain is the shared bandwidth portion of a given network. Each broadcast domain is composed of one or more collision domains. Since collisions occur at Layer 2 of the OSI Reference Model, any combination of segments and repeaters comprise a collision domain.

Repeater

A repeater is a network device that regenerates the shared media out all ports. Hubs and concentrators are considered repeaters in most network designs. Typically a repeater is used to extend the physical distance covered by a given network segment. Repeaters operate at the lowest layer of the OSI Reference Model. They do not process packets; they simply regenerate the bit patterns. A repeater extends the size of a collision domain (see Exhibit 14.2).

Bridge

A bridge is a network device that operates at Layer 2 of the OSI Reference Model. It connects to two or more LAN segments (collision domains) and

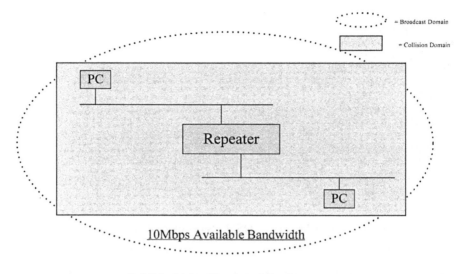

Exhibit 14.2. Repeated Environment

maintains a table describing which media access control (MAC) addresses (devices) are connected to each bridge port. Most bridges require minimal configuration; they learn where stations reside automatically.

From a bridge's perspective (Data Link—OSI Layer 2), there are only two type of packets—unicast and broadcast (see Exhibit 14.3). For unicast packets, the bridge attempts to match the destination MAC address in the frame header to one of its table entries. If the packet matches an entry *and* the destination MAC is the same port on which the packet was received, the packet is dropped. If the packet matches an entry *and* the destination MAC is on a different port than the one the packet was received, then the packet is forwarded out the destination port. Finally, if the packet does not match an entry in the table, then the packet is forwarded out all ports—similar to broadcast packets.

Bridges also forward broadcast packets. When a broadcast packet is received on a given bridge port, the packet is copied and propagated out all other bridge ports. This function can create broadcast storms in multi-bridge networks.

Router

A router is a network device that operates at Layer 3 (Network) of the OSI Reference Model. It connects two or more networks and maintains tables indicating which networks can be reached through each port. Most

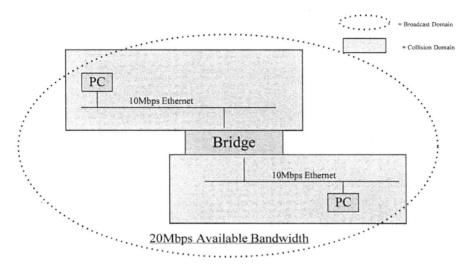

Exhibit 14.3.   Bridged Environment

---

routers require careful configuration—erroneous information entered into a router's configuration can create chaos on any network.

Routers interpret packets based upon information within the Network portion of a packet. They examine the protocol header to determine the destination network and perform a table lookup to determine the port with the most efficient path to the destination. The packet is then forwarded out the correct port (see Exhibit 14.4).

Unlike bridges, routers do not process every packet on each connected network. Only packets that need to travel from one network to another must traverse the router. In most cases, the network protocols help the sending machine determine if the destination resides on a local or remote network. If on a remote network, then the sending station will send the packet directly to the router.

Furthermore, unless specifically configured to do so, routers will not forward broadcast packets. Typically broadcast domains are bounded by router ports.

Switch

Switches function exactly like bridges, with only a few differences. Typically switches contain only LAN interfaces, while bridges may also support WAN connections. Switches may have much higher port density (e.g., 192 Ethernet ports in a single switch is not uncommon) than bridges.

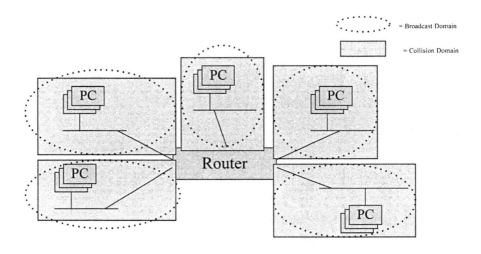

50Mbps Available Bandwidth

Exhibit 14.4.   Routed Environment

Switches are generally designed around an ASIC architecture (rather than a bridge's CPU oriented design) to provide much high levels of performance (see Exhibit 14.5).

Lastly, switches often have advanced features (such as VLANs) which allow more flexible configurations in LAN environments.

Layer 3 Switch

There is a lot of confusion regarding this new class of network devices, since Layer 3 devices have always been called routers. For the purpose of this chapter, we will consider Layer 3 switches to behave like high-speed routers with traditional switch functions.

Virtual LAN (VLAN)

Creating virtual LANs (VLAN) is a feature available on most switches sold today. A VLAN is a tool for creating broadcast domain boundaries within a set of switches. VLANs allow network administrators to control which devices are members of a particular broadcast domain. Some switches allow designers to select VLAN members based upon a variety of attributes such as: port, MAC address, protocol type. Many switches employ VLAN tagging (via 802.1Q or a proprietary protocol) so that multiple switches will be able to determine and share VLAN membership information (see Exhibit 14.6).

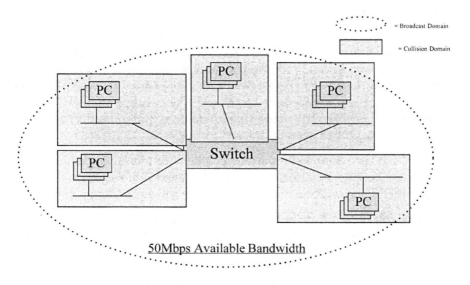

Exhibit 14.5.   Switch Environment

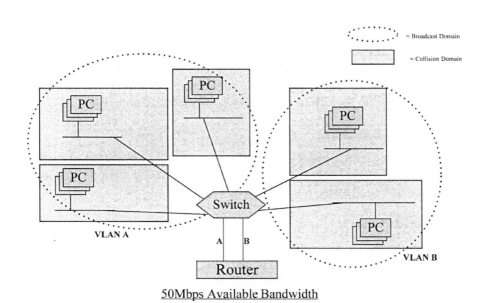

Exhibit 14.6.   VLAN Environment

VLAN Standards

Until recently, no standards have existed for VLANs and, for the most part, this has not posed a problem. Switch vendors implement VLAN tagging for packets traversing multiple switches differently, and as long as a network is composed of switches from a single vendor all is well. However, when a new vendor is introduced to a switch network, a standard tagging mechanism is required to ensure that all devices understand VLAN membership. This need has been addressed by 802.1Q.

IEEE 802.1Q provides a standard mechanism for identifying which VLAN each packet belongs to. Starting in late 1997, most Ethernet network interface cards (NIC) and Ethernet switch vendors will support this standard.

VLANs can be a powerful tool when designing networks, but without proper understanding of network protocols and topology, their use can create administrative and support difficulties—to say the least. The remainder of this chapter will discuss how VLANs, in conjunction with routing and switching, can best be implemented in modern networks.

WHEN TO USE SWITCHING

In most cases, switching is the simplest way to increase performance within a particular broadcast domain. Congested segments experiencing high collision rates can be efficiently segmented with minimal configuration changes. Installing switches typically does not require major changes to network designs, nor do end stations need to be modified. The network (broadcast domain) is simply more segmented and, therefore, provides more available bandwidth to network devices (see Exhibit 14.7).

Risk Factors—Switching

Although implementing switching does provide a performance boost to congested networks, other factors must be weighed before determining the extent to which switching should be deployed.

Management/Control

Extensive deployment of switching, without proper consideration for the size of (number of devices in) broadcast domains can create configurations that allow broadcast storms. Extensive broadcasts can congest the network by utilizing available bandwidth and preventing user data from accessing network resources. And since broadcast packets are processed by every station on a broadcast domain, workstations and servers must interrupt activities to inspect each broadcast packet — further slowing performance (see Exhibit 14.8).

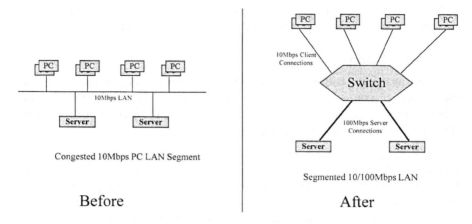

Congested 10Mbps PC LAN Segment

Segmented 10/100Mbps LAN

Before   After

Exhibit 14.7.   Switching Boosts Performance

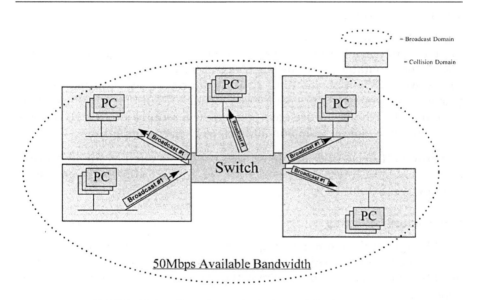

Exhibit 14.8.   Broadcasts in Switched Environment

Redundancy

Redundant switch configurations can be created with the Spanning Tree Protocol (STP). STP switches can be connected in redundant mesh topologies that will recover in the event of a link or switch failure. As with the Management/Control concerns, deploying too many switches in a spanning tree can limit the effectiveness of the redundancy. If large numbers of switches are participating in a tree, then recovery from topology changes can take significantly longer than smaller broadcast domains.

Key Design Points

When designing the switched portion of a LAN infrastructure, determining the appropriate size for each broadcast domain is fundamental. Once this decision is made, the appropriate amounts of performance (segmentation) and redundancy can be applied.

Network designers should be mindful of protocol issues when allocating broadcast domains. For example, each IP subnet should contain no more than one (switch-defined) broadcast domain because the protocol itself defines a broadcast domain within each subnet. The same is generally true for IPX networks (although a little more flexibility is possible)—each IPX network should contain no more than one broadcast domain.

When to Use Routing

Routing is the perfect complement to a switched LAN infrastructure. Routers are typically the best way to connect broadcast domains—particularly when routable protocols such as IP, IPX, and DecNet are used within the network. When connections to WAN interfaces are required, routers provide the deepest feature set for converting LAN-oriented traffic to wide area formats. Finally, secure environments will require a router to provide a measure of isolation from non-authorized user communities.

Through the use of dynamic routing protocols such as RIP and OSPF, large scale fault-tolerant networks can be created utilizing hundreds of routers (see Exhibit 14.9).

Risk Factors—Routing

Although implementing routing does provide an increased measure of management and security to switched and shared networks, other factors must be weighed before determining the extent to which routing should be deployed.

Performance

Today's highest performance routers are capable of forwarding approximately one million packets per second—a performance level more than adequate for last year's traffic. However, recent events such as the rapid adoption of Fast Ethernet (100M bps) and Gigabit Ethernet (1000M bps), combined with a traffic model oriented towards intranet architectures (where IP traffic commonly traverses subnet boundaries) are overloading traditional routers.

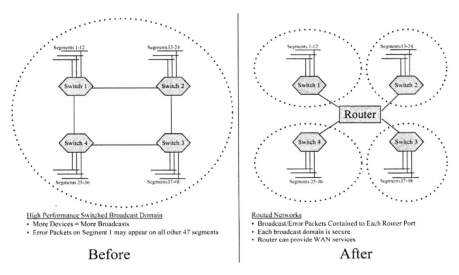

High Performance Switched Broadcast Domain
• More Devices = More Broadcasts
• Error Packets on Segment 1 may appear on all other 47 segments

Routed Networks
• Broadcast/Error Packets Contained to Each Router Port
• Each broadcast domain is secure
• Router can provide WAN services

Before   After

Exhibit 14.9.   Routing Adds Control

Because routing is an important function to network operation, a new generation of Layer 3 switches (also known as Wire Speed IP Routers), are now being offered to alleviate the IP router bottleneck. These new products can process between 5 million and 12 million IP packets per second. These performance levels allow network designers more creativity (flexibility) when determining where routing should be utilized in a network.

Key Design Points

Forgetting briefly the performance limitations of traditional routers, and thinking purely about routing functions, designers need to determine the optimal locations for routers in their networks. The same review that determined the best size for broadcast domains (in the switching section) must occur for routers as well (see Exhibit 14.10). Designers must review each protocol (IP, IPX, DecNet, etc.) and determine where traditional multiprotocol routers should reside and where high speed Layer 3 switches should complement them.

Currently, most high speed Layer 3 implementations perform limited firewall, multiprotocol (non-IP) and WAN functions. Using Layer 3 switches (wire-speed IP routers) for local IP traffic forwarding can free CPU and memory resources on traditional routers for these other tasks.

When to Implement VLANs

VLANs are probably the most misunderstood component of modern networking. Switch vendors have expended so much energy touting how

165

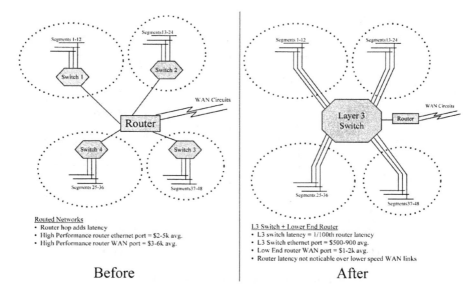

Before   **After**

Exhibit 14.10.   Layer 3 Switch Example

---

many VLANs their switches support and all the mechanisms available for creating VLANs, that many network architects feel that they must somehow implement VLANs in their designs. In fact, VLANs are not universally helpful for all networks. They can be instrumental in some situations, and this section will focus on those instances where VLANs make sense.

Protocol-Sensitive VLANs

Protocol-sensitive VLANs are one of the most powerful types of VLANs. Not all switch vendors provide the capability to create this type of VLAN, so careful research must be performed to ensure switch features can be delivered. Switches that provide protocol-sensitive VLANs read and interpret the "Protocol Type" field in the MAC frame header. Packets can then be categorized into a particular VLAN based upon the value of this field. This feature allows network designers to overlay multiprotocol networks in a manner that makes sense for each protocol (see Exhibit 14.11).

For example, a workgroup containing 300 (IP, IPX, and DecNet) users can be divided into 5 IP subnets, 1 IPX network, and 2 DecNet networks. The broadcast domain sizes can be set for each protocol according to the applications being used, the functional/security necessities of each workgroup, and the percentage of broadcast traffic generated by each protocol (see Exhibit 14.12).

166

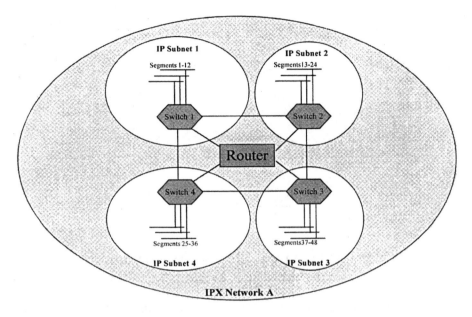

Exhibit 14.11. Protocol-Sensitive VLANs

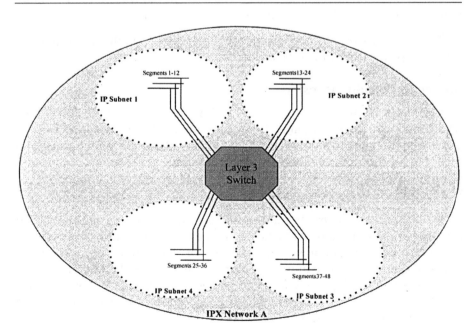

Exhibit 14.12. Protocol-Sensitive VLANs—Layer 3 Switch

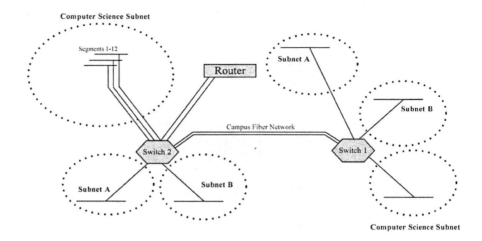

Exhibit 14.13. VLANs—Broadcast Domain Extension

Without protocol-sensitive VLANS, network designers are constrained by protocol limitations. In the example discussed previously, IP and DecNet parameters would have to be changed to sub-optimal values to accommodate the single large IPX (network) broadcast domain.

Protocol-sensitive VLANs also allow designers to limit the number of router hops for each protocol as needed.

Broadcast Domain Extension

Another powerful VLAN application is the geographical extension of non-traditional broadcast domains. Large campus environments may require broadcast domains to span multiple switches and, possibly, multiple buildings. For environments in which protocols such as IP are dominant and dynamic addressing services such as DHCP are not yet implemented, VLANs provide the best way to achieve continuity (see Exhibit 14.13).

For example, a university maintains a satellite computer science lab in the dormitories and a primary lab in the academic building. For security reasons, university administrators prefer to isolate computer science students from the general campus network. Implementing VLANs allows the computer science department to extend the same IP subnet from the academic building to the satellite lab using high speed switches rather than slower and more expensive router ports.

Without VLANs, the university's network designers would have few choices. One alternative: to create a new subnet for the satellite lab, which would require using an additional router port (expensive) and would impose an additional router hop (speed bump) on users in the satellite lab.

Risk Factors—VLANs

The majority of risks associated with VLANs have to do with over-implementing them. Designers who create too many VLANs—trying to categorize and separate every type of network user experience problems in scalability and complexity.

Redundancy

As broadcast domains, VLANs are, by definition, Layer 2 entities. Creating fault-tolerant topologies within VLANs therefore requires the use of Spanning Tree Protocol. Each VLAN requires a distinct spanning tree. So environments that have multiple overlapping VLANs require the switches to support multiple spanning trees. For many switches, the computation associated with maintaining multiple trees is too great to provide adequate performance levels—particularly in the event of a topology change.

Key Design Points

With the advent of high-speed switches that perform routing functions at wire speed, the necessity for VLANs is greatly reduced. Prior to Layer 3 switches, network designers attempted to reduce the number of router hops each packet had to traverse to reach its most common destinations. New Layer 3 switches, however, do not impose a performance penalty for crossing subnet boundaries, so routing can be deployed wherever needed.

The key point is that networks can now be designed according to the requirements imposed by protocols and applications rather than the limitations of devices that operate strictly at Layer 2 or Layer 3.

When considering VLANS, investigate the protocol mixture. Novell (IPX) environments can typically tolerate considerable larger broadcast domains than IP-based users and applications. Protocol-sensitive VLANs simplify overlapping broadcast domains for different protocols.

Also, investigate user distribution and redundancy requirements. In many cases, solutions more elegant than creating additional VLANs are available.

SUMMARY

Although demands on network managers are greater today than ever before and network complexity is at a peak, network designers have more choices at hand for developing scalable, high performance solutions. New classes of equipment allows network managers to satisfy requirements without renumbering many workstations over a weekend.

New networks can be built around real-life functional requirements rather than protocol and equipment constraints. The latest wire-speed Layer 3 switches allow network designers to implement both routing and switching functions—wherever needed—without sacrificing network performance, manageability, or scalability.

Chapter 15

Remote Access Concepts and Techniques

Peter Southwick

One of the fastest growing segments of the enterprise network is the area of remote access. Whether it is to access the Internet for fun and games or the corporate intranet for mission-critical information, the concerns and possible solutions are the same. In this chapter remote access is presented from three separate views. The first is a presentation of remote access scenarios and the concerns and solutions present in those scenarios. Each reader will recognize his own problems from those presented. The second view is an analysis of the platforms that are available today to solve those problems. The final view is of the options possible for the implementation of the solutions.

TYPICAL REMOTE ACCESS SCENARIOS

Considering the broad range of meanings that can be associated with "remote access," it is best to narrow the scope of what remote access means in this chapter. Remote access is a means by which a remote user (someone who is physically removed from direct connection to the corporate network) gains connectivity to the resources of a network. A further definition of remote access, for the principal focus of this chapter, is that the users utilize dial-up facilities for access.

Two distinct types of remote access are being used today. The first is when a user creates a dial connection to a device directly connected to the desired network. This type, which we will call direct-dial access, has been the cornerstone of remote access systems for the last decade. The second access type is when a user dials in to an intermediate service provider and is connected to the destination network via the Internet or some private network. This scenario, which we are calling indirect access, is becoming more common, especially where long distances are concerned.

Remote access is being used for a wide variety of applications today. School-age children are dialing in to schools to pick up homework assignments and perform research. College students are attending online classes, performing collaborative research and doing administrative tasks. In the corporate sector, remote access supports telecommuting, hoteling, remote (branch) offices, and Small Office/Home Office (SOHO) installations. It is said that the key to a successful telecommuting environment is access to the same resources in a similar manner as those personnel located at the corporate locations. Remote access is the key to this success. The same is true for all the applications using remote access. For the purpose of this chapter, our focus application is remote access to a corporate network. Remote access in scholastic applications have the same concerns and architecture as those described here.

In order to further define the architecture and protocols found in remote access situations, three distinct remote access scenarios must be explored. The first of these is the scenario in which the remote user has a local area network (LAN) and remotely connects this LAN to the corporate network. The second scenario is when a user has a PC in a fixed location (at their home or remote office) and via an attached communicating device (a.k.a. modem) connects to the corporate network. The final scenario is when an intermediate network provider carries the traffic between the remote access user and the corporate LAN.

LAN-TO-LAN DIRECT-DIAL SCENARIOS

In the case of the branch office, or SOHO, the typical implementation is that the office contains a LAN providing connectivity between the devices in the office (refer to the upper portion of Exhibit 15.1). The goal of the remote access is to connect the devices on this LAN to those at the corporate (main) location. At the remote location, the interconnection device of choice is the remote access router. This device is programmed to recognize a request for service for the main location and create a connection for the duration of the request. Once the request has been satisfied, the connection is terminated. At the corporate location, a similar device accepts the incoming request for service and provides connectivity to the resources of the corporate LAN. This type of remote access scenario is called dial-on-demand routing and provides an economical alternative to full period connectivity options. LAN-to-LAN scenarios have the benefit of having dedicated devices assigned to the task of providing connectivity. The remote access chore is transparent to the end users and their computers. A further benefit is that LANs are typically geographically fixed, allowing better security measures.

Fixed User-to-LAN Direct Dial Scenarios

The second scenario is that of the SOHO user who does not have a LAN (refer to the lower portion of Exhibit 15.1). The user's computer doubles as a remote access device and a computing system. When the user wishes to access information or an application on the corporate LAN, the PC cre-

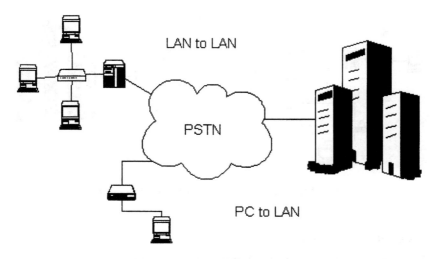

LAN to LAN

PSTN

PC to LAN

Exhibit 15.1.   Remote Access Scenarios

ates a connection to a server on the corporate LAN and a connectivity is achieved. If the operating system and the applications are savvy enough, the remote connectivity is transparent to the human user. If not, the user must establish the connection prior to the request. Two types of remote access sessions are possible in this scenario. The first is termed remote control. In a remote control session, the remote computer is acting as a remote terminal attached to the "server" or host computer attached to the corporate network. Once attached, the user has the full capabilities of the computer attached to the LAN. A possible scenario would be that you install a modem on your computer attached to the corporate LAN, leave it running, and go home. From home you dial in to this computer and run specialized, but available, software that allows you to control that computer. As one might surmise, remote control poses a great security risk. Could anyone else control this computer? For this reason, remote control has fallen out of favor for most corporations.[2] The second type of PC-to-LAN connection is called remote node. In this scenario, a remote computer is connected to a network access server or a communications server. Once verified, the user has full access to the resources of the corporate network. The remote node scenario allows the users access in a controlled fashion. A benefit of the remote node access is that the same computer can be used directly attached to the corporate LAN and remotely attached. Another benefit is that the network access server of the communication server has controlled pieces of equipment that can be secured from unauthorized access.

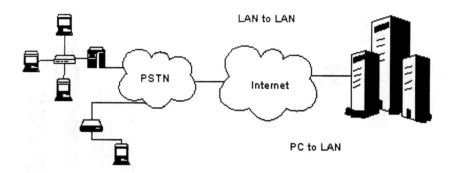

Exhibit 15.2. Indirect Dial Remote Access

Indirect-Dial scenarios

This scenario, as depicted in Exhibit 15.2, could be employed in either a LAN-to-LAN environment or a PC-to-LAN setting. In either case, the requesting device is not directly attached to the corporate LAN. Instead, the remote device connects to a network access server supplied by an Internet service provider (ISP) or an interconnect service provider. The remote access traffic is tunneled through this intermediate network (the Internet as shown in Exhibit 15.2) and delivered to the destination network. This scenario allows an assortment of equipment complements (routers or PC) to access the corporate network in a common fashion. It also allows the use of local ISPs for international remote users. In most cases, higher speed connections can be made to a local ISP than over an international direct-dialed call. Security is achieved through the use of tunneling protocols which can provide encryption and possibly compression for the remote access traffic.

CONCERNS AND SOLUTIONS

In all remote access scenarios regardless of the application, security is the number one concern. Security is followed closely by response time (speed) and, finally, a concern that has recently been giving network managers headaches, Addressing. In the following paragraphs, these concerns are discussed, along with an assortment of solutions.

Security

Today entire volumes are being written about security on corporate networks. Other chapters in this volume provide the details of firewalls and other security-related topics. For the purposes of remote access, two areas of security are discussed. These topics are presented in relationship to the threats found in remote access systems. The first threat is the uninvited

Exhibit 15.3. Security Issues

Security Threat	Network Solution
Hacking	Authentication, call back, caller ID
Spoofing	Digital signatures, digital certificates
Interception	Encryption, tunneling

user. If a modem is attached to a corporate network, it will be found by a curious user and it will be hacked. To counter this threat, authentication protocols and software can be installed. The second threat is the interception of valuable information by an eavesdropper. To counter this threat, encryption protocols are available. Exhibit 15.3 provides a summary of the security threats and their solutions.

Authentication systems today are available in two forms. The first and most common is the software-based authentication systems. The second, and more exotic, is hardware-based systems.

The software-based systems use an authentication protocol at link establishment to verify the user's identity and a digital signature associated with the information is used to verify that the information has not been tampered with. These protocols can be combined with caller identification and call-back options to create a very secure access environment. Once a user is connected and authorized, a threat still exists that someone could intercept information exchanged and insert unwanted data. To assure that what is sent is received, digital signatures are employed. The international standard for digital certificates is X.509. This system is more robust than password-based schemes.

Hardware authentication systems are based on the concept of the smart card. Each time a remote user dials in to the corporate LAN, the smart card is queried for an identifier/password. This code must match the code generated by the corporate mate to the smart card. This system, although costly, provides a very high degree of security.

Encryption is the second issue associated with securing the information requested or generated by the remote access user. Like authentication systems, encryption systems can be hardware-based or software-based. Encryption can be performed at the link level (encrypt everything going between the remote location and the corporate location) or at the data level (encrypt only the message, leaving the headers clear). The encryption key length is a critical element in the security of your information. The longer the key length, the better the security: A key of 128 bits is considered unbreakable, whereas a key of 24 bits can be broken in a matter of minutes by a determined party.

Speed

If network managers are concerned principally with security, remote access users are concerned about access speeds. A corporate user is connected to his resources by a multimegabit-per-second LAN; the typical remote user must deal with multiple kilobits per second access speeds. Recently, technologies have been introduced that are increasing the speeds possible for remote access users. Plain Old Telephone Service (POTS) modems have increased in speed and decreased in cost to the point where a 33K bps modem is the standard and 56K bps modems are readily available. The 56K bps modems offer an asymmetrical access, 56K bps in the down-stream direction and 33K bps in the up-stream direction.

An alternative to POTS is an Integrated Services Digital Network (ISDN) Basic Rate Interface access line. This technology offers speeds up to 144K bps and a combination of packet- (up to 16K bps) and circuit-switched (2 x 64K bps) access options. A new application of ISDN access is called Always-On/Dynamic-ISDN (AO/DI). In an AO/DI scenario the packet access is continuously connected to the corporate network; low-speed applications (i.e., e-mail and text-based browsing) use this access. When higher-speed access is required, the circuit-switched channels are activated, first one, then the other. When the requirements for the bandwidth are no longer needed, the circuit-switch channels are released and the packet-switched access is again used.[3]

The newest technologies for remote access are the Digital Subscriber Line (DSL) technologies. This family of access technologies is delivered to remote users on existing twisted pair (the same as POTS and ISDN). But due to specialized signaling techniques, they offer speeds that are predicted to hit 10M bps in the network-to-user direction. The common designator for the DSL technologies is xDSL, where x can be one of many letters. A (asymmetrical) DSL — one pair up to 8M bps to the user and up to 1.5M bps to the network; H (high bit rate) DSL — two pair 1.5M bps bidirectional; S (single line) DSL — one pair 786K bps bidirectional; RA (rate adaptive) DSL — one pair up to 12M bps to the user. The list is being updated and added to daily.

High speeds can also be achieved by the aggregation of multiple lower-speed circuits. This technique is generically called inverse multiplexing and can be performed in hardware as well as software. The most common hardware approach is defined by a protocol created by the Bandwidth On Demand Interoperability Working Group (BONDING). BONDING was designed around digital access technologies (i.e., ISDN) and provides the capability of aggregating multiple channels into a single high-speed access link. Software-based inverse multiplexers are based on an aggregation scheme called multilink point-to-point protocol (MP). This standard allows aggregation of channels of any type at any speed. MP can be implemented by most remote access devices, and it is by far the more common inverse multiplexing approach for remote access users.

Other options for remote access are appearing constantly; cable modems, wireless packet networks, and satellite-based networks are all possible today.

Addressing

Addressing has become a constant nag for network managers. Remote users must have a proper address, unique and with the correct network identifier in order to access the resources of the corporate network. If the network is based on the Transmission Control Protocol/Internet Protocol (TCP/IP) protocol suite, then other elements are also needed with the address, including the address mask, the address of the router, and the address of the name server. All of these addresses must be entered into the remote user's computer. If a LAN-to-LAN remote access scenario is being used, the task is lessened. But if the PC-to-LAN scenario is in use, and the PC is mobile or accessing the corporate network via the Internet, the problems increase. For the PC to LAN scenario, the problems associated with IP addresses can be resolved with the use of the Dynamic Host Configuration Protocol (DHCP). This protocol allows a remote access PC to access an address server, receive the required addresses, then access the network as a directly connected user. DHCP has an added benefit in that it allows the reuse of IP addresses (sometimes IP addresses are in short supply) between remote users. A small pool of addresses can be shared by a larger group of remote users. Another solution to the addressing problem is the use of address translation devices. With this system, the user maintains a single address and each time the user is connected to the network, the user's address is translated to a valid network address.

CHANNEL PROTOCOLS

The key to the success of the LAN has been the simplicity of the channel protocols found on the LAN. The MAC protocols provide all the services needed for access and control. In the remote access environment, no single protocol is available. Presented here are six classifications of protocols commonly found in the remote access environment. The first two classifications are used for basic transport on a single (simple protocol) channel or multiple (inverse multiplexing) channels. The third and forth classifications are security-based protocols providing authentication and encryption services to the remote access user. The final two classifications, tunneling and compression, provide value-added capabilities to a remote access environment.

Simple Protocols

The Serial Line Internet Protocol (SLIP) and the Point-to-Point Protocol (PPP) provide basic datalink protocol support for remote access users. SLIP is the minimalist's approach to a protocol. The user's information is framed with two known flag patterns, one at the beginning and another at the end. Whatever the user inserts between these two flags is transported across the access link. In certain situations, SLIP is the perfect solution for remote access. In opposition to SLIP, PPP has a suite of data link functions. PPP is based on a High-level Data Link Control frame format. As such it has bit error detection capabilities, protocol identification capabilities, and follows a strict data link initialization procedure. PPP has an additional capability of initializing network layer sessions as well. Multiple network layer protocols can be simultaneously supported on a single PPP data link. PPP has become the default and de facto standard for remote access users.

Inverse Multiplexing Protocols

When the bandwidth on a single channel is insufficient, two options exist: buy a bigger channel or add more channels. Due to economics, the second solution is often the only feasible one. If a second channel is added between the remote location and the host location, some mechanism must be employed to associate the information found on these two channels. This mechanism is called an inverse multiplexing protocol. The principal inverse multiplexing protocol is the MP. This is a frame-based inverse multiplexing protocol used in conjunction with PPP. In an MP scenario, the two ends of the connection (PC and network access server) agree on the number of channels being used and the characteristics of the channels. Once this handshake is performed, the devices statistically multiplex information over all the active channels. Modifications to MP can be found in the MP+ protocol described in RFC 1934 and in the ITU-T standard for inverse multiplexing H.323. One limitation of the MP protocol is the lack of a dynamic bandwidth allocation scheme that can add or subtract channels on an as-needed basis. To resolve this limitation, the Bandwidth Allocations Control Protocol and the Bandwidth Allocation Protocol were developed. These two protocols allow the negotiation of additional channels on the fly between a remote access device and a network access server.

Authentication and Integrity Protocols

To solve the problems associated with verifying the user's identity and the integrity of the information sent from a valid user, authentication protocols are employed. During PPP or MP session establishment, two adjunct protocols are employed to verify the identity of the users. These protocols, the Password Authentication Protocol (PAP) and the Challenge Handshake Authorization Protocol (CHAP) are used to pass user identities and passwords between remote access devices. When combined with caller identification and or a call-back scheme (the remote user dials in to the network access server, and the server releases the call and places a call back to the user) PAP and CHAP provide a very secure authorization mechanism.

An additional problem exists in that an authorized user gains access only to have his information intercepted, appended to, and resent, the appendage being some sort of a tool for later exploitation. To prevent this type of intrusion, an upper layer integrity protocol is employed. Integrity protocols are commonly called digital signatures in the sense that they seal a packet of information. Digital signatures typically employ some form of a hash algorithm that appends a binary value to the sent information that is generated by the content of the information. At the receiver, this value is verified, and if correct, the information is tamper-free. Some digital signature standards are the Secure Hash Algorithm (SHA-1) Message Digest 2 through 5 (MD2.. MD5) and the Distributed Authentication Security Service.[4]

Encryption Protocols

The principal use of remote access is for corporate network access. Often, mission-critical information is being passed between the remote locations and the corporate locations. To prevent this information from being stolen, encryption protocols are employed. Two types of encryption can be employed in a remote access scenario. The first is the use of a link level encryption device. This type of device is engaged once the remote access call is answered and encrypts all data sent between the devices. Link level encryption devices are typically hardware-based and expensive to use and deploy. The second type of encryption is an upper layer encryption protocol. This software is engaged once the remote access link is established and encrypts only the information being transmitted. Framing information is passed in the clear. These systems are the more common. Examples of upper layer encryption standards are Data Encryption Standard, Pretty Good Privacy, and Secure IP (IPsec). One final issue with encryption standards is that the U.S. federal government considers them to be national secrets and allows only the export of certain protocols. For international remote access users, this means that restrictions must be adhered to. In recognition of this restriction, most encryption protocols are available in export and U.S.-only versions, the difference being the length of the encryption keys.

Tunneling Protocols

When an Internet-based remote access scenario is used, the best security mechanism is the use of a tunneling protocol. The concept is simple: encapsulate your data in the normal full stack of corporate protocols, encrypt it, then re-encapsulate this entity in a tunneling protocol that resides in a transport layer protocol that is routed as data through the

Internet. With so many layers of protocol, who can find your data? Tunneling protocols are classified as Layer 2 or Layer 3 tunneling protocols. In a Layer two protocol, the user's information to include the Layer 2 frame (i.e. PPP) is tunneled through the Internet. In Layer 3 tunneling, only the network layer is passed between devices. Layer 2 protocols are based on the RFC-1701 description called the Generic Routing Encapsulation (GRE). GRE defines the basics of tunneling information through the Internet. Implementations of the concept defined in the GRE specification are Microsoft Corp.'s point-to-point tunnelling protocol (PPTP) and Cisco System Inc.'s L2F. These two protocols have been combined into the L2TP standard, which is currently a draft RFC. Layer 3 tunneling protocols are newer and less stable than the Layer 2 protocols. An example is IPsec, which defines a mechanism for tunneling IP traffic over the Internet.

Compression Protocols

The final classification of protocols found in the remote access environment are the compression protocols. Compression provides an increase in throughput without an increase of bandwidth. Compression standards take one of two forms, the first being the file compression standards (i.e., PKZIP from PKWare Inc.). These standards squeeze a file prior to transmission. At the destination, the file is expanded prior to use. The second type of compression system is a real-time compression. Data to be transported is compresses prior to encapsulation. At the receiver, the expansion takes place when the data is received, not when it is used. Examples of this real-time compression are Stac Inc.'s LZS compression and Microsoft's compression tunneling protocol. Both of these are proprietary in nature. A standards-based real-time compression scheme is proposed for the IPsec standard.

SECURITY AND AUTHENTICATION DEVICES

One of the most varied segments of the remote access technology market is the security segment. The technology currently spans between simple password and biometrics information (voice, finger print, face recognition). In the following paragraphs we will explore key three elements of this segment. These elements are graphically depicted in Exhibit 15.4. The first is the network access server, which is the first line of defense in any security system. The second is the authentication server. These devices allow or deny users based on stored information. Finally, key management systems allow secure transfer of information over the remote access links.

Network Access Server

Network access server is a generic term used to define a group of components that bridges the gap between remote access users and the corporate network. Components of a network access server might perform: routing, encryption, tunneling, filtering (firewall), and/or authorization. What a

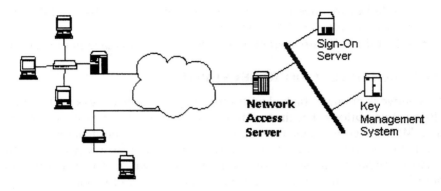

Exhibit 15.4. Security Devices

network access server definitively does is respond to a remote access request for services, verifies the identity of the user, and connects that user to the corporate network. A can also be the light at the end of the tunnel. In a remote access system using the Internet, the network access server terminates the tunneling protocol and passes the original protocol to the corporate LAN.

Single Sign-ON (SSO) Standards

A remote access system needs a standards-based remote authorization database that matches client information (i.e., user ID, password, and calling line identification) to the accessed system (corporate network). A SSO is used as opposed to a local authentication system. Two standards are supported today, the Remote Authentication Dial-In User Service (RADIUS) and the Terminal Access Control Access Control System (TACACS). Both are widely supported and feature-rich.

Key Management Systems

If encryption is required in the remote access system, then a key management mechanism is required. Key management systems are tasked with automatically keeping encryption keys updated, eliminating the need to manually update the security keys at each location of a remote access system. The key distribution is performed by the central and remote nodes establishing a secure, authenticated session and updating the key information. Examples of key management protocols are

- Internet Security Association and Key Management Protocol (ISAKMP)/Oakley — NSA — the IETF standard for key management.
- Diffie–Hellman — an encryption and key management mechanism.

- Simple Key Management for Internet Protocol (SKIP)—Sun Microsystem Inc.'s entry into key management.
- A digital certificate system that includes a key management system.

WHAT DO I HAVE TO DO TO GET STARTED?

A network manager tasked with setting up a remote access system actually has two options. The first option is to outsource the remote access system. Multiple companies are willing to provide the technical expertise to set up and install these systems. The second option, as always, is that the network manager can set up the system on his own. As the size, the number of simultaneous access scenarios, and the geographic reach of the system increase, the outsourcing option becomes more attractive. If the Internet is used as the remote access vehicle, again, outsourcing becomes an attractive option.

Outsourcing

One of the factors that goes into the selection of outsourcing is the geographic scope of the network. Outsourcing companies are typically regional, national, or international in scope. Since the competition is more severe in the smaller markets, a better deal could be made by staying with a regional or national provider. Identifying local outsource companies requires a small amount of sleuthing. Telephone companies, ISPs, retailer, and consultants all might have leads to a reputable regional company. At the national level, three established names are ANS, PSINet, and UUNet Technologies. At the international level IBM's Global Network, AT&T Corp.'s WorldNet, and MCI Communication Corp.'s Concert are all possibilities. When negotiating the outsourcing deal, be sure to do the following:

- Specify what level of security is required for your system. This is a key factor in determining the remote access scenario that is correct for your installation.
- Specify the speeds required for the remote access personnel. Test various options to determine an optimum level. Because the bandwidth bottlenecks are not always the access system, a 1M bps access speed might not provide any faster throughput than a 128K bps access line.
- Determine how many simultaneous users are required at any one time. Savings can be achieved by reducing the number of access lines, but this increases the chances of a user receiving a busy tone. Exact numbers (number of access lines and blocking probability) can be found by performing a traffic engineering study.
- Determine the functions and features provided by the outsourcing company vs. what is a customer's (your) responsibility. An example is

that if an Internet tunneling system is used, the customer typically provides the authorization hardware and software.

- Determine whether the equipment to be used for the remote access system will be dedicated to your company or shared with others. Shared equipment has a lower upgrade cost than dedicated equipment. Also determine the growth costs of the system.

Do it Yourself

If the setup of the remote access system is within your capabilities, then the preceding questions must be answered, and the answers will determine the type of software, hardware, and security to be used at the remote and central locations. As a memory aid, remember the "PASS" to remote access:

- Protocols — choose a Data Link and Network layer protocol.
- Access Lines — select one or more types and an appropriate number.
- Scenario — which is being used, LAN to LAN or PC to LAN?
- Security — determine the type and amount of authorization, integrity, and/or encryption that are required.

SUMMARY

This chapter has presented a number of critical issues surrounding a fast growing segment of the enterprise network, remote access. The concerns associated with remote access were presented along with a number of possible solutions. The goal of all remote access users is unlimited speed and ironclad security. Hopefully we have started you on a path to meet these goals.

Bibliography

Cohen, F. B., *Protection and Security on the Information Superhighway*, John Wiley & Sons, New York, 1995.
Kessler, G. and Southwick, P., *ISDN*, McGraw-Hill, New York, 1998
Cisco Systems Inc., Router Products Configuration Guide, Cisco Systems, San Jose, CA.

References and URLs

IPSec RFC 1825, RFC 1826, RFC 1827 — http://www.faqs.org/rfcs/
Key Management — HTTP://WEB.MIT.EDU/NETWORK/ISAKMP
PPTP (Point-to-Point Tunneling Protocol) — http://microsoft.com/windows95/info/pptp4w95.htm
ANS — http://www.ans.com
PSINet (Sprint Corp.) — http://www/si/com
UUNet Technologies — http://www.us.uu.net
Internet Secure Association Key Management Protocol, Oakley was added by ARPA's Hilarie Orman, http://hegel.ittc.ukans.edu/topics/internet/index.html

INTERCONNECTIVITY BASICS: PUTTING THE PIECES TOGETHER

Notes

1. Full period connectivity options include leased line circuits, frame relay, or other packet/cell access circuits.
2. In a leading high-tech company, anyone found installing a modem and remote control software on their corporate PC is dismissed.
3. Additional information on AO/DI can be found at the North American ISDN User Forum's (NIUF) Web site.
4. Further information about digital signature standards can be found in Cohen, F. B., *Protection and Security on the Information Superhighway*, John Wiley & Sons, New York, 1995.

Chapter 16
Remote Access Authentication

Ellen Bonsall

The computing world has evolved from a centralized environment consisting of single mainframes and multiple dumb terminals to a distributed client/server networking environment. Given this global change in information systems (IS), networking industry experts around the world agree that the management of information systems — particularly network security — is an increasingly difficult task for executives of today. IS managers live with the fear that a great financial loss due to an unforeseen network security breach will be blamed solely on the IS team.

Complex distributed networks have made security a critical component of network architecture. Client/server technology is delivering sensitive data and mission-critical applications directly to the desktop. Most of security products of today are designed to do one specific job, without regard to their roles in the larger security scheme. Without appropriate protection on both the Internet and enterprise sides of the network, an organization is vulnerable to even the simplest of attacks. To protect information assets of an organization, IS teams must establish security policies, procedures, and systems to support these assets.

USER AND CLIENT AUTHENTICATION

IS security professionals must combine the task of integrating worldwide authentication services across multiple networking platforms with that of securing information in the burgeoning distributed and mobile computing environment. User and client authentication must be the foundation of any viable network security plan. To compete in the global economy of today, CEOs, CIOs, and IS professionals are seeking ways to seamlessly tie employees, business and technology partners, suppliers, and customers together for information sharing — while simultaneously protecting sensitive data.

The market for remote access security and authentication products boils down to one fact: people want to know with whom they are dealing. However, as advancing technology makes complex distributed networks the norm, rather than the exception, it becomes increasingly difficult to guarantee that information will be protected from unauthorized users. It can be devastating for individuals and organizations when sensitive information falls into the wrong hands. IS professionals should track patterns of information crime, study the ways in which other organizations have dealt with network security breaches, and keep abreast of the latest products designed to protect information assets.

The specter of unauthorized local area network (LAN) remote access has caused many IS departments to consider an authentication complement for their network security schemes. Even with added protection, however, systems are vulnerable. IS security is not just about protecting electronic communications from Internet criminals. Moreover, a new range of access points in current open systems has made it possible to hack into systems from sites located anywhere in the world. To establish easy-to-use, cost-effective safeguards, IS security professionals must coordinate with CEOs, CIOs, IS staff, and users to address basic security fundamentals. Optimum solutions cannot be achieved without user cooperation and participation. Regardless of how fail-safe a system may appear, if users can disable it or gain access to information without having to comply with established security standards, the safeguard is useless. Finally, many organizations put the cart before the horse by installing the latest security panacea (e.g., an internal or external firewall) without first establishing an overall security policy. It is essential to effective access and user authentication strategies to pinpoint exactly what is being protected and from whom.

DEFINING THE SECURITY PROCESS

If an organization does not already have an official security policy that is endorsed at all levels of management, it is essential that the IS team gather the necessary parties and create one. Some departments may already have policies; the basic elements of these may be relevant to an organizational policy. The policy should be implemented as soon as possible and should, above all, mandate an enterprisewide user authentication solution that can be scaled to differing security requirements.

The IS team should develop a code of conduct for employees, and should require that employees sign a compliance document once they have read and understood the code. To further ensure compliance, the team should plan to educate employees about the importance of security and the value of information to the organization. Employee awareness programs are useful for this purpose.

Making Enterprise-Specific Security Choices

Myriad solutions exist to combat security problems of today, some of which cost more than others both in time and monetary investment. Vendors of firewalls, routers, and communications servers are continually integrating the latest technology to make their security products more reliable. IS staff who are responsible for choosing and implementing such products should carefully compare products before purchasing and implementing them. The best security solutions for an organization are not necessarily those used by other organizations in the same industry. Primary in importance is that the IS team begins the process and establishes safeguards, with the assumption that products will require constant review and updating. Before addressing specific strategies for securing servers with either native options or third-party systems, IS staff should take special care to secure any server that can be accessed remotely or that can be accessed from other remotely accessed servers on the wide area network.

When evaluating security tools, it is useful to establish the goals of the organization security system, including the user authentication facet of security. IS staff should establish exactly what the security and remote access authentication system will protect, who will be permitted access, and, relatedly, who will be denied specific access. The more specific the outline of user access requirements is, the more comprehensive remote access security will be. The success of these access objectives can be measured when the system is implemented, and the objectives can be changed as personnel, networks, and organizational goals change.

IS staff should draw up written procedures that detail how and when the security systems will be audited. In addition, an independent, internal or external audit team should look over the systems at least quarterly, and the members should be fully aware of all of the security and access objectives of the organization. When the independent audit team submits a report, any noncompliance should be addressed by the IS team immediately.

Establishing Basic Controls

A number of fundamental controls should be implemented in any organization to secure Internet and dial-up remote access.

Management Controls. Technical personnel within the organization should be trained before they are permitted to cruise the Internet or to dial in to the LAN through a remote connection. If the organization is connected to external networks, IS staff must understand the risks and manage these connections properly. In addition, a policy on the acceptable use of the Internet should be distributed to all employees. Internet access can negatively affect productivity unless reasonable limits are set and enforced.

IS staff should also establish and execute procedures for reporting and resolving detected breaches of remote access security. Procedures should include reporting breaches to management or to external organizations such as the Computer Emergency Response Team (CERT). Monitoring programs that scan the system regularly for Trojan horses, sniffers, and other undesirable programs and data are also fundamental security tools.

Inbound Traffic Controls. Inbound traffic controls include the implementation of network and node application restrictions through a firewall to limit access by remote connection to applications. Additional application controls should be installed, such as restrictions on certain types of transactions that a remote user may process. IS staff should maintain logs of all activity originating through remote access and review the logs for anomalies.

Authorization and authentication of employees must be required to view or modify internal application data. Users requesting access through an external network or remote access must also be authenticated. Proxy log-ins should be prohibited; allowing one user to act for another invites unauthorized access.

Outbound Traffic Controls. Systems security is often designed to protect an organization's networks from those who would attempt to break in. It is just as critical, however, that outbound traffic controls be established to monitor the information that leaves the organization. Implementing such controls can be very difficult, as the legal tangle of personal privacy and e-mail vs. corporate liability demonstrates. At a minimum, IS staff should maintain logs of all external network activity originated by internal users and identify and communicate to users any risks or potential threats (e.g., viruses).

File Transfer Controls. To ensure that records are transmitted and that data is received, IS staff should implement manual or automated controls to monitor file transfers. Executable code should be transmitted by only systems and applications designed to prevent unauthorized or inadvertent execution. It is usually difficult to protect against data-driven attacks, or attacks in which something is mailed or copied to an internal host and then executed. All attempts at unsolicited distribution of executable files should be called to the attention of management. Executable files are a popular way to spread viruses.

IS staff should control the use of the file transfer protocol site through a proxy server. If this is not possible, another way of restricting incoming connections to the network must be explored.

Defining Remote Access: Establishing a Common Vocabulary

Once an organizational policy has been written and fundamental controls implemented, remote access and authentication can be targeted. The security team must ensure that everyone in the organization shares a common, remote access vocabulary, so that all of the security provisions will be fully understood and complied with.

In most organizations, IS departments struggle to maintain control of information in the midst of rapidly changing strategic business and communications issues. Health care systems are an effective example of this. Instead of having users dial in to three or four different platforms and use different equipment for applications that might include claims entry, individual eligibility, and claim status verification, an IS team could purchase an integrating access server to centralize remote connections. A single dial-in access connection would allow users to access multiple hosts across diverse platforms.

AUTHENTICATION

Authentication should not be confused with identification or authorization. The IS team must agree on the definition of remote access user authentication and the tools associated with it before it makes decisions about specific technologies or products.

- **Identification.** User identification is the process by which people identify themselves to the system as valid users. The log-on process is an example of a simple user identification. Identification is not the same process as authentication, which establishes that the person logging on to the network is indeed that user.
- **Authentication.** Authentication is the process of determining the true identity of a user or an object (e.g., a communications server) attempting to access a system. It is the confirmation of the claimed identity.
- **Authorization.** Authorization is the process of determining what types of activities are permitted. In the context of authentication, once the system has authenticated a user, he may be authorized for various levels of access or different activities.
- **Authentication token.** This is a portable device (or software loaded directly on a PC) that is used for authentication. Authentication tokens use a variety of techniques, including challenge-response asynchronous, event-time-based synchronous, and time-only-based synchronous technologies.
- **Authentication tool.** An authentication tool is a software or hand-held hardware "key" or "token" used during the authentication process.

Remote Access

The generic term "remote access" is commonly applied to terminal emulation, file transfer and network management. Remote access software (such as Symantec Corp.'s PCAnywhere) makes PC drives or peripherals available to other computers. It can dial up another PC through a modem, query the hard drive of that computer, and give commands to print or to transfer files. Basic remote access software does not give as high a level of power as remote control products, which establish the PC as a node on the LAN. In using remote access software only, the access control measures provided by it are not robust enough to protect against unauthorized intrusion.

Remote Control

Remote control is the taking over of a host system with a PC keyboard and mouse and viewing its screen from anywhere in the world. The user can run programs, edit and transfer files, read e-mail, or browse a distant database. The user can dial up with a modem or a node-to-node LAN connection and take complete charge of the screen, keyboard, and mouse of another computer. The simplest remote-control scheme is a synchronous, one-to-one, dial-up connection between modems attached to two PC. Whatever mode, or combination of modes, the user's network employs, user and client authentication are vital to protecting information assets.

When a remote node connection is established, the PC is actually sitting on the LAN with which it has been connected. The PC or workstation is connected to all of the network services of the remote PC. The user has access to any services or information for which it has been authorized. Therefore, if the remote network does not have an authorization, identification, and authentication system in place, the user may roam at will.

A limited, secure connection can be established first through the use of a remote control software package and the use of any security features native to the operating system or communications hardware. If levels of security are required that are not provided by native security, third-party authentication technology should be added.

SIX COMPONENTS THAT SECURE REMOTE ACCESS

Authenticating LAN dial-up users is a starting point in evaluating user authentication technology. A variety of reasons for controlling access to the LAN and to office network workstations exist, but not all of them are about protecting the organization. Protecting the privacy of personal information is a top priority for many companies or users. Most users create personal information on their computers. No one wants such personal information made public. By controlling access, business plans and proposals, pricing figures, payroll information, and other sensitive information can be kept from prying eyes. Controlling access also reduces the chances of virus infection and slows the spread of an infection, should one occur.

Authenticating users preserves the integrity of information. By locking out unauthorized users, the chances that someone will make unwanted (or unintentional) changes to critical files are reduced. Six components are critical to secure remote access:

- Authorization
- Authentication
- Confidentiality
- Auditing
- Control
- Nonrepudiation

Authorization

The key to secure remote access is to understand and integrate the critical components without leaving anything out. Network managers must be able to authorize users (i.e., control who on the network may access which resources). Properly implemented, authorization systems prohibit the engineering department, for example, from reading the CEO's business projections. Authorization systems should provide secure, single sign-on, which allows users to log on to a network once and to gain access to all the resources that they require (but none of the ones that they are unauthorized to have).

In most cases, authorization systems are comprised of complex software packages with code that executes on specifically secured computers on the network. Some examples are: IBM's, Cygnus Support's, and Cyber-SAFE's Kerberos-based systems, and ICL Enterprises North America's SESAME-based system. However, such security is limited by the specific platforms on which they work.

User Authentication

Authentication is the process of verifying the identity of end users (and clients). It should be considered a basic building block of secure remote access. A critical component of any network architecture, user authentication employs passwords — the most common method of authenticating users. Virtually all network operating systems offer limited password protection, as do most communications servers and other applications that allow access to a network. The reusable (i.e., static) passwords that are employed are easy to use, but they offer an extremely limited degree of security. User authentication takes place after entry into the system with common ID and resuable passwords. Security is very lax. Reusable passwords have been shown over a lengthy period of time to be the least successful way to protect networks.

Why are static, reusable passwords so easy to steal or guess? Several intrinsic weaknesses are found in reusable passwords. First, most people have a difficult time remembering passwords, especially if they must remember many different passwords that are unique to each network or application that they use. Typically, they give the passwords to co-workers or paste them in visible areas for easy reference, especially if the IS staff requires them to change the passwords on a regular basis. Second, if permitted to choose their own passwords, they often pick trivial ones that are easy to remember. These may include permutations of their names, their children's names, or personal information, such as date of birth. Trivial passwords are common words that are subject to "dictionary attacks" or simply educated guesses, which is not a very secure form of authentication. Third, static passwords are vulnerable because it is possible to steal them electronically. This can be done either by unauthorized insiders or by outsiders (i.e., hackers) through a "password sniffer" or similar program designed to monitor and record the names and passwords of authorized users as they log onto a network. Because of these basic weaknesses, reusable passwords seriously jeopardize overall communications security. It is too easy to impersonate authorized users by logging on with passwords that actually are legitimate to access restricted information.

To solve this problem, network security experts are now choosing from a variety of authentication systems that generate one-time-use-only (i.e., dynamic) passwords for a greater degree of user authentication and, therefore, information security. Handheld authentication devices (e.g., tokens) employ encryption and public or proprietary algorithms to calculate these one-time-use-only passwords (or responses) to random challenges issued by authentication servers residing on the network. More specifically, there are stand-alone devices (i.e., hardware boxes) placed in front of a communications server or router to provide authentication prior to network entry; and software security servers (i.e., software running on a dedicated machine designed to operate directly on the network), for example, on a Windows NT or UNIX box. Server-based authentication software responds to requests originating from network access control points, such as firewalls, remote access servers, or O/S security software.

An Authentication Security Server. An authentication security server is not a communications server. In many cases, third-party vendors work with the manufacturers of firewalls, communications servers, and routers to integrate user authentication technology so that users may be authenticated before they pass through gateways to the LAN. Types of communications servers that integrate third-party user authentication technology include: Shiva Corp.'s LANRover; Microsoft Corp.'s NT Remote Access Service (RAS) Server; Attachmate's Remote LAN Node Server (RLN), a Cisco Systems Inc. router operating as a communications server; Checkpoint Systems Inc.'s firewall; and Atlantic Systems Group's TurnStyle firewall. The entire authentication process is dependent on the use of tokens (either hardware or software) so that one-time-use passwords used for authentication can be generated on both ends of the authentication process and then compared before access is granted. (Passwords are generated on the user's end, by the token, and at the network server end, by the authentication server.)

Authentication Tokens

Some of the tokens that work with the previously mentioned authentication servers may be used to verify dial-up users, users already on LANs, or users seeking access to a LAN through the Internet. Different tokens have different capabilities. Some products even authenticate users connecting through fax machines or telephones. Tokens can be small, handheld hardware devices, a connector-size device that sits between a computer and a modem, or software that runs on the user's PC. Some have more complex features and are considered more secure than others. However, all challenge–response tokens serve the same purpose. They generate passwords that a user's PC transmits to an authentication server that resides at an access point on a network. Alternatively, they transmit them to authentication software residing on, for example, a Microsoft NT Remote Access Server. The authentication servers (or the software residing on a PC or workstation located directly on the network) verify that the users are who they say they are when they first identify themselves.

Challenge–Response, Asynchronous Authentication

In a secure, challenge–response, asynchronous authentication process, network managers typically configure the tokens themselves — a definite benefit over factory-issued secret keys. No one except the network manager or administrator has access to the database of user secret keys and other pertinent user information. A LAN dial-up remote access can provide an example on how this works. A user dials up remotely, and before the network allows the user access, the call is intercepted by a master authentication device (or a software authentication server), which prompts the user for an ID. When the user is identified as one of the individuals allowed access to the network, the server issues a random, alphanumeric challenge to begin the process of authenticating (i.e., determining that the user is who he says he is).

That random challenge is used by both the token and the server to calculate a one-time-use password based on a secret key value stored in both the token and the server. The process typically involves the use of an encryption algorithm. The reliability of the algorithm used in the authentication solution of an organization should be carefully evaluated.

Solutions that employ the challenge–response process, secret user keys, and encryption algorithms to generate passwords result in a very high level of authentication security. The one-time-use passwords are issued only once, can be used only once, and even if stolen or captured, can never be used again. The mathematics involved in the encryption process to calculate the passwords makes it essentially impossible to reuse them.

Synchronous-Only-Based Authentication

Time-only, synchronous authentication is based on time clocks and secret keys that reside in two places: on the network (i.e., protected) side and on the user side (i.e., the side to be authenticated). On the network side, a time clock and database of secret keys operate in either a dedicated authentication hardware box or in a software authentication server. On the user side of the authentication equation, a clock, which is synchronized to the authentication server, and a secret key (corresponding to a secret key in the server) operate inside the token.

Several implementations are possible of time-only, synchronous authentication. In one specific, time-synchronous scheme, a proprietary algorithm continually executes in the token to generate access codes based on the time clock and the secret key of the token. In this case, the time is the "variable." A new access code is generated by the token approximately once a minute. The token is always activated. When the user dials in to the authentication server, the server issues a prompt to the user for an access code. The user simply attaches his or her secret Personal Identification Number (PIN) to the code currently displayed on his token at the moment access is required, and then the user transmits the combined PIN and code (which become the "one-time password"). This code is transmitted over telephone lines to the authentication server. The server uses the PIN to identify the user to compare the transmitted access code with its own current version for that user.

In a different implementation of time-synchronous authentication, the user enters his secret PIN to activate the token, which then generates a true, one-time-use password based on the token time clock and a secret key value stored inside the token. This system is more secure because the password generated does not include the PIN when it is transmitted over public telephone lines or networks. PINs should always remain secret to be considered a viable part of the "two-factor" authentication process. "Two factor" refers to something secret that only the user knows (i.e., his PIN) and something held in the user's possession (i.e., his token). For secret information to remain secret, it should not be transmitted in any way that allows unauthorized individuals to hack the information and use it at a later date. If someone captures a PIN as it is being transmitted over public telephone lines, it would be relatively easy to steal the token and use it to gain unauthorized access. It does not matter if the access code is considered a one-time-use password: if a thief has the PIN and the token, he has what is needed for unauthorized access to confidential information.

Window of Time

Time-only synchronous authentication systems are based on making available a "window of time" within which the password match must occur. The time clocks in the server and the token must remain "in sync" because the time is the variable on which the calculation depends. If the clocks are too far off, the user is denied access.

At this point, the technologies differ. When the token becomes out of sync with the server, there must be an efficient, cost-effective, user-transparent way to resynchronize the token. The user would be frustrated if he had to return his token for reprogramming before the information being requested is accessed. Centralized and remote token resetting capabilities should be considered, as well as the conditions under which tokens must be replaced. Replacing tokens or having to return them to a system administrator for resetting can be time-consuming and expensive. Authentication tokens should be "unlocked" remotely, preferably with some prearranged signal or code that only the user and the network administrator know.

Finally, the time on the token clocks gradually drifts, resulting in a lack of synchronization. If there are no provisions for unlocking or resetting, or for automatic switching of modes of operation (e.g., from synchronous to asynchronous) to back up the synchronous token, the authentication server, by necessity, will have to provide a larger "window of time" during which a user can be authenticated. Otherwise, too many tokens would go out of sync too often. The larger the window of time, the greater the security risk that someone will intercept passwords or PINs (if they are part of the transmission).

Synchronous, Event-Plus-Time Authentication

In event-plus-time synchronous authentication, the token also uses an algorithm and a secret key to generate passwords. However, it is based on two dynamic variables, instead of one, which increases the level of password security. The two variables are an event counter (i.e., the primary variable) and a time clock (i.e., the secondary variable). In one particular implementation of synchronous, event-plus-time authentication, there is also a third variable — a unique secret key that is calculated each time a password is generated by the token. This key becomes the secret key used to generate the succeeding password the next time the user activates the token. The first variable, "event," refers to the number of times a password has been generated by the token. The second variable, "time," refers to the clock counter in the token. The third variable — the new, unique key generated each time a password is issued — makes these event-time-synchronous passwords the strongest on the market.

For all synchronization authentication systems, questions should be asked about overall system management and token secret parameter programming. For example, network administrators should be able to maintain control not only of locking–unlocking procedures, but also of the user database, the setting of security parameters, and token programming. To comply with internationally recognized computer security standards, there should always be a "barrier" between the factory, which produces the tokens, and the customer, who operates those tokens. Specifically, secret parameters should be set by the customer, not by the vendor. Tokens that are programmed at the factory (or by the vendor) should be viewed with caution. It is possible that such products may result in people outside the organization having access to secret key values, user databases, and other basic token operations. These functions form the basis of secure user authentication. Such operations should remain under the auspices of the network administrators at all times.

A final point to consider with synchronous authentication systems is system management. Managing sites with a large number of users can become a daunting task under certain conditions. Questions should be asked about how the technology is going to handle distributed or centralized authentication system and token management, and how many servers will be necessary for the variety of access points or geographical locations that be must secured. The answers to these should be compared with other solutions. In the case of some technologies, cost-effective, efficient authentication system management can be impossible to achieve, and it may be necessary to purchase a larger number of authentication servers with one technology than with another. The cost of the overall user authentication system should be considered, not just the cost of the tokens, whether they hardware or software. Finally, when considering the cost of tokens, the frequency of replacement should be considered.

CONCLUSION

This article has discussed several methods of authenticating users: time-based-only synchronous authentication; event-plus-time-based synchronous authentication; and challenge–response asynchronous authentication. Each offers a different level of security and reliability when it comes to user authentication. The choice depends on the overall security policy of the organization and the depth of user authentication required. The technology of the different types of user authentication tokens should be carefully compared. The authentication technology requirements may be quite simple if security requirements are limited. On the other hand, an organization may require more reliable technology, such as two-factor, challenge–response asynchronous, or event-plus-time-based synchronous authentication. In an Internet atmosphere headed toward universal standards, the scalability and reliability of authentication systems based on technology that is not standards-based, or authentication-based on a time clock only, should be considered highly suspect.

Chapter 17
Working with Cisco Access Lists
Gilbert Held

An access list represents a sequential collection of permit and deny conditions that are applied to certain field values in packets that attempt to flow through a router interface. Once an access list is configured, it is applied to one or more router interfaces, resulting in the implementation of a security policy. As packets attempt to flow through a router's interface, the device compares data in one or more fields in the packet to the statements in the access list associated with the interface. Data in selected fields in the packet are compared against each statement in the access list in the order in which the statements were entered to form the list. The first match between the contents or conditions of a statement in the access list and one or more data elements in specific fields in each packet determines whether or not the router permits the packet to flow through the interface or sends the packet to the great bit bucket in the sky via a filtering operation.

At a minimum, router access lists control the flow of data at the network layer. Because there are numerous types of network layer protocols, there are also numerous types of access lists, such as Novell NetWare IPX access lists, IP access lists, and Decnet access lists. Due to the important role of IP in accessing the Internet and in the construction of intranets and extranets, this article focuses on the examination of access lists that support the Transmission Control Protocol/Internet Protocol (TCP/IP) protocol suite.

THE TCP/IP PROTOCOL SUITE

To obtain an appreciation for the manner by which IP access lists operate, a brief review of a portion of the TCP/IP protocol suite is in order. At the application layer, the contents of a data stream representing a particular application in the protocol suite, such as a file transfer, remote terminal session, or an electronic mail message, are passed to one of two transport layer protocols supported by the TCP/IP protocol suite — the Transmission Control Protocol (TCP) and the User Datagram Protocol (UDP).

0-8493-9838-X/00/$0.00+$.50
© 2000 by CRC Press LLC

Both TCP and UDP are layer 4 protocols that operate at the transport layer of the International Standards Organization (ISO) Open Systems Interconnection (OSI) Reference Model. Because a host computer operating the TCP/IP protocol stack can support the operation of multiple concurrent applications, a mechanism is required to distinguish one application from another as application data is formed into either TCP or UDP datagrams. The mechanism used to distinguish one application from another is the port number, with each application supported by the TCP/IP protocol suite having an associated numeric port number. For example, a host might transmit a packet containing an e-mail message followed by a packet containing a portion of a file transfer, with different port numbers in each packet identifying the type of data contained in each packet. Through the use of port numbers, different applications can be transmitted to a common address, with the destination address using the port numbers in each packet as a mechanism to demultiplex one application from another in a data stream received from a common source address. Port numbers are assigned by the Internet Assigned Numbers Authority (IANA), which maintains a list of assigned port numbers that anyone with access to the Internet can obtain.

TCP is a connection-oriented protocol that provides a guaranteed delivery mechanism. Because a short period of time is required to establish a TCP connection prior to obtaining the ability to exchange data, it is not extremely efficient for transporting applications that only require small quantities of data to be exchanged, such as a management query that might simply retrieve a parameter stored in a remote probe. Recognizing that this type of networking situation required a speedier transmission method resulted in the development of UDP. UDP was developed as a connectionless, best-effort delivery mechanism. This means that when a UDP session is initiated, data transmission begins immediately instead of having to wait until a session connection is established. This also means that the upper-layer application becomes responsible for having to set a timer to permit a period of time to expire without the receipt of a reply to determine that a connection either was not established or was lost.

Although both TCP and UDP differentiate one application from another by the use of numeric port values, actual device addressing is the responsibility of IP, a network-layer protocol that operates at layer 3 of the ISO OSI Reference Model. As application data flows down the TCP/IP protocol stack, either a TCP or a UDP header is added to the data, with the resulting segment of data containing an appropriate port number that identifies the application being transported. Next, as data flows down the protocol stack, layer 3 operations result in an IP header being prefixed to the TCP or the UDP header. The IP header contains the IP destination and IP source addresses as 32-bit numbers, which are frequently coded when configuring the protocol stack as four numerics separated by decimal points, resulting in the term "dotted decimal notation" used to reference an IP address in this format. Here, the destination IP address represents the recipient of the packet, while the source IP address identifies the originator of the packet.

Based on the preceding, there are three addresses that can be used in an IP access list for enabling or disabling the flow of packets through a router's interface: the source IP address, the destination IP address, and port number that identifies the application data in the packet. In actuality, Cisco Systems and other router manufacturers also support other IP-related protocols — such as the Internet Control Message Protocol (ICMP) and Open Shortest Path First (OSPF) protocol — as a mechanism to enable or disable the flow of predefined types of error messages and queries; an example of the latter is an ICMP echo packet request and echo packet response.

USING ACCESS LISTS

In a Cisco router environment, there are two types of IP access lists one can configure: standard or basic access lists and extended access lists.

A standard (basic) access list permits filtering by source address only. This means one can only permit or deny the flow of packets through an interface based on the source IP address in the packet. Thus, this type of access list is limited in its functionality. In comparison, an extended access list permits filtering by source address, destination address and various parameters associated with upper layers in the protocol stack, such as TCP and UDP port numbers.

Configuration Principles

When developing a Cisco router access list, there are several important principles to note. First, Cisco access lists are evaluated in a sequential manner, beginning with the first entry in the list. Once a match occurs, access list processing terminates and no further comparisons occur. Thus, it is important to place more specific entries toward the top of the access list.

A second important access list development principle to note is the fact that there is always an implicit deny at the end of the access list. This means that the contents of a packet that do not explicitly match one of the access list entries will automatically be denied. One can override the implicit deny by placing an explicit 'permit all' as the last entry in the list.

A third principle regarding the configuration of access lists concerns additions to the list. Any new access list entries are automatically added to the bottom of the list. This fact is important to note, especially when attempting to make one or more modifications to an existing access list.

This is because the addition of statements to the bottom of an access list might not result in obtaining the ability of the list to satisfy organizational requirements. Many times, it may be necessary to delete and recreate an access list instead of adding entries to the bottom of the list.

A fourth principle concerning access lists is that they must be applied to an interface. One common mistake some people make is to create an appropriate access list and forget to apply it to an interface. In such situations, the access list simply resides in the router's configuration memory area but will not be used to check the flow of data packets through the router, an effect similar to leaving the barn door ajar after spending time to construct a fine structure. Now having an appreciation for key access list configuration principles, one can focus on the creation (basic) of standard and extended Cisco router access lists.

STANDARD ACCESS LISTS

The basic format of a standard access list is:

access list number {permit|deny} [ip address] [mask]

Each access list is assigned a unique number that both identifies the specific list, as well as informs the router's operating system of the type of the access list. Standard Cisco IP access lists are assigned an integer number between 1 and 99. A new release of Cisco's router operating system permits access list names to be defined. However, because named access lists are not backward-compatible with earlier versions of router operating system, numbered lists are used in the examples presented in this article.

Because standard access lists only support filtering by source address, the IP address in the above access list format is restricted to representing the originator of the packet. The mask that follows the IP address is specified in a manner similar to the way in which a network mask is specified when subnetting an IP address. However, when used in an access list, the binary 0 in the mask is used as a "compare" while a binary 1 is used as an "unconditional" match. This is exactly the opposite of the use of binary 1s and binary 0s in a network mask to subnet an IP address. Another difference is that, in Cisco router terminology, the mask used with an access list is referred to as a wildcard mask and not as a network mask or a subnet mask.

To illustrate the use of a Cisco router wildcard mask, assume that the organization's router is to be connected to the Internet. Further assume that a World Wide Web server will be located behind the router and one wants to allow all hosts on the Class C network whose IP address is 205.131.176.0 access to the server. If using a traditional network mask, its composition would be 255.255.255.0. Writing the network and mask in binary would result in the following, where the letter 'x' represents a "don't care" condition in which either a binary 1 or binary 0 can occur in the appropriate bit position.

```
network address   205.131.176.0

11001101.10000011.10100110.00000000

network mask   255.255.255.0

11111111.11111111.11111111.00000000

-------------------------------------------------------------

       resulting address match

11001101.10000011.10100110.xxxxxxxx
```

Note that a binary 1 in the network mask represents a compare, while a binary 0 represents an unconditional match. When working with Cisco access lists, the use of binary 1s and 0s in the wildcard mask is reversed. That is, a binary 1 specifies an unconditional match, while a binary 0 specifies a compare condition. However, if one attempts to use the same mask composition instead of reversing its composition, one will more than likely obtain a result that does not meet operational requirements. This is illustrated by the following example, where a wildcard mask is used instead of a network mask.

```
network address   205.131.176.0

11001101.10000011.10100110.00000000

wildcard mask   255.255.255.0

11111111.11111111.11111111.00000000

-------------------------------------------------------------

       resulting address match

xxxxxxxx.xxxxxxxx.xxxxxxxx.00000000
```

In the above example, any value in the first three octet positions are allowed as long as the value in the last octet was all 0s. This is obviously not a satisfactory solution to the previously assumed Web server requirement. However, if 0s are placed in the wildcard mask where one would normally place binary 1s in the network mask, and vice versa, then one properly defines the wildcard mask. Modifying the masking operation one more time obtains:

network address   205.131.176.0

11001101.10000011.10100110.00000000

wildcard mask   0.0.0.255

00000000.00000000.00000000.11111111

----

resulting address match

11001101.10000011.10100110.xxxxxxxx

Note that the creation of the above mask results in specifying any host on the 205.131.176.0 network, which is the requirement one was attempting to satisfy. The use of Cisco wildcard masks can be a bit confusing at first (especially if one has a considerable amount of experience in using subnet masks); but once the concept is grasped, it is easy to apply to an access list as a subnet mask to a network address. However, it is extremely important to remember that the wildcard mask is a reverse of the network mask to include the function of binary 1s and 0s and their positioning in the mask and to apply it accordingly. With an understanding of the creation and use of Cisco wildcard masks, one can now return to the example and complete the creation of a standard access list. That access list would be constructed as follows:

access list 77 permit 205.131.176.0 0.0.0.255

In this example, the list number 77, being between 1 and 99, identifies the access list as a standard access-list to the router's operating system. Also note that the network address of 205.131.176.0 and a wildcard mask of 0.0.0.255 results in a "don't care" condition for any value in the last octet of the network address, permitting any host on the 205.131.176.0 network to have its packets flow through the router without being filtered.

A few additional items concerning access lists warrant attention. First, if one omits a mask from an associated IP address, an implicit mask of 0.0.0.0 is assumed, which then requires an exact match between the specified IP address in the access list and the packet to occur for the permit or deny condition in the access list statement to take effect. Second, as previously mentioned, an access list implicitly denies all other accesses. This is equivalent to terminating an access list with the following statement:

access list 77 deny 0.0.0.0 255.255.255.255

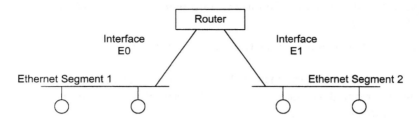

Exhibit 17.1. Using a Router to Interconnect Two Ethernet Segments

To provide another example of the use of a standard access list assume that an organization uses a router to connect two Ethernet segments together, as illustrated in Exhibit 17.1. In examining the use of the router illustrated, let's assume that Segment 1 has the network address 198.78.46.0 and one wants to enable clients with the host addresses .16 and .18 on Segment 1 to access any server located on Segment 2. To do so, the initial router configuration to include applying the access list to the outgoing interface on Ethernet 1 (E1) would consist of the following statements:

```
Interface ethernet 1
access-group 23 out
access list 23 permit 198.78.46.16 0.0.0.0
access list 23 permit 198.78.46.18 0.0.0.0
```

In the preceding example, note that the access group statement is used to define the data flow direction that is associated with an access list. Also note that the access list was applied to the outgoing interface on Ethernet 1 instead of the inbound interface on Ethernet 0 (E0) toward the router from Segment 1 as an inbound access list. While either method would work, the latter method would have the potentially undesirable effect of blocking all other traffic from leaving Segment 1. Thus, in this example this author elected to apply the access list to the outgoing interface on E1.

With an appreciation for standard IP access lists lets, one can now focus attention on their extended cousin.

EXTENDED ACCESS LISTS

A standard access list is limited to specifying a filter via the use of a source IP address. In comparison, an extended access list provides the ability to filter by source address, destination address, and upper-layer protocol information, such as TCP and UDP port values. In fact, extended access lists provide the ability to create very complex packet filters with capabilities that can significantly extend beyond the capabilities of a standard access list.

Extended access lists have the following format:

access-list number {permit|deny} protocol source IP address
source-mask destination IP address destination-mask /[operator
operand][established]

Similar to standard access lists, extended access lists are numbered. Extended access lists are numbered between 100 and 199 to distinguish them from standard IP access lists. The protocol parameter identifies a specific TCP/IP protocol, such as ip, tcp, udp, icmp, and several routing protocols that can be filtered. Examples of the latter include the Interior Gateway Routing Protocol (IGRP) and the Open Shortest Path First (OSPF) routing protocol. The arguments source IP address and destination IP address represent the source and destination IP addresses expressed in dotted decimal notation. The arguments source-mask and destination-mask represent router wildcards used in the same manner as previously described when examining the operation of standard access lists. To obtain the ability to specify additional information about packets for filtering, one can include the optional arguments operator and operand in the extended access list. When used, the operator and operand can be employed to compare tcp and udp port values. Concerning tcp and udp, the argument operators can be one of the following four keywords:

lt	less than
gt	greater than
eq	equal
neq not	equal

In comparison, the argument operand represents the integer value of the destination port for the specified protocol. For the TCP, the additional optional keyword "established" is supported. When specified, a match occurs if a TCP datagram has its ACK or RST field bits set, indicating that an established connection has occurred.

To illustrate an example of the use of an extended access list, assume that the router illustrated in Exhibit 17.1 will be connected to the Internet. Further assume that one wants to enable any host on the network behind the router whose IP address is 198.78.46.0 to establish TCP connections to any host on the Internet. However, also assume that, with the exception of accepting electronic mail via the Simple Mail Transport Protocol (SMTP), it is organizational policy to bar any host on the Internet from establishing TCP connections to hosts on the 198.78.46.0 network.

To accomplish this, one must ensure that the initial request for an SMTP connection, which is made on TCP destination port 25, occurs from a port number greater than 1023. The originator should always use destination port 25 to access the mail exchanger on the organization's network and that host using a port number greater than 1023 to respond. Based on the preceding and assuming that the address of the mail exchanger on the 198.78.46.0 network is 198.78.46.07, the following two access lists would be employed:

```
access-list 101 permit tcp 198.78.46.0 0.0.0.255 0.0.0.0
255.255.255.255
access-list 102 permit tcp 0.0.0.0 255.255.255.255 198.78.46.0
0.0.0.255 established
access-list 102 permit tcp 0.0.0.0 255.255.255.255 198.78.46.07
eq 25
interface serial 0
ip access-group 101
interface ethernet 0
ip access-group 102
```

In the preceding example, note that access list 101 is applied to the router's serial port and is constructed to enable any host on the 198.78.46.0 network to establish a TCP connection to the Internet. The second access list (numbered 102) in the above example is applied to the Ethernet 0 (E0) interface illustrated in Exhibit 17.1. The first statement in the 102 access list permits any TCP packet that represents an established connection to occur, while the second statement in the access list permits TCP packets from any source address flowing to the specific network address 198.78.46.77 with a port value of 25 to flow through the interface. Thus, an inbound connection via port 25 must occur in order for the firs statement in the 102 access list to permit succeeding packets with port numbers greater than 1023 to flow through the router.

LIMITATIONS

Although access lists provide a significant capability to filter packets, they are far from a comprehensive security mechanism. Thus, in concluding this examination of Cisco access lists, a few words of caution are in order concerning their limitations.

In examining access lists, one notes that they are constructed to filter based on network addresses. This means that they are vulnerable to address impersonation or spoofing. Another key limitation associated with the use of access lists is the fact that they cannot note whether or not a packet is part of an existing upper-layer conversation or what the conversation is about.

This means that a person could run a dictionary attack through the packet filtering capability of a router if that person's address was not barred. Similarly, a host that is allowed FTP access could issue an mget *.* command and retrieve several gigabytes of data from a server, in effect creating a denial of service attack. Due to the preceding limitations, most organizations supplement router access lists through proxy services incorporated into a firewall — which will be the subject of a subsequent article in this series.

Chapter 18
Securing Your Router
Gilbert Held

A router represents an entry point into most networks as well as the primary communications device used to move data between networks. As such, it represents a very strategic communications networking device because the inadvertent or intentional change in its configuration could have a major bearing on the ability of an organization to maintain its network in a desired state of operation. In addition, if routing tables or other parameters are altered, it becomes possible for organizational data to be directed to locations where such information could be recorded and read by third parties. Thus, it is important to understand how one can access and take control of a router and steps one can employ to secure this communications networking device.

This article examines and discusses methods of router access in both general and specific terms. The discussion of router access in general terms will be applicable to products manufactured by different vendors. However, for specific methods of access and methods one can use to secure access to a router, specific details applicable to routers manufactured by Cisco Systems will be used to supplement the generalizations. The selection of the use of examples specific to routers manufactured by Cisco Systems is based on this vendor currently having approximately a 75 percent share of the market for routers. Although specific examples of methods to protect access to routers in this article will be oriented toward Cisco routers, most routers manufactured by other vendors include similar capabilities. If an organization uses routers manufactured by another vendor, one should check the vendor's router manual for the access security functionality of that router. One should also check the specific commands supported by the router to facilitate one or more access security features for enabling, disabling, and protecting access to the device.

NEED FOR ACCESS SECURITY

When considering router security, most people automatically think of router access lists. Router access lists are used to establish restrictions on the transfer of data through router ports and are considered by many to represent the first line of defense of a network. Although router access lists are an extremely important aspect of network security, this author

0-8493-9838-X/00/$0.00+$.50
© 2000 by CRC Press LLC

considers them to actually represent the second line of defense of a network. This is because the ability to access and configure a router represents the first line of defense of a network. If other than designated personnel obtain the ability to access and change the configuration of organizational routers, this means that any previously developed access lists can be altered or removed — in effect, stripping away any previously developed network protection. Similar to the farmer who constructs a solid henhouse but inadvertently goes home at the end of the day and leaves the door ajar, failure to secure access to organizational routers permits predators of the two-legged variety to gain access to valuable resources.

Probing deeper into router access, one will note that there are several methods to bar the proverbial door to this communications device. In fact, one method to be discussed involves the use of an access lists as a mechanism to control access to the router to certain predefined IP addresses. However, prior to doing so, one must lock the door, which should be accomplished prior to the use of the access list capability of the router. Thus, the use of access lists should be viewed as a second line of defense.

ROUTER ACCESS

For the purposes of this article, the term "router access" represents the ability of a person to connect to a router and gain access to its operating system. Most routers include one or more serial ports built into the device that permits terminals or personal computers operating a specific type of terminal emulator to gain access to the router. This terminal access can occur directly via a direct cable connection or remotely via a communications path that results in a modem or DSU connected to a router's serial port. Although the use of a serial port connection is the primary method used by most organizations to provide access to a router's operating system to enable the device to be configured, it is not the only method of access. Additional methods supported by many routers include Telnet access and the use of the trival file transfer protocol (TFTP) to store and transmit system images and configurations files to and from routers and workstations.

Telnet Access

Telnet provides the ability to access a remote device to include a router as if the terminal device operating a Telnet client program was directly connected to the remote device. Telnet access to a router can occur from in front or behind a router, with the term "in front" used to reference access to a router via a wide area network connection from a station located on another network not directly connected to a specific router, while the term "behind" references a station located on a network directly connected to a routers local area network port. This means that Telnet access to a router can occur from a device located on a local organizational network or, if the router is connected to the Internet, from virtually any terminal device in the world that has Internet access. This also means that regardless of the location of the client operating the Telnet program, the operator of the program only needs to know the IP address of the network interface of the router to attempt to initiate a Telnet session to the router and gain access to the device. If the operator of the Telnet client makes a connection to the router, the operator will receive a prompt, such as routername (where routername represents the name an organization assigned to the router).

It should be noted that many organizations have an IP addressing policy where they assign low addresses to router interfaces. For example, if an organization's Class C IP network address was 205.123.124.0, it might assign 205.123.456.1 as the address of the interface from the 205 network to the router. Due to this common scheme of addressing used by many organizations, it is often easy to determine the address of a router for subsequent telnetting attempts. At this point in time, a Telnet client operator may be able to directly access all of the router's configuration capabilities and in effect take over control of the router. As an alternative, the Telnet client operator may be prompted to enter a password to gain access to the router. Concerning the latter, many routers are configured at the factory to have a default password for Telnet access. Unfortunately for many organizations that should know better, one should never use a default password. This is because such passwords are listed in the vendor's router manual, which may be available for purchase for $29.95 or available for access via the World Wide Web for free. This means that a virtually unlimited number of persons have the ability to discover the default password needed to access a router via a Telnet connection.

If the router administrator fails to change the default Telnet password or does not place any additional restrictions on Telnet access, anyone with knowledge of the IP address of the router interface can gain access to the device. As noted later in this article, if the router administrator overlooks another aspect of device access control, a security hole big enough to literally move a truck full of hackers will be opened, enabling literally millions of remote users to obtain the ability to take control of an organization's router.

TFTP Access

Most routers have two types of memory: conventional random access memory (RAM) and nonvolatile memory. Unlike conventional RAM wherein contents are erased upon the removal of power, the contents of nonvolatile memory remain in place. When configuring a router, nonvolatile memory is commonly used to store an image of router memory as well as backup or alternative router configurations. Because routers do not contain diskettes nor do they have hard drives, their ability to store more than one or perhaps a few alternative configurations is severely limited. This means that administrators that require the ability to store backup or alternative router configurations beyond the capacity of the limited amount of router nonvolatile memory typically do so on a workstation and use the trivial file transfer program (TFTP) to load and save router system images and configuration files. This also means that if TFTP access is enabled, depending on how the router supports TFTP access, it may be possible for unauthorized persons to create configuration data that, when used by the router results in a breach of security or an unintended operational environment.

Now that one has an appreciation for the main methods that can be used to gain access to a router, one can focus on the methods that can be used to either protect such access or literally lock the door on the access method, making it extremely difficult for nonauthorized persons to gain access to a router and obtain the ability to view and possibly change the configuration of the device. In doing so, this article will also, when applicable, discuss certain Cisco Systems router commands.

SECURING CONSOLE AND VIRTUAL TERMINALS

After unpacking a router and initiating its installation process, it is extremely important to consider the manner by which access to configuring the device will occur. If one only plans to enable configuration changes to occur from a directly connected terminal device, then one should ensure that Telnet and TFTP access are disabled. In a Cisco router environment, one can configure access from the console and virtual terminals via the use of the *line* command. That command has the following format:

line [type-keyword] first-line [last-line]

where information in brackets represent options. The type-keyword entry can be either *console*, *aux*, or *vty*.

The *console* entry is used to represent a console terminal line, representing a device directly cabled to a port on the router. In comparison *aux* is used to indicate an auxiliary line and allows one to specify access via a port on the router connected to a CSU, DSU, or modem, permitting serial communications from afar. The third option, *vty*, represents a virtual terminal connection for remote console access. Note that when entering the line command, the first and last lines represent a number of contiguous entries that are applicable to a specific device and can be represented and associated with a line number.

When configuring access through the use of the *line* command, it is also important to consider associating a password with the device that one enables for access. Even if one only plans to allow access to a router via a directly cabled terminal device located in a secure technical control center, every once in awhile a situation can occur that would justify password protection. In one event this author is familiar with, a tour of the technical control center of a government network by a group of Boy Scouts resulted in one extremely inquisitive individual inadvertently causing a big havoc. As the rest of the grouped moved to an area of the technical control center to view a graphical display of the status of the network, this inquisitive individual started playing with a terminal that was directly cabled to a router and that functioned as the router console. Not knowing what to enter, the Boy Scout entered a question mark (?), which resulted in the display of router commands. Within a short period of time, this Boy Scout managed to misconfigure the router while the rest of the group were on the other side of the center listening to a briefing given by the manager of the center. Needless to say, if a password was previously associated with terminal access, the unintentional misconfiguration of the router and the resulting havoc it created would not have been possible.

In a Cisco router environment, one can associate a password with a remote access method. To do so, one would use the password command? For example, the line console password "bugs4bny" would block console access until the console operator responded with the password "bugs4bny" to a prompt generated by the router for a password.

The password associated with the Cisco password command can be up to 80 characters in length. The password is case sensitive and can contain any combination of alphanumeric characters to include spaces. While this capability provides the router administrator with the ability to be innovative, it also provides the ability to make it extremely difficult for authorized users to gain access to the router. This is because selecting a password based on a large number of varying upper- and lower-case letters mixed with numerics makes it subject to erroneous entry. While this type of password will certainly be difficult to guess and should avoid the possibility of a successful dictionary attack, it is also easy for an authorized router administrator to enter incorrectly. If incorrectly entered three times, a Cisco router will return the terminal attempting access to the idle state of operation. Thus, when selecting a password, it is important to remember several password principles. First, use a mixture of alphabetic and numeric characters to alleviate the potential of a dictionary attack being successful. Second, when structuring a password, remember that as one extends the length of the password, one also increases the possibility of password entry error. In general, passwords that are between six and eight characters in length should be sufficient if they are structured to join a few abbreviated words with a sequence of numerics.

FILE TRANSFER

As previously noted, TFTP is commonly supported by routers as a mechanism to permit system image and configuration files to be stored on workstations. In a Cisco router environment, to enable the loading of network configuration files at router reboot time, one must specify the *service config* command, as fortunately the default is the disabling of this capability. If this capability is enabled, the router will broadcast a TFTP read request message and the first station to respond will have the file with a specific name based on the router's configuration loaded into the router across the network. Because a standardized file-naming scheme is used, this author believes it is best to consider leaving this feature in its disabled state instead of opening the ability for inquisitive employees with a bit of knowledge to "see what would happen" if they create a configuration file.

INTERNAL ROUTER SECURITY

Once access is gained into a router, the operating system of the device can provide a further level of protection capability that one can use for additional router access security. In a Cisco router environment, the command interpreter included in the operating system is referred to as the EXEC. The EXEC has two levels of access: user and privileged.

The user level of access allows a person to use a small subset of all router commands, such as commands that enable the listing of open router connections, commands for providing a name to a logical connection and displaying certain statistic concerning router operations. In comparison, the privileged level of access includes all user access commands as well as commands that govern the operation of the router, such as the configure command that allows a router administrator to configure the router, the reload command, that halts the operation of the device and reloads its configuration, and similar commands that have an active effect on the operational state of the device.

Due to the ability of a person gaining access to the privileged mode of operation of a Cisco router obtaining the ability to directly control the operation of the router, this level of access can also be password protected. Thus, when installing a Cisco router, it is important to use the *enable-password* configuration command to protect access to the privileged level of router access. For example, to assign the password "power4you" for the privileged command level, one would use the *enable password* command as follows:

    enable password power4you

Similar to the password associated with a serial terminal line, the password assigned to the privileged command level is case sensitive, can contain any mixture of alphanumeric characters to include spaces, and can consist of up to 80 characters. Thus, by placing a password on the serial port or on any allowed virtual terminal connections as well as on the privileged command level of the router, one protects both access into the router as well as the use of privileged commands once access is obtained.

ADDITIONAL PROTECTIVE MEASURES

If one needs to provide one or more persons on a network with the ability to configure one or more routers, one can add an additional layer of protection beyond passwords. To do so, one can program one or more router access lists. Although the use of router access lists will be the subject of a subsequent article by this author, one notes that they represent a sequential collection of permit and deny conditions that can be applied to Internet addresses. This means that if one can determine the IP addresses of stations that will require the ability to have operators configure one or more routers via a network connection, then one can use the access list capability of each router to restrict Telnet access to each router to one or more specific IP addresses. This means that not only does the terminal operator need to know the correct passwords to gain access to an appropriate router, but in addition, the operator can only perform such access from predefined locations. By combining password protection into a router with password protection to its privileged mode of operation and restricting configuration access to predefined locations via the use of one or more access lists, one can, in effect, close the proverbial door to the router.

Section 3
Advanced LAN and Interconnectivity: Building Enterprise Networks for the New Millennium

LAN and interconnectivity technologies do not stand still, nor do advances in technology move in a straight line. To build and maintain state-of-the-art LAN-based enterprise networks effectively, LAN and IT managers need to be cognizant of a number of trends. This section explores issues and solutions most likely to impact network design in the early years of the new millennium. Effective deployment of technologies such as these will position LAN and IT managers to be long-term value-added partners in their respective enterprises.

We begin our look at advanced technologies by examining an often overlooked component, the lowly network interface card (NIC). Chapter 19, "Advances in NIC Technology," considers the role NICs play in LAN performance, paying particular attention to the relationship between the NIC and the data bus architecture of the machine in which the NIC is installed.

When LANs first emerged on the scene nearly a quarter century ago, many visionaries marveled at their seemingly unlimited potential, while skeptics openly wondered how anyone could possibly need so much bandwidth. In those days, LAN speeds ranged from a few hundred kilobits to a "blazing" top end of 10 megabits per second. As the new millennium dawns, one does not have to look far to find cases where such speeds are constraining factors or even unacceptable bottlenecks. Clearly, the appetite for bandwidth continues to increase, and there is no end in sight. To assist today's LAN manager in evaluating the current options, Chapter 20, "Emerging High-Bandwidth Networks," provides a survey of the high bandwidth solutions available in support of a range of applications.

One particular high bandwidth technology, ATM, has eluded all attempts at prediction by the industry's best prognosticators for more than half a decade. Despite the fact that the oft-predicted "Year of ATM" never materialized, ATM has made steady inroads in both campus and wide area network deployments, and must be given serious consideration by any enterprise network planner evaluating high bandwidth strategies. Chapter 21, "ATM Access: The Genesis of a New Network," examines the state of ATM as it existed in the industry in 1999, and lays the groundwork for solid early-millennium planning.

Another networking trend that has confounded analysts over the years is that of voice and data integration. The business case for combining the two forms of information has always been compelling, but the solutions were too far apart technologically for any significant progress to be made. Nonetheless, many predictions have long been made that eventually data traffic would be absorbed into the already-ubiquitous voice infrastructure. At the same time, any suggestion that voice traffic would be absorbed into data networks was quickly discounted as infeasible due to the time-sensitive nature of voice traffic and the non-deterministic nature of the data network infrastructure. It now appears that the debate is essentially over, and to the surprise of many, voice over IP (VoIP) has emerged as the only serious contender for voice and data integration. International standards have solidified, and traditional manufacturers of voice infrastructure technology are now investing heavily in VoIP. Chapter 22, "Voice and Data Network Integration," takes a look at the current state of the practice, and provides practical steps today's network manager can take to prepare for and begin to take advantage of this technology.

The ever-increasing use of the Internet raises concerns among Internet service subscribers regarding the quality of service of those offerings. This issue becomes especially acute when one considers the needs of certain real time, traffic intensive applications such as voice and video. Chapter 23, "RSVP: Building Blocks of the Next-Generation Internet," examines the new resource reservation protocol, known as RSVP, and shows how RSVP can provide the quality of service management capabilities needed as internet technology evolves.

It is no secret that businesses have recently become dependent upon the Internet, and that business use of the Internet is projected to continue increasing sharply. Most solutions available today, such as RSVP, offer evolutionary, but partial solutions to some of the resulting problems, and consequently extend the useful life of the current architecture. However, today's Internet is held together by a protocol developed in 1981! Clearly, this protocol, known as IPv4, cannot continue to support the growth indefinitely. Thus, Chapter 24, "IPv6: The Next-Generation Internet Protocol," discusses the successor to IPv4, with descriptions of the new protocol's features, construction, security, and migration plan.

The next area of consideration in our survey of advanced technologies is the newly emerging ability to build virtual private networks (VPNs) on top of the public Internet infrastructure. Chapter 25, "Internet-based Virtual Private Networks," examines the history of VPNs in general, looks at the suitability of Internet-based VPNs for specific applications, and discusses the technology and service offerings currently available.

VPNs are but one specific type of solution to a more general problem, that of allowing selective external access to an enterprise's intranet. In a more general sense, such selective external access solutions can be collectively described as "extranets." Chapter 26, "Implementing and Supporting Extranets," takes a look at extranets in general, and examines some of the special concerns they create from a security perspective.

The power and flexibility of rapidly configurable extranet solutions, most notably through the use of VPN technology, has helped advance a new business model called the "virtual corporation." In this model, entire organizations are rapidly configured in response to business needs, then just as rapidly deconfigured upon completion of their intended objectives. Such a model presents an entirely new level of risk with respect to networks. Chapter 27, "Virtual Corporations: A Need for Integrated Control and Perpetual Risk Assessment," examines how to take appropriate steps to evaluate and manage these risks.

Chapter 19
Advances in NIC Technology

Gilbert Held

One of the more popular axioms in the field of networking is the fact that end-user applications tend to grow and eventually consume all available bandwidth. Although this may be a slight exaggeration, network managers and local area network (LAN) administrators are constantly challenged with the task of improving network performance. In a quest to improve network performance, network managers and LAN administrators turned to a variety of techniques. Such techniques typically include segmenting networks, adding Layer 2 and the more recently developed Layer 3 switches, and, on occasion, migrating to a new network architecture that supports a higher data transfer capacity. Although each of the previously mentioned methods represents an effective solution to the problem of network bottlenecks, they are relatively expensive solutions. In addition, implementing one or more of the previously referenced network techniques can be time-consuming and can require the modification of an existing infrastructure, which places portions of the current infrastructure in an inoperative condition for a period of time.

An alternative to modifying the current network infrastructure is available to network managers and LAN administrators that many times can enhance performance sufficiently to significantly delay an infrastructure upgrade. That alternative is the use of appropriate network interface cards (NIC) that make more efficient use of available network bandwidth. Simply stated, the ability to transmit more data onto a network and read more data off the network per unit of time enhances the use of available bandwidth. Although there are still limits on the total use of a network based upon its access method, the ability to burst increased levels of traffic will enhance the ability of users to communicate while possibly alleviating a more expensive network upgrade. For example, although a 50% level of utilization on an Ethernet network is commonly used as a base metric for considering a change in the network, the use of more efficient NICs can reduce the level of collisions. Collisions cause delays resulting from station adapters transmitting a jam signal to warn other stations of the collision and then executing a random exponential backoff algorithm which results in another delay. Thus, the ability to place more data onto a network per unit of time can

0-8493-9838-X/00/$0.00+$.50
© 2000 by CRC Press LLC

result in fewer collisions than the use of a relatively slow-performing NIC. This in turn can result in fewer delays and can make better use of available bandwidth.

In this article we will examine recent developments in NIC technology that can be effectively applied by network managers and LAN administrators to enhance LAN performance. Since an understanding of recent NIC developments requires an understanding of the evolution of the PC bus and various adapter design methods, let's turn our attention to obtaining an overview of the evolution of network adapters and computer bus technology.

COMPUTER BUS SLOTS

The bus used in the IBM PC introduced in 1981 was 8 bits externally and 16 bits internally. This bus design resulted in an 8-bit data transfer capability between adapter cards and the computer processor. Since the original IBM PC and compatible computers operated at approximately 4 MHz, this resulted in a maximum data transfer capability of 3.2M bytes. Because the bus design was in the public domain, it was referenced as an Industry Standard Architecture (ISA) bus.

The introduction of the IBM PC AT personal computer resulted in an extension of the PC bus to 16 bits, while the use of the Intel Corp. 80286 microprocessor provided a full 16-bit external and internal data transfer capability. Since the bus was extended, it is referred to as the Extended Industry Standard Architecture (EISA) bus. The development of the EISA bus was planned to provide backward compatibility with the ISA 8-bit bus. To accomplish this, the EISA bus has two connectors: a 62-line connector used by ISA adapters, and a second 36-wire connector. EISA adapters are designed to fit into both connectors. PC AT and compatible computers operate at 8 MHz. Because they transfer data 2 bytes at a time, they have a theoretical data transfer capacity of 16M byte/sec. On a bit basis, this becomes 128M bps, which is insufficient to support asynchronous transfer mode (ATM) and Gigabit Ethernet. Thus, although the EISA bus is still popular, it clearly has an insufficient capacity to support modern networks.

When IBM introduced its PS/2 product line, it also introduced a new bus architecture referred to as the Microchannel. The Microchannel bus supports an operating speed of 10 MHz instead of the 8 MHz used by the PC AT. In addition, the Microchannel included support for 16- and 32-bit data paths, and, on higher-level PCs, included a mode for which a data transfer of 64 bits could occur. Thus, a Microchannel NIC was theoretically capable of supporting data transfers of 20, 40, or 64M byte/sec. Although the Microchannel architecture is still used in some workstations, its proprietary design and license restrictions resulted in its failure to be adapted for use by the general PC industry.

THE PCI BUS

As the clock rate of PC increased, the previously developed buses functioned as bottlenecks. Recognizing this problem, Intel introduced a local bus that supports up to ten compliant expansion cards and significantly improves the flow of data through a computer. Known as the Peripheral Component Interconnect (PCI) bus, this bus exchanges information with the processor using either 32 or 64 bits. The first version of the PCI bus has an operating rate of 32 MHz and can support a data transfer capability of 132M byte/sec using a 32-bit data path, and 264M byte/sec using a 64-bit data path. An extension to the PCI bus that will result in an operating rate of 64 MHz doubles the theoretical data transfer capacity of 32- and 64-bit PCI data paths. On a bit transfer rate basis, the PCI bus is capable of supporting ATM and Gigabit Ethernet.

Two of the main advantages of the PCI bus are its enhanced throughput and automatic configuration capability. The PCI bus running at 33 MHz permits data transfer up to 132M byte/sec over a 32-bit bus and 264M byte/sec over a 64-bit bus. This is significantly faster than the data transfer capability of ISA, EISA, Microchannel, and other bus architectures.

Concerning autoconfiguration, PCI-compliant devices have predefined information embedded in them, which enables the operating system software of a PC to automatically configure and make new devices operational without requiring end-user intervention. In a networking environment, many PCI network adapters can be installed and configured by simply clicking on an "auto-configure" or "add/remove hardware" icon, facilitating plug and play to a new level. Now that we have an appreciation for the evolution of the bus structure used in personal computers, let's turn our attention to the manner by which NICs transmit and receive data to and from a network.

I/O PORT-BASED ADAPTERS

The first generation of NICs primarily used I/O ports for data transfer. Although this technique was easy to implement, processor ports are relatively slow, limiting the data transfer capability of the NIC. By the late 1980s, most NIC manufacturers abandoned the use of I/O port data transfer.

DMA-BASED ADAPTERS

Attempting to enhance the throughput of their network adapters, several manufacturers introduced direct memory access (DMA)-based products during the late 1980s through the early 1990s. DMA represents a data transfer capability originally used in minicomputer controllers during the early 1970s. At that time, DMA circuitry added $5,000 or more to the cost of minicomputer communications hardware. By the late 1980s, the incorporation of a DMA feature onto a NIC added less than $50 to the cost of the adapter while significantly enhancing its performance. Under a DMA environment, data transfers can occur concurrent with computer and NIC processor operations. A processor on the NIC initiates a DMA transfer by loading the starting address and length of data in the buffer to be passed to computer memory. Once this is accomplished, a transfer cycle is initiated, which then results in data from the NIC buffer being transferred to the PC memory. During the transfer, both the PC and the NIC's onboard processor can do other things, permitting a true concurrent operational capability. Although the use of a DMA capability enhanced the transmission and reception of data, the actual transfer of such data between the NIC buffer and the PC's memory represented a barrier to obtaining a higher data transfer capability. This barrier was removed with the development and introduction of shared-memory NIC.

SHARED MEMORY

In a quest to obtain a higher transfer rate for their WICs, manufacturers investigated a variety of techniques. One technique that actually dates to the early 1980s was improved upon during the late 1980s and early 1990s. That technique is shared memory, with the adapter being configured to share a portion of the PC's memory area. Shared memory significantly improves the data transfer capability of NICs as data in the NICs' buffer becomes immediately accessible by the computer. This alleviates the set-up and transfer time associated with the use of DMA technology, enhancing the ability of the NICs to transfer data to and from the media. Today, most modern NIC designs are based upon the use of shared memory; however, with the introduction of the PCI bus very rarely does a shared memory design achieve anywhere near the theoretical data transfer capability of the bus. Recognizing this limitation, several vendors introduced high-performance NICs during the late 1990s based upon the use of a shared-memory architecture that also incorporated parallel operations. One of the leaders in applying parallel operations is 3Com Corp. under the Parallel Tasking trademark.

PARALLEL TASKING

In 1994, 3Com introduced a series of Etherlink adapter cards, which optimize data throughput by performing read-in and transmit-out data transfers at the same time. Through this simultaneous operation, the speed to which packets are transferred from the network to the NIC is accelerated. In addition, when taken together, both operations result in a significantly higher level of throughput, which becomes necessary to realize the potential of the PCI bus and the ability to effectively use more modern 100M bps Ethernet, 155M bps ATM, and 1G bps Gigabit Ethernet LAN. In 1998, 3Com enhanced its NIC parallel tasking capability with the introduction of its Parallel

Tasking II series of NIC. 3Com's Parallel Tasking II technology was designed specifically for the PCI bus. Although the PCI bus has a theoretical capability to obtain a data transfer rate of 132M byte/sec for a 32-bit bus, and 264M byte/sec for a 64-bit bus, in actuality the achievable data transfer can be far short of this theoretical limit. Many NIC designers discovered that a common reason for the inability to realize only a fraction of the potential of the transfer capacity of the PCI bus was usually related to the burst capabilities of each path of data flow in a computer. To enhance the data flow capability of the PCI, NIC developers focused on long bursts and eliminating wait states. High PCI bus utilization is achievable only by supporting long bursts. This means that a NIC that performs parallel tasking, but it waits until a minimum amount of data is buffered prior to initiating a transfer. It will use the bus more effectively than a NIC that transmits short bursts.

Concerning wait states, it is important to burst without wait states. This is because a single wait state during bursting results in a loss of half of the available bus bandwidth. 3Com's Parallel Tasking II NIC exploits advances in PCI chip set design to include long bursts and zero wait states. This results in the elimination of PCI bus bottlenecks. For example, 3Com's Parallel Tasking II compliant adapters are capable of streaming a full packet of 1514 bytes in a single bus master operation. Previously, early PCI buses restricted data bursts to a maximum of 64 bytes, which resulted in 24 cycles to transfer one packet. The support of a long-burst capability also results in an increase in the efficiency of the PCI bus while lowering CPU utilization, since many cycles are reduced to one or a few. This also results in an enhanced throughput capability. A second area of improvement utilized by Parallel Tasking II technology involves the use of newly developed PCI bus commands. Under the newer versions of the PCI bus such commands as Memory Read Line, Memory Read Multiple, and Memory Write Invalidate became available for use. Through the use of these commands an NIC can enhance its multitasking capability. Although 3Com trademarked the term Parallel Tasking, several NIC manufacturers use the previously described techniques in their PCI-based product line. In doing so, such manufacturers typically add a small premium to the cost of their products. Vendors such as IBM, Intel Corp. Madge Networks, and Olicom introduced enhanced PCI-based NIC during the past few years.

When attempting to determine if these "turbo" NICs are appropriate for your networking environment, you should focus your attention upon their sustained transfer rate and the type of network they support. In many instances, a "turbo" NIC may provide a level of data transfer capability beyond that you can effectively use. In other instances, the acquisition of a "turbo" NIC may represent a most appropriate method to obtain the ability to effectively use the bandwidth on a high-speed LAN. For example, assume your organization operates a 10Base-T network. If you acquire a PCI 10Base-T NIC, it is highly probably that it is capable of providing an effective data transfer capacity without including a parallel tasking design. That is because the bandwidth of a 10Base-T LAN is relatively low in comparison to the theoretical transfer capacity of a PCI bus-based NIC. This means that a PCI bus-based NIC that is only 10% efficient would provide a data transfer capability of 13.2M byte/sec for a 32-bit bus. On a bit-per-second basis, this transfer rate would be 105.6, significantly exceeding the 10M bps operating rate of a 10Base-T network. This illustrates the fact that enhanced performing NICs are much more suitable for ATM and Gigabit Ethernet applications than such legacy LAN as 10Base-T and 4- and 16M bps Token Ring. Thus, a comparison of the data transfer capacity of a NIC against the operating rate of your network can provide a good indication as to whether or not an enhanced PCI bus-based NIC is actually required.

Chapter 20
Emerging High-Bandwidth Networks

Kevin M. Groom and Frank M. Groom

INTRODUCTION

Corporate users are increasingly demanding faster transport speed. This is driven by the type of media being employed and shared among workers, such as documents, images, and training material. This material is being augmented by e-mail communication and increasingly by desktop videoconferencing. Further, the access to traditional transaction data applications on servers and requests and responses from client/server applications continue to be a primary driver for network connectivity.

As personal computers (PCs) and workstations come equipped with fast Peripheral Component Interconnect (PCI) buses that can deliver data to networks at 100M bps and greater speeds; have powerful Pentium II, Power PC, or Alpha central processing units (CPUs); and have 6- to 11-Gb hard drives, the user is demanding faster transport to feed these powerful data engines. Moreover, the distribution of large data and application servers is now augmented by groupware servers such as Lotus Notes storing documents and data and World Wide Web servers storing Hypertext Markup Language (HTML) marked-up pages for access with browsers.

To transport information among increasingly diverse and distributed processors, sharply greater bandwidth is required. As the trend for workers to spend many of their hours working from home or on the road continues, fast home access to corporate information is becoming an equal partner in the high-bandwidth business environment.

Asymmetrical digital subscriber line (ADSL) high bandwidth to the home worker has emerged from trials by the Regional Bell Operating Companies (RBOCs) and is being offered in a gradual rollout in the 1998-2000 time period. ADSL is the newest and most promising high bandwidth connection technology for access from the home. Asynchronous transfer mode (ATM) of 100M bps and Gigabit Ethernet are the emerging network technologies in the office. Frame relay is the fastest growing wide area connection technology, and the beginnings of a demand for ATM is emerging. Both frame relay and ATM are the prime interexchange carrier services offered to bridge city, state, and the national locations. Finally, world high-band-width connection services are emerging as corporations attempt to meld their national networks into a blend of high-bandwidth connectivity provided by such consortiums as AT&T's World Partners Frame Relay Consortium, which partner to deliver integrated world frame relay service.

HIGH-BANDWIDTH LOCAL ACCESS FOR THE HOME

Telephone, cable, and satellite companies have concentrated significant attention on basic residential connectivity. Initially, home entertainment was the application that was expected to drive customer demand for higher speed connectivity. However, with the emergence of vast interest and usage of the Internet, industry sights have turned to Internet access, work-at-home situations, and remote access to standard business Ethernet, Internet Protocol (IP), or ATM local area networks (LANs).

The general classification for the telephone company's product direction is termed digital subscriber line (DSL) service. DSL service has a basic intent of delivering higher bandwidth transport over the in-place twisted pair telephone loop plant that extends to each residence, while placing a modem on each end of the loop, one at the subscriber's location, and one at telephone central office switch center. The local loop tends to have between 20 and 33 bridge taps along the line. About 20% of installed lines have loading coils as well.

This gives problems to other services, such as Integrated Services Digital Network (ISDN), and limits the number of telephone lines that are ISDN equitable. DSL services—due to their more modern modulation techniques, digital signal processors, and isolation of the voice traffic to the low end of the frequency spectrum—are impervious to the bridge and load coil situation, thus allowing direct usage of a large percentage of the currently existing twisted pair local loop wire. It is estimated that 85% of U.S. households could be connected through DSL service with no modification of the wire pair with an equivalent 30 to 50% of such wire being ISDN capable. Among the array of DSL services that have been defined, telephone companies have targeted ADSL and high bit–rate digital subscriber line (HDSL) services as having the most customer demand potential.

XDSL Speeds and Services

The complete array of DSL services and the traditional modem service are presented in Exhibit 20.1. These are ADSL, HDSL, very high bit-rate digital subscriber line (VDSL), and symmetric digital subscriber line (SDSL) service.

The ADSL forum has defined a standard model to be followed by telephone companies and equipment suppliers to construct an ADSL connec-

Exhibit 20.1.   Digital Subscriber User Service Array

Type	Data Rate	Mode	Use
Modem	28.8, 34.6, 56.4K bps	Duplex	Minimum remove
DSL	160K bps	Duplex	ISDN
ADSL	1.5–9M bps	Simple down	Internet
16–640K bps	Duplex up	Work home	
HDSL	768K bps	Duplex down	Symmetric
768K bps	Duplex up	Computer use	
SDSL	384K bps Up/D	Duplex	Minimum data
VDSL	13–52M bps	Duplex down	Heavy data processing
1.5–2.3M bps	Duplex up		

tion and to offer ADSL services. The loop plant twisted pair wire is expected to remain unchanged. Distances beyond 3.5 mi from a central office will be connected by means of a T1 line that will span the longer distance to arrive within a reasonable distance to a residence community. ADSL places a splitter at both ends of the local loop line as well as an ADSL transmission unit (ATU-C at the central office and ATU-R at the residence).

The purpose of the modems is to modulate higher speed data and video on the line. The splitter allows the plain old telephone service (POTS) telephone conversation to be modulated separately on the line after the data and video and to be isolated from these transmissions. At the central office, the telephone conversation is split off from the higher speed data and video and sent directly to a line module of the central office switch, such as a traditional analog transmission. These ATU modems and the splitters are portrayed in Exhibit 20.2.

The modems on each end modulate the traffic into very high speed (above 138 kHz to 1.1 GHz), medium speed (from 30 to 138 kHz) with the overlap accommodated by echo cancellation. The POTS telephone connection sits as it always has at the bottom frequency between 0 and 4 kHz. A guard band of 24 kHz separates the voice traffic from the higher speed frequencies.

ADSL is an asymmetrical connection service. The downstream traffic is designed to be significantly faster than the upstream traffic. The service is intended for an audience with asymmetrical needs. Video-on-demand service has a limited and relatively slow request traffic, followed by massive and continuous downstream flow of a video movie. Internet traffic has been observed to follow the same pattern, with a browser-based seek request for information, followed by a sizable series of text, image, video, and sound clip information flowing downstream. ADSL can have this asymmetrical connection set up in a range from 1.5M bps downstream coupled with 64K bps upstream from the residence, to 6.1M bps downstream and 640K bps upstream.

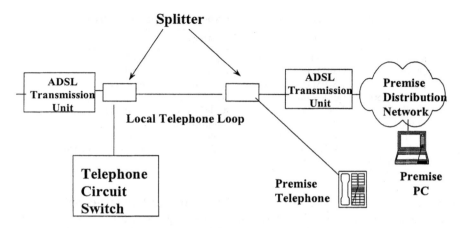

Exhibit 20.2. The Standard Reference Model for ADSL Service

There are four basic transmission modes for ADSL service:

1. Packet mode is essentially Transmission Control Protocol (TCP)/IP over a home Ethernet, which requires an Ethernet card in each home or remote office PC and twisted pair wire to connect to the ADSL home modem. This mode is ideal for home access to the Internet and for connection to a corporate network.
2. Cell-based ATM employs an ATM card in each home or remote office PC and is suited for remote office connection to a corporate ATM network by means of a telephone company ATM network. This connection is desirable for multimedia, videoconferencing, or home or office delivery of real-time training material.
3. Bit synchronization mode will be employed for streamed video to the home such as with video-on-demand service.
4. POTS mode is reserved for voice telephone traffic.

EMERGING OFFICE AND BUILDING CONNECTIVITY

Corporations are requiring increased bandwidth to connect to servers in the worker's building or across the campus, as well as to the distant location of other workers in the corporation. Simultaneously, they have an investment in older PCs, Ethernets and hubs, and software such as Novell Inc.'s NetWare. To modernize their investments and satisfy a diverse set of needs, they need to accommodate both the current network technology and the emerging high-bandwidth technology.

Current Office Connectivity and Building Backbones

Most corporations have already interconnected workgroups of users on a particular floor of an office building through an intelligent hub. Up to

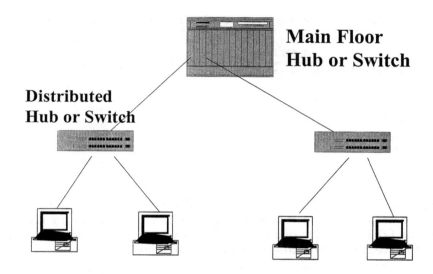

**Main Floor
Hub or Switch**

**Distributed
Hub or Switch**

Exhibit 20.3.   The Distributed Simple Hubs Connected by a Smart Switching Hub

100 or 120 users can be connected to a hub by means of category three or five twisted pair wire over distances of no more than 100 m (330 ft). These users can then be bridged to other hubs on the same or other floors. Such interconnected office workers can share common laser printers, e-mail, file servers, and applications through their shared and commonly managed LAN hub.

To minimize the investment in intelligent hubs (which cost between $10,000 and $20,000, depending on their configuration) and to extend the user's connection beyond 100-m distance limitation, cheaper "dumb" or distributed hubs supporting up to 20 PCs can be placed close to workers for their subgroup interconnection. The distributed hubs can then be linked to a more distant floor hub by means of coaxial cable or fiber. The stacking of these simple hubs and connecting them to a central switching hub for the floor is portrayed in Exhibit 20.3.

These traditional building connections are now under pressure from a number of advanced applications. In particular, the use of multimedia and desktop videoconferencing is driving bandwidth demands to the desktop for special-case users. However, the big impetus for desktop bandwidth is the movement from personal desktop computing toward network and workgroup computing. Much of desktop usage involves sending and receiving transactions over the local network to office, building, campus, and national and international servers. To meet this demand, simple office Ethernets have been upgraded first to switched 10M-bps Ethernet, which

Exhibit 20.4.   Varying Bandwidth Requirements for Media Types

Media Type	Bandwidth (bps)
Entertainment video–real-time play	3,000,000
Videoconference	128–356,000
Image visualization–real time	50–80,000
Engineering image	90,000
Voice	64,000
Sound	176,000–700,000
Stereo	1,400,000
Fax	64,000

has minimum contention, and then to 100M-bps switched Ethernet. As companies rapidly move to switched Ethernet and Token Ring LANs to reduce Ethernet collisions and the latency both experience and many move to 100M-bps Fast Ethernet on the floor, there is a general movement toward replacing the more expensive and complicated router-based fiber distributed data interface (FDDI) backbones with a single 100M-bps Fast Ethernet switch and placing a Fast Ethernet exit card in each floor hub or switch.

ATM DESKTOP CONNECTIVITY

ATM to the desktop is driven by the requirement for a variety of media to be delivered over the same connection to the desktop applications and disk storage. Exhibit 20.4 presents the range of information sizes and speeds required for the variety of multimedia that might be delivered. Sound and motion video pose the additional requirement that they must have rapid, yet unvarying delivery speed with no lags or variation. In many cases, this mixed set of media types must be delivered simultaneously in an intermixed stream over a common connection and used as a unit by the destination device.

Further, many of the individual media types require compression algorithms unique to the individual media type to be performed at the source and destination sites to squeeze the volume of information into any reasonable delivery protocol.

Only ATM provides the bandwidth reservation with guaranteed quality of service and a fast enough transfer rate to deliver these varying types of media to the desktop in a satisfactory fashion. In contrast, fast Ethernet provides high-speed and high-quality data transmission but cannot guarantee the delivery rate for individual media types. Many believe that a moderately loaded (less than 50% of capacity) 100M-bps Ethernet can carry multimedia to the desktop over the last 100 m if ATM is used for the wider backbone network.

ATM BUILDING BACKBONE NETWORKS

Unless ATM is provided all the way to ATM-equipped desktop PCs, ATM backbone networks provide only high bandwidth without the quality of service features, classes of service, and bandwidth guarantees for which ATM was created. As a backbone network, ATM competes with the newer 100M-bps and 1G-bps Ethernet and the older FDDI protocols purely on speed, simplicity of the protocol, and cost.

The simplicity and cost factors are the strength of Fast Ethernet. FDDI strength is in its embedded base and proven capability, while multimedia such as picture, video, desktop videoconferencing, and group document delivery are the features requiring ATM. If multimedia is employed locally and wide area ATM connection is provided by an interchange carrier to other distant ATM networked sites, building connectivity is moving to Fast Ethernet. ATM becomes the vehicle for interconnecting the buildings of a campus.

Where ATM is employed as building or campus backbone interconnecting 10M- or 100-bps Ethernet floor LANs, ATM acts as a bridging service and requires the employment of three LAN emulation servers, including the LAN emulation server itself, the LAN emulation configuration server, and a broadcast unknown server.

FDDI Backbone Network

The standard for campus backbone networks has been an FDDI network constructed with routers interconnected by dual fiber rings. The hubs that interconnect workgroups and workers on a given floor are connected to the FDDI by fiber links that span the greater distance from the floor to a central FDDI router. Either a passive fiber card or a full FDDI card can be placed in the hub to gain access to the backbone.

If the passive card is used, connection to the ring is at 10 or 16M bps. If the full FDDI card is placed in the hub, the connection speed from the hub to the ring router is at 100M bps. An FDDI ring is created by placing two FDDI cards (in some cases a single four-port card can be employed) in a set of routers. These routers are then interconnected by a set of dual fiber cable to form a building or campus ring. A third FDDI card or passive fiber card is placed in the router to link back to the LAN hub. Such an FDDI backbone connection is portrayed in Exhibit 20.5, with hubs serving as the office access to the backbone ring.

HIGH-BANDWIDTH CAMPUS BACKBONE NETWORKS

Looking more closely at a campus situation, we can see quite clearly how the placement of a limited set of switches can be more cost-effective than employing router-based, shared-bandwidth, FDDI backbones. The

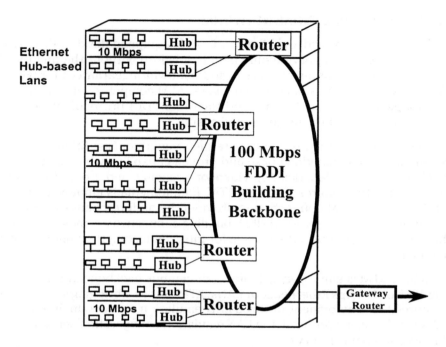

Exhibit 20.5.   Connecting Hubs to a Router-Based FDDI Building Backbone

complete FDDI campus backbone is then constructed by placing a router with two FDDI cards in the first floor of each building and stringing dual sets of multimode fiber around the campus, from building to building connected to a router in each building. One of the routers on the ring can serve as a gateway router to off-campus networks and to the Internet. Otherwise a server is connected to the ring to perform the gateway function.

Fast Ethernet Backbone Networks

To access an FDDI ring from a hub we either need to encapsulate our LAN-addressed packet inside an FDDI-addressed packet, termed "tunneling" the LAN packet, or we need to translate Ethernet to FDDI and then back to Ethernet on the other end of the ring. This complexity, delay, and cost in such translation has led to the creation of a faster version of the standard LAN protocol, Ethernet.

Although only Pentium-class computers (or PowerPC computers) workstations can make use of 100M-bps Fast Ethernet, it is quickly finding a home as a fast backbone network connecting 10M-bps Ethernet switches.

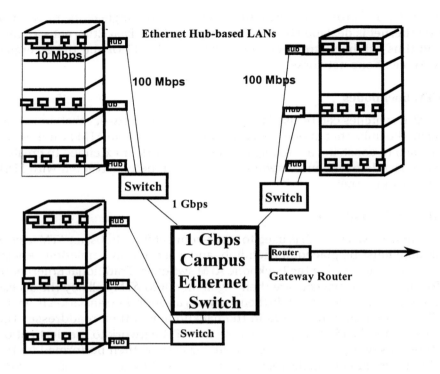

Exhibit 20.6.   1G-bps Interbuilding Campus Backbone Network

Ethernet at 100M bps can serve as fast transport between switching hubs or Ethernet switches or it can serve as a complete building backbone.

Further, Fast Ethernet can serve as fast campus backbone network interconnecting Fast Ethernet building backbones. Fast Ethernet can replace FDDI as both a building and a campus backbone, offers the same transport speed of 100M bps in a nonshared fashion, and maintains the same protocol and addressing throughout the complete campus network. The simplicity of this design as well as its low cost is quickly persuading companies to convert to this structure as an extension of what they already have installed (Exhibit 20.6).

In early release, prior to the promised 1998 standard specifications from the Gigabit Ethernet Alliance, a number of vendors have offered Gigabit Ethernet switches for campus and large building backbone networks. These switches employ a hybrid protocol with Layer 2 media access control (MAC) remaining traditional Ethernet, while Layer 1 is the fiber channel protocol using either multimode or single mode fiber. Giga-bit Ethernet is designed to interconnect 100M-bps Fast Ethernet switches and thus will be a strong competitor to existing FDDI and the emerging ATM backbone networks.

ATM Backbones

ATM switches can be used to create a backbone network that cross-connects the hubs that interconnect the floor traffic. These ATM switches can be used to construct a building backbone network or extended to create a campuswide backbone network, much as can be constructed with FDDI and Fast Ethernet.

ATM in the Building

When an ATM switch is used to cross-connect floor hubs, an ATM access module must be placed in each hub, and a set of LAN emulation servers must be connected to the backbone ATM switches. Traditional Ethernet or Token Ring LAN packets are then segmented into ATM cells by the access modules. The access module then requests an address translation from the ATM LAN emulation servers in the backbone and then readdresses the cells with ATM addresses to traverse the ATM network to the destination Ethernet segment. The reverse of this process is then performed by the ATM access module in the receiving hub. These ATM access modules, commonly called Proxy LAN emulation clients (LECs), act as bridging devices to bridge the traffic flowing from an Ethernet network to an ATM network, and bridging back again on the egress side.

ATM Campus Backbone

When the complete campus requires very high bandwidth to interconnect the buildings (155M or 622M bps) and multimedia traffic is being transported, a set of ATM switches can be placed at the heart of the campus with media, application, and file servers centrally attached to the backbone switches. These servers attract much of the traffic over the network and thus require very high entry speed between the servers and the network. LAN emulation servers are usually moved out from the building backbone to the campus ATM backbones when most of the traffic flows across campus generally supporting up to 1000 users (Exhibit 20.7).

Where larger communities are served, multiple separate LAN emulation servers can be created, specialized to a particular set of buildings. High-performance workgroups are separated from the regular LAN connections in the buildings and interconnected with their own workgroup ATM switch, which is then directly attached either to the campus or to a building ATM backbone network.

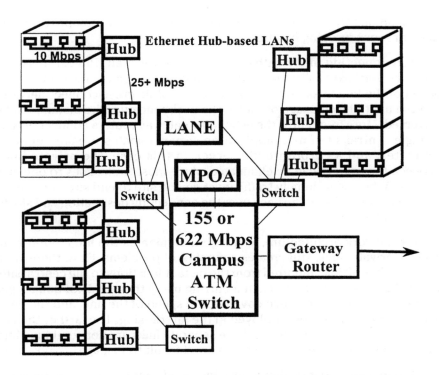

Exhibit 20.7. An ATM Switch Connecting Ethernet Switching Hubs

AVAILABLE WIDE AREA NETWORK CHOICES

Traditionally, access from the campus to wide area networking has been performed by employing a gateway router that can bridge local and wide area networks (WANs), perform required packet reformatting, and address translations and interpretations. T1 bridged routers, frame relay, and ATM networks are the current prime choices for providing high bandwidth across a wide area.

The conventional WAN is router-based, providing TCP/IP connectivity. The network is constructed as a set of autonomous networks that are interconnected by border routers. Such a network is accessed by a gateway router from individual buildings or campuses.

The individual routers that make up a TCP/IP WAN have traditionally been connected by full or fractionalized private T1 lines that have been leased from the telephone companies. Each router link requires such a connection and frequently a mesh of such lines connects all the routers. Usually the routers are located at the sending building locations, with the T1 links spanning the distance between the individual routers, providing an asynchronous bridging function.

Interconnecting many gateway routers to form an IP mesh network becomes very expensive as the distance grows. Each connection is composed of the two links on both ends to the public cross-connect network and the multiplexed usage of the public backbone over the distance to be traversed. More frequently, these building gateway routers connect only to a single central site for an application server, e-mail store-and-forward, Web sites, and a corporate file server. In this case, the private lines between the routers can be eliminated, since most traffic goes to one central site. When occasionally traffic must go end site to end site, the central router can route the traffic back over the connecting destination end site to the central router.

This network architecture, although it eliminates the interrouter connecting private lines, still creates a number of problems. First, there are a large number of links required from the distant locations to the central site. These links are very costly, each incurring many thousands of dollars per month based on the distance covered, the speed of the link, and the number of carrier companies employed in the interlinking. The farther the distance, the larger the cost. Since these separate links are not combined into a network service, these connections are difficult to manage.

A frame relay network should provide significant savings over an equivalent private line network. By employing a frame relay network to connect many locations to a central site, 20% savings should be achievable compared to a standard private line design regardless of the comparable speed used. This is regardless of whether we compare a 64K-bps private line to frame relay 64K-bps service or a 1.5M-bps private line vs. 1.5M-bps frame relay service.

Furthermore, for the many-to-many requirement, a still larger savings should be achievable approaching a 30% reduction. Frame relay service still requires the customer to lease at full price a short, private line access link to the location of the edge relay switch of the vendor. However, significant savings should be achievable over the long-haul distance with frame relay service. This results from the opportunity to statistically share the facilities and from dramatically reducing the number of individual, long-distance, end-to-end, private line links required to connect each end customer site to all the others in a many-to-many connection.

On the other hand, benefits from network management services can be achieved if the frame relay service is provided by one carrier and only short private lines connect users at each end point. Top quality network management can be achieved, since the network and its facilities are all under one carrier's control.

Using Public Frame Relay Networking to Bridge Locations

Frame relay addresses the problems raised by a national connection. Frame relay service does this by substituting a national, high-speed, public, packet-switched, shared network for the many individual private lines that would normally need to be established. Although private line links must be established from each location to the closest entry point of the national frame relay network, these links are decidedly shorter and thus much less expensive. A short T1 link to a connection may be $500 for a full 1.5M bps down to $200/month for a 32- to 64K-bps subchannel of a private line. A T1 private line from New York to Seattle, on the other hand, would cost thousands of dollars a month, mostly from the distance charges.

Charges for frame relay have been dropping. Since the public frame relay network is a shared-use network, the pricing is reduced. Ideally, frame relay is intended to be an on-demand, pay-as-you-use network with dramatically reduced price compared with building your own private network with long and leased T1 private lines. Ideally, the public frame relay network would be the equivalent of a dial-up high-speed packet network. This is considered to be a switched virtual circuit (SVC) network in terms. Such a presubscribed and pay-as-you-use public data network would require the carrier provider, on receiving a call setup message from your router, to dynamically pick each sequential link in the path of the end-to-end frame relay network that you would utilize.

Further, the carrier would need to dynamically update the route selection table in each node in the frame relay network that you temporarily use to create a virtual path for your transmission. This is projected to reduce a user's national network connectivity cost by up to 70% over a national, dedicated, private line network. Unfortunately, this dynamic update of switch tables is not yet a reality. What is offered is the ability to contract for a stated period of time a "temporarily permanent virtual path" or a permanent virtual circuit (PVC) in terms.

On placing an order with the carrier and leasing a line to the carrier's point of presence (POP) closest to each of your sites a company can have a 24-hr/day, 30 days/month, shared piece of a public high-speed network. This permanently shared piece of the network costs about 80% of what a private line network would cost. In fact, the distance portion of the private line facility is a shared portion of the carrier's digital cross-connect network anyway, with your portion being prereserved as a PVC. Exhibit 20.8 represents a frame relay network established as a set of PVCs.

To establish a "permanent circuit" between sites 1, 2, and 3, one of two modes of operation would be employed. In the standard approach, the customer would subscribe with the carrier for PVCs from site 1 to site 2, from site 1 to site 3, and from site 2 to site 3. The carrier would then provide the

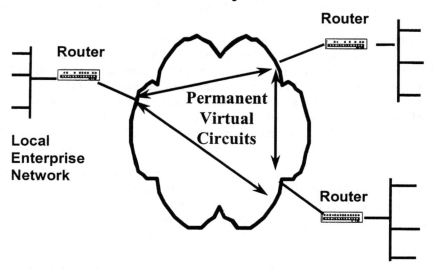

Exhibit 20.8.   Frame Relay Network Composed of Permanent Virtual Circuits

---

customer a set of frame relay addresses to place in the customer's router. This router will then translate the IP addresses to frame relay addresses and place these new addresses in each packet prior to sending them to the frame relay network to be forwarded to a specific site.

These temporary addresses are called data link control identifiers (DLCIs). Each port can specify up to 1024 DLCIs—in other words, up to 1024 PVCs per port. Fortunately, frame relay is a fully duplexed, bidirectional network requiring only one setup to establish both directions of the communication (differing from its big brother network, ATM, which requires a separate call setup for each direction of the communication path). However, like ATM, frame relay employs a different DLCI address at each end of the link (and unseen by the subscriber, a whole string of sequential DLCIs for each link along the way to the destination final leg link). To send a packet from site 1 to site 2, the customer's router must place DLCI 100 in every packet.

Customer participation in frame relay addressing has been considered enough of a hurdle that many carriers offer the preferred option of the carrier creating the frame relay addresses for the customer using the carrier's within-network router and database to perform the translation from IP to DLCI addresses. Under this option, the customer submits IP packets with IP addresses from the customer's router to the carrier's router (which is on the edge of the frame relay network). The carrier's router will then perform the address translation on both ends of the frame relay network, with the customer sending and receiving standard IP packets with which they have years of experience. As far as the customer perceives, with this approach frame relay is merely an extension of the local IP networks.

Interfacing Frame Relay with Other Networks

Since frame relay is a carrier-provided network service, existing protocols (such as the widely popular IP protocol, the IBM Systems Network Architecture [SNA], the Telco ISDN), and even voice can be carried over it with a significant reduction in cost and the added advantage of having a carrier-managed wide area linkage.

Frame Relay and ATM Interworking

The ATM and frame relay forums have approved two methods by which these two networks can be interconnected. Under network interworking, devices on the frame relay network must be knowledgeable about the ATM network and capable of performing the frame relay to ATM mapping. This includes the mapping for the frame relay service-specific convergence sublayer (FR-SSCS) functions of the ATM, AAL-5 adaptation layer at the upper portion of the ATM Layer 2 protocol. In another frame relay/ATM interworking method, the service interworking method, devices on both the ATM and frame relay networks are not required to know anything about the other network protocol.

To customer premise equipment (CPE) on a frame relay network, the entire network appears as frame relay. The same is true of CPE on the ATM network. To accomplish this protocol isolation, an FR/ATM interworking function (IWF) has been defined and performed by a device sitting as a bridge between the two networks. The IWF node must translate frame relay DLCI addresses to ATM virtual path indicators (VPIs) and virtual channel indicators (VCIs). Current public wide area frame relay and ATM offerings are provided only by setting up PVCs. In the future, it is anticipated that both frame relay and ATM networking will also be offered as "on-demand, pay-as-you-use" SVC services. Both call–setup messaging and dynamic route allocation must then be handled by the IWF interface unit for both sides of the connection.

This will be a sizable task. Exhibit 20.9 depicts frame relay connecting local networks to a wide area ATM network through a standard IWF node. This IWF node, usually a router with frame relay and ATM access cards, and the IWF address conversion and packet segmentation software.

In the early stages of ATM and frame relay interworking, most prefer to think of ATM as a low-level physical connection technology employed by frame relay service. In fact, much of public frame relay has been implemented

PUBLIC ATM
BACKBONE NETWORK

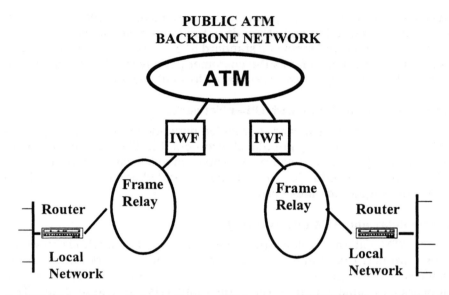

Exhibit 20.9. Frame Relay as Regional Access to an ATM Wide Area Backbone

by the RBOCs and the interexchange carriers (IE) with ATM as the actual transporting vehicle. The customer buys frame relay service, but that service is provided with an ATM backbone. Ultimately, frame relay and ATM will be considered as two services, each with its own special audience and employing IWF interconnection points as the translation and interconnection nodes between the two network protocols.

Frame relay service was designed as a data-only networking scheme due to the bursty nature of data, which in the past was incompatible with the continuous flow required for voice traffic. Now many companies are beginning to recognize the savings they could gain by employing their frame relay network to carry voice traffic along with their data traffic. Voice savings of 25 to 30% have been incurred by connecting a company's PBX to a common multimedia access switch that is shared with the company's data traffic.

The approach taken is to first convert the analog voice to digital form using sampling and pulse code modulation resulting in 8-b words at a 64-bps transfer rate. This digital representation is then compressed to remove pauses and hesitation (Bell estimates the average pause time per call at 2.5 s). This compressed, digitally represented voice set of bytes is then placed into packets (about 4000 bytes per packet), addressed to the appropriate destination, and sent forward on a 64K-bps link to the frame relay network. At the receiving end it is desirable to set up large buffers so the message can be reassembled with all the pauses and hesitations as they originally occurred. Generally, frame relay does not provide the same quality of voice as the public circuit switched telephone network, but for many businesses, the cost savings and management capability of voice over frame relay will override the modest quality degradation.

ATM NETWORKS: PUBLIC CARRIERS AS VIRTUAL CIRCUIT PROVIDERS

Where a company has achieved the speed and quality of service (QoS) control of transmission locally and wishes to connect dispersed locations and still maintain ATM speed and the QoS features, a public carrier's ATM networking service can be contracted to provide continuous ATM service that can be used in creating an end-to-end wide area ATM connection. Moreover, the complete range of ATM speeds from 51M to 622M bps can be publicly contracted for this wide area ATM connection. However, only the establishment of a permanent connection (PVC service) is currently publicly provided by most public carriers, although AT&T has announced a SVC ATM service.

With carrier-provided wide area PVC ATM service, businesses use the carrier as if it were providing a private line connection between their sites. They preestablish a 155M-bps PVC from one location to the other. The two end-point ATM switches treat the public connection as if it where a private line between the locations. Although they locally, dynamically create SVC connections, when they bridge sites using the public ATM network, they do not attempt to dynamically set up a circuit over the public network. What they do is only route the traffic to an available, preestablished PVC as if they were switching to a line connecting the sites.

The switches on each end dynamically establish their connection and disconnection locally, but the public connection is always available for use as a link between the local ATM switch port much like a permanently leased line. Either a single IXC (such as AT&T) or an RBOC telephone company (such as Ameritech) can provide the wide area ATM PVC connecting service.

PUBLIC CARRIERS PROVIDE JOINT ATM NETWORK

An RBOC can provide a local ATM PVC connection. However, when a company needs to cross the country, one has some choice in the connection. One can establish the PVC service either with an IXC—such as AT&T, Sprint, or MCI—or with a mixture of an IEC and two RBOCs. A major problem may occur when a business wishes to employ a mixture of carriers to create an end-to-end ATM network. The two local carriers need to create links to the national IXC, and the three companies need to set up a set of end-to-end PVCs that create a link across the multiple carriers to the destination. This is a difficult circuit to set up initially, and it is virtually impossible to manage as a unit today due to the reluctance of the carriers to allow management across their boundaries.

EMERGING GLOBAL OPTIONS

Partnering is the strategy employed by the carriers to create global high-bandwidth connection, such as the planned AT&T and British Telecom (BT) agreement.

Sprint, France Telecom, and Deutsche Telekom have established Globe I as their joint world communication vehicle. Beyond using the carrier consortia, organizations—such as Sandia Laboratories in Arizona—are using 155M-bps ATM satellite links to interconnect their site to a number of national supercomputer research centers such as that at the University of Illinois, and to laboratories such as Lawrence Livermore in California. Sandia establishes two one-way links (one in each direction) and can interconnect locations without the problems of establishing long fiber connections to a land-based ATM network. Motorola has announced its own satellite network for providing global 56K-bps to 155M-bps data connection to and from any location on the globe.

SUMMARY

Users continue to seek faster networks for metropolitan, national, and international connection. As users, equipped with high-performance computers seek to transport more information and multimedia over faster local networks, the push for high-speed corporate networks increases. This has led toward Fast Ethernet and ATM for the local interconnection.

Moreover, the national and global distribution of corporations and a requirement to communicate with suppliers and customers, as well as distant corporate employees at a speed equivalent to local connection, are driving the deployment of fiber-based connection locally, nationally, and globally and the employment of ATM and soon 1-Gbps Ethernet protocols. As more complicated applications with distributed databases and Web server-based information are added to corporate networks, the endless cycle requiring more speed to more locations will continue.

Chapter 21
ATM Access: The Genesis of a New Network

William R. Koss

Data communications has come a long way in the past six years. In 1992, many users deploying wide area networks (WANs) still thought in terms of 56K frame relay and fractional T1 speeds as state of the art. Some six years later, the World Wide Web (WWW) has driven most of us to deploy V.90 standard modems in the home or explore the possibilities of cable modems, ISDN, and xDSL technologies. In the enterprise network, network backbones are now primarily cell-based backbones. Long gone are shared backbones such as token-ring, Ethernet, and collapsed router backbones. FDDI is still around, but nobody is getting excited about DAS and SAS. The network core within the enterprise and within the service provider (LEC, CLEC, IAP, ISP, IXC, and CIXC) networks is using a cell-based technology called ATM (asynchronous transfer mode).

One may have heard of ATM — it was all the rage in 1994. Everyone went through a few years of ATM Year One, Year Two, Year Three, and then the marketing hype finally fizzled out. In its place came tag switching, voice over IP, IP over SONET, xDSL, and terabit routers. All this occurred while the service providers were deploying ATM within their network cores and most enterprise IT managers were completing the deployment of ATM backbones to service the growing demand for bandwidth and network performance. The purpose of this article is to explore the emergence of ATM into the wide area network and the outline the challenges and techniques that will used to deliver increased bandwidth for voice, data, and video services.

ATM TODAY: THE NETWORK CORE

For discussion purposes, existing ATM networks can be divided into two primary categories: (1) carrier class networks maintained by service providers, and (2) enterprise networks maintained by corporations and organizations and primarily intended for private use. To understand the deployment of ATM into the WAN, one can start by examining how ATM is deployed within each of the defined categories.

Not too long ago many people referred to the phone companies as the Telco or carrier markets. Today, this is an injustice. Such a large number of companies exist that offer some type of network access that the market they are part of is now referred to as service providers. Within the service provider market, many types of companies and market verticals can be defined. This article concentrates on the following acronyms that define the major vertical elements of the service provider market:

- **LEC:** Local exchange carrier that provides local access to telecommunication services; formally defined as regional Bell operating companies (RBOCs).
- **CLEC:** Competitive local exchange carrier. Companies that provide local access to telecommunication services. Most CLECs have emerged in past few years to compete for local telephone service against LECs.
- **IAP:** Internet access provider. Companies that provide wholesale Internet backbone transport and access. Examples are UUNET, ANS, SAVVIS, and Concentric.
- **ISP:** Internet service provider. Companies that provide local Internet access and Internet-based services.
- **IXC:** Interchange carrier. Companies that provide inter-LATA services between LATAs within an interstate or intrastate basis. AT&T, MCI Worldcomm, and Sprint are the primary IXCs within the United States.
- **CIXC:** For lack of a better term, competitive interchange carrier. This vertical represents companies that are developing inter-LATA services based on their own developing network infrastructure. The prominent players are Level3, Qwest, and IXC Communications.

Each service provider has developed a different type of network to meet its business and customer requirements. For discussion purposes, some generalities that encompass many of the service provider networks can be defined.

By the end of 1998, most service providers within the United States had deployed ATM within their networks. Those that have are typically well-established companies or aggressive young companies with a business strategy that depends on leveraging the technical advantages of ATM to compete for customers. For the purposes of this article, international service providers or small market players that have yet to establish themselves are not discussed here. The reason for this is that each international market is different, and the smaller market players have yet to develop enough mass to affect the market dynamics.

The existing IXCs and LECs are confronted with a series of challenges that can best described as legacy challenges. Most IXCs and LECs have created several networks to deliver customer services. They have networks for voice services, packet-based IP, frame relay, local access, and ATM. The emerging CLECs and CIXCs have bypassed legacy technologies and deployed ATM as their transport technology. The competitive nature of the service provider market requires that service providers be able to address the following challenges.

- provide the client an end-to-end network solution
- provide application services such as Internet access, global intranets, Web-based co-location, Web-based transaction and application support, and data warehousing
- unify their networks and provide a single managed service
- reduce duplicated costs and overall operational costs
- deliver integrated voice, data, and video services to the client
- provide unified billing and service-level agreements (SLAs) that guarantee quality of service

The IXCs and LECs that are the incumbent service providers are challenged to (1) reduce cost, (2) improve performance, (3) unify services, and (4) deliver higher quality services. Their plan is to achieve these objectives by leveraging the strengths of technologies such as ATM. The reason ATM is important is that it currently exists within many of the service provider core networks and ATM has several important elements that are driving ATM deployment, including:

- It solves the TDM problem; existing networks based on time-division multiplexing cannot support future network growth.
- It provides support for all services; ATM supports three primary services that service providers are concerned with: voice, data, and video.
- It exists and is proven; ATM is already deployed in the network core. It is proven, understood, and technical resources have been trained to support the technology.
- It reduces deployment and operational costs; ATM access equipment is less expensive and less complicated. The long-term support and operational costs of ATM networks is projected to provide significant long-term savings.

As the IXCs and LECs view ATM as the unifying network technology that is able to provide a solution from the carrier core to customer premises, the CLECs and CIXCs view ATM as the network infrastructure of choice. Nearly all CLECs and CIXCs have developed extensive network infrastructures that built upon ATM. ATM provides the universal network foundation to support all services and provide scalable bandwidth. As much as the IXCs and LECs view ATM as the future, CLECs and CIXCs view ATM as the technology that enables them to compete without the encumbrance of legacy networks.

Within the enterprise market, ATM has been widely deployed as the universal backbone of the network. Some users have invested in desktop ATM solutions, but many users have built successful network backbones using ATM solutions that encompass Ethernet or token-ring switching as the final connection to the desktop. Most enterprise ATM backbones are deployed within buildings and campus networks. Using a switched cell network architecture, ATM backbones running at speeds of OC3 are capable of supporting an immense amount of traffic and adequately dealing with the challenge of performance-intensive applications. Similar to the service provider market, several important elements are driving the deployment of ATM into the WAN within the enterprise market:

1. It solves the performance problem. ATM delivers the bandwidth demanded by customers in scalable increments and meters from the customer premise to the network core.
2. It provides support for all services. ATM provides the foundation for voice, data, and video support within a defined standard.
3. It exists and is proven. ATM is already deployed in the network core. It is proven, understood, and technical resources have been trained to support the technology

ATM TOMORROW: THE ATM WAN

The deployment of ATM into the WAN has been a slow process. At present, the majority of ATM WAN installations have been for DS1 speeds. Several reasons can be attributed the slow deployment of ATM technology:

- ATM has primarily been used as a backbone technology for high-speed network trunks
- emergence of possible alternative technologies such as "Everything over IP SONET"
- service providers have been slow to develop infrastructure to support ATM-based services
- continued strong demand of frame relay-based services
- market readiness and demand has been lacking as many enterprise users complete network deployments based on core technologies such as IP, 100BT, and gigabit Ethernet and frame relay
- Y2K readiness and WWW integration have consumed IT resources, inhibiting planned network upgrades

Despite these challenges, 1998 was an important milestone in the ATM WAN market. Major service providers began announcing the availability of high-speed ATM services. Sprint announced its ATM intentions in June 1998, and UUNET announced its intention to deliver high-speed ATM-based services in 1999. To understand why ATM will grow in the WAN, one must first define the business challenges that will compel both the enterprise users and service providers to deploy ATM in the WAN.

Enterprise Network Performance

This is an important concern for enterprise IT managers. Applications are driving the expansion of networks and the need to deliver high-speed services to an increasing number of users. Enterprise managers are continually faced with the challenge of supporting an increased number of applications that require an increased amount of network resources. Collaborative group documents, business presentations, and reports are routinely sent via e-mail or the Internet as the work environment becomes increasingly mobile. The demand for increased access to information at the desktop has created a demand for better network performance. Applications that have been driven out from the network core to the remote offices require more bandwidth for better performance. The ATM core of the enterprise network is and will be pushed out to the edges of the network.

Service Provider Network Performance

Service providers are challenged with the need to deliver more services other than bandwidth and network access. They are challenged to provide services such as data warehousing, data archiving, co-location of Web services, business-class Internet access (>T1), corporate intranets or VPN services, and workgroup services. To satisfy the demands of their clients, the service providers are challenged to move ATM for their network core to the customer premise. Even today, several service providers have tariffed their ATM services at the same rate that they provide frame relay service.

Quality of Service

An important technical feature of ATM is that it provides multiple levels of quality of service, and it has internal provision to address the needs of flow control and dynamic bandwidth allocation. Clients are demanding a guaranteed level of service for network dollar, and ATM enables the service provider a mechanism to provide service-level agreements (SLAs). The classic example is of two customers, one who has contracted for 6Mbps service and one who has contracted for 10Mbps service. The flow control capabilities of ATM allow the service providers to guarantee the expected level of service for each customer, although the customers may be sharing the same network link. Clients receive a different billing rate for their service, and the service provider can maximize their network bandwidth.

Inclusion, Unification, and Expansion

The conversion of the network core to ATM within the enterprise and service provider networks provides a strong impetus to expand these networks to include other users or networks. Unifying and standardizing network technology are methods of reducing cost and improving reliability and serviceability. In order to simplify the network, ATM will move from the network core to the edge of the network.

Scalability

ATM is dynamically scalable and it provides metered bandwidth that conforms to the infrastructure of networks maintained by service providers as well as enterprise users. ATM enables the service providers to deliver bandwidth that meets the demands of users. Other competing technologies such as xDSL require bandwidth services that are asymmetrical to the network. Users will demand bandwidth in increments of 1.5Mbps, 3Mbps, 6Mbps, 12Mbps, DS3, OC-3c, and OC12.

Integrated Services

ATM provides the only standardized method for unifying network services under a single network medium. ATM supports both data and voice, as well as video services. The unification of voice, data, and video is an important long-term objective for both enterprise users and service provides. Enterprise users long for the day when they can contract for one service and one bill that includes voice, data, and video services. By deploying ATM to the customer premise, Service Providers can begin to unify network functions and deliver the long-sought-after "single pipe" that provides all functions.

Outsourcing Services

ATM enables service providers to deliver high-speed, transparent LAN services (TLS). TLS services provide a simple means of providing LAN-to-LAN extension without the need to deploy a complex solution. This enables service providers to provide "outsourcing" services to clients seeking to bundle network WAN services to achieve an overall lower operational network cost.

When examining how ATM will be deployed in the future in the enterprise market, one is primarily concerned with the WAN. Although the rapid emergence of switched technologies such as 100BT Ethernet and gigabit Ethernet at low cost points successfully stunted the deployment of ATM to the desktop — ATM found a home in the network core — it was in the core of the network that ATM provided the speeds necessary to reduce network congestion. It is only now that the extensive investments made in ATM backbone technology can be leveraged to deliver "in-demand" services across the network topology. Exhibit 21.1 illustrates the deployment of ATM access services within the enterprise market.

From the service provider perspective, the ATM network of tomorrow involves migration of the ATM network from the core of the network to the customer premises. By expanding the ATM as the network transport, service providers are presented with a viable strategy to modernize the components of their networks that generate profits — but at a considerable cost. The large incumbent interchange carriers such as Sprint, Williams, MCI World-comm and AT&T have multiple networks under management. These networks include Frame Relay, voice, IP, and ATM. Expanding ATM throughout their networks allows the incumbents to (1) reduce costs, (2) deliver high-speed services, (3) unify networks, and (4) provide new CPE-based services.

Without exception, the new CLECs and CIXCs have built new networks almost entirely based on ATM as the core transport. Each of these new companies has seized on ATM as their preferred transport technology. Thus, none of these companies is encumbered with legacy networks such as Frame Relay or circuit-switched technologies. In short, when one thinks about ATM access, one is thinking about a CPE device that is designed to be an access mechanism that transports CPE services into the ATM network for delivery across the service provider network. Exhibit 21.2 illustrates ATM access into the ATM service provider backbone network from two customer sites.

KEY TECHNOLOGIES FOR THE ATM WAN

The ATM WAN of tomorrow will be a combination of "core" ATM technologies and "transition" technologies required for supporting legacy networks. When examining the deployment strategy of ATM access equipment within the ATM WAN of tomorrow, one does so from two perspectives. The first perspective is the user or CPE side and the second perspective is the network or service provider side. Using the CPE/service provider model, one can begin to define the "system" required for ATM access. On the service provider side, ATM services will be delivered at various speeds using a variety of interfaces. Typically, ATM access devices will support the following on the service provider side:

- DS1/E1 interface
- DS3/E3 interface
- OC-3c interface
- inverse muxing over ATM (IMA) interface
- add drop mux and add drop bypass

The service provider side of ATM access devices are simple compared to the variety of services that must be supported on the CPE side. The CPE side of ATM access devices must achieve two objectives: they must support the services that customers will use going forward, and they must also support a variety of legacy network technologies and services that clients have deployed over the years. It must be remembered that a motivating component of ATM is the ability to provide a consolidation of technologies and services. The following outlines the primary CPE side requirements:

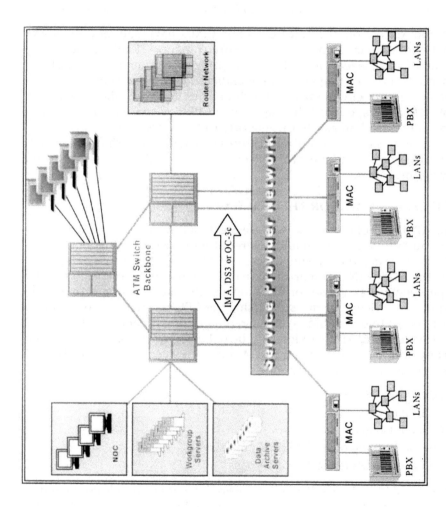

Exhibit 21.1. ATM Deployment in Enterprise Networks

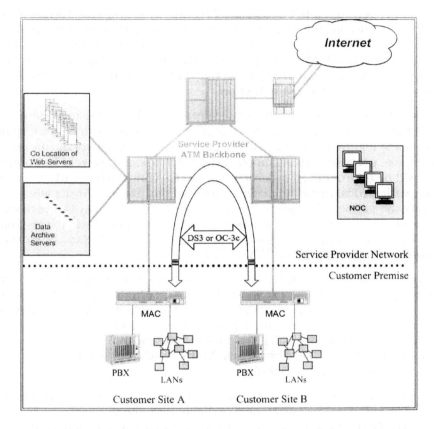

Exhibit 21.2. ATM Access from Customer Site to Service Provider

- LAN interface: 10/100 Ethernet, 4/16 Token Ring, and FDDI
- IP routing support: static routing and default gateway forwarding support
- transparent LAN service support: bridging
- LAN client support: LAN client provides support for SVCs and bandwidth management and interoperability in enterprise networks with native ATM devices

Combining the service provider and CPE side features, one creates what can be called an integrated access device (IAD) or multi-service access concentrator (MAC). The objective of this device is to provide user-to-network connectivity. It is not a router and it is not a switch — it is an access device. In simple terms, it can be considered a fast segmentation and reassembly (SARing) engine that transports voice and data into an ATM stream. The primary objective of MACs will be to balance their cost and simplicity

253

in order to leverage the benefits of ATM. Unified services or "single-pipe" strategy is a driving force behind the deployment of ATM; but if the devices used to provide ATM access are expensive or complicated, the compelling reasons to deploy ATM are diminished. Enterprise IT managers and service providers have a common objective that ATM and MACs must achieve — long-term operational cost reduction.

As enterprise networks and service providers begin the migration out from the network core, support for legacy technologies will be important in-demand features. Not only will the IXCs have legacy networks, but many enterprise users will have a mix of legacy technologies as well. The objective will be to provide an orderly transition to ATM, starting with the locations with critical needs. In order to achieve this process, MACs will need to provide support for legacy services such as Frame Relay. An essential element of this requirement will be for MACs to support Frame Relay connections from routers and FRADs, as well as FRF 5 and FRF 8 for support of Frame-to-ATM and Frame-to-ATM-to-Frame services.

As much as MACs must be data orientated to support the variety of services typically found at the remote site location, they must also be able to support a variety of voice services. A primary benefit of ATM is the integration of voice and data on a single pipe. The benefits of the technology are greatly reduced if all one can get is a faster pipe and still require a different connection for voice services. Thus, MACs need to possess strong voice services. These services include:

- circuit emulation services: structured and unstructured transmission of DS1/E1 streams for support of digital PBX interconnect
- FXO/FXS POTs: support for analog PBXs as well as dial tone, PLAR, and ring generator
- voice and silence suppression and compression
- AAL2 voice services that support dynamic bandwidth allocation through SVCs

As well as supporting a variety of services, MACs must also support a variety of network management services. MACs will be deployed by both enterprise users and service provider users. Thus, it is important for MACs to support features that enable each to manage and support the devices. The primary objective is for MACs to be "lights-out" devices that are installed, configured, and forgotten. Unfortunately, network devices rarely live up to such lofty goals and at times will be in need of management services. In this case, it will important for MACs to support a variety of "punch list" network management features. These features include:

- Web-based management
- Telnet
- SNMP

- support for popular network management platforms with MIB extensions
- CRAFT interface
- out-of-band management via modem

An important tactical capability in the deployment of MACs will be support for inverse muxing over ATM (IMA). IMA leverages two market conditions for the service provider and enterprise client. At present, many service providers are forced to deploy full DS3 circuits for clients that desire to scale above the T1 range. Unfortunately, many clients do not require a full DS3. In other cases, clients are demanding >T1 service in areas where DS3 is not readily available. The solution to this challenge can be found in IMA. IMA allows T1 lines to be bonded together to deliver access services that are >T1, but less than DS3. This elegant strategy provides a gradual scale in services and cost as network demands warrant. Exhibit 21.3 illustrates the deployment of IMA services.

ATM WAN: SHOULD YOU START NOW?

Why ATM will be important in the WAN is known; now one needs to ensure that one will be prepared to undertake the transition. From a preparation perspective, the following questions provide a starting point to determine whether or not one should initiate programs to begin transitioning the WAN transport to ATM-based services.

- Do you have remote locations that require improved performance or locations in your network that would benefit by extending your ATM backbone to include their location?
- Are you looking to reduce long-term costs and unify voice and data services?
- Do you have E-commerce, or Web-based applications that require dedicated Internet access above T1 speeds?
- Can you benefit from leveraging the infrastructure of service providers to provide data warehousing, co-location of Web servers, and high-speed intranet services?
- Do you have major application initiatives underway that will increase the demands for network bandwidth throughout your network over the next 12 to 24 months?
- Are you looking to contract for guaranteed network bandwidth for some or all of your network locations?
- Is network performance a mission-critical requirement for your business? Do you have or will you have mission-critical applications that are dependent on network performance?
- Are you interested in positioning your network infrastructure to support video-based applications such as conferencing and training?
- Are long-term cost reduction, network simplification, and performance long-term objectives for your IS organization?

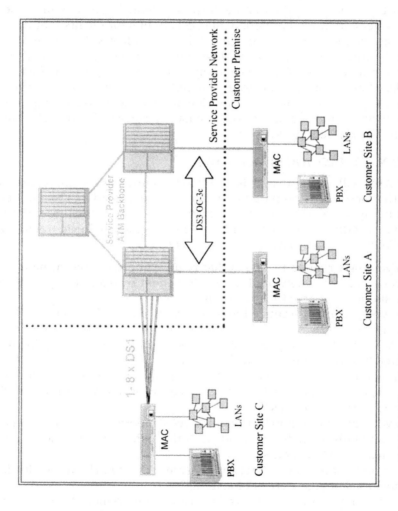

Exhibit 21.3. Deployment of Inverse Multiplexing over ATM (IMA) Services

CONCLUSION

The genesis of the new network has begun. The start has been slow — but the conclusion is inevitable. ATM is and will be deployed as the transport of choice for wide area networking. Service providers of all types are deploying ATM for solid business reasons. ATM provides key advantages not found in other WAN technologies: namely, quality of service, unification of services (voice, data, video), and superior scalability.

Enterprise networks are being deployed with public or private ATM backbones. This will be extended to remote offices and locations, where ATM access solutions will be deployed for the following reasons:

- **Cost/performance balance:** increase network performance in a manner that allows for scalable migration of services based on a cost/need ratio.
- **Simplified billing and service level agreements:** lower service cost, simplified billing statements, and guaranteed service that enable the enterprise users to purchase only what they require.
- **Leverage investments in public and private backbones:** effective use of ATM core infrastructures that are already deployed will lead to improved services and lower, long-term costs.
- **Reduce acquisition and operational costs:** deploy less-expensive technological solutions that provide long-term, low cost, "lights out" operational costs.

ATM is the only technology that is standards based and can be used to deliver multi-service networking throughout the wide area network. In addition, ATM is the only technology that can be used by enterprise users and service providers to reduce their equipment acquisition costs and ongoing operational costs over the long term.

Chapter 22
Voice and Data Network Integration

Larry Schessel

INTRODUCTION

Voice over Internet Protocol (VoIP) is the enabling technology for this service integration. In short, 64Kbps voice is converted into data packets and transferred over the data backbone. The savings of voice and data over a single corporate network can be considerable and the technology exists. But where does a company begin? This article reviews the enabling technologies and presents a viable private network evolution strategy that takes advantage of current technologies and standards. Savings are realized almost immediately.

VOICE AND DATA NETWORKS

Companies with private voice networks own one or more private branch exchanges (PBX)s to deliver the service. A PBX is the switching element that link two users together in a voice connection. PBXs can be broken done into the following basic functional components:

- Wiring: PBXs require dedicated wiring to each telephone in the company. This allows employees to call other employees connected to the PBX. To gain access to the public service telephone network (PSTN), PBXs require outside lines purchased from the local public telephone company.
- Hardware: PBX hardware includes line cards terminating the local wiring, a switch network that makes the connection between two telephones, and servers for PBX software.
- Software: PBX software controls the call setup and features such as call forwarding, call transfer, and call hold; software also provides operation and maintenance support as well as per-call statistics.

Companies with multiple locations require dedicated PBXs at each site and public leased lines connecting the multiple PBXs into a single logical network.

0-8493-9838-X/00/$0.00+$.50
© 2000 by CRC Press LLC

Private data networks are delivered using equipment known as routers and hubs. Similar to voice networks, data networks also require dedicated wiring between the different network elements and to each desktop. PCs, servers, printers, and scanners are some of the data devices that can be connected to the network to deliver specific services. Once networked, these devices communicate with each other, passing information in the form of data packets. Exhibit 22.1 compares the voice and data network topologies.

VOICE OVER INTERNET PROTOCOL

When a user picks up and dials the telephone, the PBX provides dial tone, collects digits, and routes the call based on entered digits. In routing the call, the PBX sets up a dedicated connection between the two users. As the users speak into their phones, the PBX converts the analog voice into digital signals and sends the digitized voice across the connection at a rate of 64Kbps. The PBX converts the analog signal to digital format by sampling the analog voice every 125 microseconds and converting the voice sample to an 8-bit digital representation. Digitized voice is converted back to an analog signal at the terminating end of the connection.

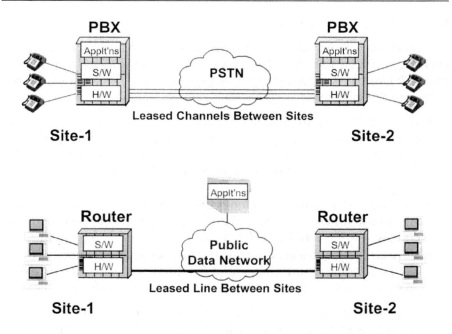

Exhibit 22.1.   Comparison Between Private Voice and Data Networks

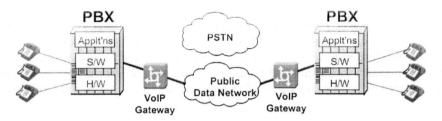

Step-1 Introduce VoIP Gateways for Inter-PBX Links

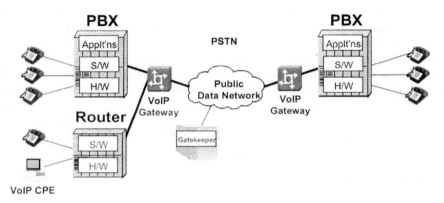

Step-2 Introduce VoIP Gatekeeper and CPE

Exhibit 22.1. **Comparison Between Private Voice and Data Networks**
(Continued)

IP data networks, on the other hand, handle device communication by packaging information into logical envelopes known as packets, addressing the packets with destination information, and routing the packets through the network. Each network node looks at the addressing information and passes the packet onto the next network node until the packet arrives at its final destination. This routing method is connectionless because there is no dedicated connection between origination and termination as there is with a voice connection. A side benefit of connectionless communication is the fact that bandwidth is only required when there is information to send.

VoIP merges voice and data technologies into one ubiquitous voice service. Analog voice signals are sampled and digitized the same as the steps performed by the voice network. However, rather than send the 64Kbps digitized signals over dedicated voice channels, the digitized voice is packetized and sent over the IP data network. Furthermore, bandwidth efficiencies can be realized if the voice signal is compressed prior to pack-etization. Voice compression can lower bandwidth demands as low as 4Kbps while maintaining near toll-quality voice. This means that a single 64Kbps channel that normally carries a single voice conversation in the voice network can carry up to 16 voice conversations in the data network.

To support call control, the International Telecommunication Union (ITU-T) has standardized the H.323 protocol. H.323 describes terminals, equipment, and services for multimedia communication over a local area network (LAN), voice being just one service supported. Other recommen-dations within the H.323-Series include H.225 packet and synchronization, H.245 control, H.261 and H.263 video codecs, G.711, G.722, G.728, G.729, and G.723 audio codecs, and the T.120-series of multimedia communica-tions protocols. Taken as a whole, these recommendations provide the standards to which many backbone, access, and customer premise equip-ment vendors are developing VoIP components and guaranteeing interop-erability. Cisco, for example, has integrated H.323 protocols and voice capabilities into each of their newest routers. Microsoft and Intel also have H.323-compatible products for voice and data communications. The next section provides an overview of product categories.

VoIP PRODUCTS

H.323 VoIP products can be broken out into the following general prod-uct categories that loosely map to network layers:

- **Customer premise equipment (CPE):** Originally, H.323 CPE was mostly developed for multimedia communication. Products such as Microsoft Netmeeting, Intel Proshare®, and PictureTel LiveLAN™ were marketed for their desktop video and data sharing capabilities. More recently, however, CPE products have been developed that are more focused on IP-voice communication. The Selsius Ethernet phone, for example, resembles a standard phone but connects to an Ethernet port rather than a PBX port. Symbol Technologies has developed a wireless H.323 telephone that also connects directly into an Ethernet port.
- **Network infrastructure:** Network equipment includes standard rout-ers, hubs, and switches. Voice, however, is very susceptible to net-work delays and packet loss. Router features such as random early drop/detect, weighed fair queuing, reservation protocol (RSVP), IP precedence, compressed real-time protocol, and multi-class multi-link PPP have been developed to address these issues and are prescribed in a converged network. Asynchronous transfer mode (ATM) network equipment also supports quality of service parameters and enables the administrator to set up dedicated private virtual connections (PVCs) between sites.

- **Servers:** A major VoIP benefit is the fact that it builds on the Internet model where there is a clear separation between network infrastructure and network applications. While network infrastructure provides the packet transport, servers support the applications. The H.323 gatekeeper server, for example, supports call control functions; an accounting, authorization, and administration (AAA) server provides billing and accounting; and network management typically requires a simple network management protocol (SNMP) server.
- **Gateways:** It will still be a long time before one sees the data network handling all voice communication. As an interim step, gateways will be necessary to link the new IP-based voice services with existing public and private voice networks. Gateways also provide a good evolutionary step for companies to selectively choose how and where they will apply VoIP for low risk and high returns.

VOICE AND DATA NETWORK INTEGRATION

So, the technology, standards, and products exist to migrate voice onto the corporate data network. But where does a company begin in order to minimize network risk and optimize savings? There are two major areas for network cost savings in a voice network: PBX private service (single location and multi-location) and public service (local and long distance). There is also another category representing value-added services that are enabled due to the voice, data, and video integration. These value-added services offer potential for companies to reengineer existing services such as automatic call distribution (ACD) services and build new services such as click-to-dial, where an Internet user can access a company's operator through the Web.

The following sections discuss each category in further detail. Included is a proposed network integration plan as well as future value-added services to consider when building the next-generation converged communication network. Refer to Exhibit 22.2 for a summary of the proposed private voice network evolution.

Private Voice Service

Purchasing a PBX is a big decision for a company. For one thing, it is expensive; and once purchased, the company is locked into the specific PBX vendor for hardware/software upgrades and maintenance. Companies are also limited to the call control features supported by the PBX so that little differentiation is possible between themselves and their competition.

In an IP world, networks are built in layers. Companies first choose the underlying infrastructure, for example, routers, switches, or ATM equipment. Then, companies choose the application protocol; IP for VoIP. Finally, they decide the specific services, servers, and CPE that they wish

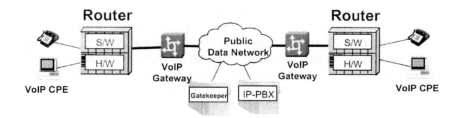

Step-3 Replace PBX with IP-PBX

Exhibit 22.2.   Stepwise Private Voice Network Evolution

---

to run over the network. Taken as a whole, the decision is just as important as the PBX decision. But taken separately, each decision is much lower in cost and risk; new technologies can be introduced with little or no impact to other network layers.

VoIP assumes that there is already a data infrastructure supporting IP services; IP data infrastructure is a mature market with many third- and fourth-generation products. VoIP, however, is in its infancy. The most mature of the products are VoIP gateways providing interworking between the voice and data networks. Gateways terminate voice interfaces from a PBX or public voice switch and convert the signaling and voice to IP protocol. Gateways then send the information across the IP network to either another gateway or a VoIP CPE.

Gateway-to-gateway communication is a good first step for a company introducing VoIP capabilities. Back-to-back gateways provide an alternative to dedicated inter-PBX trunks, typically leased lines — which are very expensive if purchased from a public carrier. Instead, gateway-to-gateway service allows the network administrator to redirect leased-line inter-PBX traffic over the internal corporate IP network. Gateway costs can be recovered in months, depending on the number of locations and distance.

Gateway-to-gateway communication can also be used to link a remote office to the corporate office PBX. The remote office would appear as one or more extensions off the corporate office PBX, and traffic to and from the remote office would be routed through the PBX. Cisco, for example, has integrated VoIP capabilities into both its small remote office routers as well as larger corporate office routers to support such an application.

Introducing H.323 CPE to the network is a good second step in the corporate network VoIP evolution. This enables IP users to originate and terminate calls directly from their PC, Ethernet phone, or wireless IP-phone. IP devices add a level of network complexity due to the potentially large number of users, security issues, and varying IP device types. The H.323 gate-keeper provides the needed user authorization and routing capabilities. Many vendors have introduced gatekeepers, both integrated into the router and contained on separate servers. Both solutions offer viable alternatives.

With the combination of gateway, gatekeeper, and IP device, companies can begin to introduce business solutions to work at home and CTI applications. Basically, the IP device can be logged into the corporate data network at the same time as calls are originated and terminated from the device. Help Desk operators working from home, for example, would require only a single link into the corporate data network to answer customer questions and access corporate information.

The third major step in evolving the private voice network is fully replacing the PBX with a next-generation IP-PBX. As discussed earlier, PBXs rely on wiring to the desktop and provide hardware and software for call control, accounting, etc. In a VoIP network, Ethernet wiring provides the desktop wiring, the data backbone provides the transport, and servers provide the PBX call control features. The wiring and data backbone exist, while companies such as Selsius and NBX are introducing the server and CPE components. It will not be long before IP-PBX features match and surpass capabilities of current PBXs and the IP-PBX becomes a viable alternative.

Value-Added Services

One area where IP-PBX features will surpass PBX capabilities will be value-added services. These are services that take advantage of voice, data, and video integration as well as IP network and device capabilities to delivery services not possible on a PBX. Some of these services offer significant cost savings, while others offer revenue-generating opportunities. Following are several value-added service examples to consider when implementing a VoIP network. Note that many other services are possible by adding new servers to the network similar to adding new Web sites to an IP network.

- **Unified messaging.** Most corporate managers receive voicemail, e-mail, and faxes on a daily basis. While timely information is one of the keys to a successful business, it is also difficult to manage the information, especially when it arrives in different forms and locations. Unified messaging consolidates the different information into a single mailbox accessible from a telephone, Web site, or pager. The unified messaging server supports media conversion so that e-mails can be read to phone users, faxes can be redirected to local fax machines, and voicemail can be converted to audio files and played back on a computer. Future enhancements may include videomail and interactive content.

- **IP call center/click-to-dial.** The number of Internet users and the amount of Internet commerce are growing faster than most estimates. Intel, for example, just announced that it is generating over $1 billion in revenue per month directly from the Internet. Cisco also generates over 50 percent of its revenue from direct Internet sales. VoIP offers further opportunity to reach customers through the Internet by enabling direct and immediate interactions with customer service representatives. The click-to-dial application enables users to click a Web site button to automatically set up a VoIP call between user and operator. IP call centers extend the model so that the call completes between IP user and IP attendant, thereby lowering 800 service costs.
- **Active directory services.** There is much electronic information within a corporation and contained on public servers. Active directories enable users to interact with the directory, potentially clicking an employee name and connecting to the user through the Internet. This service integrates the data server with VoIP capabilities and strengthens the argument for integrated voice and data services.
- **Virtual second line.** Eventually, VoIP devices will be in widespread use within the corporation and residence. Much of their success will depend on how they are addressed. Dialing an IP address to reach these devices is cumbersome and doomed to failure because it changes the way people are accustomed to making a call. The possibility exists, however, to address the IP device with a standard telephone number. This strategy merges seamlessly with today's telephones and cellular phones and provides a good evolutionary path to the next-generation communication network.
- **Follow-me/find-me.** Once the IP device has an assigned telephone number, many standard telephone features can be carried over from the PSTN. Call forwarding, call transfer, and three-way calling are examples. Follow-me service allows users to predefine a search list of telephone numbers at which they may be contacted (e.g., work number, home number, and cellular number). When an incoming call arrives, the service rings each number on the list and, once located, transfers the incoming call to one's current location. It is an intuitive step to add the IP device telephone number to the list and direct incoming calls to the IP device when active.
- **Desktop video conferencing.** VoIP specifically refers to handling voice service over the IP network. The benefits of VoIP, however, extend beyond voice. If the devices at either end of a VoIP connection support voice, video, and data, then the underlying signaling will set up a multimedia connection. No user interface change is required; the user still dials a standard telephone number. For example, a company that builds an internal VoIP network can take advantage of full multimedia communication between employees. Gateways can provide the interoperability with older telephone devices and links to the public

voice network. Not only are costs reduced because voice services are moved onto the private data network, but internal services are enhanced with video and data as well.

Public Voice Services

Public voice carriers have also recognized the potential cost savings and new revenue from VoIP solutions. Most carriers have ongoing trials to better define market segments and decide where best to apply internal resources. With the convergence of voice, data, and video, additional carriers are entering the foray. Internet service providers (ISPs), competitive local exchange carriers (CLECs), inter-LATA exchange carriers (IXCs), and cable companies have all begun investing in VoIP solutions. Some are looking to enhance existing services, while others are looking to compete with incumbent carriers.

This is all very good news to companies looking for competitive public service rates because increased competition is expected to drive down local and long-distance service rates. Already, VoIP-based companies such as ITXC have begun to offer cut-rate international and long-distance calling card services.

It is also good news for companies evolving their networks to VoIP solutions. In the short term, they can be assured that vendor priority is kept on standards and interoperability. Longer term, as carriers begin offering VoIP public services, company voice traffic can seamlessly transfer from private to public networks without the need for gateways, moving end-to-end via VoIP.

CONCLUSION

The communication paradigm is on the verge of change, signaling a new generation of lower-cost voice, video, and data services. Companies have the opportunity to take advantage of this paradigm shift in a low-risk and cost-effective manner. VoIP is the enabling technology to begin integrating voice, video, and data services onto a single data backbone network. VoIP to PSTN gateways are a good first step to begin the convergence because they are established products with many competitors. Gatekeepers and IP CPE are close behind, with the potential to introduce new value-added services. Finally, there is the opportunity to rebuild the infrastructure with IP-PBXs and public VoIP offerings. This enables ubiquitous voice, video, and data services over a data backbone and offers services one can only begin to imagine.

Chapter 23
RSVP: Building Blocks of the Next-Generation Internet

William Stallings

As the Internet and private internets grow in scale, a host of new demands march steadily into view. Low-volume Telnet conversations are leapfrogged by high-volume client/server applications. To this has more recently been added the tremendous volume of World Wide Web traffic, which is increasingly graphics-intensive. Now real-time voice and video applications add to the burden. To cope with these demands, it is not enough to increase Internet capacity. Sensible and effective methods for managing the traffic and controlling congestion are needed.

Historically, Internet Protocol (IP)-based internets have been able to provide a simple best-effort delivery service to all applications using an internet. But the needs of users have changed. A company may have spent millions of dollars installing an IP-based internet designed to transport data among LANs but now finds that new real-time, multimedia, and multicasting applications are not well supported by such a configuration. The only networking scheme designed from day one to support both traditional Transmission Control Protocol (TCP) and User Datagram Protocol (UDP) traffic and real-time traffic is asynchronous transfer mode (ATM). However, reliance on ATM means either constructing a second networking infrastructure for real-time traffic or replacing the existing IP-based configuration with ATM, both of which are costly alternatives. Thus, there is a strong need to be able to support a variety of traffic with a variety of quality of service requirements, within the TCP/IP architecture. A key tool for meeting this need has emerged: the Resource Reservation Protocol (RSVP) allows end systems to reserve internet resources to assure a given quality of service; in particular, RSVP can reserve the resources needed for real-time traffic.

RESOURCE RESERVATION: RSVP

A key task, perhaps the key task, of an internetwork is to deliver data from a source to one or more destinations with the desired quality of service,

0-8493-9838-X/00/$0.00+$.50
© 2000 by CRC Press LLC

such as throughput, delay, delay variance, etc. This task becomes increasingly difficult on any internetwork with increasing number of users, data rate of applications, and use of multicasting. To meet these needs, it is not enough for an internet to react to congestion. Instead a tool is needed to prevent congestion by allowing applications to reserve network resources at a given quality of service.

Preventive measures can be useful in both unicast and multicast transmission. For unicast, two applications agree on a specific quality of service for a session and expect the internetwork to support that quality of service. If the internetwork is heavily loaded, it may not provide the desired quality of service and instead deliver packets at a reduced quality of service. In that case, the applications may have preferred to wait before initiating the session or at least to have been alerted to the potential for reduced quality of service. A way of dealing with this situation is to have the unicast applications reserve resources in order to meet a given quality of service. Routers along an intended path could then pre-allocate resources (queue space, outgoing capacity) to assure the desired quality of service. If a router could not meet the resource reservation because of prior outstanding reservations, then the applications could be informed. The applications may then decide to try again at a reduced quality of service reservation or may decide to try later.

Multicast transmission presents a much more compelling case for implementing resource reservation. A multicast transmission can generate a tremendous amount of internetwork traffic if either the application is high volume (e.g., video) or the group of multicast destinations is large and scattered, or both. What makes the case for multicast resource reservation is that much of the potential load generated by a multicast source may easily be prevented. This is so for two reasons: (1) Some members of an existing multicast group may not require delivery from a particular source over some given period of time. For example, there may be two "channels" (two multicast sources) broadcasting to a particular multicast group at the same time. A multicast destination may wish to "tune in" to only one channel at a time. (2) Some members of a group may be able to handle only a portion of the source transmission. For example, a video source may transmit a video stream that consists of two components: a basic component that provides a reduced picture quality, and an enhanced component. Some receivers may not have the processing power to handle the enhanced component, or may be connected to the internetwork through a subnetwork or link that does not have the capacity for the full signal.

Thus, the use of resource reservation can enable routers to decide ahead of time if they can meet the requirement to deliver a multicast transmission to all designated multicast receivers and to reserve the appropriate resources if possible. Internet resource reservation differs from the type of resource reservation that may be implemented in a connection-oriented network, such as ATM or frame relay. An internet resource reservation scheme must interact with a dynamic routing strategy that allows the route followed by packets of a given transmission to change. When the route changes, the resource reservations must be changed. To deal with this dynamic situation, the concept of soft state is used. A soft state is simply a set of state information at a router that expires unless regularly refreshed from the entity that requested the state. If a route for a given transmission changes, then some soft states will expire and new resource reservations will invoke the appropriate soft states on the new routers along the route. Thus, the end systems requesting resources must periodically renew their requests during the course of an application transmission.

RSVP GOALS AND CHARACTERISTICS

The following design goals guided the development of the RSVP specification:

1. Provide the ability of heterogeneous receivers to make reservations specifically tailored to their own needs. As was mentioned, some members of a multicast group may be able to handle or may want to handle only a portion of a multicast transmission, such as a low-resolution component of a video signal. Differing resource reservations among members of the same multicast group should be allowed.
2. Deal gracefully with changes in multicast group membership. Membership in a group can be dynamic. Thus, reservations must be dynamic, and again, this suggests that separate dynamic reservations are needed for each multicast group member.
3. Specify resource requirements in such a way that the aggregate resources reserved for a multicast group reflect the resources actually needed. Multicast routing takes place over a tree such that packet splitting is minimized. Therefore, when resources are reserved for individual multicast group members, these reservations must be aggregated to take into account the common path segments shared by the routes to different group members.
4. Enable receivers to select one source from among multiple sources transmitting to a multicast group. This is the channel-changing capability that was described earlier.
5. Deal gracefully with changes in routes, automatically reestablishing the resource reservation along the new paths as long as adequate resources are available. Because routes may change during the course of the transmission of an application, the resource reservations must also change so that the routers actually on the current path receive the reservations.

271

6. Control protocol overhead. Just as resource reservations are aggregated to take advantage of common path segments among multiple multicast receivers, the actual RSVP reservation request messages should be aggregated to minimize the amount of RSVP traffic in the Internet.
7. Be independent of routing protocol. RSVP is not a routing protocol; its task is to establish and maintain resource reservations over a path or distribution tree, independent of how the path or tree was created.

Based on these design goals, the specification lists the following characteristics of RSVP:

- Unicast and multicast: RSVP makes reservations for both unicast and multicast transmissions, adapting dynamically to changing group membership as well as to changing routes, and reserving resources based on the individual requirements of multicast members.
- Simplex: RSVP makes reservations for unidirectional data flow. Data exchanges between two end systems require separate reservations in the two directions.
- Receiver-initiated reservation: The receiver of a data flow initiates and maintains the resource reservation for that flow.
- Maintaining soft state in the Internet: RSVP maintains a soft state at intermediate routers and leaves the responsibility for maintaining these reservation states to end users.
- Providing different reservation styles: These allow RSVP users to specify how reservations for the same multicast group should be aggregated at the intermediate switches. This feature enables a more efficient use of Internet resources.
- Transparent operation through non-RSVP routers: Because reservations and RSVP are independent of routing protocol, there is no fundamental conflict in a mixed environment in which some routers do not employ RSVP. These routers will simply use a best-effort delivery technique.
- Support for IPv4 and IPv6: RSVP can exploit the Type-of-Service field in the IPv4 header and the Flow Label field in the IPv6 header.

RECEIVER-INITIATED RESERVATION

Previous attempts at resource reservation, and the approach taken in frame relay and ATM networks, is for the source of a data flow to request a given set of resources. In a strictly unicast environment, this approach is reasonable. A transmitting application is able to transmit data at a certain rate and has a given quality of service designed into the transmission scheme. However, this approach is inadequate for multicasting. One reason is that different members of the same multicast group may have different resource requirements. If the source transmission flow can be divided into component subflows, then some multicast members may require only a single subflow. If there are multiple sources transmitting to a multicast group, then a particular multicast receiver may want to select only one or a subset of all sources to receive. Finally, the quality of service requirements of different receivers may differ, depending on the output equipment, processing power, and link speed of the receiver. It therefore makes sense for receivers rather than senders to make resource reservations. A sender needs to provide the routers with the traffic characteristics of the transmission (data rate, variability), but it is the receivers that must specify the desired quality of service. Routers can then aggregate multicast resource reservations to take advantage of shared path segments along the distribution tree.

DATA FLOWS

Three concepts relating to data flows form the basis of RSVP operation: session, flow specification, and filter specification. A session is a data flow identified by its destination. Once a reservation is made at a router by a particular destination, the router considers this as a session and allocates resources for the life of that session. A reservation request issued by a destination end system is called a flow descriptor, and consists of a flowspec and a filter spec. The flowspec specifies a desired quality of service and is used to set parameters in a the packet scheduler of a node. That is, the router will transmit packets with a given set of preferences based on the current flowspecs. The filter spec defines the set of packets for which a reservation is requested. Thus, the filter spec together with the session define the set of packets, or flow, that are to receive the desired quality of service. Any other packets addressed to the same destination are handled as best-effort traffic. The content of the flowspec is beyond the scope of RSVP, which is merely a carrier of the request. In general, a flowspec contains a service class, an Rspec (R for reserve) and a Tspec (T for traffic). The service class is an identifier of a type of service being requested. The other two parameters are sets of numeric values. The Rspec parameter defines the desired quality of service, and the Tspec parameter describes the data flow. The contents of Rspec and Tspec are opaque to RSVP. In principle, the filter spec may designate an arbitrary subset of the packets of one session (i.e., the packets arriving with the destination specified by this session). For example, a filter spec could specify only specific sources, or specific source protocols, or in general only packets that have a match on certain fields in any of the protocol headers in the packet. Exhibit 23.1 indicates the relationship among session, flowspec, and filter spec. Each incoming packet is part of at most one session and is treated according to the logical flow indicated in Exhibit 23.1 for that session. If a packet belongs to no session, it is given a best-effort delivery service.

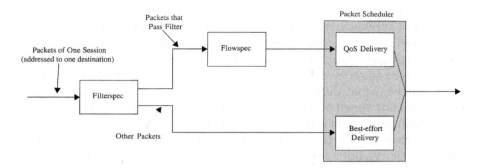

Exhibit 23.1. Treatment of Packets at One Session at One Router

RSVP OPERATION

Much of the complexity of RSVP has to do with dealing with multicast transmission. Unicast transmission is treated as a special case. An example multicast configuration is shown in Exhibit 23.2a. This configuration consist of four routers. The link between any two routers, indicated by a line, could be a point-to-point link or a subnetwork. Three hosts, G1, G2, and G3, are members of a multicast group and can receive datagrams with the corresponding destination multicast address. Two hosts, S1 and S2, transmit data to this multicast address. The heavy black lines indicate the routing tree for source S1 and this multicast group, and the heavy gray lines indicate the routing tree for source S2 and this multicast group. The arrowed lines indicate packet transmission from S1 (black) and S2 (gray). We can see that all four routers need to be aware of the resource reservations of each multicast destination. Thus, resource requests from the destinations must propagate backward through the routing trees toward each potential host.

RSVP PROTOCOL MECHANISMS

RSVP uses two basic message types: Resv and Path. Resv messages originate at a multicast group receivers and propagate upstream through the distribution tree, being merged and packed when appropriate at each node along the way. These messages create soft states within the routers of the distribution tree that define the resources reserved for this session (this multicast address). Ultimately, the merged Resv messages reach the sending hosts, enabling the hosts to set up appropriate traffic control parameters for the first hop. Exhibit 23.2b indicates the flow of Resv messages. Note that messages are merged so that only a single message flows upstream along any branch of the combined distribution trees. However, these messages must be repeated periodically to maintain the soft states. The Path message is used to provide upstream routing information. In all of the multicast routing protocols currently in use, only a downstream route,

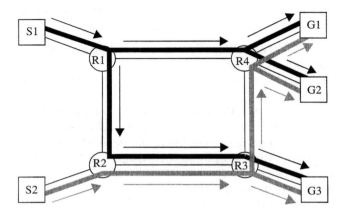

(a) Data Distribution to a Multicast Group

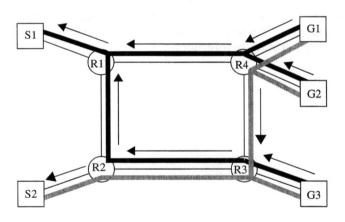

(b) Merged Resv Messages

Exhibit 23.2.   RSVP Operation

in the form of a distribution tree, is maintained. However, the Resv messages must propagate upstream through all intermediate routers and to all sending hosts. In the absence of reverse routing information from the routing protocol, RSVP provides this with the Path message. Each host that wishes to participate as a sender in a multicast group issues a Path message that is transmitted throughout the distribution tree to all multicast destinations. Along the way, each router and each destination host creates a path state that indicates the reverse hop to be used for this source. Exhibit 23.2a indicates the paths taken by these messages, which is the same as the paths taken by data packets. From the host perspective, the operation of the protocol can be described as follows:

1. A receiver joins a multicast group by sending an IGMP join message to a neighboring router.
2. A potential sender issues a Path message to the multicast group address.
3. A receiver receives a Path message identifying a sender.
4. Now that the receiver has reverse path information, it may begin sending Resv messages, specifying the desired flow descriptors.
5. The Resv message propagates through the internetwork and is delivered to the sender.
6. The sender starts sending data packets.
7. The receiver starts receiving data packets.

Events 1 and 2 may happen in either order.

SUMMARY

To meet the demands of increased volume, real-time applications, and multicasting, internets need new tools. RSVP provides a solid foundation for the next generation of internets.

Chapter 24
IPv6: The Next-Generation Internet Protocol

Gary C. Kessler

The Internet is historically linked to the ARPANET, the pioneering packet-switched network built for the U.S. Department of Defense in 1969. Starting with four nodes that year, the ARPANET slowly grew to encompass many systems across the U.S., and connected to hosts in Europe and Asia by the end of the 1970s. By the early 1980s, many regional and national networks across the globe started to become interconnected, and their common communications protocols were based on the Transmission Control Protocol/Internet Protocol (TCP/IP) suite. By the late 1980s, the number of host systems on these primarily academic and research networks could be counted in the hundreds or thousands. In addition, most of the traffic was supporting simple text-based applications, such as electronic mail (e-mail), file transfers, and remote log-in.

By the 1990s, however, users discovered the Internet and commercial use, previously prohibited or constrained on the Internet, was actively encouraged. Since the beginning of this decade, new host systems are being added to the Internet at rates of up to 10% per month, and the Internet has been doubling in size every 10-12 months for several years. By January 1997, there were more than 16 million hosts on the Internet, ranging from PC-class systems to supercomputers, on more than 100,000 networks worldwide.

The number of connected hosts is only one measure of the Internet's growth. Another way to quantify the change, however, is in the changing applications. On today's Internet it is common to see hypermedia, audio, video, animation, and other types of traffic that were once thought to be anathema to a packet-switching environment. As the Internet provides better service support, new applications will spark even more growth and changing demographics. In addition, nomadic access has become a major issue with the increased use of laptop computers, and security concerns have grown as a result of the increased amount of sensitive information accessible via the Internet.

IPV6 BACKGROUND AND FEATURES

The Internet protocol (IP) was introduced in the ARPANET in the mid-1970s. The version of IP commonly used today is version 4 (IPv4), described in Request for Comments (RFC) 791. (See the Appendix at the end of this chapter for a listing of RFCs related to IPv6.)

Although several protocol suites (including Open Systems Interconnection) were proposed over the years to replace IPv4, none succeeded because of IPv4's large and continually growing installed base. Nevertheless, IPv4 was never intended for today's Internet in terms of the number of hosts, types of applications, or security concerns.

In the early 1990s, the Internet Engineering Task Force (IETF) recognized that the only way to cope with these changes was to design a new version of IP to become the successor to IPv4. The IETF formed the IP next-generation (IPng) Working Group to define this transitional protocol, ensuring long-term compatibility between the current and new IP versions and support for current and emerging IP-based applications.

Work started on IPng in 1991, and several IPng proposals were subsequently drafted. The result of this effort was IP version 6 (IPv6), described in RFCs 1883 to 1886; these four RFCs were officially entered into the Internet Standards Track in December 1995.

Differences Between IPv4 and IPv6

IPv6 was designed as an evolution from IPv4 rather than as a radical change. Useful features of IPv4 were carried over in IPv6, and less useful features were dropped. According to the IPv6 specification, the changes from IPv4 to IPv6 fall primarily into the following categories:

- *Expanded addressing capabilities.* The IP address size is increased from 32 bits to 128 bits in IPv6, supporting a much greater number of addressable nodes, more levels of addressing hierarchy, and simpler autoconfiguration of addresses for remote users. The scalability of multicast routing is improved by adding a scope field to multicast addresses. A new type of address, called *anycast*, is also defined.

- *Header format simplification.* Some IPv4 header fields have been dropped or made optional to reduce the necessary amount of packet processing and to limit the bandwidth cost of the IPv6 header.

- *Improved support for extensions and options.* IPv6 header options are encoded to allow for more efficient forwarding, less stringent limits on the length of options, and greater flexibility for introducing new options in the future. Some fields of an IPv4 header are optional in IPv6.

- *Flow labeling capability.* A new quality-of-service capability has been added to enable the labeling of packets belonging to particular traffic "flows" for which the sender requests special handling, such as real-time service.

- *Authentication and privacy capabilities.* Extensions to support security options, such as authentication, data integrity, and data confidentiality, are built into IPv6.

Improved Terminology of IPv6

IPv6 also introduces and formalizes terminology that, in the IPv4 environment, are loosely defined, ill-defined, or undefined. The new and improved terminology includes the following:

- *Packet.* This is an IPv6 protocol data unit (PDU), comprising a header and the associated payload. In IPv4, this would have been termed "packet" or "datagram."

- *Node.* This is a device that implements IPv6.

- *Router.* This is an IPv6 node that forwards packets, based on the IP address, not explicitly addressed to itself. In former TCP/IP terminology, this device was often referred to as a gateway.

- *Host.* This represents any node that is not a router. Hosts are typically end-user systems.

- *Link.* This is a medium over which nodes communicate with one another at the data link layer (e.g., an automated teller machine, a frame relay, a switched multimegabit data service wide area network, or an Ethernet or Token Ring local area network).

- *Neighbors.* These are nodes attached to the same link.

IPV6 HEADER FORMAT

The format of an IPv6 header is shown in Exhibit 24.1. Although IPv6 addresses are four times the size of IPv4 addresses, the basic IPv6 header is only twice the size of an IPv4 header, thus decreasing the impact of the larger address fields. The fields of the IPv6 header are

- *Version.* This represents the IP version number (4 bits). This field's value is 6 for IPv6 and 4 for IPv4. This field is in the same location as the version field in the IPv4 header, making it simple for an IP node to quickly distinguish an IPv4 packet from an IPv6 packet.

- *Priority.* This enables a source to identify the desired delivery priority of the packet (4 bits).

```
+-+-+-+-+-+-+-+-+-+-+-+-+-+-+-+-+-+-+-+-+-+-+-+-+-+-+-+-+-+-+-+-+
|Version| Prio. |                    Flow Label                 |
+-+-+-+-+-+-+-+-+-+-+-+-+-+-+-+-+-+-+-+-+-+-+-+-+-+-+-+-+-+-+-+-+
|          Payload Length          |  Next Header  |  Hop Limit  |
+-+-+-+-+-+-+-+-+-+-+-+-+-+-+-+-+-+-+-+-+-+-+-+-+-+-+-+-+-+-+-+-+
|                                                               |
+                                                               +
|                                                               |
+                          Source Address                       +
|                                                               |
+                                                               +
|                                                               |
+-+-+-+-+-+-+-+-+-+-+-+-+-+-+-+-+-+-+-+-+-+-+-+-+-+-+-+-+-+-+-+-+
|                                                               |
+                                                               +
|                                                               |
+                       Destination Address                     +
|                                                               |
+                                                               +
|                                                               |
+-+-+-+-+-+-+-+-+-+-+-+-+-+-+-+-+-+-+-+-+-+-+-+-+-+-+-+-+-+-+-+-+
```

Exhibit 24.1.   IPv6 Header Format

- *Flow label.* This is used by a source to identify associated packets needing the same type of special handling, such as a real-time service between a pair of hosts (24 bits).

- *Payload length.* This is the length of the portion of the packet following the header, in octets (16 bits). The maximum value in this field is 65,535; if this field contains zero, it means that the packet contains a payload larger than 64K bytes and the actual payload length value is carried in a jumbo payload hop-by-hop option.

- *Next header.* This identifies the type of header immediately following the IPv6 header and uses the same values as the IPv4 protocol field, where applicable (8 bits). The next header field can indicate an options header, higher layer protocol, or no protocol above IP. Sample values are listed in Table 24.1:

- *Hop limit.* This specifies the maximum number of hops that a packet may take before it is discarded (8 bits). This value is set by the source

Table 24.1.   Possible Values for the Next Header Field

Value	Contents of the next header
1	Internet Control Message Protocol (ICMP)
6	Transmission Control Protocol (TCP)
17	User Datagram Protocol (UDP)
43	Routing header
44	Fragment header
58	Internet Control Message Protocol version 6 (ICMPv6)
59	nothing; this is the final header
60	Destination Options header
89	Open Shortest Path First (OSPF)

and decremented by one by each node that forwards the packet; the packet is discarded if the hop limit reaches zero. The comparable field in IPv4 is the time to live (TTL) field; it was renamed for IPv6 because the value limits the number of hops, not the amount of time that a packet can stay in the network.

- *Source address.* This is the IPv6 address of the originator of the packet (128 bits).
- *Destination address.* This is the IPv6 address of the intended recipients of the packet (128 bits).

IPv6 Addresses

To accommodate almost unlimited growth and a variety of addressing formats, IPv6 addresses are 128 bits in length. This address space is probably sufficient to uniquely address every molecule in the solar system.

IPv6 defines three types of addresses:

- A *unicast address* specifies a single host.
- An *anycast address* specifies a set of hosts, such as a set of file transfer protocol (FTP) servers for a given organization. A packet sent to an anycast address is delivered to one of the hosts identified by that address, usually the "closest" one as defined by the routing protocol.
- A *multicast address* also identifies a set of hosts; a packet sent to a multicast address is delivered to all the hosts in the group.

There is no broadcast address in IPv6 as in IPv4 because that function is provided by multicast addresses.

IPv4 addresses are written in dotted decimal notation, where the decimal value of each of the four address bytes is separated by dots. The preferred form of an IPv6 address is to write the hexadecimal value of the eight 16-bit blocks of the address, separated by colons (:), such as FF04:19:5: ABD4:187:2C:754:2B1. The leading zeros do not have to be written and each field must have some value.

IPv6 addresses often contain long strings of zeros because of the way in which addresses are allocated. A compressed address form uses a double colon (::) to indicate multiple 16-bit blocks of zeros; for example, the address FF01:0:0:0:0:0:0:5A could be written as FF01::5A. To avoid ambiguity, the "::" can only appear once in an address.

An alternative, hybrid address format has been defined to make it more convenient to represent an IPv4 address in an IPv6 environment. In this scheme, the first 96 address bits (six groups of 16) are represented in the regular IPv6 format and the remaining 32 address bits are represented in common IPv4 dotted decimal; for example, 0:0:0:0:0:0:199.182.20.17 (or ::199.182.20.17).

Address Prefix Allocation

One of the goals of the IPv6 address format is to accommodate many different types of addresses. The beginning of an address contains a 3- to 10-bit format prefix defining the general address type; the remaining bits contain the actual host address, in a format specific to the indicated address type. Table 24.2 represents an address prefix allocation (from RFC 1884).

The Provider-Based Unicast Address

The provider-based unicast address is an IPv6 address that might be assigned by an Internet service provider (ISP) to a customer. Exhibit 24.2 shows a provider-based unicast address format. This type of address contains a number of subfields, including the following:

- *Format prefix.* This indicates the type of address as provider-based unicast. It is always 3 bits, coded "010."

- *Registry identifier.* This identifies the Internet address registry from which the ISP obtains addresses.

- *Provider identifier.* This identifies the ISP. This field contains the address block assigned to the ISP by the address registry authority.

- *Subscriber identifier.* This identifies the ISP's subscriber. This field contains the address assigned to this subscriber by the ISP. The providerID and subscriberID fields together are 56 bits in length.

- *Intrasubscriber.* This contains the portion of the address assigned and managed by the subscriber.

IPv4-Compatible Addresses

Another particularly important address type is the one that indicates an IPv4 address. With more than 16 million hosts using 32-bit addresses, the

Table 24.2.   Address Prefix Allocation (from RFC 1884)

Allocation	Prefix (Binary)	Fraction of Address Space
Reserved	0000 0000	1/256
Unassigned	0000 0001	1/256
Reserved for NSAP Allocation	0000 001	1/128
Reserved for IPX Allocation	0000 010	1/128
Unassigned	0000 011	1/128
Unassigned	0000 1	1/32
Unassigned	0001	1/16
Unassigned	001	1/8
Provider-Based Unicast Address	010	1/8
Unassigned	011	1/8
Reserved for Geographic-Based Unicast Addresses	100	1/8
Unassigned	101	1/8
Unassigned	110	1/8
Unassigned	1110	1/16
Unassigned	1111 0	1/32
Unassigned	1111 10	1/64
Unassigned	1111 110	1/128
Unassigned	1111 1110 0	1/512
Link Local Use Addresses	1111 1110 10	1/1024
Site Local Use Addresses	1111 1110 11	1/1024
Multicast Addresses	1111 1111	1/256

public Internet must continue to accommodate IPv4 addresses even as it slowly migrates to IPv6 addressing.

IPv4 addresses are carried in a 128-bit IPv6 address that begins with 80 zeros (0:0:0:0:0). The next 16-bit block contains the compatibility bits, which indicate the way in which the host/router handles IPv4 and IPv6 addresses. If the device can handle either IPv4 or IPv6 addresses, the compatibility bits are all set to zero (0) and this is termed an "IPv4-compatible IPv6 address"; if the address represents an IPv4-only node, the compatibility bits are all set to one (0xFFFF) and the address is termed an "IPv4-mapped IPv6 address." The final 32 bits contain a 32-bit IPv4 address in dotted decimal form.

Multicast Addresses

IPv6 multicast addresses provide an identifier for a group of nodes. A node may belong to any number of multicast groups. Multicast addresses may not be used as a source address in IPv6 packets or appear in any routing.

```
| 3 |   5 bits   |   n bits   |  56-n bits  |    64 bits    |

+---+------------+------------+-------------+------------------+

|010| RegistryID | ProviderID | SubscriberID | Intra-Subscriber |

+---+------------+------------+-------------+------------------+
```

Exhibit 24.2. Provider-Based Unicast Address Format

```
|   8   | 4 | 4 |              112 bits                     |

+--------+----+----+------------------------------------------+

|11111111|flgs|scop|              group ID                    |

+--------+----+----+------------------------------------------+
```

Exhibit 24.3. Multicast Address Format

All multicast addresses, as shown in Exhibit 24.3, begin with 8 ones (0xFF). The next 4 bits are a set of flag bits (flgs); the 3 high-order bits are set to zero; and the fourth bit (T-bit) indicates a permanently assigned ("well-known") multicast address (T=0) or a nonpermanently assigned ("transient") multicast address (T=1). The next 4 bits indicate the scope of the address, or the part of the network for which this multicast address is relevant; options include node-local (0x1), link-local (0x2), site-local (0x5), organization-local (0x8), or global (0xE).

The remaining 112 bits are the group identifier, which identifies the multicast group, either permanent or transient, within the given scope. The interpretation of a permanently assigned multicast address is independent of the scope value. For example, if the World Wide Web server group is assigned a permanent multicast address with a group identifier of 0x77, then:

- FF01:0:0:0:0:0:0:77 would refer to all Web servers on the same node as the sender.
- FF02:0:0:0:0:0:0:77 would refer to all Web servers on the same link as the sender.
- FF05:0:0:0:0:0:0:77 would refer to all Web servers at the same site as the sender.
- FF0E:0:0:0:0:0:0:77 would refer to all Web servers in the Internet.

Finally, a number of well-known multicast addresses are predefined, including

- *Reserved multicast addresses.* These are reserved and are never assigned to any multicast group. These addresses have the form FF0x:0:0:0:0:0:0:0, where x is any hexadecimal digit.

- *All nodes' addresses.* These identify the group of all IPv6 nodes within the given scope. These addresses are of the form FF0t:0:0:0:0:0:0:1, where t =1 (node-local) or 2 (link-local).

- *All routers' addresses.* These identify the group of all IPv6 routers within the given scope. These addresses are of the form FF0t: 0:0:0:0:0:0:2, where t =1 (node-local) or 2 (link-local).

- *The dynamic host configuration protocol (DHCP) server/relay-agent address.* This identifies the group of all IPv6 DHCP servers and relay agents with the link-local scope; this address is FF02:0:0:0:0:0:0:C.

IPV6 EXTENSION HEADERS AND OPTIONS

In IPv6, optional IP layer information is encoded in separate extension headers that are placed between the IPv6 basic header and the higher-layer protocol header. An IPv6 packet may carry zero, one, or more such extension headers, each identified by the next header field of the preceding header and each containing an even multiple of 64 bits (see Exhibit 24.4). A fully compliant implementation of IPv6 includes support for the following extension headers and corresponding options:

- *The hop-by-hop options header.* This header carries information that must be examined by every node along a packet's path. Three options are included in this category. The pad1 option is used to insert a single octet of padding into the options area of a header for 64-bit alignment, whereas the padN option is used to insert two or more octets of padding. The jumbo payload option is used to indicate the length of the packet when the payload portion is longer than 65,535 octets. This option is employed when the payload length field is set to zero.

- *The routing header.* This header is used by an IPv6 source to list one or more intermediate nodes that must be visited as part of the packet's path to the destination; this option is functionally similar to IPv4's loose and strict source route options. This header contains a list of addresses and an indication of whether each address is strict or loose. If an address is marked strict, it means that this node must be a neighbor of the previously addressed node; if an address is marked loose, this node does not have to be a neighbor of the previous node.

- *The fragment header.* This header is used by an IPv6 source to send packets that are larger than the maximum transmission unit (MTU) on the path to the destination. This header contains a packet identifier, fragment offset, and final fragment indicator. Unlike IPv4, where fragmentation information is carried in every packet header, IPv6 carries only fragmentation/reassembly information in those packets that are fragmented. In another departure from IPv4, fragmentation in IPv6 is performed only by the source and not by the routers along a packet's

```
   <--- 32 bits --->      <--- 32 bits --->      <--- 32 bits --->

   +---------------+      +---------------+      +---------------+
   |  IPv6 header  |      |  IPv6 header  |      |  IPv6 header  |
   |               |      |               |      |               |
   | Next Header = |      | Next Header = |      | Next Header = |
   |     TCP       |      |    Routing    |      |    Routing    |
   +---------------+      +---------------+      +---------------+
   |  TCP header   |      |Routing header |      |Routing header |
   |      +        |      |               |      |               |
   |    data       |      | Next Header = |      | Next Header = |
   |               |      |     TCP       |      |   Fragment    |
   +---------------+      +---------------+      +---------------+
                         |  TCP header   |      |Fragment header|
                         |      +        |      |               |
                         |    data       |      | Next Header = |
                         |               |      |     TCP       |
                         +---------------+      +---------------+
                                               |  TCP header   |
                                               |      +        |
                                               |    data       |
                                               |               |
                                               +---------------+
```

Exhibit 24.4.   IPv6 Extension Header Examples

---

path. All IPv6 hosts and routers must support an MTU of 576 octets; it is recommended that path MTU discovery procedures (per RFC 1981) be invoked to discover, and take advantage of, those paths with a larger MTU.

- *The destination options header.* This header carries optional information that has to be examined only by a packet's destination node(s). The only destination options defined so far are pad1 and padN, as described above.

- *The IP authentication header (AH) and IP encapsulating security payload (ESP).* These are IPv6 security mechanisms (a section on IPv6 security appears later in this chapter).

With the exception of the hop-by-hop option, extension headers are only examined or processed by the intended destination nodes. The contents of each extension header determine whether or not to proceed to the next header and, therefore, extension headers must be processed in the order that they appear in the packet.

IPV6 QUALITY-OF-SERVICE PARAMETERS

The priority and flow label fields in the IPv6 header are used by a source to identify packets needing special handling by network routers. The concept of a flow in IP is a major departure from IPv4 and most other connectionless protocols; flows are sometimes referred to as a form of *connectionless virtual circuit* because all packets with the same flow label are treated similarly and the network views them as associated entities.

Special handling for nondefault quality of service is an important capability for supporting applications that require guaranteed throughput, end-to-end delay, and jitter, such as multimedia or real-time communication. These quality-of-service parameters are an extension of IPv4's type-of-service capability.

The priority field allows the source to identify the desired priority of a packet. Values 0 through 7 are used for congestion-controlled traffic, or traffic that backs off in response to network congestion, such as TCP segments. For this type of traffic, the following priority values are recommended:

- Zero is recommended for uncharacterized traffic.
- One is recommended for "filler" traffic (e.g., Netnews).
- Two is recommended for unattended data transfer (e.g., e-mail).
- Three is recommended for reserved traffic.
- Four is recommended for attended bulk transfer, such as FTP or hypertext transfer protocol (HTTP).
- Five is also recommended for reserved traffic.
- Six is recommended for interactive traffic (i.e., Telnet).
- Seven is recommended for Internet control traffic (i.e., routing protocols and simple network management protocol).

Values 8 through 15 are defined for noncongestion-controlled traffic, or traffic that does not back off in response to network congestion, such as real-time packets being sent at a constant rate. For this type of traffic, the lowest priority value (8) should be used for packets that the sender is most willing to have discarded under congestion conditions (e.g., high-fidelity video traffic) and the highest value (15) should be used for those packets that the sender is least willing to have discarded (e.g., low-fidelity audio traffic).

The flow label is used by a source to identify packets needing nondefault quality of service. The nature of the special handling might be conveyed to the network routers by a control protocol, such as the resource reservation protocol (RSVP), or by information within the flow packets themselves, such as a hop-by-hop option. There may be multiple active flows from a source to a destination, as well as traffic that is not associated with any flow (i.e., flow label = 0). A flow is uniquely identified by the combination of a source address and a nonzero flow label. This aspect of IPv6 is still in the experimental stage and future definition is expected.

IPV6 SECURITY

In the early days of TCP/IP, the ARPANET user community was small and close, and security mechanisms were not the primary concern. As the number of TCP/IP hosts grew and the user community became one of strangers (some nefarious) rather than friends, security became more important. As critical and sensitive data travels on today's Internet, security is of paramount concern.

Although many of today's TCP/IP applications have their own devices, security should be implemented at the lowest possible protocol layer. IPv4 has few, if any, security mechanisms, and authentication and privacy at lower protocol layers is largely absent. IPv6 builds two security schemes into the basic protocol.

IP Authentication Header

The first mechanism is the IP authentication header (RFC 1826), an extension header that can provide integrity and authentication for IP packets. Although many different authentication techniques are supported, use of the keyed message digest 5 (MD5, described in RFC 1321) algorithm is required to ensure interoperability. Use of this option can eliminate a large number of network attacks, such as IP address spoofing. This option is also valuable in overcoming some of the security weaknesses of IP source routing.

IPv4 provides no host authentication. It can supply only the sending host's address as advertised by the sending host in the IP datagram. Placing host authentication information at the Internet layer in IPv6 provides significant protection to higher-layer protocols and services that currently lack meaningful authentication processes.

IP Encapsulating Security Payload

The second mechanism is the IP encapsulating security payload (ESP, described in RFC 1827), an extension header that can provide integrity and confidentiality for IP packets. Although the ESP definition is algorithm-independent, the Data Encryption Standard (DES) using cipher block chaining mode (DES-CBC) is specified as the standard encryption scheme to ensure interoperability. The ESP mechanism can be used to encrypt an entire IP packet (tunnel-mode ESP) or just the higher-layer portion of the payload (transport-mode ESP).

These features add to the secure nature of IP traffic while actually reducing the security effort; authentication performed on an end-to-end basis during session establishment provides more secure communications even in the absence of firewall routers.

ICMPv6

The Internet control message protocol (ICMP) provides error and information messages that are beyond the scope of IP. ICMP for IPv6 (ICMPv6) is functionally similar to ICMP for IPv4 and also uses a similar message format and forms an integral part of IPv6. ICMPv6 messages are carried in an IPv6 datagram with a next header field value of 58.

ICMPv6 error messages include

- *Destination unreachable.* This is sent when a packet cannot be delivered to its destination address for reasons other than congestion
- *Packet too big.* This is sent by a router when it has a packet that it cannot forward because the packet is larger than the MTU of the outgoing link
- *Time exceeded.* This is sent by a router when the packet's hop limit reaches zero or if all fragments of a datagram are not received within the fragment reassembly time.
- *Parameter problem.* This is sent by a node that finds some problem in a field in the packet header that results in an inability to process the header.

ICMPv6 informational messages are echo request and echo reply (used by IPv6 nodes for diagnostic purposes), as well as group membership query, group membership report, and group membership reduction (all used to convey information about multicast group membership from nodes to their neighboring routers).

Migration to IPv6

When IPv4 became the official ARPANET standard in 1983, use of previous protocols ceased and there was no planned interoperability between the old and the new. This is not the case with the introduction of IPv6.

Although IPv6 is currently being rolled out for the Internet backbone, there is no scheduled date of a flash cut from one to the other; coexistence of IPv4 and IPv6 is anticipated for many years to come. The sheer number of hosts using IPv4 today suggests that no other policy even begins to make sense. IPv6 will appear in the large ISP backbones sooner rather than later, and some smaller service providers and local network administrators

```
  (-----)         -------------      (-----)      -------------     (-----)
  ( IPv6  )       | IPv4/IPv6 |      ( IPv4  )    | IPv4/IPv6 |     ( IPv6  )
  ( network )---|   router    |---( network )---|   router    |---( network )
  (        )      -------------      (        )    -------------     (        )
  (-----)                            (-----)                         (-----)
```

Exhibit 24.5.   Common Short-Term Scenario Where an IPv4 Network Interconnects IPv6 Networks

will not make the conversion quickly unless they perceive some benefit from IPv6.

The coexistence of IPv4 and IPv6 in the network means that different protocols and procedures need to be accommodated. In one common short-term scenario, IPv6 networks will be interconnected via an IPv4 backbone (see Exhibit 24.5). The boundary routers will be IPv4-compatible IPv6 nodes and the routers' interfaces will be given IPv4-compatible IPv6 addresses. The IPv6 packet is transported over the IPv4 network by encapsulating the packet in an IPv4 header in a process is called *tunneling*. Tunneling can also be performed when an organization has converted a part of its subnet to IPv6. This process can be used on host-host, router-router, or host-router links.

Although the introduction of IPv6 is inevitable, many of the market pressures for its development have been rendered somewhat unnecessary because of parallel developments that enhance the capabilities of IPv4. The address limitations of IPv4, for example, are minimized by use of classless interdomain routing (CIDR). Nomadic user address allocation can be managed by the DHCP servers and relay agents. Quality-of-sevice management can be handled by the RSVP protocol. And the IP authentication header and encapsulating security payload procedures can be applied to IPv4 as well as to IPv6.

This is not meant to suggest that IP vendors are waiting. IPv6 has already started to appear in many new products and production networks. Support for IPv6 on several versions of UNIX have been announced by such organizations as Digital Equipment Corp., IBM, INRIA (Institut National de Recherche en Informatique et en Automatique, or The French National Institute for Research in Computer Science and Control), Japan's WIDE Project, Sun Microsystems Inc., the Swedish Institute of Computer Science (SICS), and the U.S. Naval Research Laboratory.

Other companies have announced support for IPv6 in other operating environments, including Apple Computer Inc.'s MacOS, FTP Software,

Inc.'s DOS/Windows, Mentat's STREAMS, Novell Inc.'s NetWare, and Siemens Nixdorf Inc.'s BS2000. Major router vendors that have announced support for IPv6 include Bay Networks Inc., Cisco Systems Inc., Digital, Ipsilon Networks, Penril Datability Networks, and Telebit Corp.

6bone Trials

One of the important proving grounds of IPv6 is the 6bone, a testbed network spanning North America, Europe, and Japan, which began operating in 1996. The 6bone is a virtual network built on top of portions of today's IPv4-based Internet, designed specifically to route IPv6 packets. The goal of this collaborative trial is to test IPv6 implementations and to define early policies and procedures that will be necessary to support IPv6 in the future. In addition, it will demonstrate IPv6's new capabilities and will provide a basis for user confidence in the new protocol.

For most users, the transition from IPv4 to IPv6 will occur when the version of their host's operating system software is updated; in some cases, it means running dual-stacked systems with both versions of IP. For larger user networks, it may make sense to follow the model of the larger global Internet—in particular, to predesign the IPv6 network topology and addressing scheme, to build a testbed IPv6 network with routers and a DNS, and then slowly to migrate applications, users, and subnetworks to the new backbone. The lessons learned from the 6bone activity are useful for individual networks as well as for the Internet backbone.

SUMMARY

The transition to IPv6 has already started, even though most Internet and TCP/IP users have not yet seen new software on their local systems or on local networks. Before IPv6 can be widely deployed, the network infrastructure must be upgraded to employ software that accommodates the new protocol.

In addition, the new address format must be accommodated by every TCP/IP protocol that uses addresses. The domain name system (DNS), for example, has defined an AAAA resource record for IPv6 128-bit addresses (IPv4's 32-bit addresses use an A record) and the IP6.INT address domain (IPv4 uses the ARPA address domain). Other protocols that must be modified for IPv6 include DHCP, the address resolution protocol (ARP) family, and IP routing protocols such as the routing information protocol (RIP), open shortest path first (OSPF) protocol, and the border gateway protocol (BGP). Only after the routers and the backbones are upgraded will hosts start to transition to the new protocol and applications be modified to take advantage of IPv6's capabilities.

APPENDIX: THE IPV6 SPECIFICATIONS

IPv6 Core Description

IPv6 is specified in a number of RFCs. The core description of IPv6 and related protocols can be found in:

- RFC 1883: Internet Protocol, Version 6 (IPv6) Specification.
- RFC 1884: IP Version 6 Addressing Architecture.
- RFC 1885: Internet Control Message Protocol (ICMPv6) for the Internet Protocol Version 6 (IPv6).
- RFC 1886: DNS Extensions to support IP version 6.

Other related RFCs include:

- RFC 1550: IP: Next-Generation (IPng) White Paper Solicitation.
- RFC 1726: Technical Criteria for Choosing IP: The Next Generation (IPng).
- RFC 1752: The Recommendation for the IP Next-Generation Protocol.
- RFC 1825: Security Architecture for the Internet Protocol.
- RFC 1826: IP Authentication Header.
- RFC 1827: IP Encapsulating Security Protocol (ESP).
- RFC 1828: IP Authentication using Keyed MD5.
- RFC 1829: The ESP DES-CBC Transform.
- RFC 1881: IPv6 Address Allocation Management.
- RFC 1887: An Architecture for IPv6 Unicast Address Allocation.
- RFC 1888: OSI NSAPs and IPv6.
- RFC 1897: IPv6 Testing Address Allocation.
- RFC 1970: Neighbor Discovery for IP Version 6 (IPv6).
- RFC 1971: IPv6 Stateless Address Autoconfiguration.
- RFC 1972: A Method for the Transmission of IPv6 Packets over Ethernet Networks.
- RFC 1981: Path MTU Discovery for IP version 6.
- RFC 2002: IP Mobility Support.
- RFC 2003: IP Encapsulation within PPP.
- RFC 2019: Transmission of IPv6 Packets Over FDDI.
- RFC 2023: IP Version 6 over PPP.
- RFC 2073: IPv6 Provider-Based Unicast Address Format.
- RFC 2080: RIPng for IPv6.
- RFC 2081: RIPng Protocol Applicability Statement.

RFCs may be obtained over the Internet via anonymous FTP from ftp://ds.internic.net/rfc. For additional sites and mechanisms to obtain RFCs, send e-mail to rfc-info@isi.edu and put help: ways_to_get_rfcs in the message body.

Chapter 25
Internet-Based Virtual Private Networks

Nathan J. Muller

Carriers such as AT&T Corp., MCI Communication Corp., and Sprint Corp. began offering virtual private networks (VPN) in the mid-1980s as a means to recapture revenue lost to private lines that carried voice and data between far-flung corporate locations. With private networks, corporations paid a flat monthly fee for leased lines, instead of per-minute usage charges. This meant that companies could put as much traffic on the lines as they wanted — through such techniques as multiplexing and compression — without paying long-distance carriers anything extra.

The long-distance carriers responded to this situation by making it more attractive for corporations to move their traffic back to the public network. Through intelligence embedded in their networks, carriers provided a variety of access arrangements, calling features, management tools, billing options, and volume discounts that made VPNs a more attractive alternative to private networks. Since the carrier would be responsible for maintaining the "network," corporations could save even more money by cutting back on network management tools, technical staff, test equipment, and spares inventory.

Although VPNs started out as voice-oriented, they could also handle low-speed data. But in early 1997, a wholly new trend emerged in which private data is routed between corporate locations, telecommuters, and mobile employees over carrier-provided Internet Protocol (IP) networks. Basically, this type of data service lets business users carve out their own IP-based wide area networks (WAN) within the public Internet and/or a carrier's high-speed Internet backbone.

APPLICATIONS

Internet-based VPNs are suitable for a variety of applications, including remote access. At its most basic level, this type of VPN provides access to electronic mail, shared files, or the company intranet via an Internet connection. Instead of making a long-distance call to connect to a remote access server (RAS), or using an expensive private line, a remote user connects to a local Internet service provider (ISP) and then to a VPN server. The VPN server acts as a gateway between the Internet connection and the local network and handles user authentication. Once the VPN server verifies a user's name and password, access to the LAN or intranet is granted. All data — including user names and passwords — sent between the remote user and the server travel over the public Internet in encrypted form to preserve privacy.

Among the other applications of Internet-based VPNs are secure World Wide Web hosting, data warehousing, and video and voice conferencing between corporate locations. Even corporate paging services can be run over the VPN — either as the primary method of transport or as a backup to commercial satellite-based services. Such VPNs also can be used to segment groups on corporate intranets, similar to the way virtual local area networks (LAN) work. An Internet-based VPN can even be used to implement extranets between trading partners for such applications as Electronic Data Interchange.

Anything that can be done over the public Internet can be done over an IP-based VPN — only more securely and reliably. Security and reliability are especially important for supporting electronic commerce, expanding employee access to a corporate data warehouse, and making enterprise applications available to customers and strategic partners worldwide. Reliability is especially important when delay-sensitive applications must be supported, such as voice calls, videoconferencing, and SNA data.

ADVANTAGES

The current interest in implementing Internet-based VPNs is attributable to the considerable cost savings and functional benefits they offer to companies over traditional WANs. They also offer much greater adaptability when faced with changing application requirements.

Among the well-documented benefits of Internet-based VPNs are the following:

- Up-front capital costs for customer premises hardware — routers, multiprotocol frame-relay access devices, channel service units/data service units, modem pools, and access concentrators — are greatly reduced when using an Internet-based VPN vs. the traditional enterprise WAN.
- With transmission costs the single most expensive aspect of owning a WAN, companies are looking to replace dedicated point-to-point links and dial-up 800 number/toll connections with less expensive Internet connectivity.
- The greater simplicity of Internet routing compared to dedicated links means remote sites need less support, which is the second most

expensive aspect of WAN ownership. In dial access outsourcing applications, enterprise management costs fall because end user support and troubleshooting are handled by the IP backbone provider.

- Internet-based VPNs provide a single, consolidated network infrastructure for LAN-to-LAN links, client-to-LAN dial links, and enterprise access to the Internet. Eliminating duplicate or overlapping WAN infrastructures further reduces operational costs and management overhead.
- Management is greatly simplified with Internet-based VPNs. Instead of monitoring and troubleshooting the entire WAN infrastructure and user population, corporate information technology managers need only monitor the performance metrics of the IP backbone provider to ensure compliance with service agreements.
- By leveraging the expertise of the IP backbone provider, the network operations of a company can actually become more proficient. In such areas as security and broadband WAN technology, the backbone provider may have more core competency than in-house staff, resulting in better quality WAN services.
- Outsourcing one or more components of the WAN leaves IT departments more time to devote to advancing enterprise business objectives rather than to managing infrastructure.

For virtual leased-line applications, there are additional benefits of Internet-based VPNs, such as simplified network design compared to complex meshes of point-to-point links. There is no need to develop and test disaster recovery scenarios, since the IP backbone provider has the responsibility for maintaining network availability. There is also easier and faster scalability when connecting new sites, since this is done by the backbone provider, rather than by the IT department having to add and configure dedicated connections.

For global Internet access/dial access outsourcing applications, the additional benefits of Internet-based VPNs include ubiquitous access via Internet Points of Presence compared to limited coverage for local calling areas and the absence of 800 services from international locations. There is also greater ability to scale the remote user population compared to adding remote access ports and circuits at a central corporate site. Finally, inexpensive industry-standard client software is available for dialing remote networks.

IMPLEMENTATION

There are several proprietary and standard ways to implement Internet-based VPNs. Among the vendor-provided solutions are the Point-to-Point Tunneling Protocol (PPTP), the Layer 2 Forwarding (L2F) protocol, and the Layer 2 Tunneling Protocol (L2TP). These protocols are used to create tunnels, which are end-to-end connections similar to virtual circuits. Essentially, they transport Layer 3 packets such as AppleTalk, IP, and Internetwork Packet Exchange (IPX) over the Internet by encapsulating them in Layer 2 PPP (Point-to-Point Protocol) frames.

Although a single standards-based approach to Virtual IP has not yet caught on, there are two possibilities emerging: the IP Security (IPsec) protocol and SOCKS, a circuit-level proxy solution. Both are open to any form of authentication and encryption. SOCKS has been ratified by the Internet Engineering Task Force (IETF), and IPsec is in the process of being ratified. Although some vendors already support IPsec, it may not see widespread use until IPv6 — the next generation of TCP/IP.

Point-to Point Tunneling Protocol

Microsoft Corp.'s PPTP uses a process called tunneling to ensure secure data transmission over the Internet between remote clients and corporate servers. PPTP uses MS-CHAP for authentication across Windows NT domains, giving users the same access privileges they would have if they were directly connected to the corporate network. PPTP also supports data encryption, flow control, and multiple protocols, including AppleTalk, IPX/Sequenced Packet Exchange, NetBEUI and others, allowing remote users to access the corporate network with almost any protocol at hand.

Typically, a Windows NT or Windows 95 client uses a PPTP driver as its WAN driver. The client accesses a remote LAN by connecting to a PPTP-enabled Windows NT RAS at the corporate site. During initial session negotiation, a 40-bit key is exchanged between the client and server. The session — including source and destination information — is secured using RSA RC4 encryption. This level of encryption also prevents the company's own network from being able to read the destination information in the packet. This is overcome, however, by encapsulating the PPP packet within a Generic Routing Encapsulation (GRE) packet, which includes the destination information.

The large installed base of Windows NT Servers and the free distribution of the PPTP client have made PPTP the most widely used VPN technology. However, Microsoft's PPTP solution offers only one form of encryption and authentication. In addition, some routers and firewalls are not able to forward the GRE packets required by PPTP. Careful attention to compatibility issues is needed before committing to PPTP.

Layer 2 Forwarding

L2F and PPTP have the same objective: to enable organizations to move their remote access services to the Internet using tunnels. In many respects, L2F is very similar to PPTP. Although both support multiprotocol services, L2F is intended for IP-only backbones because it relies specifically on the User Datagram Protocol (UDP). L2F also does not support Dial-Out.

L2F relies on the corporate gateway to provide user authentication. By allowing end-to-end connectivity between remote users and their corporate gateway, all authorization can be performed as if the remote users are dialed in to the corporate location directly. This setup frees the ISP from having to maintain a large database of individual user profiles based on many different corporations. More importantly, the virtual dialup service becomes more secure for the corporations using it because it allows the corporations to quickly react to changes in their remote user community.

For each L2F tunnel established, L2F tunnel security generates a unique random key to resist spoofing attacks. Within the L2F tunnel, each multiplexed session maintains a sequence number to prevent the duplication of packets. Cisco Systems Inc. provides the flexibility of allowing users to implement compression at the client end. In addition, encryption on the tunnel can be done using IPsec.

Layer 2 Tunnel Protocol

Whereas Microsoft's PPTP is a software solution, Cisco's L2F is a hardware solution that requires the ISP and corporate site to have network access servers and routers equipped with the Cisco Internetwork Operating System software, which provides L2F functionality.

Because Cisco routers account for about 80% of the routers used on the Internet and corporate intranets, L2F can be viewed as a de facto industry standard in the same way as Microsoft's PPTP is viewed. The problem is that PPTP and L2F are not interoperable. The forthcoming L2TP standard is intended to rectify this situation.

L2TP is a combination of PPTP and L2F, which is under consideration as an IETF standard. It seeks to allow all functions of L2F and PPTP to be compatible, thus allowing current users and implementers to continue deploying their preferred solution with an eye toward its future interoperability.

L2TP uses many of the existing PPTP messages, slightly reformatted, over UDP, instead of using TCP for the control channel and GRE for the data channel. L2TP also retains the basic L2F authentication scheme and adds flow control. L2TP also improves on L2F by not requiring special hardware support.

IPsec

IPsec is a suite of IETF protocols that provide a high degree of security. Instead of tunneling data such as PPTP and L2F, IPsec provides packet-by-packet authentication, encryption, and integrity.

Authentication positively identifies the sender. Encryption allows only the intended receiver to read the data. Integrity guarantees that no third party has tampered with the packet stream. These security functions must be applied to every IP packet because Layer 3 protocols such as IP are stateless; that is, there is no way to be sure whether or not a packet is really associated with a particular connection. Higher-layer protocols such as Transmission Control Protocol (TCP) are stateful, but connection information can be easily duplicated or "spoofed" by knowledgeable hackers.

To implement these security features, IPsec packets use two headers: the Authentication Header (AH) and the Encapsulating Security Payload (ESP). The AH verifies that the data within the packet has not been tampered with, while the ESP encrypts the data so it remains private.

The key limitation of IPsec is that it can only carry IP packets, whereas the other tunneling protocols support IPX and AppleTalk, among others, as well as IP. Although it specifies encryption and authentication, IPsec does not include any method of access control other than packet filtering.

Although IPsec may not see widespread use until IPv6—the next generation of TCP/IP—some vendors already have products available that support it. The International Computer Security Association (ICSA) even runs an IPsec Certification Program that tests vendors' implementations of IPsec in terms of how well they support its security functions. ICSA IPsec certification indicates that the products meet at least the minimum set of required elements to prove baseline interoperability among products of different vendors.

SOCKS

Another protocol used for implementing VPN is SOCKS, an IETF standard. Because SOCKS operates at Layer 5, the session layer, it offers more functionality. For example, it has the ability to perform much finer grain access control than the lower-layer tunneling solutions, which are deployed at Layers 2 and 3. And like IPsec, but unlike the tunneling protocols, SOCKS has the ability to take advantage of a variety of different authentication and encryption mechanisms, including Secure Sockets Layer (SSL), Kerberos, Challenge Handshake Authentication Protocol (CHAP), Remote Authentication Dial-In User Service (RADIUS), and Windows NT domain authentication. Further, these methods are negotiated during the connection process.

The SOCKS solution requires each user to install software that first intercepts data from the TCP/IP stack and then passes it on to the SOCKS server for authentication. Data is encrypted at both the client and server levels.

Although SOCKS is more functional because it operates at Layer 5, it requires more overhead system resources during communications back and forth between networks. Protocols operating at the second and third layers provide less functionality but require less system overhead. In addition, the lower-layer protocols can be independent of client software, which makes for easier upgrades whenever needed.

SOCKS is a directional protocol, which means it operates in a single direction. Directional protocols are inherently more secure than tunneling protocols, which are bidirectional. Because SOCKS operates in a directional manner, the user can see other users and access shared data, but they cannot see back. Tunneling allows bidirectional communication, so all users can see and share data with one another. Directionality, however, is a compromise between flexibility and security. Directional communications are more secure because a user's data cannot be shared and redistributed. Bidirectional connections are more flexible and allow better communication between remote and local users.

At about $7,500 for a 50-client package, SOCKS can be very expensive for many companies to implement, especially when compared to Microsoft's PPTP, which is included free in Windows 95 and Windows NT.

Although PPTP and SOCKS do not integrate, both can be run on the same system. This would give users the option of using SOCKS for higher security when running such applications as e-mail, but using PPTP when they need multiprotocol support for accessing hosts or shared applications. When connecting through PPTP, they would still have RSA RC4 encryption for security.

It is becoming quite common for vendors to support multiple tunneling protocols, especially when the equipment is used to support extranets between trading partners. Bay Networks Inc., for example, offers its Extranet Switch 1000, which supports L2TP, PPTP, IPsec, and L2F. Priced at $7,000, the Extranet Switch 1000 ships with a free, unlimited user license of the client software.

VENDOR OFFERINGS

With appropriate protocol support from an ISP, companies can build their own Internet-based VPN from firewalls, routers, RAS, and other network devices. However, getting all this equipment working together to implement such things as authentication, access rights, and usage policies is often quite difficult. Companies wishing to build an Internet-based VPN are finding that they require products that are more integrated, flexible, and easy to set up and administer. Fortunately, vendors are addressing these needs with appropriate solutions so that even small companies with limited expertise can establish Internet-based VPNs.

Assured Digital

In the development of its Dynamic VPN Switching product line, Assured Digital Inc. (ADI), for example, set out with the goal of making it quick and easy for network managers to implement and manage secure VPN solutions for any type of business application over any type of access mode. The company's net-centric VPN solution is as easy to install and manage as a typical network hub and requires no manual configuration or on-site maintenance.

To make a network manager's job easier, the embedded routers in ADI's Dynamic VPN Switching network devices self-configure and automatically adapt to topology changes. Within an existing secure network ad hoc communities of interest can be created on the fly. For example, if communications suddenly increase between two branch offices, the VPN switches automatically select the optimum path based on connection policies and routing parameters. The switches reroute traffic from the central site to a direct link that efficiently uses bandwidth, reduces network traffic, and saves money.

At the heart of the automated operations of Dynamic VPN Switching is ADI's hardware/software-based Automated Operation and Security (AOS) system, which is built into each ADI device. AOS supports IPsec, PPTP, and x.509 certificates and can accommodate future network security standards. AOS delivers policy-based authorization, secures policy distribution, maintains wire-speed encryption, and it protects both data and user messages from replay. It also includes a unique cryptographic identity embedded into each device, which eliminates the complications that usually arise when trying to securely distribute encryption keys over a network or the Internet.

The integration of AOS in the ADI Management System (AMS) further automates VPN management. For example, when a new ADI device is deployed, the AMS automatically initializes, authenticates, configures, and updates all the required network and security parameters to establish multiple VPN connections. The AMS also integrates with existing authentication services, such as RADIUS.

VPNet Technologies

VPNet Technologies Inc. offers a variety of VPN products that provide flexible configuration alternatives for large enterprises, small businesses, and remote offices. The VSU-10 VPN Service Unit, for example, enables small businesses to use the Internet for real-time IPsec-compliant VPN connectivity at up to 8M bps, while VPNmanager includes all the components necessary to create VPN for up to 100 users. The company also provides enterprise versions of these products, plus client software that extends IPsec-based VPN capabilities to mobile workers and telecommuters with Windows NT-based PCs.

The VSU-10 allows users to create many types of VPN configurations, either alone or with other VPNet products, depending on the structure of the enterprise and its specific needs. Small, single-site businesses can slash remote access costs by using the VSU-10 to connect their employees, partners, and suppliers over the Internet. Companies with multiple offices can use the VSU-10 to connect each of their sites into a secure VPN. In addition, home-based telecommuters can use the VSU-10 for secure, high-capacity data communications that cost a fraction of traditional, dedicated services.

The VSU-10 can be deployed in any 10Base-T network. Two 10Base-T ports provide LAN connectivity and support a range of connection topologies. The unit can be installed to provide VPN services for an entire site. Services can also be restricted to a portion of the network or even to a single hub or server.

In addition to supporting IPsec encryption with both data encryption standard (DES) and Triple-DES, the VSU-10 provides packet-level authentication using HMAC-MD5 and features simple key management for IP-based key management. The base unit also supports packet compression in hardware to mitigate the performance-reducing effects of IPsec packet expansion and resulting packet fragmentation. The unit also can integrate with RADIUS servers.

The Java-based VPN manager brings the ease and familiarity of World Wide Web browsers to the management of VPNs. Network managers can define, configure, and manage VPNs from any location equipped with a computer hosting a Java-compatible browser. Managers can configure and check the status of VSU-10 devices, add dial-in users to a VPN, monitor the performance of private data transmissions, and troubleshoot existing configurations. SSL is used to communicate with remote VPN Service Units using either password- or certificate-based authentication.

Bay Networks

Bay Networks and Netscape Communications Corp. are developing a Directory-Enabled Networking (DEN) solution that will lower the cost of ownership for VPNs and extranets by linking administration of network hardware with enterprise-class directory software services. Netscape Directory Server embedded in Bay Networks' Contivity Extranet Switches provides the flexibility, scalability, and performance that DEN requires.

The Contivity Extranet Switch product family enables companies and partners to build VPNs and extranets for private communication, collaboration, and electronic commerce. The product family supports tunneling, authentication, directory, accounting, and connectivity protocols in a single, integrated hardware architecture.

DEN-enabled products simplify administration by enabling changes to be made in the directory only once and have them pushed out automatically to all devices on the network. This provides network administrators with the ability to customize access to the corporate network based on each user's unique profile. Netscape Directory Server can also coordinate the configuration of multiple Contivity Extranet Switches, rather than force network managers to separately configure each switch directly.

Other Vendors

Many other vendors offer Internet-based VPN solutions as well. Aventail Corp., for example, offers a secure policy-based VPN management system based on SOCKS Version 5. Essentially, Aventail allows IT managers to develop and enforce policy-based management of access to network resources on a VPN using a single application.

Internet Devices Inc. offers its Fort Knox Policy Router, which works with installed routers and delivers VPN and firewall services. Access rights, firewall filtering, and usage policies — such as limiting Web surfing for performance or to keep users away from inappropriate sites to protect the company against hostile-work-environment lawsuits — are all controlled through a single Web-based interface.

Check Point Software Technologies Ltd. offers policy-based bandwidth management and server load balancing with its firewall products. Through a partnership with Entrust Technologies Inc., Check Point offers a public key infrastructure to help companies manage encryption keys in VPN applications.

FreeGate Corp. offers software designed to let small businesses with multiple offices and remote users set up turnkey VPN. The software runs on the company's Multiservices Internet Gateway, a turnkey server designed to give small businesses Internet access and intranet services. Among the services included are IP routing, Web server functionality, firewall, e-mail, file transfer, and domain name services. The software lets users at multiple locations — each with a FreeGate server — connect to one another as if they were on a single LAN. Remote users can dial in to a FreeGate server using PPTP included with Windows clients. The server provides management software designed for nontechnical users. Configurations for local and remote users are propagated across the network of FreeGate servers.

CARRIER SERVICES

For companies that prefer to completely outsource their Internet-based VPNs, there are carriers and national ISPs that will bundle equipment and service, and manage it all for a fairly reasonable price.

The major carriers offer some compelling features with their IP-based VPN offerings. To encourage customers to consider their services, carriers also are making promises about trouble response time, network uptime, and dial port availability. The overriding concern of corporate managers, however, is end-to-end latency. If the VPN cannot get the packets through, then it is of little importance if the network is available 100% of the time.

Accordingly, latency guarantees are becoming available. UUNet Technologies, a subsidiary of WorldCom Inc., for example, guarantees 150 ms for latency and 99.9% network availability. The credit is 25% of the customer's daily bill if UUNet fails to meet one criteria, and 50% of the daily bill if it fails to meet both.

MCI claims that its OC-12 optical fiber Internet backbone averages better than 95 ms for latency cross-country roundtrip. Under MCI's service level agreement for its internet MCI VPN, customers get a 1-day credit for any 10-min outage. A 3-hour outage will result in a 3-day service credit. There are no limits to the credits that can be earned over the course of a month. Users can also access a graphical traffic report on MCI's Web page (*http://traffic.mci.com/*), which shows delay and packet loss performance in near real-time. (MCI sold its Internet infrastructure to Cable & Wireless in mid-1998 to get regulatory approval for the MCI/WorldCom merger.)

AT&T WorldNet's VPN service gives network and IT managers the ability to create closed user groups for intranets and extranets, and provides dial-up access to corporate LANs for remote users. Dedicated VPN service is provided on AT&T's frame relay network, and dial-up service uses the company's 225-node Internet backbone. The backbone can be accessed from more than 580 central offices.

AT&T enhances the reliability of its network with secure nodes and POP, a self-restoring Fastar system that minimizes the impact of cable cuts, redundant router configurations, redundant ATM switching architecture, and alternate access paths for Internet-bound packets. Network reliability for all Internet connections is 99.7%, which is slightly less than the 99.97% reliability of the public network, but high enough to persuade organizations to place daily business applications on the Internet.

Because AT&T owns and controls all of its IP network equipment and facilities, it can exercise absolute control over its backbone, a key factor in ensuring reliability. AT&T maintains a physically secure Network Operations Center (NOC), as well as an identically equipped facility in a remote location. There, systems and software have been tuned to enable the NOC staff to detect, isolate and fix any network troubles in a proactive fashion.

The IP backbone network is managed by both in-band and out-of-band network monitoring systems, allowing NOC technicians to monitor real-time status of all network elements at all times: in-band via the network and out-of-band via secure dial-up. Although Simple Network Management Protocol is the primary network management protocol used in monitoring the IP backbone network, customized alarm correlation and filtering software are also used to allow quick detection of network alarms, along with custom-built tools to monitor routing tables, routing protocols, and physical and logical circuits.

For security, AT&T uses RADIUS servers and Novell Directory Services to validate the authenticity of users dialing into the network using CHAP. Packet filters are used to prevent source address spoofing, which blocks outsiders from entering its network and closed user groups and from accessing client Web servers. All POP, modem pools, and authentication servers are in protected buildings.

AT&T does offer a service guarantee: one free day of service if the VPN goes down for more than 15 minutes. At this writing, AT&T is adding other performance guarantees, tunneling, and value-added network management services to its VPN offering.

CONCLUSION

Internet-based VPNs are rapidly shaping up as a viable option to public network services. This alternative appeals to companies that are unable or unwilling to invest heavily in network infrastructure. From the carriers' perspective, router networks cost 80% less to build than traditional circuit-switched networks of comparable capacity. This enables them to offer substantial cost savings. The major carriers even provide service-level guarantees to overcome concerns about latency and other quality of service issues traditionally associated with Internet technologies. In the long term, as performance, security, and manageability continue to undergo improvements, Internet-based VPNs could very well replace traditional private networks for many mainstream business applications within a decade or so.

Chapter 26
Implementing and Supporting Extranets

Phillip Q. Maier

Extranets have been around as long as the first rudimentary LAN-to-LAN networks began connecting two different business entities together to form WANs. In its basic form, an extranet is the interconnection of two previous separate LANs or WANs with origins from different business entities. This term emerged to differentiate previous definitions of external "Internet" connection and a company's internal "intranet." Exhibit 26.1 depicts an extranet with a Venn diagram, where the intersection of two (or more) nets formed the extranet. The network in this intersection was previously part of the intranet and now has been made accessible to external parties.

Under this design, one of the simplest definitions comes from R. H. Baker,[1] "An extranet is an intranet that is open to selective access by outside parties." The critical security concept of the extranet is the new network area that previously was excluded from external access now being made available to some external party or group. The criticality security issue evolves around the potential vulnerability of allowing more than the intended party or allowing more access than was intended originally for the extranet. These critical areas will be addressed in this document from basic extranet setup to more complex methods and some of the ongoing support issues.

The rapid adoption of the extranet will change how a business looks its security practices, as the old paradigm of a hard outer security shell for a business LAN environment now has been disassembled or breached with a hole to support the need for extranets. In many cases, the age-old firewall will remain in place, but it will have to be modified to allow this hole for the extranet to enable access to some degree for internal resources that have been deemed part of the extranet.

Recognizing the growth of extranets as a common part of doing business today is important; therefore, the business enterprise must be ready with architectures, policy, and approaches to handle the introduction of extranets into their environment. A few of the considerations are the business

0-8493-9838-X/00/$0.00+$.50

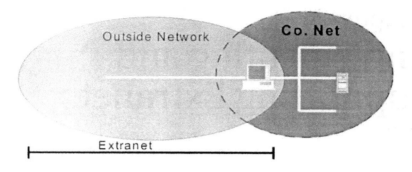

Exhibit 26.1.   Venn Diagram of an Extranet

requirements versus security balance, policy considerations, risk assess-ments, as well as implementation and maintenance costs.

From a requirements versus security balance, the issue is the initial claim by business that extranets are an immediate need and absolutely must be established, "if we are to remain competitive." But from a security standpoint, if a company makes such a drastic change to the environment, which may not have had any form of an extranet in place, they may well be throwing their financial data assets out the door with the first implementa-tion of an extranet; therefore, care must be taken from a security perspec-tive and put in balance with the claimed business need for an extranet implementation.

One of the first areas of review and possibly update is the inner com-pany's security policy. This policy most likely was not written with extra-nets in mind and thus may need modification if a common security philos-ophy is to be established regarding how a company securely can implement extranets. But the policy review does not stop with one com-pany's review of their own policy; it also involves the connecting company or companies on the outside. In the case of strategic business relationships that will be ongoing, it is important that both parties fully understand each others responsibilities for the extranet, what traffic they will and will not pass over the joined link, and what degree of access will occur and by whom over this link.

Part of any company's policy on extranets must include an initial requirement for a security risk assessment. The main question: what addi-tional levels of risk or network vulnerability will be introduced with the implementation of the proposed extranet? As well as vulnerability assess-ment, a performance assessment should be conducted to assist in the design of the extranet to assure that the proposed architecture not only addresses the security risk but also will meet performance expectations.

Some of the information needed in a combined security and performance assessment should be

- data classification/value of data
- data location(s) in the network
- internal users' access requirements to extranet components (internal access design)
- data accessibility by time of day (for estimating support costs)
- protocol, access services used to enter extranet (network design implications)
- degree of exposure by transmission mechanism (Internet, private net, wireless transmission)
- end users' environments (dial-up, Internet)
- number of users, total/expectation for concurrent users' access (line sizing)
- growth rate of user base (for estimating administrative costs)
- CONUS (Continental U.S.), international access (encryption implications)

The risk and performance assessment would, of course, be followed up with a risk mitigation plan, which comes in the form of selecting an acceptable extranet architecture and identifying the costs. The cost aspect of this plan is, of course, one of the critical drivers in the business decision to implement an extranet. Is the cost of implementing and maintaining the extranet (in a secure manner) less than the benefit gained by putting the extranet in place? This cost must include the associated costs with implementing it securely; otherwise, the full costs will not be reflected realistically.

Finally, the member company implementing the extranet must have a clear set of architectures that best mitigate the identified vulnerabilities at the least cost without introducing an unacceptable degree of risk into their computing environment. The following section reviews various extranet architectures, each with differing costs and degree of risk to the environment.

EXTRANET ARCHITECTURES

Router-Based Extranet Architecture

The earliest extranet implementations were created with network routers, which have the capability to be programmed with rudimentary access control lists or rules. These rules were implemented based solely on TCP/IP addresses. A rule could be written to allow external user A access to a given computer B, where B may have been previously unreachable due to some form of private enterprise network firewall (and in the early days,

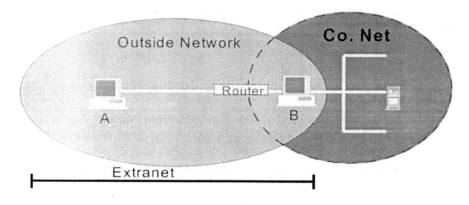

Exhibit 26.2.   Basic Extranet with Router

---

this firewall may have been a router also). Exhibit 26.2 depicts this very basic extranet.

A more realistic rule may have been written where all computers in an outside network were allowed to access computer B in a company network, thus forming an extranet. This is depicted in Exhibit 26.3.

As network security architectures matured, routers as the sole network access control device were replaced by more specific security mechanisms. Routers originally were intended as network devices and not as security mechanisms and lost functionality as more and more security rules were placed in them. Additionally, the security rules that were put into them were based on TCP/IP addresses, which were found to be subject

---

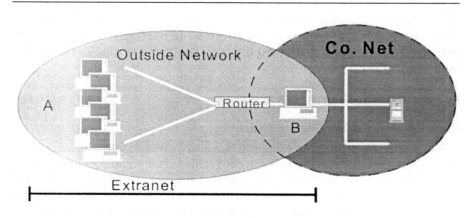

Exhibit 26.3.   More Realistic Extranet

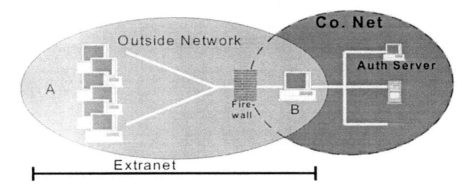

Exhibit 26.4. Extranet Using an Application Layer Gateway Firewall

---

to spoofing/masquerading and thus deemed ineffective in positively identifying the real external device being granted access. Therefore, routers alone do not provide a wholly secure extranet implementation but, when used in conjunction with one of the following extranet architectures and with other network security devices, can be a component to add some degree of security.

Application Gateway Firewalls

As network security architectures matured, the introduction of Application Layer Gateway firewalls, a software tool on a dedicated machine usually dual homed (two network interfaces, one internal, one external), became the more accepted external protection tool. These software tools have the ability not only to perform router type functions with access control rules, but also to provide user authentication services on a per-user basis. This user authentication can take the form of an internal user authentication list or an external authentication call to token-based authentication services, such as the ACE SecureID™ system. Exhibit 26.4 depicts this type of architecture setup to support an extranet using an application layer gateway firewall to enable authenticated users inward access to an enterprise in a controlled manner.

In addition to supporting access control by IP address and user, some gateways have the further capability to restrict access by specific TCP/IP service port, such as port 80, HTTP, so the extranet users only can access the internal resource on the specific application port, and cannot expose the internal machine to any greater vulnerability than necessary.

Follow-on application layer gateway implementations since have emerged to provide varying additional degrees of extranet connectivity and

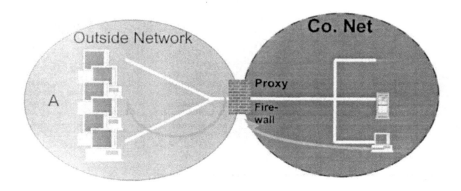

Exhibit 26.5. Outbound Proxy Architecture

security. One such method is the implementation of a proxy mechanism from an outside network to a portion of an internal company network. Normally, a proxy performs control and address translation for access from an intranet to the external Internet. These types of proxies normally reside on the firewall, and all user access to the Internet is directed through the proxy. The proxy has the ability to exert access control over who in the intranet is allowed external access, as well as where they can go on the Internet. The proxy also provides address translation, such that the access packet going to the Internet is stripped of the user's original internal address, and only the external gateway address of the enterprise is seen on the packet as it traverses the Internet. Exhibit 26.5 depicts these proxy functions.

The proxy provides both a security and network address function, though the whole process can be used in its reverse to provide an extranet architecture because of its ability to provide access rules over who can use the proxy, where these proxy users are allowed to go, or what resources they can access. Exhibit 26.6 depicts a reverse proxy extranet architecture.

Today, most proxies are set up for HTTP or HTTP-S access, though application layer gateway proxies exist for most popular Internet access services (telnet, ftp, SQL, etc.). One of the major issues with proxy servers, however, is the amount of cycle time or machine overhead it takes to manage many concurrent proxy sessions through a single gateway. With highly scaleable hardware and optimized proxy software, it can be carried to potentially handle high-user demands, but the system architecture must be designed specifically for high loads to be able to meet user response expectations, while still providing the security of an authenticated proxy architecture. On the inward proxy depicted in Exhibit 26.6, the proxy can be configured only to allow access to a single internal resource on a given TCP/IP port. Further protection can be added to this reverse proxy architecture by putting the

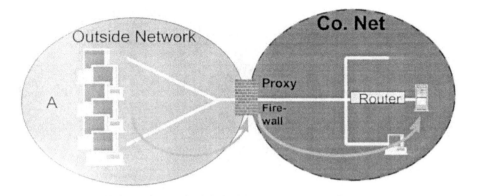

Exhibit 26.6. Reverse Proxy Extranet Architecture

target internal resource behind a router with specific access control rules, limiting the portion on the company intranet that inbound proxies can reach, which can assure limited access on the intranet should the internal machine ever be compromised. It cannot be used as a jumping-off point into the rest of company intranet.

A somewhat hybrid architecture extranet, where some firewall controls are put in place but the external user is not granted direct inward access to an enterprise's internal domain, has been evolving and put in place as a more popular extranet implementation. Under this architecture the external user is granted access to an external resource (something outside of the enterprise firewall), but still on the property of the enterprise. Then this external resource is granted access to one or more internal resources through the enterprise firewall. This architecture is based on minimizing the full external access to the intranet, but still making intranet-based data available to external users. The most popular implementation is to place an authenticating Web server outside the firewall and program it to make the data queries to an internal resource on the enterprise intranet, over a specific port and via a specific firewall rule, allowing only one external resource to have access to the one internal resource, thus reducing the external exposure of the intranet. Exhibit 26.7 depicts this type of extranet.

Issues with this type of architecture include reliance on a single user interface that safely can be placed outside the enterprise firewall, which makes it vulnerable to attack. Additionally, the issue of whether tight-enough access rules can be placed on the access method between the external user interface resource (the Web server in this example) and the internal resources that it needs access to on the protected enterprise intranet. If these two issues can be addressed safely, then this form of extranet

311

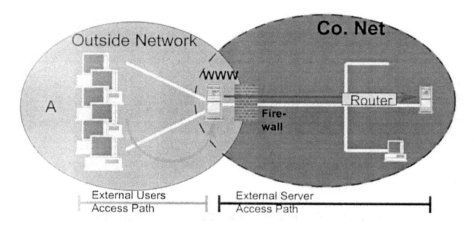

Exhibit 26.7. Extranet with Authenticating Web Server

can be very useful for an enterprise extranet with a high volume or varied user base and a large intranet-based data repository.

The user front end has been deployed as a Web server, usually SSL-enabled to ensure data integrity and protection by encrypting the data as it passes over an external SSL link. Access to this external server also is associated with some form of user authentication, either a static ID and password over the SSL link and more recently with client digital certificates, where each individual accessing the SSL-enabled site is issued his or her own unique digital certificate from an acknowledged certificate authority, validating his or her identity. Each client maintains his or her own digital certificate, with the Web server having some record of the public key portion of the client's digital certificate, either directly in the Web server internally or accessible from a stand-alone directory server (usually LDAP reachable).

The most recent entrant in the extranet architecture arena is the virtual private network (VPN). This architecture is based on a software tunnel established between some external entity, either client or external network, and a gateway VPN server. Exhibit 26.8 depicts both types of VPN architectures. External network A has a VPN server at its border, which encrypts all traffic targeted for company network C. This would be a gateway-to-gateway VPN. Or external client B may have client VPN software on his or her workstation, which would enable him or her to establish a single VPN tunnel from his or her workstation over the external network to company C's VPN server.

Although both server-to-server VPN and client-to-server VPN architectures are offered in the industry today, it is this author's experience that

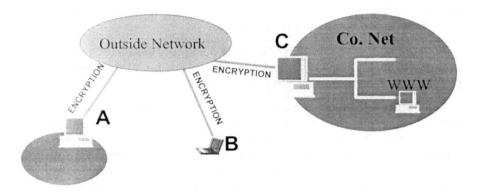

Exhibit 26.8. VPN Architecture

the more popular extranet architect is the client-to-server VPN architecture, as it offers the most flexibility for the most diverse audience of external users. Though this flexibility does add to the complexity of the implementation, as it can involve potentially a large number of external desktops, all with differing configurations. The benefits of VPNs, however, is the ability to traverse external public networks safely with some assurance of data integrity and authentication as part of the VPN implementation. This architecture shows the most promise to meet the needs of extranets and cost savings for a world hungry for connectivity over public/external networks, though it still has some growing pains to go through before reaching full product maturity.

An emerging standard for VPNs is coming out of the ITEF IPSec implementation, which draws a road map for the next generation TCP/IP security protocol. Under this protocol, standards are being drafted that will enable differing devices to securely communicate under a preagreed upon security protocol, including key exchange for encryption and standardized authentication. Today, there are IPSec-compliant products on the market, though the standard still is evolving and tests are being conducted to evaluate differing vendors' compatibility with each under the IPSec standards. One of the leading initiatives to evaluate this compliance is the Automotive Network Exchange (ANX) tests, which are intended to establish a large extranet environment between the core automotive manufacturers and their vendors.

In the meantime, there is a wide variety of VPN product vendors on the market, some touting IPSec compliance and others with proprietary implementations with IPSec in their future product road map, choosing to wait until the standard stabilizes. The recommendation is to select either a vendor offering IPSec, if it has some degree of maturity within its own product line, or one that is planning to adopt the standard, IPSec, which appears to be a viable standard once it fully matures.

Regardless of whatever VPN solution is being considered for implementing secure extranets, a few technical considerations must be understood and planned for before selecting and implementing a VPN extranet architecture.

Scalability — Similar to proxy servers, VPN servers incur a fair amount of processing overhead that consumes processing resources as high levels of concurrent VPN sessions pass through a single server. It is important to attempt to estimate projected user base and current access to appropriately size a VPN server. Some servers are established on lower-level processors for smaller environments and should not be implemented where high concurrent access rates are expected. Although there is some benefit to physical load balancing, spreading the access among multiple servers, there is also a concern about implementing too many servers to manage easily. Keeping a balance between installing a single large server and creating a single point of failure versus implementing many smaller servers creates an administrative nightmare.

Multi-homed intranets and address translation — In large intranet environments, many operate under a split domain naming structure (DNS) where intranet addresses are not advertised to the external networks, and external addresses are kept external, so as not to flood the internal network. Additionally, many larger intranet environments have multiple gateways to external networks. If one gateway is established with a VPN gateway and an external client makes a connection to the internal intranet, it is important that the tunnel comes in through the appropriate VPN gateway, but also that the return traffic goes back out through that same gateway so that it gets re-encrypted and properly returned to the external VPN client. Exhibit 26.9 depicts the correct traffic patterns for a multi-homed intranet with a single VPN gateway and an external VPN client.

VPN-based access control — Many forms of gateway VPN servers offer the ability to restrict users' access to a company intranet based on access groupings. This is especially important when intranets are being established for a diverse set of external users, and it is important to minimize their access to the intranet. This type of access control is critical in establishing secure extranets, which further highlights the importance of understanding VPN access control capabilities.

User authentication — Multiple options exist for user authentication, though the recommended option is to select a high-level authentication method, such as one-time passwords or time-synchronized password methods. Under the IPSec standard, client side digital certificates are evolving as a standard for high-level authentication. Unfortunately, initial

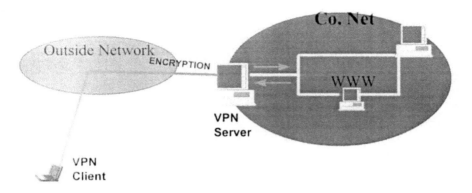

Exhibit 26.9.   Traffic Patterns for Multi-Homed Intranet with a Single VPN Gateway and an External VPN Client

implementations of client side digital certificates for user authentication are wholly software-based, eliminating the second factor authentication, the "something the user physically has" in their possession. The return to true two-factor authentication under digital certificates will not occur until physical smart cards become part of the authentication architecture. (Smart cards are credit card type tokens that have a physically embedded chip, which can be electronically read and written to, either with a portion of the client's digital certificate or the encryption algorithm used to unlock the digital certificate).

IPSec Interoperability — Ultimately, when the IPSec standard stabilizes, all vendors following the established standard will allow different vendors VPN products to interoperate. Under this environment, a company may implement vendor A's VPN server, and their acknowledged clients can purchase and use an IPSec-compliant client to gain access to the company intranet once they are authorized.

SUMMARY

Secure extranets are becoming the external network of choice in today's business world. There are multiple implementation options as depicted in this document, each with varying degrees of risk and implementation complexity. Each implementation must be evaluated against a business case, using the recommended risk and performance analysis outline. The basic router-controlled extranets are recommended only for the least valuable data environments, although the more sophisticated VPN extranet architectures appear to be the future for extranets, especially when the IPSec standard matures and gains industry adoption.

Chapter 27
Virtual Corporations: A Need for Integrated Control and Perpetual Risk Assessment

Steven Powell and Frederick Gallegos

Due in large part to dramatic advances in information technology, companies must now compete in a world of increasingly competitive, rapidly changing, unpredictable global markets. Technological forecasts suggest that this will continue well into the 21st century. It is generally thought that to take advantage of competitive opportunities in the 21st century, companies will have to compete differently from the traditional way they competed in the 20th century. The term "virtual corporation" refers to what many analysts believe will be the successful 21st century competitor.

COMPOSITION

The virtual corporation employs a mass customization strategy in which quality products are tailored to specific needs and low cost is achieved. In addition, the virtual corporation is exceedingly agile and flexible, linking a variety of organizations in an ever-changing network in which partner firms contribute to the overall enterprise based upon their core competencies. Work is performed by teams composed of members from across the functions and across the organizations in the network. Members of these teams collaborate wherever they are and whenever they are able to do so. The authority to make decisions does not reside only at the top, but is distributed throughout the organization. Finally, and very important, is the fact that the venture is based on openness, cooperativeness, and trust.

The virtual corporation is critically dependent on the timely flow of accurate information throughout the organization through the use of, but not limited to such IT technologies as E-mail, EDI, Internet/intranet/extranet, and Executive Information Systems. A good way to view how stringent the network requirements are is to analyze them in terms of the telecommunications Service Platform Map. The network must be able to reach anyone, anywhere in the world. It must support the sharing of a wide range of information, from simple voice, data, and text messages to cooperative transactions requiring the information updating of a variety of databases. Finally, it must deliver what Keen and Cummins describe as perfect service — an extremely high degree of availability, fast response time, extreme reliability, and a very high level of security.

Aside from reach, range, and service responsiveness, the network must be highly interconnective so that people, organizations, and machines can communicate at any time, regardless of location. Also, the network must be very flexible, since the organization is constantly changing. Finally, the network must be cost-effective, since low cost is one of the ingredients in the mass-customization strategy.

STRATEGIC GOAL/PLANNING

So how can this be accomplished? The ability to reach anyone, anywhere in the world requires global area networks. Clearly, the Internet and global carrier services, such as Concert, will be crucial. Also, since the intended receiver need not be in the office, or even at home, wireless networks will play a part. This will be true on-premise, such as with the use of wireless PBXs or LANs, and off-premise, with the use of cellular networks, global satellite networks such as Iridium, and Personal Communications Networks.

To support the sharing of a wide range of voice, data, and video information, bandwidth-on-demand will be required, all the way to the desktop, as well as the mobile terminal. Also, various collaborative service platforms, such as Lotus Domino, will be necessary. Finally, perfect service will have to be designed into the network. Speed can be achieved through broadband networking: locally via fast Ethernet, gigabit, and ATM LANs, and over a wide area via SMDS and ATM services; reliability through quality hardware/software and proven wired rather than wireless solutions where possible.

FUNCTIONALITY AND SECURITY: PERPETUAL CONTROLS

Backups and redundancy will increase the network's availability. The use of firewalls and encrypted communication can increase security. Increased interconnectivity can be achieved by using broadly accepted standards. Designs should be modular and open architectures such as TCP/IP and ISDN should be employed. Finally, flexibility can be achieved using software-driven solutions, such as virtual LANs and common carrier or Internet virtual private networks in which intranet, extranet, or other network reconfigurations are easily made through the software, rather than the hardware. Similarly, public networks, which can be reconfigured easily, are preferable to harder to reconfigure private networks.

Currently, some of these building blocks are not entirely capable of meeting the virtual corporation's stringent requirements. In a recent survey of network managers in Fortune 1000 firms, over 75% reported that they would not send sensitive traffic over the Internet because of lack of faith in its security. In addition to security problems on the Internet, response time is suffering from congestion on the Internet and is likely to get worse. Wireless networks also suffer from security problems and, relative to wired networks, performance problems caused by interference.

Today, wireless networks are much costlier than wired networks. Coverage and interconnectivity problems plague the off-premise wireless networks, such as cellular, packet radio, mobile satellite, and PCS. With the advent of the Information Superhighway, a number of experts suggest that many of these problems will disappear in the long term. Unfortunately, because business functions in a daily capacity, executives cannot wait for tomorrow's technology solution for maximizing profit in the competitive market.

THE MAJOR ISSUES

Even if technology permits it, there is a question as to whether or not these requirements can be satisfied due to the complexity of the management problem. In addition to the ordinary network management headaches, such as user demands for higher levels of security, shrinking budgets, inadequate training, etc., network managers in virtual corporations will have new challenges:

- First is the mission-critical nature of the network to the firm. It is the lifeblood of the firm. Perpetual assessment of risk and controls will be required.
- Second is the fact that these requirements are very stringent.
- Complexity is a major problem for network managers and it will get worse as the industry becomes more deregulated, competition intensifies, and technology offers more choices.

These are major issues facing CEOs, CIOs, and business decision-makers who want their organization to be on the cutting edge. It is especially difficult in the virtual corporation since not only is the network a multienterprise network, but one that is continually changing. Thus, the element of risk becomes another major factor for corporate and IS managers to address. Three major areas of risk are identified in the following paragraphs.

Electronic Data Interchange (EDI)

Electronic Data Interchange (EDI) has transformed entire industries through Quick Response and Point-of-Sale systems. It allows companies to exchange business data in a machine-readable, structured format. EDI software and networks link the applications of different companies. Through this system, companies exchange transactions, including purchase and payment orders, invoices, quotation requests, shipping notices, price catalogs, or planning schedules with release capabilities. Through establishment arrangements, retailers routinely transmit point-of-sale information to all of their key suppliers, and when sales figures indicate that inventories have reached specified reorder points, vendors write themselves a purchase order and ship additional goods.

With the rapid expansion of EDI use, the American National Standards Institute (ANSI) has developed a set of standards concerning the structure of an EDI transaction set and how it must be sent. ANSI's X.12 conventions govern three levels of EDI transaction set detail: 1) the formatting of transaction sets such as purchase orders or invoices, 2) the formatting of data segments such as names, addresses, and other line item details, and 3) the formatting of data elements such as prices, quantities, and product descriptions. At the same time, the EDP auditors are faced with the challenge of auditing EDI.

There are six major areas of audit/risk concern: 1) the communications software and hardware, 2) EDI translation/mapping, 3) the interface to existing application software, 4) the overall IS operating environment, 5) security and control at the VAN, and 6) implementation and maintenance of standards. Perpetual monitoring and risk assessment of an EDI system can be accomplished through the collection of many different pieces of background information. This involves identifying users and locations, EDI transaction sets being used or planned on being used, EDI message formats, the ANSI X.12 standards and any relevant proprietary standards, EDI software, communications being supported, trading agreements, current EDI volume and number of customers, and MIS problem logs.

Network managers, IS auditors, and security administrators play an important role in providing perpetual review and constant risk assessment. They must also consider the security implications of an electronic document that is transmitted over communication lines around the country or even the world. Internal encryption of at least the authentication, and ideally the message contents, appears to be a viable means to secure EDI activity. In addition to basic authentication via user ID, many value-added networks (VANs) offer password and address validation and encryption service for transactions traveling from a node through the VAN to the receiver's mailbox.

EDI has been one of the key technologies in the 1990s and is expected to grow significantly within the next decade. While significant benefits can result from the use of this technology, significant risks are also present and need to be identified. Corporate management, IS, and IS audit and control professionals are being challenged to continuously find new techniques and tools to assess risks and operational effectiveness of controls as well as audit this environment.

The Internet/Intranet/Extranet

Although the Internet has been around since the 1960s, the growth of the Internet has been formidable in the 1990s. The users of the Internet have access to a variety of services ranging from traditional electronic mail to the World Wide Web (WWW). More recently, intranets evolved to give the multienterprise organization a better way of internally sharing and communicating internal corporate information to its employees using Web technologies. Now, corporation are using extranets to pinpoint and communicate with their vendors and suppliers, as well as keep an eye on the competition.

The Internet was started by the U.S. government in a project for the purpose of creating an independent computer network capable of sustaining its function after a massive nuclear attack. For many years, the backbone of the Internet in the U.S. was supported by the National Science Foundation. The base of the modern Internet is anchored to four all-purpose network access points (NAPs). These NAPs are located in San Francisco, Chicago, New York, and Washington, D.C. The NAPs allow various computer networks within the Internet to interconnect and exchange traffic. MCI, Sprint, ANS, Alternet, and PSI are some of the network service providers (NSPs). They maintain their own large-scale wide-area networks.[1] Today, the Internet connects different computer networks worldwide and is rapidly becoming an essential communication infrastructure.

Assessing risk and effectiveness of controls as well as auditing the information superhighway (Internet, intranet, and extranet) is a new problem that requires new tools. Internet security audit software is publicly available on the Internet or similar products through commercial vendors; they include SATAN, COPS, ISS, CRACK, and Tripwire. SATAN identifies the services available and outlines the ways in which they can be misused. It also detects potential security flaws, such as bugs in the system or network utilities and poorly configured systems that lack any password. COPS checks common-procedure security programs within a Unix system. ISS checks a network for certain vulnerabilities. CRACK is a password-cracking program that uses several redefined dictionaries to identify passwords that are easily guessed or contain the user's name. Tripwire is a program that evaluates a system and checks for altered files.

There is no doubt that the Internet gives companies tremendous benefits. Although some companies only connect to the Internet because of the trend, more are moving to conducting business transactions on a daily basis. The Internet allows companies to access important information that they need to make decisions, predict sales, decide different advertising, and analyze their competitors. Each month, the Internet expands by approximately 4,000 new domains and 150,000 new hosts. The number of users is in the hundreds of millions worldwide.[2] Right now, there are approximately 22,500 separate newsgroups on the Bulletin Board System (BBS).[3] It is obvious that the Internet has become a major communications breakthrough and will continue to be so. Corporate management, IS, and IS audit and control professionals now have a chance to demonstrate their commitment to protecting corporate data and participating in the crucial phases of policy design and implementation.

Executive Information Systems (EIS)

Executive Information Systems (EIS) are designed to gather and report information created by other systems, both inside and outside the organization. Since EIS are a relatively new type of information system, there are few audit guides or risk assessment tools designed to aid the auditor or corporate user in gaining an understanding of the system and identifying control risks. Input, processing, and data are application control risks in EIS. Input control concerns are related to data and the interface that gives access to it. EIS are dependent on the input controls within the many widely dispersed source systems. EIS often contain fairly complex processing routines such as briefing books that contain prestructured reports and drill-down capabilities, preprogrammed procedures, or subroutines used to accomplish tasks. The output concerns for EIS include the accessibility of the information by unauthorized users, including E-mail, and the accuracy of visual output.

EIS are a new class of information systems that have emerged to support management's strategic and operational decision-making needs. In 1991, there were approximately 1,000 EIS in use worldwide.[4] The increased complexity of decision-making in today's business world, the reduction in middle management, and advanced computer technology have made EIS one of the most useful information systems in the organization. The utilization of these systems is expected to increase dramatically in the next decade.

CONCLUSION

Virtual corporations are fast becoming a reality in today's business world. The recently issued exposure draft by the International Federation of Accountants on "Managing Security of Information and Communication," acknowledges this leap. With this comes the reality of assessing the controls and risks within a continuously changing IT environment. The slight change to this delicate architecture provides an opportunity for added risk and possible violation. Therefore, continuous and perpetual monitoring is a critical standard that must be recognized by managers. This is especially true for applications supporting EDI, Internet/intranet/extranet, and Executive Information Systems that are integrated into the virtual corporation's mode of operation.

Notes

1. Kogan, A., Sudit, E.F., and Vasarhelyi, M., "Internet: A Technical Primer," *IS Audit & Control Journal,* Vol. I, 1996, p. 24–27.
2. http://www.nw.com/
3. Schwartau, W., "Creating Boundaries: Protecting Companies and Employees on the Information Superhighway," *IS Audit & Control Journal,* Vol. I, 1996, p. 29.
4. Hopkins, B., "Executive Information Systems Take Off," *CMA Magazine,* October, 1991, Vol. 65, p. 31–35.

Recommended Readings:

International Federation of Accountants, "Managing Security of Information and Communication, Proposed International Guideline on Information Technology," by Information Technology Committee, Exposure Draft, June 1997.

CobiT Framework, Information Systems Audit & Control Foundation, Rolling Meadows, IL, 1996.

Owen, Laura, "The Future of Information Systems Audit & Control," *IS Audit & Control Journal,* 1994, Vol. IV, pp. 62–67.

Parker, Robert, "EDP Auditing: The Heights Still Have Not Been Reached," *IS Audit & Control Journal,* 1994, Vol. IV, pp. 8–10.

Powell, Steven and Gallegos, Frederick, "Control of Wide Area Networks," Auerbach Publications: New York, 87-01-45.1, *Data Security Management,* pp. 1–16.

Powell, Steven and Gallegos, Frederick, "Strategies for Securing Wide Area Networks," Auerbach Publications: New York, 87-01-46.1, *Data Security Management,* pp. 1–16.

Section 4
Building Enterprise Infrastructures with LAN-Based Technology

Successful deployment of IT solutions is predicated upon the successful deployment of a solid IT infrastructure. Such infrastructures are increasingly built upon LAN-based technologies. In this section, we focus on several components of such an infrastructure. We first focus briefly on some operating system issues, then shift our attention to a number of other aspects of the enterprise infrastructure.

The ability to exploit LAN technology for the purpose of building or deploying applications has traditionally been dependent to some degree on the network operating system (NOS). Such solutions tended to be proprietary in nature and compatible only with a specific NOS. Later, the NOS-specific dependence began to fade as network operating systems emphasizing interoperability with multiple operating systems (OS) became the norm. More recently, the line between OS and NOS has become quite blurred as operating systems have taken on more and more networking functions.

Perhaps the most important entry into this arena in recent years is Microsoft's Windows NT operating system. Windows NT is a sophisticated OS designed specifically for the networked environment. Chapter 28, "Windows NT Architecture," takes a look at the design of this OS, enabling the LAN or IT manager to better assess the suitability of Windows NT to his or her environment.

While Windows NT is certainly one of the strongest contenders for OS dominance to come along recently, it is not the only OS on the market, and as with anything else in this industry, new challengers are always waiting around the corner. Much to the surprise of many, a relatively new operating system, whose iconoclastic business model defies all conventional wisdom, has recently come to the forefront in a very big way. Chapter 29, "A Quick Overview of Linux," answers many of the questions being asked today about this surprising challenger to NT.

To understand the direction a particular technology is headed, it is often better to look at the generic issues and trends as opposed to any particular product. As such, Chapter 30, "The Emergence of the Directory-enabled Operating System," takes a generic look at one important trend in OS evolution. A clearly significant factor in the success of a Directory-enabled Operating System is the existence of an enterprise directory service. Chapter 31, "Enterprise Directory Services," discusses this concept, beginning with a clarification of the distinction between enterprise directories and application directories. Having established the difference, the chapter discusses the essential elements of an enterprise directory, and several potential applications of such a directory.

Shifting our focus away from OS related topics, a relatively new concept in the enterprise infrastructure world has emerged in response to the enormous amount of growth in the data that must be stored on disk or tape systems. Chapter 32, "Storage Area Networks," takes a look at this new technology, which is an evolutionary extension of the concept of device sharing. The chapter will help the reader understand the reasons for implementing a SAN, the benefits of such a system, and how SANs can be used to enhance enterprise applications.

Moving from storage to transmission, one generic class of applications that is causing network planners to reassess their infrastructure strategies is that of "push technologies." Chapter 33, "Push Technology: Impact and Issues," provides a look at this technology and the issues it brings to the table. Chapter 34, "Enterprise Deployment: Building an IP PBX Telephony Network," provides a look at another application of transmission technology, and examines the way an IP PBX can fit into an organization's infrastructure.

As with each of the previous sections, the enterprise infrastructure poses its own security issues, and offers its own security solutions. In Chapter 35, "Internet Security: Securing the Perimeter," we focus on the issue of securing the infrastructure at the perimeter. The chapter assesses several types of threats that exist at the Internet boundary, and proposes methods of addressing those threats.

We conclude the section with a look at how cryptographic infrastructure components can be applied to solve a number of specific security issues for the enterprise, most notably authentication, privacy, confidentiality, integrity, and non-repudiation. Chapter 36, "Private Keys, Trusted Third Parties, and Kerberos," takes a close look at some of these issues, paying particular attention to mechanisms used to protect cryptographic keys from compromise.

Chapter 28
Windows NT Architecture
Gilbert Held

Microsoft Corp.'s Windows NT is a sophisticated operating system for workstations and network servers. This chapter helps network managers to understand the communications capability of workstations and servers running Windows NT.

INTRODUCTION

Windows NT is a 32-bit, preemptive multitasking operating system that includes comprehensive networking capabilities and several levels of security. Microsoft markets two versions of Windows NT: one for workstations — appropriately named Windows NT Workstation — and a second for servers — Windows NT Server. This chapter, which describes the workings of the NT architecture, collectively references both versions as Windows NT when information is applicable to both versions of the operating system. Similarly, it references a specific version of the operating system when the information presented is specific to either Windows NT Workstation or Windows NT Server.

ARCHITECTURE

Windows NT consists of nine basic modules. The relationship of those modules to one another, as well as to the hardware platform on which the operating system runs, is illustrated in Exhibit 28.1.

Hardware Abstraction Layer

The hardware abstraction layer (HAL) is located directly above the hardware on which Windows NT operates. HAL actually represents a software module developed by hardware manufacturers that is bundled into Windows NT to allow it to operate on a specific hardware platform, such as Intel Corp. X86, Digital Equipment Corp. (DEC) Alpha, or IBM PowerPC.

HAL hides the specifics of the hardware platform from the rest of the operating system and represents the lowest level of Windows NT. Thus, HAL provides true hardware platform independence for the operating system.

Using HAL, software developers can create new software without a lot of knowledge about the hardware platform. This allows software developers

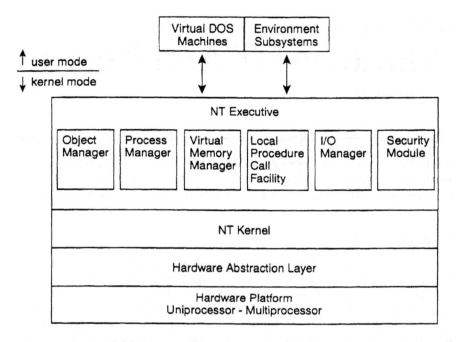

Exhibit 28.1. Windows NT Core Modules

to provide enhanced performance capabilities, such as additional device drives. Hardware vendors can provide the interface between the operating system and the specific hardware.

Kernel

The kernel represents the core of the Windows NT operating system. All operating systems have a kernel. The key difference between the Windows NT kernel and those found in other operating systems is the tasks managed.

The Windows NT kernel manages thread dispatching. (A "thread" is a basic item that can be scheduled by the kernel.) The kernel is also responsible for scheduling and processor synchronization when the hardware platform has multiple processors.

To perform scheduling, the Windows NT kernel attempts to dispatch threads for execution in a way that promotes the most efficient use of the processors in the hardware platform. The actual dispatching of threads is based on their priority, with Windows NT supporting 32 priority levels to maximize processor use.

328

The kernel always resides in real memory within the RAM of the hardware platform and is nonpayable to disk. When NT controls a multiprocessor platform, the kernel will run on all processors at the same time and communicate with each other to govern the distribution of threads.

The NT Executive

The NT Executive can be considered a common service provider because it is responsible for providing a set of services to all other operating system components. The Windows NT Executive is the highest level within the kernel mode of the operating system.

As indicated in Exhibit 28.1, the Executive consists of six core modules that provide an interface between users and computers (represented by Virtual DOS Machines and Environment Subsystems) and the kernel. Virtual DOS Machines support DOS or 16-bit Windows 3.x applications. Windows NT provides support by creating virtual machines and then implementing the required environment within such a machine, resulting in the term "virtual DOS machines."

In comparison, "environment subsystems" are environments that may be required to operate on top of Windows NT. Examples of currently supported environment subsystems include OS/2, POSIX, and Win32 (the Windows NT subsystem).

Object Manager

The object manager names, retains, and provides security for objects used by the operating system. In a Windows NT environment, an object represents physical items as well as the occurrence of defined situations. Thus, an object can represent directories, files, physical hardware ports, semaphores, events, and threads. An object-oriented approach is used to manage objects. If network managers are using Windows NT, they can view the status of event objects through the NT Event Viewer, which is provided in the operating system as an administrative tool.

Process Manager

In a Windows NT environment, a process represents an address space, a group of objects defined as a resource, or a set of threads. Thus, each of these entities is managed by the process manager. In doing so, the process manager combines those entities into a "virtual machine", on which a program executes. Here the term virtual machine represents a set of resources required to provide support for the execution of a program. Windows NT permits multiple virtual machines to be established, allowing multiprocessing capability.

Virtual Memory Manager

Windows NT uses a special file on the hard disk of the hardware platform for additional memory beyond available RAM. That file is referred to as a virtual memory paging or swap file and is automatically created when the operating system is installed.

The Virtual Memory Manager manages the use of virtual memory as a supplement to physical RAM. For example, when one program cannot completely fit into RAM because of its size or the current occupancy by other executing programs, the Virtual Memory Manager might swap one program currently in memory to disk to enable another program to execute, or it could swap portions of the program requesting execution between RAM and the hard disk to execute portions of the program in a predefined sequence.

Although the operation of the Virtual Memory Manager is transparent to programs using it, network managers can change the paging file size. To do so, they would first select the System icon in the Control Panel and then select the Virtual Memory entry from the resulting display. This action results in the display of a dialog box labeled Virtual Memory. Exhibit 28.2 illustrates the Virtual Memory dialog box with its default settings shown for a Pentium processor.

Although Windows NT automatically creates a virtual memory paging file and assigns an initial file size based on the capacity of the hard disk of the system, the operating system does not know what applications the network manager intends to run or the size of those applications. Thus, if network managers frequently work with applications that require a large amount of memory, they should consider raising the default setting.

In Exhibit 28.2, Windows NT provides a pseudo constraint on the sizes of the paging file. That constraint is in the form of a range of values defined for the size of the paging file; however, that range is a recommendation and is not actually enforced by the operating system. For example, to set the initial size of the paging file to 2M bytes, the user would type "20" into the box labeled Initial Size and then click on the Set button. Similarly, if the user wants to raise the maximum size of the paging file to 100M bytes, he would enter that value in the appropriate location in the dialog box and click on the Set button.

Local Procedure Call Facility

Programs that execute under Windows NT have a client/server relationship with the operating system. The Local Procedure Call Facility is responsible for the passing of messages among programs.

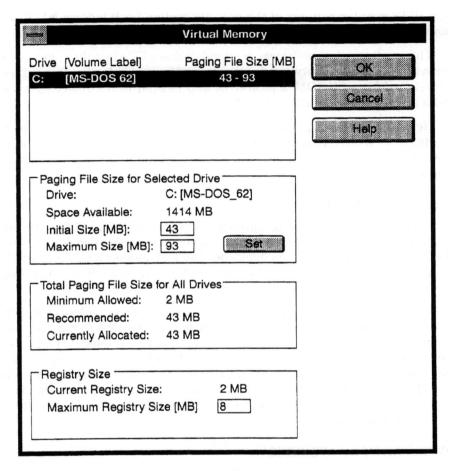

Exhibit 28.2. Virtual Memory Dialog Box

I/O Manager

The Input/Output (I/O) Manager is responsible for managing all input and output to and from storage and the network. To perform its required functions, the I/O Manager uses four other lower-level subsystems—the cache manager, file system drivers, hardware device drivers, and network drivers.

The Cache Manager provides a dynamic cache space in RAM that increases and decreases based on available memory. File system drivers provide support for two file systems, the file allocation table (FAT) and the high-performance file system (HPFS). The FAT file system provides backward support for DOS and 16-bit Windows 3.x-based programs, whereas

331

the HPFS enables support of the new file system for Windows NT 32-bit applications.

The hardware device drivers used in Windows NT are written in C++ to provide portability between hardware platforms. This allows a driver developed for a CD-ROM, a plotter, or another hardware device to work with all Windows NT hardware platforms.

Network drivers represent the fourth lower-level I/O Manager subsystem. These drivers provide access from Windows NT to network interface cards, enabling transmission to and from the network and the operating system.

The Security Module

Windows NT includes a comprehensive security facility built in to the operating system. Once the user turns on power to the hardware platform, this facility is immediately recognizable. Unlike Windows 3.x, Windows 95, or DOS, Windows NT prompts the operator for a password before allowing access to the resources of the computer.

Windows NT security works by the log-on process and a local security subsystem that monitors access to all objects and verifies that a user has appropriate permission before allowing access to an object. The log-on process is linked to the Security Reference Monitor, which is responsible for access validation and audit generation for the local security subsystem. Another component of the Security Module is the Security Account Manager. The Security Account Manager maintains user and group information on a secure database.

WINDOWS NT NETWORKING

One of the biggest advantages associated with the use of Windows NT is its built-in support of many transport protocols. The Windows NT networking architecture was established in a layered design that follows the seven-layer International Standards Organization (ISO) Open System Interconnection (OSI) Reference Model. Exhibit 28.3 illustrates the general correspondence between Windows NT layers and OSI Reference Model layers.

The environment subsystems represent virtual DOS machines as well as 32-bit applications operating on top of NT. At the presentation layer, the Network Provider module is required for each network supported through a redirector. At the session layer, the Windows NT Executive uses a server and redirector to provide capability for a server and workstation, respectively. Both components are implemented as file system drivers, and multiple redirectors can be loaded at the same time so that a Windows NT computer can be connected to several networks. For example, NT includes redirectors for Novell Inc.'s NetWare and Banyan System Inc.'s VINES,

OSI Reference Model Layers	Windows NT Layers			
Application	Environment Subsystems			
Presentation	Network Provider			
Session	Executive Services			
	Server		Redirector	
Transport	Transport Driver Interface			
Network	NetBEUI	DLC	TCP/IP	NWLink (SPX/IPX)
Data Link	NDIS			
	NIC Drivers			
Physical	NIC			

Exhibit 28.3.   Correspondence Between Windows NT and OSI Reference Model Layers

enabling an NT workstation or server to be connected to Novell and Banyan networks.

At the transport layer, the transport driver interface provides a higher-layer interface to multiple transport protocols. Those protocols, which represent operations at the network layer, include built-in NT protocol stacks for NetBEUI, used by the LAN Manager and LAN Server operating systems; Data Link Control, which provides access to IBM mainframes; Transmission Control Protocol/Internet Protocol (TCP/IP) for Internet and intranet applications; and NWLink, which represents a version of Novell's Sequenced Packet Exchange/Internet Packet Exchange (SPX/IPX) protocols. Through the use of TCP/IP, a Windows NT computer can function as a TCP/IP client, whereas the use of NWLink enables a Windows NT computer to operate as a NetWare client.

At the data link layer, Windows NT includes a built-in Network Device Interface Specification (NDIS). NDIS enables support for multiple protocol stacks through network interface card drivers. Thus, NDIS allows a network interface card to simultaneously communicate with multiple supported protocol stacks. This means that a Windows NT computer could, for example, simultaneously operate as both a TCP/IP and a NetWare SPX/IPX client.

CONCLUSION

The modular design of the Windows NT architecture makes it both portable and scalable. The hardware abstraction layer of Windows NT allows the operating system to run on different hardware platforms. Currently, Windows NT runs on Intel's X86, DEC's Alpha, MIPS reduced instruction set computing (RISC), and the PowerPC series of microprocessors jointly manufactured by IBM and Motorola Inc.

Besides being highly portable, Windows NT supports scalability, which allows the operating system to effectively use multiple processors. Thus, when network managers evaluate Windows NT Server as a platform for different applications, it is important for them to note that they have several options for retaining their investment as applications grow.

For example, because of its scalability, network managers could replace a uniprocessor Intel Pentium motherboard with a dual- or quad-processor motherboard. If this replacement does not provide the necessary level of processing power, network managers might consider migrating hardware to a high-level PowerPC or a DEC Alpha-based computer. If that migration is required and the applications continue to grow, network managers could use multiple processors to ensure scalability.

Chapter 29
A Quick Overview
Of Linux

Raj Rajagopal

Linux is a UNIX-type operating system, originally created by Linus Torvalds in 1991, that has been enhanced by developers around the world. Linux is an independent POSIX implementation and is compliant with X/Open and POSIX standards. Linux is developed and distributed under the GNU General Public License. The GNU license specifies that the source code for Linux plus any Linux enhancements should be freely available to everyone. Vendors are free to charge for distributing Linux, and the availability of source code does not apply to applications developed on top of Linux. Linux features include true multi-tasking, multi-user support, virtual memory, shared libraries, demand loading, proper memory management, TCP/IP networking, shell, file structure, utilities, and applications that are common in many UNIX implementations. A complete list of features is included in Exhibit 29.1. Linux is a candidate operating system to be evaluated by enterprise and data center managers who have any flavor of (or are considering acquiring) UNIX or Windows NT.

Sudden Surge of Interest in Linux

For an operating system invented in 1991, the interest in Linux has only recently surged. Like many other computer- and Internet-related phenomena, Linux has again proved that there is strength in numbers. Linux has reached the critical mass of users where vendors have started taking an interest in the operating system. Exhibit 29.2 shows the number of Linux users over the last five years. These numbers are estimates from Red Hat Software, one of the distributors of Linux.

The biggest customers for Linux include Internet service providers that use Linux along with the free APACHE Web server, universities, and Web developers. While Exhibit 29.2 shows cumulative numbers, analysts expect Red Hat to ship about 400,000 CDs this year. By contrast, Microsoft Corporation is estimated to have sold more than 100 million copies of Windows this year.

0-8493-9838-X/00/$0.00+$.50
© 2000 by CRC Press LLC

Exhibit 29.1. Linux Features

Feature	Description
Virtual memory	Possible to add swapping areas during runtime. Up to 16 swapping areas each of which can hold 128MB and can be used for a total of 2GB swap space.
Development languages	Supports most common languages including C, C++, Java, Ada95, Pascal, FORTRAN, etc.
UNIX commands, tools supported	Commands include ls, tr, sed, awk, etc. Tools include gcc, gdb, make, bison, flex, perl, rcs, cvs, and prof.
UNIX source/binary compatibility	Compatible with most POSIX, System V, and BSD at the source level. Through iBCS2-compliant emulation, compatible with many SCO, SVR3, and SVR4 at the binary level.
Graphical environments	X11R5 and X11R6. Motif is available separately.
Shells	All three common shells.
Editors	GNU Emacs, Xemacs, MicroEmacs; jove; ez; epoch; elvis; GNU vi; vim; vile; joe; pico; and jed.
Internationalization	Supports many localized and customized keyboards.
LAN support	Supports Appletalk server and NetWare client and server.
Internet communications	Supports TCP/IP networking including FTP, Telnet, etc.
File systems	Linux file system supports file systems of up to 4TB and names up to 255 characters long. Also supports NFS and System V. Transparent access to MS-DOS FAT partitions via a separate file system. Partition looks like a normal UNIX file system.
CD-ROM	CD-ROM file system reads all standard CD-ROM formats.
Y2K compliancy	Compliant. Linux's 32-bit data representation should handle dates until the year 2038.

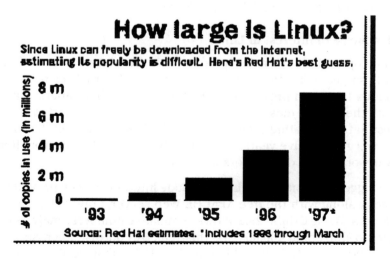

How large is Linux?

Since Linux can freely be downloaded from the Internet, estimating its popularity is difficult. Here's Red Hat's best guess.

Source: Red Hat estimates. *Includes 1996 through March

Exhibit 29.2.   Linux User Base

Exhibit 29.3. Applications Available for Linux

Application Category	Popular Products
Office applications	Star Office, Applixware, WordPerfect, XessL:ite4 spreadsheet
PDF support	Adobe Acrobat Reader
Backup	Backup/9000, BRU 2000
Video player	MpegTV Player
Database support	Sybase Enterprise Adaptive Server, Oracle DBMS, InterBase, Informix-SE
Web software	Apache Web Server, Netscape Communicator, Red Hat Web Server

Vendor Support for Linux

The growth in users has resulted in renewed interest in Linux from many vendors. Intel Corporation and Netscape Communications Corporation have announced an investment in Red Hat Software. Two venture capital firms, Benchmark Capital of Menlo Park, CA, and Boston-based Greylock, have also made investments in Red Hat.

Besides financial support, vendors have also started providing product support. Major vendors, including Sybase, Oracle, Netscape, Informix, Computer Associates, Interbase, and Corel, have announced versions for Linux. Some of the popular applications available for Linux are summarized in Exhibit 29.3.

Linux Customers

Linux is used extensively at universities and by ISPs as Web servers. Linux is also used in research and development environments and in government. The visual effects company Digital Domain used Linux in creating visual effects for the movie "Titanic." The U.S. Department of Defense uses Linux for DNS platforms and SMTP mail relays.

OPERATING REQUIREMENTS FOR LINUX

Most Linux versions run on most Intel-based machines, although other platforms are also supported (see Exhibit 29.4). Besides the Web pages of specific Linux distributors, the Web pages http://www.linux.org and http://sunsite.unc.edu/mdw/HOWTO/INFO-SHEET.html provide more detailed lists of hardware, video cards, disk controllers, etc.

LINUX SOURCES

Linux is freely available on the Internet (see Linux-related FTP sites) along with the source. Linux is also available through distributors. There are many different Linux versions, or distributions. A distribution is the compiled Linux software and source code usually combined with extra features such as configuration, installation, Web, and other applications for the specific version. Most importantly, however, distributors provide

Exhibit 29.4. Linux Operating Requirements

Component	Comments
Processor	Most Intel-based machines. Some implementations support multi-processor such as SMP. Other processors supported include Sun SPARC, Alpha, PowerPC, RS/6000, MIPS, and Macintosh.
Memory	4MB required to install most distributions; 5MB to 10MB for minimal setup; 8MB to 16MB required to run X. Requires swap partitions.
Hard disk	Hard drive required. 8MB to 16MB for swap partition. 24MB for basic installation with no X, development tools, or TeX. Most installations require 40MB to 80MB minimum, including free space. Complete systems need 60MB to 200MB.
Bus	Supports 386/486/Pentium machines with ISA, EISA, PCI, and VLB buses. VESA local bus and PCI are supported. SCSI support is available in some implementations.
Coexistence with other operating systems	Linux will coexist with DOS, MS-Windows, and OS/2 on the hard drive. Partitioning the hard disk is required for each operating system.

support for their version. Some distributions are available for download, at no charge while others are available at prices typically in the range $50 to $100 on CD-ROM from Linux distributors/vendors/retailers.html worldwide. Keep in mind that some of the distributors offer multiple distributions, which differ in price and features. When picking distributions, enterprise and data center managers need to consider the features and other applications besides evaluating the operating system itself.

Other options include purchasing Linux preinstalled on a computer, or purchasing a book that includes a complimentary CD-ROM (see Exhibit 29.5).

Linux-Related Web and FTP Sites

There are a number of Web and FTP sites that provide the Linux code as well as applications for Linux. Some of the popular ones are shown in Exhibit 29.6.

LINUX DRAWBACKS

Popular products such as Microsoft Office and some common databases will not run on Linux. Unless the Linux distribution is from a reputable vendor, support for Linux can sometimes be hard to come by. The support situation may be changing, at least for some major players. At the recent Comdex show, Red Hat Software announced 24-hour enterprise support for its Linux users starting in 1999. A similar service is also due in 1999 from another Linux distributor, Pacific HiTech. Installations planning to use Linux should be prepared to hire technically adept Linux pros to ensure that problems can be handled in a timely manner. While there are a lot of enthusiastic programmers working on the operating system itself,

Exhibit 29.5. Linux Distributors

Organization	Product	Web Address	Features and Comments
Caldera	OpenLinux	www.caldera.com	Includes a new graphical desktop called K Desktop Environment (KDE), Sybase Enterprise Adaptive Server.
Work Group Solutions	Linux Pro	www.wgs.com	The Linus Pro Plus package includes a 7 CD-ROM set, a Linux Encyclopedia, a 1,600+ page reference manual, etc. Linux Pro is aimed at the professional developer.
S.u.S.E. LLC	S.u.S.E. Linux	www.suse.com	S.u.S.E. Linux package includes 4 CD-ROMs, a reference book, and about 800 preconfigured, compiled packages. It features a menu-driven installation, hypertext help, a X11R6.3-based graphical interface, and source code.
Red Hat Software	Red Hat Linux	www.redhat.com	The Red Hat Linux Operating System, which has won many awards, can be used as a Web server, e-mail server, DNS server, or a news server for multiple sites, with virtual hosting. The package includes the Apache Web server, sendmail, publishing, calendars, Internet tools, X Window system, Netscape Navigator, and Netscape Communicator. The operating system includes disk partitioning with Disk Druid, autodetection of hardware, configuration for multiple window managers, graphical tools, and sound support.
Debian	Debian Linux	www.debian.org	Debian is not a company. Debian Linux is produced by volunteers and the primary focus is Intel-based machines. Although it is only supported through e-mail/third parties, support from the volunteers is normally very quick. Compared to other sources, the software is probably the cheapest (less than U.S. $5 for 2 CDs, or download for free).

the situation is different when it comes to peripheral device support. Peripherals typically need drivers, and details of the peripheral necessary to write the drivers are not commonly available. It is up to the peripheral vendors to come up with the drivers for the different platforms. Peripheral vendors do not always make a Linux version and, even when they do,

Exhibit 29.6.   Linux-Related Web and FTP Sites

Site	Comments
sunsite.unc.edu	Free Linux implementation at /pub/linux
tsx-11.mit.edu	Free Linux implementation at /pub/linux
ftp.ncsa.uiuc.edu	Mosaic Web browser and Web server software for Linux
ftp2.netscape.com	Netscape Web Browser for Linux
ftp.blackdown.org	Sun's Java Development Kit for Linux
sunsite.unc.com/mdw/linux.html	Linux Documentation Project Web page

it may require some effort to make the configuration work in an installation. Users accustomed to the Windows GUI may feel that the user interfaces available for Linux are not that user friendly. While Linux is UNIX-like and follows X/Open and POSIX standards, it has not been formally branded as UNIX 98 compliant. This is, in part, due to the fact that Linux is unlike a traditional UNIX offering from one manufacturer that is responsible for paying for the development and certification.

IMPLICATIONS OF LINUX

Windows NT has been able to make significant inroads into the low-end server market because it is typically priced lower than many UNIX offerings and is, in general, easier to use. Although Linux is UNIX-like in terms of ease of use, it does offer significant price advantages. This should appeal to cost-conscious customers, particularly those who do not mind the potential drawbacks listed above. While the ability of Linux to make significant inroads into the NT market is debatable, Linux is certainly bound to prove a very strong challenger to low-end UNIX solutions that are priced significantly higher than Linux.

On the high end, applications tend to be more mission-critical and customers are typically concerned about reliability, availability, and serviceability as much or more than the price. Hence, Linux may not have as much of an impact on the high end, unless one or more of the distributors establish themselves to the point that customers are comfortable about the support.

GUIDANCE FOR LINUX USAGE

Exhibit 29.7 summarizes Linux usage guidelines for enterprise and data center managers.

LINUX FUTURE OUTLOOK

The money from the venture capital and investments at Red Hat will most likely go toward creating an enterprise server group within Red Hat. Linux will follow the same path as other UNIX operating systems and Windows NT and transition to a 64-bit architecture. Intel has already indicated that the company intends to support a 64-bit version of Linux with their Merced chip

Exhibit 29.7. Linux Usage Guidance

Situations for Which Linux Is a Good Candidate	Situations for Which Linux Is Not a Good Candidate
DP environment is very cost-conscious	DP environment requires UNIX branding
DP environment has skills to make things work	Mission-critical applications
Environment that has many UNIX users and programmers	Need a wide array of peripherals
Linux-proven applications and environments such as Web servers, universities, and R&D establishments	Installations that need 24□7 support (this may change for some Linux vendors in 1999)

Exhibit 29.8. Linux-Related Newsgroups

Newsgroup	Description
comp.os.linux.announce	Announcements of Linux developments
comp.os.linux.devlopment.apps	For Linux applications development programmers
comp.os.linux.devlopment.system	For Linux operating system development programmers
comp.os.linux.hardware	Linux hardware specifications
comp.os.linux.admin	System administration questions
comp.os.linux.misc	Miscellaneous questions and issues
comp.os.linux.setup	Installation/setup problems
comp.os.linux.answers	Answers to problems
comp.os.linux.help	Questions and answers for particular problems
comp.os.linux.networking	Linux network-related questions and issues

and is working on adding to Linux its Wired for Management features, features that are aimed at making Linux easier to install in a corporation. In addition, Intel has also already disclosed details of its universal driver initiative, which aims to make developing Linux applications much easier.

All these developments and the new interest by users and vendors bode well for Linux. The potential downfall is that Linux may face the same problems as UNIX where there are multiple versions and applications are not portable from one version to another.

LINUX RESOURCES

Help on Linux is available through a variety of sources such as newsgroups (see Exhibit 29.8), publications such as the *Linux Journal,* and books. Linux International is a nonprofit consortium of Linux users and vendors.

Books on Linux include:

1. *Linux Unleashed* by Sams. Over 1100 pages and includes a CD. August 1998.
2. *Running Linux* by Matt Welsh and Lar Kaufman. O'Reilly & Associates. 650 pages, 2nd ed., August 1996.
3. *Teach Yourself Linux in 24 Hours* by Bill Ball, Stephen Smoogen, and Ryan K. Stephens. Sams Publishing. 380 pages and includes a CD.

CONCLUSION

Linux is definitely worth a serious evaluation by enterprise and data center managers who are looking for cost-effective solutions. It is a rich operating system that is gaining momentum. It is free and is being used for some specific applications. The support situation is improving. It may not however be appropriate for enterprise and data center managers who are considering mission-critical applications, who need a wide array of peripherals, or who need UNIX branding.

Chapter 30
The Emergence of the Directory-Enabled Operating System

John P. Slone

Since the advent of the computer era, operating systems have been in a perpetual state of evolution. Changes in operating systems have historically been made in response to the evolving computer hardware technology, coupled with business factors such as the relative costs of resources. In the earliest operating systems, computers were centralized and very expensive relative to other resources, especially the labor required to program and operate them. Consequently, operating systems were designed to maximize the use of the most expensive resource — the computer hardware. Operating system concepts developed during this period included multitasking, process switching, time sharing, and the like.

In recent years, the cost of hardware has plummeted to an all-time low, to the point where one computer per person is a realistic objective. At the same time, computers have been positioned to increase the productivity of those who use them, especially the group of people known as "knowledge workers." In response, the focus of operating system design has shifted to the maximization of what is now the most expensive resource — the person using the computer. Recent operating system innovations have included graphical user interfaces, multithreading, and other such innovations that make the computer easy to use and highly responsive.

Now that inexpensive computers have become ubiquitous fixtures in the business landscape, what factors will drive the next wave of innovation in operating systems? To answer this question, it is appropriate to consider how the emerging class of extremely powerful personal workstations and enterprise servers will be used, and to consider fundamental shifts in the way people are beginning to use computers as a result. In assessing this situation, one trend in operating systems is clear. Specifically, operating systems are becoming increasingly distributed, in the sense that they are making increased use of distributed resources, and in the sense that they are providing an unprecedented level of cooperation among desktop systems and enterprise servers. As such, distributed operating system capabilities are no longer limited to the most advanced, laboratory-grade computers; rather, such capabilities are being pushed out to the desktops of ordinary users. The resulting effects on operating system design issues are profound.

This chapter focuses on one specific aspect of this new class of operating systems: the role of directories. The concepts in this chapter are presented in three distinct sections. In the first section, several operating system issues related to the enterprise environment are introduced. In the second section, a number of predominant directory technologies are discussed. Finally, the ideas presented in the first two sections are tied together, illustrating how the appropriate placement and use of directories can make significant strides toward solving the identified problems.

OPERATING SYSTEM ISSUES IN THE ENTERPRISE NETWORK

In a self-perpetuating cycle, the capabilities offered by the operating systems of today and the expectations placed on the operating system are both increasing at a dramatic rate. In this section, a number of current expectations are presented in the form of issues to be solved. Questions are raised in this section, while answers are deferred until the end of the chapter.

Users and Machines No Longer Tightly Coupled

Fueled largely by the increasingly competitive business environment of today, users and machines are no longer as tightly coupled as they once were. For instance, many businesses have responded to competitive pressures by increasing their reliance on a mobile work force. Although many workers travel with their computers, a significant number do not. However, because of their dependency on applications such as electronic mail, these users are no longer content to wait until they return to their normal office. Instead, they are demanding that the operating system enable them to "log in" to someone else's computer and have access to the same services they would normally have.

In a similar fashion, many businesses are experimenting with innovative concepts that challenge traditional notions about the way people work. For instance, concepts such as job sharing, flexible work schedules, telecommuting, and rapid deployment teams create situations in which multiple people may use a single workstation or in which a single person may routinely use more than one workstation. As with the mobile workers, there is an expectation that a person will be able to access a computer and have a consistent view wherever the person happens to be. Furthermore, in the case of shared computers, each person who uses a particular computer expects to have his own view, tailored to that person's specific needs. Said another way, according to the expectations of today, things such as the desktop backgrounds, sound effects, choice and placement of icons, and menu options need to be tied to the user rather than the computer.

Such notions present a number of challenges to the operating system. For instance, how does the operating system authenticate each individual user? Once authenticated, how does the operating system know how to present the user with his individually tailored profile? Of particular importance for the travelling work force, how does a particular workstation, without any *a priori* knowledge of an individual, get informed of such things as the existence of that person, the authentication information for the individual, and that person's individual desktop profile?

Operating System Must Make Use of Distributed Resources in a Constantly Changing Environment

In the work environment of today, relatively few individuals limit their use of computing resources to those contained exclusively within their personal workstations. Rather, users make extensive use of server-based applications, remote file stores, printers attached to colleagues' computers, and so on. In a large enterprise, resources such as these tend to be in a constant state of flux. Applications get migrated from server to server as operations managers make adjustments to balance capacity and demand. New printers come on line, while others disappear or get moved to the next building. Likewise, file servers get moved to newer, larger, faster systems or get split among multiple systems to effectively handle increased storage needs.

Identifying, locating, and accessing these distributed resources is typically the job of the operating system. How does the operating system maintain a current view of the environment despite the constant change? In the case of mobile workers, how does the operating system know to access the user's normal file server and application server, while also helping the user in identifying a nearby printer?

Operating System Must Predictably Support Varying Levels of Service

Support for varying levels of service has long been a feature supported by multi-user operating systems. For instance, certain jobs were run at a higher priority than others, typically for reasons related to the billing function, and consequently received a higher level of service. Jobs with lower priority simply had to wait in most cases. With the advent of the personal computer, this notion largely disappeared from the operating system. Instead, level of service became a function of how fast a machine a particular user was provided.

With the trend toward increasingly distributed functions and increasing dependency on remote resources, coupled with the trend toward a many-to-many relationship between computers and users, level of service has once again become a valid topic of discussion. As in the mainframe era, service level is again considered an operating system issue. However, because of the distributed nature of the computing environment of today, the concept has taken on an unprecedented level of complexity.

For instance, suppose there is the need to establish a high-priority management session to handle a runaway process on a distant server. How does the local system know, first of all, that the person requesting the session has the appropriate authority to do so? Once that is established, how does the remote system also obtain that knowledge? Moreover, if intermediate systems are involved in the establishment and maintenance of the session connection, how do they also get informed of the required level of service and the basis of authority?

Scalability to Support Multiple Images of a Given Resource

It was mentioned above that operations managers often migrate server-based applications to accommodate capacity requirements. Another tool that is becoming available to manage capacity increases is the deployment of multiple images of an application on separate systems within a cluster. Conceptually, this allows traffic from a large client base to be balanced across multiple systems, while maintaining a consistent view of the application from the user's perspective.

Beyond the substantial complexity associated with simply operating multiple images of an application on a cluster, numerous issues remain. For instance, how does the existence of an additional image get communicated to the client systems so that they know how to bind to it? That is, unless those systems are informed of the new application image, what is to keep them from all continuing to bind to the original image? Moreover, if one or more images is periodically removed from service, such as for maintenance purposes, how does the client base continue to be supported by the images that remain in service during that time?

Distributed Security Complexity

The concept of distributed authentication has already been introduced in the context of traveling users logging in to systems other than their own. Authentication is but one aspect of a much broader class of problems associated with distributed security. For example, authentication merely identifies the user to the system. Once authenticated, a user's access privileges will typically vary based on the requested resources, and may often vary based on factors such as time of day.

Distributed security becomes particularly complex if these factors are coupled with location. A simple example would be the need for a user to provide a higher level of authentication, such as using a remote access card, when connecting to the network via a dial-up access line. Similarly, there may be a need to use encryption when connecting from certain locations. In other cases, access to some resources may be blocked altogether to users connecting from certain locations, even if the authenticated user would otherwise have been granted access.

Issues such as these are particularly acute in a distributed environment. In particular, it is imperative for the enterprise to ensure that all the involved systems cooperate fully, else the weakest link will become a point of vulnerability for the whole network. Given the need, and given the complexity, how does an operating system in a distributed environment consistently enforce such security policies?

Distributed policy enforcement

In addition to security, consistent enforcement of other forms of policy is also required. Increasingly, the operating system is being called upon as the enforcement vehicle. For example, suppose a company has a policy that requires all workstations to be equipped with the latest version of a certain piece of software, such as a virus scanner, a software meter, or a disk utility. Historically, user behavior tended to preclude the consistent application of such a policy. Users would be given copies of the software, then would either let them become seriously outdated or would completely eliminate them from their systems in an effort to reclaim space. Rarely would the intent of the policy be carried out in a consistent fashion.

If operating systems are being called upon to consistently enforce security policy, is it not possible for them to also enforce other policies? If so, how can this be accomplished? Furthermore, how can changes in the policy be communicated to the operating systems to ensure that the most current policy continues to be the one enforced?

In general, the answers to all the questions raised in this section can be found through the appropriate application of directory technologies. Before addressing how this can be accomplished, let us first shift our attention to the next section, which provides a discussion of some current implementations of directory technology. Using that section as a baseline, the solutions to these questions will be presented in the final section of the chapter.

DIRECTORY TECHNOLOGIES

Directory technologies have actually been around for a number of years, but it was not until very recently that they have gained significant attention. In this section, we will examine a number of industry standard directory technologies, independent of their relationship to operating systems, concluding with a look at how one major operating system manufacturer is incorporating these technologies into its own operating system product line.

In general, a directory is a computer-based system that provides two simple services. First, it provides a mapping between the names of objects and the objects themselves. Second, it provides a repository of information describing the objects in question. As the following discussion proceeds, these two roles should become clear.

Domain Name System

The Internet Domain Name System (DNS) has become so familiar that it is often overlooked in discussions concerning directory technologies. The fact is, DNS has been around for nearly a decade and a half, having first been described in RFC 882 in November 1983, and its use is fundamental to the correct operation of the Internet. As is the case for any directory, DNS provides two fundamental services. First, it provides a mapping between machine names and the machines themselves. Second, it provides a repository of information describing machines on the Internet, albeit a minimal set of information. In particular, DNS always holds the Internet Protocol (IP) address of the machine in question. It can also hold other information, such as contact information for the person responsible for managing names within the domain of the machine, alternative (alias) names for the machine, or basic routing information required for sending information to the machine.

DNS is implemented as a hierarchical system, both in terms of name structure and server deployment. Typically, a participating server is responsible only for holding information related to names in a particular domain, or portion of the name space. Client systems on the network are preconfigured to access a particular name server by default. When requiring access to a computer, client machines will present the name of the target machine to their default name server. If the server holds information about the target machine, it returns the IP address of the target machine, and the client will use that address to establish communication.

If it does not hold information about the target machine, it will return a referral, providing the IP address of a name server more likely to hold the desired information. Being a hierarchical system, the referring server always knows whether the desired name is "below" or "outside" its own name space. If it is below, the server will have been configured with information about the servers holding lower-level names and will use that information in constructing the referral. If it is outside, it can always provide a referral higher in the hierarchy. In this manner, a name server that either holds the desired name or is above the desired name will eventually be reached, thus allowing the entire domain name space to be accessible simply by knowing a starting point.

Internally, DNS uses a record-based information model, since its development predates that of object-oriented technology. Nonetheless, DNS remains an integral component of the current Internet, as well as most large-scale enterprise networks.

X.500

In the late 1980s, as part of the industrywide push toward Open System Interconnection (OSI)-based global interoperability, a general-purpose directory technology was developed. Originally published in 1988, then subsequently revised in 1993 and again in 1997, the resulting directory is now known as X.500, the nomenclature assigned by one of its sponsoring committees. The full X.500 specification occupies several hundred pages of text, diagrams, and abstract syntax notation, and constitutes a very comprehensive, robust, commercial-grade set of technologies.

At its essence, X.500 specifies a hierarchical, distributed model for an object-oriented directory. Directory services are provided by a set of interoperable Directory System Agents (DSA) and are accessed by client agents known as Directory User Agents (DUA). A DUA requesting service from the directory uses the Directory Access Protocol (DAP) to contact a DSA. The DSA responds in one of three ways. If it holds sufficient information to resolve the request, it will respond directly. If it does not hold the information, it will either send a referral, much like a DNS server sends a referral, or it will use the Directory System Protocol (DSP) to chain the request on behalf of the user to another DSA. Chaining can cascade through multiple DSAs as needed until the request is resolved. These scenarios are depicted in Exhibit 30.1.

Each object represented in the X.500 directory has an associated entry, and each entry has a globally unique name, known as a "distinguished name" (DN). Each DN is actually a concatenation of "relative distinguished names" (RDN), each of which identifies an intermediate level entry (such as a country or organization) in the directory. By ensuring uniqueness among the RDNs at any given level, globally unique naming is thus assured. Collectively, the entries in X.500 constitute a hierarchical structure known as the Directory Information Tree (DIT). A simplified DIT is illustrated in Exhibit 30.2.

As mentioned above, X.500 entries are used to hold information about objects. Such information is held in an entry in the form of a set of attributes, each of which holds its type and one or more values, as shown in Exhibit 30.3. As an example, consider an entry holding information about a person. The entry could have attributes such as the person's name, nick name, telephone number, fax number, pager number, e-mail address, security information, and so on. Similar entries could be utilized

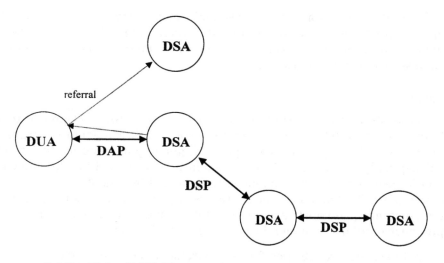

Exhibit 30.1.   X.500 Directory Services Chaining and Referral

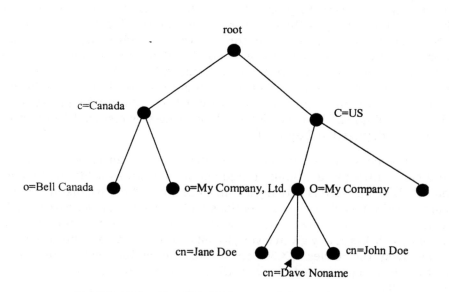

Exhibit 30.2.   Simplified Directory Information Tree

to hold information specific to other kinds of objects, such as applications, printers, computer systems, or network routers.

In addition to specifying the above concepts that make up a general-purpose directory system, X.500 also includes specifications for replication,

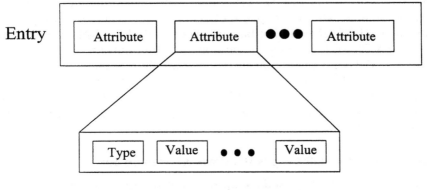

Entry

Exhibit 30.3.   X.500 Entry Structure

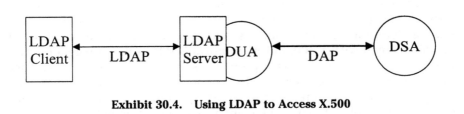

Exhibit 30.4.   Using LDAP to Access X.500

directory access control, distributed operations, distributed authentication, management, and several other features. Together these specifications constitute the most comprehensive directory system in existence today.

LDAP

In the early 1990s, in an attempt to overcome some of the complexity-related barriers to the widespread use of X.500, the Internet community developed a specification for a lightweight protocol for accessing X.500. The specification, originally published as RFC 1487 in 1993, and subsequently revised and published as RFC 1777 in 1995, for the Lightweight Directory Access Protocol (LDAP) was originally intended to be used as a front end to X.500 directories, essentially as a special-purpose DUA, as shown in Exhibit 30.4. As such, LDAP used the same naming convention, the same object model, and the same distributed operations model as X.500. The only thing that differed was the access protocol.

In 1997, the Internet community published LDAP Version 3 as RFC 2251. Unlike previous versions, LDAP Version 3 included the concept of using LDAP (the protocol) to access non-X.500 directories. Consequently, the notion of a stand-alone LDAP server came into being. In addition, the new version incorporated concepts such as LDAP referrals, operating much like X.500 or DNS referrals. For backward compatibility, LDAP Version 3 still uses the X.500-style naming convention and still relies on the X.500 information model concepts of objects, entries, attributes, and so on. However, due to the departure from the dependency on X.500, LDAP and X.500 can no longer be considered one and the same. In fact, the term LDAP has become a misnomer because the concept applies to much more than just an access protocol.

Case Study: Microsoft Corp.'s Windows NT Version 5.0

Although not yet released as a product at the time of this writing, the next version of Windows NT has been widely reported to incorporate directory technologies as integral components of the operating system. Combining elements of DNS, X.500, and LDAP, Microsoft has coined the term "Active Directory" to describe this new directory concept. As best one can determine from the information available, Active Directory is most closely aligned with X.500, but it supports LDAP as its only general-purpose access protocol. DNS is supported as if it were any other directory function, supporting standardized DNS queries, but representing domain components and computers in the same way it represents any other X.500-style directory object, using the standardized mapping between Internet-style domain names and X.500-style entry names defined in RFC 2247.

Early reports about Active Directory place it at the core of many of the NT operating system functions. In particular, it has already been mentioned that it is to be used in lieu of a more traditional stand-alone DNS server. In addition, it is reportedly to replace the current registry-based distributed authentication mechanism, and it is expected to replace the Exchange e-mail directory. Moreover, it has been reported that it will be used in support of a variety of advanced operating system functions such as remote resource location and binding, management of distributed quality of service, and distributed policy enforcement, among others.

DIRECTORY-BASED SOLUTIONS TO OPERATING SYSTEM ISSUES

Given the assortment of operating system issues identified in the first section of this paper, are the directory technologies discussed in the second section sufficient to provide a solution? In this final section, we will address not only whether or not it can be done, but also how it can be done.

To solve these issues, it is first necessary to establish and populate the directory service to be used by the operating system. In particular, the following types of objects must be defined:

- **Users** — A user object class must be defined identifying all applicable aspects relevant to individual users. In particular, identity-establishing information such as log-in ID and passwords are required, as is information pertaining to the user's desktop profile. This profile information can be stored in the directory itself, or it can be identified in the directory as a pointer to a file on a server where this information is kept.
- **Resource objects** — All types of resources will require entries in the directory. This includes printers, applications, computer systems, network resources, and the like. All information pertinent to the particular type of resource should be stored in the directory. Most important of this information is the network address of each resource.
- **Policy objects** — Of the objects listed, policy objects are the most abstract. However, it is certainly possible to represent information about practically any type of policy in a directory. For instance, required software for a given class of workstation can readily be stored in a directory entry, including a pointer to the most current version. In support of distributed security issues, objects representing security policy can also be established in this manner.

Once these directory objects have been identified and their entries have been populated in the directory, it is possible to deploy directory-based solutions to the problems identified previously.

Network Log-in

When a user logs in to any computer system, whether the normal system for that user or not, the operating system presents a standard log-in prompt, requesting the user's ID and password. Upon receipt of the ID/password combination, the operating system calls its user authentication process. However, rather than authenticating locally, the authentication process sends a query to the directory. The directory, using referrals or chaining as necessary, finds the user's entry (by searching for a matching user ID), and tests to see that the user supplied the correct password, as stored in the user's directory entry. If the two entries match, the successful result is passed back to the local operating system, which then proceeds with the log-in request.

As user information changes, the information need only be updated in one place: the user's directory entry. Of particular importance to network security administrators, upon termination of the user's employment, the entry can be simply and quickly invalidated by resetting the password to a value the user does not know. At that point, all further accesses by the user, from anywhere on the network, are then blocked.

User-specific Machine Profiles

As the log-in proceeds, the operating system obtains additional information from the user's directory entry, associating the user with a pointer to his desired machine profile, stored on a server somewhere. The server has a name, which is then resolved, via the directory, to an IP address. That address is then used to establish a connection to the server hosting the user's profile. Information in the profile is then used to obtain all the elements associated with the user's profile. Further pointers are subsequently resolved recursively until sufficient information is obtained for the local system to present the user with a familiar screen image. Although this whole process can involve significant amounts of processing and network utilization, appropriate use of caching on the user's "home" system can eliminate significant amounts of startup processing time for the normal case.

Resource Location

Assuming the user has logged in to a system as described above, the act of accessing resources follows a similar set of processes. A user typically requests a resource by name, using menu selections or mouse clicks in so doing. Once the resource has been identified to the operating system, it completes the request by sending the resource name in a query to the directory. The directory then returns information such as the network address of the resource, which the operating system uses to bind to the object.

As resources come and go, or are moved about on the network, the directory entry is updated to reflect the new information. Once updated in the directory, all participating systems immediately have access to the most current information.

Resource-Associated Access Control

Quite often, networked resources are not available uniformly to all users. For instance, a payroll application is likely to have its access restricted to a very small set of users. To accomplish this, each resource entry in the directory can be associated with a set of access control information. This information can range from very general (e.g., "permit access by any authenticated user") to highly specific (e.g., "permit access by these specified users, deny access by all others"). This access control information can be stored in the directory as part of the entry of the resource, or it can be held in a separate access control object referenced or inherited by the entry of the resource. In processing requests for any resource, the operating system, in conjunction with the directory, will verify that the user has the appropriate access rights for that particular object. A default access control policy will apply to all cases not specified otherwise.

Multiple Image Management and Load Balancing

A rather advanced scenario involving multiple images of a single resource was discussed earlier in the chapter. The directory readily supports this scenario by having the resource entry simply provide multiple values in its network address attribute. When the client-side operating system receives a response with more than one network address, it uses a random function to select among the choices, then binds accordingly. If the client receives no response from the selected address, it can select from the other values it originally received, thus providing dynamic fail-over capabilities.

Policy Enforcement

Distributed policy enforcement is accomplished primarily through the use of policy objects in the directory. Because standards do not exist for representation of such objects, the precise syntax and semantics would have to be defined for the operating system involved. However, once defined and populated in the directory, the use of the directory to enforce policy is fairly straightforward.

Suppose, for example, that a policy exists requiring every personal workstation to be equipped with the latest version of a particular virus scanner. The operating system can support the enforcement of this policy at boot time. Whenever a workstation is booted, the operating system can place a call to the directory to obtain information from the directory entry of the workstation. Among the information returned is a pointer to any applicable policy objects. By following the chain of policy object entries and pointers during system startup, the workstation can determine, for example, that it requires the particular piece of software, then check its own hard drive for the existence of the software. If the software does not exist, it can then locate a server-based copy using the information contained in the policy object, download it, install it, and even run it before the user is provided with the initial log-in prompt.

Distributed Security

Some aspects of distributed security have already been discussed. Other aspects can be similarly supported through the appropriate use of the directory. For example, suppose a user connects to the network via a remote access server. The server itself will probably require the use of a secure ID card of some sort before granting the user access to the network. Suppose, however, that a particular application the user wishes to access requires that users dialing in from the outside use an encrypted link to communicate their data. This particular aspect of the security policy of the resource can be expressed in the access control information of the resource as a function of the originating system, as opposed to the user. To express the need for encryption, the access controls for the entry of the resource could be applied, based on the originating address, in such a way that the only network address visible is one that imposes the encryption requirement. Thus, at bind time, the protocol handshake would automatically negotiate the form of encryption, supporting the needs of the distributed security policy, without inconveniencing the user in any way.

Quality of Service Management

Quality of service management is also a matter of expressing aspects of policy in directory entries. First, the user's entry must be identified as one that is permitted a certain level of service. Second, the necessary resources must have quality of service capability information identified in their entries. Finally, the needs of the user and the capabilities of the resources must be matched, subject to appropriate access controls. Of course, the individual resources themselves must support the implementation of varying levels of service; the directory merely supports matching the requirements to available resources.

CONCLUSION

In this chapter, several issues related to operating systems in the LAN-based enterprise network were presented, and several major directory technologies were introduced. When considering these operating system issues in conjunction with directory technologies, it became clear that directories can play an integral role in advancing the state of the art of operating systems. As evidenced by the early reports concerning Windows NT Version 5.0, it appears likely that at least one operating system vendor is poised to start exploiting directories in this fashion. Success of that product line will likely play a role in determining whether or not other operating system vendors follow suit. Given the increasing complexity of current LAN-based enterprise networks, LAN and IT managers are well advised to follow developments in this area.

BIBLIOGRAPHY

Chadwick, D., *Understanding X.500: the Directory,* Chapman & Hall, London, 1994.
Microsoft Corp., *Future Directions: Windows NT Server 5.0,* 1998.
Sun Microsystems Inc., JNDI: Java Naming and Directory Interface, January 1998.
Kille, S., M. Wahl, A. Grimstad, R. Huber, S. Sataluri, Using domains in LDAP/X.500 distinguished names, RFC 2247, January 1998.
Microsoft and Cisco to Collaborate to Establish Directory Services Standard, Microsoft Corp. and Cisco Systems Inc. (joint press release), Las Vegas, NE, May 7, 1997.
Mockapetris, P., Domain names — concepts and facilities, RFC 882, Internic, November 1983.
The Directory: Overview of Concepts, Models, and Services, Geneva: ITU-T Recommendation X.500, 1997.
Wahl, M. T. and Howes, S. Kille, Lightweight Directory Access Protocol, RFC 2251, December 1997.
Windows NT Server Active Directory, Microsoft Corp., 1998.
Yeong, W., T. Howes and S. Kille, Lightweight Directory Access Protocol, March 1995.

Chapter 31
Enterprise Directory Services

Martin Schleiff

Many consulting organizations, trade associations, and vendors are touting directory services as the center of the communications universe. They say enterprises will benefit as they put increasing efforts and resources into their directory services. Application directory services (e.g., the address books in today's e-mail packages) are devoted to enhancing the functional ability of a particular product, service, or application to its user community. Even though e-mail address books are capable of displaying and possibly administering some information about e-mail users, they are not geared to manage corporate-critical information and deliver it to other applications, users, and services. The predicted benefits are not realized until a company embraces the concept of an enterprise directory service.

APPLICATION VS. ENTERPRISE DIRECTORY SERVICES

Perhaps the simplest way to contrast application and enterprise directory services is to consider the community, or user base, being served. Application directory services typically have a well-defined user base. This may consist of the users of a particular calendaring or scheduling system, or an electronic messaging system. Where multiple, disparate e-mail systems are deployed, the community may consist of the users of all interconnected messaging systems, and the application directory service may include processes that synchronize directory information between each system.

Enterprise directory services focus on providing a core set of fundamental services that can be used by many environments and customer communities. The prime objective is to leverage the efforts of few to the benefit of many (see Exhibit 31.1).

The enterprise directory service provides an enabling infrastructure on which other technologies, applications, products, and services can build. It is wise to establish this infrastructure even before receiving hard requirements from specific customer environments. Two symptoms of companies that lack enterprise directory services are hindered deployment of new

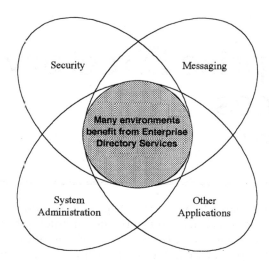

Exhibit 31.1. Enterprise Directory Services Environment

technologies and applications, and redundant processes that have been built by each environment to meet its own needs.

Another way to contrast application and enterprise directory services is to consider how they evaluate the merit of a potential new service. Providers of enterprise directory services will consider the potential for their efforts to eventually be leveraged across multiple user communities. If only one community will ever use the new service, little advantage is associated with hosting that service at the enterprise level. It might be more appropriate to encourage that community to build its own service and offer to support its efforts with managed directory information. For example, if an organization wishes to track the activities of its employees on various projects, an enterprise directory service would likely decline the request to track activities, but offer to support the project by providing access to the appropriate employee information.

WHAT GOES ON IN AN ENTERPRISE DIRECTORY SERVICE?

In a nutshell, any directory service consists of activities and processes to collect and publish information. Many directory services also add value by integrating various types and sources of information into commonly useable formats.

Services that are likely candidates to be provided as part of an enterprise directory service include the following: information solicitation, registration, naming, authentication, directory synchronization, and coordination of publication infrastructure. Each of these services is briefly described in the following paragraphs. Consideration is given to some of the issues and challenges facing the providers of directory services.

Information Solicitation Services

Providers of enterprise directory services can be characterized as data hungry; they realize that empty directories are worthless. They continually seek new and better sources of information to include in their directories. Frequently, these information sources are less than enthralled about expending any efforts and resources that do not directly benefit their own causes.

For example, the human resources department of a subsidiary may not see the benefit of including subsidiary employee information in the directories of the parent company. Likewise, a payroll organization may not fully appreciate that the information they maintain about who is authorized to sign an employee's time card could also be used to approximate the company's management hierarchy. Presenting this information in a directory provides visibility of the company's dynamic organizational structure.

Enterprise directory service providers tend to accept information in any way they can get it. Data submitted by e-mail, file transfer protocol (FTP), floppies, facsimile, phone calls, and even yellow sticky notes are readily accepted in any format. A service provider would rather bend over backward than impose the service's conventions on a hesitant supplier and risk losing their willingness to provide information. In fact, the most critical task in providing enterprise directory services is to build and maintain relationships with data providers.

Service providers also realize that directories with misleading information are worse than worthless. They therefore fret continually about the condition of the data they receive and publish.

At the system level, service-level agreements normally provide some level of confidence about the availability of systems and the quality of hardware and software support. The challenge for enterprise directory service providers is to expand this concept to include information.

Agreements with information sources help identify the quality and availability of the information that will appear in the directory. Information does not need to be perfect to be meaningful and useful, as long as the quality characteristics of the information are made known to users so they can make value judgments about how to appropriately use the information.

Registration Services

Whenever possible, enterprise directory service providers attempt to acquire directory content from other sources — they prefer to be information publishers rather than information owners. Sometimes, however, no managed source for a particular type of information can be identified. In such cases, building a registration service to collect the desired information may be considered. The following list offers examples of registration activities that may be included in an enterprise directory service:

- *Collection of workstation e-mail addresses.* In most messaging environments, e-mail address information can be collected from a well-defined group of administrators. Unfortunately, where UNIX and other workstations are abundant, administration tends to be much less defined and coordinated. In such areas, each workstation may have its own messaging system, and each user may be responsible for administration of his own system. There is probably not a single source from which to obtain address information for a large company's workstation community.
- *Primary address designation.* Many people have more than one e-mail mailbox. For example, engineers may prefer to use their UNIX systems for messaging, yet their managers may require them to maintain an account on the same mainframe used by all the managers. Individuals may require the flexibility to work with binary attachments offered by a LAN messaging system and still maintain a mainframe account to use a calendaring system that scales to enterprise levels. With frequent migrations from one messaging system to another, large groups of people may have multiple mailboxes for several weeks while they gain familiarity with the new system and transfer information from the old system. All these cases breed confusion among senders when it is not apparent which system holds the intended recipient's preferred mailbox. Registration services may be established to let individuals designate their preferred mailbox (or preferred document type or preferred spreadsheet type).
- *Information about nonemployees.* The human resources department is an obvious source of employee information to be included in a directory. The human resources department, however, probably does not track information about nonemployees who may require access to a company's computing resources and who may have e-mail accounts on the company's systems. A service to register, maintain, and publish information about contractors, service personnel, and trading partners may be considered.
- *Information about nonpeople.* Other entities that may be appropriate to display in a directory include distribution lists, bulletin boards, help desks, list servers, applications, conference rooms, and other nonpeople entities.

Caution is advised when considering to offer registration services, because such services frequently require extensive manual effort and will significantly increase the labor required to run the enterprise directory service. Also, the enterprise directory service then becomes a data owner and can no longer defer data inconsistencies to some other responsible party. Even though resources are consumed in providing such services, the benefits can far outweigh the costs of uncoordinated, inconsistent, absent, or redundant registration activities.

Naming/Identification Services

A naming service simply provides alternate names, or identifiers, for such entities as people, network devices, and resources. A prime example is domain name service (DNS), which provides a user-friendly identifier (i.e., host.domain) for a networked resource and maps it to a very unfriendly network address (e.g., 130.42.14.165).

Another popular service is to provide identifiers for people in a format that can be used as log-in IDs or e-mail addresses, and that can be mapped back to the owners. LAN-based messaging systems frequently identify and track users by full name instead of by user ID, assuming that people's names are unique across that particular messaging system. This is one of the major hurdles in scaling LAN-based messaging systems beyond the workgroup level. A naming service could manage and provide distinct full names and alleviate a major scaling problem.

Naming services should adhere to the following principles when defining identifiers.

1. *Stable and meaningless.* Identifiers, or names, are like gossip; once they become known, they are difficult to change, recall, and correct. Inherent meanings (e.g., organizational affiliation or physical location) should not be embedded in an identifier because these values change frequently, rendering the identifier inaccurate or out of date.
2. *Uniqueness.* Identifiers must be unique within a naming context.
3. *Traceable back to an individual.* To effectively manage a system, knowledge about the system's users is required.
4. *Extensible to many environments.* Many companies are striving to minimize the number of user IDs an individual must remember to gain access to myriad accounts. Others hope to eventually implement a single log-on by which their users can access any computing resource.
5. *User friendly.* Identifiers should be easy to convey, easy to type in, and easy to remember.
6. *Easy to maintain.* Algorithmically derived identifiers (e.g., surname followed by first initial) are easy to generate, but such algorithms may cause duplicate identifiers to be generated if they are not checked against some registry of previously assigned identifiers.

Some of the principles are in contention with each other, so enterprise directory service providers must identify a practical balance of desirable characteristics. A hybrid approach might incorporate some of the following rules:

- Algorithmically assign identifiers (ease of generation).
- Include a maximum of eight characters (extensible to many environments).
- Base identifiers on people's real names (semi-stable and user-friendly).
- Use numbers as needed in the rightmost bytes to distinguish between similar names (uniqueness).
- Register the identifiers in a database (traceable back to the owner and guaranteed uniqueness).
- Allow individuals to override the generated identifier with self-chosen vanity plate values (user-friendly).

Naming an entity should occur as soon as that entity is known (e.g., on or before an employee's hire date), and the identifier should immediately be published by the enterprise directory service. Then, when system administrators establish user accounts for an entity, they can find the entity's identifier in the directory and use that identifier as the user ID. Thereafter, the identifier can be used to query the directory for a user's updated contact and status information. This approach enables system administrators to focus on managing user accounts instead of employee information.

Authentication/Confidentiality Services

The swelling interest in electronic commerce has brought much attention to the need for encryption and electronic signature capabilities. The most promising technologies are referred to as public-key cryptographic systems (PKCS), which provide two keys for an individual — one a private key and the other a public key (see Exhibit 31.2). A private key must remain known only to its owner. An individual's public key must be widely published and made easily available to the community with which that person does business.

Information encrypted with an individual's public key can be decrypted only with the associated private key. Therefore, information can be sent confidentially to its recipient. Information encrypted with an individual's private key can be decrypted only with the associated public key. Therefore, a recipient can authenticate the origin of the information.

Companies are now grappling with such PKCS deployment issues as which organization will manage keys, which algorithms will be used to generate keys, will private keys be held in escrow, and will employees be allowed to use company-generated keysets for personal use. The one issue that seems clear is that public keys should be published in a directory service. Soon, enterprise directory service providers will be grappling with

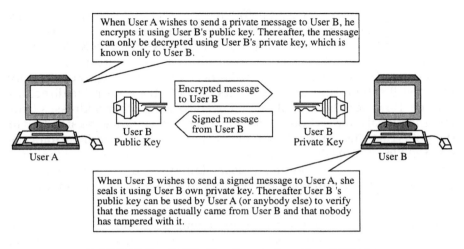

Exhibit 31.2. Public-Key Encryption: How It Works

their own issues (e.g., When should the directory actually begin to carry public keys? How to encourage vendors to build products that can query a directory for somebody's public key? How many keys should be carried for an individual? How to make these keys accessible to trading partners and other areas beyond corporate boundaries?).

Directory Synchronization Services

The press routinely represents cross-platform directory synchronization as the most difficult task in a directory service. Depending on the approach taken, this situation may be true. Several messaging system vendors provide products that can synchronize non-native address books into their own. If a company attempts to use such products to synchronize address books from more than two vendors, a true mess will result.

A much more effective manner is to synchronize each address book with a central (probably vendor-neutral) bidirectional synchronization service. The central synchronization service can pool the addresses from all participating messaging communities, translate between native and common address formats, and finally make the pooled addresses available to each community in its respective native format. The advantages of a central service over two-way address book synchronizers can be likened to the advantages of providing a messaging backbone service instead of two-way e-mail gateways. Large companies taking the centralized approach have been able to provide cross-platform synchronization services with minimal resources (e.g., one allocated headcount).

Directory standards (e.g., X.500) have the potential to further simplify cross-platform directory synchronization. If vendors ever half-embrace the standard to the point that their products actually query an X.500 service instead of (or in addition to) their local address books, directory synchronization can become a uni-directional process. Each messaging community would still submit the addresses of its users to the enterprise directory service. However, there would be no need to bring other addresses back into their local address book. If vendors ever fully embrace the standard to the point that their products actually manage their own address information right in an X.500 directory, processes for cross-platform directory synchronization are altogether unnecessary. Enterprise directory service providers ought to encourage their vendors to include these capabilities in their products.

With growing interest in electronic commerce, enterprise directory service providers are being asked to carry trading partner information in local directories. In response to such requests, and in the absence of better solutions, service providers commonly exchange files containing address information with trading partner companies and then incorporate the address information into their own processes.

A better approach would be to link the directories of the trading partner companies so that each company is responsible for its own information; there would be no need for a company to obtain a file of trading partner addresses and manage the information locally. This is yet another area where directory standards provide hope for a better future. The X.500 standards specify the technologies and protocols required for such an inter-enterprise directory. Before participating in an interenterprise X.500 directory, service providers will need to evaluate their company policies on external publication of directories, access control to sensitive information, and the readiness of trading partners to participate.

What Is X.500?

X.500 is a set of international standards jointly developed by the International Telecommunications Union-Telecommunications Standards Sector (ITU-TSS) and the International Standards Organization (ISO) that specify standards-based directory components and protocols. Some of the major components and protocols include the following:

- *Directory System Agent (DSA)*. This is where information resides. Multiple DSAs can replicate and distribute information among themselves. They can communicate among themselves to resolve directory queries.
- *Directory User Agent (DUA)*. This enables a user (or application) to access information stored in DSAs. DUAs may be stand-alone programs or incorporated into other applications (e.g., an e-mail user agent).

- *Directory System Protocol (DSP)*. This protocol is used by DSAs to communicate among themselves to resolve queries.
- *Directory Access Protocol (DAP)*. This protocol is used to communicate between DUAs and DSAs. A Lightweight Directory Access Protocol (LDAP) has been defined that is less bulky than DAP and that is appropriate for desktop devices.

X.500 Infrastructure Coordination Services

Various approaches can be taken for deployment of X.500 technology. Frequently, X.500 is included as a component of some other product the company wishes to deploy. For example, a company may purchase a new message transfer agent (MTA) that includes an X.500 DSA to manage message routing information; a company can also acquire a public-key crypto system product that includes X.500 to publish public keys, or a company may use X.500 as a distributed computing environment (DCE) global directory.

Another approach is for a company to first deploy a stand-alone X.500-based directory service and then tie in messaging, security, and other products as they are acquired. In a large company, some combination of these approaches may occur simultaneously. Setting up X.500 for a particular application is much easier than setting up a general X.500 infrastructure, but it is not the preferred approach.

It is likely that various computing communities will acquire their own X.500 directory system agents to meet their own special needs. Unless the efforts of these groups are coordinated, conflicting definitions, incompatibilities, and redundant efforts and data will emerge — foiling the potential for the efforts of the few to be leveraged to the benefit of the many.

Even though the enterprise directory service may not own all the directory components, it is the best place to organize the activities of these components. Coordination activities include acting as the company's registration authority, managing the root DSA within the company, providing a map of the company's directory information tree, registration of new DSAs, schema management, registration of object classes and attribute types, controlling where new information is incorporated into the directory, and managing replication agreements.

A SERVICE PROVIDER'S PERSPECTIVE ON X.500

These days, technologists promote technologies as directory services, vendors market products as directory services, and standards bodies represent specifications as directory services. Enterprise directory service providers must remember that all these are just tools by which to provide a directory service, and it is their responsibility to select the appropriate tools to best deliver their services. They must discern between what works in theory, what works in principle, and what works in practice.

X.500 technology is sound, but until vendors actually deliver products that use the technology, it will remain difficult to justify a serious investment in establishing X.500 infrastructure. Home-grown applications are driving X.500 deployment in some companies, but even in these companies a stronger vendor commitment would ease the burden of justification.

Information Management Issues

X.500 is frequently cast as a panacea for directory services. This is not true; the biggest challenges for enterprise directory service providers are information management issues.

X.500's strength is in information publication, not information management. In some companies, X.500 receives more attention from the security and systems administration communities than from messaging organizations. These communities have much more stringent requirements for timely and accurate data; service providers will need to revamp processes and clean up content to meet these requirements. Remembering that directories with bad information are worse than worthless, service providers will need to give as much attention to information processes and relationships with data providers as they do to X.500 technologies.

Database Issues

X.500 is often described as a type of distributed Database Management System. This can be misleading, and some applications that began building on X.500 have had to back off and use conventional database products. X.500 is well-suited for information that is structured, frequently accessed by a heterogeneous community, primarily read only, and latency tolerant. X.500, however, lacks database capabilities (e.g., referential integrity or the ability to update groups of information in a single operation). A common debate concerns whether data should be managed in X.500, or if it should be managed in a database and then published in X.500.

Directory Information Tree Structure

Most literature suggests that there are only two basic models to follow when designing the X.500 directory information tree (DIT): the DIT should reflect either a company's organizational structure or its geographical structure.

In fact, both the organizational and geographical approaches violate the first principle of naming (stable and meaningless identifiers). Frequent reorganizations and relocations will cause frequent changes to distinguished names (DNs) if either the organizational or the geographical model is followed. When designing a DIT, sources of information must be considered. For example, in companies where all employee data is managed by a central human resources organization, it may not make sense to artificially divide the information so that it fits a distributed model.

These observations are not intended to discourage use of X.500-based directory services; rather, they are intended to encourage cautious deployment. Reckless and inappropriate activities with X.500 will likely damage its chances for eventual success in a company, and this technology has far too much potential to carelessly squander away. The previously lamented lack of vendor products that use X.500 can also be taken as a window of opportunity for companies to gain X.500 experience in a controlled manner before some critical application demands knee-jerk deployment. An ideal way to start (assuming that the information is already available) is to build an inexpensive and low-risk White Pages directory service using the following components:

- *A single DSA and LDAP server.* Inexpensive products are available today; a desktop system can provide good response for thousands of White Pages users. Worries about replication agreements and getting different vendors' directory system agents to interoperate can be postponed until the service grows beyond the capabilities of a single DSA.
- *A simple Windows DUA.* Vendor-provided directory user agents can be purchased. Unfortunately, many vendor products tend to be so full-featured that they risk becoming overly complex. An in-house-developed DUA can provide basic functions, can be easily enhanced, can be optimized for the company's directory information tree, and can be freely distributed. Freeware Macintosh DUAs are also available.
- *A Web-to-X.500 gateway.* Freeware software is available.
- *A White Pages home page that resolves queries through the Web-to-X.500 gateway.* This brings the service to a large heterogeneous user community.

A precautionary note about deploying such a service is that users will consider it a production service even if it is intended only as a pilot or prototype. Support and backup capabilities may be demanded earlier than expected.

ROLES AND RESPONSIBILITIES

As companies attempt to categorize enterprise directory services, especially those that include X.500, they begin to realize the difficulty in identifying a service provider organization. An enterprise directory service is as much a networking technology as it is an information management service, or a communications enabler, or a foundation for security services. One cannot definitely predict that messaging will be the biggest customer of the service or that human resources information and e-mail addresses will be the most important information handled by the service. Possibly the best approach is to create a new organization to provide the enterprise directory service.

To build and provide effective directory services, service providers must be intimately familiar with the data so they can witness the changing characteristics of the information, recognize anomalies, and appropriately relate various types of data. Rather than assign an individual to a single role, it is preferable to assign each individual to multiple roles so that nobody is too far removed from the data and so that no role is left without a backup.

Roles and responsibilities fall into the following categories: operations management, product management, project management, and service management.

Operations Management. Directory operations management focuses on quality and availability of directory data as specified in service-level agreements. Responsibilities include the following:

1. Operate day-to-day directory processes and provide on-time availability of deliverables.
2. Ensure that the directory service is accessible by supported user agents.
3. Register information that is not available from other sources.
4. Interface with existing data suppliers to resolve inaccurate information.
5. Validate data, report exceptions, and track trends.
6. Staff a user support helpdesk.

Product Management. Directory product management focuses on the type of products and services offered to directory customers, as well as tools and processes to best provide the services. Responsibilities include the following:

1. Acquire, build, and maintain tools that enable or improve day-to-day operation of directory processes. Appropriate skills include database development, programming in various environments, and familiarity with the company's heterogeneous computing environment.
2. Establish and administer service-level agreements with information providers and customers. Negotiate formats, schedules, and methods of information exchange between the directory service and its suppliers and customers.
3. Provide and maintain approved directory user agents to the user community.

4. Promote current capabilities of directory services to potential customers.
5. Build directory products to meet customer needs.

Project Management. Directory project management focuses on the near-term future of directory services. Responsibilities include the following:

1. Conduct proof-of-concept projects to explore new uses of directory services.
2. Coordinate activities to put new uses of directory services into production.
3. Conduct proof-of-concept projects to explore the use of new technologies in providing directory services.
4. Coordinate activities to deploy new directory technologies into production.
5. Consult and assist customer environments in incorporating directory services into their applications and services (e.g., assist with LDAP coding, assemble tool kits to ease coding against directories, train application developers in use of tool kits, and provide orientation to the enterprise directory service).
6. Ascertain which projects are most needed. Possible projects include interenterprise directories, participation in global directories, authentication and access control, public keys in directories, electronic Yellow Pages, combining disparate registration services, achieving DNS functional ability with X.500, explore the use of whois++ and finger as directory user agents, partner with other groups to achieve synergy with World Wide Web and other technologies, and assist corporate communications organizations to optimize electronic distribution of information bulletins.
7. Participate with appropriate forums to define and establish international standards.

Service Management. Directory service management focuses on the soundness of current and future directory services. Responsibilities include the following:

1. Coordinate project management, product management, and operations management efforts.
2. Author and maintain service descriptions.
3. Run change boards and advisory boards.
4. Coordinate X.500 infrastructure (registration point for DSAs, object classes, and attributes).
5. Develop and gain consensus on position statements and direction statements.
6. Formulate business plans and justify required resources.

7. Act as focal point for major customer communities; collect requirements, assess customer satisfaction, and gain consensus on direction statements.
8. Represent the company's interests at external forums and to vendors.

SUMMARY

It is important to have realistic expectations of a directory service. Some who expect that a directory will provide huge payback as a single data repository and source of all corporate information may be disappointed. Others who consider directories to be of limited use beyond messaging will reap only a portion of directory benefits. It is difficult to predict which visionary ideas will become practical applications in the near future.

Probably the most vital point to consider when planning for an enterprise directory service is flexibility. In light of dynamic customer demands, new sources and types of information, increasingly stringent requirements for quality data, and emerging technologies, many service providers have elected to use a database to manage directory information (exploiting its data management capabilities) and a directory to publish managed data (capitalizing on its publication strengths).

As buzzwords proliferate, it is easy to get caught up in the glitter and pomp of new technologies. Wise service providers will realize that the important part of directory services is service and that the role of new technologies is simply to better enable the providing of a service.

Chapter 32
Storage Area Networks
Jim Morin

The enormous amount of growth in disk and tape storage is greatly complicating the life of Information Technology (IT) professionals assigned to
manage their corporation's information assets. A new concept, called Storage Area Networking (SAN), has emerged to provide an architectural
framework for storage-related applications. The SAN concept has encouraged exciting new hardware and software technology to focus on this storage management and capacity problem.

As this new technology emerges, it is important to implement tactical
projects that will lead to a strategic, new SAN infrastructure. Obviously,
this roadmap will be different for every corporation, depending on their
business, size of company, and storage management requirements. This
article provides guidance on the applications enhanced by a SAN to add to
the IT manager's knowledge and experience toolkit.

NEW FOCUS ON STORAGE

Individuals, and corporations consisting of many people, creatively
develop information related to their business every day. Often this is based
partly on data the corporation collects about its sales, market, positioning,
customers, etc. Then information is exchanged with other people to seek
confirmation or even newer ideas, based on many other sources of information. The driving force behind this creative process is to make the corporation more successful in its business.

Recently, this concept has shifted attention to how to manage the flow
of information. This management process starts at the source. If the information is in hard-copy form, the flow is relatively slow. Remember "snail
mail"? Today, more and more information is digital, greatly increasing the
potential velocity of data movement through an organization. It follows
that more timely access to information and better data management can
provide a competitive advantage. The "information at your fingertips" slogan epitomizes the concept. (If it was only that simple!)

As corporations rely more and more on this fast-paced digital flow of
information, they realize that continuous investments are required to add
capacity and streamline the arteries of transport. As the investments in

capacity have geometrically expanded — from megabytes to gigabytes to terabytes and beyond — the transport and management infrastructure struggles to keep pace.

WHAT IS A SAN?

Storage Area Networks (SANs) were envisioned to solve these "big" problems surrounding data storage and management. The original computing paradigm has the CPU shuttle data from main memory to longer-term permanent storage over an input/output (I/O) connectivity architecture and communication protocol. The CPU "owns" the storage device, and the I/O path is relatively short to ensure minimum latency of data transfers. This model works well and can be scaled to fit the size of many applications. However, it does not facilitate the exchange or protection of information and can be very limited in environments with large applications or a large number of users.

So the computing model evolved to place multiple "servers" on a network, with storage facilities that could be partitioned and shared by many users. Faster networks and network switching attempted to solve problems of scalability created by expanding the number of users. However, each server still "owned" its storage devices, limiting affordable scalability. In addition, I/O traffic is forced to contend with user application access, resulting in slower overall performance.

The next evolutionary step is the SAN. The concept is simple: enable servers and storage to independently provide their services on the network. Just like an appliance gets its power from the wall plug, a SAN provides a common plug-in connectivity infrastructure for adding processing power or storage capacity. The SAN becomes an independent, high-performance network, dedicated to I/O. (See Exhibit 32.1.)

The potential benefits of a SAN are appealing:

- independence of server and storage implementation, enabling the selection of the best technology for the application
- the ability to add new storage or server capacity as needed without impacting the existing production
- increased availability of the information with improved disaster recovery and high availability storage solutions
- improved overall performance of the information flow by implementing new channel I/O technologies that have better bandwidth, aggregate capacity, and processing speeds
- a more streamlined approach to data management tasks that results in a more productive, efficient process with better security and lower cost of ownership

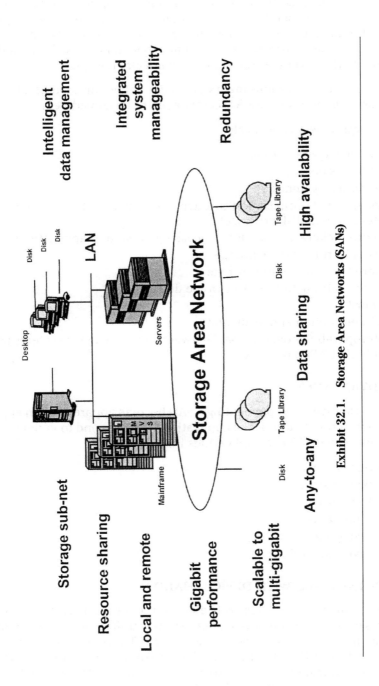

Exhibit 32.1. Storage Area Networks (SANs)

Since IT rarely has the luxury of building a computing and networking infrastructure from scratch, an important but often overlooked aspect of SANs is the need to integrate new technology and methods with existing systems. Integration protects the current investment in hardware and software and better leverages the capital dollars already spent.

Refer to the SAN requirements checklist below for several additional data management issues for SANs that need to be considered.

SAN requirements checklist:

- data management tools
- I/O protocols
- server file systems
- system-level optimization through network operating system, server interconnect, disk arrays, etc.
- record locking, transaction processing for shared applications
- virtualization of data storage
- shared data or shared storage
- device pathing (access to storage devices)
- security
- data protection and availability
- interoperability over the SAN between heterogeneous systems (S/390, multiple UNIX flavors, NT)

SAN ADVANTAGES

The advantages of implementing a SAN become apparent when applying the infrastructure to a series of applications that respond to various corporate requirements. These applications include:

- device sharing
- backup/restore
- disk mirroring
- data migration
- data sharing
- archive/retrieval

GETTING STARTED WITH DEVICE SHARING

Device sharing responds to the economic imperative that because money is scarce, an expensive resource is best utilized when shared by the optimum number of users. (See Exhibit 32.2.) This concept is as old as the idea behind the A:B switch that enabled a path to a destination to be manually switched from one source to another. However, the concept is complicated by one other important reality: diversity.

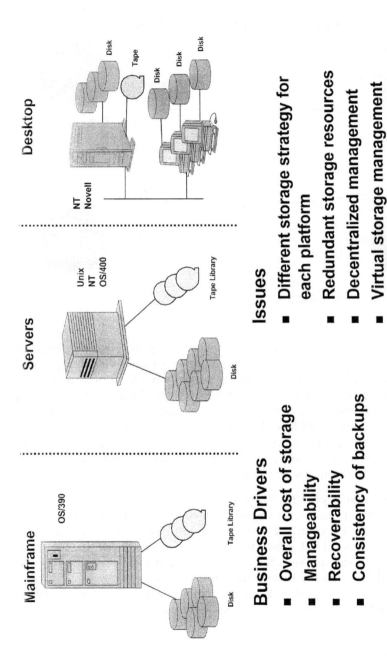

Exhibit 32.2. Shared Storage Requirements

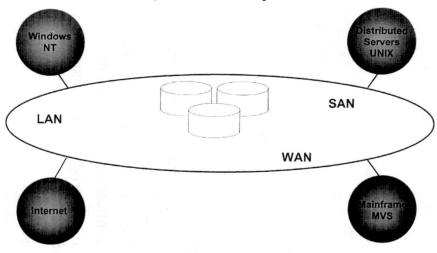

Data is accessible to any system type: locally and remotely off-site

Exhibit 32.3.   SAN: The Real Benefits

The fact is that corporate enterprise systems are diverse, comprised of mainframes, midrange systems, and popular open systems such as Windows NT and UNIX. Each kind of server has its own kind of storage systems, creating in effect islands of information. These islands are becoming more and more densely populated, growing rapidly (as much as 50 percent a year). By sheer weight, all have become critical, whether or not they were originally designed for mission-critical applications. The cost of growing these diverse storage resources and maintaining them with the same or shrinking IT staffs is a major problem.

SANs solve those problems. The SAN acts like a high-speed subnet that establishes a direct connection between storage resources and servers. (See Exhibit 32.3.) It presents a new infrastructure that liberates the storage devices, so they do not attach to particular server buses. Rather, they attach directly to the network SAN. This in essence externalizes storage resources and functionally distributes them to the organization. Storage resources, such as tape and disk libraries, can be centralized and servers can be clustered, which makes for easier access and less-expensive administration.

Specialized networking devices interface servers and storage devices to the network. These are high-speed directors, multiplexers, and gateways that possess a high order of connectivity, performance, and manageability.

Just as a LAN might use technologies such as Ethernet, Token Ring, or FDDI, a SAN can employ a wide range of local area and wide area technologies, including SCSI, ESCON, SSA, Fibre Channel, T3/E3, and SONET. All of this makes SANs suitable for corporate enterprise systems, which in addition to being diverse are spread all over the place.

Device sharing using SANs can be implemented with a slightly more automatic method than the A:B switch mentioned previously. However, the potential SAN value is greatly expanded through new software that automatically handles reserve/release protocol commands from multiple servers to the same devices.

BACKUP/RESTORE APPLICATION REQUIRES INCREASED COMPLEXITY

Once access to a shared device like a tape library is available, the first application to ensure data security is to put the data on tape via a backup application. In the event of a human-caused problem such as deleting a file, a data integrity problem like the fallout from data corruption, or a physical device problem disrupting access to the data, a copy can be restored from tape. Tape is also useful to restore files from a particular point in time, such as end-of-quarter sales figures.

A common problem in many corporate enterprise systems is varying degrees of discipline exercised in controlling and maintaining systems. Many LANs evolved from non-mission-critical applications, such as word processing, presentation development, and other personal productivity activities commonly resident on PC-based systems. Early on, these systems were indeed "personal systems" — outside the control of corporate IT staff. Individual users determined the level of discipline involved in maintenance and security. Activities like backup and restore, which were basic and integral to the maintenance strategies for mainframe-based systems and servers, were for the most part nonexistent on PC-based systems.

As PCs became common office tools, they evolved into LANs. Their importance and the importance of the information they generated and maintained increased. Now, many of the same backup disciplines of mainframe-based systems are needed for these "rogue" systems as well.

Faced with increasing responsibilities and shrinking resources, IT staffs can look to SANs to extend backup resources where needed in the corporate enterprise system. A shared backup resource in a SAN maximizes the use of tape and disk backup resources and provides consistency in the backup process.

MOVING ON TO DISK MIRRORING

Daily backups alone are not enough when companies are vulnerable to a substantial business impact from data lost between backups, or when non-stop data accessibility is required. In those cases, disk mirroring is often employed.

Disk mirroring is a method of duplicating data on separate disks in real-time to preserve the data's accuracy and make it available continuously, even in the face of disaster. Each time data is written to a primary disk, the data is duplicated — or mirrored — to a second disk. In the event that the primary disk goes down, the system can switch to the secondary disk in a matter of minutes.

Disk mirroring can be an important part of an overall disaster recovery strategy, along with backup/restore and archive/retrieval. It also can be part of a strategy to incorporate subsidiary functions, such as system development, testing, or maintenance, into a company's processing scheme without impacting mainline business operations. (See Exhibit 32.4.)

In any case, disk mirroring is employed by companies that simply cannot afford downtime for any reason, whether it is disaster related or not. These companies must have continuous operation, seven days a week, 24 hours a day. The application requires duplicate storage resources, mirroring software, interconnect facilities, and for many solutions additional processor resources. This added expense requires careful consideration before and during implementation.

SANs are a natural host for just such a storage application, making the storage resources accessible anywhere in the enterprise system and allowing efficient use of this expensive facility.

The power of the SAN can be leveraged with disk mirroring systems beyond duplicating data for disaster recovery. Increasingly, additional software provides capabilities for moving data between disk volumes as a method of data migration, file transfer, data sharing, or data warehousing. Because the SAN can be a local, campus, or remote topology, disk mirroring now becomes a very efficient method for exchanging information across the enterprise.

ANOTHER STEP — DATA MIGRATION

Another storage application that suits SANs is data migration. Data migration accompanies business change, and business change is about the only sure thing left today — besides death and taxes. Businesses alternately expand and contract due to mergers and downsizing. That, along with continual development of new technology, requires data to be migrated to new disk technology or to new locations due to data center moves and consolidations. Easy access to storage resources from remote and local sources, permanently or temporarily, is an important asset to IT managers; so is the ability to move large volumes of data quickly and safely.

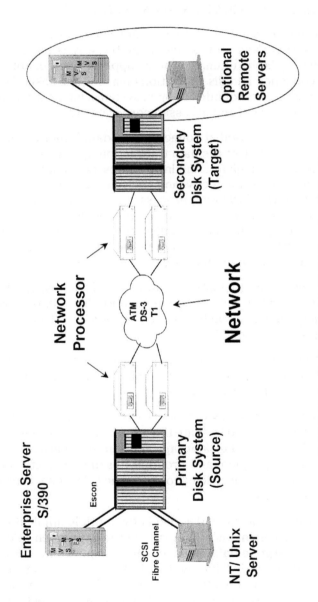

Exhibit 32.4. Typical Remote Disk Mirroring Network

SANs allow all of that — quickly, easily, and safely — among diverse systems and through many types of interconnections.

ULTIMATE STORAGE APPLICATION — DATA SHARING

Once storage devices can be shared and data can be moved quickly and safely between servers and storage facilities, the way is paved for data sharing. Data sharing is the ultimate storage application. It enables enterprisewide data collection and dissemination on a realtime basis. Access to legacy applications can be extended to open systems. Intellectual property can be collected, organized, and accessed corporatewide.

Mainframes, which are good at collecting raw data from the sources or points of transactions, collect the data transaction by transaction in realtime. The data moves through interlinking facilities, becoming deposited in databases in open systems for access and analysis. This systematic collection, extraction, and transformation process is called data warehousing. It is an emerging and widely acclaimed method of giving companies exactly the kind of relevant up-to-date information they need to run their businesses intelligently and competitively in constantly changing market-driven environments. (See Exhibit 32.5.)

SANs have exceptional capabilities to store data efficiently, interface dissimilar resources over a variety of communication links, and move large volumes of data quickly and safely between servers and storage devices. They quite simply enable effective data sharing.

Data sharing can mean either multiple applications reading and writing to the same data fields, or it can mean sending a copy of the data from the source location to another location.

Data copy services, also known as file transfer, has existed with the first creation of a file. If one wanted to share the information with someone else, one either copied the file to a disk or tape and sent the physical media, or invoked a file transfer protocol and program to send an electronic copy. Today's programs are now specialized to utilize the I/O transport protocols for much faster transport.

True data sharing of the same data fields by multiple applications and heterogeneous environments is still mostly in the experimental development stage. The enterprise data management disciplines need to evolve significantly to enable true SAN interaction. Today's operating systems still expect direct ownership of the storage devices and do not have a referee to sort out allocation requests from operating systems competing for the same storage. The Storage Networking Industry Association (SNIA) was organized to promote development of SAN industry standards and has committees working on these data management issues.

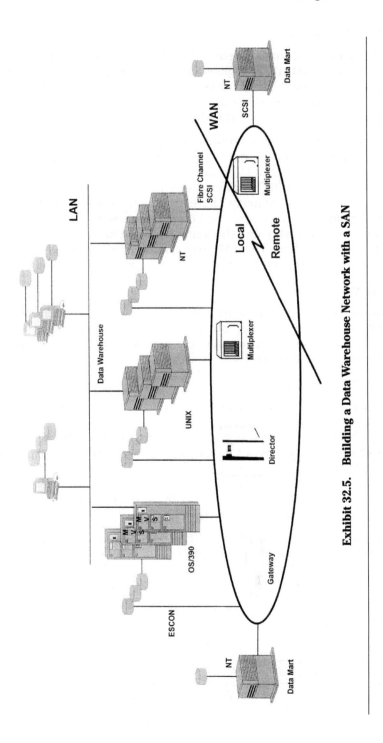

Exhibit 32.5.   Building a Data Warehouse Network with a SAN

ARCHIVE/RETRIEVAL

Finally, data sometimes needs a final resting place. Archived data is recorded on the least costly, highest capacity storage medium because the data is rarely accessed after the first month or so. Archiving data digitally offers the potential for streamlining operations, lowering costs, and improving the preservation of the stored information.

However, there is a major problem developing in many organizations as they grapple with an efficient method for archiving digital data. Selecting storage media that will stand the test of time is a major problem as tape formats and readers typically become obsolete within three to five years. For example, in the music industry, there are not too many eight-track audio tape players still around and record turntables are becoming scarce. The fast-paced tape industry has the same problem as converter machines become difficult to find. The SAN may enable more data to be stored on low-cost disk systems, avoiding some of the tape media incompatibilities.

SUMMARY

If information is the key element of the current age, then Storage Area Networks, or SANs, are the key infrastructures. The explosive proliferation of information necessitates new and creative ways of handling that information and making it accessible.

SANs meet that challenge:

- SANs provide efficient and cost-effective storage for huge and growing volumes of data.
- SANs bridge the islands of information created by diverse systems.
- SANs smooth the flow of information through diverse communications facilities.
- SANs provide an effective nonobtrusive structure for handling those storage applications so necessary for safe and secure operation of corporatewide enterprise systems.

Implementing a SAN starts with the basic need of sharing storage devices with multiple servers for more cost-effective storage. Each subsequent application can be viewed as another tactical project that leads to the strategic implementation of a Storage Area Network infrastructure.

References

1. ANSI site (http://www.t11.org)
2. Brocade (http://www.brocade.com)
3. Computer Network Technology (http://www.cnt.com)
4. EMC (http://www.emc.com)
5. Fibre Channel Association (http://www.fibrechannel.com)
6. Fibre Channel Loop Community (http://www.fcloop.org)
7. Legato (http://www.legato.com)
8. Storage Networking Industry Association (http://www.snia.org)

Chapter 33
Push Technology: Impact and Issues
Frederick Gallegos

When Windows 98 was officially released in 1998, one of its most discussed features was setting Internet Explorer 4.0 (IE 4.0) as its default Internet browser. IE 4.0 is one of the most advanced, modern browsers that can fully support the active desktop, push technology, multimedia, and much more. The other browser company, Netscape, in the release of Netscape Communicator 4.0, has included many important features, including auto-calendaring, auto-admin, the IBM Host-On-Demand interface, and other enhancements. These events set the framework for push technology. One is beginning to see the evolution of support products to ease corporate implementation of the technology into the workplace.

PUSH TECHNOLOGY BACKGROUND

From the Internet's establishment in 1969 as a scientific–academic network of four computers financed by the U.S. defense establishment, it has become a powerful, public facility accessible to tens of millions of people worldwide in various fields. The technology was designed to provide a standard means of interconnecting networks so that any system could communicate with any other system without considering the operating system's compatibility. Under this assumption, the Internet uses a subset of the total resources of all the currently existing public telecommunication networks, distinguishing the Internet as a cooperative public network that uses of a set of protocols called TCP/IP (Transmission Control Protocol/Internet Protocol).

The term "Internet" often includes the World Wide Web, electronic mail, FTP, gopher, and the growing suite of other network applications that are based on Internet communications. Standardization and wide acceptance of the Internet has stimulated many billions of dollars of broadly applicable software and network development. E-mail is the most widely used application on the Internet; and the World Wide Web is the most exciting, with its great range of content (according to *Wired* magazine in March, 1997, over 150 million individual places to go) and its powerful concept of linking the world's information as hypertext. As of January 1997, approximately nine million people were reported to be using the Web every day.

An intranet is a network that is contained within an enterprise or organization. It may consist of many internal linked local area networks and a wide area network. It may or may not include connections to the outside Internet. Typically, larger enterprises allow connection outside of the intranet to the Internet through firewall servers that have the ability to screen messages in both directions so that company security is maintained. The main purpose of an intranet is usually to share company information and computing resources among employees. An intranet can also be used to facilitate working in groups and for teleconferencing.

An intranet uses TCP/IP, HTTP (HyperText Transfer Protocol), and other Internet protocols, and in general looks like a private version of the Internet. With a new tunneling protocol that is being developed, companies will be able to send private messages through the public network, thereby tunneling through the public network from one part of their intranet to another.

An extranet is a collaborative network that uses Internet technology to link businesses with their suppliers, customers, or other businesses that share common goals (Jim Barksdale and Mark Andersen of Netscape Communications used the term). It describes software that facilitates intercompany relationships. An extranet can be viewed either as part of a company's intranet that is made accessible to other companies, or as a collaborative Internet connection with other companies. The shared information can be accessible only to the collaborating parties or it can be publicly accessible. Examples of extranet applications include (1) private newsgroups that cooperating companies use to share valuable experiences and ideas, and (2) groupware, in which several companies collaborate in developing a new application program they can all use.

WHAT IS PUSH TECHNOLOGY?

Push was created to alleviate two problems facing users of the Internet. The first problem involves information overload. The volume and dynamic nature of content on the Internet is an impediment to users and has become an ease-of-use issue. The second problem is that most end users are restricted to low-bandwidth Internet connections, such as a 28.8Kbps modem, making it difficult to receive multimedia content. Push technology addresses both of these problems.

Information Overload

Using the Internet today, without the aid of a push application, can be tedious, time consuming, and less than dependable. Users have to manually hunt down information, search out links (live and dead), and monitor sites and information sources. The advent of search engines such as Yahoo! and Alta Vista have met with tremendous success because they make it possible for the user to narrow the focus and expand the domain of information searches. Push applications and technology building blocks narrow that focus even further and add considerable ease of use.

Using push technology, an electronic publisher with content aggregated from multiple sources applies the subscriber's interest profile to select information to deliver to the subscriber on an automatic basis. For example, a news bureau can deliver articles of interest in electronic format to a PC each morning — or at any time requested.

Low Bandwidth

The bandwidth of the 28.8, or even 33.6Kbps modem provides very limited capacity to deliver multimedia content. Assuming users are willing to wait 4.16 seconds for a Web page to download means that the combined size of all elements on the page must be less than 15KB. This size limit leaves room for little more than text and small graphics. However, push technology provides the means to predeliver much larger packages of content. With an unattended connection for a half hour the previous night, an end user can receive up to 5.4MB of content to view the next day. This leaves plenty of room for multimedia content such as audio, large graphics, or short video clips. Push technology enables multimedia upon receipt.

HOW DOES PUSH WORK?

The traditional Web concept currently requires the user to poll sites for new, updated information. This manual polling and downloading process is referred to as pull technology. From a business point of view, this process provides little information about a user, and offers little control over what information is acquired. It is the user who has to keep track of the location of the information sites, and remember to continuously search for informational changes. This is a very time-consuming process and waste of valuable time.

The push model alleviates much of this medium. Interestingly enough, from a technical point of view, most push applications are still "pull" and just appear to be "push" to the user. A more accurate description of this process is called automated pull. Most push applications require a subscription and an information request profile from the user before they can begin filtering information. The software initiates the pull according to a user-defined schedule (once a day, every three hours, etc.), and the server responds with the information to match the request profile.

How Do Extranet and Intranet Relate to Push Technology?

An extranet provides non-public information to a select group of individuals, and this allows specific information to be pushed to the user's desktop in a fairly protected way. An extranet is an extension of an intranet that permits people outside the intranet to receive information within the organization's intranet.

An intranet is an internal network based on Internet protocols and technologies. An intranet enables an organization to share its resources with users without confidential information being made available to everyone with Internet access.

PUSH TECHNOLOGY PRODUCT RESEARCH

Exhibit 33.1 summarizes key features of push technology product providers. The Price column reflects the cost to the host organization (the purchaser and channel provider), from server software licenses to metered channel rates depending on the package's complexity. The Requirements column contains any information made available on the physical or system requirements of each particular software package. Finally, the Features column shows some major features, or gizmos, that make that particular product unique.

The following provides suggestions on how push technology can be used in a business environment.

Information delivery is an important requirement for business, especially within the organization. PointCast can be used for information delivery in the workplace, giving on organization the ability to broadcast company news and dramatically reduce network traffic. PointCast also provides enhanced administrative control over the broadcast, including channels and ad filtering. It also is open-channel architecture, enabling one to integrate extranet broadcasts from customers and users with optimized administration capabilities, including configuration of the PointCast Network on user desktops. The internal company channel is broadcast to users via an intranet, along with PointCast Network channels carrying public news and information.

One can capture employees' attention using SmartScreens, screen savers with up-to-the-minute company news and information. With Smart-Screens, company news headlines dynamically appear on the screen whenever a computer is in "sleep" mode. Users simply click on any headline to obtain instant access to a full news story. One can also broadcast late-breaking company news via an independent, scrolling newsflash ticker. PointCast is available with a 60-day free evaluation of the Intranet Tools beta version (all three managers included).

Extranet Use

PointCast also provides the ability to manage an extranet with broadcasts from suppliers, customers, and service providers without writing any

Exhibit 33.1. Key Features of Push Technology

Company	Product	Price	Requirements	Features
PointCast	Intranet	Free	Intel-based computer, Pentium 75 MHz 32 MB RAM 10 MB free space NT V3.51 or NT V4.0 (Server or workstation) Web browser that supports Java	Public news headlines, easy-to-create intercompany channels, administrative control, including Configuration of PointCast on users' desktops includes contents. Smart-screens deliver information in screen-saver format and scrolling newsflash ticker.
Intermind	Communicator	Range from free server licenses for noncommercial publishers to top-end licenses that cost $1500 and up, depending on number of subscribers; clients, free.	Intermind Communicator contains both publishing and client software components. Merely upload a control file that contains pointers to particular pages of content. This file — only a few kilobytes — downloads to each client.	Works well at notification but does not deliver anything other than a desktop link. Has the most channels available (over 200 and growing rapidly); has the best reporting system. Its usage and hit reports are available in HTML format directly from the client software. Can examine how many individuals downloaded your channel, what topics they viewed, and the popularity of the channel over time. The simplest tool of its kind. A notification system that points users to places around the Web. One does not get as much control over the presentation of the channel.
BackWeb	Polite Agent	Starts at $10,000 and has additional monthly per-message charges; can cost upward of $50,000. They charge a fee for every channel they deliver, which can range from $0.12 to $1.16 per subscriber.	Need at least two different computers to publish your own BackWeb channel: one for content managed by a remote console and one for a 95-only authoring tool. It requires both a UNIX and a Windows NT server on the network to deliver its "InfoPaks" or subscription channels to each user. The NT server manages the content on the UNIX server.	Channel provider and software distribution.

Exhibit 33.1. Key Features of Push Technology (Continued)

Company	Product	Price	Requirements	Features
Intel	Intercast	About $140 for the receiver	Client — (minimum) 90 MHz Pentium processor with PCI bus; 133 MHz recommended 16 MB RAM, 15 MB available hard disk (default configuration, 25 MB) 1 MB VRAM (2 MB recommended) PCI 2.0-compliance Standard CD-ROM audio port Windows 95 operating system.	Combination of Web pages and live broadcast.
Megasoft	Web Transporter	Web Transporter software distribution application starts at $20,000, with volume licensing available.	Client: Windows3.x Windows 95, Windows95/NT Solaris 2.5.1 AIX 4.x HP UX supports with an existing TCP/IP connection to the Internet or a private network. This can be a dial-up or direct connection and Netscape Navigator 2.0 or above or Microsoft Explorer 3.0 or above. Server: UNIX or Windows NT Server operating system. An HTTP server. An SQL database system. Agent-Windows 95/NT. AIX 4.x. HP UX.	Combines agents push and pull capabilities with advanced tracking, management, and version control.

First Floor	Smart Delivery	$3375 for a server module and 25 user licenses.	Client: Macintosh PowerPC Computer System 7.5 486 or Pentium PC Computer Windows version 3.1 Windows 95/NT 8 MB of RAM 5 MB of hard disk space LAN or dial-up Internet Server-Solaris 2.5 Windows NT 3.51 or later Netscape Server 1.1 Microsoft Information Server 1.0	The FirstFloor Smart Delivery system is a Web-based notification and delivery solution that streamlines the flow of corporate information. Smart Delivery allows organizations to customize information delivery, ensuring that users get the information they need, when they need it. Unlike other information management systems, Smart Delivery provides users with tools to personalize their information environment, controlling how, when, and what information they receive while automatically notifying users of what information is new or changed.
Caravelle	Ipnet WATCHER	Starting at $595	Operating System Requirements: Windows NT 3.5.1 or 4.0 120 MHz Pentium 32MB RAM 10MB hard disk space VGA or better video. Recommended Browser: Netscape Communicator 4.0.3 (4.0 minimum) or Microsoft Explorer 3.0.	Ipnet WATCHER finds and concurrently tests IP and SNMP network elements, including HTTP, FTP, DNS, NNTP, gopher, POP3, and SMTP services, server hardware, routers, printers, switches, and proxy servers. IPnetWATCHER can also monitor applications, such as Web site links, individual Web pages, and the databases behind them. When impending problems or realtime failures are identified, IPnetWATCHER Java Edition immediately notifies user-designated people through on-screen alerts, e-mail, alphanumeric pager, individual desktop icons, or the network management system.

Note: All information contained within this table was taken from the Internet, or demo CDs.

code or buying proprietary servers. The PointCast Network's new open architecture enables anyone with a Web site to broadcast content to Point-Cast's viewership by becoming a PointCast Connections™ webcaster. The Connections super-channel, which can be preconfigured to include one's extranet partners, runs seamlessly alongside other PointCast channels like CNN and Companies.

Another important requirement within business is the ability to publish, subscribe, and provide feedback. InterMind's Communicator is a Web publishing, subscribing, and feedback system. It delivers news and information via hyper-connectors. Content providers pay for licenses per unique visitor. Content providers do not need a Web site to deliver content via the Intermind Communicator.

Intermind's extranet version is not a ready-to-use product, as this product requires a large degree of customization by the user. The user and his organization must do a very good job of defining their requirements and then using Intermind's value-added customer support on all of the customizable content of the product. Furthermore, Dynamic Publisher for Domino must be installed along with Lotus Notes Domino in order to set up an intranet network.

How Is This Different from PointCast?

PointCast 1.0, introduced in February 1996, did not use channel objects. Rather, it was a client/server application that acted as a dedicated access program for the newsfeed, of which PointCast Corporation was the exclusive publisher. PointCast has patents pending on the use of this kind of application to display advertising information in a screen-saver format.

Intermind introduced channel-object technology with the launch of Intermind Communicator™ in October 1996. Like Web technology, channel objects do not limit subscribers to proprietary channels. Anyone with Web site access can become a channel publisher.

In March 1997, PointCast announced that PointCast 2.0 would support open channels based on the Channel Definition Format (CDF) specification for channel objects jointly developed with Microsoft. PointCast also said it would offer a channel-object-authoring tool, PointCast Connections, that would create CDF channel objects compatible with the new PointCast client. Today, one can even try the newest version of PointCast 2.5 (download free), with more features.

Another key requirement within business is the ability to share information. Using Megasoft's WebTransporter, one can simply load files into a Web server library, set up authentication, give users a simple, lightweight client to access the system, and let them download and install files at their convenience. It is also possible to execute download jobs on a schedule.

WebTransporter's principal functions include the following:

- enable users to scan lists of data files or software applications located on a public or private Web site, and then make requests to download any number of files
- maintain software libraries, authenticate users, and track distribution activity, including information on the number of downloads, versions and types of software, and data files requested
- prepare software and data files for online delivery; can perform automatic download and installation routines
- allow system administrators and webmasters to integrate software download capabilities into existing Web pages; can be customized with company logos, graphics, and text, providing a way to transparently link Web pages and HTML interfaces with software distribution services

The ability to combine push and pull is a key characteristic of Megasoft's product. It is not merely a tool to push files out over the network, but also to provide the technology to manage, update, and track every aspect of the process.

As mentioned earlier, getting information out to the intranet or the extranet on a timely and reliable basis can be a problem. Support systems like the FirstFloor Smart Delivery system provide a Web-based notification and delivery solution that streamlines the flow of corporate information. Smart Delivery allows organizations to customize information delivery, ensuring that users get the information they need, when they need it. Smart Delivery provides users with tools to personalize their information environment, controlling how, when, and what information they receive while automatically notifying users of what information is new or changed. The Smart Delivery line of products includes the FirstFloor Smart Publisher™, Smart Server™, Smart Subscriber™, Smart Delivery ADK, and Smart Bookmarks™.

The market leader in push technology is currently PointCast.

CONCLUSION

Businesses are looking for ways to improve their business process. For most, this means expending the least amounts of time and effort to gain the most output. The traditional pull technology has become outdated because it has more complex dynamics of information flow compared to push technology.

Push technology provides benefits such as reducing and managing the information overload and dealing with communication bandwidth bottlenecks. In addition, push technology can also easily develop an extranet solution by integrating webcasts into one's broadcasts. Some of this is seen today by subscribers to cable channels using such technology through network channels such as CNN and MSNBC. Push technology allows one to broadcast unique information by integrating one's network directory service.

Push technology makes the online experience more convincing and responsive to the needs of one's clients. Push technology is an important chemistry to push and integrate future computer communication. This chemistry cannot be complete without management's support, commitment, and future vision of a global electronic commerce environment.

For the IT professional and manager, this is a new step and horizon for which communication and teamwork with the users are key components. It can provide business with the competitive edge needed to survive. Global competition pressures have set the tone for the evolution of push technology. Those who accept the risk, plan, and communicate and work together can make it successful for the business.

Suggested Readings

1. Author unknown. BackWeb product information: http://www.backweb.com/html/products.html.
2. Author unknown. Caravelle Product Information: http://www.caravelle.com/.
3. Author unknown. Download information for PointCast product: http://www.pointcast.com/download/index.cgi?home.
4. Author unknown. FirstFloor product information: http://www.firstfloor.com/product.html.
5. Author unknown. General information about PointCast: http://www.pointcast.com.
6. Author unknown. Innergy Push Sampler: http://www.innergy.com/pushers.html.
7. Author unknown. Intermid Communicator product information: http://www.intermind.com/-prod_demo/index.html.
8. Author unknown. Intel Intercast product information: http://www.intel.com/intercast/index.html.
9. Author unknown. Megasoft Web Transporter product information: http://www.megasoft.com/wtsoc.html.
10. Author unknown. Product information for Point Cast product: http://www.pointcast.com/product/index.cgi?home.
11. Author unknown. Push: http://206.246.131.227/resources/webpub/webtips/front.shtml; http://206.246.131.227/resources/webpub/webtips/breaktime/archives/3 31 97.html.
12. Author unknown. Push Central: http://www.pushcentral.com/.
13. Castedo Ellerman. Channel Definition Format. http://www.w3.org/TR/NOTE-CDFsubmit.html.
14. David Strom. Push Publishing Technologies: http://www.strom.com/imc/t4a.html.

Chapter 34
Enterprise Deployment: Building an IP PBX Telephony Network
John Fiske

Internet telephony has been increasingly explored and implemented as a viable communication tool in large corporations. A main component of enterprise IP voice is the IP PBX, which functions the way a traditional PBX does. It allows calls to be transferred throughout the organization, it allows easy intra-enterprise calls, and it operates automatically.

An IP PBX is different in almost every other respect. Not only is it easier and less costly to operate and maintain, it operates with different technology. The IP PBX has paid off for the corporations using it through reduced manpower and by eliminating an entire (telephone) network. This article provides other payoff ideas and an explanation of the technology behind the IP PBX.

THE PBX

Yesterday's PBX fulfilled a simple need: it allowed users to talk together, and also allowed users to talk out to the PSTN (public switched telephone network). PBX (premise branch exchange) manufacturers fulfilled this need by installing a mainframe computer into the enterprise and connecting a proprietary line card interface to either analog phones or proprietary digital phones. The connection out to the PSTN was established through a trunk interface card.

Today's PC-based PBX similarly fulfills a need. Phones on the enterprise side and the PSTN on the outside can be connected together. The approach with a PC-based PBX is fundamentally the same as the mainframe PBX architecture. The big difference is the use of relatively inexpensive PCs instead of hefty mainframe computers.

The third generation, tomorrow's PBX, is the IP (Internet Protocol)-based PBX. Again, it fulfills a by-now well-known need, but with a lot of other benefits. Instead of using a line interface card and circuit-switched

0-8493-9838-X/00/$0.00+$.50
© 2000 by CRC Press LLC

card, it uses the TCP/IP network switching voice packets through an Ethernet, ATM, Frame Relay, ISDN, or whatever satisfactorily carries TCP/IP.

THE IP-PBX

Full PBX capabilities over IP LAN/WAN networks promise to substitute and replace traditional enterprise PBXs, and are an important step toward full voice and data convergence. In the IP PBX, voice traffic is digitized and compressed, placed into data packets, and transmitted across the packet network directly between the stations or WAN interfaces. End stations communicate with a call control server only when a call processing function, such as transferring a call, creating a conference call, or sending a call to voice mail, is required or requested.

Standards and the IP PBX

An IP PBX operates within the ITU (International Telecommunications Union) Standards (H.323 and T.120) that define how data equipment works in a data environment and define the signaling, call control, and audio compression for packet delivery of voice and video communications on IP networks. Without these standards in place and strictly followed, interoperability would not be possible.

Components

An IP PBX requires three components: the desktop telephone, call manager software, and a WAN/IP gateway. These three components are attached to existing LAN/WAN infrastructure.

The Desktop Telephone. Users have two desktop phone choices:

1. an IP Ethernet phone that plugs directly into an Ethernet jack
2. handsets or headsets that plug into their PC

The IP Ethernet telephone resembles a normal digital PBX set, but instead of connecting to a proprietary PBX port, it plugs into a standard Ethernet LAN jack. An IP telephone delivers audio quality comparable to that of a PBX telephone and is easy to use with single-button access to line appearances and features. The IP telephone can operate as a standard IP device with its own IP address. A fully H.323-compatible IP phone can talk to any other H.323 device. The following are key characteristics of the IP telephone.

- connects directly to any 10 Base-T Ethernet (RJ45) network
- programmable buttons for features, speed dialing, or line appearances
- IP address and signaling (TCP/IP) to call manager
- H.323 standards

- built-in compression: G.711; G.723 (ITU standards), on a call and feature basis
- IP address assignment and configuration with DHCP keypad or BootP
- administration and button configuration through a Web browser
- built-in encryption for privacy protection during voice conversation
- 3rd-pair or phantom powered to permit power backup in the event of building power failure
- one-button collaboration (T.120) with PC and NetMeeting for features such as application sharing, video, chat, and whiteboarding
- built-in repeater port for cascading Ethernet devices

The Call Manager. The call manager provides the network intelligence to enable simple-to-use and feature-rich IP communications. Call manager software is designed to work seamlessly with existing telephony systems (PBX or Centrex) or can provide full PBX functionality on its own. It can be deployed as a single IP PBX in a single office, or as a single IP PBX with multiple geographically dispersed users. With total switch and network independence, administrators can create a truly virtual campus environment utilizing a common Web browser.

By installing the call manager software on a Windows NT server in the IP network, features such as call, hold, call transfer, call forward, call park, caller identification, and multiple line appearances are provided to the IP phone. The SMDI interface on the call manager provides connectivity to various voice mail and IVR systems along with CDR reporting for call accounting and billing.

The call manager provides the call processing functionality for the IP PBX. It manages the resources of the IP PBX by signaling and coordinating call control activities. The call manager sets up a call by instructing the calling party to set up an RTP audio stream to the other device, either telephone or gateway. Once an audio stream is set up between two devices, the call manager is idle until a new request (such as transfer or disconnect) is made. In the event the call manager fails during a call, the two parties stay connected and can complete their call. Various signaling protocols, such as Q.931 for ISDN WAN control and H.225/H.245 for IP packet control, are managed and controlled by the call manager.

The call manager also manages calling zones to ensure efficient bandwidth performance at the maximum audio quality. When a call is routed over a low-bandwidth IP pipe, the call manager will instruct the IP phone to use a lower bit rate audio compression, such as G.723. For calls toward the PSTN, the call manager will have the phones use G.711, which is the compression required for PSTN calling.

The call manager offers a standard directory service that allows other applications on the network to access the call directory. It can be overseen via a Web browser and provides remote management for diagnostics and maintenance from anywhere in the world. The browser provides an intuitive interface for administrators and users. Upon administrator approval, users can access and configure their own phones. Call records are kept in a standard CDR database for billing and tracking activity.

The Gateway. IP-based telephony systems today need to connect to the PSTN and the existing PBX. Gateways are specifically designed to convert voice from the packet domain to the circuit-switched domain.

The gateway converts packetized voice to a format that can be accepted by the PSTN. Since the digitized format for voice on the packet network is often different than on the PSTN, the gateway will provide a type of conversion called transcoding. Gateways also pass signaling information.

Based on the various PSTN interfaces, there is a need for both a digital and analog trunk version. Gateways must all support supplementary services, such as call transfer and hold across subnets in the IP network and should be easily configured using the Web browser. Support for supplemental services is in the H.323 Standard and allows for the RTP audio stream to be redirected to different IP ports.

Configurations and Applications

The IP PBX is not defined by physical hardware limitations, as is a traditional PBX or even the newer "un-PBX" systems. Traditional PBXs or un-PBXs have constraints that limit scaling the system. For example, the circuit switch matrix that defines how many connections can be made at one time is based on the specific model of the PBX that has been installed. Once the limit has been reached, the entire PBX usually must be replaced.

Another limitation is the hardware line cards required for every telephone device or trunk interface. These cards fit into cabinets and, when the growth of the system requires more cards than cabinet space the entire system again must be replaced.

IP PBXs are very different in their architecture. Instead of a circuit switch matrix to make connections, the IP PBX uses LAN bandwidth to make voice connections. For telephone calls, the voice traffic does not pass through a central server or call manager. The call manager only performs signaling to set up and manage call states. Therefore, it can handle a large number of calls with fewer restrictions or limitations.

In addition, because of the scalability of LAN architectures, the IP PBX can scale linearly from one port to thousands of ports. When more ports are needed, additional hubs and switches can be added to grow the system without replacing the current investment.

IP Telephony Off an Existing PBX. This configuration extends the existing PBX within the campus using the IP network as transport. The IP PBX connects to the PBX using either an analog or digital gateway, depending on the expectations of voice traffic and the number of users. The call manager software runs on an NT server in the data center.

This application allows a business, enterprise, university, or other large organization to extend normal telephony services using the existing IP LAN. The call manager provides feature functionality to the IP telephones, with features such as transfer, secretarial call coverage, and parallel dial plan used by the PBX. With the gateway interface to the PBX, users can call users with PBX telephones or call to the PSTN with the same privileges and restraints set by the enterprise administrator.

Remote Offices over an IP Network. This application is simply an extension of the previous configuration with the inclusion of IP WAN connectivity to remote sites. The same basic rules apply for the IP PBX, just as they would for a single-site deployment. The call manager can remain on the central site, or a secondary call manager can be deployed at the remote location.

This configuration is a common initial application for the IP PBX product line. Companies with multiple sites can now easily install full telephony systems while leveraging the IP data network already in place. This saves costs for long-distance calling, as well as eliminates the cost to install a second network at each remote location. This option also enhances flexibility for growing or shrinking locations based on business conditions and making changes.

Using the analog access gateway at the remote site, the remote workers have local calling. Long-distance calling can be muted over the IP WAN link and consolidated from the central site to maximize long-distance calling costs and administration. With the IP PBX capability to configure audio compression based on call routing, calls destined to the main location would use a lower bit rate compression to conserve bandwidth.

Network Deployment

The configuration of an IP PBX as a network-based service (such as an ISP) has characteristics similar to the previous configurations, except the call manager and the gateway are located in the WAN. On premise would be IP phones and possibly a smaller analog gateway for local calling and backup, in case the IP link to the network is unavailable.

In addition to local and long-distance calling, the network provider can also provide traditional services like voice mail and call center services with the applications residing either at the remote location or in the network. The provider can also provide billing and management services for the customer: a range of telecommunications services in addition to long-distance routing and Internet access. The configuration options are based on the flexibility and power of IP networking.

PRACTICAL ADVANTAGES OF THE IP PBX

The IP PBX is expected to offer significant advantages in large-scale telephony. The earliest advantages pertain to cost. The benefits multiply, however, and include:

- *Cost.* Using the existing datacom network for voice transport, there is no need for the circuit-switched card or line interface card, and those expenses are avoided.
- *Total cost of ownership.* When one moves a phone on a circuit-switched PBX, one must call a PBX administrator, who makes an entry in a database that moves the phone from one physical port to another. It is logistical agony! IP phones are simpler and less costly in every way.
- *Maintenance.* One can plug in an IP phone directly out of the box. It automatically configures with a call management server, and it gets a directory number. Maintenance and configuration are simpler and easier.
- *Support.* There is no need for external support from field technicians from a proprietary PBX manufacturer. Additionally, there is a vast hiring pool of people who know Windows NT, TAPI, and TCP/IP — much greater than the number of people who know a particular vendor's circuit-switched PBX.
- *Extensible.* On a distributed campus with a unified dial plan and unified feature management, one can browse into the call processing server and manage the database from any point on the network.
- *Availability.* It is not necessary to pay for the extra availability the PBX vendors design into the system. One can pay a lot of money for very good PBX design work. But with an IP PBX, one does not pay for the extra capacity if it is not needed.
- *Capacity.* Using a dual Pentium Pro 300MHz server, one can run 500 to 600 phones. With the advent of inter-server signaling, it will be theoretically possible to scale the system up to 100,000 lines, or larger.

Payoffs

There are several ways an IP PBX will save a company money.

- *Long-distance charge savings.* In many international markets, especially highly regulated ones, communications carriers have artificially high tariffs, as compared to carriers in deregulated markets. Additionally, these carriers have lower tariffs for data connections. There is short-term opportunity to exploit these differences … until carriers close the gap between voice and data costs. Longer-term cost savings will come from consolidation and management of all WAN connections, the Internet, local calling, and long distance through a single gateway/router device.

- *Data and voice convergence.* Data and voice conversion will facilitate new business practices, enabling people to work more effectively. This technology will release customers from barriers imposed by proprietary solutions, allowing organizations to develop.
- Cutting acquisition and operating costs. In 1997, the capital cost of building a LAN PBX system was slightly higher than the cost of building a traditional PBX. The changing marketplace has changed this model, however. The cost of swiftly evolving LAN equipment has fallen below the also-declining cost of traditional PBX equipment.
- *Administration costs.* This is the single largest opportunity to reduce costs. One will manage a single network instead of two parallel networks. Today's PBX requires a full-time staffer to manage the PBX database. In the traditional PBX, it costs $60 to $80 to move a phone. With the IP PBX, this cost is eliminated. It is also easier and cheaper to add a phone extension. General management of the IP PBX is identical to that of the IP network, which means that the same people with the same knowledge can be used in both arenas.

CONCLUSION

Corporate IP networks are becoming increasingly pervasive and essential. Consequently, the business LAN no longer occupies a niche department. Those departments are always looking for ways to improve the network's capabilities. Rapid improvement in technology and standards is driving these efforts. It was not long ago that companies started trials for IP telephony with gateways between their PBXs and the IP networks. Now they are moving to the next step by integrating telephony services and IP telephones controlled by call manager server software. The revolution has begun, and the momentum to converge voice and data networks reveals a new value paradigm. For many companies, the real value comes not from lower (or eliminated) long distance charges, but from the reduced cost of operating and managing a separate voice network.

The IP PBX is a pillar in this revolution. Connectivity spells efficiency and productivity. The traditional PBX provided the connectivity; but the IP PBX is cheaper to acquire and easier to operate and maintain. The IP PBX, evolving still, suggests a new way for businesses to communicate. As this latest communications revolution sweeps across the land, one may want to join it.

Chapter 35
Internet Security: Securing the Perimeter
Douglas G. Conorich

The corporate community has, in part, created this problem for itself. The rapid growth of the Internet with all the utilities now available to Web surf, combined with the number of users who now have easy access through all the various Internet providers, make every desktop — including those in homes, schools, and libraries — places where an intruder can launch an attack. Surfing the Internet began as a novelty. Users were seduced by the vast amounts of information they could find. In many cases, it has become addictive.

Much of the public concern with the Internet has focused on the inappropriate access to Web sites by children from their homes or schools. A business is concerned with the bottom line. How profitable a business is can be directly related to the productivity of its employees. Inappropriate use of the Internet in the business world can decrease that productivity in many ways. The network bandwidth — how much data can flow across a network segment at any time — is costly to increase because of the time involved and the technology issues. Inappropriate use of the Internet can slow the flow of data and create the network approximation of a log jam.

There are also potential legal and public relations implications of inappropriate employee usage. One such issue is the increasing prevalence of "sin surfing" — browsing the pornographic Web sites. One company reported that 37 percent of its Internet bandwidth was taken up by "sin surfing." Lawsuits can be generated and, more importantly, the organization's image can be damaged by employees using the Internet to distribute inappropriate materials. To legally curtail the inappropriate use of the Internet, an organization must have a policy that defines what is acceptable, what is not, and what can happen if an employee is caught.

As part of the price of doing business, companies continue to span the bridge between the Internet and their own intranets with mission-critical applications. This makes them more vulnerable to new and unanticipated security threats. Such exposures can place organizations at risk at every level — down to the very credibility upon which they build their reputations.

0-8493-9838-X/00/$0.00+$.50
© 2000 by CRC Press LLC

Making the Internet safe and secure for business requires careful management by the organization. Companies will have to use existing and new, emerging technologies, security policies tailored to the business needs of the organization, and training of the employees in order to accomplish this goal. IBM has defined four phases of Internet adoption by companies as they do business on the Internet: access, presence, integration, and E-business. Each of these phases has risks involved.

- *Access.* In this first phase of adoption, a company has just begun to explore the Internet and learn about its potential benefits. A few employees are using modems connected to their desktop PCs, to dial into either a local Internet service provider, or a national service such as America Online. In this phase, the company is using the Internet as a resource for getting information only; all requests for access are in the outbound direction, and all information flow is in the inbound direction. Exchanging electronic mail and browsing the Web make up the majority of activities in this phase.

- *Presence.* In this phase, the company has begun to make use of the Internet not only as a resource for getting information, but also as a means of providing information to others. Direct connection of the company's internal network means that now all employees have the ability to access the Internet (although this may be restricted by policy), allowing them to use it as an information resource, and also enabling processes such as customer support via e-mail. The creation of a Web server, either by the company's own staff or through a content hosting service, allows the company to provide static information such as product catalogs and data sheets, company background information, software updates, etc. to its customers and prospects.

- *Integration.* In this phase, the company has begun to integrate the Internet into its day-to-day business processes by connecting its Web server directly (through a firewall or other protection system) to its back-office systems. In the previous phase, updates to the Web server's data were made manually, via tape or other means. In this phase, the Web server can obtain information on demand, as users request it. To use banking as an example, this phase enables the bank's customers to obtain their account balances, find out when checks cleared, and other information retrieval functions.

- *E-business.* In the final phase, the company has enabled bi-directional access requests and information flow. This means that not only can customers on the Internet retrieve information from the company's back-office systems, but they can also add to or change information stored on those systems. At this stage, the company is conducting business electronically; customers can place orders, transfer money (via credit cards or other means), check on shipments, etc; business partners can update inventories, make notes in customer records, etc. In short, the entire company has become accessible via the Internet.

While a company can follow this road to the end, as described by IBM, they are most likely somewhere on it — either in one of the phases or in transition between them.

INTERNET PROTOCOLS

Communication between two people is made possible by their mutual agreement to a common mode of transferring ideas from one person to the other. Each person must know exactly how to communicate with the other if this is to be successful. The communication can be in the form of a verbal or written language, such as English, Spanish, or German. It can also take the form of physical gestures like sign language. It can even be done through pictures or music. Regardless of the form of the communication, it is paramount that the meaning of an element, say a word, has the same meaning to both parties involved. The medium used for communication is also important. Both parties must have access to the same communication medium. One cannot talk to someone else via telephone if only one person has a telephone.

With computers, communications over networks is made possible by what are known as protocols. A protocol is a well-defined message format. The message format defines what each position in the message means. One possible message format could define the first four bits as the version number, the next four bits as the length of the header, and then eight bits for the service being used. As long as both computers agree on this format, communication can take place.

Network communications use more than one protocol. Sets of protocols used together are known as protocol suites or layered protocols. One well-known protocol suite is the Transport Control Protocol/ Internet Protocol (TCP/IP) suite. It is based on the International Standards Organization (ISO) Open Systems Interconnection (OSI) Reference Model (see Exhibit 35.1).

The ISO Reference Model is divided into seven layers:

1. The Physical Layer is the lowest layer in the protocol stack. It consists of the "physical" connection. This may be copper wire or fiber optic cables and the associated connection hardware. The sole responsibility of the Physical Layer is to transfer the bits from one location to another.
2. The second layer is the Data Link Layer. It provides for the reliable delivery of data across the physical link. The Data Link Layer creates a checksum of the message that can be used by the receiving host to ensure that the entire message was received.

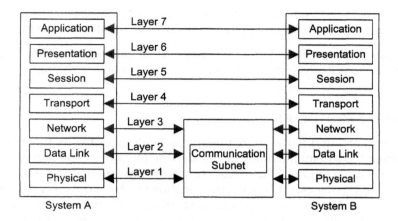

Exhibit 35.1. The ISO Model

3. The Network Layer manages the connections across the network for the upper four layers and isolates them from the details of addressing and delivery of data.
4. The Transport Layer provides the end-to-end error detection and correction function between communicating applications.
5. The Session Layer manages the sessions between communicating applications.
6. The Preparation Layer standardizes the data presentation to the application level.
7. The Application Layer consists of application programs that communicate across the network. This is the layer with which most users interact.

Network devices can provide different levels of security, depending on how far up the stack they can read. Repeaters are used to connect two Ethernet segments. The repeater simply copies the electrical transmission and sends it on to the next segment of the network. Because the repeater only reads up through the Data Link Layer, no security can be added by its use.

The bridge is a computer that is used to connect two or more networks. The bridge differs from the repeater in that it can store and forward entire packets, instead of just repeating electrical signals. Because it reads up through the Network Layer of the packet, the bridge can add some security. It could allow the transfer of only packets with local addresses. A bridge uses physical addresses — not IP addresses. The physical address, also know as the Ethernet address, is the actual address of the Ethernet hardware. It is a 48-bit number.

| **Application Layer** |
| consists of applications and processes that use the network. |
| **Host-to-Host Transport Layer** |
| provides end-to-end data delivery service. |
| **Internet Layer** |
| Defines the datagram and handles the routing of data. |
| **Network Access Layer** |
| consists of routines for accessing physical networks. |

Exhibit 35.2.   The TCP/IP Protocol Architecture

Routers and gateways are computers that determine which of the many possible paths a packet will take to get to the destination device. These devices read up through the Transport Layer and can read IP addresses, including port numbers. They can be programmed to allow, disallow, and reroute IP datagrams determined by the IP address of the packet.

As previously mentioned, TCP/IP is based on the ISO model, but it groups the seven layers of the ISO model into four layers, as displayed in Exhibit 35.2.

The Network Access Layer is the lowest layer of the TCP/IP protocol stack. It provides the means of delivery and has to understand how the network transmits data from one IP address to another. The Network Access Layer basically provides the functionality of the first three layers of the ISO model.

TCP/IP provides a scheme of IP addressing that uniquely defines every host connected to the Internet. The Network Access Layer provides the functions that encapsulate the datagrams and maps the IP addresses to the physical addresses used by the network.

The Internet Layer has at its core the Internet Protocol (RFC791). IP provides the basic building blocks of the Internet. It provides:

- the datagram definition scheme
- the Internet addressing scheme
- the means of moving data between the Network Access Layer and the Host-to-Host Layer
- the means for datagrams to be routed to remote hosts
- the function of breaking apart and reassembling packets for transmission

IP is a connectionless protocol. This means that it relies on other protocols within the TCP/IP stack to provide the connection-oriented services. The connection-oriented services (i.e., TCP) take care of the handshake — the exchange of control information. The IP Layer contains the Internet Control Message Protocol (ICMP).

The Host-to-Host Transport Layer houses two protocols: the Transport Control Protocol (TCP) and the User Datagram Protocol (UDP). Its primary function is to deliver messages between the Application Layer and the Internet Layer. TCP is a reliable protocol. This means that it guarantees that the message will arrive as sent. It contains error detection and correction features. UDP does not have these features and is, therefore, unreliable. For shorter messages, where it is easier to resend the message than worry about the overhead involved with TCP, UDP is used.

The Application Layer contains the various services that users will use to send data. The Application Layer contains such user programs as the Network Terminal Protocol (Telnet), File Transfer Protocol (FTP), and Simple Mail Transport Protocol (SMTP). It also contains protocols not directly used by users, but required for system use — for example, Domain Name Service (DNS), Routing Information Protocol (RIP), and Network File System (NFS).

ATTACKS

As previously noted, TCP is a reliable messaging protocol. This means that TCP is a connection-oriented protocol. TCP uses what is known as a three-way handshake. A handshake is simply the exchange of control information between the two computers. This information enables the computers to determine which packets go where and ensure that all the information in the message has been received.

When a connection is desired between two systems, Host A and Host B, using TCP/IP, a three-way handshake must occur. The initiating host, Host A (the client), sends the receiving host, Host B (the server), a message with the SYN (synchronize sequence number) bit set. The SYN contains information needed by Host B to set up the connection. This message contains the IP address of the both Host A and Host B and the port numbers they will talk on. The SYN tells Host B what sequence number the client will start with, seq = x. This number is important to keep all the data transmitted in the proper order and can be used to notify Host B that a piece of data is missing. The sequence number is found starting at bit 32 to 63 of the header.

When Host B receives the SYN, it sends the client an ACK (acknowledgment message). This message contains the sequence number that Host B will start with, SYN, seq = y, and the sequence number of Host A incremented, the ACK, x + 1. The acknowledgment number is bits 64 through 95 of the header.

406

The three-way handshake is completed when Host A receives the ACK from Host B and sends an ACK, y + 1, in return. Now data can flow back and forth between the two hosts. This connection is now known as a socket. A socket is usually identified as Host_A_IP:Port_Number, Host_B_IP:Port_Number.

There are two attacks that use this technology: SYN Flood and Sequence Predictability.

SYN Flood Attack

The SYN Flood attack uses a TCP connection request (SYN). The SYN is sent to the target computer with the source IP address in the packet "spoofed," or replaced with an address that is not in use on the Internet or that belongs to another computer. When the target computer receives the connection request, it allocates resources to handle and track the new connection. A SYN_RECEIVED state is stored in a buffer register awaiting the return response (ACK) from the initiating computer, which would complete the three-way handshake. It then sends out an SYN-ACK. If the response is sent to the "spoofed," nonexistent IP address, there will never be a response. If the SYN-ACK is sent to a real computer, it checks to see if it has a SYN in the buffer to that IP address. Since it does not, it ignores the request. The target computer retransmits the SYN-ACK a number of times. After a finite amount of wait time, the original SYN request is purged from the buffer of the target computer. This condition is known as a half-open socket.

As an example, the default configuration for a Windows NT 3.5x or 4.0 computer is to retransmit the SYN-ACK five times, doubling the time-out value after each retransmission. The initial time-out value is three seconds, so retries are attempted at 3, 6, 12, 24, and 48 seconds. After the last retransmission, 96 seconds are allowed to pass before the computer gives up on receiving a response and deallocates the resources that were set aside earlier for the connection. The total elapsed time that resources are in use is 189 seconds.

An attacker will send many of these TCP SYNs to tie up as many resources as possible on the target computer. Since the buffer size for the storage of SYNs is a finite size, numerous attempts can cause a buffer overflow. The effect of tying up connection resources varies, depending on the TCP/IP stack and applications listening on the TCP port. For most stacks, there is a limit on the number of connections that can be in the half-open SYN_RECEIVED state. Once the limit is reached for a given TCP port, the target computer responds with a reset to all further connection requests until resources are freed. Using this method, an attacker can cause a denial-of-services on several ports.

Finding the source of a SYN Flood attack can be very difficult. A network analyzer can be used to try to track the problem down, and it may be necessary to contact the Internet Service Provider for assistance in attempting to trace the source. Firewalls should be set up to reject packets from the external network with any IP address from the internal network.

Sequence Predictability

The ability to guess sequence numbers is very useful to intruders because they can create a short-lived connection to a host without having to see the reply packets. This ability, taken in combination with the fact that many hosts have trust relationships that use IP addresses as authentication; that packets are easily spoofed; and that individuals can mount denial of service attacks, means one can impersonate the trusted systems to break into such machines without using source routing.

If an intruder wants to spoof a connection between two computers so that the connection seems as if it is coming from B to A, using your computer C, it works like this:

1. First, the intruder uses computer C to mount a SYN Flood attack on the ports on computer B where the impersonating will take place.
2. Then, computer C sends a normal SYN to a port on A.
3. Computer A returns a SYN-ACK to computer C containing computer A's current Initial Sequence Number (ISN).
4. Computer A internally increments the ISN. This incrementation is done differently in different operating systems (OSs). Operating systems such as BSD, HPUX, Irix, SunOS (not Solaris), and others usually increment by $FA00 for each connection and double each second.

   With this information, the intruder can now guess the ISN that computer A will pick for the next connection. Now comes the spoof.
5. Computer C sends a SYN to computer A using the source IP spoofed as computer B.
6. Computer A sends a SYN-ACK back to computer B, containing the ISN. The intruder on computer C does not see this, but the intruder has guessed the ISN.
7. At this point, computer B would respond to computer A with an RST. This occurs because computer B does not have a SYN_RECEIVED from computer A. Since the intruder used a SYN Flood attack on computer B, it will not respond.
8. The intruder on computer C sends an ACK to computer A, using the source IP spoofed as computer B, containing the guessed ISN+1.

   If the guess was correct, computer A now thinks there has been a successful three-way handshake and the TCP connection between computer A and computer B is fully set up. Now the spoof is complete. The intruder on computer C can do anything, but blindly.

9. Computer C sends echo + + >>/.rhosts to port 514 on computer A.
10. If root on computer A had computer B in its /.rhosts file, the intruder has root.
11. Computer C now sends a FIN to computer A.
12. Computer C could be brutal and send an RST to computer A just to clean up things.
13. Computer C could also send an RST to the synflooded port on B, leaving no traces.

To prevent such attacks, one should NEVER trust anything from the Internet. Routers and firewalls should filter out any packets that are coming from the external (sometimes known as the red) side of the firewall that has an IP address of a computer on the internal (sometimes known as the blue) side. This only stops Internet trust exploits; it will not stop spoofs that build on intranet trusts. Companies should avoid using rhosts files wherever possible.

ICMP

A major component of the TCP/IP Internet Layer is the Internet Control Message Protocol (ICMP). ICMP is used for flow control, detecting unreachable destinations, redirection routes, and checking remote hosts. Most users are interested in the last of these functions. Checking a remote host is accomplished by sending an ICMP Echo Message. The PING command is used to send these messages.

When a system receives one of these ICMP Echo Messages, it places the message in a buffer, then re-transmits the message from the buffer back to the source. Due to the buffer size, the ICMP Echo Message size cannot exceed 64K. UNIX hosts, by default, will send an ICMP Echo Message that is 64 bytes long. They will not allow a message of over 64K. With the advent of Microsoft Windows NT, longer messages can be sent. The Windows NT hosts do not place an upper limit on these messages. Intruders have been sending messages of 1MB and larger. When these messages are received, they cause a buffer overflow on the target host. Different operating systems will react differently to this buffer overflow. The reactions range from rebooting to a total system crash.

FIREWALLS

The first line of defense between the Internet and an intranet should be a firewall. A firewall is a multi-homed host that is placed in the Internet route, such that it stops and can make decisions about each packet that wants to get through. A firewall performs a different function from a router. A router can be used to filter out certain packets that meet a specific criteria (i.e., an IP address). A router processes the packets up through the IP Layer. A firewall stops all packets. All packets are processed up through the

Application Layer. Routers cannot perform all the functions of a firewall. A firewall should meet, at least, the following criteria:

- In order for an internal or external host to connect to the other network, it must log in on the firewall host.
- All electronic mail is sent to the firewall, which in turn distributes it.
- Firewalls should not mount file systems via NFS, nor should any of its file systems be mounted.
- Firewalls should not run NIS (Network Information Systems).
- Only required users should have accounts on the firewall host.
- The firewall host should not be trusted, nor trust any other host.
- The firewall host is the only machine with anonymous FTP.
- Only the minimum service should be enabled on the firewall in the file inetd.conf.
- All system logs on the firewall should log to a separate host.
- Compilers and loaders should be deleted on the firewall.
- System directories permissions on the firewall host should be 711 or 511.

THE DMZ

Most companies today are finding that it is imperative to have an Internet presence. This Internet presence takes on the form of anonymous FTP sites and a World Wide Web (WWW) site. In addition to these, companies are setting up hosts to act as a proxy server for Internet mail and a Domain Name Server (DNS). The host that sponsors these functions cannot be on the inside of the firewall. Therefore, companies are creating what has become known as the DeMilitarized Zone (DMZ) or Perimeter Network, a segment between the router that connects to the Internet and the firewall.

Proxy Servers

A proxy host is a dual-homed host that is dedicated to a particular service or set of services, such as mail. All external requests to that service directed toward the internal network are routed to the proxy. The proxy host then evaluates the request and either passes the request on to the internal service server or discards it. The reverse is also true. Internal requests are passed to the proxy from the service server before they are passed on to the Internet.

One of the functions of the proxy hosts is to protect the company from advertising its internal network scheme. Most proxy software packages contain Network Address Translation (NAT). Take, for example, a mail server. The mail from Albert_Smith@starwars.abc.com would be translated to smith@proxy.abc.com as it went out to the Internet. Mail sent to smith@proxy.abc.com would be sent to the mail proxy. Here it would be readdressed to Albert_Smith@starwars.abc.com and sent to the internal mail server for final delivery.

TESTING THE PERIMETER

A company cannot use the Internet without taking risks. It is important to recognize these risks and it is important not to exaggerate them. One cannot cross the street without taking a risk. But by recognizing the dangers, and taking the proper precautions (such as looking both ways before stepping off the curb), millions of people cross the street safely every day.

The Internet and intranets are in a state of constant change — new protocols, new applications, and new technologies — and a company's security practices must be able to adapt to these changes. To adapt, the security process should be viewed as forming a circle. The first step is to assess the current state of security within one's intranet and along the perimeter. Once one understands where one is, then one can deploy a security solution. If one does not monitor that solution by enabling some detection and devising a response plan, the solution is useless. It would be like putting an alarm on a car, but never checking it when the alarm goes off. As the solution is monitored and tested, there will be further weaknesses — which brings us back to the assessment stage and the process is repeated. Those new weaknesses are then learned about and dealt with, and a third round begins. This continuous improvement ensures that corporate assets are always protected.

As part of this process, a company must perform some sort of vulnerability checking on a regular basis. This can be done by the company, or it may choose to have an independent group do the testing. The company's security policy should state how the firewall and the other hosts in the DMZ are to be configured. These configurations need to be validated and then periodically checked to ensure that the configurations have not changed. The vulnerability test may find additional weaknesses with the configurations and then the policy needs to be changed.

Security is achieved through the combination of technology and policy. The technology must be kept up to date and the policy must outline the procedures. An important part of a good security policy is to ensure that there are as few information leaks as possible.

One source of information can be DNS records. There are two basic DNS services: lookups and zone transfers. Lookup activities are used to resolve IP addresses into host names or to do the reverse. A zone transfer happens when one DNS server (a secondary server) asks another DNS server (the primary server) for all the information that it knows about a particular part of the DNS tree (a zone). These zone transfers only happen between DNS servers that are supposed to be providing the same information. Users can also request a zone transfer.

A zone transfer is accomplished using the nslookup command in interactive mode. The zone transfer can be used to check for information leaks. This procedure can show hosts, their IP addresses, and operating systems. A good security policy is to disallow zone transfers on external DNS servers. This information can be used by an intruder to attack or spoof other hosts. If this is not operationally possible, as a general rule, DNS servers outside of the firewall (on the red side) should not list hosts within the firewall (on the blue side). Listing internal hosts only helps intruders gain network mapping information and gives them an idea of the internal IP addressing scheme.

In addition to trying to do a zone transfer, the DNS records should be checked to ensure that they are correct and that they have not changed. Domain Information Gofer (DIG) is a flexible command-line tool that is used to gather information from the Domain Name System servers.

The PING command, as previously mentioned, has the ability to determine the status of a remote host using the ICMP ECHO Message. If a host is running and is reachable by the message, the PING program will return an "alive" message. If the host is not reachable and the host name can be resolved by DNS, the program returns a "host not responding" message; otherwise, an "unknown host" message is obtained. An intruder can use the PING program to set up a "war dialer." This is a program that systematically goes through the IP addresses one after another, looking for "alive" or "not responding" hosts. To prevent intruders from mapping internal networks, the firewall should screen out ICMP messages. This can be done by not allowing ICMP messages to go through to the internal network or go out from the internal network. The former is the preferred method. This would keep intruders from using ICMP attacks, such as the Ping 'O Death or Loki tunneling.

The TRACEROUTE program is another useful tool one can use to test the corporate perimeter. Because the Internet is a large aggregate of networks and hardware connected by various gateways, TRACEROUTE is used to check the "time-to-live" (ttl) parameter and routes. TRACEROUTE sends a series of three UDP packets with an ICMP packet incorporated during its check. The ttl of each packet is similar. As the ttl expires, it sends the ICMP packet back to the originating host with the IP address of the host where it expired. Each successive broadcast uses a longer ttl. By continuing to send longer ttls, TRACEROUTE pieces together the successive jumps. Checking the various jumps not only shows the routes, but it can show possible problems that may give an intruder information or leads. This information might show a place where an intruder might successfully launch an attack. A "*" return shows that a particular hop has exceeded the three-second timeout. These are hops that could be used by intruders to create DoSs. Duplicate entries for successive hops are indications of bugs in the kernel of that gateway or looping within the routing table.

Checking the open ports and services available is another important aspect of firewall and proxy server testing. There are a number of programs — like the freeware program STROBE, IBM Network Services Auditor (NSA), ISS Internet Scanner™, and AXENT Technologies NetRecon™ — that can perform a selective probe of the target UNIX or Windows NT network communication services, operating systems and key applications. These programs use a comprehensive set of penetration tests. The software searches for weaknesses most often exploited by intruders to gain access to a network, analyzes security risks, and provides a series of highly informative reports and recommended corrective actions.

There have been numerous attacks in the past year that have been directed at specific ports. The teardrop, newtear, oob, and land.c are only a few of the recent attacks. Firewalls and proxy hosts should have only the minimum number of ports open. By default, the following ports are open as shipped by the vendor, and should be closed:

- echo on TCP port 7
- echo on UDP port 7
- discard on TCP port 9
- daytime on TCP port 13
- daytime on UDP port 13
- chargen on TCP port 19
- chargen on UDP port 19
- NetBIOS-NS on UDP port 137
- NetBIOS-ssn on TCP port 139

Other sources of information leaks include Telnet, FTP, and Sendmail programs. They all, by default, advertise the operating system or service type and version. They also may advertise the host name. This feature can be turned off and a more appropriate warning messages should be put in its place.

Sendmail has a feature that will allow the administrator to expand or verify users. This feature should not be turned on on any host in the DMZ. An intruder would only have to Telnet to the Sendmail port to obtain user account names. There are a number of well-known user accounts that an intruder would test. This method works even if the finger command is disabled.

VRFY and EXPN allow an intruder to determine if an account exists on a system and can provide a significant aid to a brute-force attack on user accounts. If you are running Sendmail, add the lines Opnovrfy and Opnoexpn to your Sendmail configuration file, usually located in /etc/sendmail.cf.

With other mail servers, contact the vendor for information on how to disable the verify command.

```
# telnet xxx.xxx.xx.xxx
Trying xxx.xxx.xx.xxx...
Connected to xxx.xxx.xx.xxx.
Escape character is '^]'.
220 proxy.abc.com Sendmail 4.1/SMI-4.1 ready at Thu, 26 Feb 98 12:50:05 CST
expn root
250- John Doe <jdoe>
250 Jane User <juser>
vrfy root
250- John Doe <jdoe>
250 Jane User <juser>
vrfy jdoe
250 John Doe <john_doe@mailserver.internal.abc.com>
vrfy juser
250 John User <jane_user@mailserver.internal.abc.com>
^]
```

Another important check that needs to be run on these hosts in the DMZ is a validation that the system and important application files are valid and not hacked. This is done by running a checksum or a cyclic redundancy check (CRC) on the files. Because these values are not stored anywhere on the host, external applications need to be used for this function. Some suggested security products are freeware applications such as COPS and Tripwire, or third-party commercial products like AXENT Technologies Enterprise Security Manager™ (ESM), ISS RealSecure™ or Kane Security Analyst™.

SUMMARY

The assumption must be made that one is not going to be able to stop everyone from getting in to a computers. An intruder only has to succeed once. Security practitioners, on the other hand, have to succeed every time. Once one comes to this conclusion, then the only strategy left is to secure the perimeter as best one can while allowing business to continue, and have some means to detect the intrusions as they happen. If one can do this, then one limits what the intruder can do.

Chapter 36
Private Keys, Trusted Third Parties, and Kerberos

Alex Bidwell

The information superhighway is a reality. Organizations must decide whether to get on, where to go when they do get on, what to do when they get there, and how best to do it. Perhaps knowing what not to do when they get there is just as important. This article provides information to help users stay on the safe part of the highway.

CRYPTOGRAPHY BASICS AND GOALS

Basic ciphers have existed for hundreds of years. In times of war, the phrase "knowledge is power" has an obvious meaning. Keeping critical information secret is crucial. The critical issues are secrecy, integrity, and authenticity (i.e., whether the information obtained has been tampered with and who that information is from). The technologies that address these issues provide solutions to authenticating users of the system. Encryption technology has advanced so far that all users on the Internet can download programs to their PC to encrypt their files or e-mail at no cost. However, the federal government will not allow anyone to sell or use these implementations outside the U.S., except when the algorithms are sufficiently weak that encrypted messages using them can be broken in a relatively short time.

The basic function of cryptography is to convert information into something that is not understandable by those who do not have the authority or means to read it. Readable information is called plaintext, and encrypted information is called ciphertext. The function of encryption is the transformation of plaintext to ciphertext and the function of decryption is to recover the original plaintext from the ciphertext received as shown in Exhibit 36.1. People and organizations want their private information to remain private, whether it is an e-mail message, a letter, or a file of financial or sensitive data accessed by mistake or by deception.

0-8493-9838-X/00/$0.00+$.50
© 2000 by CRC Press LLC

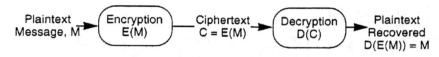

Exhibit 36.1.   Encryption and Decryption

If an effective cipher algorithm is used, the plaintext will not be easily recovered from the ciphertext unless the receiver of the message knows how to decrypt it. Users of ciphers have several goals:

- **Privacy/secrecy.** The sender does not want an eavesdropper to be able to decrypt and read the ciphertext sent or stored. The loss of the secret to "the enemy" could be damaging.
- **Integrity.** The receiver of the encrypted information does not want attackers to be able to inject false information without detection. The parties using the information do not want to be fooled by false information sent in place of the original message.
- **Authenticity.** The receiver of the information would like to be able to determine from where and from whom the information actually came. Thus, the strength and features of the cipher mechanism are important.

SECURE HASH FUNCTIONS

The values produced by secure hash functions are used to verify the integrity of a message directly. Hash values are also used as a surrogate for information that needs to be kept secret (e.g., system passwords). A shadow password file is a file of the hash values of each user's password, and a system sign on is verified if the hash value of a user's password compares with that stored on the shadow file for that user's ID. Hash functions can be used with encryption techniques to provide digital signatures, which verify not only the integrity of a message (or document), but also its authenticity. Hash functions H{M} generate a short fixed-length (i.e., typically 128 bits) representation of a message. Secure hash functions have several properties. They must produce unique output values for each arbitrary input M, such that given any other message,

$$M' [ne\ ] M, H\{M'\} [ne\ ] H\{M\}.$$

In addition, it must be impossible to reconstruct M. The likelihood of a mathematical collision or reconstruction of M should be nil.

The hash functions MD2 and MD5, designed by Rivest, and the Secure Hash Algorithm (SHA) of the National Institute of Standards and Technology (NIST) are considered secure enough to be adopted by various standards bodies and used in many implementations. MD2 is the slowest of the

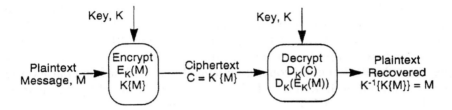

Exhibit 36.2.   Encryption and Decryption Using Shared Secret Key

---

three. MD5 was created after some partially successful cryptoanalytic attacks on MD4 were reported. SHA has been modeled after MD4 with improvements including a 160-bit hash instead of a 128-bit output.

PRIVATE OR SECRET KEY CRYPTOGRAPHY

Symmetric cryptosystems use the same private or secret key for both encryption and decryption. As shown in Exhibit 36.2, this key is shared between parties wishing to keep their communications private.

The plaintext message (M) is encrypted into ciphertext © using the algorithm directed by key (K),(K)C [larr] K{M}; and plaintext (P) is reproduced when © is decrypted or mapped using an inverse algorithm directed by (K), which is indicated by

$$(K-1).P \text{ [larr] } K\text{-}1\{C\} = K\text{-}1\{K\{M\}\} = M$$

An example clarifies which of the user's goals can be satisfied by private symmetric key cryptography and illustrates why these goals are important. Consider the simple substitution cipher. According to some predetermined scheme, one set of characters in the alphabet is used in place of other characters. If the sender uses the 36 alphanumeric characters formed by capital letters only and numbers, and the key is zero (0), no substitution is made; if the key is +1, B is used in place of A, C for B, 0 for Z, and A for 9. Examine the following ciphertext when the plaintext is encrypted with a key of -2.

Plaintext: MEET ME AT 4PM

Ciphertext: KCCR KC 8R 2NK

How well does this cipher meet the user's goals? At best, this cipher preserves secrecy for a short time only, because the enemy merely needs to examine a few paragraphs to break it. Moreover, this cipher does nothing to indicate the integrity of the message. If receivers were to use a different cipher algorithm or key with all those with whom they communicate, they might have a clue as to who sent the message. Senders could confuse the enemy by changing the cipher algorithm. For example, they could choose an 8-bit key and XOR it with each successive 8 bits of the message. This cipher can be made stronger by generalizing the algorithm and letting the key indicate which part of the algorithm to use and what to do. For example, the substitution code could be changed based on which character is being operated on in a block of plaintext, for example, eight characters. The logical operation, XOR, can also be performed with parts of the key on different blocks of plaintext. Because each unique key makes the algorithm operate differently on the message, changing the key effectively changes the algorithm.

It is much easier to generate new keys than to invent new cipher algorithms; thus, this article addresses the complexity of only that problem. Consider the number of cipher keys required to communicate securely vs. the number of parties involved. To communicate with two other people who should not be able to decipher each other's messages, two unique keys are needed. To communicate with three others, three unique keys are needed. However, six unique keys will be involved in this case for the four parties, assuming that all parties communicate and each pair of senders and receivers uses a unique key. The total number of keys involved for N parties will be $N(N - 1)/2$. Thus, if 20 parties need to communicate securely, 190 unique key pairs are involved, which is difficult to manage.

Key Management

How can all of those keys be securely generated and distributed among the parties involved? A lot of trusted couriers will be kept busy, especially if the secret keys are changed often. It is important to limit the time that an enemy has to decrypt messages intended only for the user. It is also necessary to be able to revoke keys whose security has been compromised. The security implications of key management are almost as difficult as those for generating secure ciphers.

Users need the required number of keys to be generated and distributed securely to all the parties involved. The key manager must be able to generate and securely distribute keys to all the parties involved, account for how and when keys were delivered, and certify who received a particular key. Key revocation is equally important. If an encrypted path is compromised, all parties using the keys involved must be notified in a manner they can authenticate.

Attacker's Goal

Decrypting the message requires knowledge of the cipher algorithm and the key. The attacker must discover or guess which cipher is being used and try to recover the key to break the cipher.

Strong Cipher Goal

It is desirable that the cipher algorithms be so strong that even when they are in the public domain, for example, Data Encryption Standard (DES) or International Data Encryption Algorithm (IDEA), a key is of sufficient length that guessing is very difficult, even with the most powerful computers. No matter how much plaintext or ciphertext is captured, it should be impossible to recover, short of an exhaustive search by trying all possible key values. With strong ciphers, the effort (i.e., time) required to crack the code is usually an exponential function of key length.

Cryptoanalysis

Cryptoanalysis is the science of recovering plaintext from ciphertext without prior knowledge of the key. Any of the attack techniques described here, as well as analysis to discover weaknesses in key generation or in the algorithm, are sufficient to accomplish this recovery. The news media reported "weaknesses in Netscape's encryption" in the fall of 1995. At the heart of this report was some basic detective work. From the literature provided by Netscape Communications Corp. explaining how it generated random numbers for generating keys, it became clear that a large portion of the key space was never used. This unused space significantly reduced the time of a brute force attack to hours instead of years using only a powerful personal computer. Practical cryptoanalysis refers to stealing the key by any means. When someone discovers the keys to encrypted links, these links are compromised.

TYPES OF ATTACKS

Attacks are either passive or active. In addition to good detective work, active attacks include two basic modes: an exhaustive search of the key space based on an assumed key size and cipher algorithm to find the key that converts the ciphertext to understandable plaintext, and a more clever approach, such as tricking a person or machine into including some attacker's chosen plaintext with the user's normal plaintext. The chosen plaintext and resulting ciphertext are then included in the attacker's codebook with such information as the date, day of the week, and day of the year for later correlation. If these plaintext–ciphertext pairs show up again, indicating a key value is being reused, the enemy can mount a codebook attack to decipher the values in the message that have previously been included in the codebook.

Passive Attack or Eavesdropping

Eavesdropping can be accomplished by listening to passing traffic to capture plaintext or ciphertext or to learn about the habits of the messaging parties, their systems, and the protocols that they use. Attackers can

Attack Type	Possible Effects		
	Secrecy	Integrity	Authenticity
Passive (Eavesdropping)	Yes	No	No
Active	Maybe	Yes	Yes
Brute force	Yes	No	No
Known plaintext	Yes	No	No
Chosen plaintext	Yes	Yes	Maybe
Replay	Maybe	Yes	Yes
Cut-and-paste	Maybe	Yes	Yes
Time resetting	Maybe	Yes	Yes
Man-in-the-middle	Maybe	Yes	Yes

Exhibit 36.3. Types of Attacks and Their Effects

use a sniffer on a local area network to observe e-mail sent to and from the server.

Active Attack

When mounting an active attack, the enemy inserts, deletes, or modifies legitimate messages with the purpose of deceiving the messaging parties or system administrators, thereby corrupting existing information to degrade performance or spoofing the system to gain unauthorized system entry. Exhibit 36.3 shows types of attacks and their effects. Attacks include

- **Brute force attack.** This is an exhaustive search for key value. Advances in computer technology and parallel processing have greatly reduced the time to search for key values that will crack the code. However, single-length DES keys (i.e., 56 bits) are still considered to provide acceptable protection for most applications.
- **Known-plaintext attack.** This uses one or more pairs of known plaintext, and the corresponding ciphertext is assumed to be encrypted with the same key. Obtaining and identifying such pairs are the attacker's challenges and are usually accomplished by deception or selective garbage collecting. As more samples are collected and associated with unique but unknown keys, codebook attacks form the basis for plaintext recovery or possible determination of the key.
- **Chosen plaintext attack.** This tricks the enemy into encrypting messages or embedded passages chosen by the attacker. By observing the ciphertext of several messages, the encrypted equivalent of the chosen text may be determinable and added to the attacker's codebook. The chosen plaintext attack is one of the better methods for determining whether a previously used key value is currently being used.

- **Cut-and-paste.** This involves combining two or more messages encrypted with the same key to try to produce a new message. Users may be able to trick the enemy into some action without knowing the exact message content.
- **Time resetting.** In protocols using current time, senders try to confuse the enemy as to the current time, thereby making themselves open to replay or other attacks affecting authenticity or integrity.
- **Replay.** Attackers often insert a legitimate message into the network, at a time later than originally sent, to trick the receiving party into believing the message is authentic. Attackers can request secret codes or passwords to valuable resources or they can repeat orders for transactions, which could lead to embarrassing situations.
- **Man-in-the-middle.** The enemy sits between the user and the party with whom the user wishes to communicate and impersonates each one to the other. The deception can be accomplished at a store-and-forward message node by performing unauthorized actions or by spoofing the parties into believing that the addresses or the keys that the enemy is using belong to the parties wishing to communicate.

PRACTICAL PRIVATE OR SYMMETRIC KEY ALGORITHMS

Several algorithms are used today, and they provide excellent protection for most purposes. If more protection is needed, some techniques use double- or triple-length keys.

Data Encryption Standard (DES)

The DES is the result of a proposal by scientists at IBM for a sophisticated and implementable encryption algorithm in response to several requests by the National Bureau of Standards (now the NIST) in the early 1970s. One of the key requirements was that the strength of the cipher must reside in the key; the algorithm could be made public and was. The DES algorithm has been evaluated by the National Security Agency and standards bodies and has been certified as a secure cipher through 1998 by the NIST.

DES is a block cipher and operates on 64-bit blocks of data at a time for both encryption and decryption operations using the same key. Hence, input is partitioned into 64-bit blocks of plaintext. Encryption yields 64-bit blocks of ciphertext and vice versa for decryption. The key length is 56 bits. It is usually expressed as a 64-bit number, using every least significant eighth bit as a parity bit. The algorithm is an iterated block cipher using 16 key-directed iterations. It is based on key-directed substitutions, permutations, and logical XOR operations with previous parts of the data throughout the 16 iterative levels.

Its strength is based on the enemy's ability to choose which of the possible 256 [ap] 72*1015 key values were used for this encryption. However, its strength really depends on whether the key generation facility generates truly random keys. If some of the random combinations become predictable, the cracking complexity can be greatly reduced. Export status has recently been given to versions of DES using a 40-bit key specially generated from 56-bit keys using IBM's Commercial Data Masking Facility algorithm.

Decryption in DES is done with the same algorithm as encryption; however, the key is processed in reverse order. This is an internal process; the black box merely needs to be told whether to do encryption or decryption.

Triple DES. Because the strength of DES encryption is dependent on key length, one effective way to increase key length and maintain compatibility with existing key management facilities is to consider encrypting two or three times by using two or three keys. The trade-offs are cryptographic strength and speed. Cryptoanalysts have demonstrated that double DES is no more secure than single DES. One of the better ways to implement triple DES is to use two independent 56-bit keys (or one 112-bit key) in EDE mode. This three-step encryption process uses key 1 to encrypt, key 2 to perform decryption of the output from the first encryption, followed by encryption reusing key 1. The decryption step will not produce readable plaintext because key 2 is different from key 1. The decryption process is the converse: decrypt with key 1, encrypt with key 2, followed by decryption with key 1.

International Data Encryption Algorithm (IDEA)

The IDEA was invented by James Massey and Xuejia Lai of Switzerland. It is an iterated block cipher with a structure similar to DES, but it uses only 8 iterations compared with the 16 used by DES with a 128-bit key. Its software implementations are faster than DES and much faster than triple DES. Cryptographers say that the mathematical theory on which IDEA is based makes it secure. IDEA also uses a longer key than even triple DES.

RC2

The algorithm for RC2 was designed by Ronald Rivest of RSA Data Security Inc. and has not been officially published, although details about the algorithm are available to those who sign nondisclosure agreements with RSA. RC2 is a 64-bit block cipher. It accepts keys with variable lengths from zero to the maximum supported by computers. The key is processed to generate an internal key of 1,024 bits. Special export status has been given to versions of RC2 using a 40-bit key.

RC4

The algorithm for RC4 was also designed by Ronald Rivest and has not been officially published, although someone has placed the algorithm in the public domain by posting details about implementing the code on the Internet. RSA still claims it is proprietary. Like RC2, RC4 uses a variable size key and is implemented as a stream cipher and works in output feedback (OFB) mode. Its characteristics are similar to those described for DES in OFB mode. Special export status has been given to versions of RC4 using a 40-bit key.

Symmetric Key Cipher Modes of Operation

Key cipher modes are susceptible to codebook attack or propagation of errors. Thus, the following technical information may help users understand why one mode is preferred over another. Most of these modes are applicable to other symmetric key algorithms besides DES.

Electronic Codebook Mode (ECB). ECB works best for messages with short and random data. DES is used on 8-byte blocks of data with no context information added; hence, whenever the same data blocks are encrypted, the same ciphertext results. Susceptible to codebook collection and substitution or block replay attacks, it is used primarily for sending keys and initialization vectors because the data are short and random.

Cipher Block Chaining Mode (CBC). CBC is best for encrypting files stored locally. Each block of ciphertext is made to depend on its predecessor by XORing each block of plaintext with the previous block of ciphertext before encryption. This mode prevents codebook collection problems, but it remains susceptible to block replay attacks because each block that passes through the cipher is modified by the block preceding it. It uses a shared initialization vector and last-block padding. Error propagation is as follows: 1-bit ciphertext errors become 1-block plaintext errors; ciphertext synchronization errors (i.e., dropped bits) garble all subsequent plaintext output unless blocking is provided.

Cipher Feedback Mode (CFB). CFB is best for encrypting a stream of data one character at a time (e.g., between a terminal and a host). It can be implemented as an n-bit stream cipher. With 8-bit CFB, encryption is able to start and operate on each 8-bit character. The last ciphertext block sent is fed back into the encryptor, which prevents codebook collection problems. DES is used only in encryption mode. It requires a unique initialization vector for each message to avoid being vulnerable to replay attacks. Errors will propagate. For example, 8-bit CFB will produce 9 bytes of garbled plaintext if a 1-bit error has occurred in the ciphertext.

Output Feedback Mode (OFB). OFB is best for error-prone environments. It is used for handling asynchronous data streams (keyboard input) because most of the "cipher" is performed based on prior input and is ready when the last n-bit character is typed in. OFB requires an initialization vector. This prevents codebook collection problems, but OFB remains susceptible to block replay attacks. Errors do not propagate or extend. However, several analyses have shown that unless the n-bit feedback size is the same as the block size, the algorithm strength will be significantly reduced.

Key Management Problems

The following problems often surface with the use of private, symmetric key-based ciphers.

Key Population Does Not Scale Well With User Growth. $(n)(n-1)/2$ keys are required for n people to communicate securely. For example, 19,900 keys are required for 200 people to communicate with one another securely, and 1,999,000 keys are required for 2,000 people to so communicate.

A Secret Message Cannot Be Sent Without Prior Arrangement. It is impossible for operators to send secret messages unless they already have the ability to send secret messages. In reality, senders must be able to trust the people (or their credentials) from whom they accept an encryption key. If they cannot trust them, they should not expect that messages encrypted with the key they delivered will remain secret.

Key Revocation Is Difficult. There are no mechanisms for revoking keys that have been lost or compromised (without a centric-based system). Such issues can be resolved by using secure protocols with a trusted centralized key distribution center.

CRYPTOGRAPHIC PROTOCOLS

The purpose of using a protocol with cryptography is to prevent or detect eavesdropping or cheating. Thus the parties involved can authenticate themselves to each other and establish a secret shared key with which they can encrypt their messages to preserve secrecy. If a new encryption key is established each time they need to communicate or is given a reasonably short lifetime, the amount of time a replay attack can be successfully mounted is limited. An effective protocol does not rely on the fairness or trustworthiness of the parties or the message network. Today there are several secure protocols that have been implemented experimentally. MIT's Project Athena was one of the first to tackle the tough problems associated with key management for private (symmetric secret) key cryptographic systems with a secure protocol called Kerberos. Versions of Kerberos code are available via the Internet or as supported products from several vendors. Other protocols that also perform user authentication and key management and are worth considering are Krypto-Knight, SES-AME (Secure European System for Applications in a Multivendor Environment), S-Key, Yaksha, and RADIUS.

Kerberos

The goal of Kerberos, a trusted third-party protocol, is to provide unforgeable credentials to identify principals and to provide them with shared symmetric cipher keys to preserve the privacy of any transactions during their session. The principals are users, services (applications) on servers, or hosts. The Kerberos protocol assumes all principals sit on an untrusted network, except the trusted Kerberos servers, which must reside in a secure environment. Kerberos provides two major services as a trusted third party: authentication of principals and key management. Kerberos keeps a database of each principal's secret — a hash function of each principal's password. When client machines can be used by more than a single user, network nodes or services can and should also be authenticated so session audits can indicate which workstation was involved in a user session.

Authentication of Principals. Trusted third-party functions include the following:

- **Identity-based authorization model**. Because Kerberos knows every principal's identity, it can create messages to convince one principal of another principal's identity.
- **A trusted third party performs the authentication.** The Kerberos servers are the linchpin. They must be physically and logically secure, with effective security and administration policies and procedures, to ensure they cannot be compromised. Their implementation must provide high availability.
- **Symmetric secret key exchange.** Kerberos provides one-time random session keys to both principals with a finite lifetime to limit exposure to replay attacks.
- **Principal.** This designation identifies users (user ID) or services (service ID) to Kerberos. (For discussion purposes, the principal is commonly referred to as the user.)

Key Management. The functions of key management include the following:

- **Key distribution between users and services.** Session keys are securely distributed to both parties involved.
- **Key creation.** The Kerberos implementation provides excellent random key generation. It is questionable whether or not individual users would be able to provide such a facility.

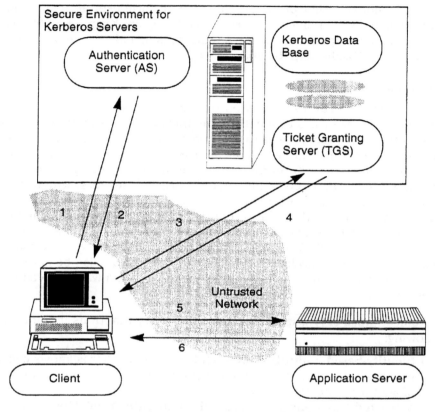

Exhibit 36.4. Kerberos Message Exchange

- **Key revocation.** If a user ID has been compromised or a session key has expired (without a renewal request), Kerberos is able to revoke all outstanding session keys established on behalf of a user.
- **Single sign-on.** Users need only remember their Kerberos ID and pass phrase. Kerberos eliminates the burdens of remembering the ID and passwords for multiple systems by passing tokens representing previously authenticated users to any system the user wishes to access.

The services provided by Kerberos are provided by an authentication server (AS) and a ticket-granting server (TGS), which reside in a secure environment as shown in Exhibit 36.4.

Kerberos Message Exchange

To obtain access to a server, s, a user must have a valid ticket and must be authenticatable to the server. To initiate the process, users identify

c	= client	K_i	= i's secret key
s	= server	$K_{c,s}$	= session key shared by c and s
IP_c	= client's network address	$K_s\{M\}$	= message M, encrypted in s's key
n	= nonce (random number)	$T_{c,s}$	= c's ticket to use s
tstmp	= time stamp of current time	$A_{c,s}$	= authenticator from c to s
chksm	= checksum	$K_s\{T_{c,s}\}$	= c's ticket to use s encrypted in s's key
expiry	= ticket start and end times	$K_{c,s}\{A_{c,s}\}$	= encrypted authenticator from c to s

Exhibit 36.5. Kerberos Nomenclature

themselves in a request to an AS to obtain credentials from the TGS. This request is represented as message 1 in Exhibit 36.4 and is not encrypted. The message flow and action scenario that follow is the same for Kerberos versions 4 and 5; the message formats shown are for Version 5. Only messages 2 and 4 are different, where double encryption of the ticket-granting ticket (TGT) has been eliminated. Exhibit 36.5 provides a key to the Kerberos nomenclature used in the following steps:

- User is prompted for ID; client sends plaintext message to the AS requesting a TGT (TGT = Tc,tgs).
- as_req = c, tgs, expiry, n
- AS looks up the hash of the user's password from the Kerberos database to form Kc to encrypt a response message and send it to the user. The response message contains a secret key, Kc,tgs, to be used to encrypt ticket request messages between the client and the TGS and the TGT, Tc,tgs, encrypted with the secret key, Ktgs, of the TGS.
- as_resp = Kc{Kc,tgs},Ktgs{Tc,tgs}.
- The user is prompted for a password, which the client uses to form Kc and decrypt the message. The value, chksm, included in the message is compared with a checksum calculated by the client. If they are the same, it is assumed that the password provided by the user is correct. If it is not correct, the user must try again.
- The secret key, Kc,tgs, is decrypted using Kc. Kc,tgs and the encrypted TGT, Ktgs{Tc,tgs}, are stored on the client so a request for services from server s can be made to the TGS. The user's password and the key Kc are erased from the client's memory to minimize exposure to snooping attacks at the client.

- The user's password was never exposed to the network. The client was able to decrypt the response from the AS because they shared a secret: knowledge of the user's password.
- Kerberos principals obtain tickets for server services from the TGS. Principals are either clients or services on servers. Tickets are encrypted in the key of the service, s.
- Encrypted Ticket $Ks\{Tc,s\}$ = $Ks\{c, s, IPc, tstmp, chksm, expiry, Kc,s\}$
- A ticket is used to securely pass the name of the client requesting service to the server. To guard against replay attacks, all tickets are sent to servers with an authenticator encrypted with the session key shared by the client and the server.
- Encrypted Authenticator $Kc,s\{Ac\}$ = $Kc,s\{c, IPc, tstmp, chksm\}$
- All messages contain a checksum that is checked to determine whether or not the message has been modified by transmission errors or malicious intent.
- When the user decides that access is required on server, s, the client does the following:
  - Sends a message containing the encrypted authenticator and the encrypted TGT requesting service from servers to the TGS.
  - tgs_req = s, expiry, n, $Ktgs\{Tc,tgs\},Kc,tgs\{Ac\}$.
- The TGS is able to decrypt the TGT because it is encrypted in its secret key. If the message chksm is correct, and the other information it previously generated is correct, the TGS extracts the client-TGS session key, Kc,tgs, from the decrypted TGT and decrypts the client's authenticator. The TGS then compares and checks the chksm and whether or not the tstmp is current enough to be considered valid. If it is valid, the following occurs:
  - The TGS sends the client an encrypted ticket to access the server, s, and an encrypted session key, Kc,s, for the client/server session. The ticket is encrypted with a key formed from the server's password which the server shares with the TGS. The encrypted ticket and the session key Kc,s is encrypted with the session key Kc,tgs, used by the client and the TGS.
  - tgs_resp = $Kc,tgs\{Kc,s\},Ks\{Tc,s\}$.
- The client then sends its authenticator and ticket to the server, s, which uses the authenticator to verify that the ticket came from the client, c, and recovers the client/server session key Kc,s from ticket, Tc,s.
- s_req = $Ks\{Tc,s\},Kc,s\{Ac\}$
- When mutual authentication is required, the server sends a message to the client encrypted with the session key containing the tmstmp generated by the client incremented by 1. This could not have been done correctly if the server did not generate the secret key, Ks, based on the server's password and shared by the server and the TGS to decrypt the ticket. The ticket contains the client/server session key.

- s_resp = Kc,s{timestmp+1}
- TGS should cache authenticators that are still valid according to their time stamp and expiry of their TGT, so they can be checked for new requests for service to guard against replay attacks.

Kerberos Shortcomings

The Kerberos protocol demonstrates several shortcomings.

- Because the AS responds without authenticating the user (based on the assumption that only the valid user would know the shared secret), an eavesdropper could record request–response pairs to form the basis of a dictionary attack. However, the nonce, n, is supposed to limit an attacker's ability to do this because it should change the appearance of the encrypted response message. Primarily, because the nonce is sent in the request message, an attacker's valid time to calculate the key is limited to the life of the nonce. This time should be much shorter than the time predicted to determine the key.
- Access control (i.e., a user's privileges on server, s) must be provided and maintained on each server that the user accesses, instead of maintained centrally.
- Most Kerberos implementations have served a relatively small population (thousands) when implemented by a university or corporation. Each implementation can be considered a realm. Interrealm authentication can be provided only as a special nonstandard feature by a few vendors. A single Kerberos server with a large user population could present problems as a performance bottleneck and a single point of failure, both of which could prevent network access. Improvements in newer versions of Kerberos will include interrealm authentication.
- Workstations used by more than one user are prime candidates for swiping session keys and TGT for current replay attacks or later dictionary attacks if a user has access to a debugger program. If the client Kerberos code is bugged so that all ID and passwords are written to hidden files for later examination of the system, these accounts will be compromised.
- The Kerberos servers present a single point of failure, which could prevent user access or whose security, if breached, could compromise the security of all user sessions. Clearly, a server implementation with high availability attributes is necessary. Alternatives utilizing distributed authentication servers may be able to limit security breaches to a smaller portion of the user population.

CONCLUSION

Protocols have been invented that provide solutions to many of the problems found with private (symmetric) key-based ciphers. Most of these protocols, such as Kerberos, are complex, and their implementations may not solve all of the problems. How does Kerberos rate in terms of the problems outlined earlier?

- **Key population does not scale well with user growth.** This problem was only partially solved. Kerberos must be able to serve n users and keeps only their n hashed passwords. It issues secret session keys only when required. However, if all users required simultaneous sessions, n(n-1)/2 secret keys would still be required — an unlikely scenario. Growth across realms remains a problem.
- **A secret message cannot be sent without prior arrangement.** This problem was solved once the "change the initial easy password" process was set in motion.
- **Key revocation difficult.** Kerberos solves this problem by administrator intervention.
- **Message originator cannot be uniquely identified.** The originator of a message cannot be identified based on knowledge of the key; it can only be narrowed down to those having knowledge of the key. The Kerberos protocol solved this problem by using a client authenticator. However, the solution was not generalized.

Section 5
Building Enterprise Solutions with LAN-Based Technology

It has always been the case that the true strength of LAN technology lies in the organization's ability to use LANs to leverage newly enabled capabilities, providing the potential for orders of magnitude increases in business productivity. In today's environment, the newly enabled capabilities center around distributed computing, including traditional distributed computing, and more recently, platform independent distributed computing. The focus of this section of the *Handbook* is on leading edge ways to apply LAN technology to make people, and by extension, the business enterprise more effective. In this section, we first focus briefly on some examples of LAN-enabled enterprise solutions, then take a look at some issues related to the development and deployment of such solutions.

When it first appeared on the scene, the World Wide Web was predominantly a publishing application, best suited to the delivery of static hypertext documents. Because of its success, it has become readily apparent that the web architecture has many additional uses. Chapter 37, "Web-to-Information-Base Access Solutions," surveys an impressive number of such applications, demonstrating clearly that the imagination is the primary limiting factor for the applicability of this technology.

Before the web existed, the most popular network-enabled application was electronic mail. Despite the immense popularity of the web, e-mail, in particular LAN-based e-mail, remains a mainstay of the enterprise network, and in many businesses it is now considered to be "mission critical." Chapter 38, "Local Area Network Messaging," discusses a number of the general issues involved with planning, implementing, and managing a LAN-based electronic messaging system.

In the next several chapters, we shift our attention to issues related to the development and deployment of applications in a LAN-based enterprise network. First, Chapter 39, "Choosing and Equipping an Internet Server," focuses on the factors one should consider when selecting a server, whether it is intended for use on the Internet or intranet. Beyond

431

the web, the chapter also discusses some basic issues concerning news and mail software based on Internet technologies.

We continue our look at development and deployment issues by focusing on the issue of language selection with respect to the development of network-based applications. The language we focus on in this section is Java, introduced by Sun Microsystems in 1995. In a few short years, Java has proven to be quite popular among programmers and in the academic community. Of particular importance to the IT manager charged with selecting a language for development of an enterprise network-based application is an understanding of Java's networking capabilities. Such is the topic of Chapter 40, "Networking Features of the Java Programming Language." Continuing the theme, Chapter 41 takes a look at "Java's Role in Distributed Computing."

Regardless what language one chooses, development of a distributed application entails a certain amount of risk and uncertainty as a result of some of the complexities not always found in traditionally developed applications. Chapter 42 examines this topic by exploring and presenting "The Pitfalls of Client/Server Development Projects."

When contemplating a new undertaking, in particular a complex one, it is often beneficial to consider what others have done and what they have encountered in the process. Chapter 43, "Creating a Paperless Workflow: A Case Study," is intended to provide such guidance for the reader contemplating a new distributed system. A particular focus of this chapter is on the need to carefully analyze the existing business process and, if necessary, to reengineer that process before designing the automated replacement.

We conclude our look at the building of LAN-based enterprise solutions by focusing on the security needs of such applications. First, we focus on an application found on virtually every networked desktop on the planet: electronic mail. Chapter 44, "Security and Control of Electronic Mail," takes a broad look at the topic, identifies several electronic mail security concerns and the general mechanisms used to address them.

Our final chapter in the section, Chapter 45, "Applets and Network Security: A Management Overview," describes the unique security issues associated with applet-based distributed applications. The chapter describes how applets work, the threats they present, and the security precautions that should be taken to minimize exposure.

Chapter 37
Web-to-Information-Base Access Solutions

Marion G. Ceruti

The purpose of this chapter is to assist managers of information systems programs who are interested in successful implementations of World Wide Web technology to access information bases, including databases and knowledge bases. This chapter also describes research efforts to extend the present capabilities in Web-based access. The Web has emerged as a form of data access middleware in some applications because of its efficiency and generality, owing to a common data transfer protocol.[3] (See, for example, References 2,7,8.) It is a key component in meeting data and knowledge access requirements. It also has become a tool for software reuse.[8] For example, databases, knowledge-base development tools, data mining tools, images, textual documents, standards, and a variety of software tools are accessible on the Web[3] to any user with a Web browser, which is defined as a client software that accesses and displays Web pages, such as Netscape Communications Corp.'s Navigator.[5]

This chapter describes case studies of Web applications in systems and research programs sponsored by the Department of Defense (DOD), and by universities as well as Web-based access products and services developed in private industry. It describes technology that military, academic, and commercial systems need to address information access requirements of the future. For example, as the tactical emphasis in the DOD shifts from platform-centric toward network-centric warfare, the issues in network utilization, the interoperability of new and legacy systems, and the reuse that the networks enable become more significant. DOD laboratories and agencies are aware of the advantages in information systems access over the Internet and have been developing programs for various purposes, all of which are aimed at sharing either data or knowledge among service components.[8]

Similarly, many advances in information access have been made in academia and industry, some of which are described below.

In Reference 5, Maurice Frank provides a good discussion of various techniques and products that enabled Web browsers to exchange data with databases as of 1995. It covers commercial Web-to-database interface products of the leading vendors of Relational Database Management Systems, such as Oracle Corp., IBM, Sybase Inc., and Informix Corp., as well as the products of several third-party vendors. The article also discusses Web-based database integration using the Common Gateway Interface (CGI). This chapter presents some additional information that has become available since then.

Web solutions that enable information access are described below in four case studies: Web-based data access, Web-based meta data access, Web-based knowledge access, and network-centric warfare. The second and third case studies include multiple examples of Web-based access, whereas the first and fourth studies describe single examples.

CASE STUDY 1 — METEOROLOGICAL AND OCEANOGRAPHIC WEB-BASED DATA ACCESS

A long-standing problem in the DOD is to provide uniform and efficient access to all users who need to view and use databases and data objects. Version control for data sets that are sent from data centers to various sites, both to headquarters and to deployed units, has been a problem because by the time the last site receives the data set, it is either out of date or different from the version received at the first site. This is also an inefficient and labor-intensive way to distribute data. Keeping all units updated with the same data simultaneously was not tractable or affordable before the use of networks.

This situation is changing because one of the most user-friendly developments in the area of data access for the database community in general has been the use of the Web. The Navy systems that provide Meteorological and Oceanographic (METOC) data will be used as examples in this discussion. (See, for example, Reference 13). Because of the dynamic nature of these environmental data, finding a solution to the problem of immediate access to timely, accurate, and consistent information is very important. For the METOC users in particular, this access solution is via the Joint METOC Viewer (JMV). (See, for example, Reference 10.) JMV is a multiplatform, client/server application suite, the design of which was based on the user interface design of the Navy Oceanographic Data Distribution System.[10] Authorized DOD users (both Navy and non-Navy) can access METOC data from most geographic locations.

The Web-accessible data on JMV is divided into two groups, data that can be transferred to another platform and data available in a read-only mode. Using JMV, METOC numerical data and products are available for downloading by geographic region. This data includes surface pressures and temperatures. Still a wider variety of data is available for display as images in windows on the screen. For example, the user can display profiles and cross sections of three-dimensional atmospheric and oceanographic data.[10]

The Web has the advantage of being independent of the hardware platform because network browsers, using a common Hypertext Markup Language (HTML) protocol for net access, are available for many platforms.[10] (See also, Reference 5). Web-based access to METOC data solves the problem of disseminating batch data sets to sites, since any site can view, and in some cases download, the data on the Web. It also solves data storage and throughput problems that were introduced when data resolutions increased from a 2.5-degree grid spacing to a 1.0-degree grid spacing. The efficiency of JMV has provided the DOD with not only enhanced capabilities, but also a substantial cost savings.[10]

DOD users may access the Naval Pacific METOC Center directly. Access to JMV for non-DOD U.S. government users is via the National Weather service. Information on JMV and the data to which it provides access is available at Web sites with the following URLs:

- http://152.80.56.202/faqs/faq_jmv_gen.html
- http://cnodds.nws.noaa.gov/jmv_man/jmvumtoc.htm
- http://www.nrlmry.navy.mil/~neith/Sigmet.html
- http://www.nlmoc.navy.mil/newpage/navigate2.html
- http://www.fnmoc.navy.mil/

CASE STUDY 2 — WEB-BASED METADATA ACCESS FOR MODELING AND SIMULATION

DOD's Modeling and Simulation Resource Repository

Modeling and simulation efforts in the DOD have grown in proportion to the shrinking defense budget because it is much more economical to run a simulation prior to field tests than it is to conduct numerous preliminary and costly field tests without the benefit of the information derived from modeling and simulation. Modeling and simulation is so important to the DOD that the Defense Modeling and Simulation Office (DMSO) has established a data repository known as the Modeling and Simulation Resource Repository (MSRR). The DMSO charter is to develop a common technical framework for modeling and simulation that includes a common, high-level simulation architecture and conceptual models of the mission space to provide a basis for the development of consistent and authoritative simulation representations. DMSO establishes data standards to support common representations of data across models, simulations, and command-and-control systems. DMSO also provides an infrastructure to meet the requirements of the developer and end users.

Part of that infrastructure includes the MSRR, the mission of which is to facilitate sharing and reuse of information by providing a service whereby resources of interest to the DOD modeling and simulation community can be registered by their owners and discovered by other potential users.

435

MSRR provides a convenient way for DOD users to search networks for resources needed in modeling and simulation projects.

The MSRR system consists of a collection of modeling and simulation resources. MSRR resources include models, simulations, object models, conceptual models of the mission space, algorithms, instance databases, data sets, data standardization and administration products, documents, tools, and utilities. MSRR users can access collections of resources utilizing a distributed system of resource servers interconnected through the Web. The MSRR system software provides for registration of resources and users, description and quality information of resources, and specialized search capabilities. The MSRR modeling and simulation resources also include information on and links to DMSO-supported projects and a DMSO document library containing various documents, briefs, and presentations relating to DMSO.

The MSRR is a DOD computer system that was designed specifically for the use of DOD members and contractors, although others may be provided access by DMSO MSRR program management on a case-by-case basis. MSRR users are divided into two categories: registered users and public users. A public user may use all areas of the MSRR except for the few areas that require a registered user's ID and password. Whereas all users may access resources, registered users can register resources on the MSRR. Registered users can be included on an access list managed by the resource provider, whereas public users cannot be included on the list.

Knowledge of and access to many modeling and simulation resources is limited given the plethora of information in the DOD community. MSRR collects at one Web site (including its links) the meta data about these diverse information resources. The resource may be in any form that can be distributed to other users. For example, it can be on a Web server or in the form of a hard copy. It can be in electronic form available for e-mailing or on a diskette that can be distributed through the U.S. mail.

An optional item in the MSRR registration process is the Web site URL. This can refer to an Internet URL for direct access to the resource, an file transfer protocol (FTP) reference for download from a FTP site, or an e-mail address of resource point of contact.

An MSRR help desk is maintained to assist users who have questions that cannot be answered solely by the modeling and simulation resources that they find while they are using the MSRR. The help desk can assist DOD members and DOD contractors with locating applicable information via the MSRR. A feedback mechanism is provided for users to submit their comments about the successes and failures of MSRR.

The DMSO Web-based meta data repositories for modeling and simulation include the following Web sites:

- http://msis.dmso.mil/
- http://www.msrr.dmso.mil/

Navy Modeling and Simulation Catalog

The Navy Modeling and Simulation Catalog, which is administered by the Navy Modeling and Simulation Management Office (NAVMSMO), is a part of MSRR that allows users to discover, access, and obtain modeling and simulation resources that support military assessments, training, and acquisition. It was established to provide leadership and guidance for the Navy's modeling policy, strategy, investment, and practices; to oversee maintenance of a model repository; to provide technical assistance to model users and developers; to review resource expenditures on new model development; to sponsor initiatives for the community good and to provide centralized coordination of U.S. Navy Modeling and Simulation.

The browse capability of the Navy Modeling and Simulation Catalog provides a method of viewing data without having to run searches or to execute complex queries against the database. In some cases, it is possible to "drill down" through the data in a systematic way. Meta data can be accessed by resource type, including data sources, modeling and simulation, references, support tools and utilities, related sites, all points of contact, and all organizations.

The resources available at the NAVMSMO Web site are described at a substantial level of detail. In some cases, the resource will be available for immediate download. In other cases, users need to follow the specific instructions. Users can capture a summary of every resource registered in the Navy Modeling and Simulation Catalog in a single report listed by category.

The Navy Modeling and Simulation Catalog includes information on data sources utilized in Navy modeling and simulation activities, models, simulations, and simulators found in the current Navy inventory. It also has references to publications and tools utilized in the support, development, and management of Navy modeling and simulation.

DMSO and NAVMSMO both provide links to service-specific, joint, and allied organizations of interest to modeling and simulation users, such as those listed in Exhibit 37.1.

CASE STUDY 3 — KNOWLEDGE-BASE DEVELOPMENT AND ACCESS USING THE WEB

What Is A Knowledge Base?

Unfortunately, a comprehensive, exclusive, and unique definition of the term "knowledge base" that will satisfy all knowledge engineers is not available. However, a working definition that will cover many cases is as follows:

Navy Modeling and Simulation Management Office (NAVMSMO)	http://navmsmo.hq.navy.mil/nmsiscat/
Air Force Communications Agency Modeling and Simulation Home Page	http://infosphere.safb.af.mil/~tnab/
Army Model and Simulation Office	http://www.amso.army.mil/
Joint Data Base Elements for Modeling and Simulation	http://208.145.129.4/
Defense Modeling, Simulation, Tactical Technology Information Analysis Center	http://dmsttiac.hq.iitri.com/
UK Simulation Interoperability Working Group	http://siwg.dra.hmg.gb/

Exhibit 37.1. Modeling and Simulation Web Sites

Unlike a database that stores information implicitly in tabular format, a knowledge base is a source of information that stores facts explicitly as declarative assertions, such as frames and slots, or in the form of probabilistic networks. (See, for example, Reference 2.) Implicit in the definition is the idea that a knowledge base is used as input into an inference engine in an expert system.

Web sites that provide access to knowledge bases can be divided into two categories: (1) those that can be accessed by Lisp or other programming languages and that could be used as input to an inference engine without extensive knowledge representation modification, and (2) those that amount to plain textual information written in nonprogramming, spoken language, such as English or French. In some cases, the distinction between the two categories is ill-defined. For example, the test of "Can the candidate knowledge base be input into an inference engine?" fails as a means to exclude what we usually think are some nonknowledge-base information sources because some software can read text, access Web sites, and extract keywords, etc., for expert systems to use. In any case, for the purpose of this chapter, all knowledge bases discussed below are assumed to be in category 1, unless otherwise noted.

High-Performance Knowledge Base

Technology has achieved more uniformity and interoperability with standard network protocols than it has with knowledge-base access because of the many ways in which knowledge representations can differ and also because of the multiple knowledge development methods that can be used to construct knowledge bases.[3] To address these and other problems associated with the construction and usage of knowledge bases, the Defense Advanced Research Projects Agency has sponsored the High Performance Knowledge Base (HPKB) program, which includes an effort to integrate via networks, knowledge base-related software, and resources.[2]

The HPKB program includes a project titled "High-Performance Knowledge Editing and Problem Solving over the Internet."[2] A key concept with this approach is that the application specialists should be able to use domain-specific editors over the Internet in a collaborative environment to develop knowledge bases. The Internet is a tool that potentially can be used to search for domain-independent, problem-solving components that can be linked to the domain-oriented knowledge bases.[2] The project will provide retrieval methods of ontologies and knowledge bases in a database system that complies with the Open Database Connectivity standards. The work is performed at the Stanford University Section on Medical Informatics, which has demonstrated access to knowledge bases over the Internet in other projects.[7]

The Knowledge-Base Infrastructure

The University of Texas has demonstrated knowledge-base access using the Internet with its Knowledge-Base Infrastructure project. It has developed tools to help domain experts encode knowledge in multifunctional knowledge bases. Its tools include a knowledge representation language (KM) and a system (KnEd) for viewing and editing knowledge bases built using KM. Written in Common Lisp and CLIM, these tools have been ported to all major implementations of Common Lisp and hardware platforms.

Whereas knowledge-base access methods are ways to locate information, many current methods are inadequate, especially for large, structured knowledge bases. To locate information about a concept using current access methods, the user would be required to provide the address (usually a frame name) of the concept within the knowledge base, which requires a level of sophistication that most users do not have. Moreover, only the concepts that already are in the knowledge base can be located, which excludes information about many concepts (meta knowledge) that is implicit in the knowledge base but that could be made explicit with the use of an appropriate inference engine. The University of Texas has developed a solution to these problems by providing an abstraction of the knowledge base in which concepts can be located by a partial description of their contents.

After locating a concept, the access methods provide an additional service: selecting coherent subsets of facts about the concept. Conventional methods either return all the facts about the concept or select a single fact. These access methods extract coherent collections of facts that describe a concept from a particular perspective. The University of Texas knowledge base developers have identified many types of viewpoints and developed methods for extracting them from knowledge bases. Their evaluation indicates that viewpoints extracted by our methods are comparable in coherence to those that people construct.

The University of Texas has made available the software (a Lisp implementation of KM), a users manual and a reference manual, all of which can be downloaded from its Web site; however, no warranty is stated or implied. The author(s) do not accept responsibility to anyone for the consequences of using it or for whether or not it serves any particular purpose or works at all. The authors are P. Clark and B. Porter, who can be contacted at *porter@cs.utexas.edu*.

Two knowledge bases of worked examples are available on the University of Texas Web site. One is the userman.km from the KM Users Manual, and the other is refman.km from the KM Reference Manual.

The URL for these knowledge bases, respectively, are

- http://www.cs.utexas.edu/users/mfkb/manuals/userman.km
- http://www.cs.utexas.edu/users/mfkb/manuals/refman.km

University of Indiana Knowledge Base

The knowledge in this Web-based information system includes databases of Standard & Poor's corporate financial statements and the Center for Research in Security Prices. Indiana University's license is restricted to students, faculty, and staff. The URL is *http://sckb.ucssc.indiana.edu/kb/data/adyx.html* and the point of contact is Lin-Long Shyu at *shyu@indiana.edu*.

The knowledge base consists of 5,000 files, each with a question and an answer formatted in Knowledge Base Markup Language (KBML), a text markup language described using Standard General Markup Language. KBML is similar to HTML with some adaptations and special features required by the knowledge base. The system features a locally written, full-text search engine called "Mindex"; a freeware Web server, Apache; several databases, including an extensible keywords database; tools and utilities for knowledge base usage reports and text maintenance, including an editing environment written in Emacs Lisp; and Web and command-line tools for searching in various modes. The system is maintained actively by consultants who work for University Information Technology Services' Support Center.

ADM Medical Knowledge Base

The ADM (Aide au Diagnostic Médical) is a system with an extensive medical knowledge base. Its two main goals are to help physicians make diagnoses and enable rapid access to medical information through telematic networks. The system can be used in many ways: diagnosis evocation, strategy in asking for complementary tests, interaction between disease and drug, interaction between disease and pregnancy, and electronic encyclopedia.

The knowledge base, which deals with all medical domain, contains the descriptions of 15,600 diseases, syndromes, and clinical presentations. It includes a data dictionary of 110,000 entities and a vocabulary dictionary with 45,000 terms. The database is implemented with a relational database management system. It is composed of several tables that physicians update regularly.

The telematics consultation system is available on a Web server. Whereas everyone may access the demonstration version, the use of the entire system is restricted to physicians who have received a password. They can use menus and text as dialogue with the system. Question types are defined, and the encyclopedic aspect has been developed. Other functions, particularly the diagnosis evocation module, are being improved and will be consulted by students and researchers on the university network using the intranet Web server. The user interface features seminatural language using dictionaries and hierarchies defined in the database. The URL that describes the ADM Medical Knowledge Base URL is *http://sunaimed.univ-rennes1.fr/plaq/proj_an/adm_an.html*.

It is available in English or French. The information in French is available at *http://www.med.univ-rennes1.fr/adm.dir/presentation.html*.

Commercial Knowledge-Base Services

This information about products and services is provided for user convenience and is not intended to be an advertisement or an endorsement by the U.S. government.

The Help Desk Institute has provided the Web-based service of describing the expert systems and knowledge base tools and services that are available in private industry. The root URL is *http://www.helpdeskinst.com/bg/contents.html*, which features links to a wide range of commercial vendors that supply knowledge base access and expert system–related services to their clients and customers, particularly in the area of online help desks. Some knowledge publishers and companies that provide knowledge bases accessible over the Internet are listed at the following URL: *http://www.helpdeskinst.com/bg/sections/knowledgepubs/index.html*.

The 1998 Support and Services Suppliers Directory also describes companies that offer expert systems and knowledge support tools at the following URL: *http://www.helpdeskinst.com/bg/sections/expertsys/index.html*. For example, some of these companies that provide the above-described services are listed on the Web site of the Help Desk Institute with their URL, as listed in Exhibit 37.2.

Advantage KBS Inc.	http://www.akbs.com
Emerald Intelligence Inc.	http://www.emeraldi.com
Intellisystems Inc.	http://www.intellisystems.com
KnowledgeBroker Inc.	http://www.kbi.com
The Haley Enterprise	http://www.haley.com
Magic Solutions Inc.	http://www.magicsolutions.com
Molloy Group Inc.	http://www.molloy.com
Product Knowledge Inc.	http://www.proknowledge.com
ServiceSoft Corp.	http://www.servicesoft.com
ServiceWare Inc.	http://www.serviceware.com
Software Artistry Inc.	http://www.softart.com
Utopia Technology Partners Inc.	http://www.utosoft.com

Exhibit 37.2.   Commercial Knowledge Base Services

The electronic document management (EDM) application management software from Amdahl Corp., enabled by Novadigm, is an automated software management product that deploys and continuously synchronizes changes to client/server software on numerous heterogeneous, distributed desktops and servers. EDM support and knowledge base access is limited to licensed customers with password. The EDM Amdahl URL is *http://amdahl.com/aplus/support/EXedm_sup.html.*

The DataWorks Corp.'s education and support services provide access to an online knowledge base of documents that contain solutions to numerous questions. Online application and technical support to customers is available through SupportNet 24 hours a day, 7 days a week. The Data-Work's URL is *http://www.dataworksmpls. com/support/.*

Some Web sites provide access to knowledge bases that are actually collections of databases or documents through a system of point-and-click queries. These fall into category 2 as described above. Technically, they are knowledge bases if they contain information stored in a declarative manner; however, the information is not necessarily stored in a format that the kind of inference engines used in expert systems can access and read. For example, Netscape provides a list of online documents that can be accessed via the Web. When Netscape describes how to browse the knowledge base, it refers to an index to lists of technical articles for various Netscape software products, current and older versions. To view technical articles, the user must select a link. Whereas this can be of considerable utility to enable users to gain information about the contents the online documents, there is no evidence that the documents have been stored using a knowledge representation that a Lisp program, for example, could read as input. The URL for Netscape's Browse the Knowledge Base is *http://help.netscape.com/browse/*.

The Visionware Ltd.'s Support URL offers its knowledge base as an exclusive and free service for Visionware customers. It is described at the following URL: *http://www.visionware.com/support.asp*. It features online product support that offers search facilities to locate known problems and problem reports in the Visionware knowledge database.

According to Verity Inc., a knowledge base consists of a set of predefined queries called "topics" that users can select to include as search criteria in their information agents. Information about Verity's knowledge base is located at their "Basic Administration Activities" Web site: *http://www.verity.com/tech-support/s97es/ent22u/ch013.htm*.

Exhibit 37.3 shows a summary of the Web sites discussed above that describe knowledge base access using the Web.

CASE STUDY 4 — NETWORK-CENTRIC WARFARE

Network-centric warfare, which is replacing platform-centric warfare and weapon-centric warfare, is one of the fastest-growing components in the DOD budget, not only because of the enhanced capabilities it provides to the warfighter, but also because of significant cost savings.[6,12,14,17] "Platformcentric" means that the purpose of a ship, submarine, airplane, or tank is defined and limited by its own sensor capabilities and ranges.[3] The advantage of network-centric warfare is that emphasis is shifted from single-platform capabilities to aggregate capabilities that provide warfighters access to an order of magnitude more information than that available on their own platform.[1,14] Future platforms will be designed around information networks.[1]

In the Navy, network-centric warfare refers to the ability to expand horizons of each ship by using computers that enable an intelligent, fast, flexible network of sensors, shooters, and command centers.[14,15] This concept is becoming reality in the U.S. fleet where the new networks make command systems several orders of magnitude more effective.[11,13,14] These systems are designed to assist in coordinating the widely dispersed forces operating in littorals that are expected to dominate future warfare because it increases the speed at which command decisions are made.[14,16] The global military multimedia network will support voice, video, data, text, graphics, and imagery transfer between all nodes, both afloat and ashore

Aide au Diagnostic Médical (ADM) Medical Knowledge Base	http://sunaimed.univ-rennes1.fr/plaq/ proj_an/adm_ an.html
DataWorks Corp.	http://www.dataworksmpls.com/support/.
EDM Amdahl	http://amdahl.com/aplus/support/ EXedm_sup.html
Help Desk Institute	http://www.helpdeskinst.com/bg/ contents.html
Netscape's Browse the Knowledge Base	http://help.netscape.com/browse/
Stanford University's Section on Medical Informatics — publications	http://smi-web.stanford.edu/pubs/
University of Indiana Compustat Knowledge-Base	http://sckb.ucssc.indiana.edu/kb/data/ adyx.html http://kb.indiana.edu/data/acte.html http://kb.indiana.edu/info/infopage.html
University of Texas Knowledge-Base Infrastructure	http://www.cs.utexas.edu/users/mfkb/ km.html
Verity Inc.	http://www.verity.com/tech-support/ s97es/ent22u/ch013.htm
Visionware Ltd.	http://www.visionware.com/support.asp

Exhibit 37.3. Knowledge Base Access Web Sites

---

sites.[11,17] This availability of information from multiple sources, including sensors on a variety of platforms on the network, will stimulate and facilitate future advances in data-fusion software.[12,13]

An example of this is a key enabling network called the Joint Deployable Intelligence Support System (JDISS). Information from JDISS can be sent via international maritime satellite (INMARSAT), for example, to portable JDISS receivers on Aegis surface-combatant ships such as the nearby USS Bunker Hill (CG 52) and USS John S. McCain (DDG 56).[15]

Another example of network-centric warfare is the Contingency Tactical Air Planning System (CTAPS), which is a network that facilitates the construction of flight plans.[15] The database, which can be updated automatically, contains the inventories of missiles, bombs, aircraft, and spares, as resources are expended.

For example, when a missile is fired, users can log on to CTAPS and automatically decrement the weapons load on the ship so that all users have accurate, up-to-date information.[15] The network provides a significant improvement in efficiency and accuracy over paper and diskette-based flight plans.[15] Other examples of technology that enable network-centric warfare are described in Reference 12.

The following Web site acts as a central location for information available to the armed forces, including links to various military and U.S. government sites: *http://www.military-network.com.*

CONCLUSION

This chapter describes successful implementations of Web access to information bases, including examples in the DOD, in academia, and in industry. The Web provides access to meteorological and oceanographic data, meta data for modeling and simulation, knowledge base development tools, and commercially available knowledge bases. It enables major paradigm shifts in the DOD such as network-centric warfare. Web technology provides solutions to growing requirements for rapid, uniform, and accurate data and knowledge access.

ACKNOWLEDGMENTS

The author thanks the Space and Naval Warfare Systems Command and the Defense Advanced Research Projects Agency for their support of the work described above. This chapter is the work of a U.S. government employee produced in the capacity of official duty and may not be copyrighted. It is approved for public release with an unlimited distribution.

References

1. Ackerman, R. K., Bandwidth demands portend revolutionary program taxes, *Signal*, 52(10), 25–29, 1998
2. Ceruti, M. G., Application of knowledge-base technology for problem solving in information-systems integration, Proc. Dep. Defense Database Colloq. '97, pp. 215–234, Sept. 1997.
3. Ceruti, M. G., Challenges in data management for the United States Department of Defense (DOD) Command, Control, Communications, Computers, and Intelligence (C4I) systems, proceedings of the Twenty-Second Annual International IEEE Computer Software and Applications Conference, Vienna, Austria, Aug. 21, 1998. In press.
4. Evers, S., Naval forces update — US Navy seeks fast track to revolution, *Jane's Defence Weekly*, International Edition (JDW), 28(21) 55, 1997.
5. Frank, M., Database and the Internet, *DBMS Mag.*, 8(13) 44–52, 1995.
6. Holland, Jr., W. J., The race goes to the swiftest in commercial, military frays, *Signal*, 52(7) 68–71, 1998.
7. Hon, L., Abernethy, N. F., Brusic, V., Chai, J., and Altman, R., MHCWeb: Converting a WWW database into a knowledge-based collaborative environment, SMI Report No. SMI-98-0724, 1998. http://smi-web.stanford.edu/pubs/SMI_Abstracts/SMI-98-0724.html
8. Lawson, R., Developing Web-based Internet applications with reusable business components, Proc. Dep. Defense Database Colloq. '96, pp. 503–520, Aug. 1996.
9. Piper, P., Defense Information Infrastructure (DII) Shared Data Environment (SHADE), Proc. Dep. Defense Database Colloq. '96, pp. 407–418, Aug. 1996.

10. Ravid, E. V., Huff, D. and Rasmussen, R., NODDS — the next generation: joint METOC viewer, Preprint volume of the 13th International Conference on IIPS for Meteorology, Oceanography, and Hydrology, pp. 203–206, Long Beach, CA, by AMS, Boston, MA, 2-7 Feb. 1997.
11. Reed, F. V., Fleet battle experiments blend naval technology with doctrine, *Signal*, 52(10) 31–34, 1998.
12. Robinson, C. A., Information dominance glitters among commercial capabilities, *Signal*, 52(10) 35–40, 1998.
13. Tsui, T. L. and Jurkevicks, A., A database management system design for meteorological and oceanograpnic applications, *Mar. Techno. Soc. J.*, 26(2), 88–97, 1991.
14. West, L., Exploiting the information revolution: Network-centric warfare realizes its promise, *Sea Power*, 41(3), 38–40, 1998.
15. Commander says untold story in gulf is about network warfare, *Def. Wk.*, 19(10), 1998.
16. Navy's future depends on secure IT and networks, *Navy News & Undersea Technology*, 14(46), 1997. http://www.pasha.com/nvy/nvy.htm
17. Pentagon arms itself with telecom weapons for 'net-centric' warfare: Nets; DOD's first line of defense, *Elec. Eng. Times*, 975, p. 1, 1997.

Chapter 38
Local Area Network Messaging
Russell Chung

Personal computer/local area network (PC/LAN)-based electronic messaging systems represent the fastest growing segment of the electronic messaging industry. This chapter will discuss the reasons for the immense popularity of LAN messaging systems, provide an overview of the components and features of a LAN messaging system, and discuss some of the issues, myths, and realities regarding LAN messaging. This is not intended to be a product comparison or a technical guide. It is meant to be a discussion of the general issues involved with planning, implementing, and managing a LAN-based messaging system.

REASONS FOR POPULARITY OF LAN MESSAGING SYSTEMS

The first LAN-based messaging systems made their appearance shortly after the introduction of LAN in 1985. Some of the top-selling products in this category include Lotus Developmental Corp.'s cc:Mail and Notes, Novell Inc.'s GroupWise, Microsoft Corp.'s Exchange Server and Microsoft Mail for PCs, SoftArc FirstClass, Da Vinci eMail, Hewlett Packard Co.'s Open Mail and CE Software QuickMail. By November 1997, there were over 79 million users of LAN messaging systems. Recent trends indicate that the growth in the overall number of LAN messaging users is continuing at the rate of more than 40% per year.[1]

Some of the major reasons for the popularity of LAN messaging systems include (1) ease of use, (2) ease of setup, and (3) low initial investment.

Ease of Use

In the early 1980s, a typical electronic-mail user prepared a message on a "dumb" terminal connected to a mainframe- or minicomputer-based e-mail system or connected to a public value-added service such as AT&T Corp.'s Mail, MCI Communication Corp.'s Mail, Compuserve, Genie, or Delphi. If a PC was involved, it was used only to emulate a "dumb" terminal. Users endured a featureless, character-based, command line interface in preparing, editing, addressing, and sending a message. With the command line interface, users worked on one line of the message at a time and had to invoke cryptic navigation commands in order to view or edit the previous lines. The single most important factor in the popularity of LAN-based messaging products is the "user-friendly" interface, which is made possible by the personal computer. With a personal computer, users running a LAN messaging program may prepare a message by filling in an on-screen form, editing the message by moving the cursor to the desired point on the screen, addressing the message by picking names from an on-screen list of users, and sending the message by pressing a key or clicking on a mouse.

Ease of Setup

The installation and setup of a LAN-based electronic messaging system on a small-business LAN or a departmental LAN is easily accomplished in a few hours by a LAN administrator. A single system can support hundreds of users. In a large company, the departmental LAN messaging systems can be linked together to form an enterprisewide messaging system. However, as the number of linked systems increases, *scalability* becomes an issue, as administrators are discovering that the management of a large, interconnected LAN-based messaging network is not a trivial task. The distributed, decentralized nature of LAN messaging systems means that a great deal of planning, training, and coordination are required to ensure reliable, timely message delivery throughout an enterprise. An electronic messaging network is like a chain; it is only as strong as its weakest link, and the distributed nature of a LAN messaging system means that it has many more links that must be managed.

Low Initial Investment

On a per-user basis, the price of a LAN messaging system and of mainframe- or minicomputer-based messaging systems are comparable. However, the initial investment for software for a mainframe- or minicomputer-based messaging system may amount to hundreds of thousands of (U.S.) dollars, whereas the initial investment for a LAN messaging system may amount to only a few thousand (U.S.) dollars. The relatively low initial investment threshold makes the establishment of a LAN-based messaging system cost-effective for small businesses and for departments of large businesses. A LAN is rarely established solely for messaging purposes. Ordinarily, a small business or a departmental workgroup makes a decision to install a LAN to facilitate access to spreadsheets, word processing documents, shared databases, or networked printers; the incremental expense of adding electronic messaging capabilities to such a LAN is a relatively modest. Recently, vendors have begun to bundle messaging client software with software office suites, further reducing the amount of the initial investment required for LAN messaging software.

COMPONENTS OF A LAN MESSAGING SYSTEM

Developers of LAN messaging systems often utilize proprietary designs and architectures that may not exactly conform to the model of a messaging system defined by the International Telecommunications Union Telecommunications Standardization Sector (ITU-TSS) (formerly CCITT) X.400 standard nor the model of a directory system defined by the ITU-TSS X.500 standard. Nevertheless, the X.400 and X.500 models provide a useful conceptual basis for describing the components of a LAN messaging system. The X.400 standard defines three components of a messaging system: user agent (UA), message store (MS), and message transfer agent (MTA).

User Agent/User Interface (UA/UI)

The user agent is the term defined in the X.400 standard for the process that is used to read, write, edit, file, send, and discard e-mail messages. From a user's standpoint, the "look and feel" and the features of the user agent are what distinguishes one vendor's product from another. In a LAN messaging system, the user agent runs on the user's personal computer. The user agent program file (or files) may be stored either on the hard drive of the user's personal computer or stored on the hard drive of the file server and loaded in the RAM of the PC when the user launches the program.

Message Store (MS)

The message store is the repository for a user's messages. Messages are placed in, and retrieved from, the message store by user agents and message transfer agents. In a LAN environment, the message store is typically located in a file server (Exhibit 38.1) or in a messaging server (Exhibit 38.2). In some cases, the message store may be located in a user's personal computer. Conceptually, the message store is the e-mail equivalent of an inbox, outbox, and file cabinet. As one might expect, the internal design of the message store varies from vendor to vendor. Some products utilize a system of hierarchical directories and separate files to store each user's messages; other products utilize a single shared file with a system of indexes and pointers to store all users' messages; still others use a combination of the two approaches.

Message Transfer Agent (MTA)

The message transfer agent (MTA) is the term defined in the X.400 standard for the process that transfers messages between messaging systems. In a typical LAN messaging environment, this message transfer agent process runs continuously on a dedicated personal computer on the LAN (Exhibit 38.1) or on a messaging server (Exhibit 38.2), regularly checking for incoming and outgoing messages and transferring them to the appropriate destinations.

449

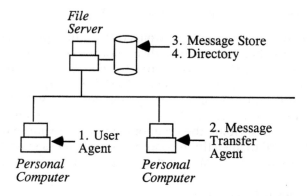

Exhibit 38.1.   Layout of a Typical File Sharing-based Lan Messaging System

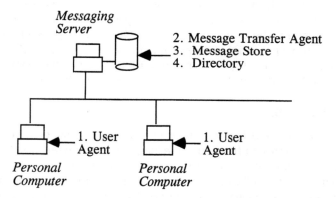

Exhibit 38.2.   Layout of a Typical Client/Server Messaging System

Directories, Directory System Agent, Directory User Agent

Messaging system directories are specialized databases that perform two functions: (1) they provide a repository of names and addresses for the purpose of routing messages and (2) they provide a place to store passwords, encryption keys, and other authentication data used to control access to the messaging system.

The X.500 model contemplates decentralized, local directories. A network of distributed, cooperating directory servers running a *directory server agent (DSA)* program responds to requests from users and from other directory servers for information from the directories. According to the X.500 model, the *directory user agent (DUA)* uses the X.500 *directory access protocol (DAP)* to submit a query to a DSA when seeking information from the directory. This model requires real-time access between users and directory servers throughout the network, or if real-time access is not always available, this model requires periodic replication of the directory information to each server.

Generally, the architecture of a typical LAN messaging directory system does not assume real-time access to directories across the network. Instead of distributed directory servers using standards-based DAP, current LAN messaging systems utilize directories that are located on each file server (Exhibit 38.1), messaging server (Exhibit 38.2), or on a user's personal computer. In current LAN messaging systems, the UA/UI program accesses the directory information that is stored on a local file server, messaging server, or on the user's personal computer using proprietary protocols instead of standards-based DAP. This approach demands that each local directory contains the names and addresses of all of the users throughout the system.

During 1997, some LAN messaging products began to offer support for the Lightweight Directory Access Protocol (LDAP), an Internet-based DAP. The use of a standard protocol to access directory information means that a user of one vendor's UA/UI program could query the directory that is stored on a different vendor's product via the Internet. In order to search an LDAP directory, the messaging server must be running the LDAP service and the UA/UI must support LDAP queries.

In order to ensure that each copy of the directory contains complete, accurate information, LAN messaging vendors have developed automated processes to update, propagate, and synchronize the information contained in the directories. Typically, this information is transmitted via store-and-forward technology rather than in real time. Despite existence of the automated processes, the maintenance and synchronization of each local directory in a large LAN messaging network continues to be one of the most challenging aspects of mail system administration.

FEATURES OF A LAN MESSAGING SYSTEM

File Sharing vs. Client/Server Architecture

A file sharing-based messaging system stores its messages in a LAN file server. The personal computers on the LAN run the user agent or the message transfer agent processes to perform the work involved in managing the message store, such as sorting, indexing, reorganizing, or verifying internal consistency. The file server performs input, output, and storage functions for the message files just as it would for any other data file, such as a spreadsheet, database, or word-processing document. Otherwise, the file server does none of the processing of the messages; *all of the work is done by the personal computer.*

Because the work of processing the messages is distributed among all of the personal computers, a modest file server can support many simultaneous users. The functionality and performance of the system depends on the power of the users' personal computers. Examples of file sharing-based LAN messaging systems are Lotus cc:Mail v.6, Microsoft Mail v.3, Novell Groupwise v.4, Da Vinci eMail, and CE QuickMail.

In November 1997, there were approximately 40 million users of file sharing-based messaging systems, approximately the same as the year before.[2]

A client/server-based messaging system stores its messages in a messaging server. All of the work involved in managing the message store, such as sorting, indexing, reorganizing, or verifying internal consistency, is performed by the messaging server. The messaging server also performs the functions of the message transfer agent. The personal computers on the LAN run the user agent and make remote procedure calls to the server to send and retrieve messages, but the management of the message store is handled by the messaging server. The communications between the client and the server may utilize propriety protocols such as Messaging Application Programming Interface or Vendor Independent Messaging, or they may utilize Internet protocols (IP) such as Point of Presence or Internet Mail Access Protocol.

Since the work of processing the messages is performed by the messaging server, a powerful messaging server is needed to support many simultaneous users. The functionality and performance of the system depends on the power of the messaging server, not on the users' personal computers. Examples of client/server-based messaging systems are Lotus Notes r.4, Microsoft Exchange, and SoftArc FirstClass v.3.

Although the number of users of file sharing-based messaging systems has remained constant over the past year, the number of users of client/server-based messaging systems has grown considerably. In November 1997, there were approximately 39 million users of client/server-based messaging systems, an increase of 120% over the previous year.[3] The popularity of client/server messaging systems is primarily due to greater scalability and reduced database maintenance requirements for these systems compared to file sharing-based systems.

Message Routing Topology

A typical mainframe-based electronic messaging system needs only a single mainframe computer to support thousands of simultaneous users. As a user sends a message to another user, the message is immediately stored in the recipient's electronic mailbox on the mainframe computer. Typical LANs are capable of supporting a few hundred simultaneous users.

In order to provide electronic messaging services to a large enterprise, a network of multiple LAN file servers or messaging servers must be employed. When a user sends a message to another user on the same server, the message is immediately stored in the recipient's electronic mailbox on the server. When users send messages to users whose mailboxes are located on a different server, the messages are routed between the servers within the network until they reach the electronic "post office" that contains the users' mailbox.

LAN messaging systems typically use either a peer-to-peer topology, a hub-spoke topology, or a combination of the two to route messages between users whose mailboxes are located on different servers.

In peer-to-peer routing (Exhibit 38.3), each post office connects to every other post office to exchange messages. As the number of post offices increases, the number of possible connections grows at a geometric rate. A network of 4 post offices must maintain 12 connection paths, a network of 6 post offices must maintain 30 connection paths, and a network of 10 post offices must maintain 90 connection paths. In a system that utilizes peer-to-peer routing, there is no single point of failure that would disrupt the entire messaging system. However, the multiplicity of routing paths is inefficient for networks that have more than a few (about a half dozen) interconnected sites.

In a hub-spoke configuration (Exhibit 38.4), one message store becomes the hub. Messages between the spokes are routed through the hub, and then on to their final destination. A failure at the hub would prevent messages from being routed throughout the system, so it is essential that redundant measures be taken to minimize hub downtime. A hub-spoke configuration provides an efficient means of routing messages in most situations.

Exhibit 38.5 depicts a combination configuration that uses two hubs. Messages between the spokes are routed through the hub, then on to another spoke or to the other hub, which relays the message to the final destination. Combinations of two, three, or more interconnected hubs provide an efficient method of routing messages between large enterprise wide messaging networks.

Gateways

Messaging gateways transfer messages between dissimilar messaging systems. They must convert the message contents from one vendor's format to the other vendor's format, and they must convert the addressing information from one vendor's format to the other vendor's format. Because of differences among vendors, some of the features of one messag-

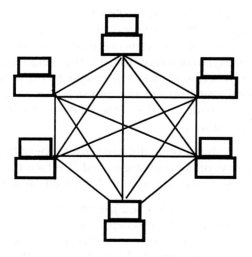

Exhibit 38.3.   Peer-to-peer Routing

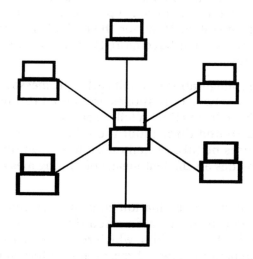

Exhibit 38.4.   Hub-spoke Routing

ing system may not be supported by the other system, and they may be lost in the conversion process.

Application Programming Interfaces (API)

Messages are placed in, and retrieved from, the message store by user agents and message transfer agents. Until recently, the proprietary design

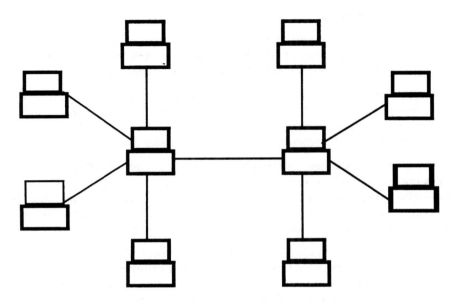

Exhibit 38.5.   Combination Configuration

of a message store prevented access except by user agents and message transfer agents from the same vendor. The development of standards-based messaging API permits user agents and message transfer agents from one vendor to access the message store of another vendor. In addition, the use of standard API permits other applications such as word processors, spreadsheets, and group calendaring programs to become "mail enabled." A mail-enabled application allows the user to send and receive messages from within the enabled application instead of leaving the application, launching the messaging application, and attaching or detaching the information.

Directory Updates and Synchronization

A mainframe-based messaging system needs only a single, centralized mail directory to provide name and address information to thousands of users. In a LAN-based messaging system, each server needs a complete copy of the mail directory with the correct e-mail address for each user. When a user is added anywhere in the network, the user's entry must be propagated to each server in the network.

In order to ensure that each copy of the directory contains complete, accurate information, LAN messaging vendors and third-party developers have produced automated processes to update, propagate, and synchronize the information contained in the directories.

Filters, Rules, Agents

As the volume of e-mail increases, users begin to encounter "information overload." A number of LAN messaging products feature filters, rules, and agents to help users manage the flow of incoming mail.

A *filter* serves as a gatekeeper; it allows messages that meet certain criteria, such as author, subject, or message size, to pass through to a user's mailbox and denies passage for messages that fail to meet that criteria. Filters are typically implemented by message transfer agents.

A *rule* examines a message that has arrived in a user's mailbox, and if the message meets certain predefined criteria, such as author, subject, or contents, the rule takes a predefined action on the message, such as filing the message, forwarding the message, or automatically replying to the message. Rules are typically implemented by a user agent.

An *agent* acts in behalf of a user and may operate on a local or a remote server to act on messages based on predefined criteria, even when a user is not logged in. Agents can also be used to generate messages to alert users upon the occurrence of certain predefined events.

LAN MESSAGING SYSTEM ISSUES, MYTHS, AND REALITIES

Reliability

Mainframe computers are designed with redundant hardware, and the operating systems are designed to be more failure-tolerant than personal computers. Therefore, mainframe-based messaging systems are considered to be more reliable than PC/LAN-based messaging systems. However, recent advances in personal computer technology and operating systems now result in a negligible difference between mainframe and personal computer reliability.

Electronic messaging system failures can be caused by a number of factors: (1) hardware failures, (2) application program failures, (3) communications failures, and (4) database corruption.

The impact of hardware failures in file servers, messaging servers, and personal computers can be reduced by the use of redundant components such as a Redundant Array of Inexpensive Disks, uninterruptible power supplies, and server mirroring (SFT level III). These measures are not inexpensive, but they will result in a level of hardware reliability that is equivalent to mainframe hardware reliability. Even without the use of these redundant components, PC/LAN components typically operate for several years without failure.

Despite extensive testing, applications do crash. The use of multitasking operating systems such as OS/2 and Windows NT reduces the possibility that the failure of one application could cause the crash of another application on the same messaging server or personal computer. When a messaging application fails, the distributed nature of LAN messaging systems limits the impact of a single failure to the local workstation or messaging server, whereas a mainframe application failure could disable the entire messaging system.

The possibility always exists that the communications links could fail. In a mainframe environment, a link failure may prevent users from gaining access to their mailboxes. The store-and-forward characteristics of a distributed PC/LAN messaging system might mean that messages would be delayed until the communications link is restored, but they would not prevent local users from accessing their mailboxes. In addition, typical PC/LAN message transfer agents offer alternative means of forwarding messages to another site, such as X.25, asynchronous dial-up, or TCP/IP.

The possibility of database corruption is greater in a file sharing-based messaging system than in a client/server-based messaging system or a mainframe-based messaging system because there are a greater number of workstations that are simultaneously writing to the message store. A user agent in a client/server or mainframe messaging system makes remote procedure calls to the server, but only the server reads from and writes to the message store. Administrators of PC/LAN-based messaging systems may reduce the possibility of database corruption by performing regular maintenance on the database and can mitigate the impact of corruption by making regular backups of the database.

SCALABILITY

A single LAN serves no more than a few hundred users. In order to meet the needs of a large enterprise, additional LAN sites must be added to the network and messages must be routed between the sites. Although this is not a concern for small networks with only a few sites, this multiplies the amount of effort for planning, coordinating, and managing the messaging system for a large enterprise. Mail administrators are learning that the management of a large enterprise LAN-based messaging network is a "nontrivial" task.[4]

Planning. The purpose of planning a large-scale PC/LAN-based electronic messaging network is to ensure that the messages arrive at their destinations quickly, efficiently, and dependably. Planners must take into consideration the underlying LAN and wide area network (WAN) infrastructure, the location and number of users, and workgroup relationships in determining where to place message stores/messaging servers ("post offices"), and which message routing topology to use to connect them.

Generally, it makes sense to locate a post office on the same LAN segment that the users are on. Ideally, in order to minimize network traffic, the message routing topology should follow the LAN/WAN infrastructure and be based on a hub-spoke topology; however, workgroup relationships must also be considered in determining message routing topology; members of workgroups that belong to the same division or department are more likely to exchange messages with one another, and for efficiency their post offices should be connected to the same hub whenever possible.

Another consideration in the design of a large-scale, distributed messaging system is the availability and deployment of administrative and support staff. Individual sites do not require the services of a full-time mail administrator, and it usually is not cost-effective to provide extensive administrative training for duties that only require a few hours per week. Instead, it is more efficient to provide training to an administrator who will manage and support a number of sites.

Management. As additional sites are added to the network, administrators are faced with two challenges: (1) they must monitor each and every link in the network to ensure that messages are flowing properly and without delay and (2) they must ensure that each local copy of the name and address book is complete and accurate.

One technique to monitoring messaging networks uses Simple Network Management Protocol (SNMP) to ensure that servers, routers, gateways, and workstations are operating properly. The use of SNMP management tools warns an operator that a machine or network component has failed, but it does not ensure that messages are actually flowing through the network in a timely manner. Another approach is to send small test messages from a post office to other post offices, using an echo program to generate a response. If a response does not arrive within a predetermined time, an alert is generated that may be forwarded by e-mail or to the mail administrator's pager. Examples of products that monitor system response are Soft*Switch Mail Monitor, cc:Mail View, and Tally (formerly Baranof) MailCheck.

Today, there is a shortage of tools for ensuring the accuracy and completeness of e-mail directories across a large organization. A few vendors have developed proprietary techniques for propagating and synchronizing directories, but they require careful configuration and monitoring for rejected entries. In a multivendor messaging environment, the problem becomes more complex, as the directories must accommodate address conversion from the format of one messaging system to the format of another system, as well as managing additions, changes, and deletions. The X.500 standard promises to solve the problem of directory access and synchronization, but it has not yet been implemented in PC/LAN messaging systems.

458

Suggested Reading

Blum, Daniel J. and Litwack, David M., The E-Mail Frontier, *Emerging Markets and Evolving Technologies*, Addison-Wesley Publishing, Reading, MA, 1995.

Morris, Larry, *New Riders' Guide to E-Mail and Messaging*, New Riders' Publishing, Indianapolis, IN, 1994.

Robinson, Philip, *Delivering Electronic Mail*, M&T Books, San Mateo, CA, 1992.

Notes

1. Electronic Mail and Messaging Systems, Nov. 17, 1997. Includes the combined total of file sharing-based systems and client/server-based systems.
2. Electronic Mail and Messaging Systems, Nov. 17, 1997.
3. Electronic Mail and Messaging Systems, Nov. 17, 1997.
4. Morris, Larry, *New Riders' Guide to E-Mail and Messaging*, p. 149.

Chapter 39
Choosing and Equipping an Internet Server

Nathan J. Muller

The Internet is a global collection of servers interconnected by routers over various types of carrier-provided lines and services. The Internet comprises databases that have a combined capacity that can only be measured in terabytes — more information than has ever been printed on paper. The Internet is accessed and navigated by PCs and workstations equipped with browser software such as Netscape Communication Corp.'s Navigator and Microsoft Corp.'s Internet Explorer. Private intranets use the same protocols, technologies, and applications found on the public Internet, but they are intended to expand access to corporate information and applications to enhance employee communication and productivity. Intranets are often linked to the public Internet to provide wide-area connectivity between far-flung corporate locations.

As of the end of 1997, there were over 20 million host computers on the Internet, more than 10 times the number of hosts in January 1992. Several studies have produced different estimates of the number of people with Internet access, but the numbers are clearly substantial and growing. Some industry studies peg the number of Internet subscribers in the U. S. at about 40 million. Although the U.S. is still home to the largest proportion of Internet users and generates the most traffic, more than 180 countries are now connected to the Internet. Estimates from numerous sources suggest as many as 200 million people will have access to the Internet by the year 2000. Intranets are experiencing rapid growth as well, with an estimated 25,000 in the U.S. alone.

INTERNET AND INTRANET SERVICES

One of the most popular and fastest growing services on the Internet is the World Wide Web. The Web is a dynamic, interactive, graphically oriented, distributed, platform-independent, hypertext information system. With browser software such as Netscape's Navigator and Microsoft's Internet Explorer, these features make it easy to find and access information published on Web servers, which can be configured for public or private access.

When configured for private access, companies can create virtual private networks or "intranets" to facilitate information exchange among employees, customers, suppliers, and strategic partners.

Of all the applications that can be run on the Web, one of the most promising is electronic commerce. With catalogs displayed on the Web, customers can order products by filling out forms transmitted to the company through e-mail. Often the transactions include buyers' credit card numbers, which calls for a secure means of transmission. Other electronic-commerce applications include online banking and stock trading.

With a Web server, an organization can also leverage the technology for internal communication on an intranet by producing online documentation and other corporate materials, automating sales force activities, providing training on demand, or using data warehousing capabilities to query a legacy database and retrieve the results.

The factor driving these activities is the same in every case: providing users access to information. As companies use the Web to deliver services, they need solutions that are capable of storing, managing, and organizing all of their existing data. Furthermore, these mechanisms need to tie in to existing applications and be reliable, scalable, and open.

Early Web implementations have focused on providing access to static data, mostly in the form of simple text and graphics. As Web-based interactions become more complex, the next step is the creation of real-world applications, which can manipulate, input, modify, analyze, and apply this content to everyday tasks. The need for live, online applications that can manipulate constantly changing data is driving the Web into the next phase of its evolution.

PLATFORM CONSIDERATIONS

The key to delivering such services over the Internet is the server. The Internet is a true client/server network. Integrating into this client/server environment requires servers with strong connectivity capabilities suitable for high-traffic and mission-critical applications. The server must have ease-of-use functionality that allows corporate constituents to access information quickly and easily. The server must have security features that enable constituents to share confidential information or conduct encrypted electronic transactions across the Internet. Finally, the server must be able to support the many applications that have become the staple of the Internet, including e-mail, file transfer, and news groups.

Processor Architecture

A high-performance server is a virtual requirement for any company that is serious about establishing a presence on the Internet. There are basically two choices of processor architectures: reduced instruction set computing (RISC)-based or complex instruction-set computing (CISC)-based. RISC processors are usually used on high-end UNIX servers, while CISC processors, such as Intel Corp.'s Pentium Pro, are used on Windows NT machines. Of note is that the performance of the Pentium Pro now approaches that of many RISC processors and costs less.

Because of the volume of service requests — sometimes tens of thousands a day — the server should be equipped with the most powerful processor available. The more powerful the processor, the greater the number of service requests (i.e., page lookups, database searches, forms processing, etc.) the server will be able to handle at any given time. In addition, if processing-intensive tasks such as encryption, packet filtering, and hostile code screening are to be performed for security purposes, a high-powered server is mandatory — these functions can diminish processor performance by as much as 20%.

SMP Servers

Servers with symmetric multiprocessing (SMP) enable the operating system to distribute different processing jobs among two or more processors. All the CPUs have equal capabilities and can handle the same tasks. Each CPU can run the operating system as well as user applications. Not only can any CPU execute any job, but jobs can be shifted from one CPU to another as the load changes. This can be very important at high-traffic sites, especially those that do a lot of local processing to fulfill service requests.

Some servers come equipped with multiple RISC or CISC processors and often can be upgraded later with additional processors. Users should be aware, however, that the added cost of an SMP server is not merely a few hundred dollars per extra processor. There are costs for additional hardware resources as well — such as extra RAM and storage space — which can add several thousand dollars more to the total purchase price. However, as needs change, SMP servers can be upgraded incrementally without having to buy a new system. In this way, performance can be increased and the original hardware investment protected. This is especially critical in the rapidly evolving Internet market of today in which organizations want to implement new applications or expand access to existing applications on their servers.

Operating System

When choosing a server, the operating system deserves particular attention. The choices are usually between a UNIX variant and Windows NT. Although some vendors offer server software for Windows 3.1 and Windows 95, these are usually intended for casual rather than business use.

The most compelling features of UNIX are its support of multiple tasks, its support of multiple users, its networking capabilities via integral support of Transmission Control Protocol/Internet Protocol (TCP/IP), and its scalability. Although most Internet servers are based on UNIX, Microsoft's Windows NT is growing in popularity, particularly among smaller companies. A Windows NT server offers nearly the performance, reliability, and functionality of a UNIX server and is much easier to set up and administer than a UNIX server. Windows NT also provides integral TCP/IP.

Like UNIX, Windows NT is a multitasking, multithreaded operating system. As such, NT executes software as threads, which are streams of commands that make up applications. At any point during execution, the NT process manager interrupts, or preempts, a thread to let another thread get some CPU time. And like UNIX, Windows NT supports multiple processors. If the server has more than one CPU, NT distributes the threads over the processors, allowing two or more threads to run simultaneously.

Although Windows NT is gaining in power and reliability, it does not scale nearly as well as UNIX on the network. UNIX can scale to hundreds of interconnected servers. Windows NT 4.0 does not scale beyond eight processors, and Windows NT 5.0 increases that number to only 16. Microsoft's NT clustering software is also limited, and multinode clustering that increases scalability through load balancing is not yet available. These may be serious limitations for large companies that may want to tie in all of their sites together over a private intranet.

Fault Tolerance

If the server is supporting mission-critical applications over the Internet or an intranet, there are several levels of fault tolerance that merit consideration. Fault tolerance must be viewed from both the systems and subsystems perspectives.

Site Mirroring. From the systems perspective, fault tolerance can be implemented by linking multiple servers together. When one system fails or must be taken off-line for upgrades or reconfigurations, the standby system is activated to handle the load. This is often called site mirroring. An additional level of protection can be obtained through features of the operating system that protect read and write processes in progress during the switch to the standby system.

Load Balancing. Another means of achieving fault tolerance is to have all hardware components function simultaneously, but with a load-balancing mechanism that reallocates the processing tasks to surviving components when a failure occurs. This technique works best with a UNIX operating system equipped with vendor options that continually monitor the system

464

for errors and dynamically reconfigures the system to adapt to performance problems.

Hot Standby. At the subsystem level, there are several server options that can improve fault tolerance, including ports, network interfaces, memory expansion cards, disk and tape drives, and I/O channels. All must be duplicated so that an alternate hardware component can assume responsibility in the event of a subsystem failure. This procedure is sometimes referred to as a hot-standby solution, whereby a secondary subsystem monitors the tasks of the primary subsystem in preparation for assuming such tasks when needed.

If a component in the primary subsystem fails, the secondary subsystem component takes over without users being aware that a changeover has taken place. An obvious disadvantage of this solution is that companies must purchase twice the amount of hardware needed, and half of this hardware remains idle until called into action when a failure occurs.

Because large amounts of data may be located at the server, the server must be able to implement recovery procedures in the event of a program, operating system, or hardware failure. For example, when a transaction terminates abnormally, the server must have the capability to detect an incomplete transaction so that the database is not left in an inconsistent state. The rollback facility of the server is invoked automatically, which backs out of the partially updated database. The transaction can then be resubmitted by the program or user. A roll-forward facility recovers completed transactions and updates in the event of a disk failure by reading a transaction journal that contains a record of all updates.

Hot Swapping. Hot swapping is an important capability that allows the system administrator or network manager to remove and replace faulty server modules without interrupting or degrading network performance. In some cases, standby modules can be brought online through commands issued at the network management work station, or automatically upon fault detection.

Uninterruptible Power Supply. To guard against an on site power outage, an uninterruptible power supply (UPS) can provide an extra measure of protection. The UPS provides enough standby power to permit continuous operation or an orderly shutdown during power failures or to change over to other power sources such as diesel-powered generators. Some UPS have Simple Network Management Protocol (SNMP) capabilities, which lets network managers monitor battery backup from the central management console. For instance, via SNMP, every UPS can be instructed to test itself once a week and report back the results.

INTERNET APPLICATION SOFTWARE

An Internet server must be equipped with software that enables it to run various applications. Some server software supports general communications for document publishing over the Web. Often called a communications server or Web server, this type of server can be enhanced with software that is specifically designed for secure electronic commerce. Server software is available for performing many different functions, including implementing newsgroups, facilitating message exchange (i.e., e-mail), improving the performance and security of communications, and controlling traffic between the Internet and the corporate network.

Sometimes a server will be dedicated to a single application such as e-mail, newsgroups, or electronic commerce. Other times, the server will support multiple Internet applications, including a firewall. The specific configuration depends on such factors as available system resources (i.e., memory, disk space, processing power, and port capacity), network topology, available bandwidth, traffic patterns, and the security requirements of the organization.

Communications Server

A communications server enables users to access various documents and services that reside on it and retrieve them via the Hypertext Transfer Protocol (HTTP). These servers support the standard multimedia document format — the Hypertext Markup Language (HTML) — for the presentation of rich text, graphics, audio, and video. Hyperlinks connect related information across the network, creating a seamless web. Hyperlinks can also provide access to various services such as e-mail and file transfer and even telephony and videoconferencing. As noted, client software such as Netscape's Navigator and Microsoft's Internet Explorer is used for navigation. Some vendors offer servers preconfigured with all the necessary Internet protocols (IP), allowing them to be quickly put into operation.

A key service performed by any Internet server is the translation of complex IP addresses to simpler server domain names. When a user requests the uniform resource locator (URL) of a certain Web page, for example, the domain name service (DNS) replies with the numeric IP address of the server the user is contacting. It does this by checking a local lookup table that cross-references server domain names and IP addresses.

For example, consider the domain name ddx, which might stand for "dynamic data exchange." This domain name might translate into the IP address 204.177.193.22. The translation capability of the DNS makes it easy for users to access Internet resources by not requiring them to learn and enter long strings of numbers. To access the Web page of Dynamic Data

Exchange, the user would enter the URL as http://www.ddx.com, which contains the domain name ddx.

If the local server does not know the IP address that corresponds with the domain name, it directs the request to a top-level DNS server, which then sends the request down the DNS hierarchy of the Internet. Once an authoritative DNS server for the domain and machine is found, the response is sent to the request originator. With this information, the client can then access the resource having that name. The whole process takes only a few seconds. Corporations use a similar system on their private intranets.

Commerce Server

A commerce server is used for conducting secure electronic commerce and communications on the Internet. It permits companies to publish hypermedia product catalogs formatted in HTML and provides connections to back-end databases and other supporting applications. There are many tool kits available to help companies create and maintain electronic commerce applications, including Web-enabling traditional Electronic Data Interchange applications. To ensure the privacy of sensitive data, the commerce server should provide advanced security features, which are available through the use of the Secure Sockets Layer (SSL) protocol or Secure HTTP (S-HTTP), among others.

SSL was developed by Netscape to provide information privacy over the Internet, preventing eavesdropping, tampering, or message forgery. SSL is under consideration by the Internet Engineering Task Force (IETF) as an official Internet standard, although many vendors, including Netscape, already support it in their products. SSL provides the following:

- Server authentication: Any SSL-compatible client can verify the identity of the sender using a certificate and a digital signature.
- Data encryption: The privacy of client/server communications is ensured by encrypting the data stream between the two entities.
- Data integrity: SSL verifies that the contents of a message arrive at their destination in the same form as they were sent.

An alternative to SSL is S-HTTP, an extension to the HTTP that provides a variety of security services, as appropriate for the application. SSL operates at the transport layer, while S-HTTP operates at the application layer. Encryption of the transport layer allows SSL to be application-independent, and S-HTTP is limited to the specific software implementing it.

S-HTTP provides confidentiality, authenticity, integrity, and nonrepudiation. The protocol emphasizes flexibility in the choice of key management mechanisms, security policies, and cryptographic algorithms by supporting option negotiation between parties for each transaction. In addition, the two protocols adopt different philosophies towards encryption, with SSL encrypting the entire communications channel and S-HTTP encrypting each message independently. S-HTTP allows a user to produce digital signatures on any message, not just specific messages during authentication, a feature SSL lacks.

There are other security protocols used in electronic commerce. One of them is Secure Electronic Transaction (SET) jointly developed by Visa International and MasterCard International Inc., with participation from leading technology companies, including Microsoft, IBM, Netscape, and RSA. The SET protocol enables consumers to securely use their credit card over the Internet without fear of another party intercepting, monitoring, or changing the transactions. The protocol secures online credit card payments involving the buyer, merchant, and bank — all of which must use the SET protocol to protect the transaction.

As with other types of Internet servers, vendors offer commerce servers that are preconfigured with the protocols necessary to support electronic commerce.

News Server

A news server lets users create secure, public and private discussion groups for access over the Internet and other TCP/IP-based networks via the standard Network News Transport Protocol (NNTP). Support of NNTP by the news server enables it to accept feeds from the popular Usenet news groups and allows the creation and maintenance of private discussion groups. Most news readers are based on NNTP and some support SSL for secure communication between clients and news servers.

A news server should support the Multipurpose Internet Mail Extension (MIME), which enables users to send virtually any type of data across the Internet. Seven basic MIME types have been defined: text, image, audio, video, application, message, and multipart. Each type has several subtypes defined: text/plain and text/html are two examples of text subtypes. MIME also provides definitions to allow character sets other than US-ASCII to be encoded as part of the header text fields or the message body. For example, MIME allows multibyte character sets needed to represent some Asian languages.

Attaching documents in a variety of formats greatly expands the capability of a discussion group to serve as a repository of information and knowledge to support workgroup collaboration. This allows colleagues, for example, to download documents sent to the group, mark them up, and send them back.

Mail Software

Client/server messaging systems are implemented by special mail software installed on a server. In essence, this software enables users to easily exchange information within a company as well as across the Internet. Mail software has many features that can be controlled by either the system administrator or each user with an e-mail account.

The mail software should conform to open standards, including HTTP, MIME, Simple Mail Transfer Protocol (SMTP), and Post Office Protocol/Internet Message Access Protocol (POP/IMAP). As noted, MIME enables organizations to send and receive messages with rich content types, thereby allowing businesses to transmit mission-critical information of any type without loss of fidelity. Secure MIME (S/MIME) is an emerging IETF standard that enables users of Web messaging clients to send encrypted messages and authenticate received messages. S/MIME offers the following basic features:

- Encryption for message privacy.
- Sender authentication with digital signatures.
- Tamper detection through a secure hashing function.
- Interoperability with other S/MIME-compliant software.
- Seamless integration into the messaging application.
- Cross-platform messaging.

S/MIME encryption helps ensure that messages remain private. S/MIME authenticates the message sender by reading the sender's digital signature. Within an S/MIME-compliant mail application the recipient can see who signed the message and view the certificate for additional detail.

The SMTP is used for sending mail from the client to the server and moving it among other servers on the Internet. SMTP ensures interoperability with other client/server messaging systems that support Internet mail or proprietary messaging systems with Internet mail gateways.

The POP is a simple store-and-forward delivery mechanism used for retrieving new mail from a UNIX server. A newer mail protocol — the IMAP — establishes a client/server relationship that allows the server to be used not only for storing incoming mail, but also for filtering it before download to the client. IMAP gives users more choices about what categories of messages to fetch from the server, where to store mail, and what the server should do with specific categories of read messages.

Proxy Server

To improve the performance and security of communications across the TCP/IP-based Internet, many organizations use a proxy server. This kind of server offers performance improvements by using an intelligent cache for storing retrieved documents.

The disk-based caching feature of the proxy minimizes use of the external network by eliminating recurrent retrievals of commonly accessed documents. This feature provides additional "virtual bandwidth" to existing network resources and significantly improves interactive response time for locally attached clients. The resulting performance improvements provide a cost-effective alternative to purchasing additional network bandwidth. Because the cache is disk-based, it can be tuned to provide optimal performance based on network usage patterns.

The proxy server should allow dynamic process management, which allows the creation of a configurable number of processes that reside in memory, waiting to fulfill HTTP requests. This feature improves system performance by eliminating the unnecessary overhead of creating and deleting processes to fulfill every HTTP request. The dynamic process management algorithm increases the number of server processes, within configurable limits, to efficiently handle periods of peak demand, resulting in faster document serving, greater throughput delivery, and better system reliability.

Some proxy servers incorporate some of the features of firewalls. For example, proxy servers can provide protection against IP spoofing, a method of attack in which an intruder spoofs or imitates the IP address of an internal computer to either send data as if he were on the internal network or to receive data intended for the machine being spoofed. The proxy server guards against this type of attack by preventing any IP packets with destination addresses not found in its local address table from entering through the Internet.

Firewall Software

A firewall acts as a security wall and gateway between a trusted internal network and such untrustworthy networks as the Internet. Access can be controlled by individuals or groups of users, or by system names, domains, subnets, date, time, protocol, and service.

Some firewalls offer real-time, automated intrusion detection to stop unauthorized activities immediately, even if the network manager is not around to intervene. With such tools, network intrusions are detected and appropriate responses are taken automatically before they can cause serious damage. Among the responses that can be implemented automatically are port reconfiguration and service denial.

Vendors of firewalls (and proxy servers) are incorporating third-party virus and applet scanning functionality into their products. The scanning software loads the suspect code into a protective buffer and compares it with a library of known viruses and hostile Java applets and ActiveX components. If a match or near match is found, the user can eliminate the code

470

before it is allowed to run. If the initial scan does not identify the code as hostile, it continues as usual. While the code runs, it is monitored for suspicious repetitive actions such as opening windows, deleting multiple files, and reallocating memory. If such behaviors are identified, the program is shut down to prevent system damage. E-mail can be scanned in the same way to identify potentially harmful code.

Firewall security is bidirectional, simultaneously prohibiting unauthorized users from accessing the corporate network while also managing internal users' Internet access privileges. Some firewalls even periodically check their own code to prevent modification by sophisticated intruders.

The firewall gathers and logs information about where attempted break-ins originate, how they got there, and what the people responsible for them appear to be doing. Log entries include information on connection attempts, service types, users, file transfer names and sizes, connection duration, and trace routes. Together, this information leaves an electronic footprint that can help identify intruders.

WEB DATABASE CONSIDERATIONS

Internet servers are the repositories of various databases. These databases may be set up for public access or for restricted intracompany access. In either case, the challenge of maintaining the information is becoming apparent to information systems professionals charged with keeping this information accurate and up to date.

Vendors are coming up with ways to ease the maintenance burden. For example, database management vendors such as Oracle Corp. offer ways of integrating an existing data warehouse with the Internet without having to reformat the data into HTML. The data is not sent until a request is received and validated.

In addition, the server supports HTTP-type negotiation, enabling it to deliver different versions of the same object (e.g., an image stored in multiple formats) according to the preferences of each client. The server also supports national language negotiation, allowing the same document in different translations to be delivered to different clients.

The database server should support the two common authentication mechanisms: basic and digest authentication. Both mechanisms allow certain directories to be protected by user name/password combinations. However, digest authentication transmits encrypted passwords, and basic authentication does not. Other security extensions that may be bundled with database servers include S-HTTP and SSL standards, which are particularly important in supporting electronic commerce applications.

471

Maintenance and Testing Tools

The maintenance of most Web databases still relies upon the diligence of each document owner or site administrator to periodically check for integrity; that is, test for broken links, malformed documents, and outdated information. Database integrity is typically tested by visually scanning each document and manually activating every hypertext link. Particular attention is given to links that reference other Web sites because they are usually controlled by a third party, who can change the location of files to a different server or directory or delete them entirely.

Link Analyzers. Link analyzers are used to examine a collection of documents and validate the links for accessibility, completeness, and consistency. However, this type of integrity check tends to be applied more as a means of one-time verification than as a regular maintenance process. This check also fails to provide adequate support across distributed databases and for situations in which the document contents are outside the immediate span of control.

Log Files. Some types of errors can be identified by the log files on the server. The server records each document request and, if an error occurred, the nature of that error. Such information can be used to identify requests for documents that have moved and those that have misspelled URLs, which are used to identify the location of documents on the Internet. Only the server manager usually has access to that information, however. The error is almost never relayed to the person charged with document maintenance, either because it is not recognized as a document error or because the origin of the error is not apparent from the error message.

Even with better procedures, log files often do not reveal failed requests that never made it to the server, nor do they always support preventive maintenance and problems associated with changed document content. With a large and growing database, manual maintenance methods become difficult and may eventually become impossible.

Design Tools. New design tools are available that address the maintenance and testing issue by providing the means to visualize the creation, maintenance, and navigation of whole collections of online documents. Where traditional Web tools such as browsers and HTML editors focus on the Web page, these tools address the Web site, which may be either physical or logical in structure. These tools include a system to identify which pages will be included in the site, and another to describe how the pages are interconnected. The construction of a site is facilitated by providing templates for creating pages and scripts and linkage to tools for editing and verifying HTML documents.

In addition to offering high-level views of a site — either graphical or hierarchical — the design tools check for stale links (either local or remote), validate the conformance level of HTML pages, and make broad structural changes to the site architecture by using a mouse to drag and drop sections of the Web hierarchy into a different location.

Agents or Robots. Although design tools address document creation and maintenance at the site level, they do not comprehensively address the maintenance needs of distributed hypertext infrastructures that span multiple Web sites. This can be handled by special software, known as agents or robots. These programs can be given a list of instructions about what databases to traverse, whom to notify for problems, and where to put the resulting maintenance information.

For example, the agent or robot may be tasked to provide the following types of information that typically indicate document changes:

- A referenced object has a redirected URL (i.e., a document has been moved to another location).
- A referenced object cannot be accessed (i.e., there is a broken or improperly configured link).
- A referenced object has a recently modified date (i.e., the contents of a document have changed).
- An owned object has an upcoming expiration date (i.e., a document may be removed or changed soon).

To get its instructions, the agent or robot reads a text file containing a list of options and tasks to be performed. Each task describes a specific hypertext infrastructure to be encompassed by the traversal process. A task instruction includes the traversal type, an infrastructure name (for later reference), the "top URL" at which to start traversing, the location for placing the indexed output, an e-mail address that corresponds to the owner of that infrastructure, and a set of options that determine what identified maintenance issues justify sending an e-mail message.

Common Gateway Interface

At a minimum, an Internet server should support the Common Gateway Interface (CGI). This is a standard for interfacing external applications with information servers, such as HTTP or Web servers. Gateway programs handle information requests and return the appropriate document or generate a document on the fly. With CGI, a Web server can serve information that is not in a form readable by the client (such as an SQL database), and act as a gateway between the two to produce something which clients can interpret and display.

Gateways can be used for a variety of purposes, the most common being the processing of form requests, such as database queries or online purchase orders.

Gateways conforming to the CGI specification can be written in any language that produces an executable file, such as C and C++. Among the more popular languages for developing CGI scripts is Practical Extraction and Report Language (PERL) and Tool Command Language (TCL), both derivatives of the C language.

A key advantage of using PERL and TCL is that they can be used to speed the construction of applications to which new scripts and script components can be added without requiring recompiling and restarting, as is required when the C language is used. Of course, the server on which the CGI scripts reside must have a copy of the program itself — PERL, TCL, or alternative program.

Increasingly, Java applets are being used to provide the interface between the Web server and back-end databases and applications. The use of Java overcomes the limitations of other languages. With a CGI program implemented in PERL, for example, there are two sources of bottlenecks. First, a process in which to run the PERL interpreter must be launched, which in turn runs the PERL program. Creating such a process once a minute is not a problem, but creating it several times a second is a major problem. Second, it takes time for the PERL program to send back the information it generates as output. Waiting for a small PERL script that does something simple such as send the contents of an HTML form via e-mail is not a problem, but waiting for a large script that does something more complicated such as allowing customers to access account information stored on a mainframe and execute financial transactions definitely is a problem.

Java application code is downloaded from server to client on demand. Java differs from the traditional CGI approach in that the applets, once downloaded, can link directly with a database server on the Internet. The applets do not need a Web server as an intermediary and, consequently, do not degrade performance. In most cases, the applications are stored in cache on a hard disk at the client location, and in others they are stored in cache memory. Either way, the application does not take up permanent residence on the client machine. Because applications are delivered to the client only as needed, administration is done at the server, assuring that users have access to the latest application release level.

CONCLUSION

The client/server architecture of the Internet and its use of open protocols for information formatting and delivery make it possible for any connected computer to provide services to any other computer. With this capability, businesses can extend communications beyond organizational boundaries and serve the informational needs of all users.

The type of services that are available is dependent upon the application software that runs on one or more servers, as well as the access privileges of each user. A server may be dedicated to a specific Internet application or multiple applications, depending on such factors as system resources and the specific needs of the organization. A careful evaluation of the hardware platform, operating system, and application software in terms of features and conformance to Internet standards ensures that the current and emerging needs of the organization and its users are met in an efficient, economical, and secure manner.

Chapter 40
Networking Features of the Java Programming Language

John P. Slone

Throughout the brief history of computer science, many programming languages have been developed. It could be argued that most have been short-lived, having little or no impact on the computer science discipline, while relatively few have profoundly affected the discipline, often surviving well beyond even the most optimistic estimations. Languages in this latter group share one significant trait: They were all purposefully designed within the context of their target environment.

For some examples consider the following. Fortran, developed in the 1950s, was purposefully designed within the context of scientific computing. The mere fact of its continued popularity among scientific programmers some four decades later is sufficient testimony to how well the designers of Fortran met their objectives. Similarly, Cobol was developed shortly thereafter with purposeful intent to address the needs of the mainframe-based business-computing environment. The dominance of Cobol in this environment is undisputed. One could just as successfully argue that C was purposefully designed to provide assembler-level capabilities in a multiplatform environment. That C was the language of choice for most early implementations of the protocols that made the Internet possible speaks volumes in this regard.

Against this backdrop, we find a new language called Java. Will Java be one of the many short-lived, low-impact languages, or will it be one of the few languages that makes a lasting impact? To answer this question, it makes sense to examine Java within the context of its targeted environment, and to assess whether or not its designers purposefully considered that environment when designing the language. The remainder of this paper will focus on one rather narrowly defined aspect of such an inquiry.

JAVA'S TARGET ENVIRONMENT

Java is the first language of significance to be developed in what could be called the "Post-Internet Revolution" environment. Although the Internet had been under development for several decades, the advent of the World Wide Web in the early to mid-1990s sparked an explosion of growth of the Internet that could only be characterized as a revolution. Consequently, the Internet became a household word and a mainstay of business computing. Industry analysts project the number of Internet-connected computers to exceed 100 million in the very near future. Among those 100 million computers, one finds a variety of computing platforms, ranging from microprocessors costing a few hundred dollars to highly specialized mainframe or supercomputers costing millions. At the low end of the cost spectrum, hardware generation life cycles are measured in months.

For languages developed prior to Java, networking was a specialty area, and the technology of networking was typically handled outside the language itself, such as through system calls. For Java, networking is a fundamental assumption, handled within the language itself. In the next section, we examine some basic concepts related to networking in this environment. In the sections that follow, we examine several networking mechanisms built into Java for the purpose of exploiting this environment.

NETWORKING BASICS

In today's era of enterprise local area networks (LAN), the predominant networking architecture is the layered architecture developed for the Internet depicted in Exhibit 40.1. This architecture provides an abstract view of networking, arranging functions according to purpose and providing a clean interface between applications software and the complexities of the network itself.

Briefly working our way from the bottom, we find these basic functions provided by each layer:

Layer 1 — Physical

This layer is where the actual transmission of data takes place. Specifications for this layer address such things as the type of communication medium (such as copper wire, optical fiber, or radio waves), signal modulation, and bitwise encoding. This layer is almost always implemented in hardware and is of no concern to the application developer.

Layer 2 — Data Link

This layer ensures that transmitted data is actually delivered across the physical medium. Typical functions include error checking and retransmission requests as needed to ensure successful delivery. In a

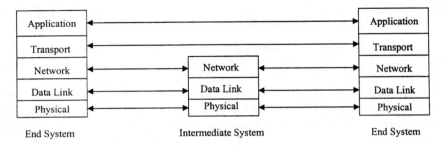

Exhibit 40.1. Layered Communications Model of the Internet

LAN environment, this layer is often used to implement forwarding of data packets between LAN segments. This layer is also typically integrated in hardware and is of no concern to the application developer.

Layer 3 — Network

The primary purpose of this layer is routing. Given the size and complexity of networks such as the Internet and LAN-based enterprise networks, protocols at this layer have been developed to handle the routing of data packets as needed to deliver data from the originating end system, through an indeterminate number of intermediate systems, and ultimately to the destination end system or systems. The most commonly known protocol at this layer is the Internet Protocol, or simply the "IP" part of TCP/IP. Protocols at this layer are implemented in a combination of hardware and software.

The only aspect of this layer that is of concern to the application developer is the IP address. The IP address is a 32-bit number, more commonly expressed in a "dotted numeric" notation such as "204.5.208.18" where each of the four numbers represents the value contained in one of the four bytes of the IP address. The IP address is analogous to a telephone number; each system has a globally unique IP address, which, when provided to the network layer, is sufficient to ensure that packets are correctly routed to the intended end system.

Layer 4 — Transport

This layer is responsible for the end-to-end delivery of data between end systems. This layer provides two fundamental services: connection-oriented and connectionless. The most common service is the connection-oriented service provided by the transmission control protocol (TCP). TCP provides for reliable delivery by maintaining a connection between the end points and by ensuring that all packets are transmitted without error and

479

in the proper sequence. When the systems are through exchanging data, the connection is torn down at the request of either end.

A less commonly known service is the connectionless service provided by the user datagram protocol (UDP). UDP provides an unreliable delivery mechanism by simply sending a packet toward the intended destination, without taking any steps to ensure successful delivery. Although this concept may seem strange at first, it actually serves a very useful purpose. The classic example is that of time synchronization. If a packet is dropped, it is more important for the next packet to get delivered than it is for the systems to take the time needed to retransmit the missing one, thus throwing the time synchronization system out of sync.

Both of these services provide the primary interface between the application and the network. From the network perspective, the interface is known as a "port." A port is essentially a 16-bit extension to the IP address. It can be thought of as providing a capability similar to that of a telephone extension. That is, while a telephone number will successfully deliver a call to a business location, an extension may need to be specified to reach the intended party. In the same fashion, the IP address will deliver the packet to the end system, but the port must be specified to reach the intended application.

From the perspective of the application, this same point of interface is viewed as a socket. A socket is an abstraction that behaves similarly to other input-output abstractions such as files or printers. A socket is made available for use by the application by binding it to an available port. The application then transmits data across the network by writing to a socket, and it receives data from the network by reading from the socket. This notion of sockets and ports is depicted in Exhibit 40.2.

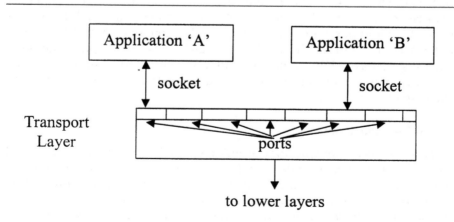

Exhibit 40.2. Socket-and-Port Transmission of Data

Layer 7 — Application

Programmers can effectively utilize network capabilities without being concerned with the application layer. However, a number of standardized network-enabled applications have been written, providing a level of network abstraction significantly higher than that of the socket. Perhaps the most familiar of such applications is the Web, which provides a high-level network abstraction known as the Hypertext Transport Protocol (HTTP). This protocol, along with other familiar protocols such as file transfer protocol (FTP), Gopher, and Telnet, is considered a Layer 7 protocol. Programmers taking advantage of these protocols can accomplish network programming tasks without being concerned with lower level details such as binding a socket to a port, opening a connection, reading from or writing to the socket, and ultimately closing the connection and unbinding the port. All this is accomplished by the Layer 7 protocol.

The Internet model is rooted historically in the Open Systems Interconnection (OSI) Basic Reference Model. In the OSI model, Layers 5 and 6 are used for "session" and "presentation," respectively, with Layer 7 defining the "application" layer. Although the Internet networking model does not generally use these two layers, the layer number designators have survived.

JAVA NETWORKING PRIMITIVES

With this application-oriented background on networking concepts, we can now discuss Java networking features within the context of these concepts. In this section, we will discuss Java networking primitives that enable the programmer to develop applications that interact directly with Layer 4. These primitives are found within the java.net package.

Connection-Oriented Networking

Connection-oriented networking employs a paradigm analogous to the telephone network. First, a connection is established between two parties. Once established, communications take place by having each party send and listen as needed. Once finished, the connection is broken. As discussed above, rather than using a telephone, each party "speaks" into and "listens" from a socket.

As with practically everything else in Java, the concept of a socket is provided as a class, thus sockets are treated just like any other object in the language. For connection-oriented networking, there are actually two classes of socket objects in Java: "Socket," which implements client sockets, and "ServerSocket," which implements server sockets. The distinction is needed to provide server applications with the processing capability of listening for and accepting connection requests from clients. Both are subclasses of SocketImpl, which is where most of the low-level methods and variables are defined. The two subclasses hide many of these details from the programmer. For example, among the constructors for the client-side socket are the following:

- Socket (InetAddress, int) — Creates a socket and connects it to the specified port on the host at the specified IP address. With this one simple constructor, the program will actually create a socket, bind it to a local port, issue a connection request to the remote IP address/port combination, and wait for an acknowledgment.
- Socket (String, int) — Creates a socket and connects it to the specified port on the host named in String. In addition to everything in the previous constructor, this one also resolves the name of the remote host specified in String to find its IP address prior to issuing the connection request.

Constructors on the server side include the following:

- ServerSocket (int) — Creates a server socket and binds it to the specified port on the local host.
- ServerSocket (int, int) — Same as above, but it allows the programmer to specify the maximum allowable backlog of pending requests.
- ServerSocket (int, int, InetAddress) – Same as the previous constructor, but it allows the programmer to specify which network interface on multi-homed machines (e.g., machines sitting on firewalls).

Similarly powerful methods are available for these classes, including fairly high-level methods such as getInputStream and getOutputStream, as well as lower-level methods such as getInetAddress, getPort, and setTcpNoDelay. Thus, between the constructors and methods, the Socket and ServerSocket classes provide programmers with a fairly powerful assortment of tools for developing networked applications.

Connectionless Networking

In contrast to connection-oriented networking, connectionless networking is accomplished by sending independent packets between the parties involved. Rather than having the notion of a connection, which is established at the beginning of the exchange and torn down following the exchange, each individual packet, called a datagram, must be provided with the necessary addressing information. This paradigm is closer to that of the postal system, in which a letter, complete with destination and return addresses, is dropped in the nearest mailbox and routed individually to its destination.

Java provides a separate type of socket class for this purpose: the DatagramSocket. In this case, there is no distinction between a server socket and a client socket, since datagrams are sent and received outside the context of a connection. Fundamentally a simpler concept, the DatagramSocket has only three constructors:

- DatagramSocket ( ) — This constructor creates a socket and binds it to any available port on the local machine.
- DatagramSocket (int) — This constructor creates a socket and binds it to the specified port on the local machine.
- DatagramSocket (int, InetAddress) — This constructor creates a socket and binds it to the specified port/interface combination on the local machine.

Note that this class of socket is associated only with the local machine. Since there is no notion of a connection, there is no association with a remote machine.

Once a datagram socket object has been created, the programmer may invoke one of several methods. Of most importance are "send" and "receive," used to send or receive datagrams, respectively. Datagrams are implemented as a separate class, known as a DatagramPacket. This class has two constructors:

- DatagramPacket (byte[ ], int) — Used to create a datagram packet for receiving datagrams of length int.
- DatagramPacket (byte[ ], int, InetAddress, int) — Used to create a datagram packet for sending packets of length int to the address and port specified.

DatagramPacket methods are provided to get or set the address, port, data, or length of the datagram as needed.

Multicast Connectionless Networking

Connectionless networking can also be accomplished among multiple parties, as opposed to the limited notion of point-to-point networking. Java provides a MulticastSocket class for this purpose as a subclass of DatagramSocket. Of particular interest are the methods joinGroup and leaveGroup, which allow the system to join and leave a particular multicast group, and the methods getTTL and setTTL, which handle the time-to-live attribute of the datagram.

HIGH-LEVEL JAVA NETWORKING ABSTRACTIONS

Up to this point, the discussion has been limited to fairly low-level networking concepts, focussed at the transport layer service interface, the socket. Although extremely powerful when compared with the networking features of most other languages, these features are little more than primitives within the context of Java networking features. The remainder of this chapter focuses on several of the higher-level networking concepts provided in Java.

URL-based programming

The first such concept discussed is that of uniform resource locator (URL)-based programming, a concept also supported within the java.net package. In general terms, URL-based programming allows the programmer to focus on the concepts associated with actually handling a remote object, rather than on all the lower-level mechanisms involved in creating a socket and binding it to a port, establishing a connection to the object machine, locating the object, and retrieving information from and/or sending information to the object. How this is accomplished should become clearer in the following paragraphs.

The fundamental class provided for this purpose is the URL. This class, uses a standard notation for representing a resource on the network. Popularized by the Web, the basic URL provides four primary components: a protocol identifier (such as http, ftp, or gopher), a machine name (such as www.yahoo.com), a port number (if not specified, a default port is assumed), and a file name (including the path to the file). The file name component can also optionally contain an internal reference to a specific named label within the file. The Java URL class provides four constructors to allow flexibility in the way a URL object is created:

- URL (String) — Allows the creation of a URL object by specifying a complete, familiar URL specification such as "http://www.yahoo.com/"
- URL (String, String, int, String) — Allows the creation of a URL object by separately specifying the protocol, host name, port, and file name.
- URL (String, String, String) — Same as the previous constructor, except that the default port is assumed.
- URL (URL, String) — Allows the creation of a URL by specifying its path relative to an existing URL object.

Once the URL object has been created, Java provides a number of low-level methods, such as those that parse the URL and return specific elements, as well as several high-level methods, providing powerful capabilities to the programmer. Examples of high-level methods include getContent, which returns the entire content of the specified URL with a single line of code. Other high-level methods include openStream, which creates a connection to the URL and opens an input stream for subsequent reading of the contents, and openConnection, which creates a connection to the URL and opens a bidirectional stream for subsequent writing to or reading from the URL. This latter method is especially important for interacting with Web-enabled applications, such as those implementing the Common Gateway Interface (CGI).

As implied by the previous paragraph, there is a concept of a URL connection, a concept that is also provided as a class known as a URLConnection. Once a URLConnection object has been created, the programmer has nearly 40 methods at his disposal for handling the connection. Among the capabilities provided by these methods are those of reading selected header fields, testing to see whether or not the URL accepts input, whether or not the URL is cached, when it was last modified, or when it expires. These methods are in addition to the methods for obvious concepts such as reading and writing.

Remote Method Invocation (RMI)

As discussed above, URL-based programming allows the Java programmer to interact at a high level with primarily non-Java resources on the network. RMI provides the Java programmer with the capability of developing truly distributed, yet fully cooperative Java-only applications. These cooperating Java components can be peer applications, client and server applications, or client applets interacting with server applications. Compared with URL-based programming, RMI allows an order of magnitude increase in the degrees of complexity and sophistication of the resulting networked applications.

To achieve this level of sophistication, it is necessary to grasp concepts that go beyond the simple definition of classes and methods, although numerous classes are defined in the java.rmi family of packages. Instead, the exploitation of RMI requires a paradigm shift in the way one thinks about network-based programming. At a very high level, RMI requires the development of two components: a Java object that implements a method through a remote interface, and a Java object that remotely invokes that method. These two objects may be on the same machine or on different machines. Conceptually, all that is necessary to make this happen is for the calling object to obtain a valid reference to the called method in the form of a specially constructed URL. In most cases, the object reference is obtained either as a parameter or as the value returned by a method. The first such reference is typically obtained from an RMI remote object registry. For clarity of discussion, the remainder of this section will assume that the object that implements the remote method is a server application, and that the object requesting the remote invocation is an applet.

Looking first at the server, the necessary ingredients are the definition of a remote interface, the definition of constructors for the remote object, and the definition of methods that can be invoked remotely. In addition, there are security requirements, but treatment of security is beyond the scope of this chapter. Finally, at least one of the remote objects must be registered in the RMI remote object registry on the server machine. At execution time, the constructor for the remote object creates an instance of the object and "exports" the object by having it listen to a socket for incoming calls.

Turning our attention to the applet side, we see that the calling object calls the remote method very much as it would any other method. However,

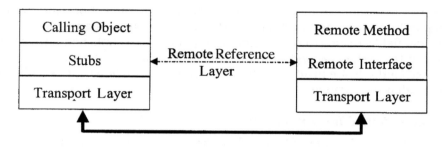

Exhibit 40.3. RMI Architecture

instead of containing a reference to the actual remote object, it contains a reference to a locally implemented stub representing the remote object interface. The stubs are generated through the use of a special compiler tool called "rmic." Thus, the actual remote method invocation is abstracted in a way that isolates the programmer from the details.

The invocation and all the necessary semantics are actually handled by the remote reference layer, and take place as follows. First, the applet calls a method making reference to a locally held stub. The stub then places the appropriate remote call, across the network if necessary, to its counterpart remote interface on the server side. That interface in turn invokes a method on the server side and passes the resulting return value back through the interface, across the network to the applet stub code, and on to the calling object. This interaction is depicted in Exhibit 40.3.

Thus it is shown that RMI provides the Java programmer with an extremely powerful set of networking capabilities. As with other high-level networking features of the Java language, RMI allows the programmer to focus on the essentials of writing and invoking methods that accomplish a certain task, while ignoring the details of the underlying network.

Java Naming and Directory Interface (JNDI)

The two high-level networking features of the Java language discussed thus far, URL-based programming and RMI, have one thing in common other than the simple fact that they facilitate the development of networked applications. Specifically, both involve the notion of binding a name to a network-based resource. With URL-based programming, this resource is either a file or a stream-based interface to an application. With RMI, the resource is a method in some remote object. Broadening our perspective to yet another dimension, we find that network programming for any purpose will inevitably involve the binding of names to resources.

At the broadest possible level, network-accessible resources can be any type of object. For example, in addition to files, stream interfaces, and methods, other valid resources could include printers, calendars, electronic mailboxes, telephones, pagers, humans, conference rooms, control valves, remote sensors, or practically anything else, limited only by the imagination. To expand programming to this broad horizon, the concept of a generalized directory is needed. In the broadest sense, a directory can be thought of as a system that provides a mapping between the name of an object and one or more attributes that describe the object.

In practice, there are multiple directories in existence in the networking environment of today. For example, the Internet Domain Name Service (DNS) is the directory that maps machine names (such as www.yahoo.com) to IP addresses (such as 204.71.200.74). Other directories, such as X.500, Lightweight Directory Access Protocol (LDAP), Network Information Services, and Novell Directory Services, provide mapping between objects named in other name spaces and their attributes. Further complicating the situation, certain objects are actually identified by compound names — those names that exist in multiple, disjoint name spaces. URLs are a prime example, since part of the URL names the machine (named in the DNS name space), and part of it names the file (named within the name space managed by the particular machine).

To provide the simplest abstraction for programmers, what is needed is a mechanism that allows objects to be identified to programs by their compound names (such as a URL), while hiding the complexities of the underlying directory structures. This is precisely the objective of the JNDI.

JNDI is implemented in three standard Java extension packages: javax.naming, javax.naming.directory, and javax.naming.spi. The first two packages comprise the JNDI Application Programming Interface (API), giving application programmers a suite of powerful classes and methods for handling object names and for interacting with the directory services. The third package makes up what is referred to as the JNDI Service Provider Interface (SPI). Conceptually, a Java application accesses the JNDI Implementation Manager through the JNDI API, while a variety of naming and directory services sit transparently behind the JNDI Implementation Manager, plugged in through the JNDI SPI. This concept is depicted in Exhibit 40.4.

Of particular interest for this chapter is the naming and directory service shown in the lower left portion of Exhibit 40.4, RMI. As shown, the RMI object registry becomes a part of a substantially larger naming and directory service and is implemented through the same classes and methods used for other network-based resources. In this manner, the entire world of network-accessible resources is placed literally at the fingertips of the Java programmer.

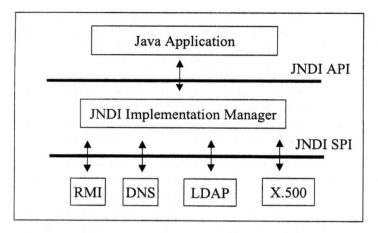

Exhibit 40.4.   JNDI Architecture

CONCLUSION

This chapter has barely begun to scratch the surface of network features built into the Java programming language. Many powerful features, including those discussed in this chapter along with many more, are built into the core Java packages; others are implemented as extensions. Through these features, Java provides programmers with the ability to write programs that implement networking concepts along a wide spectrum of abstraction levels, ranging from socket-level primitives to remotely accessing objects of any type by merely knowing the name of the object. By building upon the object-oriented nature of Java, higher and higher levels of abstraction are readily accommodated.

In the opening paragraphs of this chapter, it was suggested that the ultimate success of Java as a language would depend to an extent on how purposeful the designers were with respect to designing the language in the context of its target environment. If one considers the single aspect of "networking" as only a fundamental component of the Java target environment, one can only conclude that Java is set to profoundly impact the computer science discipline in the years to come. As such, IT managers are well advised to assess the potential role of Java in their own environments and to encourage and promote the development of Java expertise among their staffs.

Chapter 41
Java's Role in Distributed Computing

J.P. Morgenthal

Although Java is rapidly becoming the premier tool for building Internet applications, the fact that seemingly simple Internet applications, such as Web browsers, are actually distributed applications is often overlooked. Internet applications carry with them all the complexities associated with any distributed environment, although the severity of problems is admittedly lighter.

The term distributed applications encompasses many technologies and development techniques, and a clear definition of it remains elusive. For clarity, a distributed application is one in which two or more components are cooperatively operating over a process boundary. The process boundary introduces the need for concurrency and shared memory. Concurrency represents the capability to share resources in a mutually exclusive manner with all the guarantees that it implies.

A growing trend in the industry today is transitioning existing enterprise applications to Web applications. Web applications are best defined as those that present a Hypertext Transfer Protocol (HTTP) interface for operation from within a Web browser. Employing this new motif for interacting with the user has given new life to many of these applications by creating a more intuitive user interface and expanding the platforms that can access it.

Inside of the Web pages that represent this new interface are Java applets — code modules that can execute within a Java virtual machine — that enhance the Web browser's ability to interact with the user. For many, this defines the extent of Java's utility in developing distributed applications. This article presents a greater role for Java in the world of distributed computing. Java distributed computing represents a body of Java programming interfaces that enables Java applications to communicate with each other across a process boundary. The simplest form of this type of computing is two Java applications passing data over a Transmission Control Protocol/Internet Procotol (TCP/IP) network connection. The more complex form is two Java applications sending and receiving Java objects.

JAVA'S BENEFITS

Is Java hype or reality? Java is not a panacea for computing, but a very well thought out tool for building applications that need to operate in a networked environment. Like any tool, Java assists with certain jobs and is completely wrong for others. At this stage in Java's technology adoption, users are trying to see what this new tool can do.

Java has provided some immediate benefits through its use:

1. Owing to the nature of its programming language design, Java suits complex object-oriented development without some of the pitfalls associated with other languages in this category. For example, C++ requires detailed control of memory allocation and de-allocation. Java handles this automatically through garbage collection. This one small change in philosophy adds a tremendous amount of quality to software and reduces the number of problems caused with memory leaks and overruns.

2. The Java virtual machine is a widely accepted standard that is supported on all major commercial operating systems. Java's design theoretically supports the concept of write-once run-anywhere, but the mass deployment of virtual machines makes the theoretical concept a reality.

3. Java simplifies the deployment of applications in the organization. Some Java applications can be deployed as applets running on Hypertext Markup Language (HTML) pages in Web browsers. Still others can be full-blown stand-alone Java applications that automatically download their new components as a standard practice of the virtual machine. Here again, the promise of write-once run-anywhere is an important one because these types of deployments are unencumbered by hardware and operating system differences.

4. Java offers the promise of consolidated development resources. Today, many IT departments are strangled by the different hardware and system software platforms requiring support. With Java on all these platforms, many of the specialized resources can be combined to work jointly on multiplatform efforts. These combinations also help to spread understanding of the business' core applications across the development staff.

5. With companies clamoring to get at and manipulate their legacy data locked away on mainframe computers, a Java virtual machine can be a saving grace. IBM is currently porting the virtual machine for OS/390 and AS/400. Both of these machines store roughly 85% of corporate data today. Java will provide access to this data as well as offering new ways to process and distribute data throughout the organization.

In general, it could be said that Java simplifies the development, deployment, and maintenance of applications in the enterprise. Since most applications in this environment are for data entry or data retrieval, Java offers enough capabilities and performance today. For some specific applications such as computer-aided design or real-time monitoring, Java cannot provide the performance or features required. Java's strong suit is thus development of distributed applications — applications that are partitioned into multiple tasks running on different machines.

DISTRIBUTED JAVA APPLICATIONS

Network application programming is never a trivial task, but sending and receiving a simple set of data over the network using Java is greatly simplified. However, there is far more utility when the communicating components maintain context along with the data. To accomplish this, not only data needs to be transmitted, but its functional and structural components as well. Existing distributed computing middleware currently supports maintaining context by using references to running executables. Generally, these references are literal strings that identify the machine where the executable is running. Distributed Java also maintains context as references, but the references are fully functional Java objects.

To define Java distributed computing, one must understand the differences between applications running in the same address space and those running in different address spaces. Two Java applications running in the same address space can simply call functions on each other as long as the functions are programmed to be exposed publicly. In this case, there are no barriers stopping this behavior; however, when the applications are running in separate address spaces, there is a virtual barricade that surrounds each application. This barricade stops one application from seeing and being able to call functions into the other address space. The only way to subvert the virtual barricade is to make the function calls by passing the data over defined pathways into and out of it. In Java, the facility that performs this subversion is called Remote Method Invocation, or RMI.

To provide some familiar vocabulary that will help provide context for Java applications; applications that expose their functions publicly are sometimes referred to as servers, and the applications that call them are referred to as clients. Hence, the client/server paradigm that has become so popular applies again with the rise of Web applications. When discussing these terms relative to a pure-Java application, applications that expose their functions publicly are referred to as remote Java objects and the applications using them are referred to as Java clients.

Remote Method Invocation

The Remote Method Invocation facility is core to distributed Java and defines a framework for Java-to-Java application communications that extends Java over process boundaries in a natural manner. Designed using techniques learned from the experiences of the Distributed Computing Environment's (DCE) Remote Procedure Calls (RPC) and Common Object Request Broker Architecture (CORBA), Java RMI is an advanced inter-object communications system. The primary difference between inter-application and inter-object communications is the requirement for inter-object communications to support pass-by-value for objects. Pass-by-value will be explained in detail later.

As previously stated, RMI extends Java naturally over process boundaries. This means that Java communicates with remote objects — those in another address space — in a manner that is transparent to the user. That is, remote Java objects will behave in the prescribed manner of all Java objects. By upholding this contract, remote Java objects will support the same behavior of a local Java object providing the desired local/remote transparency that is one of the core focuses of distributed computing. To accomplish this level of local/remote transparency, three important requirements must be met:

1. The two communicating components must agree on a common messaging protocol.
2. The two communicating components must use the same transport mechanism, for example, TCP/IP networking protocol.
3. Code and data must be marshaled — packaged in a byte-oriented stream — in a consistent manner.

The work on behalf of JavaSoft to develop and implement these requirements represents an outstanding body of computing research and technology. Actually, points 1 and 2 are fairly simple if experienced in network programming. However, the third point requires the cooperation of multiple Java subsystems, including Introspection, Object Serialization, Garbage Collection, and Remote Method Invocation itself.

Introspection

Java's Introspection facilities allow the virtual machine to identify all of a Java object's methods and fields from the Java class description. With this knowledge, the virtual machine can "flatten" Java objects from their in-memory state to a sequential stream of bytes. Once in the latter format, the object can be stored on persistent media or transferred over a network. This facility is not exposed directly to the programmer, for this would pose an opportunity to subvert the built-in security mechanisms. Instead, this facility is exposed through the Reflection programming interface and object serialization.

Reflection is a programmatic interface for allowing Java objects to identify public, and sometimes private, methods and fields on Java objects.

492

However, the method calls to the Reflection interface are checked by the virtual machines security manager, thus allowing the security manager to restrict access. Of note, Introspection and Reflection can only be used on local Java objects. While a useful tool for building a remote procedure call mechanism, it cannot be used to examine remote Java objects. Therefore, the contract between the client and the server must be designed before the application is programmed.

Object Serialization

Object serialization uses Java's powers of introspection to store and retrieve objects from a persistent form without requiring additional programming. To accomplish this task, the serialization layer must be able to identify and read all fields on a Java object. Furthermore, the serialization layer must define a format for flattened objects that allows for identification of class type and simplified retrieval.

The data format chosen for object serialization is publicly distributed from JavaSoft with the Java Development Kit (JDK). This format implements certain required functionality for this facility. For example, if two fields within an object reference the same object, only one copy of the object is serialized along with the two individual references. This provides a level of integrity by ensuring that any changes to the object are reflected via both fields. This format also includes the class name for each object that is serialized so that the corresponding code can be associated when retrieved. Additionally, each serialized object is stored with a unique identifier that represents that object within the stream. This allows the object to be updated within the stream without having to serialize the entire graph again.

A common problem associated with persistent objects is reconciling hine. The Naming class is used by Java objects that wish to use remote Java objects and exposes an interface for finding and retrieving a reference to a remote object.

These classes allow Java applications to implement RMI in a modular manner. That is, it does not make applications that use them reliant on any particular implementation of RMI, thus allowing RMI to operate over a host of networking protocols and vendor independent implementations. The following is a sample RMI transaction.

Sample RMI Transaction

The transaction presented in the steps that follow is based on Sun Microsystems' implementation of RMI that ships with the JDK release 1.1. Again, the only parts of this transaction that are vendor independent are the parts that use the Registry and Naming classes.

Step 1. A Java client object wishing to obtain a reference to a remote Java object running on a particular machine uses the Naming class to perform a lookup on that object.

Step 2. If the remote object is running and properly registered in a RMI Registry on that machine, the Registry will return a reference. A reference in RMI is a Java object called a stub, which implements all publicly exposed methods on the remote Java object and maps the calls over the network.

Step 3. The Java client object makes a method call on the remote Java object that requires an integer parameter. The stub object uses the object serialization facility to serialize the integer object into a stream, along with the method call signature, and delivers it to a dedicated listening network service called the skeleton.

Step 4. The skeleton parses the serialized data from the client and builds a properly formatted method call on the remote Java object, which is local to itself. Any return values are serialized and passed back to the Java client. Exhibit 41.1 clarifies how the transaction operates. On machine 1, a client application uses the Java Naming class to access the Registry located on machine 2. This is done over a lookup operation. Upon successfully locating the requested object in the Registry, a Stub object is dynamically downloaded onto the client. The Stub and the Skeleton work in tandem to marshal data and method calls from the client application to the server application. The line from the Server to the Registry represents a registration process that must occur before the object can be located.

To simplify the transaction description, only an integer was passed from client to server. However, RMI implements the functionality to pass entire objects in this manner. To do this requires pass-by-value functionality for objects. This is a Herculean feat, requiring a system that can encapsulate code and data together; without both there is no assurance that an object's data will have the proper coherence. That is, pass-by-value transmits entire objects between process boundaries, including the explicit object being passed and all of its implicit objects defined as fields. When designing distributed systems, coherence will be maintained for explicitly passed objects, but implicitly passed objects may require code definition inside the remote address space.

To accomplish this feat, Java builds on the object serialization facility that stores inside the object's stream the name of the Java classes. These names are then used to request for the Java class files to be transferred if they do not exist locally. The capability to pass classes in this manner is not unusual for Java as this is exactly how Web browsers retrieve Java applets from Web servers. Indeed, the logic inside of RMI to accomplish

494

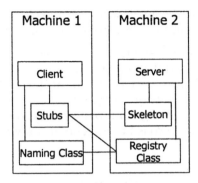

Exhibit 41.1. RMI Transaction Flow

this uses the class loader functionality associated with automatically downloading Java applets.

Ongoing debates in the industry illustrate the lack of appreciation by programmers for this capability: a severe problem for the industry's overall growth. This is most noticeable in technical discussions at industry events and over the Internet in which developers argue that Java-to-Java communications could have been handled by existing inter-object messaging protocols. However, these existing protocols do not inherently support pass-by-value for objects or distributed garbage collection — both requirements of distributed Java.

AGENT TECHNOLOGY

The new capability to pass entire objects, and the objects they contain, has bred a new type of application called the agent. Agent technology is a rapidly growing field within the Java community. The primary reason for this rise is the solution that agents provide to the problem of possible disconnected network states. Java RMI, as well as all remote procedure call mechanisms, are highly synchronous. That is, the client issues a method call and waits for a response. If the network connection is broken at any time during this waiting period, the client application will never receive its response. This could cause the applications to "hang" or to enter into exception handling logic.

Agents allow clients to send processing code to the server when the connection is up that will execute on the server. If the network connection breaks after the agent is delivered, the entire process can still continue normally. This is because agents work in an asynchronous manner; when the client wants the response to the processing, it will make a separate request to the server to return the agent and all of its collected data. Until the client receives this response, the agent will continue to exist, allowing the client to retry multiple times until it receives it successfully.

Java enables agents such as the Web browser to download an applet and call a method on it to start it running. It requires a contract between client and server to send and receive agents, but this is required of all distributed applications. The combination of synchronous and asynchronous programming allows one to design and build robust distributed applications that operate seamlessly across heterogeneous networked environments.

CONCLUSION

Many different solutions exist for distributing a task over multiple address paces and over a network. This article has presented a method for inter-object communications within a pure Java environment. For some, the simplicity provided by the distributed Java platform may be reason enough to use it over other distributed computing technologies, such as the Common Object Request Broker Architecture (CORBA), OSF Distributed Computing Environment (DEC), and Distributed Component Object Model (COM). However, even if companies choose not to use this platform, the perceptions of how to build distributed applications have been forever altered.

As this article was being written, Oracle, Netscape, IBM, and SunSoft submitted a proposal to the Object Management Group (OMG), requesting that the introspection and pass-by-value be incorporated into CORBA. Interestingly, these are the same features that provide the distributed Java platform with its power.

Chapter 42
The Pitfalls of Client/Server Development Projects
Paul Cullen

The management of client/server projects involves unique pitfalls within traditional systems development categories. This article addresses the unique characteristics of client/server development projects within the following categories:

- defining/documenting business requirements
- determining hardware/software/network requirements
- estimating
- project tracking
- defining tasks
- estimating hours required
- estimating percentage of completion
- timekeeping
- issue tracking
- developing skills with technology and tools
- security
- testing/QA process
- developing documentation
- organizational stability
- prototyping/usability
- sign-offs and approval

DEFINING AND DOCUMENTING BUSINESS REQUIREMENTS

As with a traditional development project, documenting requirements should be the start of a client/server development project. It is here that the user requirements are defined as a basis for the project estimate and cost benefit analysis. The requirements document should be detailed and include input screens, processing cycles, and output reports. The database design should also be included, defining data relationships. Not only is defining/documenting business requirements important for estimating the initial

0-8493-9838-X/00/$0.00+$.50
© 2000 by CRC Press LLC

effort of the project, it is also critical for determining changes in scope and determining what "done" is. Many times what is casually reviewed at the start of a project becomes critically important in determining a project's completion. Typical elements of a requirements document include:

- objective of the project/system
- business requirements
- input/output requirements
- affected business area
- processing requirements
- security requirements
- data or file handling requirements
- organizational impacts
- documentation requirements

It is difficult for an auditor to determine if the all requirements are comprehensive and adequately defined. However, at a minimum, the auditor should verify that the requirements are defined at a sufficient level of detail and that there is appropriate user management authorization.

DETERMINING HARDWARE, SOFTWARE, AND NETWORK REQUIREMENTS

Once user requirements are defined, hardware/software/network requirements can be established. These requirements are used to determine the processing platform and networking for the system. Factors that determine the appropriate platform(s) are existing/strategic network infrastructure, number of concurrent users, size of the database, and volume of transactions. There is typically no "right" platform to use and many IS personnel have differing opinions. In addition, vendors are always announcing new releases with new features, making it difficult to distinguish existing product features versus vaporware. Beware of technologies and methodologies that introduce new terms and vernaculars that provide a smoke screen for poor project management and lack of expertise. Hopefully, a best approach is chosen considering cost, systems performance, and ease of development. Typically, the requirements are documented in an architecture document that include:

- business requirements
- tactical considerations
- strategic considerations
- interfaces with other systems

No one hardware/software platform will "fit" all applications, just as a hammer alone will not build a house. However, no small part of the platform choice should be what platforms the developers are familiar with. Familiarity with the platforms chosen will improve the accuracy of the estimates and help ensure that "system killer" problems will not be encountered later. It is too risky to use unproven technologies as a platform for large development projects.

A potential bottleneck with client/server systems is the network capacity and traffic between the user workstation and the server. Many times, these systems are expected to perform over wide area networks (WANs) that may not provide consistent network response times.

ESTIMATING

One use of the project estimate is to determine whether management wants to fund the project based on a cost/benefit analysis. Obviously, if the estimates are not accurate, management cannot make good decisions on whether they want to do the project, assign people to tasks, or plan on when deliverables will be available. Essentially, without goods estimates, project managers cannot manage. Factors that go into good estimates are:

- *Experience with the hardware/software/network/development tools:* If the developers are not experienced with the platforms/tools, management should realize that the estimate is probably not very good and be ready to spend much more on the project and expect delays.
- *Familiarity with the requirements:* Were the developers involved in the requirements definition? If not, again the estimate is probably not very good; and be ready to spend much more on the project and expect delays.
- *Existing systems:* Is the new application a rewrite of existing systems where the reports and data requirements defined? If so, the estimate may be pretty accurate. Otherwise, additional effort may be required to re-do the system to meet user requirements.

Hopefully, a track record of similar development efforts can be used to provide a reality check for the estimates. This can also be used as a control for managing developers who may be padding their estimates. A confidence factor or range should be a part of this estimate. This would give management a best-case and worst-case scenario. This would allow management the ability to decide not to do the project if it might be too expensive or likely not meet deadlines. A final pitfall to watch out for is a target date set by senior management to be committed to by the project team. If a top-down target date is set, there is pressure on the development staff to "back into" estimates that are not based on what is required or pressure to not have estimates at all.

PROJECT TRACKING

As with all development projects, essential to avoiding or managing client/server development pitfalls is effective project management. The elements listed below are used to identify where the project is at, what is left, and the amount of effort remaining.

- *Defining tasks:* Development tasks should be defined at a size that is small enough to be easily tracked and meaningful. The project manager can effectively manage a project if there are specific deliverables with clearly defined hours and frequent due dates. Large tasks with ambiguous deliverables make it difficult to know if the project is in trouble in time to effectively manage the pitfalls. Task interdependencies and assignment of responsibilities are particularly important for projects with multiple related teams where it may be difficult to determine who is responsible for what.
- *Estimating hours required:* This should be done by someone who is experienced with what is required — hopefully the developer that will be performing the task. This would provide some ownership or commitment to task completion.
- *Estimating percentage of completion:* This can be an inaccurate guess if based on the amount of work that has already been expended to complete a task. It should be based on defined deliverables such as number of tasks, screens, or reports completed.
- *Timekeeping:* Timekeeping is frequently not used effectively. Many developers do not regularly record their time or keep an accurate estimate of the hours spent. This makes it difficult to determine the project status. In addition, the failure to record all hours for this project may cause other projects to be underestimated if the recorded hours are used for future estimates.

ISSUE TRACKING

Issue tracking can be used to refine project requirements by documenting and resolving decisions that were not contemplated during the original requirements definition. The issues log is also a good vehicle for tracking outstanding problems and ensuring that they are resolved before the system is implemented into production. A common pitfall with client/server systems is the lack of stability due to software incompatibilities, network errors, and weaknesses with the database handling concurrent updates. Issues should be weighted in severity from "show stoppers" to "nice enhancements" to prioritize the development effort. The owning user of the system should be the one to determine if an issue has been resolved, as there as a tendency for developers to claim resolution prematurely. As with any problem log, the issue log should contain who identified the issue, the date the issue was identified and communicated, severity, a description of the issue, and if resolved, the resolution text. This can also serve as an audit trail of the decisions made.

Issues should be retained after they are resolved to be used for future trending. Trend analysis should be performed to track training issues, as well as problems with hardware, operating systems software, and other application software. If each error is logged, the issues log can also be used to track the overall stability of the system. The issues log can be used to diagnose problems by pinpointing the situations where the problem occurred. The problem information can also be useful in obtaining vendor assistance in problem resolution by providing clear evidence of correlation between problems and vendor products.

DEVELOPING SKILLS WITH TECHNOLOGY AND TOOLS

On-the-job training is not the way to learn new client/server development tools and techniques. A developer should certainly take classroom or computer-based training (CBT). However, developers should not embark on large-scale projects without first having successfully completed small projects. This would reduce project risk by allowing the developers to prove themselves on a smaller scale and give them the ability to more accurately estimate the effort involved. Project managers should also be trained in managing progressively larger projects focusing on multiple teams, task interdependencies, and multiple users.

On larger projects with new technologies, there can be many people with different levels of expertise attempting to make decisions. There are many levels of knowledge. This can range from what a person read in a magazine, to what they heard from someone else, to what they know from training, to what they know from working with a system or past development experience.

The first three levels of knowledge are fairly weak but pretty common. People's roles should be managed, based on a recognition of their level of knowledge to ensure that tasks are appropriately assigned, estimates are reliable, as well as that the decisions made and directions taken are sound. Reference checks should be made for new employees and outside consultants who claim to be "experts" to verify their level of expertise.

SECURITY

A successful security implementation can be difficult in a client/server environment due to the many processing layers that must be secured:

- *Client workstation.* Historically, this has been a personal computer that has weak controls restricting who has access to programs and files. However, with the introduction of operating systems such as Microsoft's Windows NT Workstation, the controls available are rivaling the level of security available on a mainframe.

- *Application.* This level of security typically controls the menus and fields that a user is able to access. The levels of access are typically read, update, and delete.
- *Network.* This deals with securing activity on the network. Tools such as network sniffers are available to read and alter data that is transmitted over the network. There are typically two types of network controls used to prevent inappropriate disclosure or alteration of data. The first is restricting access to segments or areas of a network. This is usually done with firewall systems or screening routers that restrict traffic based on source and destination addresses. Internet connections should be controlled by firewalls. The other method for securing network traffic is encryption. This prevents the ability to read or alter data going across the network. At a minimum, passwords should be encrypted.
- *Server.* Servers typically control who can log on to the network and who can access databases and files on the network. Server security is the most common type of security used in a local area network. Access to the network is typically controlled through a userid and corresponding password. Access to files is then granted based on the assigned user or group id. Most servers provide for logging security administration and violation activity. In large client/server systems, a mainframe is performing the server function.
- *Database.* The database system can also perform security functions, requiring a userid and password and then assigning access to data based on the user or group id. In addition, databases can log security administration and violation activity.

Coordinating multiple levels of security is difficult, and many systems introduce security weaknesses by ignoring access controls on certain platforms or scripting logons on platforms that can be easily circumvented. Another typical problem with client/server systems is that they are cumbersome, requiring multiple logons with multiple userids and passwords.

Ideally, the application should be designed with a single sign-on that controls access on the application, workstation, server, and database systems, along with network controls that restrict access to the appropriate segments of the network and encrypt sensitive traffic.

TESTING

While the elements of the traditional quality assurance/testing process apply to the client/server environment, this environment contains unique challenges requiring more rigorous testing although developers may not take testing as serious because it is "only a PC system." The client/server systems development process should include test plans with expected result, actual result, and disposition of differences. If the system requirements have been well defined, they can be used to develop the test plans. Testing should include all platforms, as well as the interfaces between them and the ability to handle concurrent users. In addition to handling multiple updates through concurrent connections, many client/server systems include the ability to operate without a direct network connection through database synchronization using a process called replication. This requires unique testing steps to verify that replicated additions, updates, or deletions are handled correctly through the replication process as well as working with the system operating in a multiple-user mode. Concurrent updates to databases (two people attempting to update the same record at the same time) can create database conflicts. How the system handles conflicts should be documented and managed by the application software or manual procedures.

Poor response time is often an issue with client/server systems. Bottlenecks can be corrected by increasing network capacity, tuning database queries, or optimizing the database design.

Client/server change management also creates unique challenges with version control. Programming code is typically distributed across multiple platforms as well as embedded within databases. While PC version control packages are frequently used, change management systems that include source/object synchronization are not as sophisticated as the systems used in the mainframe environment.

DEVELOPING DOCUMENTATION

While the goal of a client/server system is to be user friendly and provide online help functions, these systems should additionally have the traditional types of documentation available to operate, maintain, and use the system. The documentation requirements should include the following:

- system overview
- user instructions/transaction codes
- system flowcharts
- system interfaces
- processing function, organization and brief description of programs.
- file descriptions/dataset characteristics (database design if applicable)
- security and control requirements of system, and implementation of those requirements in the system
- file backup and retention requirements
- user errors and messages

Documentation requirements should be included in the project plan, as well as contracts if working with an outside vendor.

ORGANIZATIONAL STABILITY

Reorganizations and staff turnover are difficult to manage, particularly in large organizations. These impacts can easily kill a project. A good project manager will anticipate the possibility of losing team members before the "two weeks notice" is given. Obviously, management should do what they can to retain key people. However, losing staff is inevitable — especially if staff is trained on "hot technologies" that are very marketable. Things that can be done to reduce the impact of staff changes are:

- *Training:* ensuring that enough people on the staff are knowledgeable with the technologies to assure that the team is not overly reliant on any one person. This could also be used to help manage personnel who are resistant to change and do not want to deal with it.
- *Establishing backups:* identifying who could fill a person's position, what it would take to get the individual up to speed, and implementing a plan before it is required. It may make sense to have designated backup individuals write parts of the system to ensure that they have the skills necessary to support it.
- *Mentoring:* identifying opportunities for more senior individuals to assist others by answering questions, assisting with reasoning, and working through problems.
- *Programming standards:* covers how code is to be written and documented to ensure that it can be supported by others.
- *Code reviews:* involves reviewing systems as they are developed to ensure that they are logically written, understandable by others, and adhere to the documentation standards.
- *Maintenance screens:* should be built to enable the modification of key system functions/parameters without programmer intervention.

PROTOTYPING

Prototyping can be useful for screen design and helpful in determining user needs. However, documentation should exist over and above the prototype. Prototyping should not be used as an excuse for not following a systems development methodology. It is crucial that the developers are involved in the requirements definition phase, as the assumptions used in the requirements definition are critical in developing the estimate. With the development of middleware, object-oriented coding, and computer-assisted software engineering (CASE) tools, it is some times difficult to determine if business requirements have in fact been adequately defined. It is crucial that project managers and auditors are certain that the development team can articulate the system requirements in "plain English" to be assured that deliverables are understood.

Prototyping is often done in cycles or iterations. It is necessary to document what will be delivered in an iteration and when it will be delivered to manage user expectations as well as avoid project slippage by pushing deliverables into future iterations.

If the client/server system is being developed to replace an existing legacy system, hopefully users of the existing system will be involved in the prototype review. In addition, user representatives who understand the workflow and are good at assessing usability should also be included.

SIGN-OFFS AND APPROVAL

Sign-offs and approval should be obtained at least at the following points of a project:

- *At the start of a project,* preferably to begin an estimate of what the project will take to complete.
- *At the completion of the requirements definition and prior to development* with an estimate of what the development effort will take in terms of development personnel, user personnel, money required for equipment, etc., as well as the timelines and task plans required to complete the project. This should be in sufficient detail to define the scope of the project, track the percentage of completion, and determine when key people need to be involved. If working with a vendor, this should be a contract.
- *At the completion of significant deliverables* to ensure that:
  - users are getting what they asked for when it was supposed to be delivered
  - the system has been tested to assure that it is performing and functioning correctly
  - the system has been developed according to programming standards and it can be supported
- *At the completion of the project* to ensure that deliverables match what was defined at the start of the project. Invariably, once the system is developed, it will be different than what the user wanted or what the developer thought the user communicated. In some cases, this begins the argument over who pays for the changes. Usually this is where it is evident that it was critical to clearly articulate and document requirements at the start of the project. Beware of the introduction of the term "phases" at the end of the project that was not mentioned at the project's beginning.

CONCLUSION

It is not easy to manage projects that are dependent on complex client/server systems. Technical problems may occur that "kill a system" that have nothing to do with project management. However, project management controls can be introduced that mitigate the risks of these problems. While auditing project management controls diverges from the traditional audit approach, corporate resources can be saved by escalating to senior management situations where these controls are not in place. As previously discussed, the most important controls to watch out for include:

- experience with the technology and similar projects
- adequately defining and documenting user requirements
- accurate estimating and establishing realistic target dates
- tracking progress and issues
- implementing effective security
- effectively documenting and testing the system
- obtaining user approval

If these controls are in place, the project manager and auditors have some assurance that the risks associated with client/server pitfalls are being effectively managed.

Chapter 43

Creating a Paperless Workflow: A Case Study

Karen C. Fox and Mark N. Folick

Businesses are, now more than ever, having to do more with less. Budgets are dwindling, needs are increasing, and demands are made to produce results faster. To meet this challenge, the workflow of organizations must change to meet the twenty-first century and information technology must be the catalyst that modifies this workflow. What does workflow have to do with information technology? Plenty, if it is about implementing work processes that improve customer response times and productivity.

The number-one workflow problem in many organizations is the flow of paper, which often takes more time and money than any other single activity. This stems from bureaucratic environments and the tendency to remain with the status quo. Bureaucratic environments tend to use paper to document processes. The processes require paper to be moved around an organization in order to gather information and approvals. Paper must move around the organization to gather information because the information is not readily available.

The paper flow problem is getting worse. As businesses demand faster results, the need for information increases. This also increases the need for approvals. One possible solution is automation. However, the tendency to remain with the status quo creates the tendency to simply automate existing systems. The automation of the paper flow in organizations requires simplification, decentralization, and automation of the approval process; but more importantly, it requires the total transformation of what organizations define as documents.

A document is a piece of paper with a signature. With increasing paper flows, organizations should examine ways to do away with paper. Organizations should rely on information instead of documents. The accessibility of information and the extent to which the process allows the utilization of this information proportionately negates the need for documents.

Universities, like corporations, must also deal with a great deal of paper. This article describes how one large university has dealt with the automation of the paper flow process and the resulting approval that accompanied much of this paperwork.

THE ORGANIZATION AND ITS PAPER FLOW PROBLEM

The University of Tennessee, Memphis, is a campus with 20,500 students and approximately 900 faculty members. Last year, the staff rolled over 100,000 multiple-part paper forms into manual typewriters. Each of these forms required administrative approval. For example, every time someone was hired, something was purchased, repairs are requested, or an employee was evaluated, an approval and authorization form had to be created. After being typed, the forms were reviewed, checked, signed, transported, entered into various databases, filed, retrieved, archived, shredded, and trashed. This scenario is all too familiar in many organizations. Shuffling forms has become the uncontested standard for conducting business and the primary means of gathering a complex series of routine administrative approvals. One recent study attributes 70 percent of organizational waste to the use of paper.[2] Such unnecessary administrative processes, however, command time and money that should be spent on more important issues.

This paper shuffling and approvals system obviously needed improvement. Historically, due to the difficulty areas had sharing information efficiently, multiple-part paper was transferred from department to department. Once the multiple-part form reached a department, information was added, a page was torn off and filed, a signature was added, and the form continued on its path. This process occurred at each department along the route. In addition, multiple approval layers were deemed necessary because auditing oversight was difficult.

With the introduction of a computing environment, the workload doubled. In addition to the paper system being kept in place as multiple-part forms flowed through the office, having information added to them along the way, the data was also entered into disparate databases. Entering the information in two places resulted in an even larger requirement for clerical support, a definite slowdown in processing, and a wide variation in the reporting of information. Because the computer systems were originally developed departmentally with no integration plans, the same information had to be reentered in each department. Due to the errors and misinterpretation resulting from this process, reporting of information lacked consistency between departments. This method of handling documents was obviously not working. Error rates were high, paper flow through the organization took far too long, and the storage of approved forms was a nightmare. This is consistent with what many organizations experience. Recent research shows that the use of paper approval forms produce a 30 percent error rate.[2] It was clear that a major system transformation had to occur — starting with the reduction of paper flow complexity.

REDUCING PAPER FLOW COMPLEXITY

The problem was much larger than simply reviewing and automating the way paper flows. The process — in and of itself — was the problem. The entire process that drove the system had to be reviewed. Simply automating paper flow would be installing a method that was cumbersome and conceived without the thought of utilizing a computing environment. Because processes should be simplified before beginning automation and because dysfunctional processes should not be automated, all processes were examined and approvals were considered with regard to the value they added.

To support the trend to decentralize management decision-making, and to promote the idea that approval and accountability should be at the operational level, more responsibility was placed on operational units and more emphasis was placed on post-payment audits rather than on centralized control. Importance was placed on the differentiation between the need for approval and the need to be aware. As a result, careful delineation was made between approvals and notifications so that the progress of a document through the system would not be impeded by someone who only needed notification. It was also noted that approvals did not always necessarily move forward, but rather became entangled in an intricate network of specific approvals and reviews. Furthermore, and perhaps most importantly, those charged with approval responsibilities merely needed easily accessible, relevant support information.

Examination of the current paper flow and approval system revealed three foundational principles to drive the development of a new process:

- employee empowerment based on decentralization of the process and accountability
- elimination of non-value-added processes
- establishment of quality at the source

The decision was made to simplify these processes as a function of implementing a new electronic approval system. These principles would be used in electronically simulating the paper flow process. Thus, the process transformation would be seen as a single change to the user.

After the current situation had been assessed and the workflow of the paper system had been analyzed and redesigned, the next step was to conduct a thorough review of the many systems available on the market to handle electronic approvals. It was discovered that mass market electronic approval systems generally fall into two categories: document management systems and databases.

DOCUMENT MANAGEMENT SYSTEMS

This category of systems can be defined as those systems that handle processing by utilizing scanned documents, electronic documents, and electronic signatures. The general flaw with these electronic approval systems is that they tend to incorporate a portion or all of the paper process. Some systems merely scan all existing documents in the paper process and route these documents along the same path as the paper was originally routed. This process simply automates a process while using expensive equipment and a great deal of network bandwidth to ship the same documents to the same places for signatures. A significant value of this process is that it eliminates paper and moves documents much faster than the paper method. While this process makes a step in the right direction, it does not come close to addressing the real problems.

Some of the better systems incorporate search engines that search on the keywords of the scanned images so that documents can be retrieved and viewed. The data, however, can only be searched by keywords. Reports, therefore, could not be generated from these documents, nor could the data be manipulated so that management reports could be derived from them. In effect, in these electronic approval systems, a move was made from typing a document on a typewriter and then reentering the data into a database, to scanning the document into an approval system and then reentering the document into a database.

These types of systems are best utilized by organizations that require storage and retrieval of scanned paper documents and find it necessary to provide a wide range of access to them. These systems, however, are not well suited to electronic approval systems. Although they eliminate paperwork, these systems do not eliminate the paper paradigm — they simply automate paper.

DATABASE SYSTEMS

In addition to reviewing document management-type approval systems, the systems based on databases were also reviewed. Some systems incorporated databases by providing the workflow algorithms. Most of those systems used the database engine for workflow and electronic approval; however, many still attached documents and did not actually keep all of the data in the system. Those that did had problems. For example, if a person was not in, the workflow would grind to a halt, because the systems did not incorporate queuing capabilities to allow the process to keep flowing. The electronic approval piece was generally incorporated as part of the system as a whole, and not as a generic part that could be added to any application and thus provide consistency.

Another type of database is based on Web-based electronic forms. This necessitates downloading forms to each individual desktop, which causes configuration problems. Some database systems tie the routing mechanism into the actual system. Several problems were found with this method. Users were entered in an authorization table, which made access cumbersome. Approval notification was also cumbersome as daily reports were required as opposed to realtime notification. Also, a user could query documents currently en-route without running the report and approving or denying a document, even if it had not been fully processed. Most of the database approval systems were tied to specific applications and were not modular enough to be adapted to any system, which was a major consideration.

While these database engines were a good idea, it was necessary to find a database solution that could be woven into other database applications. Database packages do have advantages. They are integrated and they utilize the database to detect when business rules have been triggered by other actions in the system. The workflow database was a good idea, but it needed improvement and refinement.

Problems with Commercial Products

The main flaw with the commercially available products reviewed was that they incorporated the old idea of a document. They failed to insist that the idea of a document be transformed. This philosophy seemed to only automate the old problems, instead of incorporating a new solution to the problem. For example, they make database screens look like existing documents, scan existing documents, and when utilizing electronic documents, incorporate all packages and types of electronic documents in the routing process. While these processes might by easy to implement and easy to market to the user, they are not ultimately a specific best way to solve the document routing problem. Therefore, a decision was made to design an electronic approval system specific to the needs of this organization.

DESIGNING A NEW APPROVAL SYSTEM

Due to the shortcomings of the commercially available products, the solution was to develop the system in-house. While this is not always the appropriate solution because it takes more time and money, it was deemed appropriate because there was nothing on the market that met the particular needs of this organization. In order for this electronic approval system to really work, the idea of what a document is had to be changed, as well as the way that users access the document's information. While this process took longer to design and implement, it ultimately saved an enormous amount of time.

The design philosophy of this new system was that documents should be an output of the system — not an input to the system. Users input information at the source. By inputting information at the lowest common denominator, it was found that errors decreased significantly. The system is designed around a client/server architecture with a GUI front end, which allows various departments to design their own reports and screens. This means that every department can visualize the document as they need to see it, while keeping the underlying database structure intact. This gives the departments data ownership as well as document ownership. When the document is routed to another department for approval, that department may view the document in an entirely different way. The departments are notified of the document routing via e-mail or by a to-do list built into the routing system. The departments can choose which method they prefer.

During the analysis, it was realized that there would be other campus-wide applications requiring a similar flow of documents. The decision was therefore made to create an electronic approval application generic enough to be used by all other areas. This would be a stand-alone application so that it could be added as a module of other applications and would allow the workflow analysis to be added to each application and updated as necessary.

The automated routing system developed provides the following functions:

- concurrent access by eliminating the serial paper approval cycle
- automatic generation of lists requiring approval
- notification of approval
- summarizations for faster analysis
- tailored security access
- current status and location of each document
- maintenance of audit trail

A major management step between design and implementation was to reduce the scope of the initial implementation and focus it on well-defined, proven technology. Although the system was designed to be highly scalable and platform independent, user buy-in was significant to the success of the project. An incremental approach in implementing the design was also crucial to the project's success. Recent research shows only a 27 percent success rate for software projects. This high rate of failure is largely attributable to over-ambition in regard to project scope and lack of end-user involvement.[3] To avoid problems, the system was first implemented on the organization's most widely used platform and the user team that aided in design was enlisted to spearhead implementation.

IMPLEMENTING THE NEW ELECTRONIC APPROVAL SYSTEM

To implement the system, several steps had to be taken. The data routing paths had to be determined. The organizational units and the users within these units utilizing the system had to be defined, along with their access privileges. Each organizational unit was allowed to have its own routing process tailored to its needs. The users who receive the forms and the actions they may take regarding the form are controlled by predefined tables. The system allows some users to create a form, some to approve or deny a form, some to just view the form, and still others to do more than one of these. Other features of the system include a routing history or audit trail that is kept to ensure security, the ability to set up proxies for signature purposes, the ability to attach private or permanent notes for the next person on the path, and electronic mail to inform users that there is a form waiting to be processed.

Unlike the commercially available products examined, this system allows electronic forms to be created, forwarded, and tracked, as well as approved by the users. Because the system is not a document routing system, but an approval system, the document can look different to each user who sees it, based on that user's individual needs. The system works similar to an e-mail system, with inboxes, outboxes, and document drafting areas.

The key to implementing the system was allowing the users to control the data flow, the security tables, and to departmentally have ad hoc control over the look and feel of their own screens. By designing a scalable system, the implementation could be done in increments and could grow with the user's needs. By designing a modular system, this routing system can be implemented into new as well as existing database systems, as well as tie into commercial systems.

CONCLUSION

The results of this new electronic approval system have reached far beyond the obvious response time and productivity increases. The empowerment of departments to create their own documents and enter data at the source has increased morale. Reports no longer include disparate data and concerns of data validity. The electronic approval system is a first step in the inception of a paperless organization, but a very important first step in that it changes the ideas that people have about information, the way they treat information, and the way they interact with each other when they have access to appropriate, timely information. This is nothing less than a needed revolution in the mindset of the entire process and will result in the eventual evolution in the way business is conducted.

References

1. Areu, E., Hope, B., Lemnich, J., Mcdermott, J., and Munn, T. Electronic Paper Flow: Dealing with the Realities, *CAUSE Conference Proceedings*, December 1994.
2. Blythe, K.C. and Morrison, D.L. Electronic Approval: Another Step Toward a Paperless Office, *Cause/Effect* (15:3), Fall, 1992.
3. James, G. IT Fiascoes ... and How to Avoid Them, *Datamation*, November 1997.

Chapter 44
Security and Control of Electronic Mail

Craig R. McGuffin

Systems that send and receive electronic mail (e-mail) have gained significant acceptance in business over the past few years. Many companies have discovered that e-mail systems provide an ideal method for staff to communicate by electronically sending and receiving messages and files. E-mail lets each person use the system at any given time without regard to disruptions caused by time zones or personal schedules. In addition, e-mail messages are often the most cost-effective way to transmit information. As a result, many corporate e-mail systems have taken on great significance in terms of the information they carry and the communications facilities they provide. As important information resources, e-mail systems need proper security measures (just as do more traditional business applications). The security goals of confidentiality, integrity, and availability must be met.

This chapter focuses on meeting the first two security objectives of confidentiality and integrity for e-mail systems. Important security management issues unique to e-mail applications are discussed, as is an approach to identifying security exposures and implementing controls for common e-mail architectures.

E-MAIL SECURITY MANAGEMENT ISSUES

Because of the nature of e-mail applications, security practitioners face a unique set of management issues. Security levels, policies, privacy issues, confidentiality, message integrity, and cost should be considered.

Required Security Level

A key issue in e-mail security is the level of security required, since this drives the resources needed to secure the system. E-mail systems can very quickly become key business systems, which are depended on by managers and staff for reliable and confidential communications. The system (and more importantly, the information it carries) is a business asset that must be protected.

An adequate level of security must be attained. Excessive security is unnecessary, however. Information security costs money, whether for expenditures on tangible items such as hardware and software, or simply the extra time and effort it takes on the part of users and administrators. Over-securing the system means squandering business resources.

As in most management decisions, the cost and benefits of e-mail security should be evaluated: The cost of resources spent to secure the system should not exceed the benefits obtained from a higher level of security. Unfortunately, although they are important to making a good decision, these concepts can be difficult to apply to information security, even for traditional systems. For example, the cost of a software package is usually easy to determine; however, it is often hard to arrive at the cost of a particular security procedure that requires users to change their password every 60 days. Often, rather than a strict quantification of all costs, a total for tangible expenditures coupled with an overall level for staff time and effort is estimated.

Estimating security costs and benefits of e-mail systems can be a challenge. In traditional applications (e.g., sales, receivables, and receipts system), the purpose and content is well-known; it can be determined how serious it is if invoices are lost, or if the customer file falls into the hands of a competitor. However, an e-mail system carries all types of traffic (e.g., hockey pool results, budgets, discussion documents about a planned corporate takeover, favorite recipes, client financial statements, computer jokes, and plans for employee terminations). The cost of lost confidentiality or integrity of e-mail messages varies, depending on the particular message being sent.

One possible solution is identifying the most important type of message that may be passed over e-mail in terms of its need for confidentiality and integrity, and responding to that level with the appropriate security mechanisms. This means that at least some traffic is over-secured; however, this can be viewed as an additional cost of protecting the critical messages and evaluated accordingly. Another solution is identifying discrete levels of e-mail security and segregating e-mail traffic accordingly. However, this can lead to duplication of e-mail facilities, reduced levels of e-mail connectivity, and additional work and inconvenience for users. It also increases the chance that a message that should be protected is sent by a less secure, but more convenient, method. A further approach is simply advising users that little or no security is provided by the system and that the system should not be used for critical messages. Although this is the least expensive approach in the short term, it may have a high cost in the long run. E-mail

used and the potential for loss of security. After users are comfortable with sending messages using e-mail, they rarely question whether someone else might view their mail or pretend to be them. If a lack of security allows a confidential document to become known, those responsible for the e-mail system will probably be blamed, despite advance warnings to users.

As a practical alternative, security tools can be provided to users within their e-mail systems that allow each user to select the level of security for each message. The cost associated with using the tools can be evaluated by each user and incurred as necessary. This approach often represents the best compromise between securing everything on one system and providing separate paths for different security needs.

Formalized Security Policy

One of the reasons information security efforts fail in an organization is lack of clear standards that describe the reasons and objectives for security as well as the roles and responsibilities for protecting corporate data. To address this problem, companies should create a formal security policy document intended to let staff members know what they are supposed to do and why. The policy must clearly state the importance of security to the information assets of the company and the duties each employee has to protect them. In addition, because e-mail systems can play such a key role in corporate communications, information security policies and procedures should cover e-mail systems and data. The standards should be formalized and distributed to all employees who use an e-mail system. The proper training (often neglected for any system) should be given to help make sure staff members actually understand the policies and compliance requirements.

Creating a stand-alone e-mail security policy is one option. This helps highlight the significance of e-mail security to the company. However, an existing corporate information security policy can be extended to address e-mail. For example, a policy may be written to describe high-level security standards that apply to all systems and platforms. One standard could be that all systems must uniquely identify and authenticate each user; such a high-level standard would apply to each technical environment and application. In this example, the standard would require that e-mail users be uniquely identified and authenticated by the system before they can view or send mail.

An individual e-mail security policy (or one that is integrated with an overall corporate security policy) should clearly state the following:

- The overall objectives for information security (e.g., protecting specific corporate information assets) and the criteria for making security decisions (e.g., a cost/benefit analysis).
- The roles and responsibilities for maintaining security for such key positions as the e-mail system administrator, the administrator of any computer platforms the systems run on, and individual e-mail users.

- The standards required for confidentiality, availability, and integrity, and the specific mechanisms and procedures required to meet each objective.
- The standards for acceptable use of the e-mail system, including whether or not systems may be used for items of a personal nature.
- Any cautions regarding monitoring that may take place to ensure compliance with security policy.

It is important that staff members affected by the policy read and understand the duties expected of them. In addition, they must acknowledge that understanding and the ramifications of failing to protect the system. This can be done through a brief written acknowledgment form signed by users when they receive their e-mail user ID.

Personal Privacy

A significant consideration in devising an e-mail security policy is the issue of personal privacy. As with the company telephone system, corporate e-mail systems may be used occasionally, or even regularly, for messages of a personal nature. For example, if employees are permitted to use the telephone to call home to check on their children, they do not expect the call to be monitored. There is likely the same expectation of privacy if personal messages are permitted on the corporate e-mail system. However, it is also likely that the company views e-mail as a corporate application that is to be used only for the conduct of business. Therefore, any data on the system may be subject to examination because it should be of a business nature only.

The issue of personal privacy and e-mail systems is an evolving one, without clear legal or moral answers. Corporate policy should clearly state the following:

- Whether any messages of a personal nature are permitted on the company e-mail system.
- Whether messages sent on the e-mail system are subject to examination, at any time, by corporate management or its designates (e.g., the e-mail system administrator).

Even if users are advised that administrators may examine their messages, this should be done only as part of problem resolution or for other acceptable reasons.

Confidentiality

The varying nature of e-mail traffic can make it difficult to assess requirements for protecting the confidentiality of specific transmissions. For example, although the customer file in a sales system is certainly important and its confidentiality protected, the need for securing other types of messages that can be sent on an e-mail system may be less obvious:

- **Strategic and operational plans and detailed analyses sent over an executive information system.** Because e-mail messages can include word processing documents and spreadsheets as attachments, intimate corporate details could be discovered in a message or an accompanying file.
- **Sensitive customer or client details.** Professional services firms (e.g., law firms, accounting practices, or management consulting firms) have a duty of confidentiality to their clients. Client information is often routinely transmitted over e-mail systems; this information must be protected in transit.
- **Sensitive internal matters (e.g., personnel reviews or plans for upcoming staff changes).** Premature exposure of this information may cause embarrassment, damage to reputations, and even staff revolts, each requiring damage control efforts.

Although e-mail may carry routine messages and announcements, it may also be the system that requires the highest degree of security to maintain confidentiality.

Message Integrity

The need for data integrity is easily understood for such information as customer invoices. Invoice details and totals must be correct to avoid disputes and ensure collection of all receivables. For this application, data integrity is usually maintained through such accounting controls as file balancing and reconciliation to control totals.

Examples of the types of important messages that can be conveyed by an e-mail system have been previously addressed in the section on confidentiality. Integrity is equally as critical. However, the free form of e-mail content does not seem to lend itself to traditional controls over message integrity. In addition, because a garbled word can normally be detected by the reader, the need for extra integrity control mechanisms seems low. However, consider a loss of integrity in which a portion of the message (e.g., a paragraph or the last half of the message) is lost or in which the loss of a digit may not be noticed. The integrity of the time, date, and identity of the sender must also be protected.

Despite the free form of e-mail messages, techniques can be used to detect message integrity problems. These are addressed later in this chapter. In addition, steps can be taken to ensure that a message is actually from the person identified as the sender.

Cost Control

One of the areas where e-mail systems can pose a challenge is in controlling the costs of their use. Basic costs of system use may include charges per connection, message, or kilobyte of data sent. In addition, value-added services can carry additional costs for providing gateways to outside networks and mail systems or gateways to such other services as fax and regular mail.

Although cost control is not directly tied to security concerns, security mechanisms should limit which users can access what functions. For example, not all users of the system need unlimited messaging or access to other services. Security parameters should be available to limit who can do what and how much of each service they can use. In addition, in instances in which charges for the use of e-mail and related services are incurred, security mechanisms must provide reliable identification of each user. Without this, users may claim that they did not use certain services. Although commercial third-party e-mail services normally track individual use, in-house systems may not provide these details.

REVIEWING E-MAIL SECURITY

To examine whether or not a particular e-mail implementation offers adequate protection, it is often necessary to perform a security analysis of the system following traditional review and audit techniques. Fortunately, as mentioned earlier, the security objectives of confidentiality and integrity remain the same. Therefore, a review of security for an e-mail system should follow the same basic approach as for other security reviews. However, e-mail systems bring an increased level of complexity to the review process. This is due to the number of different types of e-mail packages, computer and network operating systems, and data communications facilities that comprise a modern e-mail system. Message processing and storage can take place at many different points in the system. Different components of the system interact with end users, peer systems at other locations, and even with other types of e-mail systems. What can seem like a relatively simple application may actually be one of the more sophisticated systems the security analyst or auditor may face.

The security review can be structured by identifying and evaluating key security mechanisms.

Identification. Each user of the e-mail system should be uniquely identified. The concept of a user includes people and systems with which the e-mail system exchanges mail. Identification details must also be extended to include not only a user name, but also such network-based identifiers as host name or network node number.

Authentication. Identified users must prove their identities by supplying something that only they know or have. This is traditionally a password entered by an end user. However, this can extend to such items as knowledge of a shared key used as part of a cryptographic challenge-and-response process.

Access Control. Based on the identity of a user and a list of rules, the system should be able to permit or deny access to protected resources. In the case of an e-mail system, this includes initial access to the system, access to files (mailboxes and messages), and access to controlled services such as an external gateway.

Monitoring. The system should provide facilities to monitor system use, particularly failed attempts to access important functions (such as repeated failed log-ins). Reporting of monitoring results should be available on an exception basis.

The key to a proper evaluation of e-mail security is to first fully understand the architecture of the system. All the components involved in processing a message must be considered, from user interfaces through message transfer agents, computer and network operating systems, gateways, and data communication networks. Each layer of hardware and software may provide its own facilities for identification, authentication, access control, and monitoring. Such details as user identifiers may also pass to other system levels to enable further access control decisions. This passage must be reliable to be useful. Without understanding how the system is constructed and how each layer works, inappropriate conclusions about the state of e-mail security may be reached.

ARCHITECTURES AND SECURITY EXPOSURES

In order to identify some of the security problems found in e-mail systems, the following sections outline typical e-mail architectures and the exposures that may be found in each.

In-House Systems

An e-mail system may be as simple as an application on a single computer that offers messaging services to its users. Many operating systems include e-mail facilities as an integral part of the user environment.

In the in-house e-mail system (see Exhibit 44.1), all users log on to one system. Mail sent from one user to another never leaves the system. Messages are deposited in the mailbox of the recipient, waiting for that person to sign on and read the messages.

The security exposures of this configuration are not significantly different from those of any other single platform application. For example, the

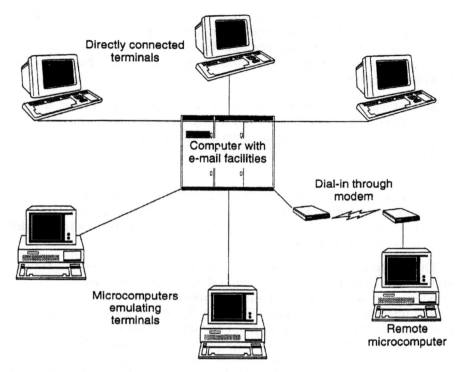

Exhibit 44.1.   Typical In-House E-Mail System

computer should require each user to go through a log-on procedure that uniquely identifies and authenticates the person, then limits access to his own mailbox. In addition, if users can access the computer from a remote location (e.g., through dial-in), further precautions should be taken to verify that the person using dial-in is authorized.

If proper operating system security is in place, e-mail can be well protected. However, this architecture may introduce a wide population of new computer users that are less well trained in using and securing computer facilities. Users may be far more casual about such details as sharing passwords or logging off when they leave a terminal unattended. These actions can expose the entire system and its users to security breaches.

Another exposure is that the e-mail system administrator may require extended security privileges in order to install and run e-mail software. For example, although it is not at all desirable, a particular e-mail package may need to be configured using an account that provides full and unrestricted access to the system. If the e-mail administrator is not experienced in the

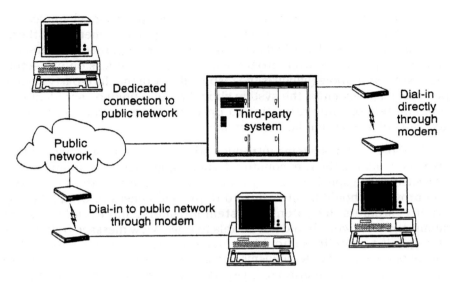

Exhibit 44.2. External E-Mail System

environment or is careless, it is possible to alter or delete key programs or files needed to keep the system functioning.

The e-mail software itself can introduce security exposures. The user interface portion of an e-mail package may offer an escape from the e-mail environment to a command-line interpreter. A user who should have access to only selected e-mail commands and facilities may be able to gain use of the full set of commands.

As a further concern, the e-mail software may require extended privileges to successfully run on the system. Any program that executes with increased privileges can present a security risk because it provides an inviting target for system intruders. One attack carried out by the infamous Internet Worm involved exploiting a security hole in an e-mail program running with extended privileges.

Third-Party Systems

Third-party e-mail systems (see Exhibit 44.2) are quite common and popular, due to the large community of users they can attract from many different organizations and different parts of the world. Although they carry regular (and sometimes hefty) user fees, they offer the convenience of a system that can be reached from many locations using simple dial-in facilities, often with an automated interface. They also free the organization of the need to install and support an individual e-mail system.

From an external user's point of view, the third-party e-mail application is essentially a large single system. The security requirements are therefore similar to those described in the last section, except that the emphasis is more on protecting users from the organization and less on protecting the system as a whole (which is the responsibility of the third-party system provider). For example, the system should require unique user identification and reliable authentication to prevent others from accessing the accounts of users from the organization.

Third-party mail systems introduce additional security concerns that are very similar to those encountered when using a service bureau for data processing. The specific security procedures taken by the third-party system provider should be investigated to prevent access to e-mail data by other customers, by potential system intruders, and even by system administrators (who should not be able to freely view message traffic). Ideally, specific guidelines should be given by the supplier regarding the nature of the security mechanisms and procedures (e.g., access control to the system and its mailboxes, regular back-ups, and monitoring for attempts at unauthorized access). The third-party e-mail system supplier may arrange for an independent review to be made of the facilities, with the results made available to current and potential customers. However, specific undertakings regarding extensive security practices may be difficult to obtain from third-party suppliers because they are not demanded by many customers. As a result, it should be assumed that the third-party system has minimal security facilities, to the extent of assuming that any message sent can be possibly viewed or altered. Security precautions should be taken to protect messages.

LAN-based Server Systems

The installation and use of LANs in the corporate environment has resulted in platforms that are well-suited to e-mail systems. Many workstation users can access a central point such as a file server that facilitates the exchange of mail messages. E-mail ties in with, and is sometimes a driving force behind, workgroup computing among LAN users.

In a LAN-based e-mail system (see Exhibit 44.3), the central file server acts as a post office, storing messages sent among users. The user, through the workstation, sends mail to others through the post office and reads messages held there.

The architecture of LANs has often confounded traditional control methods. The main problem, as addressed earlier, is the many separate components that make up a LAN, including hardware, software, and data communications facilities. Each can play a role in security by having its own security mechanisms. However, with a LAN, the quality of these mechanisms can vary widely. Although a central file server may have security

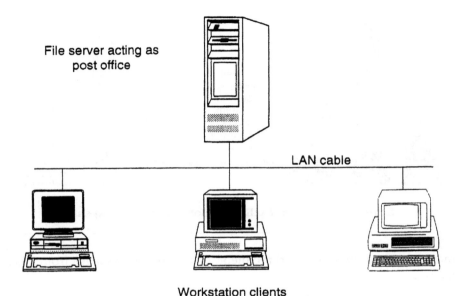

File server acting as
post office

LAN cable

Workstation clients

Exhibit 44.3.   Typical LAN-Based E-Mail System

comparable to that of mainframe computers, a workstation may have no security at all. Each user may require a password to log on to a facility, but if the password traverses the LAN cable in clear text so that anyone with the right tools can view it, security efforts may be undermined.

A LAN-based e-mail system is a good illustration of the importance of understanding the systems architecture. For example, the security reviewer must keep the following points in mind:

- Programs may reside on a file server, but they execute on a workstation. As a result, workstation security is as important as file server security.
- Configuration files containing user IDs and passwords can be held on a file server, a workstation, or both (so that work can continue off-line, even if the server is temporarily unavailable).
- Message files can be stored almost anywhere on the LAN, including the sender's workstation, the file server, and the receiver's workstation.
- Because the LAN cable is a shared medium, anyone with a workstation attached to it can view traffic as it passes across the LAN.

LANs are not usually controlled by a central point. It is normally quite easy to add nodes that can advertise such services as mail storage or routing to other networks. Existing LAN e-mail users can be tricked into sending

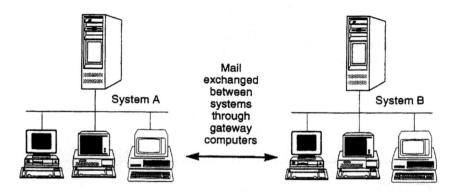

Exhibit 44.4. E-Mail Exchanged Between Transfer Agents

messages to an unauthorized recipient, or accepting messages from false sources.

None of these potential problem areas are new to someone who regularly reviews the security of LAN-based applications. They may require new techniques developed to meet the security challenges of a LAN environment.

Systems Using Transfer Agents

The utility of an e-mail system, particularly a LAN-based system, grows tremendously when it can reach other systems in the outside world. A typical example is an organization with offices at different locations.

A common approach to achieve this level of connectivity is through the use of message transfer agents (see Exhibit 44.4). A transfer agent is simply a computer on a LAN that scans a post office looking for messages destined for another LAN. The transfer agent knows how to contact the other LAN, based on its own configuration files. For example, the other LAN may be reachable through a network bridge or router, or it may use simple dial-up connections. It exchanges messages with a transfer agent on the other LAN, which arranges for final delivery on the local system. Transfer agents may also act as relays, receiving a message from one LAN and passing it on to another.

When using transfer agents between LANs, security involves the need for identification and authentication between agents. It is important that each agent ensures that it is conversing with an authorized partner before it sends messages to another LAN or accepts messages for delivery to its own users. Without specific identification and reliable authentication, there is a potential for an unauthorized transfer agent to obtain confidential traffic or originate mail from a fraudulent source.

Identification and authentication between message transfer agents can be as simple as the exchange of a user ID that uniquely identifies the agent and a password, or it can be as involved as an exchange using cryptographic techniques. However, if simple passwords are used for authentication, they should be subject to the same types of administrative controls as user passwords (e.g., aging and rules for minimum complexity).

A further security concern for transfer agents relates to administration. When messages are passed between LANs, there can be differences in the quality of administration between the different mail domains. Although one e-mail administrator may be extremely conscientious, another may not be as concerned about security. For example, it should not be assumed that every administrator takes the same precautions against unauthorized access. As a result, all mail coming from a foreign domain is not absolutely reliable or authentic, nor is that mail always well protected.

In some cases, third-party systems are used as message transfer agents. In this scenario, a local e-mail system can send messages to a third-party system, which acts as a kind of clearing house for e-mail traffic. Although using a third-party system in this manner can reduce the burden of setting up and maintaining links between private systems, it also introduces the additional security concerns raised earlier regarding a service bureau environment.

Connectivity to Heterogeneous Hosts

A growing number of e-mail systems can connect between virtually any host (see Exhibit 44.5). In this context, a host can be almost anything from a mainframe system supporting thousands of users to a single-user microcomputer. Software running on each platform establishes a connection with another host and exchanges messages on behalf of users. Key to this ability is a network communication path that permits any-to-any connectivity. The best example of this phenomenon is the worldwide Internet.

Although any-to-any connectivity provides incredible opportunities for communication, it also poses increased security threats, particularly with the Internet. A user may now interconnect with many different types of computers, operating systems, and e-mail applications, each with its own level of security in place. Attacks to the user's system may result from poor administration on a distant system or manipulation of a host. In addition, the e-mail likely travels through network nodes over which the user has no control whatsoever. As a result, protecting the security of the e-mail system becomes even more challenging, if not virtually impossible, using conventional techniques.

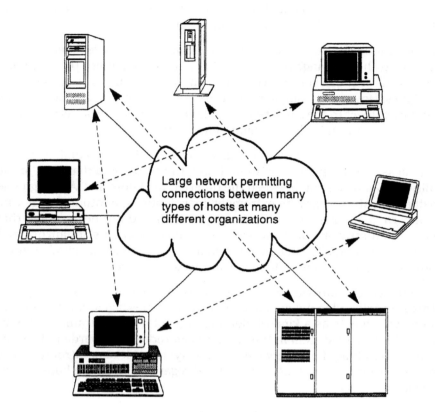

Exhibit 44.5. E-Mail Among Many Connected Hosts

One of the main methods of exchanging e-mail over the Internet is through use of the Simple Mail Transfer Protocol (SMTP). SMTP is designed to facilitate the exchange of e-mail between hosts, even if there has been no formal agreement or exchange of administrative information. As long as a host offers an SMTP server, another host can connect to it and send mail. For all intents and purposes, an SMTP host does not authenticate the name of the host that has contacted it or the name of the person who originated the message. Although this seems like a major security flaw, it is not surprising, given that the protocol allows the exchange of traffic between any host without prior arrangements. The approach is not unlike a post office, which delivers letters from anyone who correctly addresses an envelope. The post office does not ensure that the return address information is valid or authentic.

Traditional security techniques can still be used on an open network, but not when a connection from any host is accepted. Instead, a network connection can be established between known mail transfer agents that require two-way identification and authentication. Strict administrative control within each domain complements this arrangement. However, limiting connections also limits the number of correspondents with whom messages can be exchanged, which runs counter to one of the objectives of establishing the service.

More advanced security approaches are also available to users. Examples include using public-key encryption schemes, which are described later in the chapter.

APPROACHES TO SECURITY

Information security is not achieved by accident; it requires proper planning and performance of the right steps at the right time. Ensuring a secure e-mail implementation involves the same kind of process as is used for other business applications. For example:

- The need for e-mail security should be a consideration in each project phase. Whoever is managing the project must ensure that the required input is obtained from users, administrators, and security staff.
- Security criteria based on corporate standards should be formalized. E-mail packages can then be compared against the criteria to determine if they provide an acceptable level of security. Comparisons against the criteria can also be made after a planned configuration has been devised or a prototype has been installed (a pre-implementation review), and again after the system is fully functioning (a post-implementation review).
- Corporate security policy should be updated to reflect the e-mail environment. Security awareness programs for users should also be expanded, and proper training programs must be put into place.
- The e-mail system should be subject to a periodic security review.

Treating the e-mail system in the same way as other business applications can help ensure that adequate security is achieved and maintained.

Traditional Security Techniques

The particular security techniques selected for the e-mail system depends on the configuration and the mechanisms offered within the e-mail environment. As mentioned earlier, traditional security techniques can be used very effectively, particularly in single host systems. Examples of traditional techniques include

- Individual identification and authentication of each user of the system.
- Extended identification and authentication where remote access (e.g., dial-up) is permitted.

- Restrictions on access to mail directories and files so that each user can view only his own messages.
- Restrictions on access to services such as gateways to outside systems, particularly when the services incur additional cost.
- Individual identification and authentication of mail transfer agents.
- Regular monitoring of system use, particularly failed attempts to gain access to the system, a mail transfer agent, or mail files and directories. In addition, file and directory monitoring should include direct access attempts using operating system commands and utilities.

If a third-party system is used (either as the entire e-mail application or as a vehicle for transferring mail), it may be possible to reduce exposures by creating private networks. Resource constraints such as time, money, and expertise may mean that supporting an e-mail network is not possible. However, lower prices for e-mail packages coupled with decreasing communication costs and increasing speed may mean that a private network is cost-justified. Because it removes some of the concerns associated with a third-party service bureau, security may be increased.

In more complex environments, particularly where large networks are involved, it is not possible to exert this level of control over all possible participants in the e-mail system. In these cases, consideration must be given to more advanced security techniques as described in the next section.

Advanced Security Techniques

When dealing with large networks, it is not possible to know or control all participating network hosts and network paths. Although facilities may be secured, the existence of other less secure nodes renders systems more vulnerable. This requires use of more advanced security techniques to protect systems and e-mail traffic.

To increase security over network-connected e-mail hosts, emerging advanced security techniques include

- **Network firewalls and other types of traffic filtering.** These limit which foreign hosts can connect to internal computers. The main purpose is to protect internal computing resources by restricting access from outside (possibly hostile) host computers. A firewall usually includes an e-mail gateway that acts as the single point of contact for foreign hosts. The gateway then reroutes messages to internal hosts computers, as well as accepts outbound traffic.
- **Comparison of network identification information available from various protocols.** For example, a given host could be identified by an Ethernet address, a network address, and a network host name. If all three are recorded by the host, it is possible to check for consistency at a later time when a new connection is requested. If one of the items

of information varies, it may be that another node is pretending to be the known correspondent. Although this method is not totally fool-proof, it does provide an additional check that can help increase security.

- **Encryption of key network paths.** For example, a link between offices may use a public network over which there is no user control. Traffic going over the link can be encrypted and then decrypted at the other end under the user's control. If sound encryption techniques are used, the message content cannot be viewed, even if traffic is monitored or captured. In addition, message integrity is protected; if a message is somehow modified or corrupted, it will not be possible to decrypt it. Encryption offers significant advantages as an e-mail security technique because it addresses many exposures to loss of confidentiality and integrity. It also reduces the need for strict security over each e-mail system component and network path.

Using Public-Key Encryption

One approach to using encryption, known as public-key encryption, is particularly useful for the exchange of e-mail messages. Tools placed in the hands of end users allow them to exchange secure messages; the recipient has a high degree of certainty that a message comes from the person it claims to be from, it has not been altered in any way, and it has not been viewed by anyone else (including e-mail system administrators). This certainty comes at a relatively small cost (the software to encrypt and decrypt messages and the time to use them) and can operate without any changes to the e-mail system used to actually send a message.

Using public-key encryption, each user has two keys. One, known as the private key, is kept secret; the public key is given to anyone with whom the user wants to exchange messages. Knowledge of a user's public key does not allow determination of the user's private key.

The keys are used in the following manner:

- If a message is encrypted with a public key, only the private key can be used to decrypt it. Therefore, to send a message so that only the intended recipient can read it, a sender encrypts it using his public key, which has been made available.
- If a message can be decrypted with a public key, the sender must have been the one to encrypt the message with his private key. Therefore, to prove to someone that the sender sent a message, the sender would encrypt it with his private key. As a variation, if a number which uniquely characterizes the contents of the message is computed by the sender (sometimes known as a checksum or hash total, but referred to in this context as a message digest), the sender can also encrypt it and send it with the message. The recipient can then decrypt the message

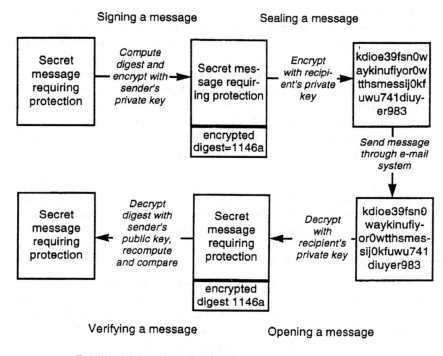

Exhibit 44.6. Four Public-Key Encryption Functions

digest, compute the value based on the message received, and compare it to the original to prove the message is unaltered.

These techniques can be combined to give us four main functions (see Exhibit 44.6) that are very similar to sending regular mail (only much more secure because of the encryption technology used):

- Signing a message to prove authorship. This involves computing a message digest, then encrypting the digest with a private key.
- Sealing a message to protect its confidentiality. This requires encrypting the message with the recipient's public key.
- Opening a message so that the contents can be viewed. Only the intended recipient can decrypt the message using his private key.
- Verifying a message to ensure it has come from the indicated sender. Using the public key of the sender is the only way to recover the message digest and check the contents.

Regardless of the path the message has been sent over, if the above steps are in place, the recipient can be assured that the message has come from the signer, that the message has not been changed in any way, and that he or she is the only person who could recover the message. The security of each e-mail system almost becomes a secondary consideration.

One complication of encryption schemes is the issue of key management. Under single-key encryption approaches, the correspondents must determine some way to securely exchange keys before communication takes place. With two-key encryption, getting the public key distributed is much simpler. Various schemes are possible, including central certification agencies, to distribute a person's public key so that a recipient can reliably authenticate a message. The problem of keeping a single key secret while communicating it between parties is greatly reduced.

Use of public-key encryption poses some problems:

- Legal restrictions may limit which encryption schemes can be used. This requires investigation for the particular jurisdiction in question.
- Networks may not be able to carry certain types of encrypted data if the results of the encryption yield nonstandard characters (e.g., those represented by an ASCII character value over 127). Fortunately, most encryption packages include a utility to convert an encrypted file to normal characters that can pass over any e-mail system or network.
- Users encrypt messages only if it is easy and fast to do. Fortunately, new encryption packages have been designed to link directly with the user interface of an e-mail system. Signing and sealing a message can be as simple as one or two additional clicks of a mouse button, eliminating the need for users to perform a separate encryption step.

Although they are not yet widely used, public-key encryption tools may become more and more prominent in the near future because of the level of protection they provide.

RECOMMENDED COURSE OF ACTION

This chapter has addressed the importance of e-mail security and control, as well as some of the exposures faced in implementing an e-mail system. Depending on the architecture, traditional security mechanisms and procedures may be adequate. Identification, authentication, access control, and monitoring can all be used to guarantee a level of security. Such emerging techniques as message encryption should be considered by the system administrator, especially when dealing with large, interconnected networks.

Chapter 45
Applets and Network Security: A Management Overview

Al Berg

Applets are small programs that reside on a host computer and are downloaded to a client computer to be executed. This model makes it very easy to distribute and update software. Because the new version of an application only needs to be placed on the server, clients automatically receive and run the updated version the next time they access the application.

The use of applets is possible because of the increasing bandwidth available to Internet and intranet users. The time required to download the programs has been decreasing even as program complexity has been increasing. The development of cross-platform languages such as Sun Microsystems, Inc.'s Java, Microsoft Corp.'s ActiveX, and Netscape Communications Corp.'s JavaScript has made writing applets for many different computers simple — the same exact Java or JavaScript code can be run on a Windows-based PC, a Macintosh, or a UNIX-based system without any porting or recompiling of code. Microsoft is working to port ActiveX to UNIX and Macintosh platforms.

APPLETS AND THE WEB

The World Wide Web is the place that users are most likely to encounter applets today. Java (and to a lesser degree, JavaScript) has become the Webmaster's tool of choice to add interesting effects to Web sites or to deliver applications to end users. Most of the scrolling banners, animated icons, and other special effects found on today's Web pages depend on applets to work. Some Web pages use applets for more substantial applications. For example, MapQuest (http://www.mapquest.com) uses Java and ActiveX to deliver an interactive street atlas of the entire U.S. *Wired* magazine offers a Java-based chat site that, when accessed over the Web, allows users to download an applet that lets them participate in real-time conferencing.

THE SECURITY ISSUE

Every silver lining has a cloud, and applets are no exception. Applets can present a real security hazard for users and network managers. When Web pages use applets, the commands that tell the client's browser to download and execute the applets are embedded in the pages themselves. Users have no way of knowing whether or not the next page that they download will contain an applet, and most of the time, they do not care. The Internet offers an almost limitless source of applets for users to run; however, no one knows who wrote them, whether they were written with malicious intent, or whether they contain bugs that might cause them to crash a user's computer.

Applets and computer viruses have a lot in common. Both applets and viruses are self-replicating code that executes on the user's computer without the user's consent. Some security experts have gone as far as to say that the corporate network manager should prohibit users from running applets at all. However, applets are becoming an increasingly common part of how users interact with the Internet and corporate intranets, so learning to live safely with applets is important for network managers.

WHAT ARE THE RISKS?

According to Princeton University's Safe Internet Programming (SIP) research team, there have been no publicly reported, confirmed cases of security breaches involving Java, though there have been some suspicious events that may have involved Java security problems. The lack of reported cases is no guarantee that there have not been breaches that either were not discovered or were not reported. But it does indicate that breaches are rare.

As Web surfing increasingly becomes a way to spend money, and applets become the vehicle for shopping, attacks on applets will become more and more profitable, increasing the risk. Sun, Netscape, and Microsoft all designed their applet languages with security in mind.

JAVA: SECURE APPLETS

Java programs are developed in a language similar to C++ and stored as source code on a server. When a client, such as a Web browser, requests a page that references a Java program, the source code is retrieved from the server and sent to the browser, where an integrated interpreter translates the source code statements into machine-independent bytecodes, which are executed by a virtual machine implemented in software on the client. This virtual machine is designed to be incapable of operations that might be detrimental to security, thus providing a secure sandbox in which programs can execute without fear of crashing the client system. Java applets loaded over a network are not allowed to:

- Read from files on the client system.
- Write to files on the client system.
- Make any network connections, except to the server from which they were downloaded.
- Start any client-based programs.
- Define native method calls, which would allow an applet to directly access the underlying computer.

Java was designed to make applets inherently secure. Following are some of the underlying language security features offered by Java:

- All of an applet's array references are checked to make sure that programs will not crash because of a reference to an element that does not exist.
- Complex and troublesome pointer variables (found in some vendors' products) that provide direct access to memory locations in the computer do not exist in Java, removing another cause of crashes and potentially malicious code.
- Variables can be declared as unchangeable at runtime to prevent important program parameters from being modified accidentally or intentionally.

JAVA: HOLES AND BUGS

Although Sun has made every effort to make the Java virtual machine unable to run code that will negatively impact the underlying computer, researchers have already found bugs and design flaws that could open the door to malicious applets.

The fact that Sun has licensed Java to various browser vendors adds another level of complexity to the security picture. Not only can security be compromised by a flaw in the Java specification, but the vendor's implementation of the specification may contain its own flaws and bugs.

DENIAL-OF-SERVICE THREATS

Denial-of-service attacks involve causing the client's Web browser to run with degraded performance or crash. Java does not protect the client system from these types of attacks, which can be accomplished simply by putting the client system into a loop to consume processor cycles, creating new process threads until system memory is consumed, or placing locks on critical processes needed by the browser.

Because denial-of-service attacks can be programmed to occur after a time delay, it may be difficult for a user to determine which page the offending applet was downloaded from. If an attacker is subtle and sends an applet that degrades system performance, the user may not know that their computer is under attack, leading to time-consuming and expensive troubleshooting of a nonexistent hardware or software problem.

Java applets are not supposed to be able to establish network connections to machines other than the server they were loaded from. However, there are applets that exploit bugs and design flaws that allow it to establish a back-door communications link to a third machine (other than the client or server). This link could be used to send information that may be of interest to a hacker. Because many ready-to-use Java applets are available for download from the Internet, it would be possible for an attacker to write a useful applet, upload it to a site where Webmasters would download it, and then sit back and wait for information sent by the applet to reach their systems.

WHAT KIND OF INFORMATION CAN THE APPLET SEND BACK?

Due to another implementation problem found in August 1996 by the Safe Internet Programming research team at Princeton University, the possibilities are literally endless. A flaw found in Netscape Navigator versions 3.0 beta 5 and earlier versions, and Microsoft Internet Explorer 3.0 beta 2 and earlier versions, allows applets to gain full read and write access to the files on a Web surfer's machine. This bug means that the attacker can get copies of any files on the machine or replace existing data or program files with hacked versions.

Giving Java applets the ability to connect to an arbitrary host on the network or Internet opens the door to another type of attack. A malicious applet, downloaded to and running on a client inside of a firewalled system, could establish a connection to another host behind the firewall and access files and programs. Because the attacking host is actually inside the secured system, the firewall will not know that the access is actually originating from outside the network.

Another bug found in August 1996 by the Princeton team affects only Microsoft Internet Explorer version 3.0 and allows applets (which are not supposed to be allowed to start processes on the client machine) to execute any DOS command on the client. This allows the applet to delete or change files or programs or insert new or hacked program code such as viruses or backdoors. Microsoft has issued a patch (available on its Web site at http://www.microsoft.com/ie) to Internet Explorer that corrects the problem.

Princeton's SIP team also found a hole that would allow a malicious application to execute arbitrary strings of machine code, even though the Java virtual machine is only supposed to be able to execute the limited set of Java bytecodes. The problem was fixed in Netscape Navigator 3.0 beta 6 and Microsoft Internet Explorer 3.0 beta 2.

JAVASCRIPT: A DIFFERENT GRIND

Netscape's JavaScript scripting language may be named Java, but it is distinct from Sun's applet platform. JavaScript is Netscape Navigator's built-in scripting language that allows Webmasters to do cross-platform development of applets that control browser events, objects such as tables and forms, and various activities that happen when users click on an object with their mouse.

Like Java, JavaScript runs applications in a virtual machine to prevent them from performing functions that would be detrimental to the operation of the client workstations. Also like Java, there are several flaws in the implementation of the security features of JavaScript. Some of the flaws found in JavaScript include the ability for malicious applets to:

- Obtain users' E-mail addresses from their browser configuration.
- Track the pages that a user visits and mail the results back to the script author.
- Access the client's file system, reading and writing files.

A list of JavaScript bugs and fixes can be found on John LoVerso's Web page at the Open Software Foundation (http://www.osf.org/~ loverso/javascript/).

ActiveX: Microsoft's Vision for Distributed Component Computing. Microsoft's entry in the applet development tool wars, ActiveX, is very different from Java and presents its own set of security challenges. ActiveX is made up of server and client components, including:

- Controls, which are applets that can be embedded in Web pages and executed at the client. Controls can be written in a number of languages, including Visual Basic and Visual C++.
- Documents that provide access to non-HTML content, such as word processing documents or spreadsheets, from a Web browser.
- The Java virtual machine, which allows standard Java applets to run at the client.
- Scripting, which allows the Web developer to control the integration of controls and Java applets on a Web page.
- The server framework, which provides a number of server-side functions such as database access and data security.

Java applets running in an ActiveX environment (e.g., Microsoft's Internet Explorer Web browser) use the same security features and have the same security issues associated with JavaScript. Microsoft offers a Java development environment (i.e., Visual J++) as well as other sandbox languages (i.e., VBScript, based on Visual Basic and JScript, Microsoft's implementation of Netscape's JavaScript) for the development of applications that are limited as to the functions they can perform.

When developers take advantage of ActiveX's ability to integrate programs written in Visual Basic or C++, the virtual machine model of Java no longer applies. In these cases, compiled binaries are transferred from the server to the Web client for execution. These compiled binaries have full access to the underlying computing platform, so there is no reason that the application could not read and write files on the client system, send information from the client to the server (or another machine), or perform a destructive act such as erasing a disk or leaving a virus behind.

USING AUTHENTICODE FOR ACCOUNTABILITY

Microsoft's approach to security for non-Java ActiveX applications is based on the concept of accountability — knowing with certainty the identity of the person or company that wrote a piece of software and that the software was not tampered with by a third party. Microsoft sees the issues related to downloading applets from the Web as similar to those involved in purchasing software; users need to know where the software is coming from and that it is intact. Accountability also means that writers of malicious code could be tracked down and would have to face consequences for their actions.

The mechanism that Microsoft offers to implement this accountability is called Authenticode. Authenticode uses a digital signature attached to each piece of software downloaded from the Internet. The signature is a cryptographic code attached by the software developer to an applet. Developers must enter a private key (known only to them) to sign their application, assuring their identity. The signature also includes an encrypted checksum of the application itself, which allows the client to determine if the applet has changed since the developer released it.

ACTIVEX: THE DOWNSIDE

This approach provides developers and users with access to feature-rich applications, but at a price. If an application destroys information on a user's computer, accountability will not help recover their data or repair damage done to their business. Once the culprit has been found, bringing them to justice may be difficult because new computer crimes are developing faster than methods for prosecuting them.

Microsoft acknowledges that Authenticode does not guarantee that end users will never download malicious code to their PCs and that it is a first step in the protection of information assets.

Further information on ActiveX can be found on Microsoft's Web site (http://www.microsoft.com/activex) and at the ActiveX Web site run by CNet Technology Corp. (http://www.activex.com).

AN OUNCE OF PREVENTION

So far, this article has discussed problems posed by applets. Following are some steps that can be taken to lessen the exposure faced by users.

Make Sure the Basics Are Covered

Users need to back up their data and programs consistently, and sensitive data should be stored on secure machines. The surest way to avoid applet security problems is to disable support for applet execution at the browser. If the code cannot execute, it cannot do damage.

Of course, the main downside of this approach is that the users will lose the benefits of being able to run applets. Because the ability to run applets is part of the client browser, turning off applets is usually accomplished at the desktop and a knowledgeable user could simply turn applet support back on. Firewall vendors are starting to provide support for filtering out applets, completely or selectively, before they enter the local network.

Users Should Run the Latest Available Versions of Their Web Browsers

Each new version corrects not only functional and feature issues, but security flaws. If an organization is planning to use applets on its Web pages, it is preferable to either write them internally or obtain them from trusted sources. If applets will be downloaded from unknown sources, a technical person with a good understanding of the applet language should review the code to be sure that it does only what it claims to.

Mark LaDue, a researcher at Georgia Tech has a Web page (available at http://www.math.gatech.edu/~mladue/HostileApplets.html) containing a number of hostile applets available for download and testing. Seeing some real applications may help users recognize new problem applets that may be encountered.

CONCLUSION

IS personnel should monitor the Princeton University Safe Internet Programming group's home page (located at http://www.cs.princeton.edu/sip) for the latest information on security flaws and fixes (under News). It is also a good idea to keep an eye on browser vendors' home pages for news of new versions.

Applets offer users and network managers a whole new paradigm for delivering applications to the desktop. Although, like any new technology, applets present a new set of challenges and concerns, their benefits can be enjoyed while their risks can be managed.

Section 6
Management of LAN-Based Enterprise Networks

Throughout this edition of the *Handbook*, we have emphasized the themes of maintaining high performance and adding value to the enterprise. Never is this emphasis more important than once a LAN-based enterprise network has been installed, and management's attention has shifted from implementation to operation and management. This section focuses on several different aspects of management, beginning with management strategy. In particular, Chapter 46 demonstrates the need for a management strategy by providing a counterexample entitled "Managing Enterprise Systems Without a Strategy: A Case Study." Given the need for a management strategy, Chapter 47 makes the case for including "Proactive Performance Management" in that strategy.

The next several chapters focus on specific management issues. Chapter 48 discusses "Issues in Managing Multimedia Networks," providing insight into the unique management challenges posed by multimedia applications.

Not all uses of LAN technology are as visible as multimedia. Some are nearly taken for granted despite the immense value they bring to an organization. An example of this is a function often provided by a LAN support department: networked data storage management. A number of tools and pieces of equipment can aid in this task, yet one element that is all too often overlooked is the definition of backup procedures. Chapter 49, "Network Data and Storage Management Techniques," discusses a number of backup strategies, along with their pros and cons.

As enterprise networks grow in scope and complexity, the ability to effectively track network assets, both hardware and software, is diminished. Fortunately, such tracking has become easier in recent years, thanks to the development of a new class of management applications. Chapter 50, "License Tracking and Metering Software," surveys the types of services currently available with such tools.

With the increasing sophistication of today's operating systems, some administrative tools are being built into the operating system, thus they need not be purchased separately. Sometimes it is all too easy to overlook the value of such tools. One particularly valuable tool is the subject of Chapter 51, "Working with NT's Performance Monitor," which discusses its general capabilities and examines its basic operation. Closely related, but more general in its focus, Chapter 52 takes a look at "Evaluating the Performance of NT-Based Systems."

The remainder of this section addresses security issues associated with the management of LAN-based enterprise networks. Chapter 53 starts this discussion by focusing on "Developing a Network Security Plan." In this chapter, the level of security and control complexity associated with distributed environments is brought into focus, and models for increasing the security, auditability, and control of such environments are presented.

Finally, while nearly every sizeable enterprise with Internet connectivity utilizes a firewall to protect its intranet, it is not clear how many of those enterprises have firewall management plans in place to protect their firewalls from attack. Chapter 54, "Firewall Management and Internet Attacks," discusses several types of firewall attacks and prescribes specific firewall management techniques that can reduce the associated risks.

Chapter 46
Managing Enterprise Systems Without a Strategy: A Case Study

Michael J. Masterson

Enterprise systems began and developed in the Clover Corporation (not the real name of the company examined in this case study) much in the same way they have in many organizations. A few standalone mainframe-based systems were initiated in the 1970s. By the 1980s, the number of incompatible standalone systems in Clover had mushroomed to more than 100 systems. These systems were linked by a network, but systems interoperability was not approached until there was a centralized LAN strategy implemented. Today, the LAN and telecommunications systems have become the backbone for the organization; but unless newer IT strategies are developed, these systems will no longer be able to keep up with the changing needs of Clover and its employees.

AN OVERVIEW OF THE ORGANIZATION AND ITS SYSTEMS

Over 2300 personnel work in the numerous structures housing this organization. Information technology (IT) provides the backbone for this task-diverse, operationally dispersed organization. The local area network (LAN) has evolved into the electronic central nervous system of the organization. Despite its importance to the company, Clover's communications and information technology policy was left to staff members best described as junior technical specialists. Senior management abdicated providing the IT vision for the Clover technological infrastructure.

MIXED AND MISMATCHED DEVELOPMENT

In about 1971, two of the first automated data program offices created and managed at Clover were for aircraft fuel systems and a system for tracking/tasking parts for aircraft maintenance. These offices functioned as stand-alone entities with host mainframe-based data and hardware to support the field-site users of these automated systems. Concurrent with the initiation of these stand-alone applications, a Field Assistance Branch

(FAB) was created to support customer requests for assistance from the users of the automated systems in the field. The FAB remains dedicated to support end-users, from basic troubleshooting to program code correction. A host mainframe system linked to the LAN and a wide area network (WAN) serves as the repository of all problem reports and effective solutions arrived at by the FAB.

More and more automated systems were placed under development at Clover, frequently as immediate solutions to immediate problems. A tremendous mismatch of systems evolved under this ad hoc, by default, strategy for information technology implementation by Clover management. Interoperability was never a consideration in systems development; consequently, the accessibility and information sharing capability (reach and range) of these automated systems — and their supporting offices — was no broader than each unique system. The result was a large number of "stovepipe" systems and offices — two automated systems created by people working literally 15 feet apart were completely incompatible.

BOSS, I HAVE A BETTER IDEA

In the early 1980s, a trio of energetic junior electrical engineers recognized the problems caused by these stovepipe systems and proposed a solution: a dual broadband network (i.e., a simplex broadband circuit, every node having separate input/output broadband feeds) for data communications. This broadband backbone was approved and built, incorporating twisted-wire pair circuits, running at 9600 bps, in use by each separate automated system office. The data network structure allowed network movement of host mainframe information within Clover, as well as allowing users in the field to network into the appropriate host mainframes. The enthusiastic response to this data network led to a medium upgrade for more bandwidth. The data communications broadband was upgraded to coaxial cable, running at 10 Mbps, allowing faster response and more user access.

Initial Failures with Implementing a LAN

After completion of the data communications network, the junior technicians understood that with a software upgrade to the existing applications, an information network could be piggybacked onto the data communications network backbone. The perceived value (by the technicians) of coordinating interoffice communications drove the creation of the information network. The LAN operated at 10 Mbps, the same speed as the data communications network. However, the diverse nature of stand-alone, office-specific software regularly overloaded the network software. In addition, conflicts between network management software and the plethora of office computer hardware led to interoperability blow-ups, resulting in a complete network shutdown. Clover's Director of Computer Operations described the technology platform as "one big kludge."

ENTERPRISEWIDE POLICY CREATES A SUCCESS

The next step in the network creation process was the designation of the LAN shop as the responsible office for network operations. Unfortunately, it took Clover senior management 23 years of fighting the Medusa of information technology within Clover before authorizing this step. With this came the authority to correct the kludged-together systems at Clover. Senior management's tasking did include support for the upgrade to a Fiber Distributed Data Interface (FDDI) LAN. Clover's FDDI LAN operates with carrier sense multiple access, with collision detection (CSMA/CD) protocol, bus configuration, and runs at 100 Mbps as the high-speed LAN for information handling in Clover. Also, the LAN office was able to collect and standardize the numerous hardware and software systems still operating within Clover. Formal office automation standards and programs were implemented to prevent a return of kludged systems. However, interoperability problems were discovered between the new versions of office software, the application programs, and the still-diverse Clover computer hardware.

Centralized LAN office authority for control of all Clover office automation, both software and hardware, has eliminated many of these problems. This control led to the installation of interoperable, 386-processor-based hardware, and Microsoft Windows 3.1 software. The LAN office now had a common body of knowledge to focus on when troubleshooting problems.

It must be noted that this brief history of the Clover LAN comes from outside the organization, with a clear view of a mature, robust network. As previously noted, a 23-year timeframe shaped the evolution of the Clover LAN. This long trip clearly demonstrates what the lack of IT vision from senior leadership created — and sustained: segmented operations, sets of stand-alone systems, and internal barriers to adaptation (Keen) for the Clover information technology platform. However, the positive aspect is the use of technology and software to overcome hardware limitations.

CURRENT LAN CONFIGURATION

An overview of the fiber optic LAN configuration is covered first, followed by the data communications network. This is a logical order since the fiber optic LAN is the most common link into the host-mainframe-based data communications network.

Desktop. Every person employed in an office at Clover has at least a 386 IBM-compatible personal computer on his/her desk. Most offices are equipped with 486sx33 machines set up with Microsoft Windows. This platform enables approximately 2100 people to have individual links into the FDDI LAN. The information network uses Novell software operating with Ethernet_2 LAN implementation. As previously mentioned, CSMA/CD broadcast protocol is used with a bus configuration. Also, a transmission control procedure/internet protocol (TCP/IP) for file transfers into the Clover Data Communications Network (DCN), a Corporate Data Network, or Internet is used. All network operations behind the desktop Windows functions are transparent to users.

Monitors. Network monitors indicate the Clover FDDI LAN handles at least 126,000 E-mail data messages per month. No estimate is available for the number of file transfers or host-mainframe data packets transfers per month. In addition, some of the layers in the FDDI LAN meet open system interconnection (OSI) model standards.

Local Gateways. From every network user node, access into the LAN is via RG-58A, a 10base2 Thinnet cable operating at 10 Mbps, connecting to the office local gateway — the multimedia access center (MMAC) (interview/briefing). MMACs isolate all traffic destined for the local office subnet, switching local subnet traffic to the correct node. Any data packets addressed outside the local subnet are managed and controlled by the MMAC. The heart of the MMAC is the intelligent repeater module (IRM). The IRM performs all repeater functions for each of the MMACs 30 ports, regardless of media type. In addition, the IRM provides the network management and control functions for the MMAC, including error detection, retiming data packets, and regenerating data preamble. A media interface module (Mim) provides the ability to use a variety of media outbound from the MMAC, to include twisted wire pair, fiber optic cable, or thick/thin ethernet coaxial cable. Of note, each MMAC can support an office LAN of up to 30 connections. However, it is LAN office policy to only have 20 individual IP addresses per MMAC. This prevents segment overload and allows flexibility for diagnostic troubleshooting.

In the Clover LAN, the MMAC Mim is set for RG-6 thicknet coaxial cable, operating at 10 Mbps, linking to the office LAN file server, a 486dx66 machine running Novell Network software. The 21 file servers in the FDDI LAN provide the shared data/programs and disk drives among the office LAN users.

Routers. In addition, the thicknet cable connects to the LAN routers. These routers operate at OSI model layer 3 and act as the traffic cops for LAN traffic (interview). Routers look at the layer 3 protocol and make decisions based on the type of media/data packet. This requires that every router in the Clover LAN be able to interpret any layer 3 protocol used in the system. The more protocols in use, the more processing time on each packet and the more of a bottleneck the router will become. The routers are multilegged, usually connecting up to four separate office LANs from one building. Routers are also called *fiber hubs* for each Clover LAN operating location. As the hub for the LAN, the router is where the switch from the information network into the broadband data communications host-mainframe computer occurs.

Bridges. The routers connect via fiber optic cable operating at 100 Mbps to the fiber bridges — the backbone of the FDDI LAN. Each Clover operating location has at least one FX 8210-N-E/fiber bridge node. These *remote bridges* transfer data between two Ethernet/IEEE 802.3 LANs over the FDDI backbone (interview). In addition, the FX 8210-N-E2 operates as a *local bridge* that transfers data between any two Ethernet/IEEE 802.3 LANs connected to it by the router. Therefore, this fiber bridge provides three data paths, controlled by the fiber bridge CPU:

- *Remote Bridging.* For LAN to FDDI and FDDI to LAN connections.
- *Local Bridging.* LAN to LAN connections.

For data handling, all LAN data frames are received by the local area network controller in the fiber bridge and stored in the bridge buffer memory (BBM). The destination addresses of the frames are checked against the addresses stored in the address table. Frames addressed to remote stations (i.e., to be transferred to FDDI) are forwarded by optical transmitters to the FDDI ring.

Gateways. One other critical level of the LAN are the gateways into other network environments. Any LAN data packets addressed for an automated system host-mainframe, the corporate information network, or Internet locations are routed to the appropriate gateway. These gateways operate at OSI layer 6 and are concerned with translating the media/data packets to allow transfer between two very different computer environments. The first is internal to Clover, e.g., linking the desktop environment to a data communications network host-mainframe. The second is external, translating out to (or inbound from) the corporate information network to work with users at field locations, or into the Internet. All data transferred from the FDDI LAN to the gateways moves at the broadband speed of 10 Mbps. There are no fiber optic gateways off the Clover LAN.

Backups. As the history of the Clover networks shows, the data communications network (DCN) was the first network created at Clover. In addition, the 10 Mbps broadband DCN functions as the backup to the FDDI LAN. If a fiber optics connection is broken, the entire Clover LAN reverts to the broadband DCN, and everything slows to 10 Mbps. Normally, the LAN office's first indication of a problem on the FDDI network originates with multiple complaints about the "slowdown" of the network.

Mainframe Access. DCN host-mainframes are the repositories of all the databases for the 147+ automated data systems developed, deployed, and managed by Clover. Several requirements must be met for a user in a desktop environment to gain access to one of the DCN host-mainframes. The user must require access to the database, be an authorized operator on the Clover FDDI LAN, have the correct host-mainframe emulation package installed on his/her desktop computer, and must be fluent in COBOL. All these factors help control (or prohibit) access to the host-mainframe. This is a valid concern for Clover program offices since once access to the mainframe is gained, permanent, undetected changes to the database can be accomplished. The LAN routers are the key to user access from the desktop, with the router sending the data packet into the 10-Mbps broadband loop to the appropriate gateway for the host-mainframe. The emulation software in the desktop environment masks all the network actions from the user. Once connected, the user operates the desktop hardware as though it was a host-mainframe-connected dumb terminal.

THE OTHER COMMUNICATION SYSTEM

One other platform at Clover is the *plain old telephone service* (POTS). Of course, there is a telephone on every employee's desk. However, Clover employees rely on the LAN almost to the exclusion of POTS. Common practice is to send an e-mail and go on to other business, and voice contact is eliminated. All too often, the result is complaints to the LAN office because "e-mail" did not go through. Occasionally, the LAN office finds a system problem. Usually, the problem is solved with the advice: "RY*!?%M" (Read Your *!?% Mail)!

FUTURE OF IT AT CLOVER: TIME FOR NEW STRATEGIES

LAN architecture at Clover is a mature, robust system. The business of Clover would be critically damaged without the technology platform currently in use. However, many concerns and decision points create uncertainty about the future information technology platform at Clover. Problems of hardware and software have already been identified by computer operations personnel. These include:

- Hard drive memory of the 21 file servers is already at maximum capacity; 6-gigabit hard drive memory units are to be installed to correct this problem.
- Prior to designation of an authorized LAN office, new versions of office automation software were impossible to implement across Clover due to inability to secure site licenses. File server-based office automation software was purchased (21 copies), and site licenses of 100 users/copy obtained. The result is easier control, upgrade, and troubleshooting of office software.

- All office automation software versions are forward compatible, but not backward compatible; for example, a file built on Microsoft Word 3.1 and sent to a machine using Word for Office 4.0 would work, but could not be sent back to the 3.1 version without special action. In some cases, there is complete incompatibility from old to new software.
- Acquisition and installation of a new Pentium-based computer systems was to commence in the spring of 1995. The increased speed and power of these machines increased the strain on the LANs slowest link — the thin/thicknet medium from the desktop to fiber optic cable. Cost estimates to upgrade to fiber optics to each desktop were estimated to be millions of dollars. No funding was available.
- Full open systems interconnection model standards were to be implemented throughout Clover. This should clear up the software compatibility difficulties mentioned previously. No completion date was set.

A serious problem is the soon-to-be reached hardware limit of available nodes on the FDDI LAN. As presently configured, the LAN can support 2250 individual users; 2100 users are on the network. However, corporate organization downsizing and restructuring means Clover will be increasing by at least 300 users in the near future. No solution is available to increase LAN capacity.

Another corporate reorganization action with serious future impact on the Clover LAN is the designation of Clover as one of four IT centers under corporate headquarters. Clover's information technology platform is not compatible or interoperable with either the other three centers or the corporate headquarters. Restructuring was finalized before the question of information technology reach and range was addressed.

Myopic Funding Strategy

A driving force contributing directly to virtually all of these current and future problems for the Clover LAN is the corporate funding and budget process. As the evolution of the network shows, funding for new systems is readily available. However, none of the 147+ automated data systems that Clover has brought online included system maintenance, training, or upgrade funding. According to one IT staff member at Clover, the senior leadership IT vision is summed up as: "Here is the new system; make it work/last/succeed." The IT funding process severely limits the IT vision of the future for Clover.

CONCLUSION

This case study of the Clover LAN clearly shows the importance of the system for current successful operations. However, senior leadership has consistently undermanaged the information technology platform at Clover. Every step of growth of the company's information systems improved

Clover business operations. Despite this importance, the Clover information technology platform will reach its limits of accessibility and interoperability by the year 2000. Without total senior management commitment to a clear information technology vision for the future, Clover as a corporate entity will be disabled for pursuit of future business options.

ACKNOWLEDGMENT

The author would like to thank all the IT staff members at Clover who helped to make this article possible.

Recommended Reading

Carr, Houston H., "Managing End User Computing," 2nd ed., Auburn University Press, 1994.
Carr, Houston H. and Snyder, Charles A., "The Management of Business Telecommunications," Auburn University Press, April, 1994.
Keen, Peter G.W., "Shaping the Future: Business Design Through Information Technology," Harvard Business School Press, 1991.
Stamper, David A., "Business Data Communications," 3rd ed., The Benjamin/Cummings Publishing Company, Inc., 1991.

Chapter 47
Proactive Performance Management

Tim Clark

Once viewed as internal utilities for interorganization communication, the networks of today are being built to deliver essential business processes to partners and to customers. It is critical for organizations to be able to proactively manage the available bandwidth and systems for effective overall performance management.

Network management is a term that encompasses many complex, interrelated disciplines. Many organizations define the elements of network management as FCAPS — fault management, configuration management, accounting/billing, performance management, and security management — and try to address each element. However, the primary emphasis in many organizations is on fault determination and event isolation and correlation. These are critical elements, obviously, but the changing nature and complexity of the network are elevating the importance of performance management.

Enterprise networks are increasingly becoming a critical delivery mechanism for the products and services of a company. Corporate intranets are being accessed by business partners and even the public to perform basic business transactions. The purchase of books, the tracking of packages, and home banking are just a few examples of goods and services being delivered over the Internet.

With this trend, the enterprise network is both more critical to the day-to-day business operations of an entity and under more stress. The bandwidth demands are skyrocketing as the usage of the new Web-based applications grows. The potential for bottlenecks grows. To meet these increasing demands, LAN and WAN switches are being deployed. Service providers are augmenting the private network. The performance of this new network is much more complex to manage than its relatively static and stable, in-house router-based predecessor.

THE CURRENT STATE OF PERFORMANCE MANAGEMENT

Organizations today often have a variety of different tools to help manage the performance of the network. Those that have mainframes deployed are running a version of TME 10 NetView. SNMP (Simple Network Management Protocol) management applications by HP, IBM, Sun, Cabletron, and others are being widely deployed. Applications from router and switch vendors help to manage those elements and devices. A wide range of specific point tools provide information limited to a particular facet of performance management.

These tools are utilized to conduct many different types of network performance analysis:

- monitor real-time network performance
- network performance threshold alarms
- historical network performance reports
- network performance service level agreements (SLAs)
- LAN capacity planning
- WAN capacity planning
- server capacity planning
- network modeling
- baselining
- benchmarking

The analysis is performed using performance reports from a very wide range of network components:

- routers
- serial links
- frame relay CIR
- Ethernet segments
- token-ring segments
- hubs
- LAN switches
- WAN switches
- servers
- workstations
- applications

Despite the plethora of tools and the variety of tasks that are undertaken in the typical enterprise network, comprehensive and proactive performance management still eludes many organizations. The barriers are numerous. In many cases, there is insufficient staff available that have the experience and training necessary to configure and administer the system, write applications to enhance the system, and maintain the system. As a result, organizations often resort to reacting to network performance problems rather than proactively managing the network's performance.

Exhibit 47.1 should be used to evaluate the current state of performance management within an organization.

Exhibit 47.1.   Performance Management Checklist

1. Do you know the exact state of the network across the enterprise at any given time?	Yes___ No___
2. Do you know the demand on network resources?	Yes___ No___
3. Do you know how and where things have changed on the network?	Yes___ No___
4. Do you know where problems are emerging — or are about to emerge?	Yes___ No___
5. Do you know who is using the network?	Yes___ No___
6. Do you have instant accessibility of real-time performance data?	Yes___ No___
7. Do you have realtime trending statistics from across the enterprise?	Yes___ No___
8. Do you have reliable access to critical information for making business decisions?	Yes___ No___
9. Are you able to identify over/under utilized resources?	Yes___ No___
10. Can you spot trouble before it starts?	Yes___ No___
11. Are you able to plan your network's growth with accurate useable information?	Yes___ No___
12. Can you see, analyze, and baseline all ports on all routers, hubs, and switches?	Yes___ No___
13. Can you provide management with the network reports it wants?	Yes___ No___

PROACTIVE PERFORMANCE MANAGEMENT

The goal of proactive performance management is to ensure that SLAs are being met and will continue to be met. To accomplish this goal, it is necessary to identify current and potential bottlenecks, inefficient or poorly performing components, and potential failures. Proactive performance management is the gathering of statistical data for monitoring and correcting the operation, and measuring the overall effectiveness of the network as well as aiding in the network planning and analysis process. Performance management is not performed in a vacuum, however. It must be integrated with other network management functions, like fault management and event correlation, to be maximally effective. Performance and fault management should be tightly integrated to ensure NMS and operations staff are aware of potential errors or trends that could impact client services.

Performance management involves establishing a set of performance objectives for resources and addressing the following steps:

1. *Monitoring:* tracks resource and communication activities in order to gather the appropriate data for determining performance.
2. *Thresholding:* sets and modifies the operational standards (e.g., threshold values) by which the system performance is monitored and judged.
3. *Reporting:* involves the presentation of gathered data.
4. *Analyzing and trending:* consists of trending and statistical analysis, which *was* performed by network operators and planners to assess the results of performance measures. New software systems now do this for you.

5. *Modeling:* imports performance data to predict where additional resources will be required to meet SLAs and to understand what impact a new application will have on current resources.
6. *Tuning:* focuses on the adjustment or reconfiguration of resources and communications activities to improve performance.

Exhibit 47.2 illustrates the relationships between these various activities and the key interaction between performance management steps and fault management.

Exhibit 47.3 lists the required elements of a proactive performance management system or set of systems.

DEVELOPING A BASELINE

In order to begin a process of enhancing the performance management capabilities of an organization, one must begin with a baseline. With today's technology, few problems are caused by equipment failure. Most are caused by the increasing demands being placed on large and complex networks. To get a jump on these problems, one needs a comprehensive picture of the network that can be used for the analysis and modeling efforts that are part of any ongoing network design task.

One must have a baseline of past activity by which to judge present and future performance. With a baseline established, network hot spots can be acted on quickly or can be predicted and prevented altogether. Developing a baseline requires the focus on the first three activities in performance management: monitoring, thresholding, and reporting.

Most organizations have implemented products and systems that are already gathering information about network performance. SNMP MIB performance metrics represent specific performance characteristics of network elements. SNMP MIB attributes are periodically polled and trend data is collected over a period of time. Some metrics are requested on a demand-only basis, while others are collected only when an alarm condition exists on the network. Networks contain a wealth of information in their SNMP MIBs and Remote Monitoring (RMON) data. However, collecting and analyzing the data can be an arduous, resource-intensive process. The development of a network baseline should pull together the relevant SNMP and RMON data that are indicators of network performance. Exhibit 47.4 illustrates these indicators.

Resource availability statistics, derived from the fault management system, are the actual measure of the accessibility of a network resource when compared to the time the resource should be available. It must be noted that there is a clear distinction between reliability and availability. Reliability is the measure of the network's ability to function without failure. Availability is the measure of the network's ability to serve the purpose for

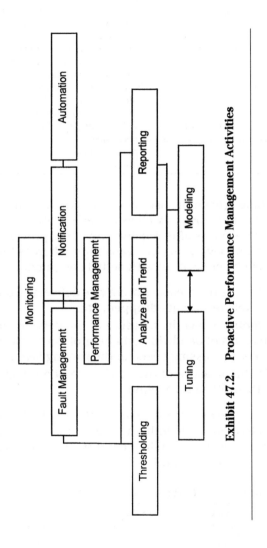

Exhibit 47.2. Proactive Performance Management Activities

Exhibit 47.3. Required Elements of a Proactive Performance Management System

Required Elements	Benefits
Monitor hardware, software, remote links, and systems	Enables shift from reactive to *proactive* network performance management
27 □ 7 collection of SNMP and RMON statistics	Enables staff to quantify network performance; improves understanding of network health and performance
Automatic notification of performance alerts	Increases end-user satisfaction and productivity; avoids additional headcount and capital expenditures
Predictive trend analysis	Predicts when next trouble spots will occur and identifies cause; solves problems before they impact network service levels
Daily reports and reviews of network performance trends and capacity trends	Enables true proactive management; provides necessary factual data and frees up IT personnel to focus on more strategic objectives

which it was installed (from the user perspective). Availability depends on the reliability of the network, as well as the efficiency of the network control staff to restore services after a failure. As noted previously, clients will primarily be concerned with service availability, whereas the network control center will also be concerned with actual component reliability.

- *Quality of service* is the measure of service delivery in terms of number of errors, packets or circuits dropped, etc.
- *Capacity* or *throughput* is the measure of the network size and can be measured in terms of bandwidth, number of WAN links in the physical layer, or packet processing speed in the routing layer.
- *Utilization* is the measure of the actual use of a resource when compared to its theoretical throughput.

Once the appropriate monitoring is set in place, thresholding allows network technicians to monitor, identify, analyze, and react to changes in system and network performance. When conditions occur that cause monitored parameters to fall outside of predetermined thresholds, the

Exhibit 47.4. Indicators of Network Performance

Network	Resource Availability	Quality of Service	Capacity	Utilization
Physical	Link status	Disrupted seconds %	Bandwidth	Bandwidth usage %
Routing	Device/interface status	Packets dropped %	Packets per second	Packet per second %
LAN (Ethernet, Token Ring)	Status	Error packets	Bandwidth	Bandwidth usage %

management system can be set to trigger alarms or monitor and report changes in system status. For each indicator of interest, thresholds must be carefully selected. Thresholds that are too rigid will result in frequent alarms, while thresholds that are too relaxed can result in performance degradation that may be overlooked by support personnel. In the development of a baseline, thresholds can identify current hot spots and potential problems.

The final step in developing a network baseline is the development of pertinent reports for communication to various constituents. This then becomes an ongoing process, particularly with new tools that allow the easy publishing of the information via corporate intranets. Performance and capacity reports can be generated using a variety of reporting tools. These tools provide an automated process to easily summarize SNMP MIB element data that has been collected from network objects. The reporting features of these tools allow for report generation as well as immediate online viewing of the data.

Performance reports are useful to clients, the network operations staff, and the network systems planning group. These reports will provide the vehicle to assist network planners in preventing future outages and drops below the minimum service levels agreements (SLAs), as well as allowing sufficient time for the network system planning to provide necessary network resources for the future. An excellent medium for providing personnel with reports is via HTML Web pages over the corporate intranet. Performance problems may be due to inadequate resources (e.g., bandwidth), inefficient processes (e.g., unnecessary encapsulation of protocols), or an inefficiently used resource (e.g., excessive noise on a circuit requiring retransmission). Some sample performance and capacity reports are described below.

- *Resource availability report:* The minimum/average/maximum availability of the network resource reported for a day/week/month; 99.91 percent availability over a period of time.
- *Resource maintainability report:* the mean time to repair (MTTR) for the network resource.
- *Resource failure report:* the number of resources reported to be unavailable for more than 'n' time.

Online Utilization Reports

The following reports can be provided online to the user community:

- LAN utilization
- interface utilization statistics
- environmental reporting

Automated Trend Analysis

A statistical analysis is needed for graphs of collected data. The analysis could contain a description of the data's behavior, including any trends. It may contain an opinion with a recommendation to change. It can provide the statistics derived from the data for those who like such numbers. The enclosed statistics should include data set minimum, maximum, average, standard deviation, and linear regression parameters. For example, the bandwidth utilization graph with an analysis tells one if the usage trend is increasing to the point of degraded performance. If so, it will predict a theoretical date that performance will hit 100 percent and it will advise one to upgrade the bandwidth speed. Separate advice should be provided to accommodate serial links, Ethernet, and token ring. However, if bandwidth utilization is normal, it should tell one that. All this information allows one to predict when upgrades will be required, if needed, rather than passively wait for some device to fail due to saturation.

Trouble Ticket Reports

Clients need to have confidence that their trouble ticket report is seriously considered as a source of identifying and attacking the problems that they are encountering. They also need to know who is handling their problem, that the problem is understood from their perspective, some projected time frame when can it be resolved, and when the problem is considered resolved by the management system. Some trouble ticket reports will be generated by conditions within the network system itself and routed to operations prior to client reports. In many cases, problems will be resolved automatically as they occur or prior to client reporting.

Reports issued for user feedback should include the following:

- number of complaints by region, system, and user group
- number of trouble tickets generated by region, system, and user group
- number of trouble tickets resolved daily, weekly, and monthly
- average time to resolve trouble ticket per category
- ratio of trouble tickets per category
- ratio of resolution per category
- types and numbers of recurring trouble tickets by region, system, and user group

A PROACTIVE PLAN

Network systems planning is the process of using historical operating data, as well as estimated future resource requirements, to determine the optimal design of the network. The ultimate goal of network systems planning is to make optimal use of network resources to ensure network services are provided at a level necessary to meet client demands and SLAs while maintaining cost-effectiveness.

An extremely important aspect of Network System Planning is network optimization. Optimization involves balancing the efficient use of network resources, client requirements, and costs. Effective network optimization requires a detailed understanding of the following areas:

- client business requirements
- client priorities (i.e., response time vs. availability)
- disaster recovery requirements
- network protocols (WIN NT, TCP/IP, AppleTalk)
- transmission methods and media (analog, digital, fiber, copper, micro-wave)
- comparison of vendor-provided services vs. in-house supported services
- application design and implementation
- component capacity and throughput (client systems as well as switches)
- component compatibility
- industry trends
- available technology and future directions
- standards efforts
- network metrics/indicators and their interpretation
- network modeling
- costs and return on investment (ROI)

The importance of having a planning group that understands all of the above items and their interrelationships cannot be overstated. A network design omitting even one of these items could result in undesirable consequences.

Input to the planning process can come from any area of network management. Specifically, these can include, but are not limited to:

- performance reports
- trouble ticket reports
- component configuration
- client resource usage estimates
- security requirements
- costs

Component configuration refers to understanding the limitations of each component in the network with regard to capacity as well as physical limitations (number of available slots, power requirements, environmental limitations, etc.). In addition, planners must be aware of future changes to vendor-supplied components such as incompatible hardware upgrades or software that will no longer be supported.

The most difficult piece of planning data to gather is an accurate list of future client resource requirements. In many cases, end users may not have the technical skills or tools to estimate network resource requirements.

This process of optimizing the network design as performed in the network systems planning function is a key to turning the performance management function from being reactive to being proactive. This is the critical function that will allow organizations to prevent problems from occurring. By utilizing the reports generated from the monitoring and thresholding activities, potential bottlenecks can be identified and the resolution of those bottlenecks can be set in place before they hamper network performance.

SUMMARY

Today's networks are becoming very critical and very visible elements in the day-to-day operation of a business. The complexity of these networks will continue to grow as the demands on them increase over time. Network performance management is an essential component of an overall strategy for these new networks. If you are a bank and your customers become frustrated with your home banking service because of network bottlenecks and long response times, they will find somewhere else to bank. It is that easy.

Today, many organizations are forced into reacting to performance issues rather than anticipating them. Often, they simply throw bandwidth at the problem although a bottleneck is caused by overutilization of a device, system, or component. Putting in place a proactive performance management system that assists in identifying current and future trouble spots will be key to the organization's ability to respond to new demands on the network.

Chapter 48
Issues in Managing Multimedia Networks

Luc T. Nguyen

With the quickened pace of technological advances in recent years, from telecommunications technologies, information technologies, and computing technologies to VLSI technologies, the telecommunications networks have become more advanced and complex than ever. To compound the issues, the traffic that is being carried on these networks is becoming more diverse. The percentage of nonvoice traffic is getting much larger, thus creating true multimedia networks. These realizations pose a challenge for many companies to look for ways to evolve their networks while still being able to manage them. To the telecommunications industry, this is both a challenge and an opportunity to provide new equipment and services.

More and more applications are being added to the networks. From intranet phone to Internet radio, from videoconferencing to entertainment video, from Web TV to movies on demand — all these will make some of the current network management methodologies obsolete. With multimedia, the definition of network performance will change; methodologies to measure and manage networks for peak performance will need to be revised.

In this chapter we will take a look at some of the issues in managing multimedia networks.

THE MULTIMEDIA NETWORKS

The network itself is changing. Service providers are widely deploying new technologies. These include very high-speed access technologies such as ADSL and cable modems, ATM switches, and ultra-fast servers that can provide instantaneous access to information. As the networks grow larger and more complex, new applications to be carried on these networks are being invented every day. Each of the new applications introduces new types of traffic characteristics that require new methodologies to manage.

With voice networks, we previously knew where the traffic came from, where it went, how long the average phone call was, and what statistical distribution could best describe its characteristics. With the introduction of data traffic, some of our knowledge of traffic engineering does not apply anymore. The average length of a data call is much longer than a voice call. The data traffic distribution is very different than that of voice traffic. In fact, each data application has its own traffic distribution that does not resemble any other. The network busy time of each type of traffic is very different, too. Voice networks tend to be busy in the morning, while Web-browsing traffic tends to peak in the early evening, and batch data transfer will pick up activities at night.

The various video applications contribute yet other types of traffic characteristics to the networks. Voice and video traffic are much more sensitive to network delay than data traffic. Video traffic also requires much higher bandwidth than either voice or data to produce a smooth picture.

When an application integrates more than one type of traffic characteristic, then the issues become even more complex. For a videoconferencing session, both the video and the voice must be sent simultaneously. Not only does each stream have to be sent in a time-sensitive manner to achieve a smoothness in delivery, they also have to be synchronized to match the movement of the picture with the appropriate sound.

To manage such multimedia networks, neither the voice network management system, the data network management system, nor the video network management system is adequate. The use of all three together is not even adequate because of the lack of coordination between the different systems. What is needed is an Integrated Network Management System.

THE INTEGRATED NETWORK MANAGEMENT SYSTEM (INMS)

As is apparent, managing a multimedia network is very complex. The network will be much faster, and the traffic mix is unpredictable. The equipment may be from multiple vendors using different technologies to support a multitude of applications. This presents a real challenge for network managers.

There are five primary areas of network management: fault management, security management, configuration management, performance management, and accounting management. Another network management area that has been receiving much interest recently is customer network management (CNM). This is when the customers are given the opportunity and tools to manage their part of the networks. We will discuss these network management areas in more detail and present options and issues involved with managing multimedia networks.

For large and complex networks, network management exceeds human capability to monitor and react to any event in the network in real time. The INMS running on high-speed computers will have to be built to keep track of the status and state changes in the numerous devices, facilities, protocols, users, and applications in the network. The INMS must be smarter, more scalable, easier to use, and more adaptable to the changes in networks and technologies than conventional management schemes. For the following sections, we will discuss the capabilities of the typical INMS.

Fault Management

Fault management is the process of locating and correcting network problems. Fault management consists of identifying the occurrence of a fault, isolating the cause of the fault, and correcting or tracking the fault.

When a fault happens in the network, generally a change of state happens in some equipment. One or more alarms are generated. Ideally, we have to capture the alarms and filter them to determine the severity, the type, the devices or services affected, and even the number of occurrences.

Often a network error results in multiple alarms. As a simple example, when a link between two devices is cut, at least two alarms are generated, one from each end device. Potentially many more may be generated, from excessive packet loss, incomplete calls, sessions disconnected, and application time-outs. The amount of data generated from one of these network faults can be overwhelming for a person to look at and will often take a considerable amount of time to determine what the real problem is. One of the roles of an INMS is to correlate all these alarms to determine their cause.

In multimedia networks, the INMS has to recognize the interdependencies of alarms between various media. A disconnect in a voice network may not affect the video network unless the voice connection is part of a video-conference. Similarly, a remote slide presentation will not be very successful if the voice and the data on the slides do not correspond satisfactorily. The INMS should be able to correlate the various parts of a multimedia connection or set of connections and monitor it for irregularities and alarms.

Sometimes an alarm is not a cause for concern. But if the same alarm happens continuously or consistently over a period of time, then it may indicate a more serious problem. The INMS should be able to count the number of occurrences of an event, either over an absolute period of time or over a sliding interval of time. These occurrences can be a specific event, or event type, or a combination of several events or event types.

Some alarms are more severe than others. The INMS should be able to recognize the severity of the alarms and react accordingly. Some alarms may be ignored with only an increase in the statistics counter. Other service-affected alarms must be dealt with immediately. Service personnel must be paged or dispatched, and management must be notified.

Alarms can be displayed on an INMS console in one of several forms. They can be displayed on a colored map of the network where each colored location can determine the severity and the location of the alarm. They can also be displayed on a list, sorted by severity, location, type, or customer. They can also be propagated to multiple monitors under different formats for different people, depending on their functions.

Security Management

Security management involves protecting sensitive information found on devices attached to a network by controlling access to that information. Sensitive information is any data an organization wants to secure. Security management protects sensitive information by limiting access to hosts and network devices, and by notifying responsible personnel of attempted or successful breaches of security. Protection via security management is achieved through specific configurations of network hosts and devices to control-access points within a network. Access points may include software devices, hardware components, and network media.

An INMS should provide a means to control the security of the network. At any time, there can be two types of users accessing the INMS: the customers and the operators. The customers access the INMS to retrieve information about their network usage, their profile, and their connectivity. The customers' login profiles should provide them with limited access to their applications and their partitions of the network. Since several competing customers can use the same network provider, it is very important for this provider to keep their data separate and only viewable by them.

The operators should be organized into several hierarchical levels depending on their authorities and responsibilities. The operator levels can be set up in their login profiles. The authority profiles will determine which operator can access what system, data, or applications. Only the INMS administrator should be permitted to change these levels of authority.

Any successful or attempted security violation, based on system or connectivity, should be reported and analyzed. Security policy should be viewed and updated often to avoid gaps and weaknesses.

Configuration Management

Configuration management is the process of obtaining data from the network and using it to manage and set up network devices. It consists of (1) gathering information about the current network configuration, (2) using the data to modify the configuration of the network devices, and (3) storing the data, maintaining an up-to-date inventory, and producing reports based on the data.

In large and complex networks, it is a tedious job to keep track of the inventory of equipment, devices, and facilities, together with their locations, network addresses, software versions, and maintenance schedules. If a device, such as a switch, fails, and a replacement switch is brought in, it is of paramount importance to bring the new switch up to the same software version of the old switch, using the same switching table, the same addresses, and the same connectivity. This must be done for the network function in the same manner as before.

When a network upgrade is necessary, especially a software version upgrade, then an INMS with this configuration management feature will become invaluable. It can save countless hours of frustrated troubleshooting to bring the network up and functioning again.

In multimedia networks, the role of the end devices becomes more important to the satisfactory connections and services. For example, the ability to control, troubleshoot, and reset the cable modems or set-top boxes will greatly enhance the up-time of the cable service. Similarly, the ability for a videoconferencing service provider to control the camera and display devices would contribute to the service quality and consistency of a videoconference. These video end devices are complex, as is the network. The complexity of these devices exceeds most users' ability to understand and operate them effectively. The INMS must reach out to these devices, check the configurations, and ensure compatibility before setting up each videoconferencing connection.

Performance Management

Performance management ensures that a network remains accessible and uncongested for maximum efficiency. Performance management should monitor network devices and associated links to determine utilization and error rates. It should also ensure that capacities of devices and links are not overtaxed to the extent of adversely impacting performance.

In multimedia networks, performance management also ensures the effective functioning of the various media making up the services. The degradation in any part of a multimedia connection means the degradation of the whole connection. Even if the video comes through flawlessly, if the audio is less than clear, a videoconference session will be less than satisfactory. The INMS should be able to collect data on the interdependencies between various media in the same connection to evaluate overall performance.

Performance management should consist of:

1. Collecting data on utilization of network devices and links.
2. Analyzing relevant data to discern high utilization trends.
3. Setting utilization thresholds.

4. Using simulation to determine how the network can be altered to maximize performance.
5. Correlating between the collected data to infer the performance levels of multimedia applications.

The INMS must provide a process or processes that can collect many types of network performance data. Some of these types of data are:

- *Response time:* Time it takes for a datum to enter the network, be processed, and leave the network.
- *Rejection rate:* Percentage of times the network cannot transfer information because of a lack of network resources and performance.
- *Availability:* Percentage of times the network is available for use, often measured as mean time between failure (MTBF).

The INMS should be able to collect performance data on demand or on schedule. Collection time should be a function of devices, links, and absolute or relative times. Information may be collected for specific devices and links or device and link types. Information should also be collected for specific applications, especially multimedia applications.

The INMS should be able to provide performance statistic reports to help the network engineer in analyzing the network. These reports will also provide a long-term view of the overall health and efficiency of the network. There are three types of performance reports:

1. *The real-time operations reports:* Provide snapshots of some part of the network at a specific time. Example: switch usage report for Christmas Day.
2. *The summary or percentage reports:* Provide the general view of the performance of parts of the network during a certain time period. Example: average switch usage report.
3. *The trending reports:* Provide the view of the performance of parts of the network over time. Example: monthly average switch usage report.

The INMS should also have a process to set performance thresholds for various parts of the network. Thresholds are boundaries within which affected devices will function normally. Violation is when one of these boundaries is exceeded. A violation will automatically trigger procedures to collect data, generate reports, or create an alarm.

Accounting Management

Accounting management is the process of measuring network usage to establish metrics, check quotas, determine costs, and bill users. Accounting management includes the gathering of data about utilization of network resources, the setting of usage quotas using metrics, and the preparing of data for billing users for their use of the network.

The INMS should have processes to measure the usage of network resources for each customer. The measurement should be on demand and/or scheduled. Since different applications may incur different costs, the INMS should also be able to measure the network usage based on applications. Example: a user may only subscribe to basic Internet access with applications such as e-mail and Web access. At any time, this user may want to communicate with the INMS of the service provider to request in real time a higher priced bandwidth for videoconferencing. The INMS should detect the request and begin measuring the video traffic when it starts so that appropriate charges can be applied.

The INMS should also allow the administration of usage quotas for each customer. The quotas define the amount of network resources a customer is allowed to use under its contracts. The use of resources beyond the quotas will trigger separate measurements and traffic may be blocked or charged at a different price. Network resources should include the INMS and other customer support functions.

Billing is a complex process that involves taxes, special pricing, promotions, and various discounting schemes that can change frequently. Billing programs should be left to specialized billing companies for those reasons and because they differ from company to company and from one industry to the next. The INMS should be flexible enough to interface with any or all billing programs, especially nonstandard legacy ones. The INMS should provide its billing data in the right format to the appropriate billing programs.

Customer Network Management

Customer network management (CNM) allows the customers access to the INMS with applications to manage their own real or virtual networks. The simplest form of CNM is an application that allows the customers to see information (e.g., billing) for their parts of the network.

Even in this simple form, many issues can be raised in a large, complex multiuser network. Some examples are how to ensure that customers can only see their own data, how to keep the data fresh and up-to-date, and what interfaces to provide to the customer. Some trends on these issues have emerged and will likely continue into the future — trends such as Web or Java user interfaces and a standard application-to-application interface using SNMP.

The INMS should provide CNM functions for the customers to manage their own parts of the network. For example, without the service provider's involvement, it should allow the customers to:

1. Change their own network routes as needed.
2. Activate high-bandwidth multimedia applications.
3. Schedule changes or updates to their network services.
4. Request specialized reports on their network usage.

To do this, the INMS must maintain a customer network data base that contains all customer information pertinent to the network. This data base may contain information about ordering, provisioning, trouble handling, operation, maintenance contracts, and billing options, as well as information about carriers and equipment vendors. Other informational data that should be included in this data base are customer contacts, vendor services, responsible organizations, types of services used or on order, etc. More specifically, the data base must contain the exact equipment that the customer has, what their capabilities are, where they are located, who made them, what software version they have, and what network addresses they have.

The INMS will maintain all these data for each customer. It must have the ability to add, delete, or modify records in this data base. Depending on the services, some of these records may be changed by the customers themselves; some may be changed only by the network operators, depending on their security levels.

The CNM should also facilitate the communications between the human operators and the human customers. Communications by faxes, e-mail, and Web sites are all possible and should be maintained and used.

As technology advances are measured in months and days, compared to years and decades, the communications network is becoming far more complex and is exceeding the capability of humans to manage it in any reasonable manner without fully integrated network management tools. The challenge we face today and in the years ahead is to build flexible and feature-rich network management systems that can help us control and administer the multimedia networks on which we all depend for our day-to-day lives. The basic network management techniques and concepts will not change, but the integration of all these techniques and concepts into an INMS will be the theme of the future. As the networks get larger and more complex, only a cohesive INMS can help an organization master its applications and its services in a cost-effective and efficient manner.

Chapter 49

Network Data and Storage Management Techniques

Lawrence D. Rogers

One of the fundamental services provided by a multi-user computer system has always been access to shared data. The shared data, once counted in megabytes, is now usually counted in gigabytes. Protecting and managing its storage is one of the most important tasks of the local area network (LAN) administrator. To protect the data and manage storage requires a combination of hardware protection, operating systems services, and software tools. There are two main problems—maintaining data integrity and storage management.

Data integrity means that systems data is always correct or can be corrected. Data integrity systems provide the ability to recover data in the face of hardware, software, and human error or from direct physical or programmatic attack. Error correcting codes (ECC) and fault-tolerant disk systems can ensure immunity to all but the most disastrous hardware failures, and corrections are performed, for the most part, invisibly. Recovery from software overwrite failures and human errors, however, relies on keeping multiple copies of files and file histories. Disaster recovery (including recovery from direct physical attack) is usually achieved by keeping copies and file histories at separate secure locations. In the latter cases, some human intervention is required, if only to make choices during the recovery process. Protection from programmatic attack requires an adequate security system and the use of virus detection or prevention programs with a file copy and history system for when serious security breaches are committed.

Storage management means optimizing the use of systems storage media with respect to both cost and performance. Moving infrequently accessed data from expensive primary storage to less-expensive storage media improves access performance and makes primary storage space available for the most commonly used data. Defragmenting disks improves performance by reducing access times. Compressing files frees disk space. Balancing the load across multiple disk drives and servers to prevent simultaneous over-utilization and under-utilization of disks in the same system smoothes performance. These and other techniques are commonly applied to storage systems to optimize performance and cost.

This chapter discusses tools and techniques used for maintaining file histories and for managing the location of files in the storage system and briefly touches on related disaster recovery techniques. The chapter does not discuss fault-tolerant systems or hardware technology for ensuring first-level data protection, nor does it discuss antivirus software or security or many other related topics. Each is beyond the scope of this chapter.

MAINTAINING FILE HISTORIES

Backup and Restore

An important technique for ensuring that data is not lost is to maintain a version history for each file. This is done by periodically copying files to a different media, such as tape or optical disk. This is usually referred to as backing up files, because it involves making backup copies of files in case an original is lost or destroyed. The versions of a file available are determined by the frequency with which these copies are made and how long the copy is kept. The two main components of a backup strategy are the type of backup performed and the media rotation strategy. This chapter first defines some different types of backup and then how these can be combined with various rotation schemes.

Full Backup. A full backup (i.e., a backup of all files) made on a regular basis allows a network administrator to recover versions of all files from the system. The available versions of any given file are determined by the interval between backups. Periodic full backups have the advantage of containing all the systems data on one backup media, or at least a minimal number of media. This can help speed recovery if a full volume must be restored. Due to the size of a full backup, and hence the time required to perform one, it may be difficult or impractical to execute full backups as often as desired. Properly combining full backups with partial backups can still give reasonable protection.

Incremental Backup. An incremental backup captures all files that have been modified since the last full or incremental backup. It requires less time to perform because less data is being copied. To restore a full volume requires two steps, first restoring from the last full backup tape and then applying each incremental backup. Generally a full backup is done each weekend and incrementals each weekday.

Differential Backup. A differential backup captures all files that have been modified since the last full backup. This means that a Monday differential captures Monday's changes after a weekend full backup. A Tuesday differential captures Monday's and Tuesday's changes. Differentials done later in the week require more space and time than incrementals, but a restore requires only the full backup restore and the latest differential.

Modified Full Backup. A modified full backup captures all files, except those for which three unmodified copies already exist on three different media. In other words, if a file has been copied three times each to a different media and it has not changed, it will not be backed up again. This reduces the time to do a full backup because files that do not change are not backed up more than three times.

If tape rotation schemes are used, precaution must be taken to see that needed copies are not overwritten. Modified full backups done on the weekend, with incrementals or differentials during the week, will ensure that the file history has copies of all files in their most recent state. Weekend backup time will be shorter, but the files will be spread across many different media. The big disadvantage is restoring a full volume or even a directory because there is a high probability the required files will be stored on many different tapes.

Continuous Backup and Transaction Tracking. The techniques described previously allow a system to be restored to its state at the time of the last backup. How often a backup is done depends on how critical the data is. A company's financial files might get backed up twice a day while routine correspondence might be copied only every two days. Some data is so critical that a business cannot afford to lose any of it. For these instances, a continuous file history can be recorded. Often this type of data is found in online database systems. Most serious database systems maintain a separate log of transactions. There are various reasons for doing this that include backing out transactions to correct errors.

This log can also be effectively used for providing continuous backup. If a consistent backup of the database is made, and then the transaction log is backed up frequently, a system can be restored to the time of the last transaction captured by restoring the backup and then reapplying each of the transactions.

It is good practice, then, to store the transaction log on a disk other than the one the data resides on, and to have it backed up frequently or even duplexed. When a full backup of the database is performed a new log file should be started. The log file itself should then be backed up repeatedly, as often as after every transaction is written to it. This same technique can be applied to important non-database files by acquiring a system that supports continuous backup. These systems basically capture a baseline backup of the files of interest and then create their own log of all the writes to those files. Using this technique, a file can be restored to the time of the last write.

Tracking the File History and Recovering Files

Knowing what media to use when recovering a whole volume is often straightforward. As described above, the last full backup is restored and then the necessary partial backups are applied, depending on what type of backup strategy has been employed. Usually the media is physically labeled and this is all that is necessary.

To recover individual files or groups of files, however, the communications manager must know what media is being used. Even if the most recent version is desired, knowing which media it is on is not always obvious and finding it without the help of the file history system can be tedious. It is important for file history or backup systems to keep an online database that tracks all versions of files and where they are stored. Various approaches to finding these files can then be supported.

When the primary file system is used, a file is referred to by its unique path name (i.e., the volume, directory, and file name used for storing it). Well-designed history databases support this same view of files and their relationships. Users can then browse the backup file history much as they would browse the directory of the primary file system.

When a particular file is selected, each of its versions and their location can be displayed. A common type of user's request is "Recover my spreadsheet; it was called BUD. . . something. I had it a few months ago." To find such a file, locating it by name or type is a good approach. The file history system should support searching by file name, by extent, and permit the use of wildcards (e.g., those supported in the DOS and Novell Inc. operating systems directories).

Another approach is to locate the file by the save set to which it was copied. A save set is a grouping of data that was all copied to a backup media together. Most backup systems that have online data support some method for tracking the files as they were stored. Tracking a file by save set allows looking for a file as it existed at a particular time.

MEDIA ROTATION SCHEMES

So far, this chapter has not discussed how long each copy of a file is to be kept. In the previous discussions, it has been implicit that when a copy has been made it is henceforth always available. This is not usually necessary, or cost-effective; it would mean always buying new storage media to replace the ones that fill up. When a file has been superseded by later versions it is, after some period of time, usually not required.

Keeping too few copies of files, however, can seriously diminish the security of the data, and so trade-offs are almost inevitable. The speed with which files can be restored, the amount of time available for backup, and the amount of data also enter into the equation.

Various schemes for reusing media are employed, both as a cost-saving measure and to keep system clutter (e.g., database size and number of tapes) under control. When media are reused, previously backed up data is overwritten. The file history database must be updated to reflect the media's new contents. Most backup databases remove all the files stored on a tape when the user indicates that a tape is to be reused. The administrator should know four things in order to make appropriate decisions about media rotation:

- The periods each day when the network is fairly dormant (the backup window).
- The amount of data on the network disks.
- The expected time that would be available to the manager to perform a full system restoration.
- How far back in time the file history must go.

Father-Son Rotation Schemes

An example would be a small manufacturing concern whose network has 120 nodes, two servers, and a total of 2G bytes on the server disks. The network is running three shifts, five days a week, and there is only one hour each night during the week to perform routine backup. The ability to restore data is crucial, but only four hours is available in which to do it. Three to four weeks of data history is sufficient. In this case, the eight-tape rotation schedule shown in Exhibit 49.1 might be chosen.

The eight-tape schedule provides for one full backup on Fridays, augmented with four incremental backups Monday through Thursday. The Friday tape is on a separate sub-schedule of four tapes. During week one, tapes one through five are used. During week two, tapes one through four are followed by tape six, and so on until tape eight is used. Then the cycle repeats. This is ideal because the daily incrementals can be done during the 60-minute window each night (which is enough time to back up at least 300M bytes of changed data) and for the Friday backup there is plenty of time before the next shift starts.

The only penalty this arrangement has is restoration time. In a worst-case scenario (i.e., restoring an entire volume), it would be necessary to load the last full backup tape, followed by every subsequent incremental tape, to ensure that the latest version of every file is restored. If more time is available at night for doing backups and less for restore, differential backups would be done in place of the incrementals. If a longer file history is required, more tapes would be included in the weekly, father tape rotation.

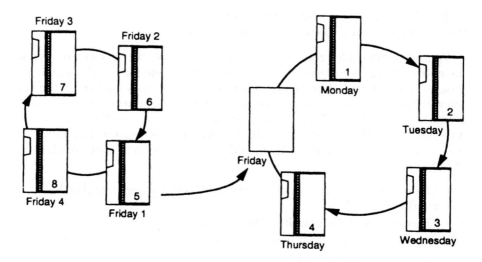

Exhibit 49.1. A Father-Son Tape Rotation Schedule

Many other father-son schemes can be constructed. Performing two full backups a week on Tuesday and Friday, with incrementals on Monday, Wednesday, and Thursday will increase confidence and restore times but will take more time at night twice a week. Keeping three weeks of history will now require 11 tapes. Performing a full backup every night is the safest method of securing data and requires the least restore time. However, it requires the most time each night and will cost as much in tapes as a father-son scheme that has one father tape being made each week, that covers the same history period.

Grandfather-Father-Son

Grandfather-father-son schemes increase the history period but leave more holes in it. Suppose the company decides that it must keep three to four months of data history. One method would be to simply increase to 16 the number of tapes used for full weekly backups. A slightly different rotation accomplishes the same coverage with six tapes, but the gaps in coverage increase as time moves on.

The grandfather-father-son scheme uses incremental or differential backups each weekday night. Four tapes are rotated for these. Each weekend for three weeks (Friday 1, Friday 2, Friday 3) a full backup is done and once every four weeks a monthly backup is performed. A new monthly tape is used each month (i.e., each four week period) for three months (Monthly 1, Monthly 2, Monthly 3) before the rotation starts over (as shown in Exhibit 49.2). Data can be recovered from any day in the most recent week,

576

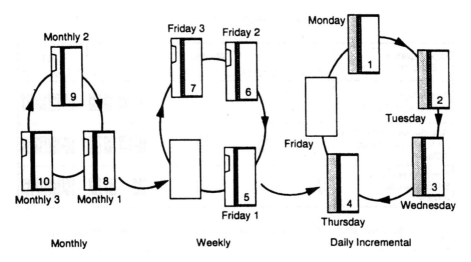

Exhibit 49.2. An Eight-Tape Grandfather-Father-Son Rotation Schedule

any of the previous four weeks, plus data that is up to 12 weeks old in four week increments. To increase the number of "months" in the history, more monthly tapes can be added.

Tower of Hanoi Tape Rotation

If economy and a long history period are required, the Tower of Hanoi algorithm can be used (at the expense of increasing the complexity of backup operations) for father weekly full backups. The usual four tape son rotation of weekday incremental or differential backups is still used, as in the schemes discussed earlier. This scheme (named for a child's toy) uses weekend tapes at exponentially growing intervals and gets up to $2^n - 1$ weeks of coverage for n tapes. Five tapes, therefore, can give up to 16 weeks' coverage, as shown in Exhibit 49.3.

The rotation is then repeated. Just before Tape 5 is reused at week 32, its data is 16 weeks old, Tape 4's data is 8 weeks old, Tape 3 is 4 weeks old, Tape 2 is 2 weeks and Tape 1 is 1 week old. This is approximately the same

Tape 1 is used weeks	1	3	5	7	9	11	13	15	17 . . .	31
Tape 2 is used weeks	2	6	10	14	18	22	26	30		
Tape 3 is used weeks	4	12	20	28						
Tape 4 is used weeks	8	24								
Tape 5 is used weeks	16	32								

Exhibit 49.3. Tower of Hanoi Tape Rotation

Age of Backups Currently on Tape

Tape Rotation Scheme	Weeks																Days				
	16	15	14	13	12	11	10	9	8	7	6	5	4	3	2	1	F	T	W	T	M
Father-Son 4 Weekly, 4 Daily Tapes													▣	▣	▣	▣	▣	▣	▣	▣	
Grandfather-Father-Son 2 Monthly, 2 Weekly, 4 Daily					▣				▣				▣	▣	▣	▣	▣	▣	▣	▣	
Tower of Hanoi 5 Exponential, 4 Daily	▣								▣				▣		▣	▣	▣	▣	▣	▣	

Exhibit 49.4. Comparison of Three Tape Rotation Schemes

coverage as grandfather-father-son with one less tape. Simplicity is probably worth the cost of an extra tape. A weakness of this scheme is the high
use and hence potential failure of tape 1. Exhibit 49.4 illustrates the length
of file history, the gaps in the file history coverage, and the number of tapes
required for these different tape rotation schemes.

MANAGING STORAGE

Monitoring Volume Use

Storage requirements are likely to change over time. An administrator
should monitor the data storage devices to determine when additional
storage is needed. Usually, filing a volume to 70% to 80% of its capacity is a
comfortable range. This depends on the size of the volume and the type of
data stored on it. More free volume space should be maintained if the data
is subject to temporary files causing rapid growth spurts, and less is
required if the data is largely stable. Deciding when a volume is full means
understanding the mix of programs that will run and their storage profiles.

For example, the month end financial program may use many intermediate temporary files and overflow the disk once a month unless this is anticipated. Understanding the storage profile of disks is key. Performance is
also influenced by a lack of available disk space. Full disks are usually fragmented—that is, the space allocated is scattered across the disk rather
than localized. The last files written are likely to be the ones most often
accessed, and these are the ones that are most heavily fragmented.

Disk fragmentation causes head movement even when clever caching
algorithms are used, resulting in a decrease in performance. Keeping sufficient disk space open allows the system to maintain performance. Adding

disks is not necessarily the answer to dwindling free space. Archiving dormant files (i.e., files that have not been accessed in some predetermined period of time) will probably free up sufficient disk space.

Archiving

Much data is transitory in nature, being active for a short period of time and then dormant for months or even years. Still, data is a valuable commodity and it is impossible to determine when it will be required. Archiving is a technique wherein a particular data set is moved from online primary storage to near-online or off-line archival storage media and then deleted from primary storage. This differs from maintaining a file history (backup), which captures copies of files that are still active and online so that they can be retrieved if they are needed. Before data can be considered safely archived and removed from primary storage, copies have to be made on multiple media (e.g., three different tapes or two optical platters).

Whether archival storage is near-online, off-line, or off-site usually depends on the age of the data. Data might be automatically archived to a near-online device after it has been dormant for three months and then taken off-line after six months. Off-site data storage is usually a disaster recovery measure, although sometimes it is convenient simply to save physical space.

Archival storage is intended to be long-term storage, so it is important to match the life expectancy of the media to the required data availability. The life span of tape depends on the environment in which it is stored (a computer room environment is recommended) and the care taken with it. Frequent retensioning, or spinning the tape from end to end, will keep it from sticking to itself.

With proper care, a ten-year life span is practical. Media vendors make available guidelines on storing tape. Optical disk is a newer technology than tape and is more expensive. Less is known about its durability, however, less environment control is necessary than for tape and a practical life span of 20 to 30 years is probable.

An archiving system should provide an easy method for locating archived data. Each tape, optical disk, or other media used for archival storage must be titled and labeled for easy retrieval. This label should be both electronic, as data on the media, and physical, attached to the cartridge, tape, or whatever media is used, in a visible location. The physical label should bear a name, archive data, and general description. The electronic label should duplicate the physical label plus provide information on the contents of the media (e.g., directories and save sets).

The same database that is used for tracking file history for backup should be used for tracking archived files, and the same search techniques should be available. Archived files are most frequently searched for by the file name or by browsing the directory tree of archived data, rather than by the time that they were archived.

Whenever data is moved from one device to another, as with archiving, it is crucial to move all directory information (name space) and security (operating system attributes) with it. The removable media used for archiving should be protected by password, physical location, or both. The number of people with physical access to archived media should be kept at a minimum to further protect the privacy of the information contained in the archive.

Combining Archiving and Backup

Archiving and backup activities are similar, and it is convenient to share the file history database between them. It is important to remember that they serve different purposes and that archived files are intended to be kept for long periods of time while backup files are maintained until they have been superseded and then discarded. Media that are used for archiving are never overwritten, while data integrity tapes are reused on a specific media rotation schedule.

The simplest and safest way to combine these two operations is to let them share a media database, but they should be kept on separate physical media and these media should be treated differently. Backup time and media cost can be reduced by combining the techniques. The modified full backup scheme described earlier reduces the time taken for a full backup by not capturing files that have been copied to three different archival media. As noted earlier, this saves backup time at the expense of restore time.

If performing modified full backups is important, it is possible to go one step further and combine backup and archiving on one media. On each weekend backup session the first thing written to a tape is the set of dormant or stable files that have not been captured three times. Then active files are written to tape. The next time this tape is used, any newly dormant or stable files would be appended to the first set of archived files, overwriting the active files. Then active files would be written. This process continues until the tape is full, at which time it is permanently stored off-site. Exhibit 49.5 illustrates this combined strategy.

Data Migration

Archiving data is an explicit action performed by a user or LAN administrator when files have been determined to be dormant. Sometimes the system will take this action according to previously published system rules. Files are removed from the primary system, and the names are removed from the primary file system directory tree. Retrieving them is

Tape After First Use

Dormant and Stable Files (First Use)	Active Files (First Use)	Unused Tape

Tape After Second Use

Dormant and Stable Files (First Use)	Dormant and Stable Files (Second Use, Overwrites Active)	New Active Files (Second Use)	Unused Tape

Exhibit 49.5. Combining Archive and Backup on One Tape

---

also an explicit act. This requires locating the desired file(s) in the file history database and then restoring them. Archiving is performed as a routine practice for maintaining files over time and to keep them from cluttering expensive primary storage.

Data migration provides an automatic method of moving data from primary to near-online storage in order to maintain more free primary storage. This is done automatically according to aging rules such as those discussed for archiving (e.g., files that have been dormant for three months would be moved to near-online storage). Exhibit 49.6 illustrates this concept.

With data migration, however, file names are not removed from the original name directory and will still appear to a user browsing those directories as if they are online. When a user attempts to access a file, the file is restored from near online to primary online storage. The user or LAN administrator does not have to do any explicit moving of data or tracking of files. These are performed automatically by the data migration system.

Data migration must make use of near-online media or retrieve times become too long, and system time-outs become a potential problem. Typically near-online storage employs high-capacity, rotating, removable media (e.g., optical or Bernoulli disks). Before installing such a system, it is important to make sure it is matched to the environment. Automatic data migration is similar to providing virtual storage for the primary disk system. The rules for when files are moved and when and how they are restored are sensitive to various virtual memory afflictions such as thrashing.

Using Hierarchical Storage

Data migration, archiving, and backup can be planned as one logical, harmonious set of actions. Archiving and data migration are used for managing storage. When using both these methods, the communications manager would set up the data migration using, for example, a near-online optical

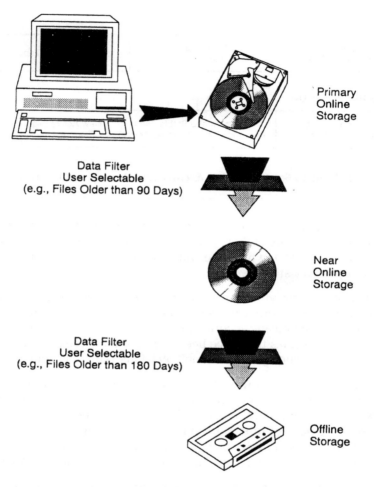

Data Filter
User Selectable
(e.g., Files Older than 90 Days)

Primary
Online
Storage

Near
Online
Storage

Data Filter
User Selectable
(e.g., Files Older than 180 Days)

Offline
Storage

Exhibit 49.6.   Schematic of Data Migration

disk jukebox. The communications manager might archive from there to an auto-loading tape device and eventually move the archive files off-site. If the archives must be kept for a long time, then specific optical media might be used for the permanent archives. Weekly and daily backups would be performed to the tape auto loader, with media being rotated from there off-site according to a schedule. The file history system would be used for tracking all copies of the files.

Such a system is called *hierarchical,* because data moves down the hierarchy from primary online storage to fast-access near-online storage, to a slower access near-online storage, to off-line and off-site storage. If all these levels of storage are to be managed, it has to be done automatically or the LAN administrator will be devoted solely to this task.

DISK FRAGMENTATION

Fragmentation has been a problem with storage systems since the introduction of direct access rotating media. When the file system needs to write data to a disk, it searches for the first available block and starts writing to this block. If the block is smaller than the amount of data that needs to be written, the storage algorithm will break up the data and store the remainder in another open block on the disk.

If, for example, a 1M-byte file is being written to disk, the disk space found may be a 500K-byte open block. The first half of the file is written to this area and then the system continues seeking. The next free space may be 300K byte, and more of the file is written. Finally, 200K bytes of open space is located and the remainder of the file is laid down on disk. The single file has been fragmented into three pieces.

If these three fragments are physically far apart on the disk, the read head will have to move to retrieve them. Moving the disk head is a relatively slow mechanical operation, thus fragmentation adversely affects performance.

Normally, a file system will try to place all information on the disk contiguously. However, after files have been written and erased, holes are left. It is unfortunate that as disks fill up they are more prone to fragmentation, and the newest, most active files are usually the most severely fragmented. The effect of fragmentation can be minimized by systems employing efficient storage allocation techniques and disk caching. Administrators can help by ensuring that ample free space is available so the system has room to manage the storage.

Even so, sometimes defragmentation is required. Defragmentation can be accomplished best using specialized utilities that have been designed for the task. These utilities rewrite data into continuous blocks to reduce disk arm movement.

An alternate method for defragmenting a volume involves the deletion and restoration of all data. When data is laid down on a fresh, unused volume, it is written contiguously; therefore, the whole volume can be backed up, the data deleted, and then a complete restore done. This should not be undertaken lightly. But with a proper full volume backup system it can be a fairly painless operation. It would be prudent to undertake multiple full backups and some restores to test the media and system before undertaking this form of defragmentation.

DATA COMPRESSION

Another technique for making better use of disk space is to compress the data stored on it. This can be done automatically in the system software or in hardware on the disk controller. The penalty paid is in performance, but this can be minimized.

One software technique is to compress only dormant files and to perform the compression automatically in off-peak hours. The data then can be expanded automatically when it is referenced. Since dormant data is referred rarely, there is little performance overhead. This technique is very similar to data migration except that data is not moved off-line, it is simply compressed. This type of data compression may be built in to future operating systems.

There are many different compression algorithms, and usually they are suited to compressing different types of data. An algorithm that is designed for compressing image data may achieve ratios as high as 50 to 1; a good algorithm designed for compressing English text may achieve ratios of 8 to 1. General algorithms applied to data without regard to type usually average only about 2 to 1 (extravagant claims by vendors aside). How much space this technique can reclaim is dependent on the type of data and the compression algorithm. Ordinarily this is less than half the disk space.

DISASTER PROTECTION

In the broadest sense, the topic of disaster recovery is well beyond the scope of this chapter. However, the chapter does focus on reconstructing a file system, assuming it has been partially or completely destroyed.

A general disaster recovery principle states that if a disaster occurs, the more accurately an environment can be reproduced the faster the system will be back up and running. The fewer changes that need to be made in bringing a system back up, the easier it will be.

Disaster recovery companies dealing with mainframes specialize in keeping duplicate environments (called hot sites) running at a separate secure location so that recovery time is absolutely minimal in the event of a disaster. A more modest position is to make sure that the environment can be reconstructed quickly.

Preparing a disaster plan is an important part of deciding what is the correct level of protection for any particular company. The first step is to have documentation that accurately catalogs the hardware environment. This means documenting the type of computer, storage media, add-on hardware, devices, network connections, and so on, as well as model numbers, time of purchase, the level of upgrade, in short, a complete journal of all the hardware for each server that has to be restored. The same applies to software. Maintaining a database (which must be backed up regularly) is a good way of keeping this information, but hard copy reports should be kept off-site in the event of the database's destruction.

The second step is to have a carefully thought out backup plan that includes off-site tape rotation. This implies installing a good set of software utilities and making disciplined use of those tools. It also includes the manual task of transporting tape off-site. When global networks are faster and less costly, this too will be automated, but at the moment a manual system is the most cost-effective.

The first step in rebuilding the system after a disaster is to reconstruct the hardware as precisely as possible. This will mean replacing whole machines or faulty components and performing hardware system tests to ensure proper operation. After restoring the hardware environment, the network operating system has to be installed, at least the minimum system sufficient to support the backup software and hardware and the file system, including any volume partitions and logical drives. Workstation-based backups require a properly configured workstation and server support for both communications and the file system. The last step is to restore the file system to the most recent state backed up. This means restoring from the most recent full backup and subsequent incrementals or differentials, according to the backup scheme. Particularly important are the security attributes of the users, groups, workgroups, and file servers. If the security and file attribute information cannot be restored, then all users, groups, and other objects specific to that server must be recreated from scratch. After the hardware, the system and data files, and their attributes are restored, the server should be tested and reviewed before putting it online. If it is put online with incorrect data or systems and customers begin using it in this configuration, there will be trouble reconciling the changes made against this restored system with the old system when its correct version is finally restored (and almost certainly it will be necessary to go back and do the correct restore). As a part of the normal backup scheme, weekend backups at least should be rotated off-site.

For more security, all backups should go off-site nightly. Fires, water damage, earthquakes, hurricanes, and other disasters happen more frequently than might be expected. Disasters also can happen to user workstations on the network. In most environments, there is at least some local storage. This storage is subject to the same risks as centralized storage. Fortunately, it also can take advantage of many of the same protective strategies. Most of today's network data management tools provide some method of backing up and restoring local workstations. Critical local data should be treated just as server data is treated.

SUMMARY

This chapter has focused on some important techniques for preserving the integrity of data and managing system storage. There are many variations on the themes presented here and the terminology used by different tool and system vendors may vary slightly. This chapter should make it possible to sort through the different options available and choose and operate the ones that are most appropriate for a given network.

Chapter 50
License Tracking and Metering Software

Nathan J. Muller

In the business environment of today, it has become necessary to track computer assets — both hardware and software — for determining cost of ownership and depreciation, as well as for aiding departmental budgeting and theft deterrence. Tracking computer assets has become easier in recent years with the advent of management applications that periodically scan network-attached devices to compile a complete inventory of hardware and software. Even when a mobile user dials in to the corporate local area network (LAN) via modem, a complete inventory of the portable computer can be taken during the connection process at the remote access server.

Software monitoring is particularly important. Not only is software usually the most expensive asset, it also often determines how much an organization spends in other areas such as hardware, staff training, and support. There are several compelling reasons why small and large organizations should monitor software usage:

- Minimize software costs by not overspending for software licenses and upgrades.
- Eliminate exposure to litigation and financial penalties by ensuring compliance with vendor licensing agreements.
- Reveal patterns of usage that can aid in capacity planning, training, and budgeting.
- Limit the amount of time personnel are engaged in using nonessential applications.
- Minimize exposure to viruses and other hostile code that may be lurking in bootleg copies.

In general, there are two types of functions provided by monitoring programs: software metering and license tracking. Both functions are closely related and are usually included in the same product, along with such related functions as automated software distribution and installation. Software monitoring functionality may come in the form of a standalone product such as CentaMeter from Tally Systems Corp. or it may be embedded in a larger systems management package, such as Intel Corp.'s LANDesk and Microsoft Corp.'s System Management Server (SMS). All provide scanning capabilities and management reports of varying degrees of flexibility and detail.

OPERATION

Monitoring software allows the information technology administrator to control the number of concurrent users of stand-alone applications as well as those in a software suite. In the case of a software suite, the metering software tracks each application in the suite individually to automatically allow the correct number of concurrent users, per the vendor's license agreement. In addition, information is provided on which applications have been used, which users have accessed them, and how long users have accessed them.

The metering software automatically discovers what applications are being used on each system on the network by scanning local hard drives and file servers for all installed software. The executable files of each application are examined to determine the product name and the publisher. Files that cannot be readily identified are listed as found but are flagged as unidentified. Once the file is eventually identified, the administrator can supply the missing information.

Each application in the software inventory is automatically assigned a unique name or tag, which is used for metering. When a user launches a metered application, the tag is checked to determine if there are available copies (licenses). When a user starts an application, one less copy is available to run. Likewise, when the application is closed the copy becomes available again. Before users are granted access to an application, the software inventory is checked to determine whether or not there are copies available. If all copies are being used, a status message is issued to the requesting user, indicating that there are no copies available. The user can then decide to wait in queue for the next available copy or try again later.

FUNCTIONALITY

The IT administrator can choose to be notified of the times when users are denied access to particular applications because all available copies are in use. If this happens frequently, it may help justify the need to purchase additional copies of the software or pay an additional license charge to the vendor so more users can access the application.

Some software metering packages allow application usage to be tracked by department, project, workgroup, and individual for charge-back purposes. Charges can be assigned on the basis of general network use, such as time spent logged on to the network or disk space consumed. Reports and graphs of workgroup or department charges can be printed out or exported to other programs, such as an accounting application. Even if workgroups and departments are not actually required to pay for application or network usage, the charge-back feature can still be a valuable tool for identifying operations costs and for budget planning.

Metering software can also be used for capacity planning. For example, if a company has accounting software running on six different servers, it might want to consolidate applications down to fewer servers. To do this properly, the company needs to know which servers are getting accessed the most and from what locations. With this information, a decision can be made as to which servers can safely handle the redistributed load without imposing undue performance penalties on frequent users.

Another function performed by some metering products is automated software distribution. After a software inventory is compiled, this information can be used to create a software distribution list that includes workstation addresses. When an upgrade or patch becomes available from the vendor, the IT administrator can send it to all the workstations appearing on the distribution list.

Some metering products not only automate software distribution, but they facilitate remote installation as well by enabling the administrator to add conditional logic to customize mass installations across the network. Ordinarily, it would take considerable effort for the administrator to develop a script to automate software installations because he would first have to anticipate all of the changes an application makes when it is installed. With the right installation package, however, the administrator can concentrate on adding the customization logic and let the installation component of the metering software figure out the hundreds of files that are changed by an individual installation.

LICENSE TRACKING

In monitoring the usage status of all software on the network, each application can be identified by total licenses, licenses used, licenses inactive, licenses free, and users queued for the next available copy (Exhibit 50.1). This and other information is used to monitor software license compliance and optimize software usage for both network and locally installed software packages.

Some products, including CentaMeter from Tally Systems, even provide an analysis of software usage by time of day (Exhibit 50.2).

Microsoft's SMS 2.0 is among the systems management products that feature dynamic license sharing across servers and domains. SMS also has extensive license metering capabilities, letting users with laptop computers check out licenses, providing pools of licenses or static licensing, and

CentaMeter Manager - Hanover, NH

File View Application Suite License Options Reports Help

WordPerfect 6.0a

Application	License File	Total	Used	Inactive	Free	Queued
WordPerfect 6.0a	WP	19	19	4	0	0
Microsoft Office 4.2	MSOFFICE	5	3	1	2	0
Microsoft Excel for Windows 5.0a	EXCEL	5	3	1	2	0
WordPerfect 5.1+	WPDOS	3	3	1	0	
Lotus SmartSuite	SMART	5	2	1	3	0
Microsoft Project for Windows 4.0	WINPROJ	3	1	1	2	0
Corel CorelDRAW 5.0	CORELDRW	5	5	2	0	0
Borland Paradox 4.5	PDOXDOS	2	1	0	1	0
Fifth Generation FastBack Plus 6.0	FB	1	1	0	0	
Computer Select 3.0	COMPSEL	2	0	0	2	0

Ready

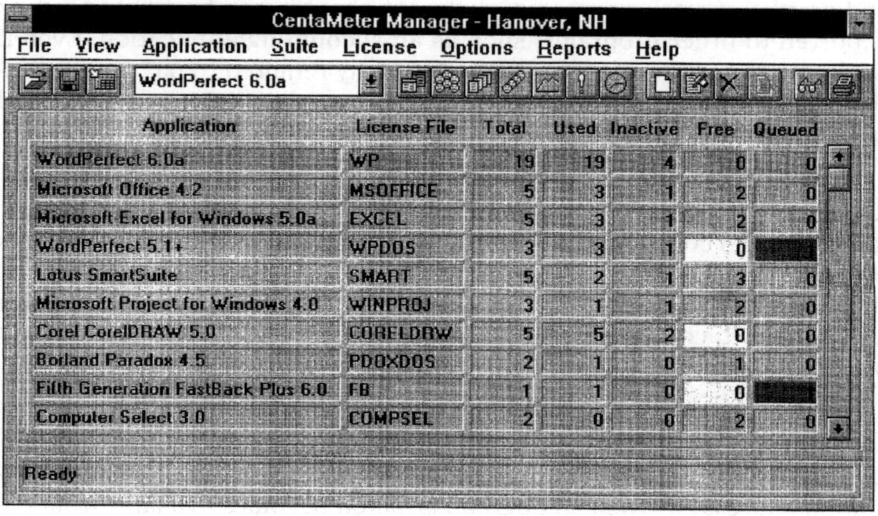

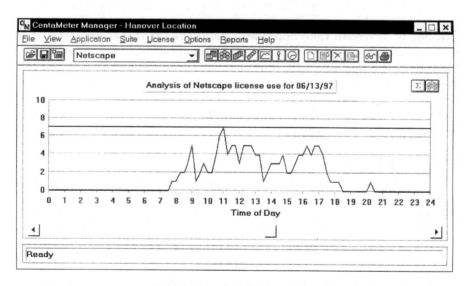

Exhibit 50.1. Analysis of License Usage by Application From Tally Systems' CentaMeter

Exhibit 50.2. Tally Systems' Centameter Manager Provides a Visual Indication of Software Usage By Time Of Day. In This Analysis of Netscape Browser Usage, For Example, the Peak Hour Was 11:00 A.M., When 7 of the 10 Browser Licenses Were In Use At the Same Time

supporting accounting for charge-back on application usage. SMS can also search for unsupported applications on the network and report their existence to the administrator, or even disable them so they cannot be run. It also has tamper-resistant features that report when a malicious user attempts to disable client software or rename applications.

FEATURES

Some software metering products issue a warning if the limit on the number of legal copies in use has been exceeded. Depending on the product, the tracking program may even specify the directories in which these files were found. This saves the IT administrator from having to track down any illegal copies by visiting suspect machines to delete them. Some of the advanced features of current software metering products include

- Custom suite metering with optimization capability: Allows the administrator to monitor the distribution of software suites in compliance with license agreements. This ensures that a suite will never be broken up illegally. The metering software automatically monitors the usage of individual components by end users and switches whole suite licenses to users working with more than one suite application at a time, leaving stand-alone licenses available whenever possible. With the optimization capability, single and suite licenses are used efficiently and legally — automatically.

- Interactivity tracking and reminders: Allows the administrator to track the amount of time open applications are inactive and reminds users to close inactive applications to make those resources available to others.

- License allocation: Allows the administrator to allocate licenses to an individual, group, machine, or any combination of these. Access to applications is given on a priority basis to users who need it most. Overflow pool licenses can be created for common access.

- Priority queuing: Gives users the option of joining a queue when all eligible licenses for an application are in use. Different queuing arrangements and access limits can be implemented for each application. High-priority users can jump ahead in the queue, while VIPs can get immediate access to an application regardless of license count restrictions.

- Point-of-execution metering: Allows tracking of applications, regardless of where they are executed — even on a local disk drive where users think they have privacy and can get away with ignoring company policy. Unauthorized programs can be shut down wherever they reside — even for VIP users.

- License sharing across locally connected servers: The metering software can be installed on any server for tracking applications across multiple servers. Access to licenses for a product installed on more than one server can be pooled together.

- Enterprise management capabilities: Allows licenses for applications to be transferred to remote locations across wide area network (WAN) connections, facilitating configuration changes and organizational moves.
- Local application metering: Tracks software usage and restricts access to unauthorized applications installed on local hard drives.
- Unregistered applications logging: An IT administrator can log all executions of local applications that do not have license profiles defined. For example, this feature can be helpful for learning what downloads are being used and/or who may be using unregistered software on a network, further preventing software piracy and the spread of harmful viruses.
- Enhanced application identification: Allows the administrator to use a variety of categories to identify an application for metering, including file name, size, date, drive, and path, or any combination of these.
- Dynamic reallocation of licenses: Allows the administrator to transfer licenses between groups and users to accommodate special access needs.

A relatively new feature, offered by Tally Systems, is "files-tracked" metering in which storage hierarchy decisions are made based on files that are frequently or infrequently used. An infrequently used file might be archived to tape, for example, while a frequently used file would stay on a local hard disk. Files can be tracked by any extension and reports are generated on usage. This feature can save money by minimizing the need for more disk drives or other types of online storage.

REPORTS

Application use can be metered on a global basis or selectively, according to such parameters as users, workgroups, workstations, hardware configuration, and networks. The information gathered by the monitoring software can be reported in a variety of ways, including

- Graphs: A graph is created daily for each application showing peak usage over a 24-hour day Administrators can also view usage by group or user, as well as queuing patterns over time.
- Error report: An error report describes users who have been denied access to an application, attempted unauthorized access, or who have restarted their applications in mid-operation.
- Color-coded status screen: A single screen displays the ongoing status of each metered application, and administrators may select different colors to indicate that a license limit has been reached or that users are in the queue.

- Color-coded user screen: Displays which users are active and which are inactive on any application.
- E-mail alerts: Messages can be sent via any mail application to a designated address when an unauthorized user attempts to access an application, when a user has been denied access to an application, or when license limits have been exceeded.
- Pager alerts: Messages that are deemed critical by the administrator can be sent to a pager so immediate action can be taken. For example, a pager alert can be sent whenever unauthorized software has been installed on a workstation. Since this can cause problems on the network, as well as unwanted legal trouble, immediate notification by pager allows the offending user to be tracked down as soon as possible.

Vendors provide different kinds of reports. The standard usage report calculates the number of users that have started applications during a specified time period. Another type of report shows peak usage over a 24-hour period. There is even a report that shows all unmetered applications that are running on the network. Examples of unmetered applications are freeware and beta programs, demo software, and internally developed applications.

A license report offers an enterprisewide view of license usage by calculating usage for each application by location in order to determine whether more or fewer licenses should be allocated. This also helps determine how software license load should be balanced among servers.

There are also reports that provide historical data on such events as total number of executions, total time the application has been in use, and the total number of reject/queue occurrences.

Some vendors include a built-in report writer in their monitoring products to help the administrator summarize historical data. Seagate Technology Inc., for example, provides trending reports through its Crystal Reports engine, an application that is included as part of its Desktop Management Suite. More than 15 types of reports can be generated, including one that shows compliance with Microsoft's Select Agreement. Hewlett-Packard Co. includes a copy of the Crystal Reports engine in its Desktop Administrator.

GLOBAL LICENSING

A global license is created by defining the total number of purchased licenses for any given product. The monitoring software keeps track of users' demand for each application and will automatically move unused licenses from a server with excess counts to a server in need of a license. When a global license is defined, one server is designated as the dispatcher for that license.

In the case of Elron Software Inc.'s SofTrack, for example, messages between servers keep each other informed of user demand for various applications. If a server on the network runs out of licenses for a particular application, it will request one from the dispatch server. The dispatch server in turn will borrow a license from the server with the most available licenses. The communication continues so that the server in need of a license borrows it, and the maximum concurrent user counts for that application are automatically updated on each server. From the user's perspective, it looks as if he is just waiting in queue for the next available license.

SofTrack is also useful for organizations that are in the process of migrating their networks from Novell Inc.'s NetWare to Windows NT. In addition to running over Transmission Control Protocol/Internet Protocol (TCP/IP) and Internetwork Packet Exchange (IPX) nets, it provides concurrent global license sharing between the two types of servers under central administration. This gives organizations the ability to share licenses between the different server platforms to ensure license compliance and maximize license availability, while allowing them to migrate at their own pace.

Another product that spans multiple operating environments and also works over TCP/IP nets is KeyServer from Sassafras Software Inc. The license metering tool can run on a Windows NT/Windows 95 computer or on a Macintosh/Power Macintosh computer. Regardless of which platform and operating system is actually running KeyServer, its license management services can support thousands of clients on both platforms with negligible traffic overhead. Using a common console from the Windows or Macintosh platform, all the features of KeyServer can be configured locally or remotely, enabling global administration via a corporate intranet or the Internet (Exhibit 50.3).

A key advantage of products that work over WAN is that they allow the IT administrator to distribute and meter software to remote IP servers that are not part of the local network. Depending on the specific product, software usage can be monitored and controlled across file servers for Windows, OS/2, UNIX, and Macintosh clients.

The IT administrator can tag applications or suites for metering and can set several properties, such as maximum concurrent users, rules for license borrowing between servers, program files to meter, and the amount of time a user waits in a queue. With the ability to monitor all of the metered servers in the enterprise and print comprehensive reports, the IT administrator is saved the time-consuming chore of collating reports from many different locations.

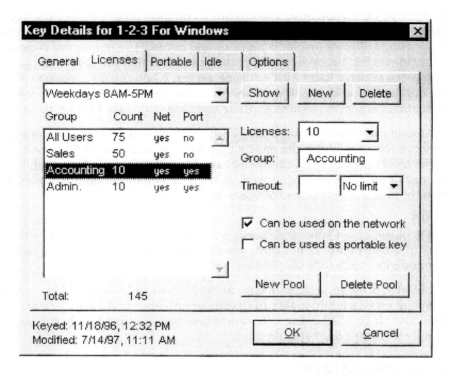

**Exhibit 50.3.   Using the Key Details Window in Sassafras Software's Key-
server, the It Administrator Can Set Up Permissions for
Multiple Groups of Users Via TCP/IP Nets**

LICENSE REGISTRATION STANDARD

Almost all legitimate computer software use is regulated by an explicit
license. The license typically states who may use the software and under
what conditions. There are many different types of licenses, each of which
reflects the intended use of the software.

Up until a few years ago, software use licenses were often nothing more
than a printed license statement included in the product packaging. Software vendors relied on the integrity of their customers to not violate the
license; in many cases, this was sufficient to protect the vendor's investment in developing the software. However, in an attempt to further reduce
losses that result from illegal software distribution and use, a group of software companies cooperated in developing the Licensing Service Application Programming Interface (LSAPI).

The LSAPI specification was developed in 1994 by a consortium of vendors including Sassafras, Microsoft, Novell, Apple Computer Inc., Digital

Equipment Corp., and others to provide a common programming interface to licensing services while hiding the underlying details. The LSAPI lets supporting software products monitor and control the number of concurrently in-use instances of those applications. Through the LSAPI, an application can register itself with a license server. When run on a workstation, the application asks the license server if the license agreement recorded in the license server permits another instance of the application to run.

Among the vendors supporting LSAPI is Novell. Its NetWare Licensing Services (NLS) provides the means by which applications that are written to the LSAPI specification can be managed in a NetWare environment. NLS is a distributed, enterprise network service that enables administrators to monitor and control the use of licensed applications on a network.

NLS is tightly integrated with the Novell Directory Services technology and is based on an enterprise service architecture. This architecture consists of client components that support different platforms and system components that reside on NetWare servers.

NLS also provides a basic license metering tool and libraries that export licensing service functionality to developers of other licensing systems. To take advantage of NLS, the software in use on a company network must comply with the LSAPI specification.

LEGAL RAMIFICATIONS

Another way to use metering software is for auditing purposes. It lets companies know if more copies of programs are being used than were paid for under each vendor's licensing agreement. An audit can also spot software that has been installed by individual users without company authorization, but for which the company is ultimately responsible.

The ability to identify and locate unauthorized software is important because it is a felony under U.S. federal law to copy and use (or sell) software. Companies found guilty of copyright infringements face financial penalties of up to $100,000 per violation.

The two leading trade associations of the software industry are the Software Publisher's Association (SPA) and the Business Software Alliance (BSA). Both organizations run antipiracy campaigns and provide opportunities for whistleblowers to report software piracy through toll-free numbers and forms posted on their Web pages.

Software piracy is actually commonplace among businesses. In a 1997 study of global software piracy jointly sponsored by the SPA and BSA, it was estimated that of the 523 million new business software applications used globally during 1996, 225 million units — nearly one in every two — were pirated. This figure represented a 20% increase in the number of units pirated over the 1995 estimate of 187 million units. Revenue losses to the worldwide software industry due to piracy were estimated at $11.2 billion in 1996, a 16% decrease over the estimated losses of $13.3 billion in 1995. However, the decline was attributed to lower software prices rather than a decrease in piracy.

The 1,200-member SPA represents companies that develop and publish software applications and tools for use on the desktop, client/server networks, and the Internet. The SPA claims to receive about 40 calls a day from whistleblowers over its toll-free hotline. It sponsors an average of 250 lawsuits a year against companies suspected of software copyright violations. Since 1988, every case the SPA has been involved in has been settled successfully.

The BSA is another organization that fights software piracy. The BSA membership includes the leading publishers of software for personal computers such as Adobe Systems Inc., Lotus Development Corp., Microsoft, Novell, and Symantec Corp. According to the BSA, software piracy cost U.S. businesses $6 million in fines and legal fees in 1997. In the U.S. alone, software piracy cost 130,000 jobs in 1996 and by 2005, piracy is expected to cost another 300,000 jobs.

Both the SPA and BSA offer free audit tools that help IS managers find licensed and unlicensed software installed on computer systems. BSA offers Softscan for Windows and MacScan for Macintosh. SPA offers SPAudit by McAfee Associates Inc. (now part of Network Associates Inc.) and KeyAudit by Sassafras Software. SPAudit does hardware and software audits on both network and standalone Windows NT and NetWare machines utilizing a catalog to identify over 4,400 software applications. KeyAudit works on Macintosh machines.

One of the most comprehensive and accurate audit tools available is GASP from Attest Systems Inc. This is the tool that SPA, BSA, Microsoft, and other software companies use for conducting enforcement audits worldwide. Its database of applications exceeds 7,000 and is user-expandable. Most audits are completed in less than 2 minutes. GASP comes in two versions. GASP Net is compatible with Windows NT, SMS, NetWare, VINES and other network operating systems. GASP Audit is compatible with Windows NT, Windows 95, Windows 3.x, DOS, and Macintosh.

CONCLUSION

When software metering arrived on the scene, it was primarily used to prevent the unauthorized use of software and manage concurrent-use software licenses. Today, information — not control — is the primary use of software license metering programs. Knowing what users are doing at their desktops promotes effective asset management. Specifically, the focus is on reporting of actual usage, trends in usage site to site, and what software packages are being used effectively and what ones are not being used at all.

Gathering all license usage information in one place allows companies to see the big picture and use the information for decision support. Among other things, this can save money on software, support, and training. It can also aid capacity planning and budget development. The use of asset management information as decision-support criteria is a trend that will likely become stronger in the future.

Chapter 51
Working with NT's Performance Monitor

Gilbert Held

One of the more valuable administrative tools built in to Microsoft Corp.'s Windows NT Workstation and Windows NT Server is the Performance Monitor program. Although the design goal of Performance Monitor is to assist network managers and LAN administrators in performing capacity planning operations, this program can also be used to facilitate a variety of troubleshooting activities to include network troubleshooting. Since the best way to obtain an appreciation for Performance Monitor is by its use, we will examine its basic operation through the use of a few screen displays to obtain an appreciation for its capability. However, prior to doing so, let's first obtain an overview of the general capabilities of this graphical tool and information concerning potential differences between its implementation in Windows NT Version 4.0, along with information on how it is implemented in the beta release of Windows NT 5.0.

OVERVIEW

Performance Monitor is a graphical tool that provides both Workstation and Server users with the ability to measure the performance of their computer along with other computers on a network, with the latter capability based upon a user on one computer having a valid account on another computer accessed via a network.

Performance Monitor is accessed through the Start-Administrative Tools sequence. As an alternative for persons that still like to use command line entries, you can enter the command perform at the command prompt. Both Windows NT Version 4.0 and Windows NT Version 5.0 support both methods of invoking Performance Monitor.

Once Performance Monitor is active, you can use it to view performance metrics for objects on your computer or another computer on the network, create alerts with predefined thresholds that are invoked when the thresholds are exceeded, export data from charts, logs, and Alert Logs maintained by Performance Monitor to spreadsheet or database programs for manipulation. Our discussion of Performance Monitor is applicable to both

0-8493-9838-X/00/$0.00+$.50
© 2000 by CRC Press LLC

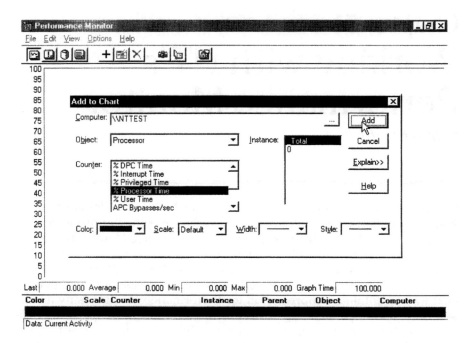

Exhibit 51.1. **Using the Performance Monitor "Add To Chart" Dialog Box
to Chart the Percentage Of Processor Time Being Used**

Windows NT Version 4.0 and the beta release of Windows NT Version 5.0. Where appropriate, I will indicate differences between the two.

USING THE GRAPHIC INTERFACE

Upon selecting Performance Monitor from the Administrative Tools bar, or entering the appropriate command line entry, Performance Monitor displays a screen with a graphical area that is blank. That blank area is used for charting the performance of selected objects and object counters.

Exhibit 51.1 illustrates the initial blank Performance Monitor screen display in the background of the figure. The foreground shows the dialog box labeled "Add to Chart," which is displayed as a result of clicking on the plus (+) symbol icon on the toolbar of the background screen display. Since the "Add to Chart" dialog box is the key to the use of Performance Monitor to display metrics concerning the operation of your computer or another computer on the network, let's examine the entries in this dialog box.

The computer entry provides you with the ability to chart the performance of one or more objects on your computer or a different computer that is connected to your network. The object, counter, and instance entries provide you with a mechanism to specify exactly what is to be monitored or charted.

In Windows NT, an object represents a mechanism used to identify a system resource. Objects can represent individual processes, sections of shared memory, and physical devices. Clicking on the downward pointing arrow associated with the object window results in a display of a series of objects to include memory, processor, paging file, and physical disk. Under the beta version of Windows NT Version 5.0 several new objects were added to Performance Monitor. The new objects include a network object and a logical disk object. For each object, Performance Monitor maintains a unique set of counters that, when selected, produce statistical information. This is illustrated by the selection of the Processor object in Exhibit 51.1. Note that the counter window illustrates six counters associated with the Processor object. In actuality there are more than six Processor counters, since you can scroll through additional counter entries that are not directly visible in the Counter window. For illustrative purposes, we will select the % Processor Time counter because that counter indicates the percentage of elapsed time that a processor is busy executing a nonidle thread. When attempting to isolate poor server performance, it is important to determine if the bottleneck is the server or the network. By examining the value of the % Processor Time counter over a period of time, you can obtain a valuable insight as to whether or not the server load is causing the bottleneck.

Returning to Exhibit 51.1, note the window labeled Instance. Each object type can have one or multiple instances. For example, a multiprocessor-capable server could have multiple processors installed on its system board. This means that a mechanism is required to provide you with the ability to examine each processor. That mechanism is obtained by the window labeled Instance. Some object types, such as Memory and Paging File, do not have instances. If an object type has multiple instances, each instance will produce the same set of statistical information because the counters are the same for each instance. That is, counters vary only by object type.

The lower portion of the "Add to Chart" dialog box provides you with the ability to specify or customize the manner by which counters are charted. You can select a particular color, scale, line display width, and line style for your chart. If you do not select any particular value or set of values, Performance Monitor will cycle through a predefined default set of values if you plot multiple counters. In doing so, Performance Monitor will assign different default values to each counter you wish plotted, enabling you to easily distinguish one plot from another.

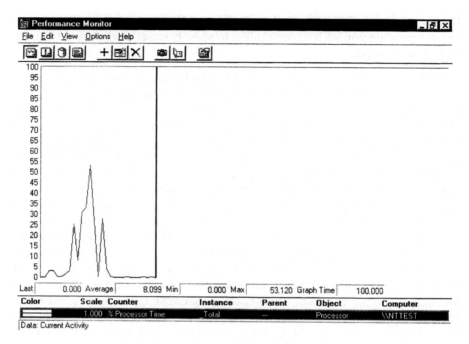

Exhibit 51.2. Observing the % Processor Time Utilization

Exhibit 51.2 illustrates the initial plotting of the % Processor Time counter on the author's NT computer. Note that at the time the screen was captured, the % Processor Time counter value had a maximum of slightly over 53%, a minimum value of 0, and an average value of 8.099%. During the monitoring interval this author executed several programs to ascertain their effect upon processor performance, which resulted in the spike of activity shown in Exhibit 51.2. Through the use of Performance Monitor in a similar manner, you can determine the effect of different workloads being placed upon the processing capability of an NT-based system. This, in turn, provides you with a mechanism to determine if you should consider upgrading a uniprocessor system to a more powerful microprocessor, assuming that it is upgradable, or adding one or more processors to a multiprocessor-based computer. Thus, the use of Windows NT Performance Monitor can be a valuable tool for capacity planning purposes.

WORKING WITH MULTIPLE OBJECTS

Very often it is difficult to determine the culprit for poor performance. This is due to the complexity of modern computers and networks for which many areas of activity interact upon one another, resulting in the possibility that a hardware, software, or network bottleneck could be

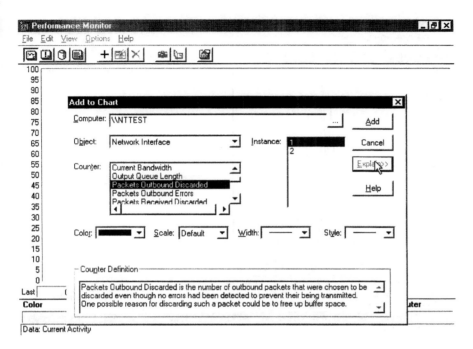

Exhibit 51.3. **The Beta Version of Windows Nt 5.0 Includes Several New Network-related Objects and Associated Counters to Include Objects for the Network Interface, TCP, and IP**

adversely affecting the level of performance being complained about by a remote user. Recognizing the necessity to provide a mechanism to view the values of multiple counters, the designers of Performance Monitor permit you to simply specify additional counters for display.

Exhibit 51.3 illustrates one of several new objects and related object counters added to the beta version of Windows NT 5.0. In Exhibit 51.3, the network interface object is shown selected. Several additional objects added to the beta version of Windows NT Version 5.0 that are not included in Version 4.0 include Transmission Control Protocol (TCP), Internet Protocol (IP), and Internetwork Package Exchange (IPX), providing an enhanced ability for network capacity planning operations.

In examining Exhibit 51.3, note that the Instance window shows the values 1 and 2. This results from the fact that the computer used by this author has two network adapters installed. Through the use of the "Add to Chart" dialog box, statistics could be obtained for either or both network adapters. Also note the counter definition at the bottom of the dialog box. One of the more helpful features of Performance Monitor is the ability to

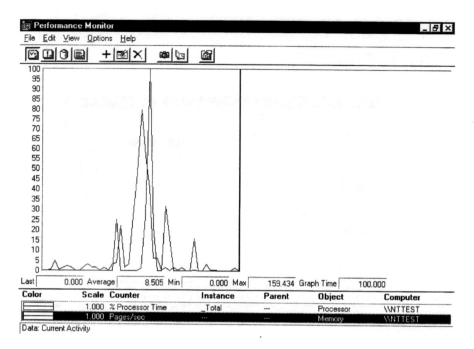

Exhibit 51.4.   Viewing the Display of Multiple Counters on a Performance Monitor Screen

---

click on a button labeled "Explain," which results in the display of a short definition of a highlighted counter. This can be an extremely useful feature due to the large number of counters associated with many objects, as well as because of the use of counter names that, upon occasion, are difficult to relate to a particular activity. Both Windows NT Version 4.0 and the beta version of Windows NT 5.0 include the Explain button capability.

Exhibit 51.4 illustrates the charting of two counters. Although the illustration is shown in black and white, making a discrimination between the two counter charts difficult, on a color monitor the plotting of each counter is in a different color, which facilitates the ability of users to view the charting of multiple counters. However, if you closely examine Exhibit 51.4, you can still differentiate between the two plots. To do so you would first examine the color indicated for each counter, which shows the plotting style used for plotting. Doing so you will note that the pages/sec counter display uses a dotted line. Although a bit difficult to discern in black and white, the use of different styles enables you to discriminate among plotted objects. To make it easier to differentiate among multiple plots, you can use the width window previously shown in Exhibit 51.1 to adjust the width of the lines used to plot different counters. In addition, you can select more pronounced styles, such as dots, dashes, and other symbols to better differentiate one plot from another.

Because there is only one row in Performance Monitor to indicate the last, average, minimum, and maximum values for a plotted counter, a mechanism is required to select the display of such data when multiple counters are displayed. That mechanism is obtained through scrolling a highlighted bar among the counter information displayed at the bottom of the Performance Monitor display. For example, in Exhibit 51.4 the highlighted bar is shown placed over the Pages/sec counter previously selected from the Memory object. Thus, the values in the last, average, minimum, and maximum windows are associated with the Pages/sec counter. If you move the highlighted bar upward over the % Processor Time counter, the previously described windows would reflect values for the % Processor Time counter.

USING ALERTS

Although Performance Monitor provides a valuable visual display of data concerning previously defined counters, most persons have more important things to do than sit before a console for a long time waiting for an event that may never happen. Recognizing this fact, Performance Monitor includes a built-in alert facility that enables users to set predefined thresholds. Once those thresholds are reached, Performance Monitor will automatically place an appropriate entry into the Windows NT Alert Log. In addition, if you desire, you can enter the name of a program that will be automatically executed when an alert situation occurs.

Exhibit 51.5 illustrates the use of the "Add to Alert" dialog box of Performance Monitor. In this example, the % Processor Time counter for the Processor object is shown selected. In the box labeled "Alert If," the "over" button is shown selected and the value 50 is shown entered in the "Alert If" window. This means that an alert will be generated if the % Processor Time counter value should exceed 50%.

In the lower right portion of the "Add to Alert" dialog box is a window with the label "Run Program on Alert." Note the entry "notify.exe." This entry results in the automatic execution of the previously mentioned program when the % Processor Time value exceeds 50%. In addition, since the button labeled "Every Time" is shown selected, this means that the program will be executed each time the previously defined alert occurs.

The program notify.exe represents an e-mail shell that was developed by this author to transmit a predefined message to technicians. You can also obtain commercial programs that can generate a paging message, send an e-mail, and even dial a telephone number and generate a predefined voice

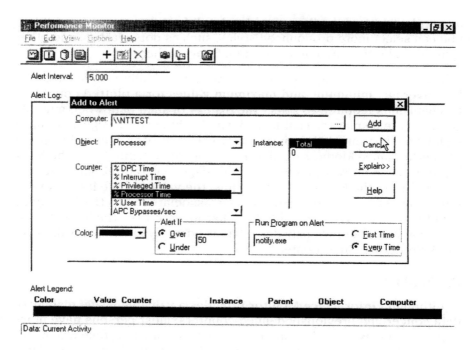

**Exhibit 51.5.   Creating an Alert That Will Execute the Program Notify.exe
When the % Processor Time Exceeds 50%**

message. Through the use of such programs combined with the Run Program on the Alert window, you can really alert your staff to different conditions when human intervention may be necessary. For example, by setting an alert to be generated upon the occurrence of a predefined number of network transmission errors, you would alert networking technicians to check the network. Doing so may enable potential problems to be noted and fixed prior to such problems adversely affecting network users, or even resulting in an eventual network failure if left unchecked.

In concluding this article on the use of Windows NT, Exhibit 51.6 shows the Performance Monitor Alert window. The Alert Log at the point in time the screen display was captured is empty, since it was extremely difficult to exceed a 50% Processor time level of utilization to coincide with a screen capture operation. If one or more alerts occurred, they would be time-stamped and listed in sequence of occurrence in the Alert Log window.

SUMMARY

Performance Monitor provides an easy-to-use statistical reporting capability that also enables you to define alert conditions. Through the use of

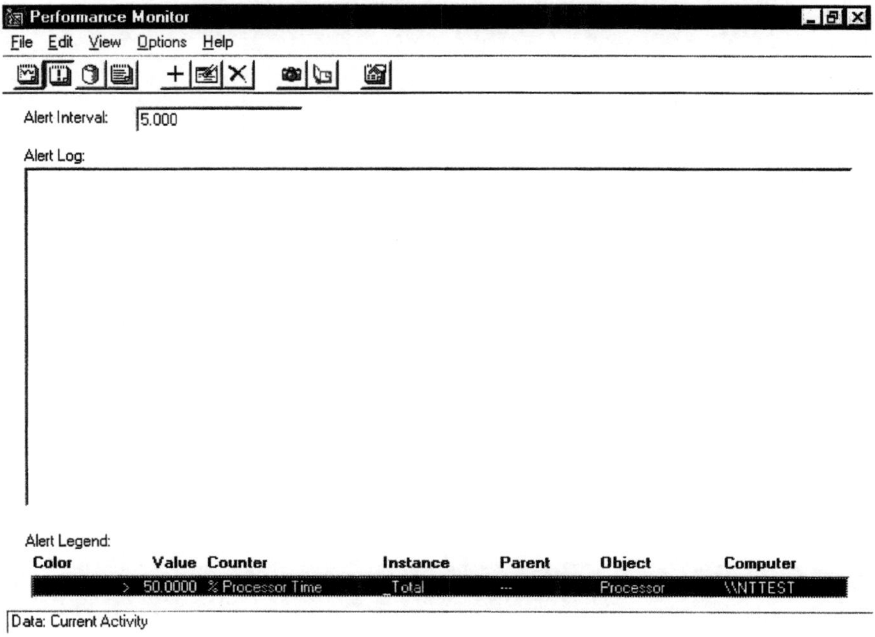

Exhibit 51.6.   The Performance Monitor Alert Log

this built-in utility program, you can note the growth or contraction in the use of system resources and plan hardware and network upgrades accordingly. Since Performance Monitor is included with each copy of Windows NT, it provides an ideal mechanism to identify and correct bottlenecks, plan for increased processor and network workloads, and troubleshoot a variety of computer- and network-related problems. Thus, network managers and LAN administrators that support Windows NT clients should become conversant with the capabilities of this utility.

Chapter 52
Evaluating the Performance of NT-Based Systems

Gilbert Held

Computer performance represents a topic that in one area is very similar to a discussion of the weather — that is, many people can be expected to talk about both topics. However, unlike the weather, which is normally beyond one's control, one does have some latitude when it comes to tailoring the performance of a computer system. By changing hardware components, adding additional memory, swapping a fixed disk for a faster one, and tuning software components, one can usually enhance the performance of a computer. Unfortunately, until recently it was difficult to evaluate the benefits derived from changing hardware or modifying software settings. Fortunately for Microsoft Windows NT users, this operating system includes a built-in performance monitor that can be used to determine the existing level of performance of a computer, as well as for ascertaining the impact of hardware and software changes. Thus, by understanding how to use the Windows NT built-in Performance Monitor utility — either by itself to ascertain the performance of various computer components or in conjunction with hardware and software changes — one obtains the ability to evaluate the performance of an NT computer. In doing so, one might be able to determine that a simple and easy-to-perform operation may be all that is required to eliminate a performance bottleneck, alleviating the necessity to replace or upgrade an existing computer. Thus, in addition to providing a mechanism to examine the level of performance of existing hardware and software, the use of the Windows NT Performance Monitor may enable one to postpone or avoid an expensive equipment upgrade.

OVERVIEW

There are several key components of a Windows NT computer system that can affect its performance. Those components include the amount of memory installed in the computer, the access time and data transfer rate of hard disks, the type of processor or processors installed on the computer's motherboard, and the type of network adapter card used for a connection to a LAN. In addition to hardware, there are also several software component settings that can have a major effect on the performance of an NT-based computer system. Two of those software settings are the use of virtual memory and the operation of a screen saver. Concerning the latter, one of the most overlooked facts about computers is the fact that the use of a screen saver requires CPU cycles. This means that the simple act of removing a screen saver from a heavily utilized server will enhance its performance.

Unfortunately, the simplicity associated with enabling and disabling the use of a screen saver does not carry over to other hardware and software changes. That is, while the decision to activate or disable a screen saver is a binary decision, the decisions associated with altering hardware or changing system properties are more complex. Thus, in many instances, one will want to consider making an initial hardware or software change and then use the NT Performance Monitor to access the results of the change on computer performance. Recognizing the old adage that "the proof of the pudding is in the eating," one can now focus on the use of virtual memory and its potential effect on the performance of a computer.

VIRTUAL MEMORY

Both Windows NT Workstation and Windows NT Server are similar products, with the key difference between the two being the fact that the server version is optimized to support more users accessing its resources. Thus, although this discussion of virtual memory is applicable to both versions of Windows NT, it is more applicable for Windows NT Server because the use of virtual memory has a greater impact on a computer running multiple applications accessed by many persons than a computer operating multiple applications operated by one or a few persons.

Virtual memory is a term used to reference the use of disk storage as a temporary storage area for program code and other information normally stored in random access memory (RAM). When the RAM storage requirements of applications programs and various NT operating system modules exceed physical RAM, NT will temporarily swap data to virtual memory. When that information is required again, Windows NT will retrieve it from disk and, if necessary, swap other information to virtual memory. Although virtual memory swapping is transparent to the user, it has a significant effect on computer performance.

PERFORMANCE EFFECT

When Windows NT uses its virtual memory capability, it transfers data to and from a special file on the hard disk, referred to as a virtual-memory paging file. This file is also commonly referred to as a swap file. The transfer of information to and from disk occurs at electromechanical speed, with the movement of disk read/write heads over an appropriate disk sector contributing to a major portion of the delay in reading from or writing to a disk. Although modern disk drives are relatively fast devices, they still operate at 1/50th to 1/100th the speed of computer memory in terms of data transfer capability. While paging will always adversely affect the performance of a computer, the size of the paging file on the computer can have a more profound impact. If the size of the paging file is too small for the amount of activity on the server, one can experience a "thrashing" condition, with the operating system repetitively reading and writing small portions of RAM to and from disk.

As this occurs, the performance of the computer will be significantly impacted because additional input/output (I/O) operations are occurring that contribute to delays in processing application data. For example, if operating a database application on the server, the paging operations will delay access to the database. While an individual paging operation will hardly be noticeable, when thrashing occurs, the delays can become significant, especially if the server supports hundreds of employees. Although one could alleviate this condition via the installation of additional RAM, one could also considerably enhance the performance of the server by making an adjustment to the size of the system's virtual memory paging file. How this is done is the focus of the next section.

CHANGING THE PAGING FILE

Since the introduction of Windows NT version 3.5, Microsoft has considerably changed the interface and components of the operating system. However, one component that has retained both its location and general properties is the System Properties dialog box in the NT Control Panel. Through NT version 5.0, one can use the Performance tab in the System Properties dialog box to review the computer's current virtual memory page file settings as well as to change those settings.

Exhibit 52.1 illustrates the screen display of the System Properties dialog box selected from the Control Panel under Windows NT version 5.0. Note that the middle portion of the dialog box displays the current size of the paging file and provides the ability to change the size of that file.

Under Windows NT, a virtual memory paging file is automatically created on the computer when the operating system is installed. The size of the paging file initially created is based on the amount of RAM installed in the computer, and is typically set by the operating system to equal that amount plus 12 MB. However, the size of the file also depends on the amount of available free space on the hard drive when the paging file is created. Thus, if one installs Windows NT over a prior version of the operating system, or over a different operating system, and then changes the hard drive or removes obsolete files, the size of the paging file may vary from the Microsoft recommendation. In addition, the recommendation is merely a

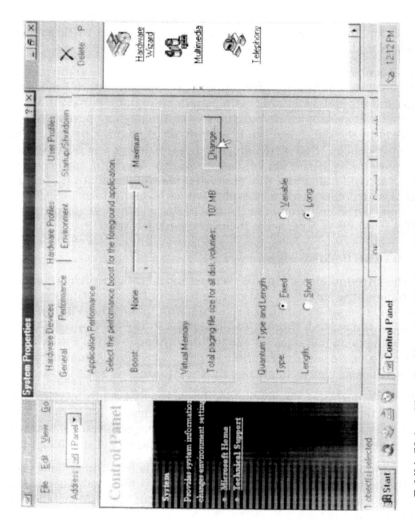

Exhibit 52.1. View the Size of the Windows NT Paging File from the Performance Tab in the System Properties Dialog Box

recommendation and may not be suitable for the traffic expected to be supported by the server. Thus, one can now examine how to change the size of the paging file and then observe changes in performance resulting from changing the size of the paging file.

Exhibit 52.2 illustrates the screen display resulting from selecting the button labeled "change" in the Performance tab in the System Properties dialog box. Note that the Virtual Memory dialog box displays the initial size of the paging file, which represents the recommended size of the file and its maximum size. The latter setting permits an area on disk to be reserved to enable the size of the paging file to grow. In this example, the paging file is shown set to 107 MB and can grow to 157 MB.

Although Microsoft's default settings for the computer's paging file will be sufficient for many users, it is a fact of life that very rarely are two computers used in a similar manner. This means that for some Windows NT users, an adjustment to the size of the paging file may be in order. However, how can one determine if sluggish performance is being caused by an improper allocation of paging file space, the inability of the computer's processor to support current operations, a lack of RAM, or another factor? The answer to this question can be obtained through the use of the Windows NT Performance, Monitor which provides the key for evaluating the performance of an NT computer.

EVALUATING NT PERFORMANCE

Exhibit 52.3 illustrates the initial display of the NT Performance Monitor after the plus sign (+) button in the icon bar across the top of the display was clicked. That action results in the display of the dialog box labeled "Add to chart," which enables one to display in realtime metrics associated with different counters, which are in turn associated with different NT objects. Under Windows NT, an object is a higher layer component, such as a processor or paging file. The counters represent performance elements whose values are tracked. If the computer contains two or more objects, such as a multiprocessor computer with two or more processors installed on the motherboard, each processor will have an instance associated with it. One would then be required to select the instance to identify the particular processor for which one wants a counter to be displayed.

Returning to Exhibit 52.3, note that the counter "% Processor Time" was selected. This will result in the display of the percentage of processor time being used once the "Add" button is clicked. By observing this metric, one would be able to note whether or not the processor was a bottleneck. Also note that if that computer is connected to a network and one has an appropriate account on another NT computer, one can use Performance Monitor on the computer to monitor the performance of a distant computer. Thus, a supervisor or user with a series of appropriate accounts on different

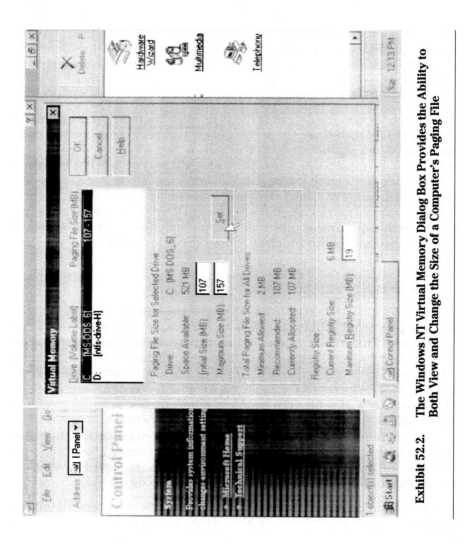

Exhibit 52.2.   The Windows NT Virtual Memory Dialog Box Provides the Ability to Both View and Change the Size of a Computer's Paging File

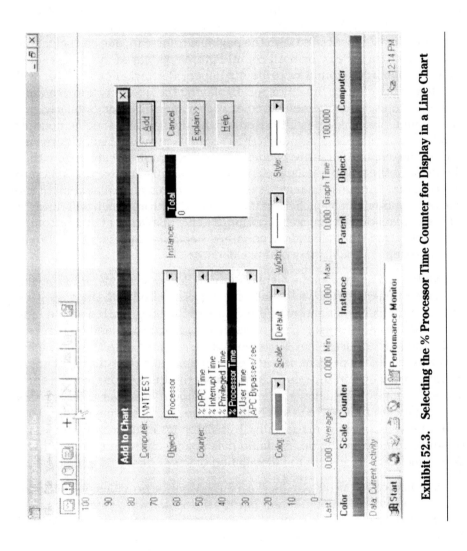

Exhibit 52.3. Selecting the % Processor Time Counter for Display in a Line Chart

computers could periodically monitor the performance of a network of NT computers from one location.

The previous concern about the size of the NT paging file can now be addressed. Exhibit 52.4 illustrates the selection of the "Paging File" object in the Performance Monitor utility program. In examining Exhibit 52.4, note that Performance Monitor does not provide a direct indication of the amount of usage associated with the paging file. Instead, one can select the % Usage, % Usage Peak, or both counters to be displayed over a period of time. As one adds counters to be displayed, Performance Monitor will automatically change the color for displaying the counter; however, one can elect to override the default color with a specific color. Similarly, one can change the scale linewidth used for the display of a specific counter and the style of the line. Although those options provide the ability to customize the display of a series of counters on a common screen display, they do not alter the ability to display any counter, as all counters are built into the program and must be used as-is. If one requires an explanation of the use of a counter, one can click on the "Explain" button, which will result in a brief explanation of the use of a counter being displayed at the bottom of the screen. Once the selection of counters is complete, pressing the "Done" button results in the display of those counters.

Exhibit 52.5 illustrates the display of the % Processor Time, % Usage and % Usage Peak, the latter two counters being associated with the paging file object. A careful examination of the colors of the lines plotted would indicate that the % Processor Time periodically spiked to 40 and 60 percent, while the percent usage and % Usage Peak associated with the paging file never exceeded 10 percent. If you were running a mixture of typical applications and monitored performance during the busy hour (which represents the hour of the day with the highest amount of server activity), this would indicate that one can safely reduce the size of the paging file. This could be valuable information that translates into the bottom line of an organization if it is low on available disk space and wishes to defer the downtime associated with the installation of a new drive.

As indicated in this article, Performance Monitor provides one with the ability to view the use of different hardware and software components. By using Performance Monitor, one can observe the existing performance of hardware and software as a mechanism for the adjustment of computer components. Then one can reuse Performance Monitor to evaluate the effect of those changes as well as to periodically monitor the performance of the computer. In doing so, one may be able to note potential problems before they occur and initiate corrective action prior to the user community experiencing the effect of performance bottlenecks.

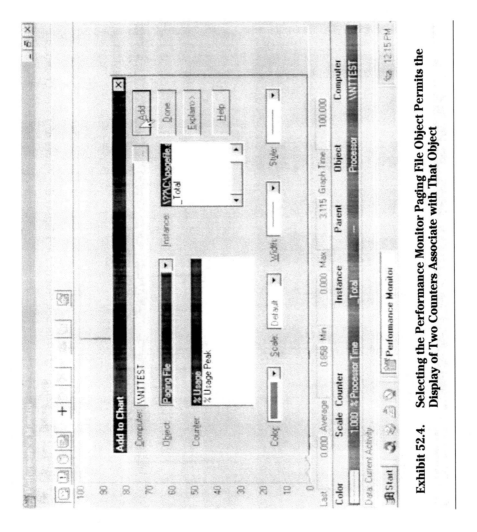

Exhibit 52.4. **Selecting the Performance Monitor Paging File Object Permits the Display of Two Counters Associate with That Object**

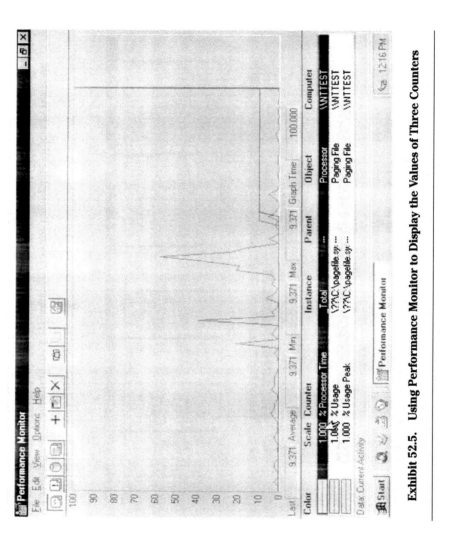

Exhibit 52.5. Using Performance Monitor to Display the Values of Three Counters

Chapter 53
Developing a Network Security Plan

Frederick Gallegos and Stephen Tanner

Distributed environments security is becoming one of the greatest areas of concern for organizations around the world. The convergence and growing use of the Internet, mirocomputer-based networks, wide area networking, intranets, extranets, and electronic mail have increased the security exposure of most organizations.

In this environment, IS managers and executives rely on the assistance of security and audit personnel to devise plans that effectively monitor the complex distributed environments of today and tomorrow. This article reviews the changing role of audit and security in distributed environments, the types of threats present in these environments, the range of methodologies available for securing a sample Novell network, and some of the current technologies and tools available for maintaining network security.

SECURING THE NEW DISTRIBUTED ENVIRONMENT

Over the years, the definition of distributed environments has changed. Technology has produced hardware and software to meet the needs of organizations to integrate automation of their work processes and data collection and storage. For the purposes of this discussion, a distributed environment is defined as follows:

A collection of computer hardware components joined together within a building or spread over a geographically diverse area with telecommunications software and cabling. The goal is to allow the sharing of data, software applications, communications, and hardware to automate the manual processes of an organization in the realization of its mission and objectives.

An organization's information assets have differing levels of value. On one level, there are the costs of hardware, software, and technology used to develop and store data to generate information. On another level, there are the human resource costs of actually collecting and interpreting data in order to store meaningful information for ongoing decision making. Finally,

0-8493-9838-X/00/$0.00+$.50
© 2000 by CRC Press LLC

there is the value of keeping the information confidential and secret from outside entities.

The importance of network security is its goal of preserving the varying levels of investment, maintaining trustworthy and accurate data, and ensuring a sustainable level of trust in the automated systems used to collect, store, and disseminate accurate, reliable information.

REVIEW OF SECURITY AND CONTROL THREATS

Security threats take on many forms.[1] The goal of developing this list is not to provide exhaustive sources, but to provide a framework for evaluating exposure in the major categories outlined. These areas present new roles for audit and security personnel in conducting their reviews and providing the IS executives and managers with assurances that controls are in place and working effectively.

The four main security categories are as follows:

1. Physical security (including hardware)
2. Operating system-level security
3. Communications security
4. Procedural security

Physical Security and Control Threats

Following are some of the areas of physical vulnerability:

- *Hardware attack.* In a hardware attack, someone attaches a device to the network to gather and siphon off data. Typical invasions include the installation of trojan horses and viruses.
- *Software attack.* In a software attack, workstation modules (operating systems, TSRs, and application software) are modified to gather data from the system and save it for later retrieval, or to deny network or data access.
- *Masquerade attack.* Here, the perpetrator uses the identity of an authorized user to obtain access to the network, and then reviews its structure and data.
- *Unauthorized copying of software and data.* In this case, the perpetrator installs unlicensed software or violates the licensing agreement through unauthorized copying of software; the person may also breach company confidentiality through the extraction of company data and information.

Operating System-Level Security Threats

This type of network attack results from unauthorized individuals installing software that circumvents operating-system-level security and allows them to go around restrictions designed into the operating system.

Often, exposure to this threat is through commercially available software that has been written to take advantage of inherent bugs or loopholes in the operating system.

Communications Security Threats

These types of threats come in two forms:

1. *Tapping*. Tapping means that an open telephone line in a data communications system is accessed for the purpose of tracking data flow.
2. *Spoofing*. In this case, an outside party pretends to be a server or peer authorized for data or network access.

Procedural Security Threats

Although procedural security threats cover an enormous range of topics, the category can be broken down into four main elements:

1. How effectively has software been installed?
2. How well is the system being administered?
3. How are user rights and privileges being managed?
4. How is the system restored after a failure?

COUNTERING SECURITY AND CONTROL THREATS

Developing countermeasures to security threats can be a daunting task if attempted without a well-thought-out methodology. The initial phase is to begin developing a network security plan. According to the Gartner Group,[2] several issues must be addressed in developing such a plan. The most important issue is to establish a policy that is endorsed by upper management and draws from security experts, CIS auditors, network managers, business-unit managers, and users from across the enterprise.

A security policy should address methods of achieving the following goals:

- Confidentiality: making information available only to authorized entities and ensuring the privacy of communications.
- Authentication: determining whether information is genuine (whether the source and destination entities are what they claim to be).
- Access control: permitting or denying access based on a variety of parameters. These include the identity of the source and destination, and the nature of the business relationship if the potential users are outside parties.
- Data integrity: ensuring that data is accurate.
- Nonrepudiation: providing proof of transmission and receipt.

A complete security policy also contains provisions for ongoing updating, such as the indoctrination of security awareness among all users and the establishment of standards and procedures for security training.

In addition to a strong security plan, an organization must look at its particular environment and technology to develop specific approaches for countering possible security threats inherent within that technology. In the following sections, general principles to address a typical Novell network environment are reviewed. This illustration reflects the current majority of microcomputer-based networks in North America and in many parts of the world. The general principles and audit, security, and control steps outlined are transferable to all network environments.

APPLYING METHODOLOGIES IN A NOVELL ENVIRONMENT[3]

In securing a network, specifically a Novell network, different models of security can be identified to meet the various levels of maintenance costs and security requirements appropriate to a particular organization. Five such models are presented in the sections that follow; each subsequent model builds on and enhances the level of security of the preceding model. Again, the resources to perform such functions can come from consulting services, security staff, and CIS auditors.

The Simple Model (Minimum Security)

The simple model comprises the following steps:

- Buy an antivirus package for the network that can be auto loaded in the login script.
- Give every user a log-in script.
- Always install network application software to specification.
- Place the server in a safe area (where it will not be tampered with inadvertently, bumped, or otherwise interfered with).
- Choose a password for ADMIN that is not common or easily discernible by anyone. Require that end users do the same with their own passwords.
- Place the server and backup device in a secure area. Keep the backup devices and backup software in a secured location apart from the server.
- Make regular backups.
- Restore the first backup to another directory as a test just after it is made.
- Move backups and a copy of backup software off site on a regularly scheduled basis.
- Lock the file server console from within the MONITOR.NLM.
- Do not store the file server console password in the AUTOEXEC.NCF file.
- Set up some form of education about computer security.

Basic Model

The basic model includes the simple model and the following additional steps:

- Educate the organization about passwords and computer viruses.
- Require users to log out and lock up stations not in use.
- Test the backup process by creating a directory, filling it with nonessential data files, backing up the files, deleting them, and restoring them from the backup device.
- Maintain a second archive of all data and applications off site for disaster recovery.
- Learn and understand the file system directory and file attributes.
- Install software in its own directory.
- Remove DOS from the server by typing REMOVE DOS at the console.
- Ensure that the console password is different from the ADMIN's password.

The Protected Model

The protected model comprises the basic model and the following steps:

- Implement proper security education.
- Implement a premise key distribution system.
- Require passwords for print servers.
- Make sure all users exit from the system log-in script or use their own personal log-in scripts (an empty log-in script is better than no log-in script).
- Limit the number of concurrent connections.
- Provide the system administrator with the capabilities and security equivalencies of the ADMIN user object and then delete the user ADMIN.
- Check access control list (ACL) rights in NDS for all users other than ADMIN.
- User accounts of terminated employees or otherwise unused accounts should be disabled or deleted.
- Keep a list of detailed accounts, users, and other pertinent information for use when restoring backups.
- Use only Novell-certified and tested NLMs.
- Enable intruder detection.
- Enable the SECURE CONSOLE feature on the server to restrict the loading of NLMs.
- Disable all remote console capabilities or assign RCONSOLE a unique password.
- Set network time restrictions.

- Remove write and create rights for the MAIL directory from the [Public] trustee.
- Use a network analyzer to produce a list of clear-text passwords.
- Train users to log out whenever they leave their computer, or provide some kind of automatic locking utility for everyone's computer.
- Require regular password changes for all accounts.
- Do not allow reuse of a password.
- Verify size for installed executables with the manufacturer. Check them periodically to ensure they have not changed size.

Audited Model

The audited model builds on the protected model. It includes the following additional steps:

- Have the network audited regularly by CIS auditors.
- Monitor access to the server room, cable, and workstations.
- Monitor executable files.
- Provide security training for end users and administrators with annual refreshers.

Secured Model

The secured model is the most secure. Its high level of security is derived from the audited model and the following steps:

- Remove disk drives from workstations when not in use.
- Restrict physical station addresses.
- Ensure that only trusted users have workstation access.
- Eliminate untrusted user accounts from trusted networks.
- Secure all workstations.
- Institute trusted-connectivity components in the network.

These models review the main areas of security in a local area network (LAN) or a zone within a wide area network (WAN). Additional issues must be considered when dealing with outside access to the network through the Internet, intranet, extranet, E-mail, or telephony. These include confidentiality, authentication, access control, data integrity, and nonrepudiation.

Access control continues to be the serious concern among organizations using telecommunications to connect their networks across geographically diverse operations. The point of a distributed environment is to facilitate the transfer of information between systems; however, things get complicated when connecting to systems outside the organization. The challenge is to restrict access to hackers and viruses without degrading the overall performance of the network for those authorized to use it.

FIREWALLS

Firewalls are becoming the method of choice for organizations determined to maintain security from outside intruders. A firewall is a compilation of hardware and software components designed to work together in maintaining security of an internal network from attacks from outside. Their use and implementation varies, but the principle by which they are designed is to place a gateway between the internal network and the outside world.

The firewall can restrict traffic that is not explicitly permitted, or allow traffic that is not explicitly blocked. For maximum safety, the first option is more secure because it allows services to be enabled on a case-by-case basis after a careful assessment of need and risk. Furthermore, the network administrator knows what accesses are permitted.

Firewall vendors such as Raptor describe five domains of network security:[4]

1. Internet security
2. Workgroup security
3. Mobile PC security
4. Remote site security
5. Integrated enterprise security

CIS auditors and IS security personnel can play a key role in monitoring the integrity of the firewall and ensuring operational and security compliance. Each of these domains has specific requirements, but common elements among firewall installations include suspicious activity monitoring, encryption, multiple authentication options, proxy software to foil spoofing attacks, real-time alarms to catch hackers in the act, tools to secure remote data communications, and network management tools.

SECURITY TOOLS

As security risk exposures have increased in distributed environments, so have tools to monitor and correct them. Diagnostic tools can be used to assist an organization in identifying specific security weaknesses within its distributed environments. One example is the Security Administrator Tool for Analyzing Networks (SATAN).[5] This is a public domain software security tool released through the Internet. This tool has many administrators concerned about its availability to potential hackers, but it can be more of an aid if used before a hacker attempts to attack a distributed environment.

SATAN gathers information about Internet-connected hosts and detects the presence of Unix services such as remote log-in and file transfer. The program then outlines the ways in which these services can be misused, and identifies other security flaws such as bugs in system or network utilities. It also identifies poorly configured systems that lack passwords or other basic precautions, and unauthorized activities by inside users such as opening unprotected Internet connections. SATAN then displays information about the nature and seriousness of the flaws it finds and offers suggestions on how to correct them.

From a management standpoint, vulnerabilities identified by SATAN should not be tolerated. They are normally elementary weaknesses that any competent hacker can circumvent. A network that is vulnerable to SATAN is not protected from the most casual intrusion.

CURRENT ISSUES AFFECTING SECURITY

As technology continues to become more pervasive, and end users become more sophisticated, internal and external security risks will likely increase. End users are able to navigate and access databases as never before. Available technologies becoming industry standards include Windows 95, open database connectivity (ODBC), object linking and embedding (OLE), client/server technology, and other desktop technologies. The challenges to organizations attempting to implement network security are becoming even greater than they have been in the past.

Many security experts are suggesting that distributed environments are becoming virtually impossible to fully secure. Network security has become a dynamic process as new technologies allow the breach of existing security measures. The use of CIS audit and CIS security expertise can help monitor the quality of security and control within the distributed environment and aid IS executives in determining the relative importance of the necessary adjustments, modifications, and improvements needed for planned strategic systems of the future.

CONCLUSION

Though the challenges of securing a network are becoming greater than ever, it is not too late to begin formalizing a plan to secure an organization's current environment. CIS auditors and security consultants and staff can play key roles in helping managers maintain a secure and controlled environment. By developing a network security policy that becomes the framework for a proactive plan, IS executives and managers can integrate the skills and resources of audit and security personnel in maintaining the plan. Vendors, such as Novell, are working with clients and security professionals to develop new and improved tools to assist in securing networks developed with their products.

Network security administrators and CIS auditors are using tools such as SATAN in their fight against common security infiltration by hackers and others. The Internet is providing a tremendous medium for those researching issues specific to their circumstances. It is also allowing professionals to share information with each other on reducing and eliminating security risks within their network environments.

Network security can be approached by following the guidelines outlined in this article. Once a network has reached a certain level of security, managers must continue looking for ways to keep up with other potential security risk exposures. Network security is a dynamic process with continuous opportunities for its improvement.

Notes

1. Novell Application Notes — Special Edition — *Building and Auditing a Trusted Network Environment with Netware 4,* Provo, UT: Novell Publishing, April 1994, p. 30–34.
2. Gartner Group Advisory Services Point to Point, April 28, 1995 — *Network Security, Part 2: Policy Should Come First.*
3. Novell Application Notes — Special Edition — *Building and Auditing a Trusted Network Environment with Netware 4* — Figure 3.1 p. 48.
4. Raptor Web Page — http://www.Raptor.com.
5. Gartner Group Advisory Services Point to Point, April 28, 1995 — *Network Security, Part 1: SATAN Makes Debut.*

Chapter 54
Firewall Management and Internet Attacks
Jeffery J. Lowder

Network connectivity can be both a blessing and a curse. On the one hand, network connectivity can enable users to share files, exchange e-mail, and pool physical resources. Yet network connectivity can also be a risky endeavor if the connectivity grants access to would-be intruders. The Internet is a perfect case in point. Designed for a trusted environment, many contemporary exploits are based on vulnerabilities inherent to the protocol itself. According to a recent dissertation by John Howard on Internet unauthorized access incidents reported to the Computer Emergency Response Team (CERT), there were 4567 incidents between 1989 and 1996, with the number of incidents increasing each year at a rate of 41 to 62 percent. In light of this trend, many organizations are implementing firewalls to protect their internal network from the untrusted Internet.

LAYING THE GROUNDWORK FOR A FIREWALL

Obtaining management support for a firewall prior to implementation can be very useful after the firewall is implemented. When a firewall is implemented on a network for the first time, it will almost surely be the source of many complaints. For example:

- Organizations that have never before had firewalls almost always do not have the kind of documentation necessary to support user requirements.
- If the firewall hides information about the internal network from the outside network, this will break any network transactions in which the remote system uses an access control list and the address of the firewall is not included in that list.
- Certain types of message traffic useful in network troubleshooting (e.g., PING, TRACEROUTE) may no longer work.

All of these problems can be solved, but the point is that coordination with senior management *prior to* installation can make life much easier for firewall administrators.

Benefits of Having a Firewall

So how does one obtain management support for implementation of a firewall? The security practitioner can point out the protection that a firewall provides: protection of the organization's network from intruders, protection of external networks from intruders within the organization, and protection from "due care" lawsuits. The security practitioner can also list the positive benefits a firewall can provide:

- *Increased ability to enforce network standards and policies.* Without a firewall or similar device, it is easy for users to implement systems that the Information Services (IS) department does not know about, that are in violation of organizational standards or policies, or both. In contrast, organizations find it very easy to enforce both standards and policies with a firewall that blocks all network connections by default. Indeed, it is not uncommon for organizations to discover undocumented systems when they implement such a firewall for the first time.
- *Centralized internetwork audit capability.* Because all or most traffic between the two networks must pass through the firewall (see below), the firewall is uniquely situated to provide audit trails of all connections between the two networks. These audit trails can be extremely useful for investigating suspicious network activity, troubleshooting connectivity problems, measuring network traffic flows, and even investigating employee fraud, waste, and abuse.

Limitations of a Firewall

Even with all of these benefits, firewalls still have their limitations. It is important that the security practitioner understand these limitations because if these limitations allow risks that are unacceptable to management, it is up to the security practitioner to present additional safeguards to minimize these risks. The security practitioner must not allow management to develop a false sense of security simply because a firewall has been installed.

- *Firewalls provide no data integrity.* It is simply not feasible to check all incoming traffic for viruses. There are too many file formats and often files are sent in compressed form. Any attempt to scan incoming files for viruses would severely degrade performance. Firewalls have plenty of processing requirements without taking on the additional responsibility of virus detection and eradication.
- *Firewalls do not protect traffic that is not sent through it.* Firewalls cannot protect against unsecured, dial-up modems attached to systems inside the firewall; internal attacks; social engineering attacks; or data that is routed around them. It is not uncommon for an organization to install

a firewall, then pass data from a legacy system around the firewall because its firewall did not support the existing system.

- *Firewalls may not protect anything if they have been compromised.* Although this statement should be obvious, many security practitioners fail to educate senior management on its implications. All too often, senior management approves — either directly or through silence — a security posture that positively lacks an internal security policy. Security practitioners cannot allow perimeter security via firewalls to become a substitute for internal security.

- *Firewalls cannot authenticate datagrams at the transport or network layers.* A major security problem with the TCP/IP is that any machine can forge a packet claiming to be from another machine. This means that the firewall has literally no control over how the packet was created. Any authentication must be supported in one of the higher layers.

- *Firewalls provide limited confidentiality.* Many firewalls have the ability to encrypt connections between two firewalls (using a so-called virtual private network, or VPN), but they typically require that the firewall be manufactured by the same vendor.

A firewall is no replacement for good host security practices and procedures. Individual system administrators still have the primary responsibility for preventing security incidents.

FIREWALLS AND THE LOCAL SECURITY POLICY

Cheswick and Bellovin (1994) define a firewall as a system with the following set of characteristics:

- All traffic between the two networks must pass through the firewall.
- Only traffic that is authorized by the local security policy will be allowed to pass.
- The firewall itself is immune to penetration.

Like any security tool, a firewall merely provides the capability to increase the security of the path between two networks. It is the responsibility of the firewall administrator to take advantage of this capability; and no firewall can guarantee absolute protection from outside attacks. The risk analysis should define the level of protection that can be expected from the firewall; the local security policy should provide general guidelines on how this protection will be achieved; and both the assessment and revised policy should be accepted by top management prior to firewall implementation.

Despite the fact that, according to Atkins et al.,[1] all traffic between the two networks must pass through the firewall, in practice this is not always technically feasible or convenient. Network administrators supporting legacy or proprietary systems may find that getting them to communicate through the firewall may not be as easy as firewall vendors claim, if even possible. And even if there are no technical obstacles to routing all traffic through the firewall, users may still complain that the firewall is inconvenient or slows their systems down. Thus, the local security policy should specify the process by which requests for exceptions[1] will be considered.

As Bellovin[2] states, the local security policy defines what the firewall is supposed to enforce. If a firewall is going to allow only authorized traffic between two networks, then the firewall has to know what traffic is authorized. The local security policy should define "authorized" traffic, and it should do so at a somewhat technical level. The policy should also state a default rule for evaluating requests: either all traffic is denied except that which is specifically authorized, or all traffic is allowed except that which is specifically denied.

Network devices that protect other network devices should themselves be protected against intruders. (If the protection device were not secure, intruders could compromise the device and then compromise the system[s] that the device was supposed to protect.)

FIREWALL EVALUATION CRITERIA

Choosing the right firewall for an organization can be a daunting task, given the complexity of the problem and the wide variety of products from which to choose. Yet the following criteria should help the security practitioner narrow the list of candidates considerably.

- *Performance.* Firewalls always impact the performance of the connection between the local and remote networks. Adding a firewall creates an additional hop for network packets to travel through; if the firewall must authenticate connections, that creates an additional delay. The firewall machine should be powerful enough to make these delays negligible.
- *Requirements support.* A firewall should support all of the applications that an organization wants to use across the two networks. Virtually all firewalls support fundamental protocols like SMTP, Telnet, FTP, and HTTP; strong firewalls should include some form of circuit proxy or generic packet relay. The security practitioner should decide what other applications are required (e.g., Real Audio, VDOLive, S-HTTP, etc.) and evaluate firewall products accordingly.
- *Access control.* Even the simplest firewalls support access control based on IP addresses; strong firewalls will support user-based access control and authentication. Large organizations should pay special attention to whether a given firewall product supports a large number of user profiles and ensure that the firewall can accommodate increased user traffic.

- *Authentication.* The firewall must support the authentication requirements of the local security policy. If implementation of the local security policy will entail authenticating large numbers of users, the firewall should provide convenient yet secure enterprisewide
  management of the user accounts. Some firewalls only allow the
  administrator to manage user accounts from a single console; this
  solution is not good enough for organizations with thousands of users
  who each need their own authentication account. Moreover, there are
  logistical issues that need to be thought out. For example, suppose the
  local security policy requires authentication of all inbound telnet connections. How will geographically separated users obtain the proper
  authentication credentials (e.g., passwords, hard tokens, etc.)?
- *Physical security.* The local security policy should stipulate the location of the firewall, and the hardware should be physically secured to
  prevent unauthorized access. The firewall must also be able to interface with surrounding hardware at this location.
- *Auditing.* The firewall must support the auditing requirements of the
  local security policy. Depending on network bandwidth and the level
  of event logging, firewall audit trails can become quite large. Superior
  firewalls will include a data reduction tool for parsing audit trails.
- *Logging and alarms.* What logging and alarms does the security policy
  require? If the security policy dictates that a potential intrusion event
  trigger an alarm and mail message to the administrator, the system
  must accommodate this requirement.
- *Customer support.* What level of customer support does the firewall
  vendor provide? If the organization requires 24-hour-a-day, 365-days-a-
  year technical support, is it available? Does the vendor provide training courses? Is self-help online assistance, such as a Web page or a
  mailing list, available?
- *Transparency.* How transparent is the firewall to the users? The more
  transparent the firewall is to the users, the more likely they will be to
  support it. On the other hand, the more confusing or cumbersome the
  firewall, the more likely the users are to resist it.

FIREWALL TECHNIQUES

There are three different techniques available to firewalls to enforce the
local security policy: packet filtering, application-level gateways, and circuit-level gateways. These techniques are not mutually exclusive; in practice, firewalls tend to implement multiple techniques to varying extents.
This section defines these firewall techniques.

Packet Filtering

Packet filters allow or drop packets according to the source or destination address or port. The administrator makes a list of acceptable and

Exhibit 54.1. Sample Packet Filter Configuration

Rule Number	Action	Local Host	Local Port	Remote Host	Remote Port
0	Allow	WWW server	80	*	*
1	Deny	*	*	*	*

unacceptable machines and services, and configures the packet filter accordingly. This makes it very easy for the administrator to filter access at the network or host level, but impossible to filter access at the user level (see Exhibit 54.1).

The packet filter applies the rules in order from top to bottom. Thus, in Exhibit 54.1, rule 0 blocks all network traffic by default; rule 1 creates an exception to allow unrestricted access on port 80 to the organization's Web server.

But what if the firewall administrator wanted to allow telnet access to the Web server by the Webmaster? The administrator could configure the packet filter as shown in Exhibit 54.2. The packet filter would thus allow telnet access (port 23) to the Web server from the address or addresses represented by <machine room>, but the packet filter has no concept of user authentication. Thus, unauthorized individuals originating from the <machine room> address(es) would be allowed telnet access to the WWW server, while authorized individuals originating from non-<machine room> address(es) would be denied access. In both cases, the lack of user authentication would prevent the packet filter from enforcing the local security policy.

Application-Level Gateways

Unlike packet filters, application-level gateways do not enforce access control lists. Instead, application-level gateways attempt to enforce connection integrity by ensuring that all data passed on a given port is in accordance with the protocol for that port. This is very useful for preventing transmissions prohibited by the protocol, but not handled properly by the remote system. Consider, for example, the Hypertext Transmission Protocol (HTTP) used by WW servers to send and receive information, normally on port 80. Intruders have been able to compromise numerous servers by transmitting special packets outside the HTTP specification. Pure

Exhibit 54.2. Packet Filter Configuration to Allow Telnet Access from <machine room> to <www-server>

Rule Number	Action	Local Host	Local Port	Remote Host	Remote Port
0	Allow	WWW server	80	*	*
1	Allow	WWW server	23	<machine room>	*
2	Deny	*	*	*	*

packet filters are ineffective against such attacks because they can only restrict access to a port based on source and destination address; but an application gateway could actually prevent such an attack by enforcing the protocol specification for all traffic on the related port.

The application gateway relays connections in a manner similar to that of the circuit-level gateway (see below), but it provides the additional service of checking individual packets for the particular application in use. It also has the additional ability to log all inbound and outbound connections.

Circuit-Level Gateways

A circuit-level gateway creates a virtual circuit between the local and remote networks by relaying connections. The originator opens a connection on a port to the gateway, and the gateway in turn opens a connection on that same port to the remote machine. The gateway machine relays data back and forth until the connection is terminated.

Because circuit-level gateways relay packets without inspecting them, they normally provide only minimal audit capabilities and no application-specific controls. Moreover, circuit-level gateways require new or modified client software that does not attempt to establish connections with the remote site directly; the client software must allow the circuit relay to do its job.

Still, circuit relays are transparent to the user. They are well-suited for outbound connections in which authentication is important but integrity is not.

See Exhibit 54.3 for a comparison of these firewall techniques.

DEVELOPING A FIREWALL POLICY AND STANDARDS

Reasons for Having Firewall Policy and Standards

There are a number of reasons for writing formal firewall policies and standards, including:

- Properly written firewall policies and standards will address important issues that may not be covered by other policies. Having a generic corporate policy on information systems security is not good enough. There are a number of specific issues that apply to firewalls but would not be addressed, or addressed in adequate detail, by generic security policies.
- A firewall policy can clarify how the organization's security objectives apply to the firewall. For example, a generic organizational policy on information protection might state that, "Access to information is granted on a need-to-know basis." A firewall policy would interpret this objective by stating that, "All traffic is denied except that which is explicitly authorized."

Exhibit 54.3. Advantages and Disadvantages of Firewall Techniques

Firewall Technique	Advantages	Disadvantages
Packet filtering	Completely transparent Easy to filter access at the host or network level Inexpensive: can use existing routers to implement	Reveals internal network topology Does not provide enough granularity for most security policies Difficult to configure Does not support certain traffic Susceptible to address spoofing Limited or no logging, alarms No user authentication
Application-level gateways	Application-level security Strong user access control Strong logging and auditing support Ability to conceal internal network	Requires specialized proxy for each service Slower to implement new services Inconvenient to end users No support for client software that does not support redirection
Circuit-level gateways	Transparent to user Excellent for relaying outbound connections	Inbound connections risky Must provide new client programs

- An approved set of firewall standards makes configuration decisions much more objective. A firewall, especially one with a restrictive configuration, can become a hot political topic if the firewall administrator wants to block traffic that a user really wants. Specifying the decision-making process for resolving such issues in a formal set of standards will make the process much more consistent to all users. Everyone may not always get what he or she wants, but at least the issue will be decided through a process that was adopted in advance.

Policy and Standards Development Process

The following process is recommended as an efficient, comprehensive way to develop a firewall policy. If the steps of this process are followed in order, the security practitioner can avoid making time-wasting oversights and errors in the policy. (See also Exhibit 54.4.)

1. *Risk analysis.* An organization should perform a risk analysis prior to developing a policy or a set of standards. The risk analysis will not only help policy-makers identify specific issues to be addressed in the document itself, but also the relative weight policy-makers should assign to those issues.
2. *Identify list of topics to cover.* A partial listing of topics is suggested under Policy Structure later in this article; security policy-makers should also identify any other relevant issues that may be relevant to the organization's firewall implementation.
3. *Assign responsibility.* An organization must define the roles and responsibilities of those accountable for administering the firewall. If

necessary, modify job descriptions to reflect the additional responsibility for implementing, maintaining, and administering the firewall, as well as establishing, maintaining, and enforcing policy and standards.

4. *Define the audience.* Is the policy document intended to be read by IS personnel only? Or is the document intended to be read by the entire organization? The document's audience will determine its scope, as well as its degree of technical and legal detail.

5. *Write the policy.* Because anyone can read the document, write without regard to the reader's position within the organization. When it is necessary to refer to other organizational entities, use functional references whenever possible (e.g., Public Relations instead of Tom Smith, Public Relations). Be sure to list a contact person for readers who may have questions about the policy.

6. *Identify mechanisms to foster compliance.* A policy is ineffective if it does not encourage employees to comply with the policy. Therefore, the individual(s) responsible for developing or maintaining the policy must ensure that adequate mechanisms for enforcement exist. These enforcement mechanisms should not be confused with the clause(s) of a policy that specify the consequences for noncompliance. Rather, enforcement mechanisms should include such administrative procedures as awareness and training, obtaining employee signatures on an agreement that specifies the employee has read and understands the policy and will comply with the intent.

7. *Review.* New policies should be reviewed by representatives from all major departments of the organization — not just IS personnel. A special effort should be made to resolve any disagreements at this stage: the more low- and mid-level support that exists for a policy, the easier it will be to implement that policy.

After the policy has been coordinated with (and hopefully endorsed by) department representatives, the policy should be submitted to senior management for approval. It is extremely important that the most senior-level manager possible sign the policy. This will give the IS security staff the authority it needs to enforce the policy.

Exhibit 54.4. Policy Development Process

1. Risk analysis
2. Identify list of topics to cover
3. Assign responsibility for policy
4. Define the audience
5. Write the policy
6. Identify mechanisms to foster compliance
7. Review

Once the policy is adopted, it should be reviewed on at least an annual basis. A review may have one of three results: no change, revisions to the policy, or abandoning the policy.

Policy Structure

A policy is normally understood as a high-level document that outlines management's general instructions on how things are to be run. Therefore, an organizational firewall policy should outline that management expects other departments to support the firewall, the importance of the firewall to the organization, etc. The structure of a firewall policy should look as follows:

- *Background.* How does the importance of the firewall relate to overall organizational objectives (e.g., the firewall secures information assets against the threat of unauthorized external intrusion)?
- *Scope.* To whom and what does this policy apply?
- *Definitions.* What is a firewall? What role does it play within the enterprise?
- *Responsibilities.* What resources and respective responsibilities need to be assigned to support the firewall? If the default configuration of the firewall will be to block everything that is not specifically allowed, who is responsible for requesting exceptions? Who is authorized to approve these requests? On what basis will those decisions be made?
- *Enforcement.* What are the consequences for failing to meet the administrative responsibilities? How is noncompliance addressed?
- *Frequency of review.* How often will this policy be reviewed? With which functions in the organization?
- *Policy coordinator.* Who is the point of contact for this policy?
- *Date of last revision.* When was this policy last revised?

Firewall Standards

Firewall standards can be defined minimally as a set of configuration options for a firewall. (Although firewall standards can and should address more than mere configuration issues, all firewall standards cover at least this much.) Exhibit 54.5 presents a sample outline for firewall standards. Because all firewalls come with default configurations, all firewalls have default standards. The job of the security practitioner is to draft a comprehensive set of standards governing all aspects of firewall implementation, usage, and maintenance, including but not limited to:

- protection of logs against unauthorized modification
- frequency of logs review
- how long logs will be retained
- when the logs will be backed up
- to whom the alarms will be sent

Exhibit 54.5.   Sample Outline of Firewall Standards

I.   Definition of terms
II. Responsibilities of the firewall administrator
III. Statement of firewall limitations
   a. Inability to enforce data integrity
   b. Inability to prevent internal attacks
IV. Firewall configuration
   a. Default policy (allow or deny) on network connections
   b. Physical location of firewall
   c. Logical location of firewall in relation to other network nodes
   d. Firewall system access policy
      1. Authorized individuals
      2. Authentication methods
      3. Policy on remote configuration
   e. Supported services
      1. Inbound
      2. Outbound
   f. Blocked services
      1. Inbound
      2. Outbound
   g. Firewall configuration change management policy
V.   Firewall audit trail policy
   a. Level of granularity (e.g., we will have one entry for each FTP or HTTP download)
   b. Frequency of review (e.g., we will check the logs once a day)
   c. Access control (e.g., access to firewall audit trails will be limited to the following individuals)
VI. Firewall intrusion detection policy
   a. Alarms
      1. Alarm thresholds
      2. Alarm notifications (e.g., e-mail, pager, etc.)
   b. Notification procedures
      1. Top management
      2. Public relations
      3. System administrators
      4. Incident response teams
      5. Law enforcement
      6. Other sites
   c. Response priorities (e.g., human safety, containment, public relations)
   d. Documentation procedures
VII. Backups
   a. Frequency of incremental backups
   b. Frequency of system backups
   c. Archive of backups (e.g., we will keep backups for one year)
   d. Off-site backup requirements
VIII. Firewall outage policy
   a. Planned outages
   b. Unplanned outages
      1. Reporting procedures
IX. Firewall standards review policy (e.g., this policy will be reviewed every six months)

Exhibit 54.6.   Sample Warning Banner

Per AFI 33-219 requirement:

Welcome to USAFAnet
United States Air Force Academy

This is an official Department of Defense (DoD) computer system for authorized use only. All data contained on DoD computer systems is owned by DoD and may be monitored, intercepted, recorded, read, copied, or captured in any manner and disclosed in any manner by authorized personnel. THERE IS NO RIGHT TO PRIVACY ON THIS SYSTEM. Authorized personnel may give any potential evidence of crime found on DoD computer systems to law enforcement officials. USE OF THIS SYSTEM BY ANY USER, AUTHORIZED OR UNAUTHORIZED, CONSTITUTES EXPRESS CONSENT TO THIS MONITORING, INTERCEPTION, RECORDING, READING, COPYING, OR CAPTURING, AND DISSEMINATION BY AUTHORIZED PERSONNEL. Do not discuss, enter, transfer, process, or transmit classified/sensitive national security information of greater sensitivity than this system is authorized. USAFAnet is not accredited to process classified information. Unauthorized use could result in criminal prosecution. If you do not consent to these conditions, do not log in!

Legal Issues Concerning Firewalls

If firewall audit trails need to be capable of being presented as evidence in a court of law, it is worthwhile to provide a "warning banner" to warn users about what sort of privacy they can expect. Many firewalls can be configured to display a warning banner on telnet and FTP sessions. Exhibit 54.6 shows an example of such a warning.

FIREWALL CONTINGENCY PLANNING

Firewall Outage

What would be the impact on an organization if the firewall was unavailable? If the organization has routed all of its Internet traffic through a firewall (as it should), then a catastrophic hardware failure of the firewall machine would result in a lack of Internet connectivity until the firewall machine is repaired or replaced. How long can the organization tolerate an outage? If the outage were a catastrophic hardware failure, do you know how you would repair or replace the components? Do you know how long it would take to repair or replace the components?

If the organization has a firewall, the odds are that a firewall outage would have a significant impact on that organization. (If the connection between the two networks was not important to the organization, why would that organization have the connection and protect it with a firewall?) Therefore, the security practitioner must also develop contingency plans for responding to a firewall outage. These contingency plans must address three types of failures: hardware, software, and evolutionary (failure to keep pace with increasing usage requirements).

In the case of a hardware failure, the security practitioner has three options: repair, replacement, or removal. Firewall removal is a drastic measure that is not encouraged, it drastically reduces security while disrupting any user services that were specially configured around the firewall (e.g., Domain Name Service, proxies, etc.). Smaller organizations may choose to repair their hardware because it is cheaper, yet this may not always be an option and may not be quick enough to satisfy user requirements. Conversely, access can be restored quickly by swapping in a "hot spare," but the cost of purchasing and maintaining such redundancy can be prohibitive to smaller organizations.

Significant Attacks, Probes, and Vulnerabilities

To be effective, the firewall administrator must understand not only how attacks and probes work, but also must be able to recognize the appropriate alarms and audit trail entries.

There are three attacks in particular with which every Internet firewall administrator should be familiar.

Internet Protocol (IP) Source Address Spoofing. IP Source Address Spoofing is not an attack itself. It is a vulnerability that can be exploited to launch attacks (e.g., session hijacking). First described by Robert T. Morris in 1985 and explained in more detail by Steven Bellovin in 1989, the first known use of IP Source Address Spoofing was in 1994. Since then, hackers have made spoofing tools publicly available so that one need not be a TCP/IP expert in order to exploit this vulnerability.

IP Source Address Spoofing is used to defeat address-based authentication. Many services, including rlogin and rsh, rely on IP addresses for authentication. Yet, as this vulnerability illustrates, this form of authentication is extremely weak and should only be used in trusted environments. (IP addresses provide identification, not authentication.) By its very nature, IP allows anyone to send packets claiming to be from any IP address. Of course, when an attacker sends forged packets to a target machine, the target machine will send its replies to the legitimate client, not the attacker. In other words, the attacker can send commands but will not see any output. As described below, in some cases, this is enough to cause serious damage.

Although there is no way to totally eliminate IP Source Address Spoofing, there are ways to reduce such activity. For example, a packet filter can be configured to drop all outbound packets that do not have an "inside" source address. Likewise, a firewall can block all inbound packets that have an internal address as the source address. However, such a solution will only work at the network and subnet levels. There is no way to prevent IP Source Address Spoofing within a subnet.

TCP Hijacking. TCP Hijacking is used to defeat authenticated connections. It is only an attack option if the attacker has access to the packet flow. In a TCP Hijacking attack, (1) the attacker is located logically between the client and the server, (2) the attacker sends a "killer packet" to the client, terminating the client's connection to the server, and (3) the attacker then continues the connection.

Denial of Service. A strength of public networks like the Internet lies in the fact that anyone can create a public service (e.g., a Web server or anonymous File Transfer Protocol [FTP] server) and allow literally anyone else, anonymously, to access that service. But this unrestricted availability can also be exploited in a denial-of-service attack. A denial-of-service attack exploits this unrestricted availability by overwhelming the service with requests. Although it is relatively easy to block a denial-of-service attack if the attack is generated by a single address, it is much more difficult — if not impossible — to stop a denial-of-service attack originating from spoofed, random source IP addresses.

There are two forms of denial-of-service attacks that are worth mentioning: TCP SYN Attack and ICMP Echo Flood.

1. TCP SYN Attack. The attacker floods a machine with TCP "half-open" connections, preventing the machine from providing TCP-based services while under attack and for some time after the attack stops. What makes this attack so significant is that it exploits an inherent characteristic of TCP; there is not yet a complete defense to this attack.

Under TCP (used by Simple Mail Transfer Protocol [SMTP], Telnet, HTTP, FTP, Gopher, etc.), whenever a client attempts to establish a connection to a server, there is a standard "handshake" or sequence of messages they exchange before data can be exchanged between the client and the server. In a normal connection, this handshake looks similar to the example displayed in Exhibit 54.7.

The potential for attack arises at the point where the server has sent an acknowledgment (SYN-ACK) back to the client but has not yet received the ACK message. This is what is known as a half-open connection. The server maintains, in a memory, a list of all half-open connections. Unfortunately, servers allocate a finite amount of memory for storing this list, and an

Exhibit 54.7. Normal TCP Handshake

Client	Server
SYN ---------------->	Server
<-----------------------	SYN-ACK
ACK ---------------->	
Client and server may now exchange data	

attacker can cause an overflow by deliberately creating too many partially open connections.

The SYN Flooding is easily accomplished with IP Source Address Spoofing. In this scenario, the attacker sends SYN messages to the target (victim) server masquerading a client system that is unable to respond to the SYN-ACK messages. Therefore, the final ACK message is never sent to the target server.

Whether or not the SYN attack is used in conjunction with IP Source Address Spoofing, the effect on the target is the same. The target system's list of half-open connections will eventually fill; then the system will be unable to accept any new TCP connections until the table is emptied. In some cases, the target may also run out of memory or crash.

Normally, half-open connections timeout after a certain amount of time; however, an attacker can generate new half-open connections faster than the target system's timeout.

2. Internet Control Message Protocol (ICMP) Echo (PING) Flood. The PING Flood Attack is where the attacker sends large amounts of ICMP ping requests from an intermediary or "bounce" site to a victim, which can cause network congestion or outages. The attack is also known as the "smurf" attack because of a hacker tool called "smurf," which enables the hacker to launch this attack with relatively little networking knowledge.

Like the SYN attack, the PING Flood Attack relies on IP Source Address Spoofing to add another level of indirection to the attack. In a SYN attack with IP Source Address Spoofing, the spoofed source address receives all of the replies to the PING requests. While this does not cause an overflow on the victim machine, the network path from the bounce site to the victim becomes congested and potentially unusable. The bounce site may suffer for the same reason.

There are automated tools that allow attackers to use multiple bounce sites simultaneously. Attackers can also use tools to look for network routers that do not filter broadcast traffic and networks where multiple hosts respond.

Solutions include:

- disabling IP-directed broadcasts at the router
- configuring the operating system to prevent the machine from responding to ICMP packets sent to IP broadcast addresses
- preventing IP source address spoofing by dropping packets that contain a source address for a different network

CONCLUSION

A firewall can only reduce the risk of a breach of security; the only guaranteed way to prevent a compromise is to disconnect the network and physically turn off all machines. Moreover, a firewall should always be viewed as a supplement to host security; the primary security emphasis should be on host security. Nonetheless, a firewall is an important security device that should be used whenever an organization needs to protect one network from another.

The views expressed in this article are those of the author and do not reflect the official policy or position of the United States Air Force, Department of Defense, or the U.S. government."

Notes

1. Atkins, Derek et al. *Internet Security Professional Reference,* 2nd edition, New Riders, Indianapolis, IN, 1997.
2. Bellovin, Steven M. *Security Problems in the TCP/IP Protocol Suite, Computer Communications Review,* 19:2, April 1989, pp. 32–48. Available on the World Wide Web at ftp://ftp.research.att.com/dist/-internet_security/ipext.ps.Z

References

Bernstein, Terry, Bhimani, Anish B., Schultz, Eugene and Siegel, Carol . *Internet Security for Business,* John Wiley & Sons, New York, 1996.
Cheswick, W.R. and Bellovin, S.M. *Firewalls and Internet Security: Repelling the Wily Hacker,* Addison-Wesley, Reading, MA, 1994.
Garfinkel, Simson and Spafford, Gene. Practical Unix & Internet Security, Sebastopol, CA, 1995.
Huegen, Craig A. The Latest in Denial of Service Attacks: 'Smurfing', Oct. 18, 1998. Available on the World Wide Web at http://www.quadrunner.com/~chuegen/smurf.txt.
Howard, John D. An Analysis of Security Incidents on the Internet 1989–1995, Ph.D. dissertation, Carnegie Mellon University, Pittsburgh, PA, 1997.
Morris, Robert T. A Weakness in the 4.2BSD Unix TCP/IP Software, *Bell Labs Computer Science Technical Report #117,* Feb. 25, 1985. Available on the World Wide Web at ftp://ftp.research.att.com/-dist/internet_security/117.ps.Z.
Wood, Charles Cresson. Policies from the Ground Up, *Infosecurity News,* March/April 1997, pp. 24-29.

About the Editor

John P. Slone is a Principal Engineer in the Computing Infrastructure Engineering department at Lockheed Martin Enterprise Information Systems in Orlando, FL, a member of the adjunct faculty of the Florida Institute of Technology, and a consulting editor for Auerbach Publications. He has worked in the information technology industry since 1978, published numerous technical articles, presented at technical conferences, participated in various domestic and international standards committees, and received a number of corporate and industry awards. He is a member of Upsilon Pi Epsilon, an international honor society for computer science, and a member of Kappa Delta Pi, an international honor society for education. He holds an M.S. in Computer Information Systems from Florida Institute of Technology in Melbourne, FL, and a B.S. in Mathematics from Georgetown College in Georgetown, KY.

Index

A

AAA, see Accounting, authorization, and administration

Access control, resource-associated, 354

Access lists, 201, 202

    Cisco, 207

    extended, 205

Access security, need for, 209

Accounting, authorization, and administration (AAA), 263

Accounting management, 568

Active attack, 40

Active Directory, 352

Adapter cards, 43

Address

    prefix allocation, 282, 283

    resolution protocol (ARP), 109, 291

ADI, see Assured Digital Inc.

ADI Management System (AMS), 300

ADM medical knowledge base, 440

ADSL, see Asymmetrical digital subscriber line

Advanced Technology (AT), 33

AFS, see Andrew File System

Agent technology, 495

Aggregate Route-Based IP Switch (ARIS), 151

AH, see Authentication header

Alta Vista, 385

American National Standards Institute (ANSI), 320

AMS, see ADI Management System

Andrew File System (AFS), 112

ANSI, see American National Standards Institute

ANX, see Automotive Network Exchange

AOS, see Automated Operation and Security

API, see Application Programming Interface

Applets, network security and, 535–541

    ActiveX, 540

    applets and Web, 535

    Authenticode for accountability, 540

    denial-of-service threats, 537–538

    holes and bugs, 537

    information sent back, 538

    JavaScript, 539–540

    ounce of prevention, 541

    risks, 536

    secure applets, 536–537

    security issue, 536

Application

    bandwidth table, 20

    gateway firewalls, 309

    Programming Interface (API), 454, 487

    -specific integrated circuits (ASIC), 137, 141

Archival storage, 579

ARIS, see Aggregate Route-Based IP Switch

ARP, see Address resolution protocol

AS, see Authentication server

ASIC, see Application-specific integrated circuits

Assured Digital Inc. (ADI), 299

Asymmetrical digital subscriber line (ADSL), 227

Asynchronous transfer mode (ATM), 19, 146, 227

  backbones, 245, 248

  building backbone networks, 233

  campus backbone, 236

  desktop connectivity, 232

  networks, 230, 243

  speeds, 243

  WAN, 248

AT, see Advanced Technology

AT&T frame relay network, 303

ATM, see Asynchronous transfer mode

ATM access, 245–257

  ATM WAN, 248–251

    enterprise network performance, 249

    inclusion, unification, and expansion, 249–250

    integrated services, 250

    outsourcing services, 250–251

    quality of service, 249

    scalability, 250

    service provider network performance, 249

    starting point, 255

  key technologies for ATM WAN, 251–255

  network core, 245–248

Attacks, types of, 420

Authentication, 73

  event-plus-time, 195

  header (AH), 94

  process, two-factor, 194

  server (AS), 196, 426

  token, 189, 193

Authenticode, 540

Automated Operation and Security (AOS), 300

Automatic call distribution, 263

Automotive Network Exchange (ANX), 313

Auto-Negotiation, 22, 23

Autonomous System, 133

B

Backup(s)

  establishing, 504

  software, 622

  workstation-based, 585

Basic Input Output System (BIOS), 37, 45

Bay networks, 301

BBM, see Bridge buffer memory

BBS, see Bulletin Board System

BGP, see Border gateway protocol

BIOS, see Basic Input Output System

Block ciphers, 74

BNC, see British Naval Connector

Border gateway protocol (BGP), 291

BPDU, see Bridge protocol data unit

Bridge

  buffer memory (BBM), 549

  environment, 159

  protocol data unit (BPDU), 13

British Naval Connector (BNC), 57

British Telecom (BT), 244

Broadcast domain

  boundaries, 160

  by-product, 155

  extension, 168

Broadcast traffic, 154

Browser company, 383

BSA, see Business Software Alliance

BT, see British Telecom

Bulletin Board System (BBS), 322

Bus

  loads, 44

speed, 41

Business Software Alliance (BSA), 596

C

CA, see Certification authorities

Cache

disk-based, 470

memory, 34

Caldera, 339

Call forwarding, 266

CASE, see Computer-assisted software engineering

CBT, see Computer-based training

CD-ROM, 46, 48

Cell Switch Router, 150

Central office (CO), 12

Central processing unit (CPU), 147, 227

cycle, 136

heat and, 36

Centrex, 395

CEO business projections, 191

CERT, see Computer Emergency Response Team

Certification authorities (CA), 78

CGI, see Common Gateway Interface

Challenge Handshake Authentication Protocol (CHAP), 81, 178

Channel protocols, 177

CHAP, see Challenge Handshake Authentication Protocol

CIDR, see Classless interdomain routing

CIP, see Classical IP

Cipher

algorithms, 418

block chaining mode, 423

CISC, see Complex Instruction Set Computers

Cisco

Internetwork Operating System software, 297

password command, 213

router environment, 214

wildcard mask, 204

Cisco access lists, working with, 199–208

extended access lists, 205–207

limitations, 207–208

standard access lists, 202–205

TCP/IP protocol suite, 199–201

using access lists, 201–202

Classical IP (CIP), 148

Classless interdomain routing (CIDR), 290

Client/server development projects, pitfalls of, 497–506

business requirements, 497–498

developing documentation, 503

developing skills with technology and tools, 501

estimating, 499

hardware, software, and network requirements, 498–499

issue tracking, 500–501

organizational stability, 504

project tracking, 499–500

prototyping, 504–505

security, 501–502

sign-offs and approval, 505

testing, 502–503

CLNS, see Connectionless Network Service

Clock rate, 2, 36

CNM, see Customer network management

CO, see Central office

Cobol, 477

Code reviews, 504

Collision domain, 157

Commerce, secure, 73

Common Gateway Interface (CGI), 434

Common Object Request Broker
  Architecture (CORBA), 492, 496

Communications
  networking device, 209
  server, 189, 466

Complex Instruction Set Computers (CISC),
  31, 463

Computer(s)
  -assisted software engineering (CASE),
    504
  -based training (CBT), 501
  Emergency Response Team (CERT), 187,
    629
  Power PC, 234
  printer-based, 70
  science, history of, 477
  system, DOD, 436
  von Neumann, 142

Configuration management, 553, 566

Connectionless Network Service (CLNS),
  136

Connectionless virtual circuit, 287

Consulting organizations, 357

Contingency Tactical Air Planning System
  (CTAPS), 444

CORBA, see Common Object Request
  Broker Architecture

Corporate networks, implementing routing,
  switching, and VLANs in modern,
  153–169
  network design evolution, 154–156
    management, 155
    network device evolution, 156
    performance, 154–155
    redundancy, 155–156
  technology overview, 156–162
    bridge, 157–158
    broadcast domain, 156–157

collision domain, 157
  Layer 3 switch, 160
  repeater, 157
  router, 158–159
  switch, 159–160
  virtual LAN, 160–161
  VLAN standards, 162
  when to use switching, 162–169
    broadcast domain extension,
      168–169
    implementing VLANs, 165–166
    key design points, 164, 165, 169
    management/control, 162
    performance, 164–165
    protocol-sensitive VLANs, 166–168
    redundancy, 163–164, 169
    routing risk factors, 164
    switching risk factors, 162
    VLAN risk factors, 169
    when to use routing, 164

CPE, see Customer premise equipment

CPU, see Central processing unit

CRC, see Cyclic redundancy check

Cryptoanalysis, 419

Cryptographic methods, overview of, 73–84
  cryptographic algorithms in action,
    78–84
    password protection, 80–82
    pretty good privacy, 82–84
  purpose of cryptography, 73–78
    hash functions, 76–77
    public key certificates, 78
    public-key cryptography, 75–76
    reason for three encryption
      techniques, 77
    secret key cryptography, 74–75

CTAPS, see Contingency Tactical Air Planning System

Customer

    network management (CNM), 564, 569

    premise equipment (CPE), 241

Cyclic redundancy check (CRC), 414

D

DAP, see Directory Access Protocol

Data

    archived, 382

    classification, 307

    communications network (DCN), 549

    Encryption Standard (DES), 74, 288, 301

    flows, concepts relating to, 273

    integrity, 519

    link control identifiers (DLCIs), 240

    Link Layer function, 124

    migration, 378, 580, 581, 582

    sharing, 380

    transfer capacity, 226

Database

    engineer, for workflow approval, 510

    full backup on, 573

    maintaining, 585

    support, 337

Datagram

    Delivery Protocol (DDP), 127

    socket object, 483

DCE, see Distributed Computing Environment

DCN, see Data communications network

DDP, see Datagram Delivery Protocol

Debian Linux, 339

Debugger program, 429

DEC, see Digital Equipment Corp.

Default router, 52, 128

Defense Modeling and Simulation Office (DMSO), 435

Denial-of-service threats, 537

Department of Defense (DOD), 433

DES, see Data Encryption Standard

Desktop videoconferencing, 231, 266

Destination options header, 286

Development languages, 336

Device

    communication, 261

    sharing, 374

DHCP, see Dynamic Host Configuration Protocol

DHCP, dynamic IP addressing with, 49–53

    additions to DHCP protocol, 53

    dynamic host configuration protocol, 51–52

    planning for DHCP, 53

    reverse ARP, 49–50

    working of DHCP, 52–53

Dialup service, virtual, 297

Dictionary attacks, 192

DIG, see Domain Information Gofer

Digital Equipment Corp., (DEC), 327

Digital Signature Standard (DSS), 76, 79

Digital Subscriber Line (DSL), 176

Direct-dial access, 171

Direct memory access (DMA), 223

Directory

    Access Protocol (DAP), 349, 450

    Information Tree (DIT), 349, 350, 366

    server agent (DSA), 450

    services, 266

        management, 369

        White Pages, 367

    synchronization, 358, 363

    System

Protocol (DSP), 349

vendor, 367

technologies, 347

updates, 455

User Agents (DUA), 349, 450

Directory-enabled operating systems,
emergence of, 343–356

directory-based solutions to operating
system issues, 352–356

distributed security, 355–356

multiple image management and
load balancing, 355

network log-in, 353

policy enforcement, 355

quality of service management, 356

resource-associated access control,
354

resource location, 354

user-specific machine profiles, 354

directory technologies, 347–352

domain name system, 348–349

LDAP, 351–352

Microsoft Windows NT version 5.0,
352

X.500, 349–351

operating system issues in enterprise
network, 344–347

distributed policy enforcement, 347

distributed resources, 345

distributed security complexity,
346–347

scalability to support multiple
images of given resource, 346

support of varying levels of service,
345–346

users and machines no longer
tightly coupled, 344–345

Disaster protection, 584

Disk

drives, 45

failure, 465

fragmentation, 578, 583

mirroring, 378

utility, 347

Distance vector (DV), 131, 132

Distributed computing, Java's role in,
489–496

agent technology, 495–496

distributed Java applications, 491–495

introspection, 492–493

object serialization, 493

remote method invocation, 491–492

sample RMI transaction, 493–495

Java's benefits, 490–491

Distributed Computing Environment (DCE),
365, 492

Distributed policy enforcement, 347

DIT, see Directory Information Tree

DLCIs, see Data link control identifiers

DMA, see Direct memory access

DMSO, see Defense Modeling and
Simulation Office

DNS, see Domain name system

Document management systems, 510

DOD, see Department of Defense

Domain Information Gofer (DIG), 412

Domain name system (DNS), 111, 291, 349,
466

proxy server for, 410

server addresses, 52, 120

services, basic, 411

DSA, see Directory server agent

DSL, see Digital Subscriber Line

DSP, see Directory System Protocol

DSS, see Digital Signature Standard

DUA, see Directory User Agents

Dumb terminal, 447

DV, see Distance vector

Dynamic Host Configuration Protocol
(DHCP), 49, 51, 285

Dynamic Publisher, 390

Dynamic routing, 109

E

E-commerce, 255, 364, 392

E-mail, 277, 317

   accounts, on company systems, 360

   address, 82, 360

   alerts, 593

   company view of, 518

   customer support via, 402

   data submitted by, 359

   exchange of between transfer agents,
      526

   messages, 88

   network, 530

   package, 357

   security, 520

      management, 515

      policy, 518

   system(s)

      in-house, 521, 522

      LAN-based, 525

      minicomputer-based, 447

      third party, 523

Eavesdropping, 419

ECC, see Error correcting codes

EDI, see Electronic Data Interchange

EDM, see Electronic document management

EISA, see Extended Industry Standard
      Architecture

Electronic codebook mode, 423

Electronic Data Interchange (EDI), 319

Electronic document management (EDM),
      442

Electronic forms, Web-based, 511

Electronic mail, security and control of,
      515–533

   approaches to security, 529–533

      advanced security techniques,
         530–531

      traditional security techniques,
         529–530

      using public-key encryption,
         531–533

   architectures and security exposures,
      521–529

      connectivity to hetergeneous hosts,
         527–529

      in-house systems, 521–523

      LAN-based server systems, 524–526

      systems using transfer agents,
         526–527

      third-party systems, 523–524

   e-mail security management issues,
      515–520

      confidentiality, 518–519

      cost control, 520

      formalized security policy, 517–518

      message integrity, 519

      personal privacy, 518

      required security level, 515–517

   recommended course of action, 533

   reviewing e-mail security, 520–521

      authentication, 521

      identification, 520

      monitoring, 521

Employee empowerment, 509

Encapsulating security payload (ESP), 288

Encapsulation, translation vs., 144

Encrypted session payload, 94

Encryption, 175

function of, 415

protocols, 179

techniques, 77

Enhanced Small Device Interface (ESDI), 46

Enterprise deployment, 393–399

    IP-PBX, 394–398

        components, 394–396

        configurations and applications, 396–397

        network deployment, 397–398

        standards and, 394

    PBX, 393–394

    practical advantages of IP PBX, 398–399

Enterprise directory services, 357–370

    activities included in enterprise directory service, 358–365

        authentication/confidentiality services, 362–363

        directory synchronization services, 363–364

        information solicitation services, 359

        naming/identification services, 361–362

        registration services, 359–361

        X.500, 364–365

    application vs. enterprise directory services, 357–358

    roles and responsibilities, 367–370

        operations management, 368

        product management, 368–369

        project management, 369

        service management, 369–370

    service provider's perspective on X.500, 365–367

        database issues, 366

        directory information tree structure, 366–367

        information management issues, 366

Enterprise infrastructures, building of with LAN-based technology, 325–326

Enterprise network(s)

    management of, 543–544

    performance, 249

Enterprise solutions, building of with LAN-based technology, 431–432

Enterprise systems, management of without strategy, 545–552

    better idea, 546–547

    current LAN configuration, 547–550

        backups, 549

        bridges, 549

        desktop, 547–548

        gateways, 549

        local gateways, 548

        mainframe access, 550

        monitors, 548

        routers, 548–549

    enterprisewide policy, 547

    future of IT at Clover, 550–551

    mixed and mismatched development, 545–546

    other communication system, 550

    overview of organization and systems, 545

Error correcting codes (ECC), 571

ESDI, see Enhanced Small Device Interface

ESP, see Encapsulating security payload

Ethernet, 42, 105, see also Gigabit Ethernet

    address, 128, 404

    categories of, 55

    elegant, 139

    environments, collisions particular to, 157

    fast, 318

hub, 58

MAC, 20, 21

multicast packets, 13

phone, 264

segments, using router to interconnect, 205

technology, secure, 93

Extended Industry Standard Architecture (EISA), 222

Extranet(s)

architectures, 307

company policy on, 306

implementing and supporting, 305–315

application gateway firewalls, 309–315

router-based extranet architecture, 307–309

relation of to push technology, 385

with router, 308

Venn diagram of, 306

F

FAB, see Field Assistance Branch

Fast Ethernet backbone networks, 234

FAT, see File allocation table

Father-son rotation scheme, 575

Fault

management, 553, 565

tolerance, 1, 464

FDDI, see Fiber distributed data interface

FDR, see Full-duplex repeaters

Fiber distributed data interface (FDDI), 19, 232

Fiber-optic media, 10

Field Assistance Branch (FAB), 545–546

File

allocation table (FAT), 331

handling requirements, 498

histories, maintaining, 572

server(s), 345

connection, 65

print connection data flow, 66

program residing on, 525

sharing, 451

transfer protocol (FTP), 103, 281, 406

access, 208

data submitted by, 359

sites, Linux-related, 337

URL access to, 436

Firewall(s), 409

application gateway, 309

benefits, 630

company building of, 299

Internet connections controlled by, 502

limitations of, 630

local security policy and, 631

outage, 640

proxy services incorporated into, 208

software, 470

vendors of, 470

VPN with link encryption between, 92

Firewall management, internal attacks and, 629–644

developing firewall policy and standards, 635–640

firewall standards, 638–639

legal issues concerning firewalls, 640

policy and standards development process, 636–638

policy structure, 638

reasons for having firewall policy and standards, 635–636

firewall contingency planning, 640–643

firewall outage, 640–641

significant attacks, 641–643

firewall evaluation criteria, 632–633

firewalls and local security policy, 631–632

firewall techniques, 633–635

    application-level gateways, 634–635

    circuit-level gateways, 635

    packet filtering, 633–634

laying groundwork for firewall, 629–631

    benefits of having firewall, 630

    limitations of firewall, 630–631

Flow label, 280

Frame relay addressing, 240

FTP, see File transfer protocol

Full-duplex repeaters (FDR), 25

Funding strategy, myopic, 551

G

Garbage collection, distributed, 495

Gatekeepers, 265, 267

Gateway(s)

    application-level, 634

    back-to-back, 264

    -based sniffer, 89

    circuit-level, 635

    default, 119

    local, 548

    messaging, 453

    routers, building, 238

    signaling information passed by, 396

GEA, see Gigabit Ethernet Alliance

Generic Routing Encapsulation (GRE), 180, 296

Gigabit Ethernet, 19–30

    building networks with, 25–26

    cabling and topology rules, 24–25

    enabling technologies, 27–28

    management of, 26

    supporting organizations, 26–27

    technical overview, 20

    working of, 20–24

        adoption of fiber channel, 21–22

        Auto-Negotiation, 22–23

        1000Base-X signaling systems, 20–21

        half-duplex/full-duplex, 23–24

Gigabit Ethernet Alliance (GEA), 26

Gigabit Media Independent Interface (GMII), 22

GMII, see Gigabit Media Independent Interface

GNU General Public License, 335

Grandfather-father-son rotation scheme, 576

GRE, see Generic Routing Encapsulation

H

HAL, see Hardware abstraction layer

Hard disks, data transfer rate of, 609

Hardware

    abstraction layer (HAL), 327

    authorization, 183

    -based systems, 175

    costs of, 619

Health care industry, 3

High Performance Knowledge Base (HPKB), 439

High-bandwidth networks, emerging, 227–244

    ATM building backbone networks, 233

    ATM desktop connectivity, 232

    ATM networks, 243

    available wide area network choices, 237–243

        frame relay and ATM interworking, 241–243

interfacing frame relay with other networks, 241

public frame relay networking, 239–241

global options, 244

high-bandwidth campus backbone networks, 233–236

ATM backbones, 236

ATM in building, 236

ATM campus backbone, 236

Fast Ethernet backbone networks, 234–236

high-bandwidth local access for home, 228–230

office and building connectivity, 230–232

public carriers, 243–244

High-performance file system (HPFS), 331

Hot backup, 53

Hot standby, 465

HPFS, see High-performance file system

HPKB, see High Performance Knowledge Base

HTML, see Hypertext Markup Language

HTTP, see HyperText Transfer Protocol

Hub(s)

power supply, 6

with redundant power supply, 9

switching, 58

Hypertext link, 472

Hypertext Markup Language (HTML), 227, 435, 472, 490

HyperText Transfer Protocol (HTTP), 384, 481, 489, 634

I

IAD, see Integrated access device

IANA, see Internet Assigned Numbers Authority

IAP, see Internet access provider

ICMP, see Internet Control Message Protocol

ICMP, see Internet Control Message Protocol

ICSA, see International Computer Security Association

IDEA, see International Data Encryption Algorithm

IETF, see Internet Engineering Task Force

IGP, see Interior Gateway Protocol

IGRP, see Interior Gateway Routing Protocol

IMA, see Inverse muting over ATM

Indirect dial remote access, 174

Industry Standard Architecture (ISA), 41, 222

Information

assets, 619

crime, 186

management, 366

overload, 384

security (InfoSec), 85

solicitation services, 359

superhighway, 415

systems (IS), 185

professionals, 186

team, 186, 187

Technology (IT), 371, 545

InfoSec, see Information security

Initial Sequence Number (ISN), 408

INMS, see Integrated network management system

Integrated access device (IAD), 253

Integrated network management system (IMS), 564

Integrated Services Digital Network (ISDN), 55, 176

Intelligent Drive Electronics, 47

Intel Pentium processor, 67

Interconnectivity

advanced LAN and, 217–219

basics, 99–101

Interior Gateway Protocol (IGP), 133

Interior Gateway Routing Protocol (IGRP), 134, 206

International Computer Security Association (ICSA), 298

International Data Encryption Algorithm (IDEA), 419, 422

International Federation of Accountants, 322

International Standards Organization (ISO), 200

International Telecommunications Union (ITU), 394

Internet

    access provider (IAP), 246

    application software, 466

    Assigned Numbers Authority (IANA), 117, 200

    Control Message Protocol (ICMP), 289, 409

    Engineering Task Force (IETF), 27, 50, 152, 467

    Packet Exchange, 14

    service provider (ISP), 52, 63, 174, 267

        address assigned by, 282

        connection to local, 294

Internet Protocol (IP), 49, 106, 403

    address(es), 113

        administration, 115

        requirements, 114

    authentication header, 286, 288

    data networks, 261, 397

    end stations, 129

    Mobility Support, 292

    network(s)

        corporate, 398

        number, 107

        subdivision of, 118

packet, 108, 110

radio, 563

resource reservation scheme, 271

sniffer attacks on, 89

source address spoofing, 641

stacks, 104

subnetwork number, 126

virtual private networks, 318

voice over, 260

Internet security, 401–414, 625

    attacks, 406–409

        ICMP, 409

        sequence predictability, 408–409

        SYN flood attack, 407–408

    DMZ, 410–411

    firewalls, 409–410

    Internet protocols, 403–406

    testing perimeter, 411–414

Internet server, choosing and equipping, 461–475

    Internet application software, 466–471

        communications server, 466–467

        commerce server, 467–468

        firewall software, 470–471

        news server, 468

        mail software, 469

        proxy server, 469–470

    Internet and intranet services, 461–462

    platform considerations, 462–465

        fault tolerance, 464–465

        operating system, 463–464

        processor architecture, 462–463

        SMP servers, 463

    Web database considerations, 471–474

        common gateway interface, 473–474

        maintenance and testing tools, 472–473

Internetwork Packet Exchange (IPX), 126, 594, 603

Intranets, 385, 462

Inverse muting over ATM (IMA), 251, 256

I/O cards, 137

IP, see Internet Protocol

IPv6, 277–292

    background and features, 278–279

        differences between IPv4 and IPv6, 278–279

        improved terminology of IPv6, 279

    IPv6 extension headers and options, 285–287

    IPv6 header format, 279–285

        address prefix allocation, 282

        IPv4-compatible addresses, 282–283

        IPv6 addresses, 281–282

        multicast addresses, 283–285

        provider-based unicast address, 282

    IPv6 quality-of-service parameters, 287–288

    IPv6 security, 288–291

        6bone trials, 291

        ICMPv6, 289

        IP authentication header, 288

        IP encapsulating security payload, 288–289

        migration to IPv6, 289–291

    IPv6 specifications, 292

IPX, see Internetwork Packet Exchange

IS, see Information systems

ISA, see Industry Standard Architecture

ISDN, see Integrated Services Digital Network

ISN, see Initial Sequence Number

ISO, see International Standards Organization

ISP, see Internet service provider

Issue tracking, 500

IT, see Information Technology

ITU, see International Telecommunications Union

J

Java

    applets, 538

    application(s)

        code, 474

        distributed, 491

    client object, 494

    Development Kit (JDK), 493

    naming and directory interface (JNDI), 486

    networking

        abstractions, 483

        capabilities, 432

        primitives, 481

Java programming language, 477–488

    high-level Java networking abstractions, 483–487

        Java naming and directory interface, 486–487

        remote method invocation, 485–486

        URL-based programming, 484–485

    Java networking primitives, 481–483

        connectionless networking, 482–483

        connection-oriented networking, 481–482

        multicast connectionless networking, 483

    networking basics, 478–481

        application, 481

        data link, 478–479

        network, 479

        physical, 478

        target environment, 478

transport, 479–480

JDISS, see Joint Deployable Intelligence
Support System

JDK, see Java Development Kit

JNDI, see Java naming and directory
interface

Job sharing, 344

Joint Deployable Intelligence Support
System (JDISS), 444

K

KBML, see Knowledge Base Markup
Language

Kerberos, 425, see also Private keys, trusted
third parties, and Kerberos

    message exchange, 426

    nomenclature, 427

    protocol, 429

    server, 429

Key revocation, 430

Knowledge

    Base Markup Language (KBML), 440

    -base services, commercial, 441

    representation language, 439

    workers, 343

L

LAN, see Local area network

LANE, see LAN Emulation

Laptop computers, 2

Law enforcement, 3

Layer 2 and 3 switching, evolution to,
139–152

    Layer 2 switching, 141–146

    Layer 3 switching, 146–152

LDAP, see Lightweight Directory Access
Protocol

LEC, see Local exchange carrier

Legacy technologies, 254

License tracking and metering software,
587–598

    features, 591–592

    functionality, 588–589

    global licensing, 593–594

    legal ramifications, 596–597

    license registration standard, 595–596

    license tracking, 589–591

    operation, 588

    reports, 592–593

Licensing Service Application Programming
Interface (LSAPI), 595

Lightweight Directory Access Protocol
(LDAP), 351, 451, 487

Link

    analyzers, 472

    state (LS), 131

Linux, overview of, 335–342

    customers, 337

    drawbacks, 338–340

    future outlook, 340–341

    guidance for Linux usage, 340

    implications of Linux, 340

    operating requirements for Linux, 337

    resources, 341

    sources, 337–338

    sudden surge of interest in Linux,
335–336

    vendor support, 337

Local area network (LAN), 139, 154

    adapter, 71

    administrator, 113, 116

    ATM, 228

    basics, 1–2

    connectivity options, 64

    corporate, 173, 587

    dial-up users, authenticating, 190

Emulation (LANE), 148

clients, 236

configuration server, 233

full-duplex, 142

infrastructure, switched, 164

interconnectivity, 100

-to-LAN communication, 62, 63

legacy, 226

messaging system

features of, 451

myths, 456

model, 5

rates, 146

routers, 550

servers, multiple, 453

speeds, 217

standalone, 99

switch(es), 100, 145

distinguishing factor between, 143

first, 141

technology, strength of, 431

Token Ring, 279

types of, 55

virtual, 27

Local exchange carrier (LEC), 246

Logical sniffer, 90

Login script, 622

Lookups, 411

Lotus Notes Domino, 390

LS, see Link state

LSAPI, see Licensing Service Application Programming Interface

M

MAC, see Media access control

MacScan, 597

Mail transfer agent, 111

Mainframe

access, 550

computers, design of, 456

era, service level in, 346

Maximum transmission unit (MTU), 285

Mean time between failure (MTBF), 4, 568

Media

access control (MAC), 140, 158, 235

addresses, 158

protocols, 177

schemes, 145

converters, 57

rotation schemes, 574

Memory

buses, 33

cache, 34

expansion cards, 465

shared, 224

speed, 32

virtual, 336

Mentoring, 504

Message

integrity, 519

originator, 430

routing topology, 452, 458

store, 449

transfer agent (MTA), 365, 449

Messaging

servers, 453

unified, 265

Messaging, local area network, 447–459

components of LAN messaging system, 449–451

directories, 450–451

message store, 449

message transfer agent, 449

user agent/user interface, 449

features of LAN messaging system, 451–456

   application programming interfaces, 454–455

   directory updates and synchronization, 455

   file sharing, 451–452

   filters, 456

   gateways, 453–454

   message routing topology, 452–453

LAN messaging system issues, myths, and realities, 456–457

reasons for popularity of LAN messaging systems, 447–448

   ease of setup, 448

   ease of use, 447–448

   low initial investment, 448

scalability, 457–458

   management, 458

   planning, 457–458

Microsoft

   ActiveX, 535

   Internet Explorer, 461

   Office, 338

   Outlook, 82

   System Management Server, 588

Modems, 45

MPC, see Multiprotocol over ATM clients

MPLS, see Multiprotocol Label Switching

MPOA, see Multiprotocol over ATM

MPS, see Multiprotocol over ATM servers

MTA, see Message transfer agent

MTBF, see Mean time between failure

MTU, see Maximum transmission unit

Multicast transmission, 270

Multimedia networks, issues in managing, 563–570

integrated network management system, 564–570

   accounting management, 568–569

   configuration management, 566–567

   customer network management, 569–570

   fault management, 565–566

   performance management, 567–568

   security management, 566

multimedia networks, 563–564

Multiplexing, 110

Multiprotocol Label Switching (MPLS), 152

Multiprotocol over ATM (MPOA), 151

   clients (MPC), 151

   servers (MPS), 151

Multiservices Internet Gateway, 302

Multitasking, 343

N

Naming/identification services, 361

NAPs, see Network access points

NAT, see Network Address Translation

National Institute for Standards and Technology (NIST), 76, 79

Navy Modeling and Simulation Catalog, 437

NDIS, see Network Device Interface Specification

Netnews, 287

Netscape

   Communicator, 383

   Directory Server, 302

   JavaScript, 535, 539

   Navigator, 433, 461

NetWare, 67, 134

Network(s)

   -based programming, 485

   Access

      Layer, 405

points (NAPs), 321

server, 178

adapter cards, 58

Address Translation (NAT), 410

administrators, 86

application programming, 491

assets, tracking of, 543

AT&T frame relay, 303

building corporate, 64

-centric warfare, 443

communications, 403

corporate, 153, 172, 181

design evolution, 154, 156

Device Interface Specification (NDIS), 334

e-mail, 530

engineer, 5

Fast Ethernet backbone, 234

firewalls, 530

General, 94

interface card (NIC), 13, 19, 162

LAN-to-LAN, 305

Layer, 404

address, 124

protocols, 125

software, 123

log-in, 353

manager, 116, 621

mask, 203

Monitor (NM), 90

multiple servers on, 372

Operating Center (NOC), 303

operating system (NOS), 59, 325

paths, encryption of key, 531

private data, 260

redundancy, 16

security architectures, 308

service providers (NSPs), 321

shared media, 93

troubleshooting, 629

types of, 86

Networks, building highly reliable computer, 3–17

business justification, 16

device reliability metrics and ratings, 4–6

link layer issues, 12–14

local area networks, 12–14

wide area networks, 12

network layer, 14–15

network management and testing, 15–16

physical layer issues, 6–11

environment, 6–7

power, 7–11

redundancy, 6

ultimately reliable network, 16–17

Network security plan, developing, 619–627

applying methodologies in Novell environment, 622–624

audited model, 624

basic model, 623

protected model, 623–624

secured model, 624

simple model, 622

countering security and control threats, 621–622

current issues affecting security, 626

firewalls, 625

review of security and control threats, 620–621

communications security threats, 621

operating system-level security threats, 620–621

physical security and control
threats, 620

procedural security threats, 621

securing new distributed environment,
619–620

security tools, 625–626

Network Services Auditor (NSA), 413

Newsgroups, Linux-related, 341

News server, 468

NIC, see Network interface card

NIC technology, advances in, 221–226

computer bus slots, 222

DMA-based adapters, 223–224

I/O port-based adapters, 223

parallel tasking, 224–226

PCI bus, 223

shared memory, 224

NIST, see National Institute for Standards
and Technology

NM, see Network Monitor

NOC, see Network Operating Center

NOS, see Network operating system

Notebook computer, 53

Novell

environments, 169, 622

Ethernet, see Ethernet

NSA, see Network Services Auditor

NSPs, see Network service providers

O

Object

linking and embedding (OLE), 626

Management Group (OMG), 496

ODBC, see Open database connectivity

OFB, see Output feedback

OLE, see Object linking and embedding

OMG, see Object Management Group

Online classes, 171

Open database connectivity (ODBC), 626

Open Shortest Path First (OSPF), 135, 206

Open Systems Interconnection (OSI), 4, 103

-compliant systems, 99

model standards, 548

network layer, 104

Reference Model, 123, 157, 481

Operating systems (OS), 325

Operations management, 368

OS, see Operating systems

OS/2, 329

OSI, see Open Systems Interconnection

OSPF, see Open Shortest Path First

Output feedback (OFB), 423, 424

Outsourcing, 182

applications, 295

services, 250

P

Packet

filtering, 633

switching, 106

Pager alerts, 593

PAP, see Password Authentication Protocol

Paperless workflow, creating, 507–514

database systems, 510–511

designing new approval system,
511–512

documenting management systems, 510

implementing new electronic approval
system, 513

organization and paper flow problem,
508–509

reducing paper flow complexity, 509

Parallel tasking, 224

Password

Authentication Protocol (PAP), 178

captured, 88

command, Cisco, 213

encryption of, 77

inspecting, 95

one-time, 97

for print servers, 623

protection, 61, 73, 80, 191

reuse, 624

schemes, one-time, 92

sniffer, 192

Telnet, 211

Path message, 276

Payroll organization, 359

PBX, see Private branch exchange

PC, see Personal computer

PCI, see Peripheral Component
  Interconnect

PCS, see Physical Coding Sublayer

PDU, see Protocol data unit

Pentium-class computers, 234

Pentium Pro processors, 34

Performance management, proactive,
  553–562

  current state of performance
  management, 553–555

  developing baseline, 556–560

    automated trend analysis, 560

    online utilization reports, 559

    trouble ticket reports, 560

  proactive plan, 560–562

Performance Monitor, see Windows NT
  Performance Monitor, working with

Peripheral Component Interconnect (PCI),
  35, 223

PERL, see Practical Extraction and Report
  Language

Personal computers (PCs), 227

card, 44, 58

connection, remote printer via, 65

drives, first, 46

high-speed file server, 60

keyboard, 190

/LAN, 447

remote printing on, 68, 69

Personal Identification Number (PIN), 194

PGP, see Pretty Good Privacy

Physical Coding Sublayer (PCS), 29

Physical sniffer, 90

PIN, see Personal Identification Number

PKC, see Public-key cryptography

PKCS, see Public-key cryptographic
  systems

Plain old telephone service (POTS), 176,
  229, 550

Plaintext, 74, 81, 415

Plug and play systems, 99

Point-of-execution metering, 591

Point-to-Point Tunneling Protocol (PPTP),
  92, 180

Point of presence (POP), 239

PointCast, 390, 391

Pointing device, 45, 48

POP, see Point of presence

POTS, see Plain old telephone service

Power PC, 32, 42

PPTP, see Point-to-Point Tunneling Protocol

Practical Extraction and Report Language
  (PERL), 474

Premise branch exchange, 393, 395

Pretty Good Privacy (PGP), 82, 179

Printer(s)

  -based computers, 70

  connection methods, LAN, 71

  networked, 448

Printing techniques, LAN, 65–71

    connection method, 65–66

    direct connection, 71

    file server attachment problems, 66–67

    print job traffic, 66

    print server connection, 67–68

    problems addressed, 65

    recommended course of action, 71

    remote printing on PC, 68–70

Priority queuing, 591

Private branch exchange (PBX), 259

    advantages of IP, 398

    IP telephony off existing, 397

Private keys, trusted third parties, and Kerberos, 415–430

    cryptographic protocols, 424–429

        Kerberos, 425–426

        Kerberos message exchange, 426–429

        Kerberos shortcomings, 429

    cryptography basics and goals, 415–416

    practical private or symmetric key algorithms, 421–424

        data encryption standard, 421–422

        International Data Encryption Algorithm, 422

        key management problems, 424

        RC2, 422

        RC4, 423

        symmetric key cipher modes of operation, 423–424

    private or secret key cryptography, 417–419

        attacker's goal, 418

        cryptoanalysis, 419

        key management, 418

        strong cipher goal, 419

    secure hash functions, 416–417

types of attacks, 419–421

    active attack, 420–421

    passive attack or eavesdropping, 419–420

Processor types, 31–39

    balance, 38–39

    BIOS, 37

    cache, 34–35

    heat, 36–37

    memory buses, 33–34

    memory speed, 32–33

    pipelining, 37–38

    speed doublers and triplers, 35–36

Product management, 368

Project tracking, 497, 499

Protocol data unit (PDU), 279

Proxy server, 314, 469, 470

PSTN, see Public switched telephone network

Public key certificates, 78

Public-key cryptographic systems (PKCS), 362

Public-key cryptography (PKC), 75

Public switched telephone network (PSTN), 393, 396

Push model, 385

Push technology, 383–392

    background, 383–384

    defined, 384–385

        information overload, 384–385

        low bandwidth, 385

    features of, 387–389

    market leader in, 391

    product research, 386–391

        extranet use, 386–390

        PointCast, 390–391

    relation of extranet to, 385

working of, 385–386

Q

Qualcomm Eudora, 82

Quality of service management, 356

R

RADIUS, see Remote Authentication Dial-In User Service

RAID, see Redundant Arrays of Inexpensive Drives

RAM, see Random access memory

Random access memory (RAM), 211

RAS, see Remote access server

Reconciliation Sublayer (RS), 30

Red Hat Software, 339

Reduced Instruction Set Computers (RISC), 31, 463

Redundant Arrays of Inexpensive Drives (RAID), 47

Redundant physical conditions, 11

Remote access authentication, 185–197

  authentication, 189–190

    remote access, 189–190

    remote control, 190

  components securing remote access, 190–196

    authentication tokens, 193

    authorization, 191

    challenge–response, asynchronous authentication, 193–194

    synchronous, event-plus-time authentication, 195–196

    synchronous-only-based authentication, 194–195

    user authentication, 191–193

    window of time, 195

  defining security process, 186–189

    basic controls, 187–188

defining remote access, 188–189

enterprise-specific security choices, 186–187

user and client authentication, 185–186

Remote access concepts, 171–184

  channel protocols, 177–180

    authentication and integrity protocols, 178–179

    compression protocols, 180

    encryption protocols, 179

    inverse multiplexing protocols, 178

    simple protocols, 178

    tunneling protocols, 179–180

  concerns and solutions, 174–177

    addressing, 177

    security, 174–175

    speed, 176–177

  getting started, 182–183

    outsourcing, 182–183

    self-starting, 183

  LAN-to-LAN direct-dial scenarios, 172–174

    fixed user-to-LAN direct scenarios, 172–173

    indirect-dial scenarios, 174

  security and authentication devices, 180–182

    key management systems, 181–182

    network access server, 180–181

    single sign-ON standards, 181

  typical remote access scenarios, 171–172

Remote access server (RAS), 293

Remote Authentication Dial-In User Service (RADIUS), 62

Remote control, 190

Remote method invocation (RMI), 485, 491

Remote Monitoring (RMON), 556

Remote Procedure Calls (RPC), 492

Resource objects, 353

Resource Reservation Protocol (RSVP), 269–276, 287

    data flows, 273

    goals and characteristics, 271–272

    operation, 274, 275

    protocol mechanisms, 274–276

    receiver-initiated reservation, 272–273

    reservation request messages, 272

    resource reservation, 269–271

Return on investment (ROI), 561

RIP, see Routing Information Protocol

RISC, see Reduced Instruction Set Computers

RMI, see Remote method invocation

RMON, see Remote Monitoring

Robots, 473

ROI, see Return on investment

ROM code, 71

Router(s), 62, 155, see also Router, securing; Routing

    access, 210

    default, 128

    security, internal, 214

    Wire Speed IP, 165

Router, securing, 209–215

    file transfer, 214

    internal router security, 214–215

    need for access security, 209–210

    protective measures, 215

    router access, 210–212

        Telnet access, 210–211

        TFTP access, 211–212

    securing console and virtual terminals, 212–213

Routing

    algorithm, 109

    dial-on-demand, 172

    direct, 128

    header, 281, 285

    indirect, 128

    Information Protocol (RIP), 15, 133, 145

    multilayer, 149, 150

    process, 129

    Table Maintenance Protocol (RTMP), 135

    topology, 109

Routing protocols, routing and, 123–137

    conventional router implementations, 136–137

    routing in network layer, 125–130

    routing protocols, 130–133

    survey of major routing protocols, 133–136

RPC, see Remote Procedure Calls

RS, see Reconciliation Sublayer

RSVP, see Resource Reservation Protocol

RTMP, see Routing Table Maintenance Protocol

S

Safe Internet Programming (SIP), 536

SAN, see Storage area networks

SAP, see Service Advertising Protocol

SATAN, see Security Administrator Tool for Analyzing Networks

SDSL, see Symmetric digital subscriber line

Secret key cryptography, 74, 417

Secure Electronic Transaction (SET), 468

Secure Hash Algorithm (SHA), 416

Secure Hash Standard (SHS), 77

Secure Sockets Layer (SSL), 298, 467

Security, see also Applets, network security and; Electronic mail, security and control of; Network security plan, developing

Administrator Tool for Analyzing Networks (SATAN), 625

distributed, 346, 355

E-mail, 515

Internet, see Internet security

IPv6, 288–291

management, 553, 566

need for access, 209

policy, formalized, 517

requirements, 498

server, 502

systems, 188

techniques, 529

threats, 620

Sendmail, 413

Serial Line Internet Protocol (SLIP), 178

Server(s)

AAA, 263

authentication, 196

communications, 189, 466

data bus structures

    peripherals, 45

    RAID, 47

DHCP, 114

DNS, 120

file, 345

interconnect, 374

Kerberos, 429

LAN emulation configuration, 233

messaging, 453

Microsoft NT Remote Access, 193

multiple, 372, 453

Netscape Directory, 302

network access, 178

news, 468

proxy, 314, 469, 470

RADIUS, 304

remote access, 293

security, 502

System Management, 588

ticket-granting, 426

VPN, 314

Web, 311

Windows NT, 90, 599

Server data bus structures, 41–48

bus loads, 44–45

CD-ROMs, 48

data buses, 41–42

disk drives, 45

displays, 48

evolution of data buses, 42–44

historical origins, 46

IDE, 47

keyboard and pointing device, 48

network cards, 47–48

ServerSocket, 482

Service Advertising Protocol (SAP), 135

Service-level agreements (SLAs), 247, 249, 257

Service provider network performance, 249

SET, see Secure Electronic Transaction

SHA, see Secure Hash Algorithm

Shared storage requirements, 375

SHS, see Secure Hash Standard

Sign-offs, 505

Simple mail transfer protocol (SMTP), 103

Simple Network Management Protocol (SNMP), 50, 59, 458

Single sign-ON (SSO), 181

Sin surfing, 401

SIP, see Safe Internet Programming

Site mirroring, 464

SLAs, see Service-level agreements

SLIP, see Serial Line Internet Protocol

Small business, LAN connectivity options
for, 55–64

    cabling, 56–57

    client/server, 60–62

    getting started, 63–64

    hubs, 58–59

    media converters, 57

    network adapters, 57–58

    network operating system, 59

    peer-to-peer, 59–60

    routers, 62–63

Small Office/Home Office (SOHO), 100, 172

Smart cards, 315

SmartScreens, 386

SMP, see Symmetric multiprocessing

SMTP, see Simple mail transfer protocol

SNA, see Systems Network Architecture

SNIA, see Storage Networking Industry
Association

Sniffer(s)

    attacks, 89, 91

    deployment of unauthorized, 85

    device, fingerprints on, 96

    gateway-based, 89

    logical, 90

    physical, 90

    -related incidents, response to, 95, 96

    in shared media network, 87

    in Token-Ring network, 87

Sniffer threat, assessing and combating,
85–98

    extent of problem, 88–91

        outbreak of sniffer attacks on
Internet, 89

        unauthorized gateway-based sniffer
in large corporation, 89–91

nature of threat, 86–88

    concern, 86–88

    how sniffers work, 86

    types of sniffers, 86

responding to sniffer-related incidents,
95–97

solutions, 91–95

    education of users, 94–95

    encryption, 91–92

    Ethernet technology, 93

    IPv6 protocol, 94

    password authentication, 92–93

    policy, 91

    secure e-mail, 94

    system administrators, 93

    third-party authentication, 94

    unauthorized physical sniffers, 94

SNMP, see Simple Network Management
Protocol

Software

    authorization, 183

    backup, 622

    Cisco Internetwork Operating System,
297

    copyright violations, 597

    costs of, 619

    firewall, 470

    Internet application, 466

    license compliance, monitoring of, 589

    metering products, 591

    Network Layer, 123

    package, cost of, 516

    problem, troubleshooting, 538

    support, physical paths with, 11

SOHO, see Small Office/Home Office

Spanning Tree Protocol (STP), 156, 163

Speed dialing, 394

Speed doublers, 35

Spreadsheets, 448

SQL database, 473

SSL, see Secure Sockets Layer

SSO, see Single sign-ON

Standalone systems, incompatible, 545

Star topology, collapsed, 10

Storage area networks (SAN), 371–382

    advantages of, 374

    archive/retrieval, 382

    data migration, 378–380

    data sharing, 380–381

    definition, 372–374

    getting started with device sharing, 374–378

    new focus on storage, 371–372

Storage management techniques, network data and, 571–586

    maintaining file histories, 572–574

        backup and restore, 572–573

        tracking file history and recovering files, 574

    managing storage, 578–583

        archiving, 579–580

        combining archiving and backup, 580

        data migration, 580–581

        monitoring volume use, 578–579

        using hierarchical storage, 581–583

    media rotation schemes, 574–578

        father-son rotation schemes, 575–576

        grandfather-father-son, 576–577

        Tower of Hanoi tape rotation, 577–578

Storage Networking Industry Association (SNIA), 380

STP, see Spanning Tree Protocol

Stream ciphers, 74

Subnet mask, 118

Subnetting, 107

Subnetwork, 123

Subsystem failure, 465

SVC, see Switched virtual circuit

Switched virtual circuit (SVC), 239

Switching, see Corporate networks, implementing routing, switching, and VLANs in modern; Layer 2 and 3 switching, evolution to

Symmetric digital subscriber line (SDSL), 228

Symmetric multiprocessing (SMP), 463

Synchronization authentication systems, 196

SYN flood attack, 407

System(s)

    flowcharts, 503

    killer problems, 499

    Network Architecture (SNA), 49

    security, 188

T

TCP, see Transmission Control Protocol

TCP/IP, see Transmission Control Protocol/Internet Protocol

TCP/IP essentials, 103–112

    history, 105–106

    Internet protocol, 106–111

        fragmentation and reassembly, 108–109

        IP addressing, 106–107

        IP packet format, 107–108

        routing, 109–110

        transport protocols, 110–111

    process and application protocols, 111–112

        DNS, 111

FTP, 111

HTTP, 112

remote file sharing, 111–112

SMTP, 111

Telnet, 111

protocol models, 103–105

Telecommunications Service Platform map,
317

Telecommuting, 344

Telephony systems, 395

Telnet, 103, 111

access, 210, 215

connection, 146

password, 211

Terminate and stay resident (TSR) program,
68, 69

TFA, see Transparent file access

TFTP, see Trivial file transfer protocol

TGS, see Ticket-granting server

TGT, see Ticket-granting ticket

Thrashing, 581

Ticket-granting server (TGS), 426

Ticket-granting ticket (TGT), 427

Time sharing, 343

TISC platforms, 38

TLS, see Transparent LAN services

Token resetting capabilities, remote, 195

Token Ring, 55, 145

Topology rules, 24

Tower of Hanoi tape rotation, 577–578

T1 private lines, 239

Trade associations, 357

Traffic filtering, 530

Traffic Peek, 90

Transmission Control Protocol (TCP), 199,
269, 479, 603

Transmission Control Protocol/Internet
Protocol (TCP/IP), 49, 103, 383, 403

application, 121

connectivity, 237

for intranet applications, 33

network connection, 489

protocol

architecture, 405

suite, 122, 177, 199

Transmission

errors, 428

technology, 1

Transparent file access (TFA), 111

Transparent LAN services (TLS), 250

Transport layer protocols, 110

Triggering, topology-based, 149

Tripwire, 93

Trivial file transfer protocol (TFTP), 210, 212

Trouble ticket reports, 560

TSR program, see Terminate and stay
resident program, 68

Tunneling protocols, 179

U

UA, see User agent

UDP, see User Datagram Protocol

Unicast transmission, 270

Unified messaging, 265

Uniform resource locator (URL), 466, 484

Uninterruptible power supply (UPS), 7, 8,
465

University of Indiana knowledge base, 440

UNIX, 80, 93

Unshielded twisted-pair (UTP) cable, 56

UPS, see Uninterruptible power supply

URL, see Uniform resource locator

User

agent (UA), 111, 449

authentication, 191

Datagram Protocol (UDP), 104, 199, 269, 480

errors, 503

UTP cable, see Unshielded twisted-pair cable

V

Value-added networks (VANs), 320

Value-added reseller (VAR), 64

VANs, see Value-added networks

VAR, see Value-added reseller

VCIs, see Virtual channel indicators

Videoconferencing, 294, 563

Video-on-demand service, 230

Video traffic, 564

Virtual channel indicators (VCIs), 241

Virtual corporation, 219, 317–323

composition, 317–318

functionality and security, 318–319

major issues, 319–322

electronic data interchange, 319–321

executive information systems, 322

Internet/intranet/extranet, 321–322

strategic goal/planning, 318

Virtual dialup service, 297

Virtual LANs (VLANs), 150, 155

broadcast domain extension, 168

environment, 161

operations, standard for, 28

protocol-sensitive, 166, 167

risk factors, 169

standards, 162

Virtual machine, 329

Virtual memory, 336, 610

afflictions, 581

dialog box, 613

Manager, 330

Virtual path indicators (VPIs), 241

Virtual private network (VPN), 91, 219, 462

architecture, 313

server, 314

Virtual private networks, Internet-based, 293–304

advantages, 294–295

applications, 293–294

carrier services, 302–304

implementation, 295–298

Layer 2 forwarding, 296–297

Layer 2 tunnel protocol, 297

point-to-point tunneling protocol, 296

socks, 298–299

vendor offerings, 299–302

assured digital, 299–300

bay networks, 301–302

VPNet technologies, 300–301

Virtual terminals, securing, 212

Viruses, 347, 587

VLANs, see Virtual LANs

Voice and data network integration, 259–267

private voice service, 263–265

public voice services, 267

value-added services, 265–267

voice over Internet protocol, 260–263

Voice over Internet Protocol (VoIP), 218, 259

Voice telephone traffic, 230

VoIP, see Voice over Internet Protocol

von Neumann computer, 142

VPIs, see Virtual path indicators

VPN, see Virtual private network

W

Wait states, 225

WAN, see Wide area network

Web

    database, 471, 472

    implementations, early, 462

    server, 311

    sites, modeling and simulation, 438

Web-to-information-base access solutions, 433–446

    knowledge-base development and access using Web, 437–443

        ADM medical knowledge base, 440–441

        commercial knowledge-base services, 441–443

        high-performance knowledge base, 438–439

        knowledge base defined, 437–438

        knowledge-base infrastructure, 439–440

        University of Indiana knowledge base, 440

    meteorological Web-based data access, 434–435

    network-centric warfare, 443–445

    Web-based metadata access for modeling and simulation, 435–437

        DOD's modeling and simulation resource repository, 435–437

        Navy modeling and simulation catalog, 437

Western Digital, 42

White Pages directory service, 367

Wide area network (WAN), 12, 140, 457, 624

    connections, redundant, 12

    deployment of ATM into, 248

    gateways located in, 397

    router-based, 237

    switches, 554

Wildcard mask, 203

Windows NT architecture, 327–334

    architecture, 327–332

        hardware abstraction layer, 327–328

        I/O manager, 331–332

        kernel, 328–329

        local procedure call facility, 330

        NT Executive, 329

        object manager, 329

        process manager, 329

        security module, 332

        Virtual Memory Manager, 330

    networking, 332–334

Windows NT-based systems, evaluating performance of, 609–618

    changing paging file, 611–613

    evaluating NT performance, 613–618

    overview, 609–610

    performance effect, 610–611

    virtual memory, 610

Windows NT computer, configuring TCP/IP on, 113–122

    advanced IP addressing, 119

    DNS tab, 119–121

    IP address requirements, 114–119

        IP address, 117–118

        default gateway, 119

        subnet mask, 118

    overview, 113

    Windows NT configuration, 114

Windows NT Performance Monitor, working with, 599–607

    alerts, 605–606

    graphic interface, 600–602

    multiple objects, 602–605

    overview, 599–600

Wire Speed IP Routers, 165

Word processing documents, 448

Work Group Solutions, 339

World Wide Web (WWW), 245, 321, 410

WWW, see World Wide Web

X

Xerox Network Services (XNS), 14

XNS, see Xerox Network Services

Y

Yahoo!, 385

Z

Zone transfers, 411

Milton Keynes UK
Ingram Content Group UK Ltd.
UKHW021934071024
449327UK00022B/1808